Dana Facaros

flying visits ITALY

CADOGANguides

Contents

About the authors

Dana Facaros and **Michael Pauls** have written over 30 books for Cadogan Guides, including all the Italy series. For three years they lived in a tiny Umbrian hilltop village, where they suffered massive overdoses of food, art and wine, and enjoyed every minute of it. They have since lived all over Europe, but have recently hung up their castanets in a farmhouse surrounded by vineyards in the Lot Valley.

Authors' acknowledgements

We would like to say a huge and sincere thank-you to the noble and talented **Justine Montgomery**, who saved the bacon and devoted 25 hours a day to editing this book even while packing her bags; we both wish her all the best in Oz.

Cadogan Guides
165 The Broadway,
Wimbledon, London
SW19 1NE, UK
info.cadogan@virgin.net
www.cadoganguides.com

The Globe Pequot Press
246 Goose Lane, PO Box 480, Guilford,
Connecticut 06437–0480, USA

Cover design by Jodi Louw
Book design by Andrew Barker
Cover photographs by John Ferro Sims (back), and John Ferro Sims and Kicca Tommasi (front)
Maps © Cadogan Guides, drawn by Map Creation Ltd
Managing Editor: Christine Stroyan
Series Editor: Linda McQueen
Editor: Justine Montgomery
Design: Sarah Gardner
Proofreading: Catherine Bradley
Indexing: Isobel McLean
Production: Navigator Guides Ltd

Printed in Italy by Legoprint
A catalogue record for this book is available from the British Library
ISBN 1-86011-896-8

Please help us to keep this guide up to date. We have done our best to ensure that the information in this guide is correct at the time of going to press. But places and facilities are constantly changing, and standards and prices in hotels and restaurants fluctuate. We would be delighted to receive any comments concerning existing entries or omissions. Authors of the best letters will receive a copy of the Cadogan Guide of their choice.

Introduction and Themes

Tradition may have it that all roads – and most flights – lead to Rome, but that was a conceit of the Romans rather than any reflection on what the rest of the country had to offer, and it's all set to change. A host of new cheap flight destinations has put a whole range of Italy's cities at your fingertips. And they're only a couple of hours from London, ideal for a flying visit, a short break...or more, should you find that the place has stolen your heart and feel compelled to acquire an Italian retreat of your own.

Italy's charms are no secret. The Leaning Tower, Pompeii, the Sistine Chapel or the reflections of a moonlit Venice are no less fascinating than they have been for centuries, and they all find their way into these pages. Some, such as Leonardo da Vinci's *Last Supper*, continue to draw attention to themselves today, courting controversy as we juggle the desire to conserve with the desire to restore. But for every one of its clichés, Italy has a hundred other natural wonders and artistic showpieces that any other nation would die for. Some cities will put you in reach of the Italy you feel you already know through brochures and holiday programmes, now possible to discover at first-hand; others will introduce an Italy you never knew existed.

Flying Visits Italy is the perfect opportunity to rediscover old favourites and open your eyes to new places – places that, while they remain off the Grand Tour of the average foreigner, have certainly not been lost on the locals. You'll find each regional capital is distinguished by a great civic pride; each will have its story to tell, its famous son(s), its unique craft – a history more often than not etched into its very stones, bearing eloquent witness to the twists and turns of fortune it has weathered. Sumptuous churches testify to the wealth of popes and dukes; municipal museums hoard treasures from prehistory to the present day; great leaps in art can be charted as you are introduced to first one, then another school of local talent. And at the core of each city beats the heart of every Italian town, large or small: its *piazza*, the social forum of old, its cafés, market stalls and *gelaterie* buzzing with voices and vitality, while history bounces off the walls of the *palazzi* on all sides.

We've divided these varied pockets of Italy into regional chapters, treating each new destination in turn as a gateway to the attractions of the surrounding region. Several pages introduce the key sights, monuments and museums in the gateway city, while a practical section provides the essentials on how to get around, where to stay, eat and shop while you're there. Then come suggestions for day trips or overnighters that you can make from the city by public transport, a chance to glean an insight into the fabric of the region. And in most cities you'll find we've included a five-day touring itinerary you can do from the city by hiring a car, picking out some of the hidden and not-so-hidden gems of the Italian provinces for you to explore at your own pace.

The guide reflects the diversity of the country, however, and is arranged according to the special strengths of each region. Where the gateway cities are very close together, for instance, they've been coupled to share a touring itinerary, as with Venice and Treviso, both of which make a perfect springboard for touring the grand villas of the Veneto. Other regions lend themselves better to individual trips than to touring around. Emilia-Romagna, for instance, helpfully clusters its jewels in towns easily accessible from Bologna and Forlì, so you'll find it most inspiring simply to make a beeline for Ravenna, its mosaics gleaming from the Dark Ages; Faenza, city of faïence-

What to Go For...

	Art City	Beaches	Gastronomy	Scenery	Shopping	Architecture	Archaeology
Alghero		●	●	●	●		★
Ancona		●	●	●		★	
Bergamo	●			●	★	●	★
Bologna	●		●		●	●	
Brescia	●			★	★	●	●
Forlì	★	★	★			●	
Genoa		★	●	★		●	
Milan	●		●	★	●	●	
Naples	●	●	●	●	●		●
Pescara		●		★			★
Pisa	●			★	★	●	
Rome	●		●		●	●	●
Treviso	●			●		●	
Trieste	★	★	●	★			●
Turin				★		●	●
Venice	●	●		●	●	●	

● In the gateway city itself ★ Within easy reach of the gateway city

ware; or bright, brash Rimini, with sun-trap beaches and a Renaissance pearl... By the same token, we reckon that excavating the riches of **Rome** will keep you busy for a short stay (or many), but in case you feel like surfacing from its myriad strata of Italian civilization, we suggest a few trips out: to its ancient port at Ostia; to stunning Orvieto, famous for its wine; to the surrounding lakes and villas, offering a breather from the city today just as they did for the dukes and and cardinals who built them.

In the northwest, **Turin** lies at the heart of Piemonte – literally, at the 'mountains' feet' – a quirky, Baroque city set against an ethereal backdrop of snowy peaks. Step beyond and you'll find table-flat rice paddies, the vinous delights of Asti Spumante, and the Valle d'Aosta, with its Alpine playgrounds and stunning scenery. **Genoa**, Italy's greatest port, is only just over the Alps, but it seems a world away, riddled with narrow alleys and restless energy, crammed with the spoils of merchant ventures. Seafood and *pesto* alone are reason enough to linger, but on either side shimmer famous resorts such as Portofino and the magnificent Cinque Terre. East of here, Lombardy offers not only Italy's romantic lakes *par excellence* – Garda, Como and Maggiore – but the gems of the Lombard plain: scholarly Pavia, curlicue violin-making Cremona and Renaissance Mantua. These days, you can take your pick of where to stay, too. There's **Milan**, of course, feverish centre of fashion and finance; but you could opt instead to base yourself in **Bergamo** or **Brescia**, fine cities that have somehow escaped the limelight up to now, unaffected by tourism yet both boasting their own schools of art. Bergamo, piled on its promontory, is the gateway to the Bergamasque valleys, some of the most serene and undiscovered pockets of Lombardy. Brescia, meanwhile, conserves some of the best Roman remains in northern Italy, while, less than an hour away, rosy Verona will lure you in with her irresistible charms.

To the east lie the three regions of the Veneto, governed or influenced for centuries by that Most Serene Republic, **Venice**, a fairy-tale city which only becomes more remarkable with every visit. Drop in just to the north, though, and you'll find her little sister, **Treviso**, one of the Veneto's best-kept secrets: a charming walled town brightened by exterior frescoes and patterned by lovely waterways. Neoclassical **Trieste**, meanwhile, lies at the heart of the Friuli wine lands, a rich ethnic mix wedged between Austria and Slovenia, sweetened with delicious pastries and a stone's throw from Aquileia, the most important archaeological site in northern Italy.

Loosen your belt and indulge in **Bologna**, Italy's capital of gastronomy, with a generous helping of medieval art and architecture on the side; and if that doesn't satisfy you, there's elegant Parma, city of cheese and ham, an hour away, or Modena, home of Ferrari, balsamic vinegar and Lambrusco. If that all sounds too rich, head for **Forlì**, closer to the coast. It tends to get bypassed, but it's an attractive old town with a distinct Mussolinian quarter in its midst – a perfect place to sample Emilia-Romagna's delicious cities and beach resorts while escaping the crowds.

In central Italy, **Pisa** needs no introduction, but you can extend the sphere of its Field of Miracles to take in Florence, the 'art city' that coined the term; the Chianti wine lands; or the charming hill towns that adorn the rolling, civilized landscape in all directions. Further east, the salty old port city of **Ancona**, famed for its seafood, marks the way into the Marches. This is Tuscany without the tourists: dotted with pleasant hill towns and bordered by a string of beach resorts, it boasts the fine Renaissance city of Urbino, set amid bristling castles in the mountains of the Montefeltro.

Land in prosperous **Pescara**, Abruzzo's biggest resort, and you'll be able to stretch your limbs upon mile upon mile of sand, edged by a score of restaurants and bars; but you'll also be within reach of territory more familiar to the Abruzzo bear than the visitor: the Alpine grandeur of the Gran Sasso, the loftiest peaks of the Apennines.

Besides the spectacular Amalfi Drive, **Naples** and its bay offer an embarrassment of riches: Pompeii, Sorrento, the island idyll of Capri, not to mention some of the finest marine delicacies you'll ever eat. Hold on to your valuables and venture into the tangle of the city itself; here you'll find Italy's greatest archaeological collection, pizza to die for and a gritty, vital bazaar atmosphere quite unlike anywhere else.

And should you want something less Italian, step off the plane into **Alghero**, the beautiful old Sardinian port where the locals speak archaic Catalan, where beautiful coves skirt transparent seas and uncrowded beaches, and where Pisan Romanesque churches share space among ancient volcanic hills with a fascinating prehistoric network of dolmens, menhirs and *nuraghi*.

They say you cry twice in Italy: when you first arrive, and when you have to leave. But now, with flying visits made so easy, there's no need – for you can simply return again and again.

Travel and Practical A–Z

02

Travel

Getting There

By Air: the Lowdown on Low-cost Flights

Over the last few years the airline industry has undergone a revolution. Inspired by the success of the easyJet company, many smaller airlines – Buzz, Ryanair, go, Bmibaby – flocked to join it in breaking all the conventions of air travel in a remarkable attempt to offer fares at rock-bottom prices. After September 11th, just when major carriers were hitting the ropes, these budget airlines experienced unprecedented sales and have responded by expanding their list of destinations.

No Frills, No Thrills

The ways in which these low prices are achieved sometimes affect the experience of the traveller, but sometimes can actually be a bonus. First, the airlines have made use of a range of **smaller regional airports**, both in the UK and in Europe, where the landing fees and tarmac-time charges to the airline are at a minimum.

The **planes** are small and all of the same type to save maintenance costs.

Fares are one-way – dispensing with the traditional need to stay over on a Saturday night to qualify for a low fare – and vary widely; easyJet (go) sells the seats in price blocks, the cheapest seats being sold first.

You will not be issued with a **ticket** when you book, and you will be encouraged, sometimes even by a price discount, to book on-line. When you check in, you will be issued with a boarding card, but you may not have an **assigned seat**; in this case, you board on a first-come, first-served basis.

There are no 'air miles', no discounts on top of the low ticket price and no formal **meal** will be served, though there will usually be snacks for sale on board. There are no refunds, but some of the companies will allow you to **change** your destination, date of travel or the named traveller for a fee of around £15. Note that there are charges for **excess baggage**. You may find that **staffing levels** are kept very low: at booking stage, in the air and on the ground.

Who Flies Where?

	page	Ryanair	easyJet/go	Bmibaby
Alghero	261	•		
Ancona	197	•		
Bergamo	78	•		•
Bologna	147		•	
Brescia	86	•		
Forlì	162	•		
Genoa	39	•		
Milan	58		•	
Naples	243		•	
Pescara	211	•		
Pisa	172	•		
Rome	222	•	•	
Treviso	126	•		
Trieste	132	•		
Turin	23	•		
Venice	107		•	

Airline Carriers

Alitalia, London, **t** (0870) 544 8259; Dublin, **t** (01) 677 5171, *www.alitalia.co.uk*.

Bmibaby, t 0870 264 2229 (**British Midland t** 0870 6070 555), *www.flybmi.com*.

British Airways, t 0845 773 3377, *www.britishairways.com*.

easyJet, t 0870 6000 000, *www.easyJet.com*.

go, t (0870) 607 6543, *www.go-fly.com*.

KLM, t (0870) 507 4074, *www.klm.com*.

Meridiana, t (020) 7839 2222, *www.meridiana.it*.

Lufthansa, t (08457) 737 747, *www.lufthansa.com*.

Aer Lingus, Dublin, **t** (01) 886 8888, *www.aerlingus.com*.

Ryanair, t (0871) 246 0000, *www.ryanair.com*.

Note that **easyJet** and **go** have recently merged. This will not result in changes to **go**'s departure airports and destinations; details listed here are correct at the time of going to press. Check either airline's **website** for all the latest news relating to the merger.

Making it Work for You: 10 Tips to Remember

1 Whichever airline you are travelling with, the earlier you book, the cheaper the seats will be. EasyJet, for example, divides its planes into blocks, with the first 10 per cent of seats sold at the lowest price.

2 Book on-line for the best prices, and often for a discount of between £2.50 and £5.

3 Be prepared to travel at less convenient times. Early morning and late evening flights will be the last to fill up. But ensure you check that there is a means of getting from your destination airport if you arrive in the evening, and allow for at least an hour's delay. Will that force you to get a taxi rather than a local bus service, and does that eat up the saving you make by travelling late?

4 Think hard whether you want to book by credit card. You will have the consumer protection that offers, but there will be a supplement of anything up to £5. Consider using a debit card instead.

5 Check whether airport taxes are included in the quoted price; they are usually extra.

6 If you intend to travel often and can go at short notice, sign up for airlines' email mailing lists to hear news of special offers.

7 Check the baggage allowance and don't take any excess. If you can travel light, take hand baggage only, as at busier airports your airline may be low priority for the baggage handlers and this can cause a long wait.

8 If you want to avoid paying for overpriced airport food or unsatisfying snacks, take your own food and drink, allowing for delays.

9 Make sure you have your booking reference and confirmation with you when you check in. (This reference will have been emailed or posted to you.)

10 Never ignore the advised check-in times, which can vary from 30mins to 2hrs. Don't be tempted to cut it fine; if you arrive too late you won't be allowed on the plane even if it is visible on the tarmac, as cheap flights depend on the airline keeping tarmac time short. If you care where you sit, or are travelling in a group, either check in even earlier (seats are often allocated at check-in), or go to the departure gate as early as possible to be ahead of the bunch.

What's the Worst that Can Happen?

From time to time the press ripples with stories of a 'holiday hell' caused by low-cost air travel. These range from people ending up a four-hour journey from their destination, via falsely advertised destinations (Malmö as Copenhagen, Brescia as Verona, etc.), to lost baggage and no one to look for it, to queues and cancellations and so many hidden extras to be paid for – taxes, supplements, expensive food, travel to and from outlying airports – that it would have been cheaper to go by private jet. There are no 'spare' planes, so if one breaks down, the day's schedules tend to collapse like a house of cards. Surprisingly, however, the overall punctuality record is no worse than that of major carriers.

Of course disasters can always happen, but an awareness of the way the system works and why the fares are cheap can go a long way towards avoiding mishaps or being caught out – *see* the box above. And, while corners are cut in many ways, there is no evidence that those corners are related in any way to safety. Always take out good travel insurance.

Note also that as the market for cheap travel takes off, major carriers such as BA and British Midland have begun to compete directly, with targeted advertising, offering one-way fares that do not require a Saturday night stay.

Entry Formalities

Passports and Visas

To get into Italy you need a valid passport. EU nationals do not need a visa. US, Canadian and Australian nationals do not need a visa to enter Italy for stays of up to 90 days. If you mean to stay longer, you must get a *permesso di soggiorno*: you will need to state your reason for staying and be able to prove a source of income and medical insurance. According to Italian law, you must register with the police within eight days of your arrival. If you check into a hotel this is done automatically. Should you come to grief in the mesh of rules and forms, you can get someone to explain it to you in English by calling the Rome Police Office for visitors, **t** 06 4686, ext.2987.

Getting to Italy Cheaply from North America

US and Canadian citizens will be able to find flights direct to some of the larger Italian cities listed in this guide. But it is also possible for North Americans to take advantage of the explosion of cheap inter-European flights, by taking a charter flight to London, and booking a London–Italy budget flight on the airline's website. This will need careful planning: you're looking at an 8hr flight followed by a 3hr journey across London and another 1½–2hr hop to Italy; it can be done, and you may be able to sleep on a night flight, but you may prefer to spend a night or two in London.

Direct to Italy

There are frequent flights to Rome and Milan from North America on most of the major airlines. Delta flies from New York to Rome, Venice and Milan, and in summer you may also be able to get non-stop charters to some of the regional destinations. During off-peak periods (the winter months and fall) you should be able to get a scheduled economy flight from New York to Rome for around $520–600 (round-trip), and for an extra $100 or so a transfer to one of the regional airports.

Air Canada, **t** (1 888) 247 2262, *www.aircanada.ca*.

Alitalia, **t** (800) 223 5730, *www.alitaliausa.com*.

American Airlines, **t** (800) 433 7300, *www.aa.com*.

British Airways, **t** (800) AIRWAYS; TTY **t** (877) 993 9997, *www.britishairways.com*.

Continental, **t** (800) 231 0856, Canada **t** (800) 525 0280, *www.continental.com*.

Delta, **t** (800) 241 4141, *www.delta.com*.

Northwest Airlines, **t** (800) 225 2525, *www.nwa.com*.

United Airlines, **t** (800) 241 6522, *www.ual.com*.

Via London

Start by finding a cheap charter flight or discounted scheduled flight to London; check the Sunday-paper travel sections for the latest deals and, if possible, research your fare on some of the US cheap-flight websites: *www.priceline.com* (bid for tickets), *www.expedia.com*, *www.hotwire.com*, *www.bestfares.com*, *www.travelocity.com*, *www.eurovacations.com*, *www.cheaptrips.com*, *www.courier.com* (courier flights), *www.fool.com* (advice on booking over the net).

When you have established the availability and arrival times for possible London flights, match up a convenient flight time on the website of the budget airline that flies to your chosen Italian city (*see* p.6). *Be careful if using easyJet to opt for its flights from Luton, not Liverpool, and note also that Bmibaby's hub, East Midlands airport, is not near London and would be impractical for a single day's journey.*

You will most likely be arriving at Heathrow terminals 3 or 4 (possibly Gatwick), and may be flying out from Stansted (Ryanair/go), Luton (easyJet/go) or Gatwick. To get between them you will have to travel through central London. Add together the journey times and prices for Heathrow into central London and back out again to your departure airport. You could mix and match – the Tube to Victoria and the Gatwick Express, or a taxi from Heathrow to Liverpool Street and a train to Stansted – but don't even think of using a bus or taxi at rush hours (7–10am and 4–7pm); train and/or Underground (Tube) are the only sensible choices. Always add on waiting times and delays in London's notoriously creaky transport system; finally, although the cheapest budget airline fares are early morning and late at night, make sure your chosen transport through the city is still operating.

Airport to Airport Taxis

A taxi directly between airports might avoid central London but it is an expensive option:

Heathrow–Gatwick: 1hr 30mins, £85–100.

Heathrow–Luton: 1hr 15mins, £80–90.

Heathrow–Stansted: 2hrs 15mins, £140–160.

Customs

EU nationals over the age of 17 can now import a limitless amount of goods for their personal use. Arrivals from non-EU countries have to pass through Italian Customs. Duty-free allowances have now been abolished within the EU. For travellers entering the EU from outside, the duty-free limits are 1 litre of spirits or 2 litres of liquors (port, sherry or champagne), plus 2 litres of

Heathrow

Heathrow is about 15 miles west of central London. **Airport information: t** 0870 0000 123.

By Tube: Heathrow is on the Piccadilly Line. Tube trains depart every 5–9 mins from 6am to midnight and the average journey time to the city centre is 55mins. A single (one-way) fare to the city centre costs £3.60.

By bus: The Airbus A2 (**t** 0870 575 7747) departs from all terminals every 30mins and makes several stops before terminating at King's Cross after 1hr 45mins. Tickets cost £8 single.

By train: The Heathrow Express is the fastest option: trains every 15 mins between 5.10am and 11.40pm to Paddington Station, which is on the Tube's Bakerloo, Circle, District and Hammersmith and City Lines, taking 15mins. Tickets cost £13 single.

By taxi: There are taxi ranks at all terminals. Fares into central London are about £35–50.

Gatwick

Gatwick, **t** 0870 000 2468, is about 20 miles south of London. There are 2 terminals, North and South, linked by a shuttle service.

By train: The fastest service is the Gatwick Express (**t** 0870 530 1530), which runs from Victoria Station to the South Terminal every 15mins (taking about 30mins). Tickets cost £11 for a single. Two slower train services run from Victoria and from London Bridge.

By taxi: Fares to and from the centre of London with a black cab are about £40–60 depending on traffic.

Luton

Luton is about 30 miles north of London. **Airport information: t** (01582) 405 100.

By bus: Greenline bus 757 (**t** 0870 608 7261) runs roughly every 30mins between Luton Airport and bus stop 6 in Buckingham Palace Road, near Victoria Station, via Marble Arch. Tickets cost £7 single. The journey takes 1hr 15mins.

By train: Between 8am and 10pm, Thameslink (**t** 0845 330 6333) runs frequent trains from King's Cross Thameslink Station (10mins' walk from King's Cross Station), via Blackfriars, London Bridge and Farringdon, to Luton Airport Parkway. Tickets cost £10 single. At Luton a free shuttle bus takes you on to the airport; the journey takes 55mins.

By taxi: A black cab will cost you around £40–60 from central London.

Stansted

Stansted is the furthest of the airports from London, about 35 miles to the northeast. **Airport information: t** 0870 000 0303.

By bus: Airbus A6 and Jetlink coaches (**t** 0870 575 7747) run every 30mins from Victoria Station, Marble Arch and Hyde Park Corner, taking 1hr 40mins. Less frequent services run throughout the night. Tickets cost £8 single.

By train: The Stansted Express (**t** 0870 530 1530) runs every 30mins (every 15mins at peak times) between 5am and 11pm to and from Liverpool Street Station, in the City, taking 45mins. Tickets cost £13 single.

By taxi: A black cab from central London will cost £45–£65.

Sample Journeys

Heathrow–Luton: get to Heathrow Express from terminal 15mins; wait for train 10mins; journey 15mins; go from Paddington Station down into Tube 10mins; Tube to Farringdon 15mins; go up and buy Thameslink ticket 10mins including queueing; train and shuttle to Luton 55mins. **Total journey time** 2hrs 10mins, plus 45mins for delays and hitches, so 3hrs would be safest.

Heathrow–Stansted: get to Tube station from terminal 10mins, wait for Tube 5mins, Piccadilly Line to King's Cross 1hr 10mins, change to Circle Line and continue to Liverpool Street Tube Station 15mins, up into main line station and buy Stansted Express ticket 10mins, wait for train 20mins, train journey 45mins. **Total journey time** 2hrs 55mins, plus 45mins for delays and hitches, so 3hrs 40mins would be safest.

wine, 200 cigarettes and 50ml of perfume. Much larger quantities – up to 10 litres of spirits, 90 litres of wine, 110 litres of beer and 800 cigarettes – bought locally and provided you are travelling between EU countries, can be taken through customs if you can prove they are for private consumption only and that taxes have been paid in the country of purchase. Under-17s are not allowed to bring tobacco or alcohol into the EU. **Pets** must be accompanied by a bilingual Certificate of Health from your local vet. You may not bring meat, vegetables or plants into the UK.

Canadians can take home $300-worth of goods in a year, plus their tobacco and alcohol allowances.

Residents of the USA may each take home US$400-worth of foreign goods without attracting duty, including the tobacco and alcohol allowance. For more information, US citizens can telephone the US Customs Service, **t** (202) 354 1000, or look at *www.customs.gov*.

Getting Around

By Train

FS national train information: ***t*** *1478 88 088 (open 7am–9pm)*; www.fs-on-line.com.

Italy's national railway, the **FS** (Ferrovie dello Stato) is well run and often a pleasure to ride. There are also several private rail lines that may not accept rail passes.

There is a strict hierarchy of **trains**. The cheapest are the slowest, making the most stops. Faster trains often carry an obligatory seat reservation requirement and usually require a supplement. Train **fares** have increased greatly over the last couple of years and only those without extra supplements can still be called cheap. The FS offers several passes and discounts for day returns, families, senior citizens and those aged under 26.

On Friday nights, weekends and in the summer, **reserve a seat** in advance (*fare una prenotazione*). The fee is small and can save you hours of standing. **Tickets** may be purchased at the station or at many travel agents; it's wise to buy them in advance as queues may be long. Do check when you purchase your ticket in advance that the date is correct; tickets are only valid the day they're purchased unless you specify otherwise.

Always remember to **stamp your ticket** (*convalidare*) in the not-very-obvious yellow machine at the head of the platform before boarding the train. Failure to do so will result in a fine. If you get on a train without a ticket you can buy one from the conductor, with an added 20 per cent penalty.

Be sure you ask which **platform** (*binario*) your train will come in to; the big boards in the stations are not always correct.

Refreshments on long-distance routes are provided by bar cars or trolleys. Station bars often have good take-away travellers' fare.

FS stations also have other services. Most offer a *depòsito*, where you can leave luggage for a small fee. Some even have an *albergo diurno* (with showers, shaving facilities, etc.), currency exchanges open at weekends (not the best rates), hotel-booking services, etc. You can also arrange to have a hire car awaiting you at your destination – Avis, Hertz and Maggiore provide this service (*see* opposite).

Details on tickets, discount passes and advance reservations are available at:

CIT (UK), Marco Polo House, 3–5 Lansdowne Rd, Croydon, Surrey, **t** (020) 8686 0677, *www.citalia.co.uk*.

CIT (USA), 15 West 44th Street, 10th Floor, New York, NY 10036, **t** (212) 730 2121.

CIT (Canada), 80 Tiverton Court, Suite 401, Markham, Toronto L3R O94, **t** (905) 415 1060.

By Coach and Bus

Inter-city coach travel is sometimes quicker than train travel, but also a bit more expensive. You will find regular coach connections only where there is no train. In many regions they are the only means of public transport and well used, with frequent departures. Coaches almost always depart from the vicinity of the train station, and tickets usually need to be purchased before you get on, from a booth or one of the nearby bars. If you can't get a ticket before the coach leaves, get on anyway and ask the driver.

City buses are the traveller's friend. Most cities label routes well; all charge flat fees for rides within the city limits and immediate suburbs (about €1). Bus tickets must always be purchased before you get on, either at a tobacconist, a newspaper kiosk, a bar, or from ticket machines near the main stops. Once you get on, 'obliterate' your ticket in the machines at the front or back of the bus; controllers stage random checks to make sure you've punched your ticket. Fines for cheaters are about €25.

By Car

While virtually all the day trips we propose are easily accessible by public transport, you may decide to hire a car if you plan to follow the touring itineraries suggested in this guide.

Hiring a Car

Hiring a car (*autonoleggio*) in Italy is simple but not particularly cheap. Some companies require a deposit amounting to the estimated cost of the hire. A small car (e.g. Fiat Punto) with unlimited mileage and collision damage waiver, including tax, will cost around €40 per day although, for longer rentals, this will decrease slightly pro rata. The minimum age limit is usually 25 (sometimes 23) and the driver must have held their licence for over a year – this must be produced, along with the driver's passport and credit card, when hiring the car. It is probably easiest to arrange your car hire with a domestic firm before you depart and, in particular, to check out fly-drive discounts, which may be much better value.

If you are taking a budget flight and decide to hire a car once you get to your destination, local tourist offices can provide information on car hire agencies. Car hire firms are also listed for the larger towns in this book, and most major rental firms have offices in airports or main train stations.

Car Hire

In the UK

Avis, **t** (0870) 606 0100, *www.avis.co.uk*.
Budget, **t** (01442) 280 181, *www.budget.co.uk*.
Europcar, **t** (0870) 607 5000, *www.europcar.com*.
Hertz, **t** (0870) 599 6699, *www.hertz.co.uk*.
easyCar, *www.easyCar.com*.

In the USA

Auto Europe, **t** (888) 223 5555, *www.autoeurope.com*.
Avis Rent a Car, **t** (800) 331 1084, *www.avis.com*.
Europcar, **t** (877) 940 6900, *www.europcar.com*.
Europe by Car, **t** (800) 223 1516, *www.europebycar.com*.
Hertz, **t** (800) 654 3001, *www.hertz.com*.

Driving in Italy

Italians are famously anarchic behind the wheel and the only way to beat them is to join them, by adopting an assertive and constantly alert driving style. Bear in mind that he/she who hesitates is lost. In many historical cities, you'd be better off not driving at all.

If you are undeterred, you may in fact enjoy driving in Italy, at least away from the congested tourist centres. Signposting is generally good, roads are well maintained, and for touring the countryside a car gives immeasurable freedom.

Buy a good road map (the Italian Touring Club series is excellent). The **Automobile Club of Italy** (ACI) is a good friend to the foreign motorist. They can be reached from anywhere by dialling **t** 116 – also use this number to find the nearest service station. If you need major repairs, the ACI can ensure the prices charged correspond to their guidelines.

Petrol (*benzina*: unleaded is *benzina senza piombo*, and diesel *gasolio*) is still expensive in Italy (around €1/litre). Many petrol stations close for lunch in the afternoon, and few stay open late at night, although you may find a 'self-service' where you feed a machine nice, smooth notes. Services can be hard to find in remote areas and are generally closed all afternoon. Motorway (*autostrada*) tolls are quite high, but rest stops and petrol stations along the motorways stay open 24hrs.

Rules and Regulations

Third-party **insurance** is a minimum requirement in Italy. Extend your cover if necessary to ensure you are fully covered for driving in Italy, and keep your documents to hand as proof. Also get hold of a **European Accident Statement** form, which may simplify things if you are unlucky enough to have an accident. Always insist on a full translation of any statement you are asked to sign. Break-down assistance insurance is a sensible investment.

Speed limits (generally ignored) are officially 130km/hr on motorways, 110km/hr on main highways, 90km/hr on secondary roads and 50km/hr in built-up areas. Speeding **fines** may be up to €250, or €50 for jumping a red light.

Europ Assistance, Sussex House, Perrymount Road, Haywards Heath, W. Sussex RH16 1DN, **t** (01444) 442 211. Helps with car insurance while travelling abroad.

Practical A–Z

Climate and When to Go

'*O Sole Mio*' notwithstanding, all of Italy isn't always sunny; it rains just as much in Rome every year as it does in London.

Summer comes on dry and hot in the south and humid and hot in much of the northern lowlands and inland hills. The Alps and high Apennines stay fairly cool, while the coasts are often refreshed by breezes, except for Venice, which tends to swelter. You can probably get by without an umbrella, but take a light jacket for cool evenings. Overall, August is probably the worst month: transport is jammed to capacity, prices are at their peak and the cities are abandoned to hordes of tourists; many shops and restaurants close at this time, too.

Spring and **autumn** are the loveliest times to go; spring for the infinity of wildflowers in the countryside, autumn for the colours of the hills and the vineyards. The weather is mild, places aren't crowded and you won't need your umbrella much, at least until November.

Winter (Dec–Mar) is a time for skiers and opera buffs, or for those who want the art and museums to themselves. The Riviera has the mildest climate, but elsewhere it can rain and rain, and mountain valleys can lie for days under banks of fog.

Crime and the Police

Police: **t** 113.

In Italy, there is a fair amount of petty crime – purse-snatchers, car break-ins, etc. – but violent crime is rare. Nearly all mishaps can be avoided with adequate precautions.

Be particularly careful in crowded places and stations, don't leave valuables in hotel rooms and don't carry too much cash; split it so you won't lose the lot at once. Beware of beggars; the classic trick is for one child to thrust a placard at you while other children rifle your pockets. If you are targeted, grab sharply hold of your possessions and shout furiously – Italian passers-by or police may come and help you if they realize what is happening.

If you are using a **car**, park it in garages, guarded car parks or on well-lit streets.

There are three types of **police** in Italy: the national, quasi-military *Carabinieri*, clad in black; the more local *Polizia Urbana*; and the *Vigili Urbani*, who are mainly concerned with directing traffic and handing out fines.

Average High Temperatures in °C (°F)

	Jan	April	July	Oct
Ancona	6 (42)	14 (56)	25 (77)	17 (62)
Bologna	7 (44)	17 (62)	27 (81)	19 (66)
Florence	6 (42)	13 (55)	25 (77)	16 (60)
Genoa	8 (46)	14 (58)	25 (76)	18 (64)
Milan	2 (35)	13 (55)	25 (77)	14 (56)
Naples	9 (47)	14 (58)	25 (77)	14 (58)
Rome	7 (44)	14 (58)	26 (79)	18 (63)
Treviso	-3 (26)	7 (44)	18 (64)	9 (48)
Trieste	5 (41)	13 (55)	24 (75)	16 (60)
Venice	4 (38)	13 (54)	24 (74)	15 (59)

Electricity

Your electrical appliances will work if you adapt them to run on 220 AC with two round prongs on the plug. American appliances need transformers as well.

Health and Insurance

Ambulance (*ambulanza*): **t** 113.

Fire: **t** 115.

In an **emergency**, call an ambulance or ask for the nearest hospital (*ospedale*). Less serious problems can be treated at a *pronto soccorso* (casualty department) at any hospital clinic (*ambulatorio*), or at a local health unit (Unita Sanitarial Locale – USL). Airports and major train stations also have **first-aid posts** and pharmacists are trained to advise on minor ills. Dispensing **chemists** (*farmacie*) are usually open 8.30–1 and 4–8. Big towns will have a 24hr *farmacia*; others take turns to open overnight (the address rota is posted in the window).

EU citizens who carry their **E111 form** are entitled to reciprocal health care on Italy's National Health Service and a 90 per cent discount on prescriptions. The E111 should cover you for emergencies, but does not cover all medical expenses (e.g. no repatriation costs and no private treatment). If you have to pay for any treatment, make sure you get a receipt, so that you can claim for reimbursement later.

Non-EU citizens should check that they have adequate insurance for any medical expenses plus the cost of returning home. Alternatively, consider a special travel insurance policy, covering cancelled flights, theft and losses and offering 100 per cent medical refund; check to see if it covers your extra expenses if you get caught in airport or train strikes. Sporting accidents are rarely covered by ordinary insurance.

Money and Banks

The **euro** is the official currency in Italy (and 10 other nations of the European Union) and the official exchange rate was set at **1 euro = L1,936.27**. Since February 2002, the Lira has no longer been legal tender. Euros come in denominations of €500, €200, €100, €50, €20, €10 and €5 (banknotes) and €2, €1, 50 cents, 20 cents, 10 cents, 5 cents, 2 cents and 1 cent (coins).

It's a good idea to have a wad of euros to hand when you arrive in Italy, the land of strikes, unforeseen delays and quirky banking hours. Take care how you carry it, however (don't keep it all in one place).

Most ATMs (Bancomats – automatic cash dispensers) will spout cash with your bank card and PIN number – for a significant commission – but check with your bank first. They also take Eurocheque cards and credit cards. Large hotels, resort area restaurants, shops and car-hire firms will accept plastic as well; smaller places may not. Visa, American Express and Diner's are more widely accepted than MasterCard (Access).

Obtaining money is often a frustrating task, involving much queueing and form-filling. The major banks and exchange bureaux licensed by the Bank of Italy give the best exchange rates for currency or traveller's cheques. Hotels, private exchanges in resorts and FS-run exchanges at train stations usually have less advantageous rates, but are open outside normal banking hours. In addition there are exchange offices at most airports. Below are a few **weekend exchange offices**:

Florence: Thomas Cook, Lungarno Acciaioli 6r.
Milan: Banca Ponti, Piazza del Duomo 19.
Naples: CIT, Piazza Municipio 72.
Rome: Banco Nazionale delle Comunicazione, Stazione Termini.
Venice: CIT, Piazza S. Marco.

Opening Hours, Museums and National Holidays

Although it varies between regions, most of Italy closes down at 1pm until 3 or 4pm. Afternoon hours are from 4–7, often 5–8 in the summer. Some cities (eg. Milan) close down completely during August. Don't be surprised if a place is unexpectedly closed (or open), whatever its official stated hours.

Banks: Open Mon–Fri 8.30–1 and 3–4. They close on weekends and on local and national holidays (*see* below).

Shops: Open Mon–Sat 8–1 and 3.30–7.30. Some supermarkets and department stores stay open all day. Hours vary according to season and are shorter in smaller centres.

Museums: Italy has a hard time financing the preservation of its cultural heritage, so it's wise to check at the tourist office to find out exactly what is open and what is 'temporarily' closed before setting off on a wild-goose chase. We have listed the hours of important sights and museums, and specified those that charge admission. Entrance charges vary widely; major sights may be €6 or more, others may be free. EU citizens under 18 and over 65 get free admission to state museums, at least in theory.

Churches: All churches, except for the biggest cathedrals and basilicas, close in the afternoon at the same hours as the shops, and the little ones tend to stay closed. If there's no caretaker to keep an eye out, churches are usually locked. If you've come for the art, don't come during services, always keep some small change for the light machines

National Holidays

Most museums, as well as banks and shops, are closed on the following national holidays:

1 January (New Year's Day)
6 January (Epiphany)
Easter Monday
25 April (Liberation Day)
1 May (Labour Day)
15 August (Assumption, or *Ferragosto*, the climax of the Italian holiday season)
1 November (All Saints' Day)
8 December (Immaculate Conception)
25 December (Christmas Day)
26 December (*Santo Stefano*, St Stephen's Day)

(in case the work you want to see needs to be illuminated) and note that during the week before Easter paintings and statues may be covered with mourning shrouds.

In general, Sunday afternoons and Mondays are dead periods for the sightseer. Places without specified opening hours can usually be visited on request – but usually before 1pm.

Post and Telephones

Open Mon–Sat 8–1; in large cities 8–6 or 7.

La posta italiana is one of the most expensive and slowest **postal services** in Europe. Note, however, that the Vatican City has a special speedy and efficient postal service (which requires special Vatican stamps), so if you're anwhere in Rome, make sure you post your cards from the Holy See.

Stamps (*francobolli*) are available in post offices or at tobacconists (*tabacchi*, identified by blue signs with a white T). Prices fluctuate.

Most **phone booths** now take either coins or phone cards (*schede telefoniche*); the latter are available at tobacconists and news-stands – snap off the small perforated corner or they won't work. In smaller villages you can usually find *telefoni a scatti*, with a meter attached, in at least one bar (usually charging a small fee). Try to avoid telephoning from hotels; smaller hotels don't usually rip you off, but others may add 25 per cent or more to the bill.

To make a reverse charge call (*a erre*), you need to go to the offices of Telecom Italia. To **call Italy from abroad**, the international dialling code is 39. For **international calls** from Italy, dial 00, then dial the country code (UK 44; USA and Canada 1; Ireland 353), then the local code (minus the 0) and number. Calls within Italy are cheapest after 10pm; international calls after 11pm.

Price Categories

The hotels and restaurants listed in this guide have been assigned categories reflecting a range of prices.

Restaurant categories are for set menus or a two-course meal for one without wine.

Hotel prices are for a double room with bath/shower in high season.

Restaurant Price Categories

very expensive over €45
expensive €30–45
moderate €20–30
cheap below €20

Hotel Price Categories

luxury €225–400
very expensive €150–225
expensive €100–150
moderate €60–100
cheap below €60

Tipping

When you eat out, mentally add to the bill (*conto*) the bread and cover charge (*pane e coperto*, €2–4), and a 15 per cent service charge. This is often included in the bill (*servizio compreso*); if not, it will say *servizio non compreso* and you'll have to do your own arithmetic. Additional tipping is at your own discretion, but never do it in family-run places as you may offend.

Tourist Information

Tourist information offices: *open 8–12.30 or 1 and 3–7, possibly longer in summer. Few open on Saturday afternoons or Sundays.*

Known as EPT, APT or AAST, information booths provide hotel lists, town plans and information on local sights and transport. They should also be able to inform you about local sporting events, leisure activities, wine estates and festivals. Queues can be maddeningly long. If you're stuck, you may get more out of a friendly travel agency than an official tourist office. Nearly every city and province has a web page, and you can often book your hotel direct through the Internet.

UK, Italian State Tourist Board, 1 Princes Street, London W1R 8AY, **t** (020) 7408 1254, **f** (020) 7493 6695, *www.italiantourism.com*.

USA, 630 Fifth Ave, Suite 1565, New York, NY 10111, **t** (212) 245 5095/4822, **f** (212) 586 9249; 12400 Wilshire Blvd, Suite 550, Los Angeles, CA 90025, **t** (310) 820 1898/9807, **f** (310) 820 6357; 500 N. Michigan Ave, Suite 2240, Chicago 1 IL 60611, **t** (312) 644 0996, **f** (312) 644 3019, *www.italiantourism.com*.

Food and Drink

There are those who eat to live and those who live to eat, and then there are the Italians, for whom food has an almost religious significance, unfathomably linked with love, *la Mamma* and tradition. In this singular country, where millions of otherwise sane people spend much of their waking hours worrying about their digestion, standards both at home and in the restaurants are understandably high. Few Italians are gluttons, but all are experts on what is what in the kitchen; to serve a meal that is not properly prepared is tantamount to an insult.

For the visitor this culinary obsession is an added bonus – along with Italy's remarkable sights and music, and the warm sun on your back, you can enjoy some of the best tastes and smells the world can offer.

Restaurant Generalities

Breakfast (*colazione*) in Italy is an early morning wake-up shot to the brain: a *cappuccino* (*espresso* with hot foamy milk), a *caffè latte* (white coffee) or a *caffè lungo* (a generous *espresso*), accompanied by a croissant-type roll (*cornetto* or *briosca*) or a fancy pastry. Breakfast in most Italian hotels seldom represents great value.

Lunch (*pranzo*), generally served around 1pm, is the most important meal of the day, with a minimum of a first course (*primo piatto* – any kind of pasta dish, broth or soup, or rice dish or pizza), a second course (*secondo piatto* – a meat dish, accompanied by a *contorno* or side dish), followed by fruit or dessert and coffee. You can, however, begin with a platter of *antipasti* – ranging from seafood delicacies to raw ham, *salami* in a hundred varieties, vegetables, olives, and many, many more. Most Italians accompany their meal with wine and mineral water, concluding with a *digestivo* liqueur.

Cena, the **evening meal**, is much the same as *pranzo* although lighter, without the pasta: a *pizza* and beer, eggs or a fish dish. In restaurants, however, they offer all the courses, so you can still have a full meal in the evening.

The various terms for types of **restaurants** – *ristorante, trattoria* or *osteria* – have been confused, so that a *trattoria* or *osteria* can be just as elaborate as a restaurant, though a *ristorante* is rarely as informal as a *trattoria*. Invariably the least expensive eating place is the *vino e cucina*, serving simple cuisine for simple everyday prices. The fancier the fittings, the fancier the **bill**, though neither of these has anything to do with the quality of the food. If you're uncertain, look for lots of locals. *See* p.14 for the price ranges used in this book to guide you in your choice of establishment.

Eating out in Italy is not the bargain it used to be, but in many places you'll find a choice of set menus which are cheaper than eating *à la carte*. A *menu turistico* offers full, set meals of usually meagre inspiration for a reasonable set price; a *menu degustazione* is the gourmet option, featuring the chef's specialities and seasonal dishes.

The original Italian *tavola calda* (hot buffet), is becoming harder to find among the fast food chains; bars often double as *paninotecas* (serving sandwiches or *tramezzini*, little sandwiches on plain white bread – nicer than they look), and *pizza* by the slice (*al taglio*) is common in city centres. At any grocer's (*alimentari*) or market (*mercato*) you can buy the materials for picnics; some will make the sandwiches for you.

Regional Specialities

What comes as a surprise to many visitors is the tremendous regional diversity at the table; often nothing on the menu looks familiar, once disguised by a local name.

In **Northern Italy**, look for heavier dishes prepared with butter and cream. *Pasta all'uovo* and *risotto* are favourite first courses, while game dishes, liver, *bollito misto* (mixed boiled meats), *fritto misto* (mixed fried meats), sausages and seafood appear as main courses. **Piemonte** is a gourmet region, renowned for its white truffles and cheeses. It also serves *bagna cauda,* a rich hot dip made with butter, olive oil, garlic, anchovies and cream, or roasted meats. **Liguria**'s cuisine is the *cucina povera* of olive oil, lots of vegetables, a little cheese and wine, and seafood; it also gave the world *pesto.* The **Lombards** again like their food substantial: *antipasti* include raw *carpaccio,* or *bresaola*; popular *primi* are saffron-tinted *risotto alla milanese* or pasta stuffed with pumpkin and cheese; meat courses include *ossobuco alla milanese* (veal knuckle braised with white wine and tomatoes) and the hearty pork and cabbage stew, *cazzoela* or *cassuoela*. If you're really hungry, plump for brick-heavy *polenta,* a cake of yellow maize flour, with various sauces.

In the **Veneto**, a typical seashore meal might include oysters or *sarde in saor* (marinated sardines) followed by *risi e bisi* (rice and peas, cooked with Parma ham and Parmesan) or Venice's favourite pasta, *bigoli in salsa* (thick spaghetti, served with a piquant onion, butter and anchovy sauce). *Secondi* range from *fegato alla veneziana* (liver and onions) to *seppie alla veneziana* (cuttlefish in its own ink). Inland, the rivers yield fish for the famous *brodetto di pesce* (fish soup). Towards the **Trentino-Adige** the cooking displays hearty Austrian influences; desserts in **Friuli** are an epiphany: poppy-seed strudel, or Slovenian-style *gibanica* (ricotta, honey, poppyseeds and pinenuts).

Emilia-Romagna ranks as Italy's gourmet region *par excellence*, the land of *tortellini* and *lasagne*, Parmesan cheese, Parma ham and balsamic vinegar. A typical *antipasto* would be a selection of *salumi* (cured pork) cuts. Pasta is the classic *primo*: *tortelli* filled with pork, ham and Parmesan; or *tortellini d'erbetta* filled with herbs and *ricotta*. Alternatively there's *tagliatelle with ragù* (or *alla bolognese*), a smooth sauce of very finely minced pork and veal, prosciutto, onions, carrots, celery, butter and tomato – the lofty origin of the humble British 'spag bol'.

Central Italy is the land of beans and chick peas, game, tripe, salt cod (*baccalà*), *porchetta* (whole roast pork with rosemary), Florentine steaks, *saltimbocca alla romana* (veal scallops with ham and sage) and freshwater fish. **Tuscan and Umbrian** cooking uses fresh, simple, high-quality ingredients flavoured with herbs and olive oil, and the local *porcini* mushrooms or truffles. Seafood is prominent in the **Marches**, along with a fancier version of lasagne called *vincisgrassi* and stuffed fried olives. **Rome** is an excellent place to delve into any style of regional cooking, with dozens of restaurants from all over Italy. You can easily get a taste of the **Abruzzo** there, a region known for its game dishes, sheep cheese, saffron and its quality pasta.

The further south you go, the spicier things get, and the richer the puddings and cakes. **Southern Italy** is the land of home-made pasta, vegetables and superb seafood; its specialities are often seasoned with condiments like capers, anchovies, lemon

Italian Menu Vocabulary

Antipasti (Starters)

These treats can include almost anything; among the most common are:

antipasto misto mixed *antipasto*
bruschetta garlic toast (with olive oil and sometimes with tomatoes)
carciofi (sott'olio) artichokes (in oil)
frutti di mare seafood
funghi (trifolati) mushrooms (with anchovies, garlic and lemon)
gamberi ai fagioli prawns (shrimps) with white beans
mozzarella (in carrozza) soft cow/buffalo cheese (fried with bread in batter)
prosciutto (con melone) raw ham (with melon)
salsicce sausages

Minestre (Soups) and Pasta

agnolotti *ravioli* stuffed with meat
cappelletti small *ravioli*, often in broth
crespelle crêpes
frittata omelette
orecchiette ear-shaped pasta
panzerotti *ravioli* with *mozzarella*, anchovies and egg
pasta e fagioli soup with beans, bacon and tomatoes
pastina in brodo tiny pasta in broth
polenta cake or pudding of corn semolina
ravioli flat stuffed pasta parcels
spaghetti all'Amatriciana with spicy bacon, tomato, onion and chilli sauce
spaghetti alle vongole with clam sauce
stracciatella broth with eggs and cheese
tortellini crescent-shaped pasta parcels

Carne (Meat)

agnello lamb
anatra duck
arrosto misto mixed roast meats
bollito misto mixed boiled meats, or stew
braciola chop
brasato di manzo braised beef with vegetables
bresaola dried raw meat
carpaccio thinly sliced raw beef
cassoeula pork stew with cabbage
cervello brains
cervo venison
coniglio rabbit
costoletta/cotoletta chop
lumache snails
manzo beef
osso buco braised veal knuckle
pancetta bacon
piccione pigeon
pizzaiola beef in tomato and oregano sauce
pollo chicken
polpette meatballs
rognoni kidneys
saltimbocca veal, prosciutto and sage, in wine
scaloppine thin slices of veal sautéed in butter
stufato beef and vegetables braised in wine
tacchino turkey
vitello veal

Pesce (Fish)

acciughe or ***alici*** anchovies
anguilla eel
aragosta lobster
baccalà dried salt cod
bonito small tuna
calamari squid
cappe sante scallops
cozze mussels
fritto misto mixed fried fish
gamberetti shrimps
gamberi prawns
granchio crab
insalata di mare seafood salad
merluzzo cod
ostriche oysters
pesce spada swordfish
polipi/polpi octopus
sarde sardines
sogliola sole
squadro monkfish
stoccafisso wind-dried cod
tonno tuna
vongole small clams
zuppa di pesce fish in sauce or stew

Contorni (Side Dishes, Vegetables)

aglio garlic
asparagi asparagus
carciofi artichokes
cavolo cabbage
ceci chickpeas
cetriolo cucumber
cipolla onion
fagiolini French (green) beans
fave broad beans

funghi (porcini) mushrooms (boletus)
insalata (mista/verde) salad (mixed/green)
lenticchie lentils
melanzane aubergine
patate (fritte) potatoes (fried)
peperoncini hot chilli peppers
peperoni sweet peppers
peperonata stewed peppers
piselli (al prosciutto) peas (with ham)
pomodoro(i) tomato(es)
porri leeks
rucola rocket
verdure greens
zucca pumpkin
zucchini courgettes

Formaggio (Cheese)

bel paese soft, white cow's cheese
cacio/caciocavallo pale yellow, sharp cheese
caprino goat's cheese
parmigiano parmesan cheese
pecorino sharp sheep's cheese
provolone sharp, tangy cheese; *dolce* is less strong
stracchino soft white cheese

Frutta (Fruit, Nuts)

albicocche apricots
ananas pineapple
arance oranges
banane bananas
ciliege cherries
cocomero watermelon
fragole strawberries
frutta di stagione fruit in season
lamponi raspberries
limone lemon
macedonia di frutta fruit salad
mandorle almonds
mele apples
more blackberries
nocciole hazelnuts
noci walnuts
pesca peach
pesca noce nectarine
pompelmo grapefruit
prugna/susina prune/plum
uva grapes

Dolci (Desserts)

amaretti macaroons
crostata fruit flan
gelato (produzione propria) ice cream (home-made)
granita flavoured ice, usually lemon or coffee
panettone cake with candied fruit and raisins
semifreddo refrigerated cake
spumone a soft ice cream
torta cake, tart
zabaglione eggs and Marsala wine, served hot
zuppa inglese trifle

Bevande (Beverages)

acqua minerale mineral water
con/senza gas with/without fizz
aranciata orange soda
birra (alla spina) beer (draught)
latte (intero/scremato) milk (whole/skimmed)
succo di frutta fruit juice
vino (rosso, bianco, rosato) wine (red, white, rosé)

Cooking Terms (Miscellaneous)

aceto (balsamico) vinegar (balsamic)
affumicato smoked
bicchiere glass
burro butter
conto bill
coltello knife
cucchiaio spoon
forchetta fork
forno oven
fritto fried
ghiaccio ice
griglia grill
in bianco without tomato
lumache snails
marmellata jam
menta mint
miele honey
olio oil
pane (tostato) bread (toasted)
panini sandwiches (in roll)
panna cream
pepe pepper
ripieno stuffed
rosmarino rosemary
sale salt
salvia sage
tavola table
tovagliolo napkin
tramezzini sandwiches (in sliced bread)
uovo egg
zucchero sugar

juice, oregano, olives and fennel. **Campania**'s favourites are simple: *pasta e fagioli* (pasta and beans) or *spaghetti alle vongole* (with baby clams); its seafood is exceptional – mussels (*zuppe*) appear frequently, along with mackerel and sardines. Aubergines and courgettes make their way into many dishes, especially *melanzane parmigiana* (aubergine baked with tomato and mozzarella). Naples, of course, invented both *pizza* and *spaghetti*; a genuine Neapolitan pizza cooked in a wood-fired brick oven is the archetypal local eating experience.

Sardinia stands a little apart, with its own piquant cheeses and pasta varieties; bread is as much an art form as a staple; look out for the distinctive, twice-baked *pane carasau*. As in Campania, clams (called *arelle* or *còcciule*) are a favourite, but the coasts are also rich in spiny lobster and provide such delicacies as *bottarga* (Sardinian caviar). For *secondi*, the Sards like to dine on roasted meats: *proceddu* (suckling pig) is one of the island's most famous dishes. They also have a sweet tooth; try *sebadas*, pastries filled with ricotta cheese, bran and orange peel, then fried and doused in bitter honey.

Wine and Spirits

Italy is a country where everyday wine is cheaper than Coca-Cola or milk. There is a bewildering array of regional wines, many of which are rarely exported because they are best drunk young. Unless you're at a restaurant with an exceptional cellar, do as the Italians do and order the local wine (*vino locale* or *vino della casa*).

Most Italian wines are named after the grape and the district they come from. If the label says DOC (*Denominazione di Origine Controllata*) it means that the wine comes from a specially defined area and was produced according to a traditional method. *Riserva, superiore* or *speciale* denotes a wine that has been aged longer and is more alcoholic; *recioto* has a higher sugar and alcohol content. Other Italian wine words are *spumante* (sparkling), *frizzante* (pétillant), *secco* (dry), *dolce* (sweet), *amabile* (semi-sweet), *abbocato* (medium dry) and *liquoroso* (fortified and sweet). *Rosso* is red, *bianco* white; between them lie *rubiato, rosato, chiaretto* or *cerasuolo. Vendemmia* means vintage or wine harvest, a *cantina* is a cellar, and an *enoteca* is a wine-shop or museum where you can taste and buy wines.

The regions of Piemonte, Tuscany and Veneto produce Italy's most prestigious red wines (king of the Tuscans is the mighty *Brunello di Montalcino*), while Friuli-Venezia Giulia and Trentino-Alto Adige are the greatest regions for white wines (*Pinot Grigio* and *Tocai* make some of the best). But almost every other corner of Italy has its vinous virtues, be it the *Lambrusco* of Emilia-Romagna (much nicer than the stuff that gets exported), the *Taurasi* of Campania, the *Frascati* of Lazio or the *Turriga* of Sardinia.

Italy turns its grape harvest to other uses, too. Italians are fond of post-prandial brandies – Stock or Vecchia Romagna appear on the best-known Italian bottles. *Vermouth* is made of wine flavoured with Alpine herbs and spices, while *grappa* is a rough, Schnapps-like spirit drunk in black coffee after a meal (a *caffè corretto*). Other drinks include *Campari*, a red bitter drunk on its own or in cocktails; *Fernet Branca, Cynar* and *Averno* (popular aperitif/digestifs); and a host of liqueurs like *Strega*, almond *Amaretto*, cherry *Maraschino*, aniseed *Sambuca*, or Sardinian myrtle *Mirto*.

Piemonte

04

Piemonte and Valle d'Aosta

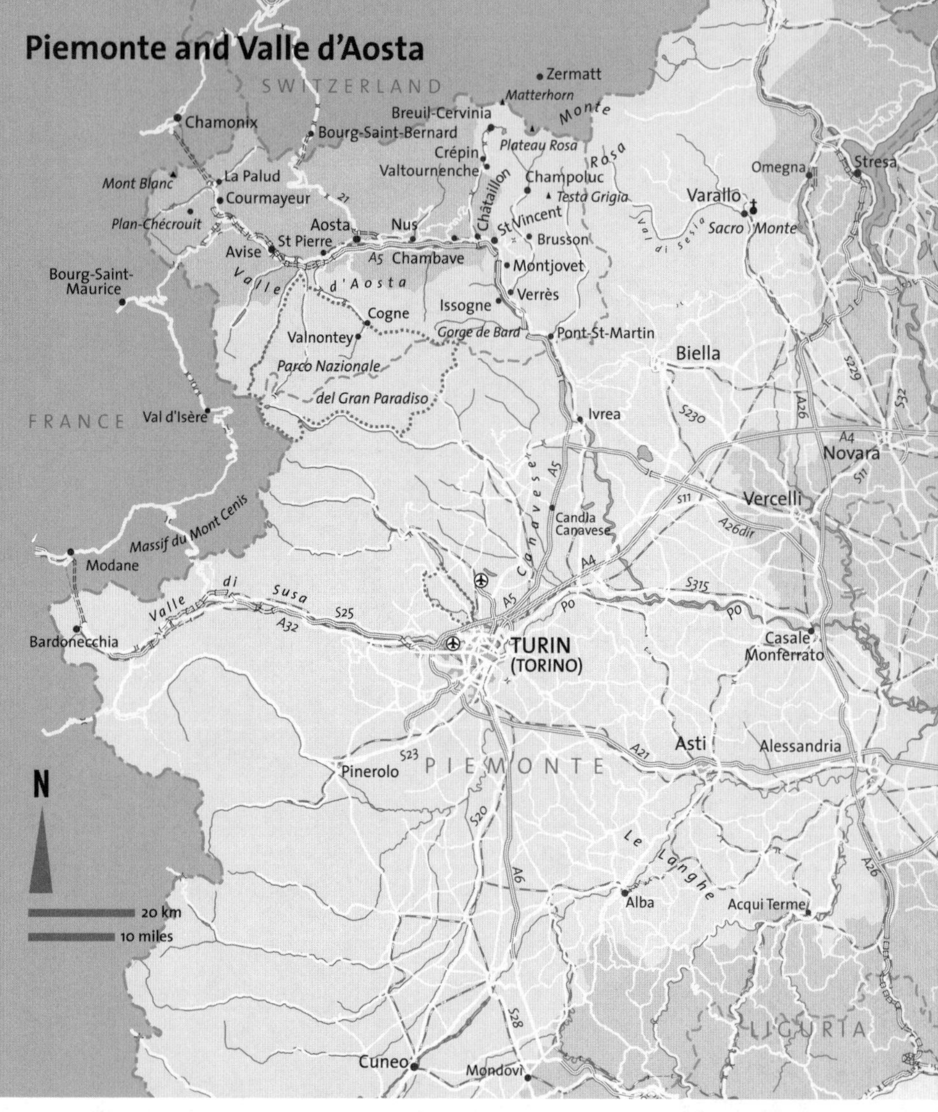

Piemonte (Piedmont), 'the foot of the mountains', is not only the birthplace of the modern Italian state, the cradle of its industry, and the originator of such indispensable Italian staples as vermouth, Fiats and breadsticks, but also a beautiful region full of surprises. Towering to the north and west are such famous peaks as Gran Paradiso and Monviso, while the small, autonomous Valle d'Aosta is home to such world-class heavyweights as Mont Blanc and the Matterhorn. The south is walled off from Liguria by the lush green Maritime Alps which, like the rest of Piemonte, are ill-equipped with the amenities of international tourism, and utterly delightful. South of the River Po, rolling hills are clad in the noble pinstripe of some of the world's most prestigious vineyards, while to the north lies a flat plain criss-crossed by a web of small canals that feed Europe's most important rice fields. And in the midst of it all lies Turin, not the industrial by-product one might suppose, but Baroque and strange.

Turin (Torino)

The aristocratic capital of the Savoys, Turin is an elegant Baroque city of arcades and squares. Its historic centre has the air of a courtly drawing room (no other Italian city looks anything like it), but the glitter and sleekness of the shops are thanks mostly to Fiat money; it's a local cliché that the big corporation – Europe's largest car manufacturer – replaced the Savoys as Turin's modern dynasty. Home of the famous shroud, of Juventus and vermouth, and reputedly the centre of black magic in the Mediterranean, Turin makes a rather unexpected 'Gateway to Italy'. Standing on the Po, the longest and most benighted of Italy's rivers, its cuisine is influenced by France; its winters are colder than Copenhagen's; its most renowned museum is Egyptian.

Along Via Roma

Just north of Porta Nuova station, fashionable **Via Roma** leads from the manicured **Piazza Carlo Felice** into the heart of the city, laid out in a stately rhythm of porticoed streets and squares. On its way it passes through an impressive 'gateway' of twin churches, behind which lies Turin's finest square, **Piazza San Carlo**, a 17th-century confection centred around a flamboyant equestrian bronze of Duke Emanuele Filiberto of Savoy, 'the Iron Head', by local sculptor Carlo Marochetti (1838). Stop to sip a cappuccino in the most celebrated of Turin's hallowed cafés, the 19th-century **Caffè Torino**, a veritable palace of java, with chandeliers and frescoed ceilings.

The Museo Egizio (Egyptian Museum) and Galleria Sabauda

Museo Egizio *open Tues–Sun 8.30–7.30; adm exp.*
Galleria Sabauda *open Tues–Sun 8.30–7.30; adm.*

These two treasure troves, just off Piazza San Carlo, share the ponderous **Palazzo dell'Accademia delle Scienze**, designed by the remarkable Guarino Guarini, an architect priest who came to work in Turin in 1668 and changed the face of the city.

The **Museo Egizio** began as a collection of curios back in 1628 and has been growing ever since; today it claims to be second only to that of the museum in Cairo. On the **ground floor** is a reconstruction of the 15th-century BC Temple of Ellessya, and an excellent collection of monumental public sculpture, notably the 13th-century BC black granite Rameses II, the 15th-century BC Thothmes III, and the sarcophagus of Ghemenef-Har-Bak, a vizier of the 26th Dynasty. **Upstairs** is an immense papyrus library, including copies of the *Book of the Dead* and the *Royal Papyrus*, listing all the kings of Egypt. Elsewhere you can spend hours wandering through the essentials and the trivialities of ancient Egypt: mummies in various stages of déshabille, statuettes, jewellery, textiles, and a reconstructed 14th-century BC tomb, where even the bread and beans prepared for the afterlife remain intact. The **basement** holds finds from excavations made between 1905 and 1920, with painted sarcophagi, reconstructed tombs, and dozens of beautiful wooden models: boats with crews, kitchens and granaries, servants performing everyday tasks, as well as scale models of the dead.

Turin
to Stazione Dora
Porta Palatina
Palazzo Reale
Teatro Romano
Duomo
Giardino Reale
Armeria Reale
S. Lorenzo
Teatro Regio
Palazzo Madama
Università
Mole Antonelliana
Giardino Zoologico
Fiume Po
S. Consolata
Giardino Cittadella
Palazzo Carignano
SS. Annunziata
Museo Egizio e Gall. Sabauda
S. Filippo Neri
Gran Madre di Dio
Sta Cristina
S. Carlo
Museo Regionale di Scienze Naturali
Museo Nazionale della Montagna Duca degli Abruzzi
Stazione Porta Susa
Stazione Porta Nuova
Air Terminal
Galleria Civica d'Arte Moderna e Contemporanea
Orto Botanico
Parco del Valentino
Ponte Vittorio Emanuele I
Ponte Umberto I
Piazza della Repubblica
Piazza Castello
Piazza Vittorio Veneto
Piazza San Carlo
Piazza Carlo Felice
Piazza Solferino
Corso Regina Margherita
Corso Vittorio Emanuele II
Via Po
Via Roma
Via Garibaldi
N
250 metres
250 yards

On the **top floor**, the **Galleria Sabauda** houses the principal collections of the House of Savoy. The Savoys liked Flemish and Dutch art just as much as Italian, which gives the Sabauda a variety most Italian galleries lack. Among the Italians are two fine Florentine works: *Tobias and the Archangel Raphael* by Antonio and Piero del Pollaiuolo, and a study of Botticelli's newborn *Venus*; other works are by Mantegna, Taddeo Gaddi, Il Sodoma, Tintoretto, Titian, Veronese and Bergognone. Among the northerners are Jan Van Eyck, Memling, Van Dyck and Rembrandt. The French have a room to themselves, with works by Poussin, Claude and Clouet.

Palazzo Carignano

Across from the Egyptian museum, Guarini's **Palazzo Carignano** was begun in 1679 for the Savoy-Carignano branch of the royal family. Of its two façades, one is a fine, undulating Baroque concoction, the other dull and neoclassical. The palace is full of Italian historical fossils: the bedroom where King Carlo Alberto died; Cavour's study; and the chamber of the Piemontese Subalpine Parliament preserved as it was during its final session in 1860 – full of gilt and red plush. The palace also hosted the first Italian Parliament, which on 14 March 1861 proclaimed Vittorio Emanuele II King of Italy. The themes are covered in more depth in the **Museo Nazionale del Risorgimento** (*open Tues–Sun 9–7; adm*), one of the more interesting of Risorgimento museums.

Around Piazza Castello and Via Po

Parallel to Via Accademia Valentina, the **Galleria Subalpina** (*see* Shopping, p.26) leads to the huge expanse of **Piazza Castello**, Turin's main square. In the middle, behind a beautiful, serene façade by Juvarra (1718), the **Palazzo Madama** keeps the **Museo Civico dell'Arte Antica** (*closed until 2004*), with copies of the Duc de Berry's *Book of Hours* and the superb *Portrait of an Unknown Man* (1476) by Antonello da Messina among a notable collection of manuscripts and medieval and Renaissance works. Under the arcade on the north of the piazza, the **Armeria Reale** (*open Tues–Sun 8.30–7.30; adm*) boasts one of the finest collections of medieval and Renaissance arms in the world; its library contains a famous self-portrait in red ink by Leonardo da Vinci.

Just off Piazza Castello stands the dark apricot **Palazzo Reale** (*open Tues–Sun 8.30–7.30; adm*), the main residence of the princes of Savoy from 1646 until 1865. The guided tour shows that they lavished much of their subjects' taxes on chandeliers and fluffy frescoes, making the palace's **Giardino Reale** a far more pleasant place to while away a few hours. On the corner stands the chapel of **San Lorenzo**, its bland exterior giving no hint of Guarini's idiosyncratic Baroque fantasia within (1668–80).

Around the corner, just off Via XX Settembre, is Turin's plain **Duomo di San Giovanni**, built by three dry 15th-century Tuscan architects. What it lacks in presence it makes up for with one of the most provocative relics of Christendom: the **Turin Shroud**, brought here in the 16th century by Emanuele Filiberto. To house the relic properly, Guarini designed the striking black marble **Cappella della Sacra Sindone** (Chapel of the Holy Shroud; *closed for restoration, but much can be appreciated from the outside*), crowned by a bold dome zig-zagging to a climax of basketweave arches full of restless energy. The shroud is kept in a silver casket in an iron box in a marble coffer in the

Getting to Turin

Ryanair flies from London Stansted (2hrs).

Getting from the Airport

Turin's Caselle airport (**t** 011 300 0611) is 15km north of the city. Every 30mins an **airport bus** stops at Porta Susa Station, at the main bus terminal on Corso Inghilterra (**t** 011 300 0611), and at Porta Nuova Station, taking 30–40mins (5am–10.30pm). **Tickets** (€4.13) can be bought from a kiosk in the arrivals hall or at Café Negrita on the corner of Via Sacchi and Corso Vittorio Emanuele II (opposite Porta Nuova).

A **taxi** to the centre (30mins) is €26–42.

Getting Around

Turin is not a big city: most of its sites are clustered within **walking** distance of each other. Otherwise, its regular grid of streets is served by old-fashioned **trams** and **buses**. The city transport office at Porta Nuova Station (**t** 848 888 088) provides a good free transport map (also available from tourist offices). There is also a **tourist bus** offering city tours starting from outside the tourist office in Piazza Castello (one tour daily except Tues, at 2.30pm). The **Porta Susa Station**, on the west side of town, can be a convenient getting-off point, while a third station, **DORA**, serves the regional line to Cirié, Lanzo and Ceres. The SADEM **bus terminal** (Corso Inghilterra) serves Aosta's ski resorts and towns in the province.

Taxi ranks are in many of the main piazzas (**t** 011 5730, or **t** 011 3399).

Car Hire

The airport offices open all day every day, while those in town open in the mornings.

Avis, Corso Turata 37, **t** 011 50 1107.
Hertz, Via Magellano 12, **t** 011 50 2080.
Europcar, Via Madama Cristina 72, **t** 011 650 3603.

Tourist Information

Turin: Piazza Castello 161, **t** 011 535 181/535 901, **f** 011 530 070 (*open Mon–Sat 9.30–7, Sun 9.30–3*). This office has a free room-finding service; other branches are at Porta Nuova Station, **t** 011 531 327; Via Garibaldi 25, **t** 011 443 1806, **f** 011 442 3838; and Caselle Airport.

For information on concerts, film times and so on, check out the listings in *La Stampa*, or visit the **InfoCulture** booth, Piazza San Carlo 159, freephone **t** 800 015 475. Ask for the *Torino Cultura Brochure*, translated into English.

Market Days

For bargains, don't miss the Saturday morning **'Balôn' flea market** (Piazza della Repubblica). The much bigger **'Gran Balôn'** joins it every second Sunday of the month.

Festivals

The **Turin Film Festival** (*Nov*) is a popular showcase for up-and-coming independent art-house movies (**t** 011 562 3309). **Settembre Musica** (*Sept*) is entirely devoted to classical music, featuring two concerts a day in the city's theatres and churches. **St John's Day** (*24 June*) is Turin's big folklore festival.

Shopping

Turin is a good city for shopping, particularly for **clothes**, with the smartest shops located around **Via Roma** and **Piazza Castello**. Two of the best places for window shopping are the great *gallerie* off the Via Roma: **Galleria San Federico** and **Galleria Subalpina**. A good buy in Turin is fine chocolates, ***gianduiotti***, named after Gianduia, a comic figure associated with St John's Day; try them at Giordano, Piazza Carlo Felice 69. A few doors down is a shop selling Alessandria's famous **Borsalino hats**. Turin is still Italy's top producer of **vermouth**: Carpano, the oldest house (1786), bottles the popular bittersweet Punt e Mes, while the competition, Martini & Rossi and Cinzano, are known for their classic dry *bianco* and the reddish elixir of many an Italian happy hour.

Sports

Football is Italy's second religion (season Sept–May) and Turin's vast **Stadio delle Alpi**, Strada Altessano 131 (tram no.9) is home to **Torino**, in the Italian second division, and

Juventus, reigning first division champions. It is generally said that the Italian league produces the highest standard of football played anywhere in the world and that no one (except emergent Roma and Lazio, or perhaps AC Milan in a good year) plays it better than Juventus. (**t** 011 65631 for tickets).

Where to Stay

Turin ✉ 10100

Turin's hotels tend to be either expensive and designed for business, or cheap and fairly seedy. Most are near Porta Nuova Station.

★★★★**Turin Palace**, Via Sacchi 8, **t** 011 562 5511, **f** 011 561 2187 (*luxury*). A traditional grand hotel across from Porta Nuova Station, in operation since 1872 and with the deserved reputation of being Turin's top hotel. The public rooms are sumptuous, the restaurant elegant and expensive, and the sound-proofed bedrooms luxurious.

★★★★**Grand Hotel Sitea**, Via Carlo Alberto 35, **t** 011 517 0171, **f** 011 548 090 (*very expensive*). In a quiet street near the centre, this offers pleasantly luxurious bedrooms (half-price at weekends). Its restaurant **Carignano** (*expensive*) serves Piemontese fare.

★★★**Victoria**, Via Nino Costa 4, **t** 011 561 1909, **f** 011 561 1806 (*expensive*). The hotel is furnished with a delightful hotchpotch of screens, tables and sofas, while the bedrooms are all determinedly singular; one is decorated in leopard skin. The staff are friendly and helpful. A superb, bright and airy breakfast room overlooks the garden. Excellent value.

★★★**Roma & Rocca Cavour**, Piazza Carlo Felice 60, **t** 011 561 2772, **f** 011 562 8137 (*moderate*). This is somewhat impersonal; though some of its rooms are lovely, with old-fashioned fittings and furnishings, others are merely adequate. All prices drop out of season.

★★**Sila**, Piazza Carlo Felice 80, **t** 011 544 086 (*cheap*). A great location and views, although the hotel itself is slightly gloomy. It's very handy for the airport bus stop.

★**Kariba**, Via San Francesco d'Assisi 4, **t** 011 534 856 (*cheap*). Comfortable and cheap, with clean and welcoming bedrooms (without bathrooms). *Closed Aug.*

Eating Out

Vecchia Lanterna, Corso Re Umberto 21, **t** 011 537 047 (*very expensive*). Turin's temple of fine cuisine is a subdued and classy turn-of-the-century restaurant. Specialities include quail pâté, duck-filled *ravioli* in truffle sauce, stuffed trout – enhanced by a perfect wine list. Book ahead. *Closed Sat lunch and Sun.*

Cambio, Piazza Carignano 2, **t** 011 546 690, or **t** 011 543 760 (*very expensive*). Opened in 1757, this offers a taste of the old royal capital: the décor, frescoes, mirrors and even the waiters' costumes have all been carefully preserved. On Fridays, you're invited to try dishes once served by the Savoys, though recipes have been adapted to modern tastes. Specialities include *agnolotti*, beef braised in Barolo, trout with almonds and *finanziera* (made of veal, sweetbreads, cock's combs and *porcini*, cooked in butter and wine). Top it off with home-made *tarte tatin*, all for a kingly bill. *Closed Sun, Aug and first week of Jan.*

Montecarlo, Via San Francesco da Paola 37, **t** 011 888 763 (*moderate*). One of Turin's most romantic restaurants, in the atrium of the Contessa di Catiglione's *palazzo*. Under the stone arches a delectable variety of *antipasti* (marinated swordfish, a flan of scampi) may be followed by well-prepared *secondi* such as baked liver, lamb or duck. Excellent wines and desserts. *Closed Sat lunch, Sun and Aug.*

L'Arcimboldo, Via Santa Chiara 54, **t** 011 521 1816 (*moderate*). Pick from over 100 sauces to accompany your pasta; the hare *ravioli* and lemon sorbet with vodka are recommended. *Closed Mon, Aug and first 10 days of Jan.*

Arcadia, Galleria Subalpina 16, **t** 011 561 3898 (*cheap*). Popular for excellent *antipasti*, pasta and country-style meat dishes. *Closed Sun.*

Lullaby, Via XX Settembre 6, **t** 011 531 024 (*cheap*). Serves delicious, filling local fare in a still-smart but unpretentious atmosphere; and there's no *coperto*. *Closed Sun and Aug.*

No visitor should pass over Turin's distinctive and seductive 19th-century **cafés**. They're not cheap, but their sweets and sandwiches are usually superb, and they're very much a part of the city. Try **Baratti & Milano**, Piazza Castello, much as it was in 1873; **Caffè Torino**, Piazza San Carlo 204, famed for its cocktails; or the beautiful **Mulassano**, Piazza Castello 15.

urn on the chapel altar, and shown only on special occasions. An exact replica is on display, along with an explanation of the scientific investigations which tried to determine whether it was possible that the shroud was used at Christ's burial; it flunked a carbon-dating test in 1989, and is now believed by many to date from the 12th century. Besides the shroud, the cathedral contains a fine polyptych of *SS. Crispin and Crispinian* by Defendante Ferrari, and a copy of Leonardo da Vinci's *Last Supper*, painted when the original began to crumble.

Near the campanile are the remains of a Roman theatre, while across the piazza, the Roman **Porta Palatina** has two 16-sided towers. You can see more of Augusta Taurinorum on Via XX Settembre in the **Museo delle Antichità** (*open Tues–Sun 8.30–7.30; adm*).

The Mole Antonelliana

***Lift** operates Jan–Feb Tues–Sun 11–5, Sat 11–11; Mar–Dec Tues–Sun 10–8, Sat 10am–11pm; **museum** open Tues–Sun 9–8, Sat 9am–11pm; guided tours in Italian; adm, cheaper combined ticket available.*

Turin's idiosyncratic landmark, the **Mole Antonelliana** on Via Montebello, was begun in 1863 by the quirky Piemontese architect-engineer Alessandro Antonelli. Some 549ft high, it is a considerable engineering feat, at once harmonious and bizarre. Sporting a vaguely Greek temple façade, it is stacked with a colonnade, windows, a majestic glass pyramid, a double-decker Greek temple, and a pinnacle crowned by a star. A lift to the terrace (282ft up), affords a fine view of Turin and the Alps, while inside, the **National Museum of Cinema** focuses on Italian film from the 1940s to the present.

South of Corso Vittorio Emanuele II

Stretching along the west bank of the Po is Turin's largest park, **Parco del Valentino**, where the city's **Orto Botanico** (Botanical Garden) is laid out beneath the French-style Castello del Valentino (1660). As part of its 1884 Exhibition, Turin built itself another castle, complete with a mock medieval hamlet, the **Castello e Borgo Medioevale** (***castle tours** Tues–Sun 9–7; adm; **borgo** open Mon–Sun 9–8*), with houses modelled on traditional Piemontese styles. Three kilometres south of the Parco del Valentino, the **Museo Nazionale dell'Automobile Carlo Biscaretti di Ruffia** (*Corso Unità d'Italia 40; open Tues–Sun 10–6.30; adm*), showcases the great age of Italian car design, while west of Porta Nuova station, the **Galleria Civica d'Arte Moderna e Contemporanea** (*Via Magenta 31; open Tues–Sun 9–7; adm*) has one of Italy's best collections of modern art, with works by Klee, Chagall, Modigliani, Picasso and others.

Basilica di Superga

From Corso Casale, take bus no.79 northeast along the Po.

Juvarra's Baroque masterpiece, the Basilica di Superga, was built atop a commanding 2,205ft hill on the fringes of the town to fulfil a vow made by Vittorio Amedeo II during the French siege of Superga (1706). Two fine towers flank a magnificent drum dome, set above a deep neoclassical porch; the crypt holds the tombs of Vittorio Amedeo II and subsequent kings of Sardinia, and the views stretch across to the Alps.

Day Trips from Turin

Vercelli and its Rice Paddies

Vercelli is surrounded by an endless patchwork of paddies, dating back to the 15th century. In summer, they become magical, an irregular chequerboard of mirrors bordering on the abstract. As a minor 'city of art', Vercelli is an old, atmospheric place, and its chief marvel, the **Basilica di Sant'Andrea**, looms up just across from the station. Begun in 1219 by Cardinal Guala Bicchieri, it was completed using money given to Bicchieri by Henri III to thank him for his aid in obtaining the throne. Though basically Romanesque, signs of the new Gothic style from the Île-de-France whisper in Sant'Andrea's twin bell towers, the flying buttresses, the vaulting and the plan of the church. Beyond the Romanesque portals, the lofty interior is majestic and striking in its simple red and white decoration, while the lovely cloister, with its cluster columns and sculptural details, offers the best view of the unusual cupola and the basilica's Romanesque and Gothic features.

Vercelli's grand 16th-century **cathedral**, a short way away in the Piazza Sant'Eusebio, has an especially valuable library of *codices*, including 11th-century Anglo-Saxon poems. From here, Via Duomo leads past the **Castello d'Amedeo**, then to Via Gioberti and Via Borgogna, site of the **Pinacoteca Borgogna** (*open Tues–Fri 3–5.30, Sat and Sun 9.30–12; adm*), featuring works by Vercelli's 16th-century school of painters: most famously Il Sodoma, Gaudenzio and Defendante Ferrari. Gaudenzio's masterpiece, the *Madonna of the Oranges*, is among the famous series of his frescoes (1529–33), which adorn **San Cristoforo** on Via Lucca.

Via Borgogna gives on to old Vercelli's main street, the Corso Libertà, distinguished by the lovely courtyard of the 15th-century **Palazzo Centori** at no.204. The Corso continues to the main Piazza Cavour and then on into the newer part of town, where, in Piazza Zumaglini, rice prices are decided in the **Borsa Risi**.

Getting There

The best way to reach Vercelli is by rail. Frequent **trains** (around two each hour) travel to Vercelli on the Turin–Milan line, taking about 1hr.

Tourist Information

Vercelli: Viale Garibaldi 90, **t** 0161 58002, **f** 0161 257 899.

Market Day

Markets are held in the Piazza Cavour under the Palazzo Municipio.

Eating Out

Il Paiolo, Via Garibaldi 72, **t** 0161 250 577 (*expensive*). The province isn't known for its cuisine in spite of its rice, but you can dine well on hearty *risotti* at 'the cauldron'. *Closed Thurs.*

*****Il Giardinetto**, Via Sereno 3, **t** 0161 257 230, **f** 0161 259 311 (*moderate*). Vercelli's little hotel also has an attractive restaurant and bar, serving dishes such as *carpaccio di razza con fave*, onion soup and *filetto di manzo in casseruola* (beef casserole) mushrooms and plenty of local cheeses. *Closed Mon and 9–24 Aug.*

Asti

Former rival of Milan, Asti is an old and noble city. Although today synonymous with fizzy wine, the town's greatest pride is its poet, Vittorio Alfieri (1749–1803); Corso Alfieri is the main street, and all of the sites are within a block of its length. At its end, the 15th-century church and cloister of **San Pietro in Consavia** (*open April–Sept Tues–Sun 10–1 and 3–7; Oct–Mar Tues–Sun 10–1 and 3–6*) houses a small archaeological collection. More intriguing, however, is its round baptistry, perhaps as old as the 10th century, supported by eight thick columns with cubic capitals.

Six streets further west, the Corso passes by the large **Piazza Alfieri**, in front of the **Campo del Palio**, the scene of Asti's bare-back horse race (*see* Festivals, below). A short way from Piazza Alfieri is the attractive Romanesque-Gothic **Collegiata di San Secondo**, home of the relics of Asti's patron saint, the *Palio Astigiano* (the banner awarded at the horse race) and a polyptych by Asti's greatest Renaissance artist, Gandolfino d'Asti. Medieval towers loom over the rooftops: the tall, elegant **Torre Troyana**, and further down, the swallowtail merlins of the **Torre Comentina**; beyond that rises the octagonal **Torre dei De Regibus**. Nearby is the Gothic **cathedral**, a 14th-century monument with Baroque frescoes, paintings by Gandolfino d'Asti and Holy Water stoups constructed from Roman and Romanesque capitals.

Back on the Corso, Vittorio has a wild-eyed bust and a whole museum devoted to him in the **Casa Alfieri** (*Corso Alfieri 375; closed for restoration; ask at the tourist office for an update*). Opposite, on Via Mazzini, the **Palazzo Malabayla** is the city's finest Renaissance palace. Asti's Corso comes to end by another medieval tower, the **Torre Rossa**, an unusual cylinder on a Roman foundation, with a chequerboard crown.

Getting There

Frequent **trains** serve Asti from Turin's Porta Nuova station, taking 30mins–1hr.

Tourist Information

Asti: Piazza Alfieri 29, **t** 0141 530 357, **f** 0141 538 200.

Festivals

Asti's **Palio** (*third Sun in Sept*) combines medieval pageantry, daredevil riding, and much feasting and celebration. A tradition of neighbourhood rivalry dating back to 1275, it was revived in 1967 and coincides with Asti's great **wine fair**. A week beforehand, the *Festival delle Sagre* sees people parade in 19th-century costumes, and recreate cooking and working practices of that era. Their produce is on sale in the Campo del Palio.

Eating Out

Asti ✉ 14100

Gener Neuv, Lungo Tanaro 4, **t** 0141 557 270 (*very expensive*). Overlooking the river, this is an elegant gourmet haven where you can enjoy a superb *menu* based on traditional Piemontese fare and prepared in an imaginative and exquisite manner. The desserts are light and beautiful; the list of Piemontese wines matchless. Book ahead. *Closed Mon and Aug.*

Falcon Vecchio, Via Mameli 9, **t** 0141 593 106 (*moderate*). Another favourite haunt, set in a wonderfully atmospheric old building; all the dishes are *tipici Astigiani* – try the truffles or local meats. *Closed Sun eve and Mon.*

Monna Laura Pizzeria, Via Cavour 30, **t** 0141 594 159 (*cheap*). This place buzzes at the weekends with people who come for the well-prepared if standard fare. *Closed Mon.*

Overnighter from Turin

Varallo and Sacro Monte

Varallo is a fine, friendly town embraced by wooded slopes; the River Sesia froths and tumbles here, making for exciting white-water kayaking. A good **Pinacoteca**, with works by the Vercelli school, shares space with the Natural History Museum in the **Palace of Museums** (*t 0163 51424; open June–Sept Tues–Sun 10–12.30 and 2–6; Oct–May by request; adm*). There's also a fine church, **San Gaudenzio**, artistically piled up on top of a stair, housing a polyptych by Gaudenzio Ferrari. An entire wall of his work, depicting the Life of Christ, decorates the church of **Santa Maria delle Grazie**, at the foot of the steps up to Sacro Monte.

A very stiff walk (or cable car ride) will bring you to **Sacro Monte**, Varallo's five-star attraction, with singularly beautiful views over the lush woodlands. It was founded as the Sanctuary of New Jerusalem in 1491 by the Blessed Bernardo Caimi, who wanted to recreate the Holy Shrines of Palestine. The idea caught the fancy of St Charles Borromeo, the Archbishop of Milan, and when the two holy men were done, the result is nothing tub-thumping less than the Disneyland of the Counter-Reformation: 45 chapels, set in beautifully manicured grounds, containing the world's first dioramas: 16th-century 3D scenes from the Bible with fresco backgrounds, featuring some 1,000 statues and 4,000 painted figures. More holy hills of this genre crop up around the lakes of Lombardy (*see* p.73 and p.75).

When you can pull yourself from this sincere but slightly nutty extravaganza, visit the **Piazzale della Basilica**, a little gem of porticoes, palm trees and a fountain under a pavilion. The Basilica itself is a gilded explosion of Baroque; the crypt, its walls covered in heart-rending tributes to dead children, provides the final flourish of religious fervour.

Getting There and Around

Buses from Turin's Porta Susa station serve Varallo (more frequently in summer), taking 2hrs. **Shuttle buses** to Sacro Monte leave from Varallo's train station.

Tourist Information

Varallo: Corso Roma 38, **t** 0163 51280, **f** 0163 53091.

Where to Stay and Eat

Varallo ✉ **13019**

*****Albergo Italia**, Corso Roma 6, **t** 0163 51106, **f** 0163 54145 (*moderate*). A former Ursuline convent until the 18th century, this has hosted kings and noblemen in Belle Epoque splendour and its rooms retain some of its original architectural features. There's also a pleasant garden and a restaurant serving typical Valsesian fare.

*****Vecchio Albergo Sacro Monte**, Loc. Sacro Monte 3, **t** 0163 54254 (*moderate*). Built in 1594, this attractive hotel offers pleasant, fully renovated rooms with bath, TV and phone, but has not lost its old-fashioned charm. The restaurant serves typical local specialities. *Open Mar–Oct.*

***Monte Rosa**, Via Regaldi 4, **t/f** 0163 51100 (*cheap*). A wonderful little family-run hotel. Behind the red façade wait large, old-fashioned, beautifully furnished rooms, with balconies and lovely views.

Touring from Turin

Day 1: Chivalric Castles and Alpine Heights

Morning: Take the A5 north of Turin, entering the semi-autonomous Valle d'Aosta at **Pont-St-Martin**, a fine old town with a remarkable bridge from the 1st century BC. From here, go along the S322 through the narrow Gorge de Bard to the old town of **Verrès**, at the junction of the Val d'Ayas, defended by the massive **Castello di Verrès** (*open Mar–June and Sept 9–7; July and Aug 9–8; Oct–Mar 10–12.30 and 1.30–5; closed Tues; adm*). More enchanting is the nearby residence of the Challant lords, just across the river in Issogne: the **Castello di Issogne** (*open Oct–Mar 10–12.30 and 3.30–5; Mar–Aug 9–8*) has a frescoed courtyard that lacks only knights dallying by the fountain; the upper apartments, with their period furnishings and tapestries, are equally evocative.

Lunch: In Issogne, or Verrès, *see* below.

Afternoon: Drive north through the thick pines and chestnut groves of the Val d'Ayas, a walker's paradise dotted with traditional Alpine chalets and ruined castles. From Brusson, the road climbs steeply to **Champoluc**, where you can take the cable car to the slopes just below **Testa Grigia** (10,875ft), one of the grandest belvederes of the western Alps. An ascent to the summit (*guide recommended*) is rewarded with a breathtaking view of Gran Paradiso and Monte Rosa, towering over a sea of peaks.

Dinner and Sleeping: In Champoluc, *see* below.

Day 1

Lunch in Issogne

Al Maniero, 50m from the castle, **t** 0125 929 219 (*cheap*). A friendly restaurant serving typical *valdostano* cuisine, with an emphasis on its home-made pastas and desserts. *Closed Mon.*

Lunch in Verrès

Da Pierre, Via Martorey 73, **t** 0125 929 376 (*expensive*). Elegant dining, with a menu that varies by season, as does the favoured spot to dine – in winter by the blazing hearth, in summer in the garden. Try the *agnolotti alla savoiarda* and venison in blueberry sauce, topped off by a warm slice of apple pie smothered in cream. *Closed Tues.*

Dinner and Sleeping in Champoluc

Quite often your best bet for dining is in the hotel restaurants.

***Villa Anna Maria**, Via Croues 5, **t** 0125 307 128, **f** 0125 307 884 (*expensive*). A lovely old mountain chalet, brimful of charm and simple, rustic bonhomie in a magnificent setting; the food is also delicious. *Open all year.*

***Castor**, Via Ramey 2, **t** 0125 307 117, **f** 0125 308 040 (*moderate*). An enchanting setting in Champoluc, with breathtaking views of Monte Rosa, panelled rooms with all mod cons, plenty of space and a very nice restaurant (*moderate*). English-run. *Open all year.*

***Hotel de Champoluc**, Via Ramey 65, **t** 0125 308 088, **f** 0125 307 985 (*moderate*). Located right by the ski slopes, this is a modern place with all the facilities you might wish for, including satellite TV and a fully equipped fitness centre, solarium and whirlpool. *Open all year.*

***Hotel Breithorn**, Via Ramey 27, **t** 0125 308 734, **f** 0125 308 398 (*moderate*). This long-established hotel dates from 1903 but has recently been beautifully renovated; its stylish, comfortable rooms have wood-beamed ceilings and there's a Turkish bath, jacuzzi and sauna.

Day 2: Healing Waters, Walks and the Matterhorn

Morning: Drive back down the Val d'Ayas to the crossroads at **Brusson**. Turn right to drive through the scenic pine forests of the Colle di Joux to **St Vincent**, an élite albeit slightly shabby spa for the rich and dissipated since the 18th century, boasting more than a mild climate and waters these days, with one of Europe's largest casinos (*open all year daily 3pm–3am; adm exp, half price weekdays; hotel guests usually get in for free; bring your passport*). Besides one-armed bandits, St Vincent offers excursions through the chestnut groves to **St Germain Castle** in Montjovet; or up the funicular to the **Terme di St Vincent**, a health spa built around a mineral spring, the *Fons Salutis*; or you can make a cultural call at St Vincent's frescoed Romanesque **church** (*closed 12–2*), built over the baths of a Roman villa.

Lunch: In St Vincent, *see* below.

Afternoon: Take the road to **Châtaillon** and turn right towards Italy's picture window on the Matterhorn, **Valtournenche**. The valley capital, it is the hometown of the renowned Matterhorn guides – memorial plaques posted around the church are a grim reminder of the dangers they face. Catch a cable car up the **Cime Bianche**, or take a dramatic walk along the specially constructed galleries through the **Gouffre des Buserailles**, a narrow gorge carved out by the River Marmore above Crépin. The valley road ends at sparkling, smart **Breuil-Cervinia**, one of Italy's most renowned ski resorts, enjoying a uniquely grand setting – the Matterhorn to the north, the sweep of the **Grandes Murailles** to the west, and the **Fruggen Massif** to the east.

Dinner and Sleeping: In Breuil-Cervinia, *see* below.

Day 2

Lunch in St Vincent

Batezar da Renato, Via Marconi 1, **t** 0166 513 164 (*very expensive*). The place to celebrate a lucky streak at the roulette tables: in easy walking distance of the casino, with such delicacies as salmon mousse flavoured with wild fennel, duck with peaches, or pigeon stuffed with *funghi*, and a classy wine list. *Closed Wed, May and late June to mid-July.*

Le Grenier, Piazza Monte Zerbion 1, **t** 0166 512 224 (*expensive*). In an old granary, this serves *valdostano* specialities, including fresh fish, fondues and pasta, all washed down by local and Piemontese wines. *Closed for lunch Tues and Wed, also 10–26 Jan and 1–15 July.*

La Rosa Bianca, Via Chanoux 38, **t** 0166 512 691 (*moderate*). On a more modest note, you can try this small friendly diner in the centre.

Dinner and Sleeping in Breuil-Cervinia

******Cristallo**, Viale del Piolet 6, **t** 0166 943 411, **f** 0166 948 377 (*luxury*). The top hotel here, standing above the town in all its smart, modern glory. It has bold bright colours and styling, extremely comfortable rooms, a sauna, indoor swimming pool for rainy days and tennis courts. *Closed June and Sept–Nov.*

****Les Neiges d'Antan**, **t** 0166 948 775, **f** 0166 948 852 (*expensive*). The superbly named 'Snows of Yesteryear', 4km away at Perrères, is a pretty chalet in tranquil surroundings where the resort's skyscrapers are hidden from view. The **restaurant** (also *expensive*) is the best in the area, so even if you don't stay at the hotel you may decide to drop by for a traditional meal of salt beef, polenta, cheeses, Valdostana wines and home-made desserts. *Open Dec–May and July–mid-Sept.*

La Maison de Saussure, behind the church, **t** 0166 948 259 (*expensive–moderate*). The place to come for wholesome mountain fare such as polenta and *camoscio* (chamois). They have a fine selection of local spirits, including *grappa*, and you can sit out on a terrace in summer. *Open eves only Mon–Thurs Nov–May.*

Day 3: More Mountain Views and a Fairy Castle

Morning: Breuil-Cervinia dates from the 1930s, and although it may look like a frontier boom town, the mountains are everything, with 190km of ski runs, and summer skiing on the glacier at **Plateau Rosa** (11,482ft); a cable car and lift from here can take you to the top of **Piccolo Cervino** (12,739ft), from where fantastic ski trails continue down to Zermatt, or along the valley to Valtournenche. Other winter sports on offer are ice skating, bob-sledding and hockey. An easy hike from Plateau Rosa takes you over the Colle Superiore delle Cime Bianche, either to emerald **Lago Goillet** and its view encompassing the Val d'Ayas, or to the summit of the **Breithorn** (13,684ft).

Lunch: In Breuil-Cervinia, *see* below.

Afternoon: Drive back down the valley to Châtaillon and turn right onto the S26 towards Aosta. The road passes **Chambave**, under a crag draped with the ruined **Castello di Cly**; the surrounding vineyards produce a prized golden dessert wine called Passito di Chambave. More wine and modest tourism are the industries of **Nus**, the next town, where the medieval Viscounts of Aosta built their **Castello di Fénis** (*open Mar–June and Sept 9–7; July and Aug 9–8; Oct–Mar 10–12.30 and 1.30–5; closed Tues only Oct–Feb; adm*). More of a residence than a fortress, this is a genuine fairy-tale castle, all turrets and swallowtail crenellations, its rooms and alcoves filled with medieval and modern furniture. It all culminates in a beautiful courtyard with wooden balconies and a 15th-century fresco. From Nus you can visit two remote valleys – the **Val Clavalité**, or the **Val St-Barthélemy** – or continue 13km to Aosta.

Dinner and Sleeping: In Aosta, *see* below.

Day 3

Lunch in Breuil-Cervinia

Le Bistrot de L'Abbé, **t** 0166 949 060 (*moderate*). A typical *valdostano* bistro/wine bar, serving raclette and *fondue* alongside a decent selection of wines. *Closed Mon.*

Alternatively, pop into **Alimentari Furggen** (**t** 0166 948 904; *closed Thurs in low season*) or **Macelleria Marquis**, Piazza Jumeaux, (**t** 0166 949 556; *closed Thurs and Sun afternoon in low season*) to pick up a *valdostano* picnic of fine charcuterie, cheese and wine.

Dinner in Aosta

Vecchia Aosta, Piazza Porta Praetoria 4, **t** 0165 361 186 (*moderate*). This is built into the Roman walls, with the most striking dining room in town. The food is good, too; home-made pasta, cured venison, trout with almonds – and lots of wines to help it down. *Closed Wed and two weeks in Feb and Nov.*

Papa Marcel's, off the main drag on Via Croix de Ville. Good place for a nightcap – the only place with any character, with graffiti all over the walls and hundreds of bottles full of weird liquids on the shelves. A must.

Sleeping in Aosta

********Europe**, Via Ribitel 8, **t** 0165 236 363, **f** 0165 40566 (*expensive*). An excellent, friendly hotel in the centre, with all mod cons, as well as a restaurant and piano bar.

*****Rayon de Soleil**, above Aosta in Saraillon, Viale Gran San Bernardo, **t** 0165 262 247, **f** 0165 236 085 (*moderate*). A pleasant hotel, with fine views, a garden and an indoor pool. *Closed Oct–mid-Dec.*

*****Bus**, Via Malherbes 18, **t** 0165 236 958, **f** 0165 236 962 (*moderate*). Back in town, a good choice in a quiet street off Via Aubert, with comfortable, tastefully decorated rooms and a good restaurant (*cheap*).

***Monte Emilius**, Via G. Carrel 9, **t/f** 0165 35692 (*cheap*). With its lovely/terrible views of mountains/railway tracks, this little gem has some large Art Deco-style rooms with balconies. The restaurant is also good.

Day 4: Aosta and the Gran Paradiso Massif

Morning: Enchanting mountains wrap Aosta in a great, shimmering blueness at the crossroads of France and Switzerland; there's more French spoken here than Italian. Explore its charming core, scattered with grand Roman monuments and medieval towers. In Place Emile Chanoux is the IVAT, where arts and crafts are displayed; Aosta is renowned for its skilled woodwork. Off the main **Via Sant'Anselmo**, the Romanesque-Gothic hybrid **Collegiata dei SS. Pietro ed Orso** (*open daily April–Sept 9–7; Oct–Mar 10–5*) is famous for rare Ottonian frescoes and for the carved capitals in its cloister (1133). The **Cathedral** features 15th- and 16th-century stained-glass, finely inlaid 15th-century choir stalls and two excellent mosaics. The huge wooden cross is the work of local craftsmen from the end of the 14th century. The **Museo Archeologico** on Piazza Roncas contains some good local finds (*open daily 9–7*).

Lunch: In Aosta, *see* below.

Afternoon: Drive west from Aosta to St Pierre, and turn left into the Val di Cogne. A breathtaking drive leads past the stunning **Grand Eyvia** gorge to the pleasant *comune* of **Cogne**, gateway to the Parco Nazionale del Gran Paradiso, a refuge for ibex, chamois and golden eagles. The flowers are most spectacular in early June, all labelled in the **Giardino Alpino Paradisia** (*open mid-June–mid-Sept 10–5.30; July and Aug until 6.30; adm*) in the lovely **Valnontey** near Cogne. There are well-marked trek routes through the park, from flat meanders to lung-bursting hikes up mountain sides; the Cogne tourist office (36 Place Chanoux) can provide maps and advice.

Dinner and Sleeping: In Cogne, *see* below.

Day 4

Lunch in Aosta

Vecchio Ristoro, Via Tourneuve 4, **t** 0165 33238 (*expensive*). Housed in a windmill that functioned until only a few years ago. The hot *antipasti*, smoked trout and salmon, and an especially good selection of local cheeses are all excellent. *Closed Sun, and Mon lunch.*

Piemonte, Via Porta Praetoria 13, **t** 0165 40111 (*cheap*). A traditional favourite in the heart of town, featuring excellent, home-style Piemontese and French cuisine – *bagna cauda* upon request in the winter, boar steaks in the autumn, *crêpes* and apple pie, all at reasonable prices. *Closed Fri.*

Dinner in Cogne

Lou Ressignon, Via Mines de Cogne, **t** 0165 74034 (*moderate*). Serves good, honest Valdostan specialities in an attractive chalet – chamois (*camoscio*) with *polenta* – topped off by home-made desserts. *Closed Tues and Nov.*

Brasserie du Bon Pec, Rue Bourgeois 72, **t** 0165 749 288 (*moderate*). An excellent cosy little diner where big meaty grills and *fondues* are served by waiters in Cogne national dress. There is an extensive and expensive wine list. It's very popular, so book ahead. *Closed Mon only, Nov–mid-Dec.*

Sleeping in Cogne

********Bellevue****, Rue Grand Paradis 22, **t** 0165 74825, **f** 0165 749 192 (half board *expensive –moderate*). The best location in Cogne, if not all the Valle d'Aosta, with majestic views of a glacial valley – carpeted with flowers in summer and littered with skiers in winter – from the excellent restaurant. It's family-run and the super-friendly staff dress in Cogne traditional costume. There's limousine service, and a pool and jacuzzi in the basement. *Open Christmas hols–Oct.*

*****Sant'Orso**, Via Bourgeois 2, **t** 0165 74821, **f** 0165 749 500 (*moderate*). Enjoys splendid views, at slightly more affordable prices, and has an excellent restaurant (*moderate*).

Day 5: Fortified Valleys and the Apex of the Alps

Morning: Drive back down to St Pierre and head west along the main valley road; pass **Villeneuve**, sprawled under the ruined, 12th-century **Châtel-Argent**, then **Arvier**, which makes a helluva wine, *Vin de l'Enfer*. Charming **Avise**, with two medieval castles, lies at the foot of a romantic gorge, where the **Pierre Taillée** has remains of the Roman road cut into the rock. Above the road to the left, **Derby** has a fine collection of fortified medieval houses, a little Gothic church and a waterfall, the **Cascata di Linteney**. The Valle d'Aosta reaches its climax in **Courmayeur**: at the foot of Mont Blanc, this is perhaps Italy's most fashionable winter and summer resort; the skiing is matchless, the scenery mythic, the facilities among the best in the Alps.

Lunch: In Courmayeur, *see* below.

Afternoon: Take your pick of activities: in winter, there is magnificent downhill and cross-country skiing, ice skating and an indoor swimming pool. In summer there is skiing on the **Colle del Gigante**, rock-climbing, golf, tennis, riding, hang-gliding, fishing and spectacular walks. Take an unforgettable trip on the thrilling cable car from **La Palud**, just north of Courmayeur, to Chamonix over Mont Blanc (*€55, €26 to Punta Helbronner; summer only; returning by bus; passports required*), or go part-way to **Punta Helbronner** (11,358ft), stopping off at an **Alpine botanical garden**. Or take the **Funivia Courmayeur** from the west of town to the **Plan Chécrouit**, and from there up to Col Chécrouit. At the top of town, a little **Alpine museum** (*closed for restoration*) houses the diaries, drawings and equipment of Alpine pioneers.

Dinner and Sleeping: In Courmayeur, or splurge on a meal in La Palud, *see* below.

Day 5

Lunch in Courmayeur

Ristorante Pierre Alexis 1877, Via Marconi 54, **t** 0165 843 517 (*expensive–moderate*). This offers refined Italian cuisine, including venison and duck in creative, fruity sauces, as well as a good selection of home-made desserts. *Closed Mon and low season.*

Pizzeria-Ristorante Du Tunnel, Via Circonvallazione 80, **t** 0165 841 705 (*cheap*). A warm rustic place which prides itself on simple but well-prepared regional fare, and above all for traditional wood-fired pizzas. *Closed Wed off season, two weeks June and two weeks Nov.*

Du Parc, Via Circonvallazione 88, **t** 0165 844 609 (*cheap*). Nearby, this serves both international and regional dishes. *Closed Thurs.*

Dinner in La Palud

Maison de Filippo, **t** 0165 869 797, **f** 0165 869 719 (*moderate*). *The* place to dine: people come over the border to feast at this jovial temple of Alpine cuisine. The rustic décor is charming – but not fussy – and in summer you can dine in the garden. The food, from the *antipasti*, to ravioli stuffed with porcini, to fondue, trout or game, and the *grand dessert finale*, is all delicious. *Closed Tues.*

Dinner and Sleeping in Courmayeur

Reservations are a must at Christmas, Easter, July, Aug, and second week Feb–end Mar.

****Royal E Golf**, Via Roma 87, **t** 0165 831 611, **f** 0165 842 093 (*very expensive*). This has all the facilities and service you could wish for, and the views are fantastic, especially from the excellent restaurant. Rooms are beautifully furnished and there's an indoor pool and piano bar. *Open Dec–April and July–Sept.*

*****Del Viale**, Viale Monte Bianco, **t** 0165 846 712, **f** 0165 844 513 (*expensive*). An old-fashioned chalet with nice views. The folksy lobby and restaurant have stripped wooden floors and an open fire. Most rooms have a balcony or terrace. *Closed May, Oct and Nov.*

Venezia, Via Delle Villette 2, **t/f** 0165 842 461 (*cheap*). Large rooms with fantastic views.

Liguria

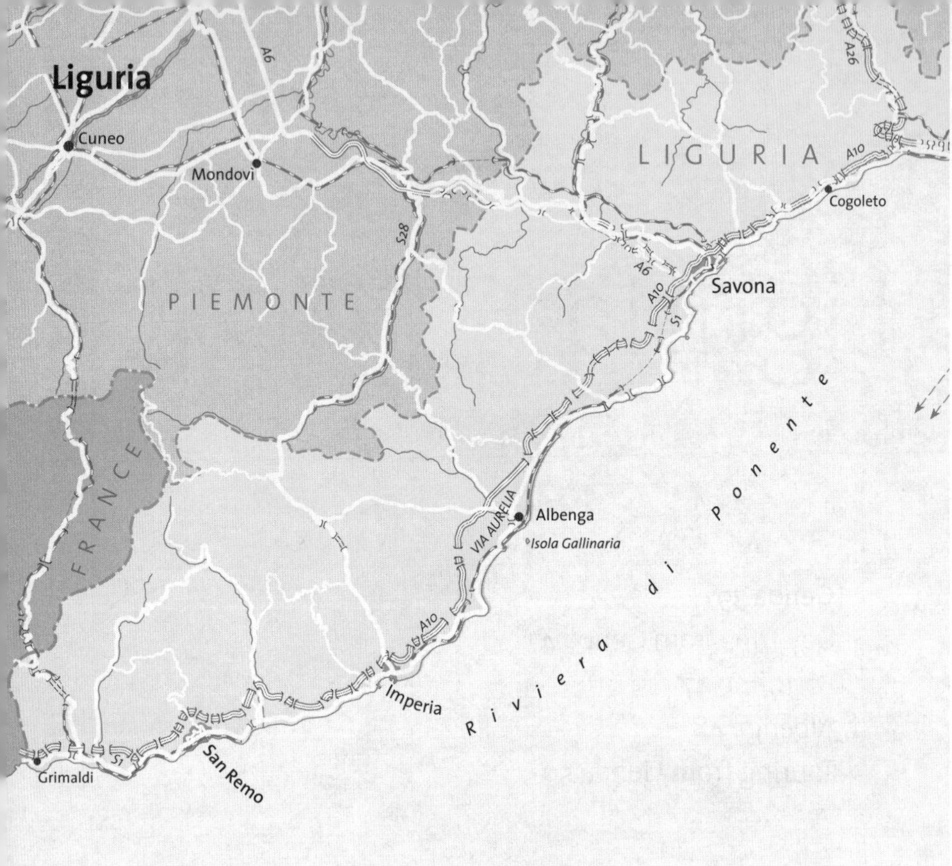

'Riviera' in Italian simply means shore, but in Liguria the shore is *the* Riviera, a rugged, rock-bound rainbow of coast linking France to Tuscany, endowed with one of the rarer Italian commodities: beautiful beaches. Rather than large, buxom, sandy beaches, these are usually refined, slender strands in magical settings – beneath steep cliffs and hanging gardens, backed by old fishing towns squeezed between the rock, or palm-fringed resorts that fit like an old pair of shoes.

Sheltered by the Maritime Alps and Apennines from the fogs and chills of the north, Liguria has a sensuous growth of lemons, oranges and flowers; the olive oil from its ancient groves is legendary. Bathed in a luminous, warm light, the Riviera's colours are dazzling, the reds, blues, yellows like glistening newborns. The delights of sun and sea are only part of what the region has to offer. Just a few dozen hairpin turns up into the hinterland, and you're in another world altogether, lush and cool and green; Liguria is the most forested region of Italy. Long isolated from the rest of the country because of the mountains, Liguria has a distinct identity all its own. After the Crusades, the Republic of Genoa grew to become a seapower and east-west wheeler-dealer rivalled only by Venice, and in the 17th century it became the wealthiest corner of Europe. Such experiences shaped the Ligurian character; tough, shrewd, adventurous and independent. Columbus, of course, came from Liguria, as did the great admiral Andrea Doria, and the Risorgimento heroes Garibaldi and Mazzini.

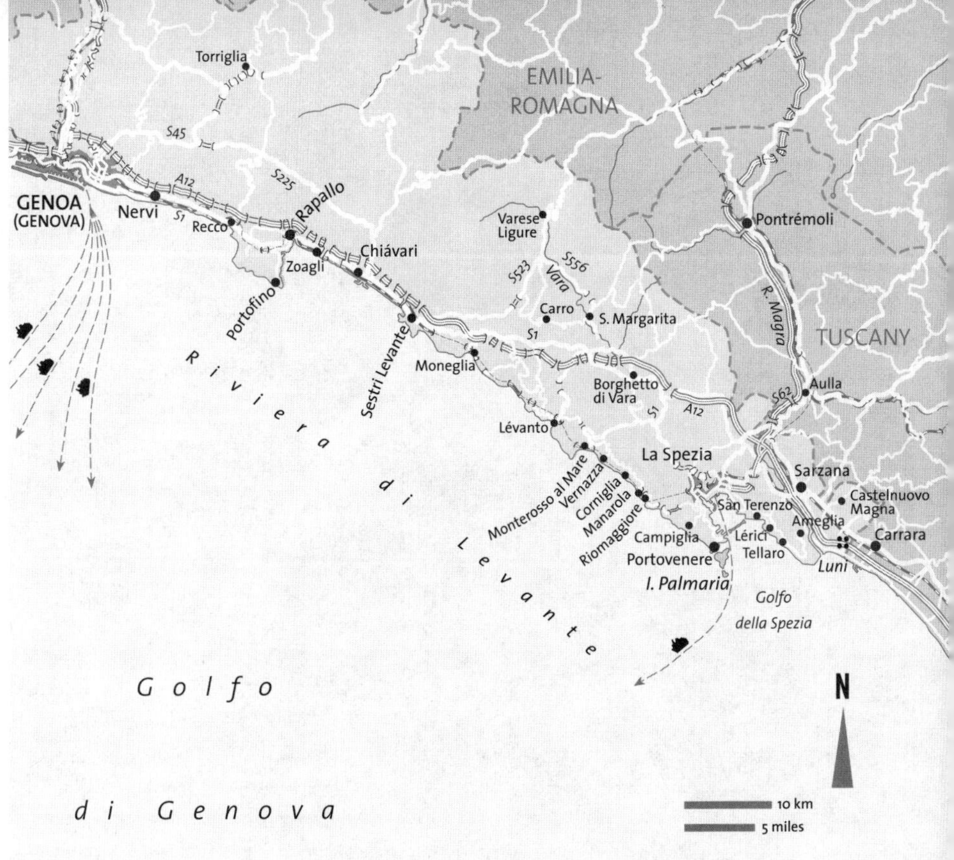

Genoa (Genova)

There's always a tingling air of excitement, unexpected fortune or sudden disaster in real port cities. Genoa is Italy's largest port, and it has allowed any scenic potential to be snuffed out by the more pressing affairs of its sea trade. But behind the godawful elevated highway, huge docks and stacks of containers, dishevelled alleys wind about, lined with typical piquant portside establishments catering to weaselly old men of indeterminate nationality and discreetly tattooed ladies. Counterbalancing this fragrant zone of stevedores is the Genoa that Wagner, Dickens and countless others have marvelled at, Petrarch's 'Superb City' of palaces, gardens and art; the city whose merchant fleet once reigned supreme from Spain to the Black Sea; the New York City of the late 16th and 17th centuries, flowing with money and populated by entrepreneurs. Modern Genoa (pop. 680,000) is a kinetic antidote to the Riviera's resortarama. Even its impossible topography is exciting: tunnels bore under its very centre, penthouses hang over the hills at street level, and the old quarter is a vertical warren of *caruggi* – miniature canyons under eight-storey tenements, streaming with banners of laundry. There are stately streets of late-Renaissance and Baroque palaces, fine art collections and one of the most amazing cemeteries on earth. And, since the 1992 Columbus exhibition, Genoa has a new razzmatazz, concentrated in the Porto Antico.

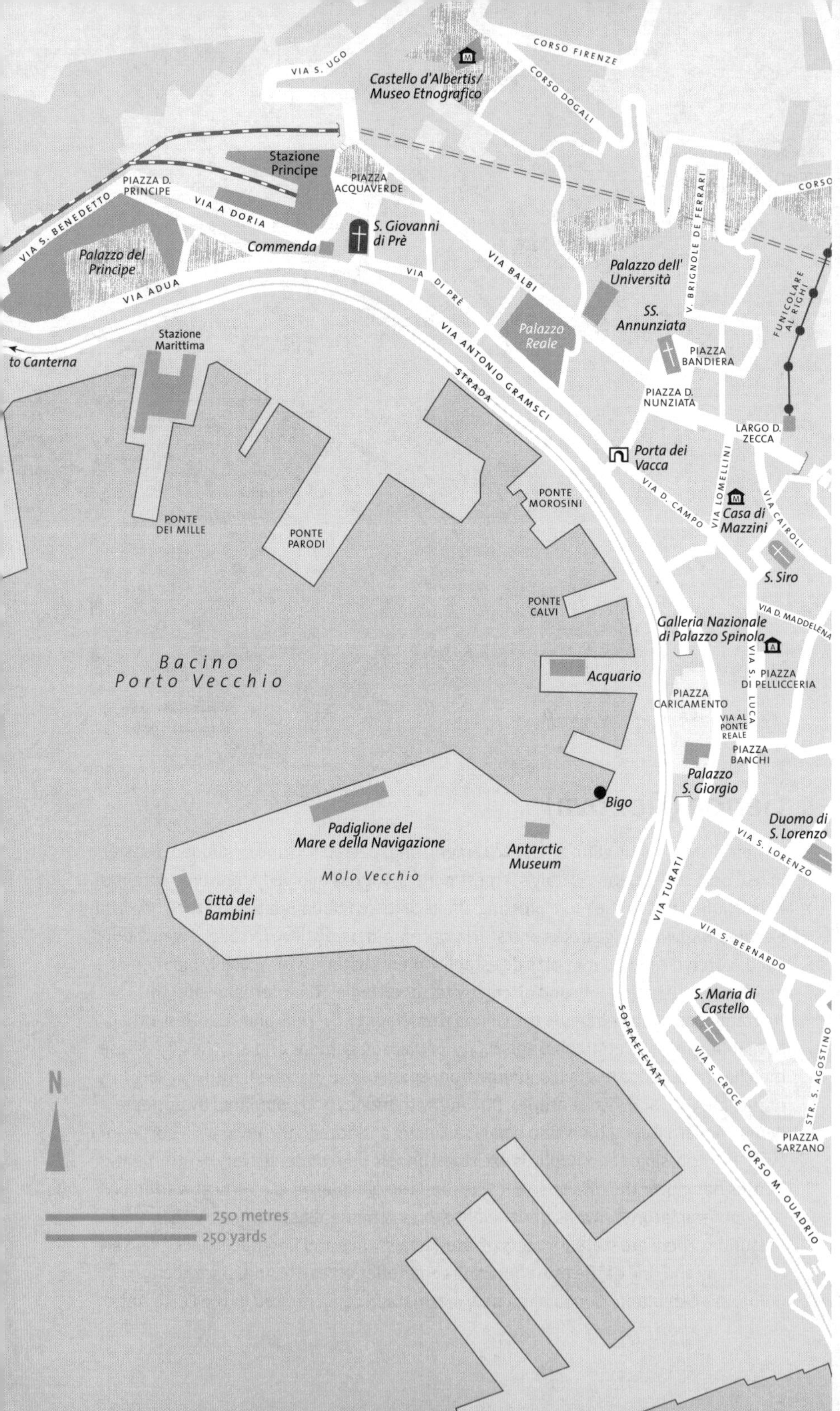

VIA S. UGO
Castello d'Albertis/
Museo Etnografico
CORSO FIRENZE
CORSO DOGALI
Stazione
Principe
PIAZZA D.
PRINCIPE
VIA S. BENEDETTO
VIA A DORIA
PIAZZA
ACQUAVERDE
S. Giovanni
di Prè
Commenda
Palazzo del
Principe
VIA ADUA
VIA DI PRÈ
VIA BALBI
Palazzo dell'
Università
V. BRIGNOLE DE FERRARI
CORSO
FUNICOLARE
AL RIGHI
SS.
Annunziata
Palazzo
Reale
PIAZZA
BANDIERA
Stazione
Marittima
to Canterna
VIA ANTONIO GRAMSCI
STRADA
PIAZZA D.
NUNZIATA
LARGO D.
ZECCA
Porta dei
Vacca
PONTE
MOROSINI
VIA D. CAMPO
VIA LOMELLINI
Casa di
Mazzini
VIA CAIROLI
PONTE
DEI MILLE
PONTE
PARODI
S. Siro
PONTE
CALVI
VIA D. MADDELENA
Galleria Nazionale
di Palazzo Spinola
Bacino
Porto Vecchio
Acquario
VIA S. LUCA
PIAZZA
DI PELLICCERIA
PIAZZA
CARICAMENTO
VIA AL
PONTE
REALE
PIAZZA
BANCHI
Palazzo
S. Giorgio
Bigo
Duomo di
S. Lorenzo
Padiglione del
Mare e della Navigazione
Antarctic
Museum
VIA S. LORENZO
Molo Vecchio
Città dei
Bambini
VIA TURATI
VIA S. BERNARDO
S. Maria di
Castello
SOPRAELEVATA
VIA S. CROCE
STR. S. AGOSTINO
N
PIAZZA
SARZANO
CORSO M. QUADRIO
250 metres
250 yards

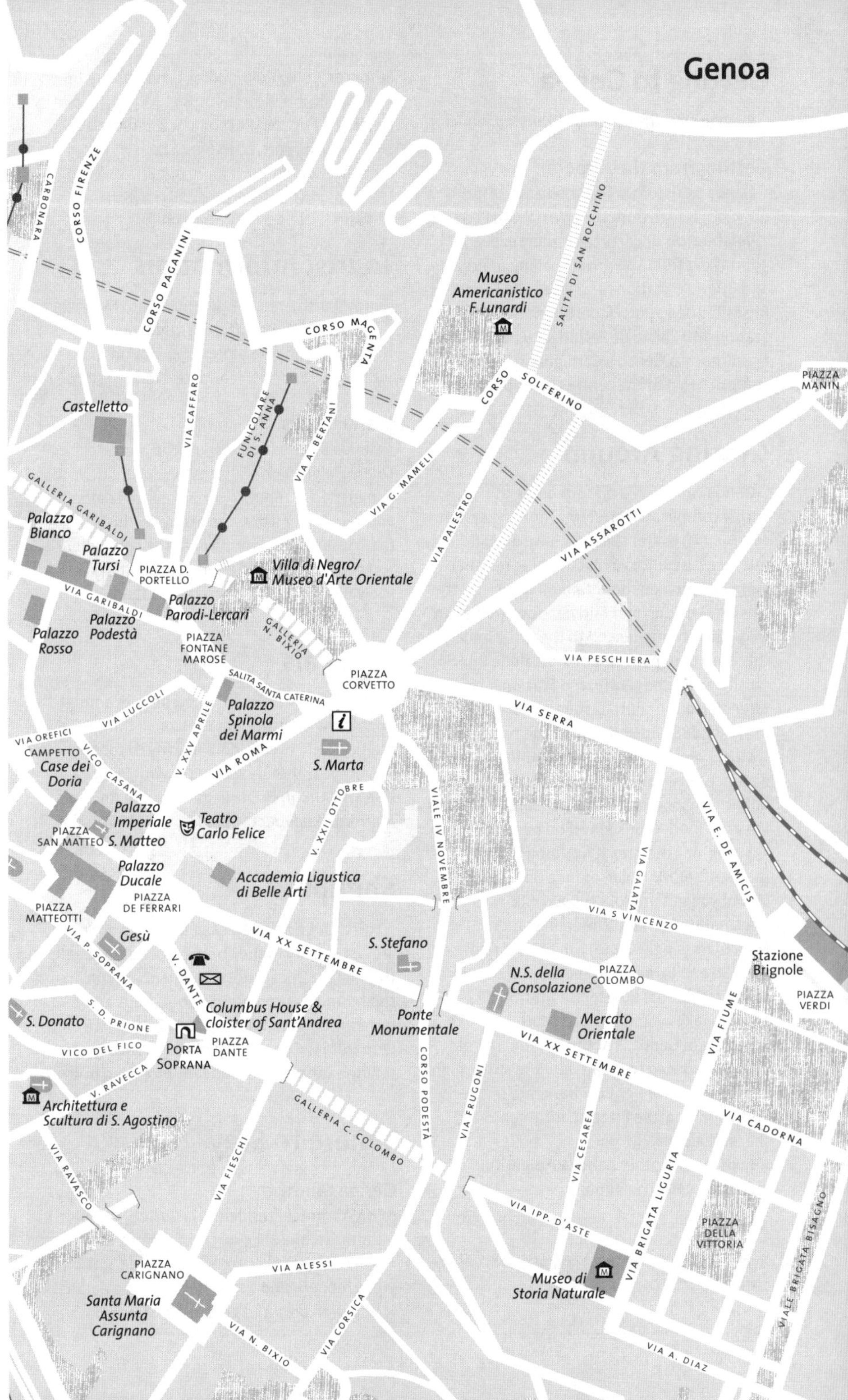

Genoa
Carbonara
Corso Firenze
Corso Paganini
Corso Magenta
Salita di San Rocchino
Museo Americanistico F. Lunardi
Corso Solferino
Piazza Manin
Castelletto
Via Caffaro
Funicolare di S. Anna
Via A. Bertani
Via G. Mameli
Via Palestro
Via Assarotti
Galleria Garibaldi
Palazzo Bianco
Palazzo Tursi
Piazza D. Portello
Villa di Negro/ Museo d'Arte Orientale
Via Garibaldi
Palazzo Parodi-Lercari
Palazzo Podestà
Palazzo Rosso
Galleria N. Bixio
Piazza Fontane Marose
Via Peschiera
Piazza Corvetto
Salita Santa Caterina
Palazzo Spinola dei Marmi
Via Serra
Via Lucoli
Via Orefici
Campetto
Vico Casana
V. XXV Aprile
Via Roma
S. Marta
Case dei Doria
Palazzo Imperiale
Teatro Carlo Felice
Piazza San Matteo
S. Matteo
V. XXII Ottobre
Viale IV Novembre
Via E. De Amicis
Via Galata
Palazzo Ducale
Accademia Ligustica di Belle Arti
Piazza De Ferrari
Piazza Matteotti
Via S Vincenzo
Via P. Soprana
Gesù
Via XX Settembre
S. Stefano
Stazione Brignole
V. Dante
N.S. della Consolazione
Piazza Colombo
Piazza Verdi
Via Fiume
S. Donato
S. D. Prione
Columbus House & cloister of Sant'Andrea
Ponte Monumentale
Mercato Orientale
Vico del Fico
Porta Soprana
Piazza Dante
Corso Podestà
Via Frugoni
V. Ravecca
Architettura e Scultura di S. Agostino
Galleria C. Colombo
Via Cadorna
Via Cesarea
Via Ravasco
Via Fieschi
Via Ipp. D'Aste
Via Brigata Liguria
Piazza della Vittoria
Viale Brigata Bisagno
Piazza Carignano
Via Alessi
Museo di Storia Naturale
Santa Maria Assunta Carignano
Via N. Bixio
Via Corsica
Via A. Diaz

Getting to Genoa

Ryanair flies from London Stansted (2hrs 10).

Getting from the Airport

Genoa's Cristoforo Colombo airport (**t** 010 601 5410) is 6km from the city in Sestri Ponente.

Volabus 100 departs the airport every 30mins (€2 from the driver), calling at Principe and Brignole Stations and Piazza de Ferrari. Buses to the airport depart from Brignole Station and Piazza de Ferrari. City bus 151 links the airport to Genoa's **Cornigliano** train station. A **taxi** to the centre costs approx €14.

Getting Around

Genoa can seem a bit forbidding at first, with a complicated street-numbering system: commercial establishments have a red (r) number; residences a black or blue number. Trapped between mountains and the sea, the city is 30km long and fairly narrow. **Trains** run frequently from one end to the other and there are two main stations: **Stazione Principe**, northwest of the centre, and **Stazione Brignole**, to the southeast (rail information **t** 147 888 088). Bus no.37 links the two.

Most points of interest are within walking distance between the two train stations, but public transport is relatively cheap, and **tickets** are valid for 90 mins' travel on bus (ATM: **t** 010 558 2414, or **t** 010 599 7892), urban FS train, metro, lift or funicular; or for a day. Buy them before you get on from tobacco shops or from information kiosks at the train stations. **Funiculars** (single €0.30) run from Piazza Portello and Largo della Zecca up to the city's upper residential quarters. A **lift** from Piazza Portello takes you up to Castelletto.

Driving in Genoa is not much fun. The old quarter is closed to traffic, and the street plan is chaotic. Convenient **car parks** are by the Porta Soprana, the Piazza Caricamento and the Piazza della Vittoria.

Taxis, on the other hand, are plentiful. For a radio taxi, call **t** 010 5966.

Car Hire

Avis, Via della Casacce 3, **t** 010 650 7280, or at the airport, **t** 010 540 906.

Europcar, Corso Colombo 33, **t** 010 301 447, or at the airport, **t** 010 650 4881.

Hertz, Via Eugenio Ruspoli 1/3r, **t** 010 570 2625, or at the airport, **t** 010 651 2422.

Maggiore, Corso Sardegna 275/281, **t** 010 839 2153, or at the airport, **t** 010 651 2467.

Tourist Information

Genoa: Porto Antico–Palazzina Santa Maria B5, **t** 010 24871, **f** 010 246 7658, *aptgenova@aptgenova.it*. Also at Principe Station, **t** 010 246 2633, and at the airport, **t** 010 241 5247.

Market Days

Genoa's huge **food market**, the Mercato Orientale on Via XX Settembre, is a great place to experience Liguria's cornucopia of seafood and vegetables. For more exotic produce, try the bazaar-like **Sottoripa** near the port, where you can buy shark's fins and ouzo. There's a lively **flea market** in Piazzetta Lavagna.

Festivals

Genoa's premier cultural event is its annual **Boat Show**, a vast celebration of all things nautical held over 10 days in early October.

Every year the city competes with Venice, Pisa and Amalfi in the **Regatta of the Ancient Maritime Republics** (Genoa to host in 2004).

Shopping

You won't find any lack of shops. **Antiques** are a speciality in the streets around Garibaldi; the Palazzo Ducale hosts frequent antique shows and has some good bookshops and fashion showrooms. Drogheria Torielli (Via San Bernardo) is Genoa's last old-fashioned **grocer**, selling exotic Mediterranean spices and nuts.

Where to Stay

Genoa ✉ 16100

******Starhotel President**, Via Corte Lambruschini 4, **t** 010 5727, **f** 010 553 1820 (*very expensive*). In front of Brignole Station; big, modern and super-sleek, it has a palatial reception area and gourmet restaurant.

★★★★**Jolly Hotel Marina**, Molo Ponte Calvi 5, **t** 010 25 391, **f** 010 251 1320, *www.jollyhotels.it* (*very expensive*). New in 2002 and superbly positioned on one of the old port wharves, opposite the aquarium; its elegant rooms have all mod cons, including Internet access.

★★★★**Bristol Palace**, Via XX Settembre 35, **t** 010 592 941, **f** 010 561 756, *astorige@tin.it* (*very expensive*). Near the Carlo Felice theatre, with sumptuous antique furnishings, beautiful rooms (a/c) and a pleasant bar.

★★★★**Savoia Majestic**, Via Arsenale di Terra 5, **t** 010 261 641, **f** 010 261 883, *info@hotel-savoiagenova.com* (*expensive*). An elegant 19th-century place with a charming hall and American-style bar; it has spacious rooms, helpful staff and a big breakfast buffet.

★★★**Agnello d'Oro**, Via Monachette 6, **t** 010 246 2084, **f** 010 246 2327 (*moderate*). Although most of the 17th-century charm is focused in the lobby, the rooms are very comfortable.

★★★**Bellevue**, Salita Providenza 1, **t** 010 246 2400, **f** 010 265 932 (*moderate*). Smart, modern rooms with a/c and a wonderful view of the port, but no restaurant.

The area around Brignole is the better area for budget accommodation; avoid the cheapest places near the port.

★★★**Vittoria & Orlandini**, Via Balbi 33, **t** 010 261 923, **f** 010 246 2656, *vittorin@mbox.vol.it* (*cheap*). A charming, slightly eccentric hotel with comfortable rooms around an inner garden and a pretty breakfast room with views over the old town.

★★**Cairoli**, Via Cairoli 14/4, **t** 010 246 1454, **f** 010 246 7512, *cairoli@rdn.it* (*cheap*). Very central, with sparkling, modern rooms and a relaxed, friendly and personal atmosphere.

Eating Out

Focaccia, topped with olive oil and salt, is sold throughout the city. *Farinata* (made of chick-pea meal, olive oil and water, and baked) and *panissa* (similar, but fried) are a bit more specialized. Genoa's *confetterie* highlight a long love affair with sweets and candied fruit.

Toe Drue, Via Corsi 441, **t** 010 650 0100 (*expensive*). One of the most famous restaurants in Genoa, serving an array of delightful and unusual Ligurian specialities, many featuring seafood. Booking essential.

Zefferino, Via XX Settembre 20, **t** 010 570 5939 (*expensive*). Something of a local institution, run by the same family since 1939, offering a taste of 1960s glamour with its delicious Ligurian dishes and 'transatlantic cuisine' and a huge array of desserts. *Closed Wed.*

Trattoria Da Vittorio, Via Sottoripa 59, **t** 010 247 2927 (*moderate*). If the beautiful displays of fish and shellfish can't entice you in, the fact that half a lobster with linguine, wine and coffee comes in under €20 may do. Book or be prepared to wait. No credit cards.

Archivolto Mongiardino, no.2, in the street of the same name, **t** 010 247 7610 (*moderate*). Excellent seafood, in the maze of streets in the southern old city. *Closed Sun and Mon.*

Mannori, Via Galata 70/r, **t** 010 588 461 (*moderate*). Excellent home cooking: the pots simmer all morning to create hearty soups and other dishes that a good Ligurian *mamma* might make. *Closed Sun and Aug.*

Ostaja Do Castello, Salita Santa Margherita del Castello, **t** 010 246 8980 (*cheap*). Some of the best cheap food in town, with good Genoese specialities. *Closed Sun.*

La Taverna Di Colombo, Vico Della Scienza 6, **t** 010 246 2447 (*cheap*). With a warm, inviting atmosphere and two courses for under €7.50, it's hard to beat this popular tavern.

Da Bedin, Via Dante 56/r, **t** 010 580 996. Famed for its pizza and *farinata*, by Columbus' house.

Antica Sciamadda, Via S. Giorgio 14/r. A classic for local snacks near the old port: *farinata*, pies and *frisceu di baccalà* (fish croquettes).

Profumo, Via del Portello. Has the best *pandolce*.

Pasticceria Traverso, Via Pastorino 116–188/r, **t** 010 745 0065. Founded in 1893, the official supplier of sweets to the Italian Senate; the home-made Paganini chocolates are a must.

The main centre of **café and bar life** is around the Via XX Settembre, though a choice of noisier, seamier places lie around the port.

Entertainment

Paganini's home town has no shortage of music. The Teatro Carlo Felice, in Piazza de Ferrari, is home to the **Genoa Opera** (main season Jan–June), which in summer sponsors the prestigious **Ballet Festival** (**t** 010 589 329 or **t** 010 591 697). A good source of **listings** for entertainment is the daily paper, *Il Secolo XIX*.

Western Genoa: Stazione Principe to Via Garibaldi

Visitors emerge from Genoa's palatial **Stazione Principe** to be greeted by a Statue of Columbus and a view of the port from Piazza Acquaverde. Between here and the port lies the **Palazzo del Principe Doria Pamphili** (*open Sat 3–6, Sun 10–3; adm; guided tours outside opening hours,* **t** *010 255 509*), built for Andrea Doria, Prince of Melfi. The Dorias were Genoa's proudest clan, and Andrea had the palace frescoed with stories of the rulers of Rome and the heroes of the Doria family. In the 1930s the family's private quay was made into the **Stazione Marittima**, an elegantly eclectic departure point for transatlantic liners. West of here, Genoa's slender, 386ft **Lanterna** (*guided tours by appointment only,* **t** *010 246 5396*) welcomed home the fleet in medieval times.

From Piazza Acquaverde, aristocratic **Via Balbi** stretches east towards the old city, lined by stately Baroque residences. The vestibule and courtyard of the remarkable **Palazzo dell'Università** (1630) are an architectural triumph; opposite, the massive yellow and red **Galleria Nazionale di Palazzo Reale** (*open Sun–Tues 9–1.45, Wed–Sat 9–7; adm*) introduces the style to which Genoa's oligarchs became accustomed: hanging gardens and superb mosaics; *quadratura* frescoes; a gallery of mirrors; rooms sprinkled with Gobelin tapestries and paintings by Veronese, Guercino and Van Dyck.

East of here, the **Largo della Zecca** offers a choice of views: take a thrilling funicular ride up to **Righi** for a view of Genoa's hinterlands, or walk through the tunnel to Piazza Portello and take the lift up to the Castelletto belvedere. Alternatively, browse through Via Cairoli's antique shops as it curves round to Genoa's most famous street, **Via Garibaldi**, an elegant Millionaires' Row of uninterrupted late-16th-century *palazzi*. Among them, the **Galleria di Palazzo Bianco** (*No.11; open Tues, Thurs and Fri 9–1, Wed and Sat 9–7, Sun 10–6; closed Mon; adm*) has the city's most noteworthy art collection. A good assortment of Italian paintings includes works by Filippino Lippi, Pontormo and Veronese, and there's an even more impressive collection of Flemish art, particularly Hans Memling's *Christ Blessing* and Gerhard David's *Madonna della Pappa*. Other artists represented include Rubens, Cranach, Van der Goes and Van Dyck, Murillo and Zurbarán. Another section features some of the best canvases by the Genoese.

Across the street at no.18, the **Galleria di Palazzo Rosso** (*under renovation, but still open Tues, Thurs and Fri 9–1, Wed and Sat 9–7, Sun 10–6; adm*) is the apotheosis of Genoese domestic Baroque, with its gilt stucco and woodwork, a hall of mirrors by Filippo Parodi, and frescoes of the Four Seasons by Domenico Piola and Gregorio De Ferrari. Besides excellent portraits of the Brignole family by Van Dyck, there are works by Pisanello, Dürer, Rubens, Veronese and Genoa's Bernardo Strozzi.

Via Garibaldi continues past more fine *palazzi*, each characterized by something different, to the romantic **Piazza delle Fontana Marose**, where the **Palazzo Spinola** (1543) still bears the exterior frescoes once common in Genoa. From the nearby **Piazza Corvetto**, Galleria N. Bixio climbs to the **Villa di Negro**, an urban oasis which takes full advantage of Genoa's crazy topography, with streams, cascades, grottoes and walkways. It culminates at the top with the **Museo d'Arte Orientale** (*open Tues, Thurs, Fri and Sat 9–1; adm*), Italy's finest hoard of Oriental art. Here you'll find a lovely collection of statues, paintings and theatre masks, combined with an extraordinary set of Samurai armour.

Back in Piazza Corvetto, Via Roma leads down to the tumultuous **Piazza de Ferrari**, where the neoclassical **Teatro Carlo Felice** (1829) holds a year-round programme of opera, dance and theatre. Behind the black and white mass of the Palazzo Ducale (*see* below) lies Piazza Matteotti, reached by a monumental staircase.

The Old City

From Piazza de Ferrari you can descend along Via Dante into the skein of medieval Genoa, passing through **Piazza Dante** to the imposing twin-towered **Porta Soprana**, where the **Casa di Colombo** (*guided tours by appointment only,* ***t*** *010 246 5346*) stakes a dubious claim to being Christopher's 'boyhood home'. The old town is ideal for exploring, full of atmosphere and fascinating architectural details. The tall houses are sliced by corridor-like alleys (*caruggi*), many of which live in perpetual shade; some houses have striped white marble and black slate portals, an honour permitted only to families who performed a good deed for the city. Corners and wall niches are decorated with hundreds of little shrines known as *madonnette*, 'little madonnas'. Among the highlights is the 13th-century Gothic monastic church of **Sant'Agostino** (*Via Ravecca; museum open Tues–Sat 9–7, Sun 9–12.30*), its bell tower coated with colourful majolica tiles. The triangular cloisters have been converted into the well-designed museum containing fragments salvaged from Genoa's demolished churches, including the 1312 fragment of the tomb of Margherita of Brabant, wife of Emperor Henry VII, sculpted by Giovanni Pisano. The collection also features Romanesque sculpture, frescoes and later sculptures by the Gagini, Parodi, Pierre Puget and Antonio Canova. To the west, the Roman castle (reached by way of a striking tower house, the **Torre degli Embriaci**) provided the foundations for Genoa's most venerable church, **Santa Maria di Castello**, incorporating Roman columns and stones in its Romanesque structure. Fairest of its artworks is the 15th-century fresco of the *Annunciation* in the cloister, while the strangest is the *Crocifisso Miracoloso* in a chapel near the high altar – miraculous in that the Christ's beard is said to grow whenever Genoa is threatened with calamity.

An alternative entrance into the historic centre from Piazza de Ferrari is by way of Piazza Matteotti, dominated by the yellow and red façade of the **Palazzo Ducale** (*open Tues–Sun 9am–9pm; adm; call to book a guided tour of the* ***Monumental Rooms, t*** *010 562 440; adm exp*), once the seat of Genoa's doges. Beautifully refurbished for 1992, today it is filled by restaurants, bars and shops, and hosts frequent exhibitions. Sharing the square is the 17th-century church of the **Gesù**, its interior a pure Baroque fantasia of lavish stuccoes, frescoes and *trompe-l'œil* stage effects that highlight its frothy treasures: paintings by Rubens, the 'Divino' Guido Reni and Simon Vouet.

Just off Piazza Matteotti stands the jauntily striped **Duomo di San Lorenzo**, begun in the 12th century. Odds and ends from across the centuries embellish the exterior, including an early Gothic carving of St Lawrence toasting on his grill, above the central portal. The rather morose interior also wears jailbird stripes; on the left, the sumptuous **Cappella di San Giovanni Battista** has fine sculptures and marbles by Domenico and Elia Gagini (1451), and a 13th-century sarcophagus that once held the Baptist's relics. In the vaults off the nave to the left, the subterranean **Museo del**

Tesoro della Cattedrale (*open Mon–Sat 9–12 and 3–6; guided tours only, every half hour; adm*) is an Ali Baba-like cavern of genuine treasures: a basin that was part of the dinner service of the Last Supper; the blue chalcedony dish on which John the Baptist's head was served to Salome; the golden, jewel-studded 12th-century Byzantine *Zaccaria Cross*; and an elaborate 15th-century silver casket holding John the Baptist's ashes, which goes on an outing through the city in a procession on 24 June.

North of Piazza Matteotti lies the beautiful **Piazza San Matteo**, completely clothed in the honourable black and white bands of illustrious civic benefactors. This was the public foyer of the Doria family, encompassed by their proud *palazzi*, charming private **cloister**, and the family church of **San Matteo**, rebuilt in the early 14th century along with the rest of the square, and inscribed with their great deeds.

Between Via San Lorenzo and Via Garibaldi

This northern section of the historic centre, built up mostly in the Renaissance, has survived better than the area around Porta Soprana, and has, amid its monuments, fine shops, pubs, restaurants and cafés. From Piazza San Matteo it's a short walk to the **Campetto**, a lovely square adorned with the ornate 16th-century **Palazzo di Gio Imperiale**; in the nearby Piazza Soziglia you can take a break at one of the oldest coffee-houses in Genoa, **Kainguti** (no.98/r), or **Romanegro** (no.74/r), both founded at the beginning of the 19th century. From here, pretty Via degli Orefici meanders down to the ancient core of Genoa, **Piazza Banchi**, where bankers and merchants met in the late-16th-century Renaissance **Loggia dei Mercanti**. Running through the square, **Via San Luca** was the principal thoroughfare of medieval Genoa and home turf of another prominent Genoese family, the Spinola; one of their palaces houses the **Galleria Nazionale di Palazzo Spinola** (*Piazza di Pellicceria; open Tues–Sat 9–7, Sun 2–7*), complete with lavish 16th–18th-century décor. The paintings, still arranged as in a private residence, include Antonello da Messina's sad, beautiful *Ecce Homo*, Joos Van Cleve's magnificent *Adoration of the Magi* and works by Van Dyck, Genoa's masters, and Rubens. The lovely citrus-filled terrace has views over Genoa's slate roofs.

Along the Seafront

West of Piazza Banchi, Via al Ponti Reale descends to the **Piazza Caricamento**, lined with the evocative medieval arcades of Via Sottoripa. In 1298, the Genoese snatched a certain Marco Polo and imprisoned him in the gaudy **Palazzo di San Giorgio**; here he met Rustichello of Pisa, who was to ghostwrite his famous book, *Il Milione* (*The Travels*), of which Columbus possessed a well-thumbed copy. Today's occupants, the Harbour Board, will let you in to see the rooms refurbished in their original 13th-century style.

Seawards from Piazza Caricamento, Genoa's long-neglected old port was dusted off and redeveloped for the 1992 celebrations, and has been expanding ever since. It's tallest attraction is the **Bigo** (Crane; *adm*), which can be scaled on a panoramic lift, but there's also a marina, an ice rink, a giant swimming pool, a huge cinema complex and the **Città dei Bambini** (*open 10–6; closed Mon and Sept; adm*), the largest children's educational play area in Italy, designed for ages 3–14. The **Padiglione del Mare e della Navigazione** (*open Mon–Fri 10.30–6, Sat and Sun 10.30–7; adm*) contains artefacts from 16th- and 17th-century ships, as well as a reconstruction of a medieval shipyard; behind it, the grand military **Porta del Molo-Siberia** (1553) hints at the opulence of the Molo Vecchio, the main quay of old Genoa. There's also Europe's largest **Aquarium** (*www.acquario.ge.it; open Tues–Fri 9.30–6.30, ticket office closes at 5; Sat and Sun 9.30–8pm, ticket office closes at 6.30; adm exp, under 3s free*).

East Genoa

East of Piazza de Ferrari, another side of La Superba awaits in the city's chief shopping street, **Via XX Settembre**, adorned with Liberty-style flourishes and plenty of good old-fashioned neon. The long avenue leads under the **Ponte Monumentale** towards the huge, Fascist-era Piazza della Vittoria; on its way it passes Genoa's main market, the **Mercato Orientale** (1889), occupying the cloister of the 18th-century church **Nostra Signora della Consolazione**.

Staglieno Cemetery

Take bus no.34 from Piazza Acquaverde or Piazza Corvetto; open daily 8–5.

Below Piazza Manin, up along the Torrente Bisagno, is the extraordinary last port for the Genoese, the great **Staglieno Cemetery**. Founded in 1844, the necropolis is so extensive it even has its own internal bus system. The Genoese have a reputation for being canny and tight-fisted, but they have few peers when it comes to post-mortem self-indulgence. Staglieno is a veritable Babylon of the dead, a fantastic, surreal city of miniature cathedrals, Romanesque chapels, Egyptian temples and Liberty-style palaces and statuary. In the centre, Giuseppe Mazzini lies in a simple tomb behind two massive Doric columns, surrounded by inscriptions by Tolstoy, Lloyd George, D'Annunzio, Carducci and others. Mrs Oscar Wilde is buried in the Protestant section.

Day Trips from Genoa

Portofino

One of Italy's most romantic little nooks, **Portofino** was discovered long ago by artists; then by the yachting brotherhood, who fell in love with its delightful little port framed by mellowed, narrow houses; and then by the rich and trendy, who fell in love with its spectacular beauty and seclusion, which made it a favourite setting for illicit trysts, far – or so they hoped – from the clicking cameras of the paparazzi. Linked to the rest of the Riviera only by the narrow coastal road, Portofino is certainly a difficult place to reach. Despite this, its hard-fought-for seclusion vanishes by day in summer when thousands of trippers pour in for an afternoon's window-shopping in the smart boutiques (some selling the district's famous lace), a drink in the exquisite *piazzetta* or a portside bar, or perhaps a walk in the cypress-studded hills. In the evening, the yachtsmen and the residents of the hillside villas descend once again to their old haunts and reclaim Portofino as their own.

Getting There

The Genoa–Pisa **railway** hugs the coast, though often you only get glimpses of the scenery between the tunnels. Frequent trains run from Genoa's Principe station to **Santa Margherita-Ligure** (journey 30mins approx.), from where buses continue to Portofino (18–20mins). There are also trains from Brignole station.

Tourist Information

Portofino: Via Roma 35, **t** 0185 269 024.

Eating Out

Dining here can be a rarefied experience. Most of the restaurants are clustered around the piazza and port; the Hotel Eden and Hotel Splendido Mare also have good restaurants.

Il Pitosforo, Molo Umberto I 9, **t** 0185 269 020 (*very expensive*). The Ligurian cuisine is among the finest anywhere, whether you order *bouillabaisse*, spaghetti with prawns and mushrooms, the red mullet or sea bream with olives. A tree grows out of the middle of the dining room, and one whole wall is lined with a collection of spirits from around the world that will make any serious drinker's eyes glaze over in delight. Every night at 10pm all the lights are switched off to highlight the magical view of the golden lights in the port. *Closed Tues*.

Da Puny, Piazza Martire Olivetta 7, **t** 0185 269 037 (*expensive*). Delicious pasta and seafood to start, and well-prepared main fish dishes, such as sea bass baked in salt. *Closed Thurs*.

Taverna del Marinaio, Piazza Martire Olivetta 36, **t** 0185 269 103 (*moderate*). By no means cheap, but this is as reasonable a place as you'll find here, serving excellent fish and pasta. *Closed Tues*.

Portofino's name is derived from the Roman *Portus Delphini*, which had a *mithraeum* (an initiatory sanctuary dedicated to the Persian god Mithras) on its isthmus. On the site stands the church of **San Giorgio**, housing the supposed relics of the defrocked St George; as often as not there's a cat sleeping on the altar. Further up, **Castello Brown** (*open Tues–Sun 10–6; adm*), built in the 1500s as a defence against the Turks, converted into a residence, then reconverted into a castle, affords enchanting views of the little port. Another lovely walk, beyond the castle, is to Punta del Capo and the old lighthouse, taking in magnificent views of the Gulf of Tigullio through the pine forest.

Albenga

Albenga is the most historic and interesting town on the Riviera del Ponente, owing its centuries of good fortune and prestige to the river Cento and its tributaries, which formed the most fertile alluvial plain in all Liguria. Originally a port, Albenga's harbour shifted with the course of the Cento river, and nowadays the town stands a kilometre from the sea, using the fertile soil of the old river bed in which to grow asparagus.

Albenga's evocative and urbane centre retains its *castrum* grid plan from Roman times. Via Enrico d'Aste was the Roman *decumanus* and Via Medaglio d'Oro the *cardo*. The beautiful main square, **Piazza San Michele**, was for centuries the seat of civil and spiritual authority, all in the shadow of an impressive collection of 13th-century brick towers. Few Italian cities have preserved so many of these proto-skyscrapers (a dozen, of which seven are perfectly intact). Thanks to the marshy soil, three stand like tipsy bridesmaids around the elegant campanile (1391) of the Romanesque **Cattedrale di San Michele**, within which is a Carolingian crypt and an enormous 19th-century organ.

Steps from the nearby **Loggia Comunale** (1421) lead down to Albenga's celebrated 5th-century **baptistry** (*open Tues–Sun 10–12 and 3–6*). Emperor Constantine set the fashion for geometrical baptistries with his octagonal baptistry of St John Lateran in Rome, and Albenga's is a minor *tour de force* of the genre, combining an unusual 10-sided exterior with an octagonal interior. Within, some of the windows are covered with beautiful sandstone transennas, carved with stylized motifs. There are also fine granite columns topped with reused Corinthian columns, early-medieval tombs carved with Lombard-style reliefs and a font for total immersion. One niche retains its original blue and white mosaics, depicting 12 doves, symbols of the Apostles – the only surviving example of Byzantine art in northern Italy outside Ravenna (*see* p.165).

Next to the Baptistry stands the tower (*c.* 1300) of the **Palazzo Vecchio del Comune**, where the **Museo Civico Ingauno** (*open Tues–Sun 10–12 and 3–6*) displays Roman and medieval finds, and a lovely view over Albenga from the top floor. The third tower, from the same era, adjoins the **Palazzo Peloso Cipolla** ('Hairy Onion Palace'), containing the **Museo Navale Romano** (*open Tues–Sun 10–12 and 3–6*), with wine amphorae and other items salvaged from a 1st-century BC Roman shipwreck near the Isola Gallinaria, as well as 16th–18th-century pharmacy jars from Albisola. A section on prehistory is being arranged on the ground floor.

Just north of the cathedral's buxom apse, Piazzetta dei Leoni is named after three 17th-century stone lions, brought here from Rome by the wealthy Costa family to embellish their handsome **Palazzo Costa Del Carretto di Balestrino** (1525); the family also owned the medieval house and tower with swallowtail crenellations. Nearby on Via Episcopio, the striped **Palazzo Vescovile**, with exterior frescoes, houses the **Museo Diocesano** (*open Tues–Sun 10–12 and 3–6*), a handsome collection of 17th-century tapestries, paintings and illuminated manuscripts. Beyond, the 13th-century **Loggia dei Quattro Canti** marks the centre of the Roman town, where three more tower houses stand, or rather, tilt.

Getting There

Regular trains (roughly one each hour) serve **Albenga** from Principe station, taking 1hr–1hr 25 mins, depending on the type of train.

Tourist Information

Albenga ✉ **17031**: Viale Martiri Della Liberta 1, **t** 0182 558 444, **f** 0182 558 740, *iatalbenga@italianriviera.com*.

Eating Out

Hotel Italia, Via Martiri della Libertà, **t** 0182 50405 (*moderate*). Near the old town and the station. Take a trip back to the 1930s, and dine well in the same classy old atmosphere (*restaurant open to non-guests*).

Cristallo, Via Cavalieri di Vittorio Veneto 8, **t** 0182 50603 (*expensive*). Small, simple family-run restaurant in the centre, renowned for the freshness of its fish, prepared with a knowing touch in the kitchen. *Closed Mon.*

Antica Osteria dei Leoni, Via Mariettina Lengueglia 49, **t** 0182 51937 (*expensive*). Near the cathedral, this offers Ligurian seafood with a Neapolitan twist – try the lasagne with aubergines and clams. It also has tables outside. *Closed Mon and two weeks in Oct.*

Puppo, Via Torlaro 20, **t** 0182 51853 (*cheap*). Join the crowds at the long wooden tables for pizza and the best *farinata* in Albenga.

Touring from Genoa

Day 1: Swathes of Velvet, Macramé and Sand

Morning: Use the elevated *Sopralevata* to get out of Genoa, taking the scenic coastal Via Aurelia (S1) east along the the Riviera di Levante. Pause at **Zoagli**, which produces handmade patterned velvets, silks and damasks as it did back in the Middle Ages. See how it's done at **Giuseppe Gaggioli** (*Via Aurelia 208A, **t** 0185 259 057*). From the beach, follow the rock-cut path along the shore for lovely views over the gulf, then drive on to browse through the lively morning market in **Chiávari**'s Piazza Mazzini. Orchids are a speciality here, as is the craft of macramé, used to adorn linen with intricate fringes and tassels. Visit the **Museo Archeològico** (*open 9–1.30*) with finds from a nearby 8th–7th-century BC necropolis.

Lunch: In Chiávari, *see* below.

Afternoon: Continue as far as Sestri Levante, then leave the S1 where it delves inland, opting for the S370 and its arduous coastal tunnels, as the Apennines move in and crowd the coast. Stop at **Monéglia** to see the beautiful *risseu* pavement (1822) in the church of Santa Croce, then drive on to **Lévanto**, set in an amphitheatre over the sea. It can claim not only a lovely long sandy strand in a pretty garden setting amid chunks of its old walls, but also the last petrol station before La Spezia. Next comes **Monterosso al Mare**, the westernmost and largest (pop. 1,730) of the Cinque Terre.

Dinner and Sleeping: In Monterosso al Mare, *see* below.

Day 1

Lunch in Chiávari

Lord Nelson Pub, Corso Valparaiso 27, **t** 0185 302 595 (*very expensive*). Amid the dark wood and bottles you can dine on the most elegant gourmet cuisine in town, with delicate seafood such as ravioli with smoked ricotta and shrimp, and *dentice* (like sea bream) with pine nuts, olives and potatoes. Save room for exquisite desserts. *Closed Wed.*

Felice, Via L. Risso 71, **t** 0185 308 016 (*moderate*). Serves delicious *zimino* (fish soup) and other Ligurian fare; it's small, so book. *Closed Mon.*

Dragut, smack on the marina, **t** 0185 324 828 (*moderate*). Nothing but meat and chicken dishes served here, and plenty of both, along with fashion videos. *Closed Wed.*

Dinner in Monterosso al Mare

Il Gigante, Via IV Novembre, **t** 0187 817 401 (*moderate*). The best food in Monterosso. Especially good Ligurian specialities – *pansotti, trenette al pesto* and fresh fish.

Ristorante Belvedere, Piazza Garibaldi 38, **t** 0187 817 033 (*moderate*). Just below the rail line, but the beachside view of the setting sun more than compensates. The house speciality, the *anfora belvedere*, is a gargantuan platter of the best the sea has to offer.

Sleeping in Monterosso al Mare

******Porto Roca**, Via Corone 1, **t** 0187 817 502, **f** 0187 817 692, *www.portoroca.it* (*very expensive*). The top choice, on the headland, with lovely views of the sea from all the rooms.

******Palme**, Via IV Novembre 18, **t** 0187 829 013, **f** 0187 829 081 (*expensive*). A modern hotel in a large garden 5mins from the sea.

*****Hotel Baia**, Via Fegina 88, **t** 0187 817 512, **f** 0187 818 322 (*moderate*). On the water's edge, with light, airy rooms (ask for a balcony), that enjoy sunshine from dawn till dusk.

*****Degli Amici**, Via Burranco 36, **t** 0187 817 544, **f** 0187 817 424 (*moderate*). A good budget option, in the old town, 150m from the beach. Rooms are light and airy, some with balcony, and there's an excellent **restaurant**.

Day 2: Hanging Over the Sea in the Cinque Terre

Morning: Explore Monterosso, the most touristy of the five towns, with picturesque beaches (free and 'organized') and boats to hire for tours of the coast. Most of the facilities are in the new town, Fegina, separated from the old by a hill crowned with the **Convento dei Cappuccini** (1622), encompassing the medieval **Torre Aurora** and church of **San Francesco**, home to some surprisingly fine art: Strozzi's *La Veronica*, a *Crucifixion* by Van Dyck and two works by Luca Cambiaso. The striped church of **San Giovanni** has an exquisite marble rose window with lace-like edges. Walk or drive to the 18th-century **Sanctuary of Soviore** and, if you have the puff, don't miss the climb to the breathtaking (literally) **Punta Mesco**. Take a momentary train ride, drive or walk (1hr30) to the next town, **Vernazza**, guarded by two imposing Saracen towers on a rocky spit. It is the only one of the five towns to have a little port. The apse of the church of **Santa Margherita d'Antiochia** (1318) overlooks the main piazza.

Lunch: In Vernazza, *see* below.

Afternoon: Spend the afternoon in Vernazza, or continue to **Corniglia** (1hr30 by foot – one of the most strenuous 'link' walks), set high up on the cliffs, though it has the longest (albeit pebbly) beach way down below. Corniglia has been the centre of the Cinque Terre's winemaking since Roman times; an amphora bearing its name was excavated from the ash at Pompeii. The parish church of **San Pietro** has a handsome Gothic façade pierced by a lovely rose window. In the evening, drive on to **Riomaggiore** and sleep there, or return to Monterosso, reaching Riomaggiore the next morning.

Dinner and Sleeping: In Riomaggiore, *see* below, or Monterosso (*see* facing page).

Day 2

Lunch in Vernazza

Gambero Rosso, Piazza Marconi 7, **t** 0187 812 265 (*moderate*). Well-known restaurant that's partly carved out of the rock; try the *tegame di acciughe*, made with the Cinque Terre's special anchovies.

Da Capitano, **t** 0187 812 201 (*moderate*). Fine fish fare on the square – try the *linguine ai granchi*, washed down with a glass of the genial Captain's own wine.

Dinner in Riomaggiore

Ristorante La Lanterna, Via San Giacomo 10, **t** 0187 920 589 (*cheap*). With a beautiful terrace overlooking the harbour and a menu that includes some 20 pasta dishes, among them *spaghetti alla botarga* (roe) and *spaghetti ai ricci di mare* (sea urchins).

Ripa del Sole, Via de Gasperi 4, **t** 0187 920 143 (*moderate*). Specializes in home-made pasta, including *chicche* (mini gnocchi). *Closed Mon and second half of Nov.*

Cappun Magru, Loc. Groppo di Manarola, **t** 0187 920 563 (*moderate*). A tiny place that relies on the day's catch for its fishy *secondi*, washed down by a great choice of local, Piemontese and Tuscan wines. Do book. No credit cards. *Closed Mon, Tues, Dec and Jan.*

Sleeping in Riomaggiore

****Villa Argentina**, Via A. De Gasperi 39, **t/f** 0187 920 213 (*moderate*). Arty hotel in one of the prettiest corners of town, with a good optional buffet breakfast that will set you up for walking the Via dell'Amore (*see* Day 3).

Locanda Ca'dei Duxi, Via Pecunia 19, **t/f** 0187 920 036 (*moderate*). In the centre of town, this *locanda* has six entirely restored, colourful rooms with satellite TV, mini bar, safe and a/c. Ideal for young families, as several rooms have bunk beds. The gregarious owner is a font of local knowledge.

*****Due Gemelli**, Via Littoranea 9, **t/f** 0187 731 320 (*cheap*). A low-key choice 9km from the centre at Campi, in a lovely setting among the pines and olives, overlooking the sea.

Day 3: Lovers and Verticality in the Cinque Terre

Morning: Explore Riomaggiore, one of the prettiest towns of the Cinque Terre, which sees plenty of visitors crowding its lively cafés and rocky beaches. The church here also has a good 14th-century rose window, surviving in a neo-Gothic façade; inside there's a lifesize wooden *Crucifixion* by Anton Maria Maragliano. Other pretty walks are up to the ruins of the castle and to the spectacular view point of the **Madonna di Montenero**, 1,120ft over the sea (there's also a road). Then you can walk the most popular and singular section of the footpath between the towns, the **Via dell'Amore** (Lovers' Lane), carved into the living rock over the sea. In 20 minutes or so you'll be in **Manarola**, an astonishing sight, piled like a dream on a great black rock by the sea.

Lunch: In Manarola, *see* below.

Afternoon: Stroll through the colourful fishing village of Manarola, founded in the 12th century. The outer walls of the houses follow the lines of the original castle, while the Gothic church has another superb rose window. From here, an hour's walk through splendid scenery leads you back to **Corniglia**. Return to Riomaggiore and drive on across the rocky peninsula towards La Spezia, at the head of the 'Gulf of Poets' (*see* Day 4). The road meets the S530 just south of La Spezia; turn right and drive along towards Portovénere. You can detour west up a little road to **Campiglia**, hanging like a balcony over the stupendously vertical landscapes of the Tramonti, or continue winding along the narrow S530 to the tip of the peninsula. Here stands ancient, fortified **Portovénere**, one of the most beautiful towns on the Riviera.

Dinner and Sleeping: In Portovénere, *see* below.

Day 3

Lunch in Manarola

Aristide, Via Roma, **t** 0187 920 000 (*moderate*). The choice *trattoria*, serving a delicious *minestra* and fish dishes, also rabbit, game and other meat in season.

★★★**Marina Piccola**, **t** 0187 920 103, **f** 0187 920 966 (*cheap*). A good place to get away from it all, with a very nice restaurant.

Dinner in Portovénere

La Taverna del Corsaro, Lungomare Doria 182, **t** 0187 790 622 (*expensive*). In one of the most delightful locations in town at the beginning of the promontory, where you can savour delicacies like prawn in bell pepper sauce and *zuppa di datteri* (razor clams).

Ristorante La Marina, Piazza Marina 6, **t** 0187 790 686 (*expensive*). Enjoy stuffed squid followed by the creamiest of pannacottas with blackberry coulis whilst watching the little ferries potter between the island of Palmaria and the mainland. *Closed Thurs.*

Sleeping in Portovénere

★★★★**Grand Hotel Portovénere**, Via Garibaldi 5, **t** 0187 792 610, **f** 0187 790 661, *ghp@village.it* (*expensive*). In a 17th-century convent, set by the sea with views across the gulf and Palmaria. The former cells have been converted into stylish rooms with a/c; there's a fitness and beauty centre, parking and a pretty restaurant with a terrace.

★★★★**Hotel Royal Sporting**, Via dell'Ulivo 345, **t** 0187 790 326, **f** 0187 777 707, *www.royal-sporting.com* (*expensive*). A large, modern hotel built in the Mediterranean style in a fantastic location overlooking sea and town; it has a salt-water pool, beach, garden and tennis courts. There is also a place to park. *Closed Nov–Mar.*

★★★**Paradiso**, Via Garibaldi 34, **t** 0187 790 612, **f** 0187 792 582 (*moderate*). A little family-run hotel with lovely sea views from its terrace, and cosy, well-equipped rooms; pay parking.

★★**Genio**, Piazza Bastreri 8, **t** 0187 790 611 (*cheap*). The cheapest rooms in town, and a nice little garden, too.

Day 4: Around the Bay of Poets

Morning: Wander through Portovénere's narrow, cat-crowded lanes, and climb up to the 16th-century **Castello** for its marvellous views. The town was named after the port of Venus, whose temple stood at the tip of the promontory, by the little zebra church of **San Pietro**. From the cove below, Byron swam across to Lérici and Shelley's villa. You can take a boat trip across the channel to **Isola Palmaria** to visit its famed Grotta Azzura, but it's cheaper to do it from La Spezia. Drive back along the S530 to **La Spezia** for a stroll down the promenade of swaying palms and beautiful gardens. Visit the excellent **Naval Museum** (*open Tues–Thurs and Sat 9–12 and 2–6, Mon and Fri 2–6; adm*) or, above on the hill, the **Museo del Castello** (*Via XXVII Marzo; open summer daily 9.30–12.30 and 5–8; winter daily 9.30–12.30 and 2–5; closed Tues; adm*), with prehistoric finds from Palmaria's Grotta dei Colombi, Roman material from Luni and, best of all, ancient Ligurian statue-*steles* from the Bronze and Iron Ages.

Lunch: In La Spezia, *see* below.

Afternoon: Continue around the gulf on the S331 to Lérici, passing **San Terenzo**, beloved of Percy Bysshe Shelley, who lived at Casa Magni. In **Lérici**, you can swim in the pretty Baia di Maralunga, below the castle, or go south (in summer take the bus, there's no place to park), to the tiny, tranquil cove of **Fiascherino**, once home to D.H. Lawrence; beyond is the quintessentially Ligurian fishing hamlet of **Tellaro**, with its tall medieval houses and pink Baroque church. From Lérici, the road wends its way around the promontory up to **Ameglia**, the gourmet vortex of this end of the Riviera.

Dinner and Sleeping: In Ameglia, *see* below.

Day 4

Lunch in La Spezia

Parodi, Viale Amendola 210, **t** 0187 715 777 (*expensive*). An elegant restaurant just off the seafront, serving the best gourmet dishes in the city, featuring market-fresh ingredients and all the best from the land and sea; there's also a great choice of wines and spirits. *Closed Sun*.

Osteria All'Inferno, Via Lorenzo Costa 3, **t** 0187 29 458 (*moderate–cheap*). Housed in an old coal cellar, this inconspicuous restaurant has been run by the same family since 1905. Though originally just an *enoteca* (wine bar), they have been serving local delights such as *mesciua* and *porcetta al forno* since 1945. *Closed Sun and whole of Aug*.

There are a good number of low-price restaurants around Via del Prione.

Dinner and Sleeping in Ameglia

Ameglia is the gastronomic capital of the eastern Riviera, and well worth a splurge.

★★★**Paracucchi Locanda dell'Angelo**, at Ca' di Scabello, Viale V Aprile 60, **t** 0187 64391/2, **f** 0187 64393 (*moderate*). The pioneer establishment, comprising a modern, stylish and slick hotel, with a pool and the sea only minutes away; the **restaurant** (*very expensive*), founded by one of Italy's most famous chefs, Angelo Parcucchi – now run by son Marco – is top notch, although not as good as Tamerici (*see* below); the menu changes often, but each dish is superb and often amazingly simple. Great desserts, especially the fruit flambée, and excellent wine list. *Closed Sun eve and Mon out of season*.

★★★**Locanda delle Tamerici**, Via Litoranea 116, **t** 0187 64262, **f** 0187 64627 (*rooms moderate, restaurant very expensive*). Also down by the sea at Fiumaretta, with cosy, adorable, tranquil rooms and a romantic flower-filled garden. The restaurant rivals Angelo's for its lovely, flavour-enhanced seafood and vegetable dishes. A few days here on full board, unwinding by the sea, is one of the nicest possible cures for stress. *Closed Tues*.

Day 5: Ancient Luni, its Wine and the Val di Vara

Morning: From Ameglia, cross the bridge over the Magra (S432) and turn left for **Luni**, ancient Portus Lunae, a Roman colony founded in 177 BC, which once thrived as a marble port. Excavations have revealed a 2nd-century AD amphitheatre capable of seating 5,000, a forum, houses (some with frescoes and mosaics), temples and the Palaeochristian basilica. Visit the **museum** (*open April–Sept Tues–Sun 9–12 and 3–7; Oct–Mar Tues–Sun 2–7; adm*), with its collection of statuary, coins and jewellery; it also has a display of archaeological techniques used in excavating ancient Luni. On leaving, take the by-road north of Luni (crossing the S1) towards **Lama**. As you enter the village, turn left to **Castelnuovo Magra**, a long town stretched along a hill with a castle on one end. Try the local Vermentino dei Colli di Luni in the *enoteca*.

Lunch: In Castelnuovo Magra, *see* below.

Afternoon: Drive back down to join the S1 and head west back beyond La Spezia along the Val di Vara. Look out for little stone heads with primitive faces outside the houses, used to ward away evil. From **Borghetto di Vara**, take a detour north along the S556 as it skirts the river, passing picturesque hamlets half-abandoned in the chestnut forests. Turn left just before S. Margarita, cutting west via **Carro** to meet the S523 just north of Velva. Follow the S523 back down to the coast to rejoin the S1 by Sestri Levante, and end the day in genteel **Rapallo** with a ride on the *funivia* (*Mar–Oct 8–sunset; Nov–Feb 8.30–5; cars leave every 30 mins*), which climbs 7,707ft to the **Santuario di Montallegro**, affording a heavenly view of the Tigullio Gulf.

Dinner and Sleeping: In Rapallo, *see* below.

Day 5

Lunch in Castelnuovo Magra

Armanda, Piazza Garibaldi 6, **t** 0187 674 410 (*expensive–moderate*). People make special trips just for the house speciality: stuffed lettuce in broth (*lattughe ripiene in brodo*), *cima*, an exquisite, delicate *torta* filled with zucchine and artichoke hearts, rabbit deboned and stuffed, and other authentic dishes. It's minute, so book. *Closed Wed.*

Canale, the Mulino del Cibus, **t** 0187 676 102 (*moderate*). Wine bar in an old working mill, with a wide selection of wines and tasty dishes to match, whether you just feel like nibbling cheese and salami or need something more filling like lasagne or duck's breast in vinegar and honey. *Closed Mon.*

Dinner in Rapallo

Churrascaria Brasileira, Corso Assereto 13, **t** 0185 614 16 (*expensive–moderate*). The simple menu here is carnivore heaven: as much of all the different cuts of meat as you can eat for €22.50 excluding wine and dessert. *Open for dinner only. Closed Mon.*

Osteria U Bansin, Via Venezia 105, **t** 0185 231 119 (*cheap*). Open since 1907, this truly authentic *osteria* attracts everyone due to its quick service and wonderfully good local food. *Closed Sun.*

Sleeping in Rapallo

********Eurotel**, Via Aurelia Ponente 22, **t** 0185 60981, **f** 0185 50635, *www.tigullio.net/eurotel* (*very expensive*). Bright red hotel on the outskirts of town, with great views of the hills and harbour, large well-appointed rooms with balconies, smart lounge areas and a heated outdoor pool.

*****Minerva**, Corso Colombo 7, **t** 0185 234 472, **f** 0185 234 474 (*moderate*). A good value, up-to-date hotel near the seashore, with tasteful décor, garden and bar.

***Pensione Bandoni**, Via Marsala 24/3, **t** 0185 50423, **f** 0185 57206 (*cheap*). A good value, comfortable, simple hotel close to the seafront and right in the middle of town.

Lombardy

06

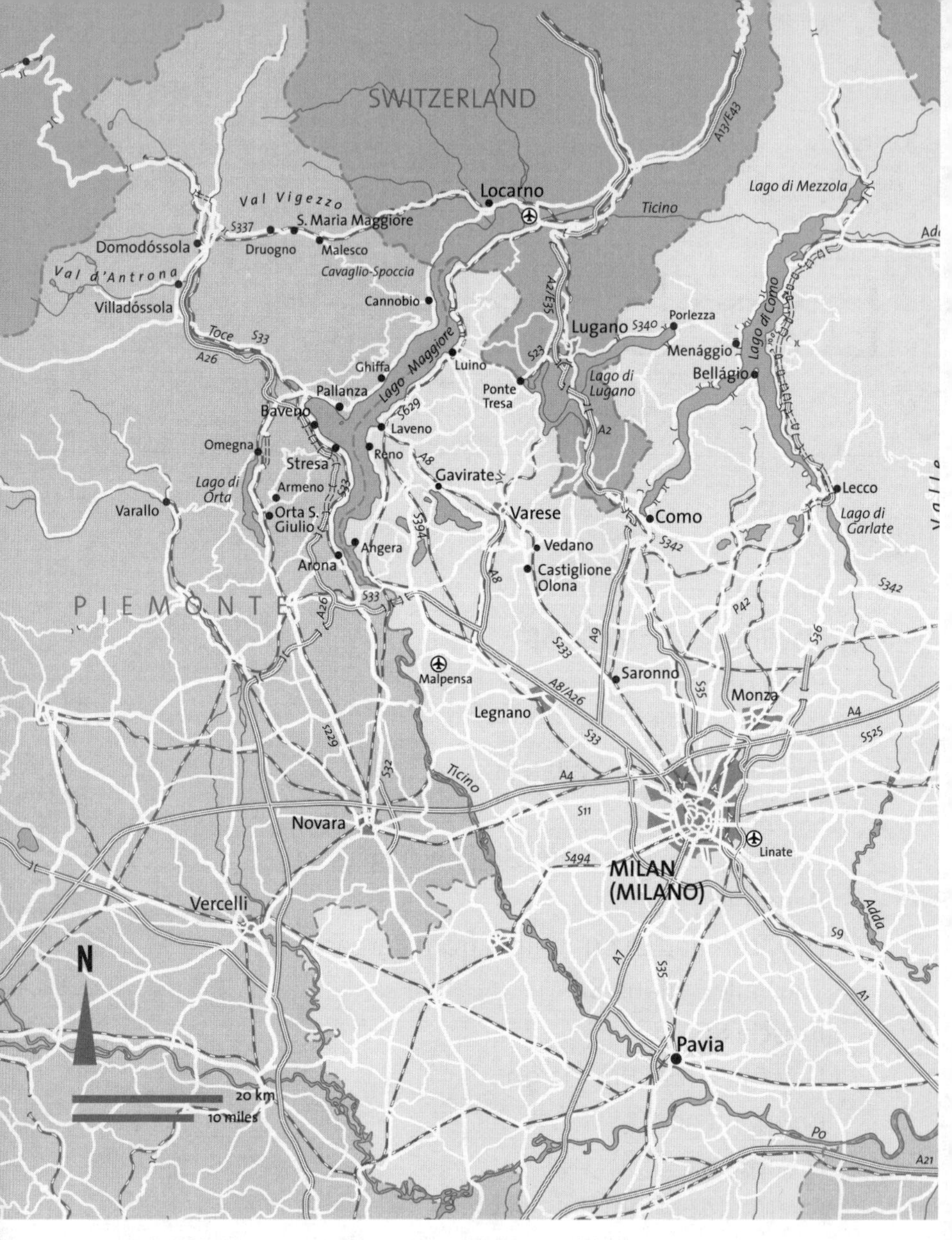

Of all the barbarians who desecrated the corpse of the Roman Empire, none was more barbaric than the Lombards (or Longobards), a tall Germanic tribe who bled much of the peninsula dry before settling down in the region that still bears their name. Even today the Milanese are taller than the average Italian, although whether that's because of their Lombard blood or plain prosperity is anyone's guess. Since the Middle Ages Lombardy has been the economic powerhouse of Italy. The complaint that Milan makes money while Rome wastes it is almost as old as the city itself.

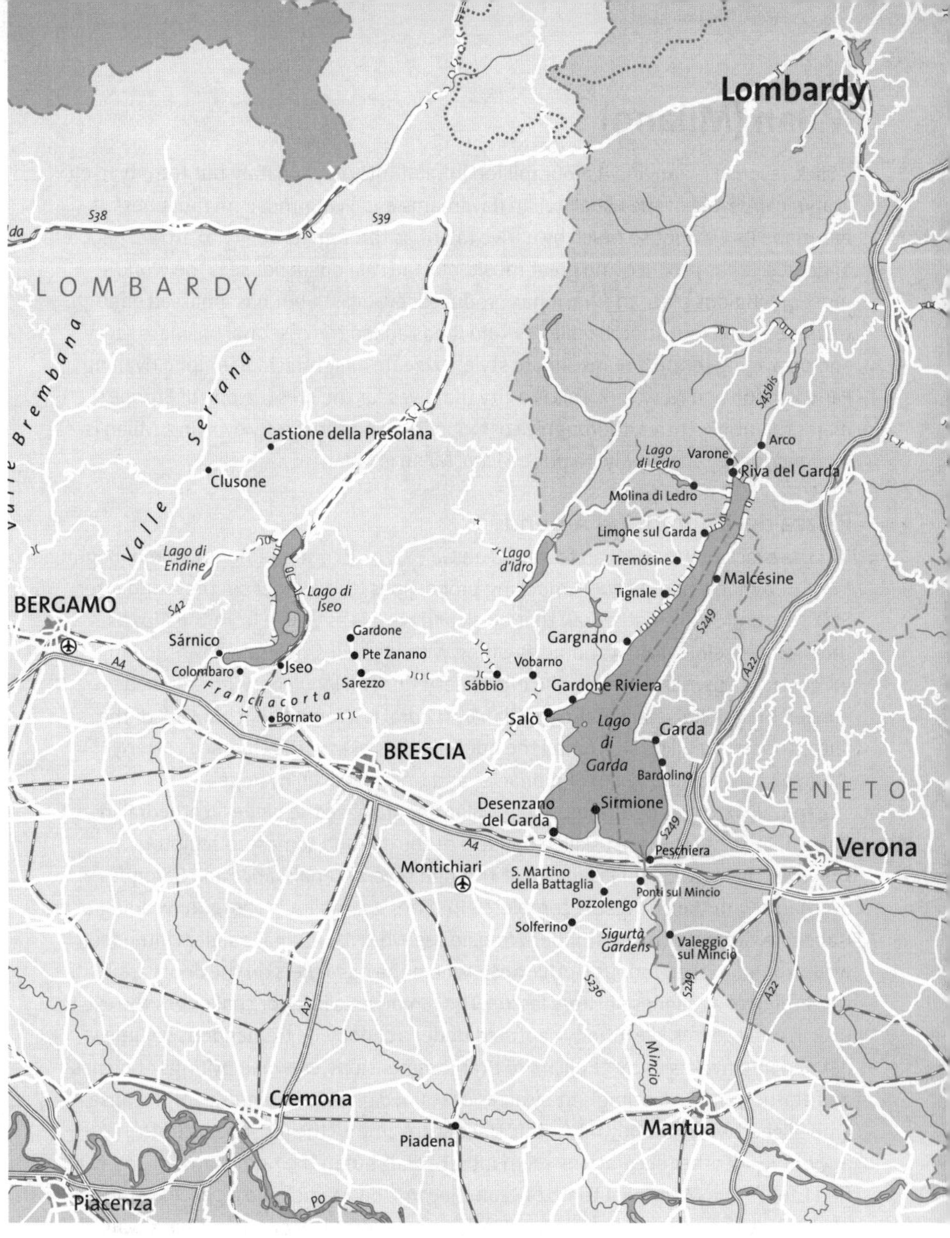

Frenetic Milan, the pounding, racing economic heart of modern Italy, is the centre of gravity for the entire north. The destinies of empires and kingdoms have been decided here, not to mention religions – Christianity was made the religion of the Roman Empire in the Edict of Milan, in 303. Lombardy has its gentle side as well. This was the homeland of poets Virgil and Catallus, of composers Monteverdi and Donizetti, of the great violin masters, Amati, Guarneri and Stradivarius. And since the 18th century countless poets, composers and weary aristocrats have come for the peace and beauty of the Italian Lakes.

Milan (Milano)

Slick, feverish Milan and its four million inhabitants may run Italy, but the city itself is atypical, devoid of the usual Italian daydreams and living-museum mustiness. It has made its way not so much by native talent as through its ability to attract people of genius: it has produced no great music, but La Scala opera house is the world's most prestigious place to sing; it has produced few artists, but has amassed enough treasures to fill four superb galleries. And it has added the essential business savvy and packaging to the Italians' innate style, to create a high-fashion empire rivalling Paris, London and New York. This is a city that lives for the present: one of Europe's major financial centres, thoroughly cosmopolitan and constantly evolving. Milan is *sui generis*; they say simply, *Milan l'e Milan*, Milan is Milan.

Piazza del Duomo and Around

In the exact centre of Milan towers Gian Galeazzo Visconti's famous **Duomo** (begun in 1386), a monument of such imposing proportions (third largest in the world after St Peter's and Seville Cathedral) that on clear days it is as visible from the Alps as the Alps are visible from its dome. Bristling with 135 spires, defended by 95 leering gargoyles, 2,244 marble saints and one cheeky sinner (Napoleon, who crowned himself King of Italy here in 1805), Milan Cathedral is a remarkable bulwark of the faith. And yet for all its size, for all the hubbub of its *piazza*, the Duomo is utterly ethereal, a rose-white vision of pinnacles and tracery woven by angels.

Gian Galeazzo was determined that Milan should have the biggest cathedral in Italy, calling in all the most skilled builders of the day and some 300 sculptors. However, the bewildered façade went through several Renaissance and Baroque overhauls with the end result, completed in 1809, resembling a shotgun wedding of Isabelline Gothic with Christopher Wren. To see what its original builders intended, walk around to the glorious Gothic **apse**, where the bas-reliefs on the doors are something of a Milanese history lesson. The remarkable **interior** challenges the eye to take in what seems like infinity captured under a canopy. Its tremendous volume is defined into five aisles by 52 pillars of titanic dimensions, crowned by rings of niches and statues, and is dazzlingly lit by acres of stained glass; the windows of the apse, embellished with flamboyant Gothic tracery, are among the most beautiful anywhere. All other decorations seem rather small, but in the right transept you will find Leoni's fine Mannerist tomb of Gian Giacomo de' Medici, and a peculiar statue of San Bartolomeo holding his own skin. For a splendid view of Milan, take a walk through the enchanted forest of spires and statues on the **cathedral roof** (*open Nov–Feb daily 9–4.45; Mar–Oct daily 9–5.45; steps or lift from outside the cathedral; adm; combined ticket with Museo del Duomo*). On the south side of the cathedral, the neoclassical **Palazzo Reale** (*closed for restructuring*) was for centuries the headquarters of Milan's rulers.

North of the Duomo

Around Piazza della Scala and Via Manzoni

The king lent his name to Milan's elegant **Galleria Vittorio Emanuele** (1878) a glass-roofed arcade filled with elegant bars and some of the city's finest shops. It opens up to the Piazza della Scala, home to one of the world's great opera houses, the **Teatro alla Scala** (*under restoration*). Inaugurated in 1778 with Salieri's *Europa Riconosciuta*, La Scala saw the premières of most of the 19th-century classics of Italian opera.

In front of La Scala runs one of Milan's busiest and most fashionable boulevards, **Via Manzoni**. At no.10, the lovely 17th-century **Museo Poldi-Pezzoli** (Ⓜ *Monte Napoleone; open Tues–Sun 10–6; adm; combined adm for Poldi-Pezzoli and Bagatti-Valsecchi museums*) has an exquisite collection of 15th- to 18th-century paintings, including Antonio del Pollaiuolo's famous 15th-century *Portrait of a Young Woman*, depicting an ideal Renaissance beauty. She shares the Salone Dorato with other gems: Mantegna's Byzantine-style *Madonna*, Giovanni Bellini's *Pietà*, Piero della Francesca's *San Nicolò* and Guardi's *Grey Lagoon*. Besides more outstanding paintings, the collection is also rich in Islamic metalwork and rugs, Flemish tapestries, Murano glass and lace.

Just up Via Manzoni is the entrance to Milan's high-fashion vortex, concentrated in the palace-lined **Via Monte Napoleone** and elegant **Via della Spiga**. Even if you're not after astronomically priced designer clothes, they make for good window-shopping and even better people-watching.

The Giardini Pubblici

From Piazza Cavour, Via Palestro curves through the two sections of Milan's Public Gardens. In the romantic **Giardini di Villa Reale** (Ⓜ Palestro) the Villa Reale houses the **Civica Galleria d'Arte Moderna** (*open daily 9.30–5.30*) where you can see the Vismara collection of paintings (works by Picasso, Matisse, Modigliani, de Pisis, Tosi, Morandi and Renoir) and sculptures by Marino Marini (d. 1980), generally acknowledged as the top Italian sculptor of the 20th century. The first floor hosts Italian art of the 1800s, and, temporarily, paintings by Picasso, Klee, Kandinsky and Modigliani (*from the Civico Museo d'Arte Contemporanea, displayed here while the Palazzo Reale is closed for restructuring*). The second floor hosts French painters Gaugin, Bonnard, Manet and Toulouse Lautrec and assorted Italian Futurists.

The **Giardini Pùbblici** proper is a good place for kids, with its zoo, swans, pedal cars and playgrounds. Here, too, is Italy's premier **Natural History Museum** (*open Mon–Fri 9.30–6, Sat–Sun 9.30–6.30*), near the Corso Venezia, a street lined with neoclassical and Liberty-style (Art Nouveau) palaces. Close by, the **Società per le Belle Arti ed Esposizione Permanente** (*Via Turati 34,* Ⓜ *Turati; open Tues–Fri 10–1 and 2.30–6.30, Thurs until 10pm; Sat, Sun and hols 10–6.30; adm exp*) currently displays 20th-century works from the Civico Museo dell'Arte Contemporanea, including some by Boccioni, De Chirico and Modigliani. Northwest of the park, the **Piazza della Repubblica** has many of the city's hotels and the Mesopotamian-scale **Stazione Centrale** (1931).

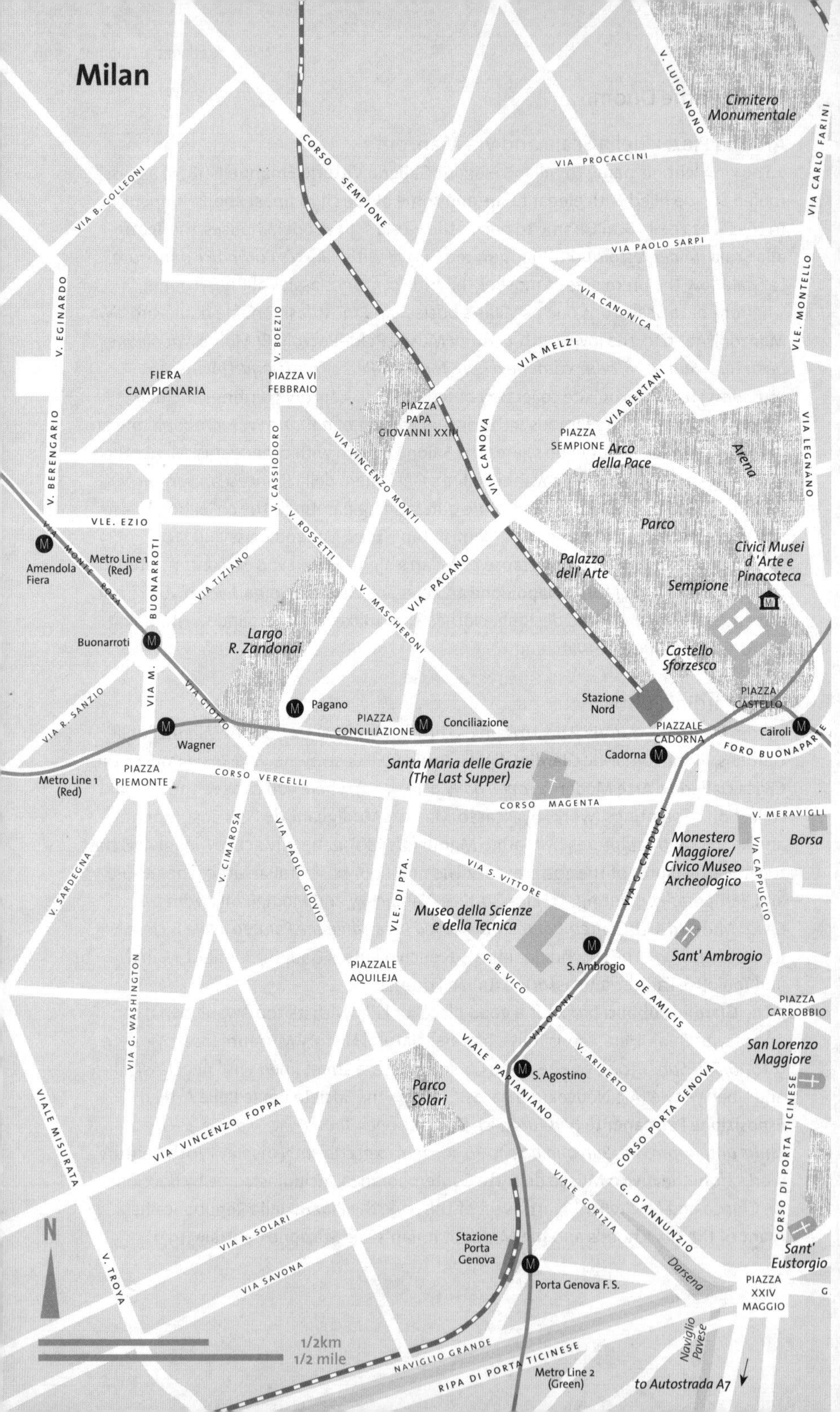

Milan
Cimitero Monumentale
V. Luigi Nono
Via Carlo Farini
Via Procaccini
Corso Sempione
Via B. Colleoni
Via Paolo Sarpi
Vle. Montello
Via Canonica
V. Eginardo
V. Boezio
Via Melzi
Fiera Campignaria
Piazza VI Febbraio
Piazza Papa Giovanni XXIII
Via Bertani
Piazza Sempione
Arco della Pace
Arena
Via Legnano
V. Berengario
Via Cassiodoro
Via Vincenzo Monti
Via Canova
Parco
Vle. Ezio
Amendola Fiera
Metro Line 1 (Red)
Via Monte Rosa
Buonarroti
Via Tiziano
V. Rossetti
Via Pagano
Palazzo dell' Arte
Civici Musei d 'Arte e Pinacoteca
Sempione
V. Mascheroni
Largo R. Zandonai
Castello Sforzesco
Via M. Buonarroti
Via R. Sanzio
Via Giotto
Pagano
Piazza Conciliazione
Conciliazione
Stazione Nord
Piazza Castello
Wagner
Piazzale Cadorna
Cairoli
Foro Buonaparte
Cadorna
Santa Maria delle Grazie (The Last Supper)
Metro Line 1 (Red)
Piazza Piemonte
Corso Vercelli
Corso Magenta
V. Meravigli
Monestero Maggiore/ Civico Museo Archeologico
Borsa
Via Cappuccio
V. Sardegna
V. Cimarosa
Via Paolo Giovio
Vle. di Pta.
Via S. Vittore
Via G. Carducci
Museo della Scienze e della Tecnica
Sant' Ambrogio
S. Ambrogio
Via G. Washington
Piazzale Aquileja
G. B. Vico
De Amicis
Piazza Carrobbio
Via Olona
San Lorenzo Maggiore
V. Ariberto
Viale Papiniano
S. Agostino
Parco Solari
Viale Misurata
Via Vincenzo Foppa
Corso Porta Genova
Corso di Porta Ticinese
Viale Gorizia
G. D'Annunzio
N
Via A. Solari
Stazione Porta Genova
Sant' Eustorgio
V. Troya
Via Savona
Porta Genova F. S.
Darsena
Piazza XXIV Maggio
1/2km
1/2 mile
Naviglio Grande
Naviglio Pavese
Ripa di Porta Ticinese
Metro Line 2 (Green)
to Autostrada A7

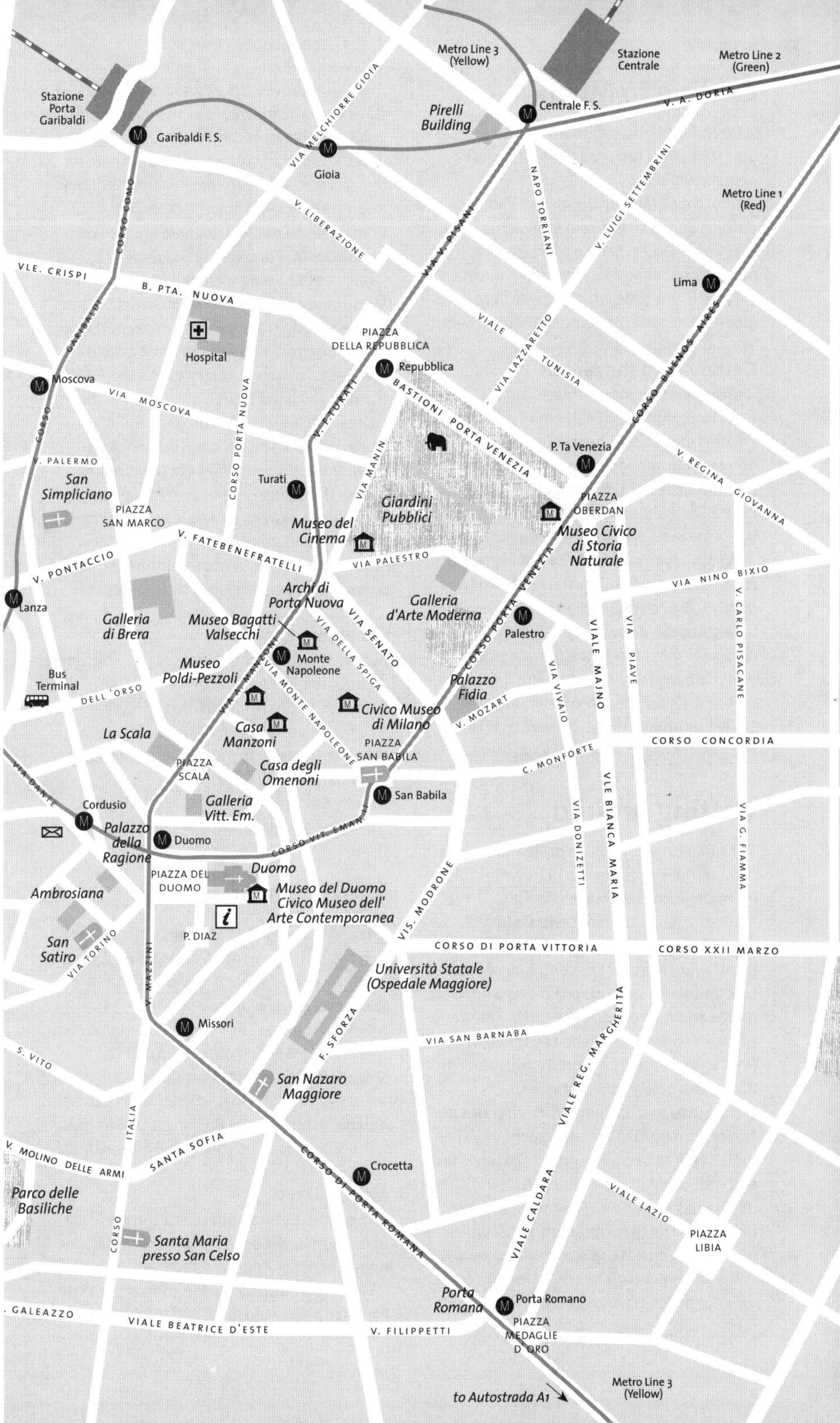

Stazione Porta Garibaldi
Garibaldi F. S.
Metro Line 3 (Yellow)
Stazione Centrale
Metro Line 2 (Green)
Pirelli Building
Centrale F. S.
V. A. Doria
Via Melchiorre Gioia
Gioia
Corso Como
V. Liberazione
Napo Torriani
V. Luigi Settembrini
Via V. Pisani
Metro Line 1 (Red)
Vle. Crispi
B. Pta. Nuova
Lima
Hospital
Piazza della Repubblica
Viale Tunisia
Via Lazzaretto
Corso Garibaldi
Moscova
Via Moscova
Repubblica
Bastioni Porta Venezia
Corso Buenos Aires
V. F. Turati
Via Manin
P. Ta Venezia
V. Palermo
Corso Porta Nuova
V. Regina Giovanna
San Simpliciano
Turati
Giardini Pubblici
Piazza Oberdan
Piazza San Marco
Museo del Cinema
Museo Civico di Storia Naturale
V. Fatebenefratelli
V. Pontaccio
Via Palestro
Corso Porta Venezia
Via Nino Bixio
Lanza
Archi di Porta Nuova
Galleria d'Arte Moderna
Galleria di Brera
Museo Bagatti Valsecchi
Via Senato
Palestro
Viale Majno
Via Piave
V. Carlo Pisacane
Via della Spiga
Monte Napoleone
Museo Poldi-Pezzoli
Via A. Manzoni
Via Vivaio
Bus Terminal
Dell 'Orso
Via Monte Napoleone
Civico Museo di Milano
Palazzo Fidia
V. Mozart
La Scala
Casa Manzoni
Piazza San Babila
Corso Concordia
Piazza Scala
Casa degli Omenoni
C. Monforte
San Babila
Via Dante
Cordusio
Galleria Vitt. Em.
Vle Bianca Maria
Via Donizetti
Via G. Fiamma
Palazzo della Ragione
Duomo
Corso Vit. Eman. II
Ambrosiana
Piazza del Duomo
Museo del Duomo
Civico Museo dell' Arte Contemporanea
Vis. Modrone
P. Diaz
San Satiro
Via Torino
Corso di Porta Vittoria
Corso XXII Marzo
Università Statale (Ospedale Maggiore)
V. Mazzini
Missori
F. Sforza
Via San Barnaba
Viale Reg. Margherita
S. Vito
San Nazaro Maggiore
Italia
V. Molino delle Armi
Santa Sofia
Corso di Porta Romana
Crocetta
Parco delle Basiliche
Viale Lazio
Corso
Santa Maria presso San Celso
Viale Caldara
Piazza Libia
Porta Romana
Porta Romano
Galeazzo
Viale Beatrice d'Este
V. Filippetti
Piazza Medaglie d'Oro
Metro Line 3 (Yellow)
to Autostrada A1

Getting to Milan

Go flies to Milan Linate from London Stansted (2hrs) (**t** 02 7485 2200; *www.sea-aeroportimilano.it*).

Note that **BMIbaby** (from East Midlands and Cardiff) and **Ryanair** (from Stansted) also fly to Bergamo's Orio al Serio airport (**t** 035 326 323), only an hour or so away (*see* p.87). Buses (**t** 035 318 472) link it to Milan's Stazione Centrale (approx €7), corresponding to regular flights.

Getting from the Airport

Milan has two main airports, **Linate** (8km from the centre) and **Malpensa** (50km west).

From Linate, **STAM buses** (€2.50) run every 30mins (5.40am–9pm) to Stazione Centrale (20mins approx.). **City bus 73** (€0.75) runs to Piazza San Babila (Ⓜ line 1) every 10mins (5.30am–2am). A **taxi** costs about €15–20.

From Malpensa, the **Malpensa Express** (**t** 02 20222) runs to Cadorna North Railway Station (Ⓜ Cadorna) every 30mins (5am–11pm; taking approx. 40mins; €7). **Air Pullman** buses (**t** 02 5858 3185) run to the Stazione Centrale every 20mins (4.15am–midnight; 1hr approx; €6.50). An hourly bus service stops at the Trade Fair upon request. Beware that **taxis** from Malpensa to Milan cost a fortune.

Getting Around

Milan is only difficult to navigate in a car: most of the sights are in a highly walkable inner circle, the Cerchia dei Navigli.

Milan's main **Stazione Centrale** (Ⓜ lines 2, 3; **t** 147 888 088, 7am–11pm) is on Piazza Duca d'Aosta northeast of the centre. Here you can pick up a very useful **map** showing all the bus routes and metro stops, the *Guida Rete dei trasporti pubblici*, published by the ATM (Milanese transport authority, freephone from Italy **t** 800 016857, *www.atm-mi.it*).

The **buses** and dashing Art Deco **trams** and trolleys run by ATM are convenient and their routes well marked. The **metro** (Ⓜ) too is fast and well run, with three lines: Red (Ⓜ 1), Green (Ⓜ 2), and Yellow (Ⓜ 3). The metro and most bus routes run 6am–midnight, after which **night buses** operate reasonably frequently.

The same **tickets** (€1 each; 10 for €9.20) are valid for buses, trams and the metro. Buy them in advance from newsagents, metro stations or the machines at the main stops, and stamp them in the machines on board. A ticket is valid for 75mins' travel anywhere on the network **above ground**, regardless of how many transfers you make. Tickets cannot be used twice on the metro. There are also **one-day passes** (€3) or **two-day passes** (€5.50).

Milanese **taxis** are white and generally reliable. There are ranks in the Piazza del Duomo, by the Stazione Centrale, and in several other central *piazzas*. Alternatively, call **t** 02 8383, **t** 02 6767, **t** 02 3100 or **t** 02 5353. On entering the taxi you pay a charge of €3.

Driving in Milan is no fun and requires chutzpah, luck and good navigation skills. If you must, there are ATM **car parks** on the outskirts. Parking is permitted for up to 2hrs in the areas marked by a **blue line**, provided you display a '*Sostamilano*' card (from *tabacchi*, bars or news kiosks; €1.30/hr until 8pm, €2.60 cumulatively 8pm–midnight).

Car Hire

Avis, at Linate airport, **t** 02 715 123; at Stazione Centrale **t** 02 669 0280.

Europcar, at Linate airport, **t** 02 7611 0258, or **t** (freephone within Italy) 800 014 410.

Hertz, at Linate, **t** 02 7020 0256; at the station, Via Galvani, **t** 02 6698 5151.

Italy By Car, Via Vittor Pisani 13, **t** 02 670 3151, or **t** (freephone within Italy) 800 846 083.

Tourist Information

Piazza del Duomo, Via Marconi 1, **t** 02 7252 4301/2/3, **f** 7252 4350 (*open Mon–Fri 8.30–7, Sat 9–1 and 2–6, Sun 9–1 and 2–5*).

Stazione Centrale (*open Mon–Sat 8–7, Sun 9–12.30 and 1.30–6*). Provide accommodation lists, city maps and other information.

Milan Hoteliers Association, Corso Buenos Aires 77, **t** 02 674 8031, *www.traveleurope.it*.

Milano Hotels Central Booking, **t** 02 805 4242, *www.hotelbooking.com*. Hotel reservations.

Market Days

The tourist office publishes a complete list of markets: most open 9–1 and nearly all are non-existent in August.

The huge Saturday clothes markets in **Viale Papiniano** (Ⓜ S. Agostino) and **Via Osoppo**

(Ⓜ Gambara) go on until 6pm. Flea markets include **Fiera di Senigallia** (Viale D'Annunzio, Sat 8.30–5; Ⓜ S. Agostino) and **San Donato** (Sun mornings; Ⓜ San Donato). For antiques, try the **Mercatone dell'Antiquariato** (Naviglio Grande, last Sun of month except July; Ⓜ Porta Genova) or the **Mercato Antiquariato di Brera** (Via Fiori Chiari, third Sat of month; Ⓜ Lanza).

Festivals

The **Carnival of Sant'Ambrogio**, Milan's patron saint, takes place in March.

Shopping

Shopping Hours: *most shops close all day Sunday, on Monday morning and in August. Food stores close on Monday afternoons.*

Fashion is a national obsession, and Milan is Italy's best shopping city hands down, most especially for clothes and designer goods of every kind. The artsy window displays are a shopper's paradise. The big **sales** begin the second week of January and around 10 July.

Many of the big names have their 'headquarters' in the **Quadrilatero**, defined by Via Monte Napoleone, Via della Spiga, Via S. Andrea and Via Borgospesso (Ⓜ Monte Napoleone). Most also have branch offices elsewhere.

On Monte Napoleone, you'll find the latest of the latest designs, as well as the classic jewellers. **Buccellati** (no.4), is considered by many the best jewellery designer in Italy. Other classics on Monte Napoleone are **Faraone** (no.7a), **Martignetti** (no.10), **Cartier** (corner Via del Gesù), **Damiani** (no.16), **Cusi** (no.21a) and **Calderoni**, the oldest (no.23); for **Bulgari** go to Via della Spiga (no.6).

When it comes to fashion and leather goods, Monte Napoleone has **Alberta Ferretti**, **Ferragamo**, **Fratelli Rossetti**, **Gucci**, **Missoni**, **Nazareno Gabrielli**, **Prada**, **Roccobarocco**, **Ungaro** and **Versace**. Via della Spiga boasts the likes of **Bottega Veneta**, **Byblos**, **Dolce e Gabbana**, **Krizia** and **Luciano Soprani**; try **Mercatino Michela** for second-hand designer fashions. On Via S. Andrea are **Chanel**, **Fendi**, **Ferré**, **Helmut Lang**, **Prada**, **Trussardi**, as well as **Moschino**. **Valentino** is at Via Santo Spirito 3; **Armani** is at Via Durini 23–25. **Armani's Megastore**, Via Manzoni 31, has just opened, complete with three floors, a sushi bar and a Mediterranean café and restaurant.

Besides the **Galleria Vittorio Emanuele**, several minor *gallerie* branch off the Corso Vittorio Emanuele, each lined with good quality and reasonably priced shops.

The shops on busy **Via Torino** have some of Milan's more affordable clothes and footwear, while **Via Paolo Sarpi** (Ⓜ Moscova) also has excellent merchandise and reasonable prices. **Corso Buenos Aires** (Ⓜ Lima), one of Milan's longest and densest shopping thoroughfares, offers something of every variety and hue. **Brera** has some of Milan's most original shops and boutiques, and the big COIN department store, Piazza 5 Giornate 1/a, is a good bet for reasonably priced fashions. The biggest, oldest department store is La Rinascente, in **Piazza del Duomo**, with especially good clothing and domestic sections. Near the Duomo, **Via Spadari** and **Via Speroni** are a food shopper's heaven, beginning with the Casa del Formaggio, Via Speroni 3. At Via Spadari 9 stop at Peck, the home of Milanese gastronomy.

Where to Stay

Milan ✉ 20100

Milan offers smart hotels for expense accounts, and seedy dives for arrivals from the provinces. Book ahead. (*See* above for booking services). During the trade fairs (especially Mar, April and autumn) you may find no room.

*******Four Seasons**, Via Gesù 8, ✉ 20121, **t** 02 77088, **f** 02 7708 5000, *www.fourseasons.com* (*luxury*). A beautiful hotel in a 15th-century monastery. The church is the lobby, breakfast is served in the refectory, and most of the spacious rooms look over the cloister; enormous bathrooms and great plush sofas around the blazing fire in the winter.

*******Principe di Savoia**, Piazza della Repubblica 17, ✉ 20124, **t** 02 6230, **f** 02 659 5838 (*luxury*). Built in 1927, this is elegant, prestigious and has been lavishly redecorated. Evita Peron, Maria Callas and the Aga Khan have all stayed here; it also has a divine restaurant (**La Galleria**, *see* below).

*******Grand Hotel et de Milan**, Via Manzoni 29, ✉ 20121, **t** 02 723 141, **f** 02 8646 0861, *www.grandhoteletdemilan.it* (*luxury*). A favourite with everyone from Verdi to Hemingway and, these days, Kate Moss and Naomi Campbell. Rooms are individually furnished with antiques, and the ambience is grand and gracious without being stuffy.

★★★★**Sheraton Diana Majestic**, Viale Piave 42, ✉ 20129, **t** 02 20581, **f** 02 2058 2058; Ⓜ Porta Venezia (*very expensive*). A fashionable, stylish hotel in the Liberty (Art Nouveau) style, built at the turn of the century, with charming rooms, views over a garden and a lovely breakfast buffet.

★★★**Antica Locanda Dei Mercanti**, Via San Tomaso 6, ✉ 20121, **t** 02 805 4080, **f** 02 805 4090, *www.locanda.it* (*very expensive*). A discreet, charming inn on a pedestrian street an easy walk from the main sites. Rooms are individually and classically furnished in with fine white fabrics.; the top floor ones have dramatic canopy beds and roof terraces.

★★**Antica Locanda Solferino**, Via Castelfidardo 2, ✉ 20121, **t** 02 657 0129, **f** 02 657 1361 (*expensive*). An atmospheric 19th-century inn with 11 rooms, all different, though the baths are spartan; breakfast is brought to your room. Book well ahead. *Closed Aug.*

★★**Casa Mia**, Viale Vittorio Veneto 30, ✉ 20124, **t** 02 657 5249, **f** 02 655 2228, *hotelcasamia@libero.it* (*moderate*). An excellent value hotel just north of the Giardini Pubblici, recently renovated with all amenities.

★**Alba d'Oro**, Viale Piave 5, ✉ 20129, **t** 02 7602 3880 (Ⓜ Palestro/Porta Venezia) (*moderate*). Small and safe; baths down the hall.

San Francisco, Viale Lombardia 55, ✉ 20131, **t** 02 236 1009, **f** 02 2668 0377 (*moderate*). A safe and acceptable choice close to Ⓜ Loreto.

Eating Out

Moneyed Milan boasts some of Italy's finest restaurants and a wide range of international cuisine. Saffron is Milan's fetish spice, appearing in most dishes *alla milanese*.

La Scaletta, Piazzale Stazione Porta Genova 3, **t** 02 5810 0290 (*very expensive*). The workshop of the *nuova cucina* sorceress, Pina Bellini, who does exquisite things to pasta and risotto, fish and rabbit. Excellent wines and desserts complement a memorable meal. *Closed Sun and Mon; booking advised.*

Peck, Via Victor Hugo 4, **t** 02 876 774 (*very expensive*). Synonymous with the best in Milan for over a hundred years, either in its delicatessen at Via Spadari 9, or here at its cellar restaurant, which offers such a tantalizing array of delights that you hardly know where to begin. Their unctuous *risotto alla milanese* is hard to beat. *Closed Sun and hols and 3 weeks in July, but open in Aug.*

La Galleria, Piazza della Repubblica 17, **t** 02 6230 2026 (*very expensive*). The restaurant of the Hotel Principe di Savoia serves gourmet Paduan food amid polychrome marble, crystal and *trompe-l'œil*. *Open all year.*

Aurora, Via Savona 23 (in the Navigli), **t** 02 8940 4978 (*expensive*). Lovely *belle époque* dining rooms and equally lovely Piemontese cuisine, with an emphasis on mushrooms and truffles. Exceptional value. *Closed Mon.*

Antica Trattoria della Pesa, Viale Pasubio 10, **t** 02 655 5741. Close to Porta Comasina (*expensive*). Here you can dine on original Italian cuisine academy *risotto alla milanese*, *ossobuco* and *casseuola* with polenta, or try 'new' dishes such as home-made *cappelletti* and *tagliolini* with truffle. *Closed Sun.*

Centro Ittico, Via Aporti 35, **t** 02 614 3774 (Ⓜ Loreto, Buemos Aires) (*expensive*). Fish comes directly from the market counter to your plate. Expect only a lemon sorbet for dessert. *Closed Sun and Mon.*

The **Ticinese** quarter has several restaurants offering good, affordable regional dishes.

Ponte Rosso, 23 Via Ripa di Porta Ticinese, **t** 02 837 3132 (*moderate*). Soak in a romantic old-world bistro atmosphere, mixing excellent Veneto and Lombard specialities. *Closed Sun and Wed eve.*

Tipica Osteria Pugliese, Via Tadino 5, **t** 02 2952 2574 (*moderate*). Eat cheaply by filling up on *antipasti* from a selection of 40 from Puglia, including *burrata* (mozzarella with creamy core) and *nodini* (hard knots of mozzarella). Also try the pasta, meat and fish cooked in a wood oven. *Menus from €18 (antipasti only).* Friendly atmosphere and service. *Closed Sun.*

Tre Pini, Via Tullio Morgagni 19, **t** 02 6680 5413 (*moderate*). The place to go for roasted meat and fish. Try '*focaccetta dell'accoglienza*' (greeting bun), and then enjoy ribs, roasted *fiorentinas* (steaks) or *tagliata di branzino* (sea bass) with cherry tomatoes. *Closed Sat.*

The best places to find cheaper restaurants are the streets in the Brera, Ticinese and Navigli districts. Milan is well endowed with fast-food places; Brek and Pastarito come highly recommended.

Da Rino Vecchia Napoli, Via Chavez 4 (between Stazione Centrale and Parco Lambro), **t** 02 261 9056 (*cheap*). A vast selection of prize-winning championship pizzas. They also do good *antipasti*, gnocchi and fish; it's best to book. *Closed Sun lunch and Mon.*

Geppo, Viale Brianza 30, **t** 02 284 6548 (*cheap*). Fifty kinds of pizza, including a Milanese with saffron, rocket and porcini mushrooms (Ⓜ Loreto). *Closed Sun.*

Osteria Tagiura, Via Tagiura 5, **t** 02 4895 0613 (*cheap*). In the San Siro area; open at lunch only. At this friendly family-run *osteria*, the menu is very affordable and very good. Fish on Fridays, home-made pasta every day, different daily traditional dishes; unparalled *testaroli al pesto. Closed Sun, no credit cards.*

Joya, Via P. Castaldi 18, **t** 02 2952 2124 (*cheap* at lunch, more expensive in the evening). One of the best vegetarian restaurants in Italy. *Closed Sat lunch and Sun.*

Milan is also the home of the ***panini***.

Bar Quadronno, Via Quadronno 34. The oldest panini bar, from 1966. *Open 8–2; closed Mon.*

Panino del Conte, Via Brioletto corner Via dei Bossi 7. Noble sandwiches in Brera, where you can try the famous *piadina del Conte*, and warm *focaccia*. *Open 7–2am; closed Sun.*

Entertainment

Check listings in the daily *Corriere della Sera* and *La Repubblica*'s Wednesday *Tutto Milano* magazine. Other sources include the free *Milano Mese*, available at the tourist office. Tickets are sold at the **Virgin Megastore**, Piazza Duomo 8; **Ricordi**, in Galleria Vittorio Emanuele at Corso Buenos Aires 33; **La Biglietteria**, Via Molino delle Armi 3; **Box Ticket**, Largo Cairoli; and in Stazione Cadorna.

Key venues are listed below:

La Scala, 24hr booking line **t** 02 860 775; *www.teatroallascala.org*. For many, La Scala is the reason for visiting Milan. The opera season runs 7 Dec–mid-July and mid-Sept–mid-Nov. Note that you can only order two tickets at a time, although you can make consecutive reservations. Finding a good seat at a moment's notice is all but impossible; try asking your hotel concierge, or show up at the box office an hour before a performance starts to see what's available.

Anteo, Via Milazzo 9, **t** 02 659 7732 (Ⓜ Moscova). Regularly shows films in English. *Closed Aug.*

Auditorium di Milano, Corso San Gottardo, Navigli, **t** 02 8942 2090. Venue for classical concerts, jazz, choral and chamber music.

Giuseppe Verdi Conservatorio, Via del Conservatorio 12, **t** 02 762 1101 or **t** 02 7600 1854. For classical music. *Closed July–mid-Sept.*

Piccolo Teatro, Via Rovello 2, **t** 7233 3222, *www.piccoloteatro. org*. Italy's best theatre company; book in advance as far as possible.

Teatro Nazionale, Piazza Piemonte 12, **t** 02 4800 7700, *www.teatronazionale.com*. Puts on both plays and musicals.

Nightlife

The *aperitivo* is an old Milanese tradition, so Milan has adopted the happy hour in style and has some good, lively **bars**.

Atiemme, Bastioni Porta Volta 15. Brera's Corso Garibaldi/Corso Como area jumps at night: in spots include this fashionable former train station with good cocktails and music.

Bar Basso, Via Plinio 39 (Città Studi area). Happy hour heaven: over 500 cocktails and home-made ice creams. *Closed Tues.*

Blues Canal, Via Casale 7. Has a Sunday brunch (12–4) with live classical music and top live jazz in the evenings too. Spot Louis Armstrong's trumpet on the walls.

Cocquetel, Via Vetere 14. Very popular, with hundreds of cocktails.

Grand Café Fashion, Corso di Porta Ticinese. One of the most popular bars in town.

Havana, Viale Bligny 50. Has live music, salsa and *merengue* every night.

The **club** scene in Milan is often concerned more with appearance than dancing and having a good time. Generally, clubs open every day until 3am, and the expensive admission entitles you to one free drink. At the time of writing, two discos are hot among fashion victims, models and designers: **Hollywood**, Corso Como 15 (*closed Mon*) and **Shocking**, Via Bastioni di Porta Nuova 12 (*closed Sun and Mon*).

Brera and its National Gallery

From La Scala, Via G. Verdi leads into the **Brera District**. This old neighbourhood maintains some of its original flavour, but it's rapidly becoming trendy, full of antique shops, late night spots and galleries. At the corner of Via Brera and Via Fiori Oscuri is the **Galleria Nazionale di Brera** (Ⓜ *Lanza or Monte Napoleone; open Tues–Sun 8.30–7.15, may close by 6pm in winter; adm*), one of world's finest hoards of art. The collection was compiled by Napoleon, who stripped northern Italy's churches and monasteries to form a Louvre-like collection for Milan, the capital of his Cisalpine Republic.

Perhaps the best known of scores of masterpieces is Raphael's *Marriage of the Virgin*, a Renaissance landmark for its evocation of an ideal, rarefied world. Piero della Francesca's last painting, the *Pala di Urbino*, hangs in the same room. The Venetian masters are well represented: Carpaccio, Veronese, Titian, Tintoretto, Jacopo Bellini and the Vivarini, but especially Giovanni Bellini; there are luminous works by Carlo Crivelli and Cima da Conegliano and several paintings by Mantegna, including his remarkable *Cristo Morto*. Other famous works include Bramante's *Christ at the Column*, Caravaggio's striking *Supper at Emmaus* and a polyptych by Gentile da Fabriano. Outstanding among the non-Italians are Rembrandt's *Portrait of his Sister*, El Greco's *St Francis* and Van Dyck's *Portrait of the Princess of Orange*. The new 20th-century wing is populated mainly by Futurists, who believed that to achieve speed was to achieve success, and the followers of De Chirico, who seem to believe just the opposite.

Castello Sforzesco

Damaged and rebuilt numerous times, the **Castello Sforzesco** (Ⓜ Cairoli or Cadorna) is one of Milan's best-known landmarks, and houses the excellent **Civici Musei d'Arte e Pinacoteca del Castello** (*open Tues–Sun 9–5.30*), storing intriguing fragments of Milanese history. Leonardo designed the ilex decorations of the Sala delle Asse; the Sala degli Scarlioni contains the museum's finest sculptures, including Michelangelo's unfinished *Rondanini Pietà*, a haunting, late work that repudiates all of his early ideals of physical beauty in favour of blunt, expressionistic figures. Lombards predominate in the **Pinacoteca**: Foppa, Solario, Magnasco, Bergognone and Bramantino, and Milanese proto-surrealist Giuseppe Arcimboldo (1527–93), whose *Primavera* depicts a woman's face made up entirely of flowers. The castle also holds an extensive Egyptian collection, Iron-Age items and a beautiful collection of musical instruments.

West of the Duomo

Santa Maria delle Grazie and the *Last Supper*

Ⓜ Cadorna, then Via Boccaccio and left on Via Caradosso. Open Tues–Sun 8.15–6.45; in summer until 10pm on Thurs and Sat; adm exp; booking compulsory, ***t*** *02 8942 1146; only 15 visitors are admitted at a time.*

The convent of Santa Maria delle Grazie has a beautiful 15th-century church, its interior graced with a majestic tribune and choir designed by Bramante, and its refectory decorated with nothing less than Leonardo da Vinci's *Last Supper* (*Cenacolo*) in the refectory, completed in 1498. Seizing the moment when Christ announces that one of his disciples will betray him, it is a masterful psychological study, the apostles' gestures of disbelief and dismay captured intuitively by one of the greatest students of human nature. Unfortunately for posterity, Leonardo was not content to use proper fresco technique (where the paint is applied quickly to wet plaster) but painted with tempera on glue and plaster, enabling him to achieve the subtlety of tone and depth he desired. The result was exceedingly beautiful, but almost immediately the moisture in the walls began flaking off particles of paint. Numerous restorers have tried to save it, most recently Pinin Brambilla, whose Olivetti-funded labours of 22 years (in which she removed all traces from former restorations and painted in the gaps) were revealed in 1999 to near universal outrage from critics.

The Monastero Maggiore and Milan's Financial District

From Santa Maria delle Grazie the Corso Magenta leads back towards the centre; at no.71 is the new home of the fascinating collection of opera memorabilia of the **Museo Teatrale alla Scala** (*open Tues–Sun 9–6, adm*). Further along, on the corner of Via Luini, the Monastero Maggiore has the 16th-century church of **San Maurizio** (*open Sept–June 4–6pm*), with exceptional frescoes by Bernardino Luini. The former convent (*Corso Magenta 15*) houses Etruscan, Greek and Roman collections in the **Civico Museo Archeològico** (*open Tues–Sun 9–5.30*). East of the museum, the area between Sant'Ambrogio and the Duomo has for centuries been the headquarters of Milan's merchant guilds and financiers, concentrated in the **Piazza Cardusio** (Ⓜ Cardusio), Via degli Affari and Via Mercanti.

In Piazza Pio XI, the **Ambrosiana** (***library** open for study; occasional visits for special exhibits or for an appointment, call **t** 02 8645 1436; **pinacoteca** open Tues–Sun 10–5.30; adm*) is Milan's most enduring legacy of its leading family, the Borromei. Cardinal Federico Borromeo's great library, founded in 1609, contains 30,000 rare manuscripts, including a 5th-century illustrated *Iliad*, Leonardo da Vinci's famous *Codex Atlanticus*, and much, much more. The Cardinal's **pinacoteca** ranges from the sublime to the peculiar, showing a marked preference for the Dutch. Here are Botticelli's lovely *Tondo*; paintings by Bergognone (including the altar from Pavia's San Pietro in Ciel d'Oro, *see* p.69), as well as works by Luini, Ambrogio da Predis and Leonardo. The first Italian still-life, Caravaggio's *Fruit Basket*, is also here; further on is Titian's *Adoration of the Magi*, painted for Henri II of France. A small room, illuminated by a stained-glass window of Dante, contains the glove Napoleon wore at Waterloo.

Sant'Ambrogio

*Ⓜ Sant'Ambrogio; **church** open daily 9–12 and 2–8; **museum** open Mon–Fri 10–12 and 3–5, Sat and Sun 3–5; closed Tues; adm.*

Located just off San Vittore and Via Carducci, a stern 12th-century gate guards the last resting place of Milan's patron saint, the beautiful **church of Sant'Ambrogio**. Ambrose was Bishop of Milan between 374 and 397, and his eloquence is given much of the credit for preserving the unity of the Church; he left such an imprint on Milan that to this day genuine Milanese are called Ambrosiani. Founded by Ambrose in 379 and rebuilt in the 1080s, it was the original model for the Lombard Romanesque style. On the left, note the 10th-century bronze serpent and the vigourously sculpted pulpit (1080). The apse is adorned with 10th–11th-century mosaics of the Redeemer and saints, while the sanctuary contains the 9th-century *Ciborium*, and a magnificent gem-studded altarpiece (835). At the end of the south aisle the 4th-century **Sacello di San Vittore in Ciel d'Oro** has brilliant 5th-century mosaics in its cupola and a presumed authentic portrait of St Ambrose. Bramante spent two years working on Sant'Ambrogio, contributing the unusual Portico della Canonica and the two cloisters.

Southern Milan

Southwest of the city centre, Via Torino leads into the artsy Ticinese quarter (*tram 3 from Via Torino*), where pieces of Roman *Mediolanum* can be still seen, most notably the **Colonne di San Lorenzo** on Corso di Porta Ticinese. Here you'll find the oldest church in Milan, the **Basilica di San Lorenzo Maggiore**, housing the beautiful Cappella di Sant'Aquilino (*adm*), with 4th- or 5th-century mosaics of Christ and his disciples. Across the Parco delle Basiliche, the **Basilica di Sant'Eustorgio** is famous for its pure Tuscan Renaissance Cappella Portinari from 1468 (*open Tues–Sun 9.30–12 and 3.30–6; adm*), attributed to Michelozzo and admired for its cubic simplicity and proportions.

The colourful **Navigli** district (Ⓜ *Porta Genova, tram 2 or 14*) is named for its canals, the Naviglio Grande and Naviglio Pavese, that meet to form the docks near Porta Ticinese. Like any good port, the Navigli was once a funky working-class district of warehouses, workshops and sailors' bars; today it's a relaxed, fashionably bohemian zone, attracting many of the city's artists and cheaper restaurants.

Day Trips from Milan

Pavia

Pavia saw its brightest days in the Dark Ages, when it served as capital of the Goths, but later found favour with Gian Galeazzo Visconti, who built the castle to house his art collection and founded the striking Certosa di Pavia. Pavia's core retains its old Roman street plan; much of its northeast quadrant is occupied by the **University of Pavia**. The old *cardus* (Corso Cavour) and *decumanus* (Corso Strada Nuova) intersect by the **Duomo**, possibly the ugliest church in all Italy, which owes its corrugated cardboard façade to an understandable lack of interest in ever finishing it. The Strada Nuova continues to a pretty **Covered Bridge**, leading over the river to **Borgo Ticino**.

East of the Strada along Via Capsoni lies Pavia's most important church, the **Basilica di San Michele Maggiore**, rebuilt in the 12th century and mellowed into a fine golden hue. Intricate – if weatherworn – friezes cross its front like comic strips, depicting an 'apocalyptic vision' of medieval bestiary, monsters and human figures. The interior, where Frederick Barbarossa was crowned with the Iron Crown of Italy, contains more fine carvings on the capitals of the columns.

Getting There

Buses from Milan run roughly every 30mins to the modern station-cum-shopping centre in Via Trieste. There are also frequent **trains** (journey 30mins); the train station is a 10-min walk from the centre, at the end of Corso Cavour and Viale Vittorio Emanuele II.

Tourist Information

Pavia: A couple of streets from the station, at Via Filzi 2, **t** 0382 22156, **f** 0382 32221, *info@apt.pv.it*, *www.apt.pv.it*. Churches are generally open daily, but closed 12–3pm.

Eating Out

Pavia's specialities include frogs, salami and *zuppa pavese* (a raw egg on toast drowned in hot broth); good local wines are from the Oltrepò Pavese region, one of Lombardy's best.

Locanda Vecchia Pavia al Mulino, Via al Monumento 5, **t** 0382 925 894 (*expensive*). A gourmet choice in the restored 16th-century mill of the Certosa, with refined dishes such as truffle-filled home-made ravioli, or prawn with *lardo* of Colonnata and porcini , and delicate desserts. *Closed Mon and Wed lunch.*

Antica Osteria del Previ, Via Milazzo 65, **t** 0382 26203 (*moderate–cheap*). On the Ticino, this old-fashioned place serves home-made salami, risotto with frog or radicchio and speck, and river-fish, frog and snails for *secondi*. A good selection of meats includes kidney, pork, goose and kid. *Closed Sun.*

Osteria del Naviglio, Via Alzaia 39, **t** 0382 460 392. A gourmet wine bar/restaurant on the Naviglio after it bends behind the Castello. Try a vast selection wines alongside *sformato* (a hearty mousse) of potato and porcini, or pappardelle with duck. Excellent desserts include sorbets and *semifreddo*. You can have the *menu degustazione* (*moderate*) or dine cheaply at the wine bar. *Closed Mon.*

At the top of Strada, three sides of the mighty **Castello Visconteo** survive to house Pavia's **Museo Civico** (*open Tues–Fri 10–1.30, Sat and Sun 10–7; Dec–Jan and July–Aug open Tues–Sun 9–1 only*), containing Roman and Gaulish finds, robust Lombard and medieval carvings and colourful mosaics. On the first floor are works by Giovanni Bellini, Foppa, Van der Goes and others. Behind the castle, Via Griziotti leads to **San Pietro in Ciel d'Oro** ('St Peter in the Golden Sky'), built in 1132 and named for its once-glorious gilded ceiling. It has a key work of 14th-century Lombard sculpture: the Campionese Masters' **Arca di Sant'Agostino**, sheltering the bones of St Augustine.

The Certosa di Pavia

Open Tues–Sun, Oct–Mar 9–11.30 and 2.30–4.30; April 9–11.30 and 2.30–5.30; May–Sept 9–11.30 and 2.30–6. If you come on the Milan–Pavia bus, the Certosa is a 1½km walk from the nearest stop.

The Charterhouse of Pavia is the pinnacle of Renaissance architecture in Lombardy. Gian Galeazzo Visconti laid the cornerstone in 1396, with visions of the crown of Italy dancing in his head, and the desire to build himself a fittingly splendid pantheon. It bears the greatest imprint of Giovanni Antonio Amadeo, who, with his successor Bergognone, worked on its sculptural programme for 30 years and contributed the design of the lavish façade. Today's monks still maintain vows of silence, though a couple are released to take visitors around the complex. Once through the **vestibule** a large grassy court opens up; at the far side rises the sumptuous façade of the **church**, a marvel of polychromatic marbles, medallions, bas-reliefs, statues and windows covered with marble embroidery from the chisel of Amadeo. The interior decoration is

Renaissance, with Baroque additions. Outstanding works of art include Bergognone's statues of saints in the chapel of Sant'Ambrogio; the tombs of Lodovico il Moro and his bride, by Cristoforo Solari; the beautiful inlaid stalls of the choir; and the tomb of Gian Galeazzo Visconti, all works of the 1490s. The sacristry contains a magnificent early *cinquecento* ivory altarpiece, with 94 figures and 66 bas-reliefs.

Piacenza

Piacenza is a quiet old town, with two superb Baroque bronze horses by Francesco Mochi in its centrepiece square **Piazza Cavalli**. From here, the main Via XX Settembre leads to the Lombard–Romanesque **Duomo** (1122–1233), a picturesque confusion of columns, caryatids and galleries, in the shadow of an unusual octagonal cupola and a mighty campanile (1333). The Romanesque–Gothic interior features a striking striped floor and some good 15th-century frescoes, while reliefs on columns in the nave show the work of various local guilds. The cupola has frescoes of *Old Testament Prophets* by the Milanese Morazzone; most of the dome and the *Sibyls* below were done by Guercino.

East of the Duomo on Via G. Alberoni, **San Savino** (*if closed, try* **t** *0523 322 661*) is Romanesque (1107) behind its late-Baroque façade, and has two remarkable original mosaics. One, in the presbytery, shows a classically allusive Time, or Fate, spinning, surrounded by the cardinal virtues: Justice, Fortitude, Temperance and Prudence. The other, in the crypt, depicts the signs of the zodiac and the labours of the months.

Getting There

There are around two trains per hour from Milan's Stazione Centrale (40–50mins) to Piacenza's **station** on Piazzale Marconi, a 10-min walk from the centre.

Tourist Information

Piacenza: Piazza Cavalli 7, **t** 0523 329324, **f** 0523 306727, *www.piacenzaturismi.it*.

Eating Out

Piacenza follows Parma in the kitchen, offering similar meats – *coppa* and *pancetta* – and equally similar *tortelli caudati*, filled with ricotta, Parmesan and herbs. *Pisarei e faseu*, which appears on some menus, is a dish of dumplings in saucy beans.

Antica Osteria del Teatro, Via Verdi 16, near Sant'Antonino, **t** 0523 384 639 (*very expensive*). One of Italy's very best restaurants, where local recipes merge delectably with French nouvelle cuisine: the *tortelli del Farnese* with butter and sage are as light as a summer's breeze; *secondi* include seafood, heavenly *foie gras* in pastry, layered with honey and Calvados, or a bit of Sardinia in the roast suckling pig perfumed with myrtle; for dessert, splurge on one of the heavenly chocolate concoctions. There's a choice of two *menus di degustazione*. Be sure to book. *Closed Sun, Mon and Aug*.

La Carozza, Via 10 Giugno, north of the station off Viale S. Ambrogio, **t** 0523 326 297 (*moderate*). You can get a fine plate of spaghetti *alle vongole* and a grilled fish or mixed grill here. *Closed Sun*.

La Pireina, Via Borghetto 137, **t** 0523 338 578 (*cheap*). A traditional *trattoria* near the old city walls, serving typical local dishes in a simple, unpretentious way: *tortelli d'erbette* (stuffed with spinach and ricotta), *tagliolini al ragù*, or *faldia* (a type of schnitzel made with horse steak). *Closed Sun, Mon eve, and first half of Aug*.

From Piazza Cavalli, Corso Cavour leads to the pachydermic **Palazzo Farnese**, former residence of the Farnese family but now home to the **Musei Civici** (*open Tues, Wed and Thurs 8.30–1, Fri, Sat and Sun 8.30–1 and 3–6; closed Mon; guided tours at 9.30, 10.15 and 11; adm*), a complex of four museums, with lavishly decorated rooms, numerous paintings of the Farnese family and some excellent detached 14th-century frescoes. The highlight among the paintings upstairs is Botticelli's *Tondo* (1480s), but pride of place goes to Ilario Spolverini, a specialist in Farnese-flattering ceremonial scenes and biblical extravaganzas worthy of Cecil B. de Mille. In the Hall of Sculptures, five good Renaissance reliefs of the Apostles share space with the most famous Etruscan bronze of all, the *Fegato di Piacenza*, a model of a liver diagrammed and inscribed with the names of Etruscan deities. The Etruscans regarded the liver as a microcosm of the sky, divided into 16 houses and each ruled by a god; the augurs looked in the liver for blemishes to see which deity had anything to communicate.

Overnighter from Milan

Como

Sapphire Lake Como has been Italy's prestige romantic lake ever since the early days of the Roman Empire. The city itself is small and lively, with a bent for science, silk and architecture. In AD 23 it gave us Pliny the Elder, compiler of antiquity's greatest work of hearsay, the *Natural History*, and later it produced his nephew Pliny the Younger, whose letters are one of our main sources for information on Roman life of the time.

Como's historic centre opens up to the lake at **Piazza Cavour**, with its cafés, hotels, steamer landing and pretty views. In the park just to the west stands the striking **Monumento ai Caduti**. It was designed by the Futurist architect Antonio Sant'Elia of Como (1888–1916), but built by local Giuseppe Terragni (1904–34), the most inspired Italian architect of the Fascist period, whose buildings are spread throughout Como.

From Piazza Cavour, Via Plinio leads to Como's elegant Piazza Duomo, where the **Torre del Comune** is attached to the **Broletto**, and this in turn to the magnificent **Duomo** (1396), the most harmonious example of transitional architecture in Italy. Gothic dominates in the façade, rose window and pinnacles. The sculpture and reliefs are mainly by the Rodari family (late 15th–early 16th century). Pliny the Elder and Pliny the Younger flank the central door; Renaissance humanists regarded all noble figures of antiquity as honorary saints. Inside, the three Gothic aisles combine happily with a Renaissance choir and transept, crowned by a late Baroque dome by Filippo Juvarra. Most of the art is from the Renaissance: in the right aisle are scenes from the Passion by Tommaso Rodari, and fine canvases by Gaudenzio Ferrari (*Flight into Egypt*) and Luini (*Adoration of the Magi*); the latter's famous *Madonna with Child and Four Saints* adorns the high altar. The left aisle has works by Rodari, Ferrari and Luini.

For a contrast, go behind the Duomo to the Piazza del Popolo, where Terragni's **Palazzo Terragni** stands out in all its functional, luminous beauty. Built in 1931, the palace is 50 years ahead of its time, an essay in light and harmony. It is a masterpiece of the only coherent architectural style Italy has produced in the 20th century.

Como's Romanesque gem, **Sant'Abbondio**, is a short walk from the **Porta Vittoria**, a 72ft skyscraper-gate from 1192. With its lofty vaults and forest of columns, it offers a kind of preview of great events in Italian architecture. Its clean, unadorned majesty is relieved by the rich bands of reliefs around the windows, imitating the intricate patterns of damasks from the Near East. The elegant apse is decorated with 14th-century frescoes: note the knights in armour arresting Christ in Gethsemane.

Como is framed by beaches: one lies on the west end of town in Via Cantoni; the other at the east end, by the **Villa Genio**. Nearby, in the Piazza De Gasperi, funiculars wind up to **Brunate**, a mountain village with famous views across the lake as far as Monte Rosa (*trains every 15–30 mins; call* **t** *031 303 608; combined ticket ferry/funicular*).

Getting There and Around

Frequent FS **trains** from Milan's Centrale or Porta Garibaldi stations take some 40mins to reach Como's main San Giovanni station (**t** 147 888 088). Slower trains on the Milano-Nord line go to the lakeside station of Como-Lago.

A **steamer** (July and Aug), motor boats and hydrofoils are run by Navigazione Lago di Como, Piazza Cavour, **t** 031 304 060, **t** (free) 800 551 801. Some services stop in winter.

Tourist Information

Como: Piazza Cavour 17, **t** 031 269 712, **f** 031 240 111, *lakecomo@tin.it*, *www.lagodicomo.com*. Provides maps for **walkers**; the trek from Como to Bellágio is exceptionally pretty.

Where to Stay

Como ✉ 22100

★★★★**Le Due Corti**, Piazza Vittoria 15, **t** 031 328 111, **f** 031 265 226 (*expensive*). A converted monastery offering characterful rooms around the cloister; all preserve much of their original architecture and are furnished with antiques. Modern concessions include a/c, satellite TV, minibar and jacuzzis in some bathrooms, and a small outdoor pool. There's also an Art Deco bar, a wine bar, a good restaurant and piano bar.

★★★**Park Hotel**, Viale Fratelli Rosselli 20, **t** 031 572 615, **f** 031 574 302 (*moderate*). Recently renovated and welcoming, near the lake and close to S. Giovanni railway station.

★★★**Marco's**, Via Lungo Lario Trieste 62, **t** 031 303 628, **f** 031 302 342 (*moderate*). Has small rooms with TV, phone and balcony, near the lake front and the cableway to Brunate.

★★**Posta**, Via Garibaldi 2, **t** 031 266 012, **f** 031 266 398, *www.hotelposta.net* (*cheap*). This was designed in 1930 by Terragni, although refurbishment has altered the interiors.

Eating Out

Villa Flori's Ristorante Raimondi, **t** 031 573 105 (*expensive*). For an elegant splurge, join Como society at the Villa Flori hotel, where exquisite renditions of classic Italian cuisine are served on the lakeside terrace or in the luminous dining room. *Closed Mon.*

Le 7 Porte, Via A. Diaz 54, **t** 031 267 939 (*expensive*). Within the walls, featuring Italian delicacies imaginatively mixed with unusual ingredients, such as ravioli with carrots and yoghurt. Good salads, fish and meats in two stylish vaulted rooms. *Closed Sun.*

Osteria Angolo del Silenzio, Via Lecco 25, **t** 031 337 2157 (*expensive; cheap one-course lunch on weekdays*). Just outside the walls; it has home-made pasta, fish and meat, game and mushrooms in season, and a nice courtyard. A good cellar for wine tasting. *Closed Mon.*

Villa Olmo Parco, Via Cantoni 1, **t** 031 572 321 (*moderate*). Serves well-prepared food with fine wines near the beach. *Closed Tues.*

Ristorante Teatro Sociale, near the cathedral on Via Maestri Comacini, **t** 031 264 042 (*cheap*). Post-theatre traditional inn, with a good €15 menu including wine. *Closed Tues.*

Touring from Milan and Bergamo

Day 1: An Ideal Citadel, a Holy Hill and a Doll House

Morning: Drive to **Castiglione Olona**. From **Milan**, take the S233 north via Saronno towards Varese; from **Bergamo**, take the S342 west, passing Como and turning left at San Salvatore onto the road to Vedano Olona. Beyond Vedano, the road meets the S233 just north of Castiglione. In Castiglione, find the ghastly new church and take the steep road into the valley to find Cardinal Castiglioni's **Borgo**, an 'ideal citadel' nearly unchanged since the 15th century. Visit the **Palazzo Branda Castiglioni** (*open April–Sept Tues–Sat 9–12 and 3–6; Sun and hols 10.30–12.30 and 3–6; Oct–Mar Tues–Sat 9–12 and 3–6; Sun 3–6*) and the **Collegiata** (*open Oct–Mar Tues–Sun 10–12 and 2.30–5; April–Sept Tues–Sun 9.30–12 and 3–6.30*), filled with Masolino's masterly frescoes.

Lunch: In Castiglione Olona, or continue up the S233 into Varese, *see* below.

Afternoon: Wander through **Varese**'s gardens and take bus C to the **Sacro Monte** (*see* p.31), with 14 chapels filled with Baroque art. Head to Lake Maggiore, following the road west from Varese to Gavirate, then cutting across via Besozzo and Brébbia to the S629, which leads south to the **Rocca di Angera** (*open April–Oct daily 10.30–12.30 and 4–6; Jul and Aug 9.30–12.30 and 3–7; adm*). See its fabulous doll collection (*open Mar–Oct 9.30–12.30 and 3–7; adm*), and the vast **Sala della Giustizia**, frescoed with astrological fancies and battle scenes. Drive on around the lake to **Stresa** on the S33.

Dinner and Sleeping: In Stresa, *see* below.

Day 1

Lunch in Castiglione Olona

La Cantina del Borgo Osteria degli Artisti, Via Roma 32, **t** 0331 859 021 (*moderate*). In the city centre. A nice place to eat local *brasati*, risotti and polenta. *Closed Mon.*

Lunch in Varese

Lago Maggiore, Via Carrobio 19, **t** 0332 231 183 (*expensive*). In an 18th-century palace on the edge of the city centre. Has been one of Varese's best restaurants for decades, using top-notch ingredients in regional and more exotic dishes; the cheeseboard alone may revolutionize your ideas about Italian cooking. *Closed Sun and Mon lunch.*

Dinner in Stresa

Piemontese, Via Mazzini 25, **t** 0323 30235 (*expensive*). Find a table in the garden to tuck into the divine spaghetti with melted onions, basil and pecorino and the excellent fish dishes. *Closed Mon, Jan and half of Feb.*

The Irish Bar, Via Passeggiata Margherita 9, **t** 0323 31054. An institution for years, run by the hospitable Giovanni and Brigid Zawetta.

Sleeping in Stresa

*****__Des Iles Borromées__**, Corso Umberto I 67, **t** 0323 938 938, **f** 0323 32405, *www.stresa.net/hotel/borromees* (*luxury*). Opened in 1861; stylish in its aristocratic Belle Epoque furnishings and its mod cons. Overlooking the islands and a lovely, flower-decked, palm-shaded garden; there's a pool, beach, tennis, a gym and a 'well-being' centre.

***__Moderno__, at Via Cavour 33, **t** 0323 933 773, **f** 0323 933 775, *moderno@hms.it* (*expensive–moderate*). Rooms are set round an inner patio; all have TV, and there are also two very good restaurants. *Open Mar–Oct.*

*__La Locanda__, Via Leopardi 19, **t/f** 0323 31176 (*cheap*). Near the Mottarone cableway, this is a quiet family-run hotel: all 14 rooms are comfortable, with bath, and most have their own balcony, although with no lake view. *No restaurant; private parking.*

Day 2: Luxuriant Villas, Gardens and Views

Morning: Explore Stresa, Maggiore's most beautiful town, bursting with flowers and sprinkled with fine old villas, and famous for its mild climate. The little triangular **Piazza Cadorna** is Stresa's social centre, swollen in August and September by music lovers attending the *Settimane Musicali di Stresa*. Visit the 1850 **Villa Pallavicino** (*open Mar–Oct, daily 9–6; adm*) and its colourful gardens, where saucy parrots rule the roost, and the 18th-century **Villa Ducale** (*open daily 9–12 and 3–6; donation requested*), once the property of Catholic philosopher Antonio Rosmini. Drive up the beautiful, villa-lined road to **Baveno**, where in 1879 Queen Victoria spent a summer at the Villa Clara, now **Castello Branca**.

Lunch: In Baveno, *see* below.

Afternoon: Take a boat trip – or row yourself – to the islands of the Borromei to see their sumptuous gardens and villas on **Isola Bella** and **Isola Madre** (*guided tours daily end Mar–end Oct: end Mar–end Sept 9–12 and 1.30–5.30; Oct 9.30–12 and 1.30–5; adm exp*), which between them offer fine collections of art, tapestries and 18th-century marionettes, artificial grottoes and a luxuriant botanical garden (*be sure to pick up the free guide to the plants*). Between Baveno and Stresa, a road winds west via Gignese and Alpino up to **Monte Mottarone** (4,920ft). Drive up to enjoy its famous views, taking in not only all seven Italian lakes, but also glacier-crested peaks from Monte Viso in the west to the Adamello in the east. Continue down to **Armeno**, from where a road leads southwest to **Orta San Giulio**, on the shore of Lake Orta.

Dinner and Sleeping: In Orta San Giulio, *see* below.

Day 2

Lunch in Baveno

★★★**Al Campanile**, Via Monte Grappa, **t/f** 0323 922 377 (*moderate*). A pretty old villa-hotel in a lush garden in the centre, with a nice restaurant on the garden terrace with local seasonal dishes. *Closed Wed out of season.*

★★**Serenella**, Via 42 Martiri 5, Feriolo, **t** 0323 28112, **f** 0323 28550 (*moderate*). Just north of Baveno, serving delicious home-made pasta, risottos, and fresh fish or meat *secondi*; has a summer garden. *Closed Wed, Jan and Feb.*

Dinner and Sleeping in Orta San Giulio

★★★★**Villa Crespi**, Via G Fava 8/10, **t** 0322 911 902, **f** 0322 911 919, *www.lagodortahotels.com* (*very expensive*). In a garden at the top of town, this Moorish folly was built in 1880 and painstakingly restored and furnished with period pieces. Rooms have romantic canopied beds, marble baths and jacuzzis. The elegant dining room offers ravishing dishes mixing Mediterranean and alpine flavours: macaroni with lobster ragout or pigeon breast stuffed with foie gras and wrapped in savoy *labrage*. The wine list has over 400 labels. Menus are surprisingly good value. *Closed Tues in winter, Jan and Feb.*

★★★**Orta**, Piazza Motta, **t** 0322 90253, **f** 0322 905 646, *www.orta.net/hotelorta* (*moderate*). Brimming with old-fashioned character, the Orta has been run by the same family for over a century, with big rooms and bathrooms and a charming dining terrace on the lake.

★★**Olina**, Via Olina 40, **t** 0322 905 656, **f** 0322 90377 (*moderate*). Very pleasant rooms, some with whirlpool shower, and an elegant restaurant whose specialities are home-made pasta, lake fish and meat cooked on a earthenware pot (*moderate*). *Closed Wed.*

Taverna Antico Agnello (*moderate*). A cosy and charming place with lake fish and venison *cotoletta* with juniper; also a good selection of cheeses, sliced hams and salami, delicious *torte di verdura*, home-made pasta, *confiture* and desserts and a good wine list; book in advance and if ordering risotto. *Closed Tues.*

Day 3: Dragon Island Haunts and Folkloric Valleys

Morning: Wend your way through the narrow lanes in Orta San Giulio, known for its flower festival (*April/May*). Walk from the Via Motta (*40–60mins*) along the shoreline around the promontory, catching a glimpse of the patrician villas through their gardens. You can drive up to Orta's **Sacro Monte** (*park always open but chapels open summer 9–5.30; winter 9–4.30*), one of the best of its kind, with life-sized statues in 17th-century costume enacting scenes from St Francis' life. Alternatively, jump on a ferry (*every 15–20 mins*) to **Isola San Giulio**, inhabited by dragons until AD 390 when Giulio showed up and sent them packing. Take a look in his **basilica** (*open daily 9.30–12.15 and 2–6.45 (5.45 in winter); Mon closed until 11*) with its striking **pulpit**, and take in the view of the opposite shore over a drink on the restaurant terrace. Drive round the lake to its northern tip, pausing for lunch near **Omegna**.

Lunch: Around Omegna, *see* below.

Afternoon: Drive north of Omegna along the S229/S33, following the River Toce; here the Ossola valleys cut deep into the Alps, sculpted by moody rivers. At **Villadòssola**, take a detour up the pretty wooded **Val d'Antrona**, famed for its old-fashioned ways: the older women still wear traditional costumes every day and make Venetian lace. At **Domodòssola**, take the S337 east along the **Val Vigezzo**, a romantic haven of hills and velvet pastures, known as 'the Valley of Painters', who, inspired by the landscape, left exterior frescoes behind in the villages. Note the pretty frescoed chapels scattered through **Druogno** on your way to **Santa Maria Maggiore**.

Dinner and Sleeping: In Santa Maria Maggiore, *see* below.

Day 3

Lunch around Omegna

Ponte Bria, Via Ponte, Bria, **t** 0322 863 732 (*moderate*). In the woods a few km from Omegna near the hamlet of Cireggio di Omegna, this restaurant has a little artificial lake for trout fishing. Specialities include home-made *crespelle*, ravioli and gnocchi, grilled trout directly from the lake, grilled venison and meat fillets served on a hot stone. *Closed Mon out of season, Nov–Feb.*

***Leone**, Forno, **t/f** 0323 885 112 (*cheap*). Family run, peaceful and cosy. The restaurant serves typical local dishes such as young goat with polenta and homemade salami. Try the special *torta del pane* cake.

Da Libero, Fornero, **t** 0323 87123 (*cheap*). A favourite rendezvous for its authentic, well-prepared trout, polenta, rice dishes and more, served on a lovely terrace in the summer. Rice dishes with champagne or mushrooms are the specialities. Book in advance. *Closed Tues and Jan.*

Dinner and Sleeping in Santa Maria Maggiore

*****Miramonti**, Piazzale Diaz 3, **t** 0324 95013, **f** 0324 94283, *www.miramontihotels.com* (*moderate*). You can sleep and eat in style up near the station here, preferably at the cosy chalet with flowers flowing over the balconies. Dine in candlelight at the hotel restaurant on finely prepared local dishes, including the traditional cake *pane e latte* (stale bread, milk, raisins), and indulge yourself afterwards with the local *digestivo* S. Giacomo, poured from tall narrow bottles (*menu vigezzino at €21*).

*****Delle Alpi**, **t/f** 0324 9490 (*moderate*). Another family-run hotel opposite the pedestrian centre, with a nice front terrace.

Locarno, next to the church, **t** 0324 95088 (*cheap for pizza, moderate for restaurant*). This serves good pizzas in the evening. *Closed Tues.*

Da Brianin, in front of the church, **t** 0324 94933 (*moderate*). This offers local dishes, fish and home-made cakes served in a sober and elegant dining room.

Day 4: A Politician's Villa and a *Danse Macabre*

Morning: Continue up the Val Vigezzo to the picturesque, higgledy-piggledy village of **Malesco**. Turn right onto a road that will keep you in second gear as you wind down the wild, sparsely populated **Val Cannobina** to Lake Maggiore, passing a cluster of wee hamlets known as **Cavaglio-Spoccia**. Pause in **Cannobio**, an ancient town with steep, medieval streets, where every Sunday morning sees the entire lake front given over to a bustling market. Look into the **Santuario della Pietà** to see the altarpiece by Gaudenzio Ferrari, one of his finest. Next continue south to **Verbania-Pallanza**, passing by way of pleasant, quiet **Ghiffa**, famous for its felt hats. Stop for lunch in pretty **Pallanza**.

Lunch: In Pallanza, *see* below.

Afternoon: Visit the celebrated **Villa Taranto** (*if the prime minister is not in, open April–Oct daily 8.30–7.30; adm exp*), planted with 20,000 different kinds of plants; the aquatic plants, spring tulips and autumn colour in particular are exceptional. Catch the car ferry from **Intra** to **Laveno-Mombella** and drive south down the S629 to visit the deserted convent of **Santa Caterina di Sasso** (*open 8.30–12 and 2–6; follow the signs from the shore road and walk down from the car park*), hanging – literally – on the cliffs between Cerro and Reno, with its medieval frescoes; don't miss the 16th-century *Danse Macabre* in the loggia. Drive north along the lake shore, turning right in **Luino** to reach **Ponte Tresa**. Here, take the S23 north to **Lugano** for a Swiss interlude.

Dinner and Sleeping: In Lugano, *see* below.

Day 4

Lunch in Pallanza

Milano, Corso Zanitello 2, **t** 0323 556 816 (*expensive*). In a fine old lake-front villa, with dining out on the romantic terrace. The food is some of the finest on Maggiore: wonderful *antipasti* and lake fish prepared in a number of delicious styles. *Closed Tues.*

Osteria dell'Angolo, Piazza Garibaldi 35, **t** 0323 556 362 (*moderate*). On the lake front, with lovely food: *crespelle* stuffed with *scamorza* cheese, and various risottos (book the latter in advance). *Closed Mon.*

Dinner in Lugano

Antica Osteria Gerso, Piazzetta Solaro 24 at Massagno, **t** 966 1915 (*moderate*). An intimate, simple restaurant serving a limited but discriminating menu: onion soup with tangy pecorino cheese, *tortelli di zucca alle mandorle* and duck with oranges, with wine from the adjacent *enoteca*. Book a day or two ahead. *Closed Sun and Mon.*

Parco Saroli, Via Stefano Franscini 6, **t** 923 5314. This fashionable eaterie serves excellent and unusual home-made pasta, seafood, superb breads, cheeses, desserts and an award-winning wine list: *menu* SF47.50, a 6-course *menu degustazione* SF65. *Closed Sat and Sun.*

Sleeping in Lugano

*****__Villa Principe Leopoldo__, Via Montalbano 5, **t** 985 8855, **f** 985 8825, *www.leopoldo-hotel.com* (*luxury*). A 19th-century Relais & Châteaux in a beautiful hillside park overlooking the city; the restaurant has gourmet Mediterranean and international cuisine.

__Fischer's Seehotel__, Sentiero di Gandria 10, **t 971 5571, **f** 970 1577 (*expensive–moderate depending on room*). Simple and pleasant; smack on the lake far from the traffic. It has a nice restaurant (kitchen closes at 8.30pm).

*__Montarina__, Via Montarina 1, **t** 966 7272, **f** 966 1213, *www.montarina.ch* (*cheap*). Hotel/hostel in a 19th-century villa in a palm garden, with lake views, parking, a pool and chicken farm. Comfortable rooms with bath a bit extra.

Day 5: An Arty Swiss City and *Bella* Bellágio

Morning: Spend the morning in warm, palmy Lugano, an arty city with sumptuous lake views and a sumptuous Renaissance gem in waterfront Piazza Luini: the church of **Santa Maria degli Angioli**, frescoed in 1529 with an enormous *Crucifixion* by Luini, thought to be his masterpiece. Choose between art from the late Gothic period and 19th and 20th centuries in the **Museo Cantonale d'Arte** (*entry in Via Canova 10; open Wed–Sun 10–5, Tues 2–5; adm*), or the **Villa Favorita** (*open Easter–Oct, Fri–Sun 10–5; adm exp*) where the Thyssen collection of European and American modern art has an emphasis on the Luminists and Hudson River School. Drive east out of Lugano, following the S340 along the shore back to Italy and pausing in **Porlezza** for lunch.

Lunch: In Porlezza, *see* below.

Afternoon: Drive on past the tiny, enchanting Lago di Piano to the shore of Lake Como at **Menággio**, a pleasant resort with a beach. Take the car ferry across to **Bellágio**, spectacularly set at the tip of the mountainous Triangolo Lariano. Explore its steep, stepped lanes of handsome houses, spilling over with flowers, or linger on the waterfront watching the ferries glide to and fro. There are two fine villas to visit: the spectacular grounds of the **Villa Serbelloni** (*guided tours April–Oct Tues–Sun at 11 and 4; tickets available from the tourist office up to 10mins beforehand*); and the **Villa Melzi** (*open late Mar–Oct daily 9–6.30; adm*), its immaculate lawns, banks of flowers and water-lily pond all decorated with Egyptian, Roman and Hellenistic sculpture.

Dinner and Sleeping: In Bellágio, *see* below. In the morning, take the S583 south to Lecco; then take the S36 for Milan, or the S639 south to join the S342 to Bergamo.

Day 5

Lunch in Porlezza

★★★**Regina**, Lungolago Matteotti 11, **t** 0344 61228, **f** 0344 72031, *www.hregina.com*, (*moderate*). The hotel restaurant features good home-made pasta, excellent fish and breast of duck with grapes, and a very convenient 2-course menu (€15). *Closed Mon.*

Il Crotto del Lago, in Cima di Porlezza hamlet, Via Fontanella 3, **t** 0344 69136 (*moderate*). For outdoor dining on a terrace above the lake, specializing in fish (sea and lake).

Dinner in Bellágio

Barchetta, Salita Mella 13, **t** 031 951 389 (*expensive*). Feast on creative Lombard cuisine on a terrace over Bellágio's narrow streets. Try the foie gras and pasta, rigorously home-made, or lake delicacies. The wine list is unparalleled. *Set menus from €30. Closed Tues, Nov–Feb.*

Bilacus, Salita Serbelloni 9, **t** 031 95080 (*moderate*). On a romantic terrace in the centre; feast on excellent, intense *spaghetti alle vongole*, saffrony mushroom risotto, or simple grilled fish. *Closed in winter.*

Sleeping in Bellágio

★★★★★**Grand Hotel Villa Serbelloni**, Via Roma 1, **t** 031 950 216, **f** 031 951 529, *www.villaserbelloni.it* (*luxury*). A magnificent, ornate hotel set in a flower-filled garden at the tip of the headland. The frescoed public rooms are glittering and palatial, and there's a heated pool and private beach, tennis, gym, boating and water-skiing, and evening dancing to the hotel orchestra. *Open April–Oct.*

★★**Silvio**, Via Carcano 12, **t** 031 950 322, **f** 031 950 912, *www.bellagiosilvio.com* (*moderate*). A few km from the centre in Loppia, on the road to Como. An absolute must for good value accommodation, friendly service, peaceful surroundings and excellent home cooking. Rooms are comfortable, and all with lake or garden view. Try the lovely fish ravioli and *tiramisù* which have been approved by Pavarotti, Chancellor Kohl and Robert de Niro.

Bergamo

Bergamo mixes a rugged edge with delicate refinement; it has given the world not only a great peasant dance, the *bergamasque*, but also the maestro of *bel canto*, Gaetano Donizetti, the Renaissance painter of beautiful women, Palma Vecchio, and the great master of the portrait, Gian Battista Moroni. And, in the 16th century, the city became so prosperous that another Bergamo, Bergamo Bassa, grew up on the plain below.

Bergamo Bassa

The heart of Bergamo's pleasant Città Bassa, laid out in the 1920s, is wide, stately, lined with trees and always full of cars. Viale Giovanni XXIII goes up from the station to the elongated **Piazza Matteotti**, flanked by cafés, the 18th-century **Teatro Donizetti** and the church of **San Bartolomeo**, housing an altarpiece by Lorenzo Lotto. To the west is the city's shopping area, around the Piazza Pontida, while a few blocks east, **Via Pignolo** is lined with 16th-century *palazzi* and three churches, each with paintings by Lotto. Via Pignolo continues north to Piazzale Sant'Agostino, where the 16th-century **Porta Sant'Agostino** is the main gate to the Città Alta. From just inside the gate, the Viale delle Mura circles the top of the mighty **Venetian walls** (1561–1588).

Off Via Pignolo, just outside the walls of the Città Alta, Via della Noca leads east to the **Accademia Carrara** (*open daily 9.30–12.30 and 2.30–5.30; adm; adm free Sun*), one of the top provincial art museums in Italy. It has exquisite portraits: Botticelli's haughty *Giuliano de' Medici*, Pisanello's *Lionello d'Este*, Gentile Bellini's *Portrait of a Man* and Lotto's *Portrait of Lucina Brembati* with a vicious weasel under her arm and a sickly moon overhead. Other portraits (especially the *Young Girl*) are by Bergamo's Giovanni Battista Moroni (1520–78), the master to whom Titian sent the *Rectors of Venice*, with the advice that only Moroni could 'make them natural'. There are beautiful *Madonnas* by Giovanni Bellini, Mantegna, Fra Angelico, Landi and Crivelli. Other paintings are by Cariani, Fra Galgario, Palma Vecchio and Previtali (all from Bergamo), Bergognone, the Venetians Carpaccio, Vivarini, Titian, Veronese, Tintoretto, Tiepolo and Guardi; the Brescian school; also Cosmè Tura, Van Dyck and Bruegel.

Opposite, at Via S. Tomaso 53, the **Galleria d'Arte Moderna e Contemporanea** hosts temporary exhibitions, mostly of 20th-century art (*open Mon, Wed–Fri 9.30–12.30 and 3–7, Thurs till 10.30, Sat and Sun 10–7; hours may vary according to exhibitions*).

The Città Alta: Piazza Vecchia

The view of the Città Alta, its domes and towers rising boldly on the hill against a background of mountains, is one of the most arresting urban views in Italy. Bus no.1 stops at the **funicular**, built in 1887 to ascend to the heart of the Città Alta. From here, a short walk takes you to the beautiful **Piazza Vecchia**, encased in a magnificent ensemble of medieval and Renaissance buildings. At the lower end, the white **Biblioteca Civica** was modelled after Sansovino's famous library in Venice; among its treasures is Donizetti's autograph score of *Lucia di Lammermoor*. Next is the 12th-century **Torre Civica** (*open April–Sept daily 9–12 and 2–8, Fri and Sat till 11pm,*

Sun 9–8pm; March daily 10–12 and 2 to 6; Oct weekends and hols only 10–12 and 2–6; Nov–Feb weekends and hols only 10–12 and 2–4; adm), with a 15th-century clock and curfew bell that still vainly orders the Bergamasques to bed at 10pm; visitors can walk up the stairs for the views over the city. Closing the square, the 12th-century **Palazzo della Ragione** has some interesting capitals and a relief of the Lion of St Mark, added in 1800 to commemorate Bergamo's golden days under Venice.

The dark tunnel arches of the Palazzo della Ragione afford glimpses into a second square, **Piazza Duomo**, and what appears to be a jewel box. This reveals itself to be the sumptuous façade of the 1476 **Colleoni Chapel** (*open daily 9–12 and 2–6.30; Nov–Mar till 5.30; closed Mon*), designed by Giovanni Antonio Amadeo. Bartolomeo Colleoni was born just around the corner in 1395. At the height of his fame as a *condottiere* he was given complete control of Venice's armies and, after his death, he received the unique honour of an equestrian statue in Venice, which as a rule never erected personal monuments. The chapel is a crazy quilt of medieval motifs and flourishes that spits in the face of the usual Renaissance aims of proportion and serenity. Amadeo also sculpted the tombs within, a double-decker model for Colleoni and his wife, although the golden equestrian statue by Sixtus of Nuremburg on top does the *condottiere* no favours. The fine paintings under the dome were done by G.B. Tiepolo in 1733.

Flanking the chapel are the octagonal **Baptistry** of 1340 (*open by appointment, **t** 035 278 111*) in white and red marble, and the colourful porch (1353) of the **Basilica of Santa Maria Maggiore**. The basilica, from 1137, is one of the finest Romanesque churches in Lombardy; the palatial late 16th-century interior hits you like a gust of old perfume. Sumptuous tapestries hang from the walls, including scenes from the *Life of the Virgin* by Alessandro Allori, but the best art is off limits in the chancel and choir, where Lorenzo Lotto designed a series of 33 Old Testament scenes, beautifully executed in *intarsia* in 1552 by Capodiferro di Lovere. At the back of the church, Donizetti's spirit hovers over a keyboard at his tomb, along with mourning putti.

Piazza Vecchia is also the site of the insipid **Duomo**, which was given a pseudo late Baroque façade in 1886. Inside there is a *Martyrdom of St John* by Tiepolo, a boxwood bishop's throne by Fantoni, *SS. Fermo, Rustico and Procolo* by Sebastiano Ricci (all 1700s) and Cariani's early 16th-century *Madonna of the Turtle Doves*.

Around the Città Alta

The rest of the Città Alta deserves a stroll. The Visconti, who ruled Bergamo until the Venetians snatched it in 1428, built the 14th-century **Rocca** (*tower open Sat and Sun 12–2.30*) at the highest point in the Città Alta, affording a fine view from the park. Below, Via Porta Dipinta curves around to the Porta Sant'Agostino, passing two churches: neoclassical **Sant'Andrea**, housing a superb altarpiece by Moretto; and Romanesque **San Michele al Pozzo Bianco**, its solemn interior illuminated with frescoes from the 1200s and 1500s. Further along, the **Convento di Sant'Agostino** contains more frescoes, from the 14th and 15th centuries, including some by Vicenzo Foppa.

To the west of the Rocca, Via Colleoni leads up past the *condottiere*'s house at no.9 (*call **t** 035 217 185 to visit*) to the 14th-century **Cittadella**, the former residence of the

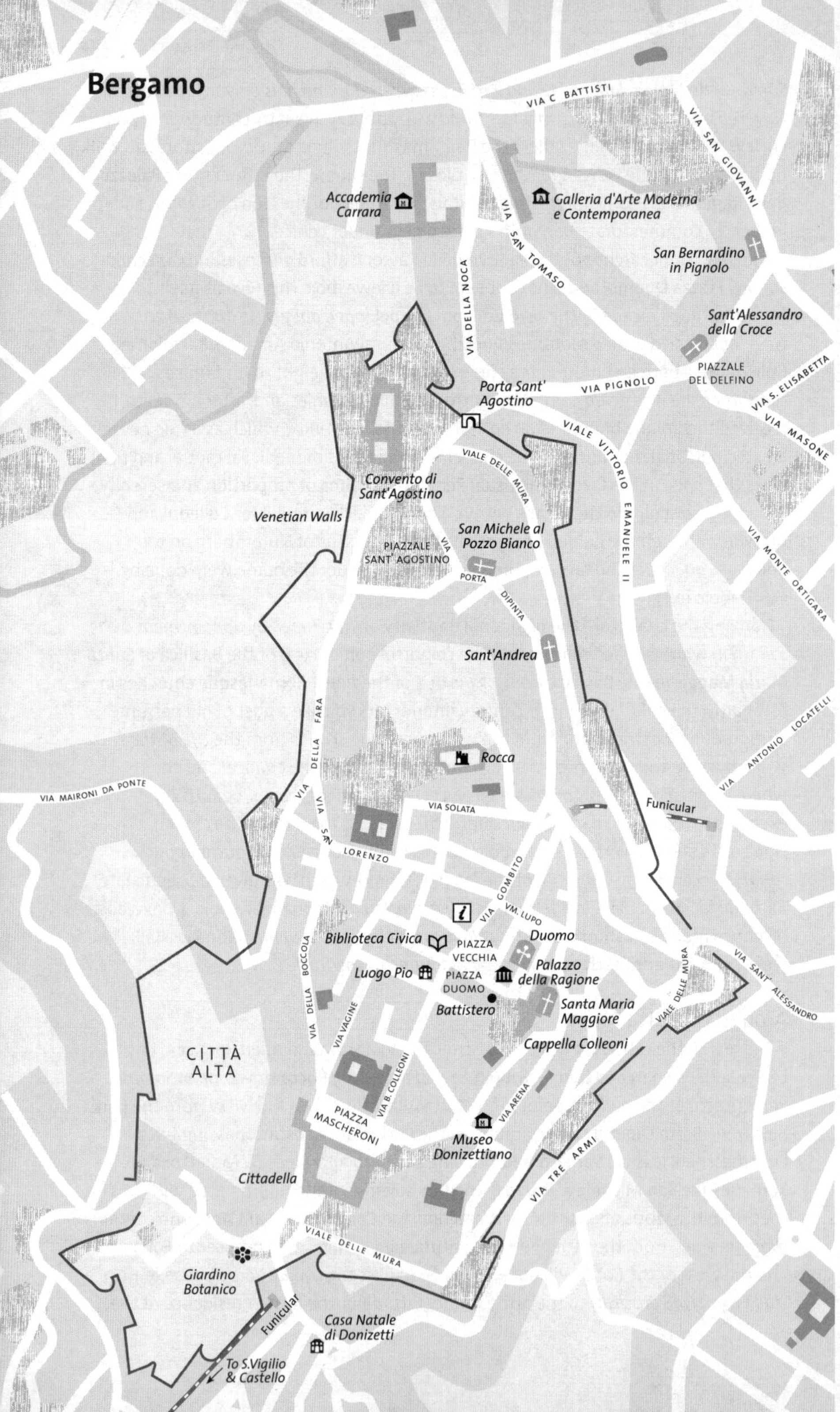
Bergamo
VIA C BATTISTI
VIA SAN GIOVANNI
Accademia Carrara
Galleria d'Arte Moderna e Contemporanea
VIA SAN TOMASO
VIA DELLA NOCA
San Bernardino in Pignolo
Sant'Alessandro della Croce
PIAZZALE DEL DELFINO
VIA PIGNOLO
Porta Sant' Agostino
VIA S. ELISABETTA
VIA MASONE
VIALE VITTORIO EMANUELE II
VIALE DELLE MURA
Convento di Sant'Agostino
Venetian Walls
PIAZZALE SANT' AGOSTINO
San Michele al Pozzo Bianco
VIA PORTA DIPINTA
VIA MONTE ORTIGARA
Sant'Andrea
VIA DELLA FARA
Rocca
VIA ANTONIO LOCATELLI
VIA MAIRONI DA PONTE
VIA SOLATA
Funicular
VIA SAN LORENZO
VIA GOMBITO
VM. LUPO
Biblioteca Civica
PIAZZA VECCHIA
Duomo
Luogo Pio
PIAZZA DUOMO
Palazzo della Ragione
Battistero
Santa Maria Maggiore
VIA SANT' ALESSANDRO
VIALE DELLE MURA
VIA DELLA BOCCOLA
VIA VAGINE
Cappella Colleoni
CITTÀ ALTA
VIA B. COLLEONI
VIA ARENA
PIAZZA MASCHERONI
Museo Donizettiano
Cittadella
VIA TRE ARMI
VIALE DELLE MURA
Giardino Botanico
Funicular
Casa Natale di Donizetti
To S.Vigilio & Castello

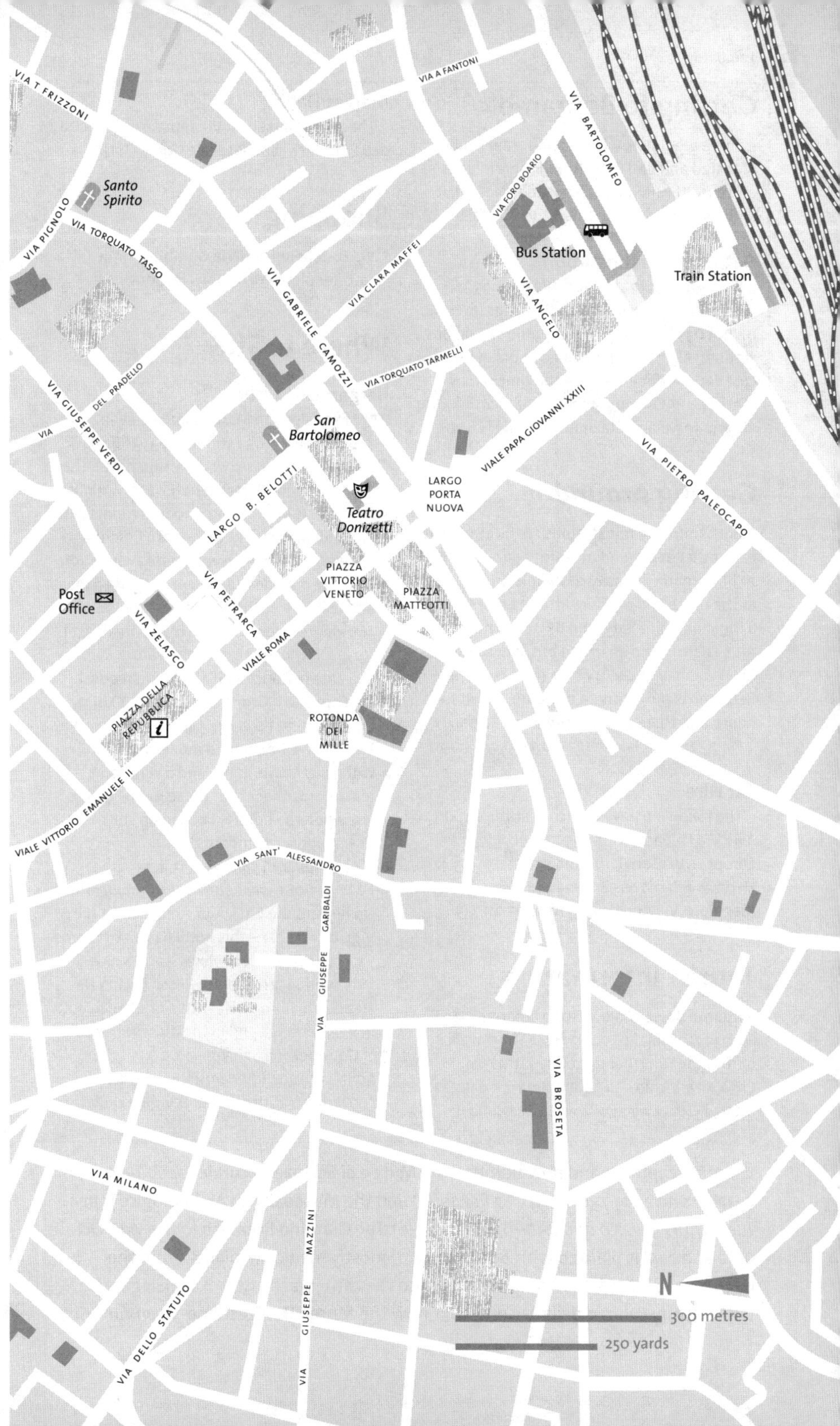
VIA T FRIZZONI
VIA A FANTONI
VIA BARTOLOMEO
VIA FORO BOARIO
Santo Spirito
VIA PIGNOLO
VIA TORQUATO TASSO
Bus Station
Train Station
VIA CLARA MAFFEI
VIA GABRIELE CAMOZZI
VIA ANGELO
VIA TORQUATO TARMELLI
VIA DEL PRADELLO
VIA GIUSEPPE VERDI
San Bartolomeo
VIALE PAPA GIOVANNI XXIII
VIA PIETRO PALEOCAPO
LARGO PORTA NUOVA
LARGO B. BELOTTI
Teatro Donizetti
PIAZZA VITTORIO VENETO
PIAZZA MATTEOTTI
Post Office
VIA PETRARCA
VIA ZELASCO
VIALE ROMA
PIAZZA DELLA REPUBBLICA
ROTONDA DEI MILLE
VIALE VITTORIO EMANUELE II
VIA SANT' ALESSANDRO
VIA GIUSEPPE GARIBALDI
VIA BROSETA
VIA MILANO
VIA GIUSEPPE MAZZINI
VIA DELLO STATUTO
N
300 metres
250 yards

Getting to Bergamo

There are flights with **Ryanair** from London Stansted and **BMI Baby** from East Midlands and Cardiff (1hr20 from Stansted). Note that airlines may advertise this airport as Milan.

Getting from the Airport

Bergamo's Orio al Serio airport (**t** 035 326 323) is 5km from Bergamo. ZANI **buses** (every 30 mins; **t** 035 678 611) go to Bergamo's main bus station, taking around 5mins (€1.05). A **taxi** will cost €20–25 depending on the time of day.

AUTOSTRADALE buses, **t** 035 318 472, link Orio al Serio to **Milan**'s Stazione Centrale (€6.70).

Getting Around

Both **train** and **bus stations** are located near each other at the end of Viale Papa Giovanni XXIII. Bergamo is easily navigable on foot, and at the north end of Viale Vittorio Emanuele II, a **funicular** joins Bergamo Basso to the Città Alta. There is also an **urban bus** service (**tickets** €1). If you have a **car**, try to leave it elsewhere. Bergamo is purgatory to navigate, hell at rush hours, and there's hardly anywhere to park.

For a **taxi**, call Taxi Bergamo, **t** 035 451 9090.

Car Hire

The following have branches at the airport:

Avis, Via Paleocapa 3, **t** 035 271 290.
Europcar, Via San Bernardino 133, **t** 035 315 428.
Hertz, Via Camozzi 38, **t** 035 248 186.
Maggiore, Via Angelo Maj 16, **t** 035 211 333.

Tourist Information

Bergamo Basso: Viale Vittorio Emanuele 20, **t** 035 210 204, **f** 035 280 184, a short walk from the funicular up to the Città Alta.

Città Alta: Vicolo dell'Aquila Nera 3, **t** 035 242 226, **f** 035 242 994, *www.apt.bergamo.it*.

Market Days

There are markets in **Via Morale** (*Fri*), **Piazza della Città** (*Fri*) and **Piazzale Goisis** (*Sat*).

Shopping

Via B. Colleoni and **Via Gombito**, in the Città Alta, offer plenty of options for souvenirs.

Where to Stay

Bergamo ✉ 24100

******Excelsior San Marco**, Piazzale della Repubblica 6, **t** 035 366 111, **f** 035 366 175, *www.hotelsanmarco.it* (*very expensive*). The city's most comfortable hotel, a few minutes from the funicular, with modern rooms with a/c, and an excellent restaurant Colonna (*expensive; set menus moderate*), where you can dine outside (June–Sept) on grilled meat and fish. The beautiful roof terrace has a 360-degree view over the town; breakfast is served in the terrace's conservatory. Rooms at a cheaper price available upon request.

******Cappello d'Oro**, Viale Giovanni XXIII 12, **t** 035 232 503, **f** 035 242 946 (*expensive*). This has well-equipped modern rooms with lovely bathrooms, and a very good **restaurant**. Check that those rooms rented out when the hotel is booked up still meet the category's standards.

*****San Vigilio**, Via S. Vigilio 15, **t** 035 253 179, **f** 035 402 081, *www.sanvigilio.it* (*moderate*). Up beyond the Città Alta – reached by the S. Vigilio cable car – this hotel has just 7 rooms – 5 with magnificent views – and a nice olde-worlde atmosphere. Host Tiziana De Franceschi is an artist with a fine touch both in her paintings and in the dishes she cooks.

*****Gourmet**, Via San Vigilio 1, **t** 035 251 610, **f** 035 437 3004 (*moderate*). Family-run and convenient, at the foot of S. Vigilio cablecar.

Venetian captains, and now home to the **Museo di Scienze Naturale** (*open Tues–Sun 9–12.30 and 2.30–7.30; until 5.30 in winter*) and the **Museo Civico Archeològico** (*open Tues–Thurs 9–12.30 and 2.30–6; Fri–Sun 9–6*). The **Giardino Botanico** (*open Mar–Oct 9–12 and 2–5*) is planted with 600 species of mostly medicinal plants. From the Cittadella, medieval Via Arena leads back to the cathedral by way of the elegant 13th-century Palazzo della Misericordia, now the **Museo Donizettiano** (*open Tues–Sat*

There's a nice terrace for outdoor dining and the restaurant (*expensive*) offers gourmet cuisine ranging from fish to meat and delicacies such as Iranian caviar. *Closed Tues.*

****Agnello d'Oro**, Via Gombito 22, **t** 035 249 883, **f** 035 235 612, *www.agnellodoro.it* (*moderate*). The most atmospheric hotel in the Città Alta was built in 1600, although rooms are modern, all with bath and TV. The excellent **restaurant** (*moderate*) offers regional dishes including *casoncelli, maize foiade* and rice dishes, beef stew, sausages and quails with polenta. Dine out in a little square in front in the summer. *Closed Mon.*

****San Giorgio**, Via S. Giorgio 10, **t** 035 212 043, **f** 035 310 072, *san_giorgio@infinito.it* (*cheap*). Near the station, this has quiet rooms with private bath, TVs and other comforts.

***Caironi**, Via Toretta 6, **t** 035 243 083, **f** 035 236 938 (*cheap*). A friendly, family-run traditional *locanda* in Bergamo Bassa, a 20-min walk from the station (bus 5, 7 or 8). It has a nice garden for summer dining, and rooms have shared bathrooms on each floor. The **restaurant** (*cheap*) looks promising. *Closed Mon.*

Eating Out

Bergamo prides itself on its cooking: look for *casoncelli* (ravioli of tangy sausage-meat, in butter, bacon and sage), *polenta taragna* (with butter and cheese), and risotto with *funghi*. It is also a major inland fish market. In August, though, you might have to resort to a picnic.

Da Vittorio, Viale Papa Giovanni XXIII 21, **t/f** 035 218 060 (*expensive*). The classic for fish and exquisitely prepared seafood, as well as a variety of meat dishes, polenta, risotto and pasta. *Closed Wed, and three weeks in Aug.*

Taverna del Colleoni, Piazza Vecchia, **t** 035 232 596, **f** 035 231 991 (*expensive*). A celebrated restaurant featuring exquisite classical Italian cuisine, including delicate dishes such as ravioli filled with leek and potato in a pine nut pesto. Slightly cheaper menu at lunch. *Closed Mon and two weeks in Aug.*

Baretto di San Vigilio, Via Castello 1, **t** 035 253 191 (*expensive*). Just off the exit of San Vigilio cablecar, a fine restaurant with a stylish and secluded atmosphere. Fish a speciality, but also mouthwatering pasta (black tagliolini with shrimps), soups, meat dishes – try the *maialino* (pork) on an aubergine tarte – great *antipasti* and a good choice of wines and cigars. Best to book. *Closed Mon.*

Da Ornella, Via Gombito 3, **t** 035 232 736 (*moderate*). The place for *polenta taragna* with rabbit, chicken and *porcini*, served in hot cast-iron bowls, and *casoncelli*, local *affettati* and braised meats. *Closed Thurs.*

La Colombina, Borgo Canale 12, **t** 035 261 402 (*moderate–cheap*). A near perfect restaurant near Donizetti's birthplace, with stunning views from its dappled terrace, and a pretty Liberty-style (Art Nouveau) dining room. Try the salad of local *taleggio* cheese with pear, a plate of cured meats, and the best *casoncelli* in town. Leave room for the caramelized apple cake. *Closed Mon and Aug; may also be closed one week in Jan and June.*

Bar Donizetti, Via Gombito 17a, **t** 035 242 661. A nice wine bar with tables in the arcaded market; it serves gourmet snacks – *crostini* with gorgonzola, honey and truffle – and hot dishes. *Closed Fri, and mid-Oct–mid-Nov.*

San Vigilio, Via San Vigilio 34, **t** 035 251 388. For pizzas with a view: an enchanting panorama of the Paduan plain; a good choice at all times and for all purses. *Closed Wed.*

Marianna, by the Porta S. Alessandra. The place to go for ice cream, where you can sit on the shady terrace gorging on fig, apricot, rose petal or peach flavours. Also good for Tuscan cuisine. *Closed Mon in winter.*

Caffè Balzer, Portici Sentierone 41. A historical café in Bergamo Bassa, facing the Teatro Donizetti, selling *pâtisserie*.

10–1 by appointment; Sun 10–1 and 2.30–5), with a few wistful sticks of Donizetti's furniture, his little piano, portraits and daguerreotypes. You can also visit his birthplace, the **Casa Natale di Donizetti** (*open Sat and Sun 11–6.30, or call* **t** *035 320 472*), on Via Borgo Canale, just outside the walls near Bergamo's second funicular. This rises up to **San Vigilio** and another fortress, the **Castello**, with superb views over the green Parco dei Colli.

Day Trips and Overnighters from Bergamo

The Valle Seriana

Northeast of Bergamo, the Valle Seriana plunges into the stony heart of the Orobie Alps. Industrial in its lower half and ruggedly alpine in the north, the valley is Bergamo's favourite summer retreat, and is also known for the whirling Baroque wood sculptures and carvings by the Fantoni and Caniana families. **Clusone**, in the middle of the valley, is the prettiest town and capital of the Valle Seriana. In central Piazza dell'Orologio, the 11th-century **Palazzo Comunale** is covered with secular frescoes – the most joyfully decorated building in Lombardy – and bears a beautiful astronomical clock called the **Orologio Planetario Fanzago** (1583); come on a Monday when the market in the *piazza* overflows with cheeses and sausages. Near the clock, the **Oratorio del Disciplini** is adorned with an eerie 1485 fresco of the *Danse Macabre* and the *Triumph of Death*, where one skeleton mows down the nobility and clergy with arrows, while another blasts them with a blunderbuss (at the time of writing undergoing major restoration). There are more frescoes inside from the same period, especially a superb *Crucifixion*; the *Deposition* is another work by the Fantoni, who also contributed works in the late 17th-century **Santa Maria Assunta**. But it's the exterior frescoes and porticoes that lend Clusone so much of its charm; in the 1980s others were reclaimed from under the grimy stucco, including one glorious, grinning Venetian lion.

Further up the valley, **Castione della Presolana** is the biggest resort of the Valle Seriana, surrounded by striking dolomitic mountain scenery: the population in August

Getting There

There are regular **bus** services (**t** 035 289 011) from Bergamo's main bus station to the Valle Seriana, taking about 1hr to reach **Clusone** and 1hr20 or so to **Castione**. Buses leave hourly on weekdays, every 1–2hrs on Sun and hols.

Tourist Information

Clusone: Piazza dell'Orologio, **t** 0346 21113.

Castione della Presolana: Piazza Roma, **t** 0346 60039, or **t** 0346 31146.

Eating Out

Clusone ✉ 24023

Antica Locanda Hotel, Piazza Uccelli 1, **t** 034 621 413 (*moderate*). The hotel restaurant prides itself on its regional cuisine, including local wines, *salumi* and cheeses. *Closed Tues.*

Albergo Ristorante Alpino, Via Querena 22, **t/f** 034 621 314 (*moderate*). Another hotel restaurant to try for its genuine Bergamasque mountain dishes.

Castione della Presolana ✉ 24020

★★★★**Milano**, at Bratto, **t** 0346 31211, **f** 0346 36236 (*expensive in season, otherwise moderate*). A large complex in a park designed for families, complete with two restaurants (the Caminone is especially good) as well as an *enoteca*. *Closed Oct and Nov.*

★★★**Prealpi**, also at Bratto, **t/f** 0346 31180 (*top of cheap range*). Older hotel with rooms with bath, and disabled access; the restaurant serves regional specialities. *Closed mid-Sept to mid-Oct.*

Getting There

By Train

Regular trains from Bergamo serve **Milan**'s Stazione Garibaldi (Ⓜ 2), taking one hour. There are also services to Milan's Stazione Lambrate (Ⓜ 2), on the east side of the city.

There are also frequent rail services to **Brescia** (1hr). For rail information, call **t** (toll-free from Italy) 1478 88088.

By Bus

There are regular bus services (**t** 035 289 011) to both **Milan** and **Brescia**.

Tourist Information

Milan: Piazza del Duomo, Via Marconi 1, **t** 02 7252 4301/2/3, **f** 7252 4350 (*open Mon–Fri 8.30–7; Sat 9–1 and 2–6; Sun 9–1 and 2–5*).

Brescia: Corso Zanardelli 34, **t** 030 43418/ 45052, **f** 030 293 284, *promobs@tin.it*, *www.bresciaholiday.com*.

Where to Stay and Eat

See the listings for **Milan** (pp.62–5) and **Brescia** (pp.87–8) for details on selected hotels and restaurants in these two cities.

leaps from 3,000 to 30,000. The pulpit in the parish **church** was sculpted by the Fantoni workshop. One of the biggest attractions is the lovely **Passo della Presolana** (3,691ft), with its near sheer dolomite walls, and **Monte Pora**, a ski resort, with tremendous views over Lake Iseo.

Milan

Should you require a dose of designer retail therapy, cosmopolitan Milan (*see* pp.58–68) is just an hour's train ride from Bergamo. What's more, if you can tear yourself from the shops, the city is amply endowed with older treasure troves: La Scala, a host of masterpieces by the likes of Leonardo, Raphael and Botticelli, and the third largest cathedral in the world, to name a few.

Brescia

Equally close, but in the other direction, Brescia (*see* pp.86–90) has outstanding relics and remains from its days as Roman Brixia, as well as fine Lombard architecture, and churches and galleries decorated by its own school of Renaissance artists, namely Vincenzo Foppa, Romanino and Moretto. As Italy's leading producer of firearms, the city also has a gun or two to show.

Touring from Bergamo

See pp.73–7 for a trip around Lake Orta, Lake Maggiore and the Ossola Valleys, or pp.100–104 for Lake Garda and its surroundings.

Brescia

Brescia is a busy and prosperous place, but somehow it's no one's favourite town. Perhaps it's the vaguely sinister aura of having been Italy's chief manufacturer of arms for the last 400 years. Perhaps it's because the local Fascists saw fit to punch out the heart of the old city and replace it with a *piazza* as frosty and heavy as an iceberg. Or perhaps it's because this region of Italy is so rich in tempting towns that most people yield instead to the charms of Verona, Milan or Bergamo. Nevertheless, Brescia has a full day's supply of fine art, architecture and historic attractions, and its Roman and Lombard relics are among the best preserved in northern Italy.

The Central Squares

Hurry, as the Brescians do, through the deathly **Piazza della Vittoria**, a frigid, Fascist square designed in 1932 by Marcello Piacentini. Behind the post office is a far more elegant display of power, the **Piazza della Loggia**, named for the 1492 **Palazzo della Loggia** (*public areas open in office hours*), its great white roof swelling over the old city like Moby Dick. Looming up behind the **Torre dell'Orologio** is the lead-roofed crown of the **Duomo**, built in 1602 by Gianbattista Lantana (*open Mon–Sat 7.30–12 and 4–7.30, Sun 8–1 and 4–7.30*); from the interior you can visit the adjacent **Duomo Vecchio** or

Getting to Brescia

Ryanair flies from London Stansted (2hrs10).

Getting from the Airport

Gabriele D'Annunzio airport (**t** 030 965 65110) is 11 miles east of Brescia at Montichiari. **Buses** to Brescia's bus station depart from outside Arrivals, connecting with regular flights (6.10am–8.45pm; journey 30mins). You can buy **tickets** (€5) on board. A **taxi** will be €35 or so.

If you're on your way to **Verona**, *see* p.96.

Getting Around

Brescia is easy to make your way around on foot. The **bus** and **railway** stations are next to each other just south of the city centre: on Viale Stazione, the railway station and the SIA bus station serving the Brescia province, **t** 030 377 4237; around the corner, in Via Solferino 6, the other bus services serving all other destinations including Garda, Cremona, etc., **t** 030 34915. Bus C goes to the city centre, a 10-min walk up the Corso Martiri della Libertà.

For a **taxi**, call Radiotaxi, **t** 030 35111.

Car Hire

The following have branches at the airport:
Avis, Via XXV Aprile 16, **t** 030 295 474.
Europcar, Viale della Stazione 49, **t** 030 280 487.
Hertz, Via XXV Aprile 4C, **t** 030 45132.
Maggiore, Viale della Stazione 88, **t** 030 49268.

Tourist Information

Brescia: Corso Zanardelli 34, **t** 030 43418 or 45052, **f** 030 293 284, *www.bresciaholiday.com*, near the Piazza del Duomo.

Museum Ticket (€6): Includes the Museums of Santa Giulia, Risorgimento, Pinacoteca Tosio Martinengo and Ancient Arms Luigi Marzoli.

Market Days

The main market is held in the **Piazza Loggia** (*Sat*). An antiques market is held in the Piazza della Vittoria (*second Sun of the month*).

Events

The *Mille Miglia* vintage car race across Italy gets under way in Piazza della Vittoria in May.

Shopping

Brescians are proud of their wines, olive oil and fish from the surrounding region. This is not a touristy town, but the main shopping area is along **Corsos Zanardelli** and **Magenta**, **Via Gramsci** and **Via X Giornate**.

Where to Stay

Brescia ✉ 25100

Brescia caters mainly to business clients, and its best hotels are comfortable if not inspiring.

*******Vittoria**, Via X Giornate 20, **t** 030 280 061, **f** 030 280 065 (*very expensive*). The city's premier hotel has large, sumptuous rooms, palatial bathrooms, banqueting suites, and liberal marble and chandeliers, but the Fascist-era architecture is a bit soulless.

*****Master**, Via L. Apollonio 72, **t** 030 399 037, **f** 030 370 1331 (*expensive–moderate*). By the castle, this is family run and offers spacious if simple rooms, a nice gazebo in the garden and a cheap menu in the restaurant.

La Rotonda (*open April–Oct Wed–Mon 9–12 and 3–7; Nov–Mar Sat and Sun only, 9–12 and 3–6*). Built in the 11th century over the ancient Roman baths, this is shaped just like a top hat: low and rotund, with a massive cylindrical tower. Inside, its form is broken only by a 15th-century raised choir; the altarpiece, by Moretto, is one his greatest works. Several medieval bishops are entombed around the walls, while the treasury holds two relics: the 16th-century *Stauroteca* containing a bit of the True Cross, and the 11th-century banner once borne on the *carroccio* (ox-cart) of the Brescian armies.

On the other side of the new Duomo stands the vast 12th-century **Broletto**, its formidable tower predating it by a century. Behind the new Duomo, the **Biblioteca Queriniana** (*closed to the public*) contains 300,000 rare books and manuscripts.

★★★★**Ambasciatori**, Via Crocifissa di Rosa 92, **t** 030 399 114, **f** 030 381 883 (*moderate*). A bit further out and very modern; this is family-run and offers a warm welcome, very good rooms, all with a/c, private bath and TV.

★★★**Antica Villa**, Via San Rocchino 90, **t** 030 303 186, **f** 030 338 4312 (*moderate*). A little further outside the centre, this offers warm hospitality in a secluded 18th-century villa at the foot of the Ronchi hills. Soundproofed rooms with a/c; car park.

★★★**Astron**, Via Togni 14, **t/f** 030 48220 (*moderate–cheap*). This offers clean, simple rooms overlooking the station, making it convenient for the city centre, although its proximity to the station is a disadvantage.

★★**Trento**, Piazzale Cesare Battisti 31, off Porta Trento, **t** 030 380 768 (*moderate–cheap*). Fairly new and conveniently located within walking distance of the city centre and castle. Rooms have all mod cons including a/c, and the restaurant has a cheap menu.

Eating Out

Brescians are rather conservative at table: stews, polenta, skewered meat and risotti have been in vogue since the Renaissance.

La Sosta, Via San Martino della Battaglia 20, **t** 030 295 603 (*expensive*). An elegant restaurant, set in a restored 17th-century stable; the menu features prestige fish and Italian classics. *Closed Mon, Sun eve, and Aug.*

Castello Malvezzi, Via Colle San Giuseppe 1, **t** 030 200 4224 (*expensive*). A lovely medieval place just north of the centre, serving delicious food to go with a superb selection of wines (€45 average meal). *Closed Mon and Tues, 15 days Aug and Jan.*

I Templari, Via Matteotti 19, **t** 030 375 2234 (*expensive*). Fresh seafood with a Tuscan touch. *Closed Sat lunch, Sun and Mon lunch.*

Duomo Vecchio, Via Trieste 3, **t** 030 40088 (*moderate*). An intimate place near the Duomo Vecchio, serving excellent southern Italian dishes. Try the reasonably priced lunch menu. *Closed Tues.*

Locanda dei Guasconi, Via Beccaria 11/G, **t** 030 377 1605 (*moderate*). A medieval setting in the centre for traditional polenta and lamb, but also more unusual fare such as ostrich meat. Very popular with young people. Book in the evening. *Closed Mon.*

Giovita, Via San Faustino 63, **t** 030 290 6513 (*moderate*). Serves a range of soups, risottos, boiled meats and other local specialities. It also offers cheap and hearty single-dish menus at lunch. *Closed Sun.*

Al Graner, Piazzale Arnaldo, **t** 030 375 9345 (*moderate*). A popular meeting place in this lively *piazzale*, specializing in meat, including Fiorentina steak. *Closed Mon.*

Bersagliera, Corso Magenta 38, **t** 030 375 0569 (*cheap*). A good, popular pizzeria. *Closed Mon.*

La Vineria, Via X Giornate 4, **t** 030 280 477 (*cheap*). Feast here on excellent cured meats and salami, herby risotto, *casoncelli* and home-made tarts. *Closed Mon.*

Due Stelle, Via San Faustino 48, **t** 030 42370 (*cheap*). One of Brescia's oldest *osterias*, with a nice wine-tasting cellar and a courtyard with a fountain for dining in the summer. It serves tripe, *casoncelli* and peasant dishes, such as chicken dumplings in broth. Dried cod from Thurs to Sun; good *antipasti*. *Open Tues–Wed lunch only, Thurs–Sun all day.*

Osteria dell'Elfo, Piazza Vescovato 1/b, **t** 030 377 4858. A popular spot for an aperitif and snack in the evening. *Closed Mon.*

Roman and Lombard Brixia

Flanking the Broletto, the ancient *Decumanus Maximus* (Via dei Musei), leads to the heart of Roman Brixia. Its forum, the **Piazza del Foro**, lies under the mighty columns of the **Capitoline Temple**, erected in AD 73 and preserved by a medieval mud-slide that covered it until 1823. A Republican-era Capitoline temple has since been discovered beneath, with unusual mosaics of natural stone. The Temple is divided into three *cellae*, containing the lapidarium, tablets, altars and architectural fragments of the Roman age. Next to it is the unexcavated **Roman Theatre**, while in Piazza Labus you can make out the columns of the **Senate**, imprinted like a fossil in the wall of a house.

From Piazza del Foro, Via dei Musei continues to the **Monastero San Salvatore-Santa Giulia** (*open end Oct–May Tues–Sun 9.30–5.30; July–Sept Tues–Sun 10–6; adm: see combined ticket, p.87*), where the **Museo della Città** documents the various layers of Brescian history, from prehistory through the Roman, Lombard, Carolingian, Middle Ages to the Venetians. At the heart of the complex is the 8th-century **Basilica of San Salvatore**; in the nave, the capitals are either ancient Roman or made of stucco, an art at which the Lombards excelled. Some Carolingian frescoes remain under the arcades; others were painted by Girolamo Romanino in 1530. The semi-circular crypt contains vigorous capitals sculpted by the school of Antelami: the one on the life of St Giulia is a serene masterpiece. Two other churches, added in the 12th and 16th centuries, contain frescoes by Floriano Ferramola (1480–1528).

The **Civico Museo Romano** (*open winter Tues–Sun 9–12.30 and 3–5; summer Tues–Sun 10–12.30 and 3–6; adm*) holds a considerable Roman collection. Among the treasures are six gilded bronze busts of emperors and a 6ft bronze *Winged Victory*, all found in the temple; a gilt bronze figurine of a Gaulish prisoner, believed to be Vercingetorix; a beautiful Greek amphora (6th century BC); and a facsimile of the 25ft-long Peutringer Map of Vienna, itself a 12th-century copy of a Roman road map. Other exceptional pieces are an 8th-century golden *Cross of Desiderius*, studded with 212 gems and cameos, and a 4th-century ivory coffer adorned with beautiful scriptural bas-reliefs. Lombard jewellery, medieval art and Renaissance medals round out the collection.

The Cydnean Hill

The hill behind Via dei Musei formed the core of Gaulish and early Roman Brixia. Up on top, an imposing Venetian gate marks the entrance to the **Castello** with its round 14th-century Mirabella Tower. The dungeon houses the **Museo Civico delle Armi Antiche Luigi Marzoli** (*open June–Sept Tues–Sun 10–5; Oct–May 9.30–1 and 2.30–5; adm*), with one of Italy's most extensive collections of arms and armour; it features a special display of 15th–18th-century firearms. The castle granary holds the **Museo del Risorgimento** (*same hours*), with more weapons, paintings, uniforms and decrees, while the gardens are a favourite refuge from the car-filled city below.

The Pinacoteca

From the Capitoline Temple, Via Crispi descends to Piazza Moretto and the **Pinacoteca Civica Tosio-Martinengo** (*open June–Sept Tues–Sun 10–5; Oct–May 9.30–1 and 2.30–5; adm*), housed in a 16th-century patrician palace. It showcases Brescia's local talent, including Vincenzo Foppa (1485–1566), Giovanni Girolamo Savoldo (1480–1548), Alessandro Bonvoncino (or Moretto; 1498–1554), Girolamo Romanino (1485–1566) and Giacomo Antonio Ceruti (1698–1767). Foppa's monumental paintings were among the first to evoke a single, coherent atmosphere, while Moretto contributed the first Italian full-length portrait. Savoldo is recognized for his lyrical use of light, while Ceruti's un-romanticized genre paintings of Brescia's humble, demented and down-and-out were a unique subject for the time. Among the non-Brescians represented are Moroni of Bergamo (taught by Moretto); Lorenzo Lotto (a lovely *Adoration of the Magi*); Tintoretto; Clouet; and two early works by Raphael.

West Side Churches

The piquant quarters west of the Piazza della Loggia are worth exploring for their interesting old churches, many of which contain good frescoes by the Brescian school. Among them, two are strikingly unusual: **San Faustino in Riposo** (*open Mon–Sat 7.30–11 and 3–7, Thurs 7.30–10 only, Sun 7.30–12 and 3.30–7*), a cylindrical, steep-roofed drum of a church from the 12th century (west of Via S. Faustino, near Via dei Musei) and, further up, on Contrada Carmine, the 14th-century **Santa Maria del Carmine** (*open summer Tues–Sun 10–12 and 4–7; shorter hrs in winter*), crowned with Mongol-like brick pinnacles; it contains some of Foppa's finest frescoes, and a 15th-century terracotta *Deposition* by Mazzoni. Further south on Corso Matteotti, the 18th-century **Santi Nazzaro e Celso** (*open during Mass, Sat 6pm and Sun at 9, 10, 11 and 6; or call **t** 030 375 4387*) houses the Averoldi polyptych (1522), considered the masterpiece of Titian's youth, with a gravity-defying *Risen Christ* in the centre that soars overboard into the numbing bathos of spiritual banality. The chapels hold works by Moretto.

Day Trips from Brescia

Cremona

Cremona is famous for four things that have added to the sum total of human happiness: its Romanesque cathedral complex, Claudio Monteverdi, nougat and violins. Walking around you can easily pick out in the curves and scrolls on the palaces that inspired the instrument's form. Today some 50 *liutai* (violinmakers) keep up the tradition, and every third October (in 2003) the city hosts a festival of stringed instruments. You can have an introduction to the cream of the industry at the **Museo Stradivariano**, near the station on Via Palestro (*no.17; open Tues–Sat 8.30–6, Sun and hols 10–6; closed Aug; adm*), featuring casts, models and drawings explaining how Stradivarius did it. Around the corner at Via U. Dati 4; bypass the dreary paintings in the **Museo Civico** (*same hours*) for the archaeology section, which has a fine labyrinth mosaic featuring Theseus and the Minotaur (*c.* 2nd century AD) from the Roman *colonia* at Cremona.

South of the museum, Via Palestro continues into the heart of town as Corso Campi, passing just west of **Piazza Roma**, where Stradivarius' red marble tombstone lies on Corso Mazzini. As you approach the seductive medieval **Piazza del Comune**, you may glimpse the curious pointed crown of the tallest belltower in Italy, the 370ft **Torrazzo** (***tower** open April–Oct Tues–Sun 10.30–12 and 3–6, till 7pm Sun and hols; Nov–Feb weekends and hols only 10.30–12 and 3–6; adm; visits to **clock room** and **violinmaker's shop** by appointment only, **t** 0372 27633; adm exp*). Built in the 1260s, it has battlements, bells and a fine astronomical clock added in 1583.

Linked to the Torrazzo by a double loggia, the **Duomo** is the highest and one of the most exuberant expressions of Lombard Romanesque, with a trademark local flourish in the graceful scrolls added to the marble front. The main **Porta Regia** remains in its

Getting There and Around

Cremona's **train** station is delightful: there are train services roughly hourly from Brescia, taking 45mins. The station lies north of the centre, at the end of Via Palestro. Buses arrive at and depart from the bus station in Via Dante, next to the train station. **Boating** on the Po is possible at Portour, Via Roncobasso 8 (Porto Canale area), **t** 0368 7413636.

Tourist Information

Cremona: Piazza del Comune 5, **t** 0372 23233, freetoll **t** 800-655511 (from Italy), **f** 0372 534 080, *www.cremonaturismo.com*.

To visit a **violin workshop**, ask for their free list of *Botteghe Liutarie*.

Shopping

Local producers of Cremona's famous nougats include **Sperlari**, Via Sperlari 25 and **Vergani**, Corso Matteotti 112. **Lanfranchi**, Via Solferino 30, offers traditional Pan Cremona, soft with almonds, honey and chocolate.

Eating Out

Ristorante Il Violino, Via Sicardo 3, **t** 0372 46101 (*expensive*). A classy place behind the baptistry, enjoying an enviable reputation for its regional dishes: melt-in-the-mouth *antipasti*, *tortelli di zucca* and zesty *secondi* featuring meat or seafood. Book ahead. *Closed Mon eve and Tues.*

Trattoria Mellini, Via Bissolati 105, **t** 0372 30535 (*moderate*). On the west end of town, this more traditional restaurant features dishes such as casseroled donkey and baby horse; less controversial dishes include a kind of risotto with salami and savoy cabbage, fresh pasta with sausage, and other hearty regional fare. *Closed Sun eve, Mon and Aug.*

Porta Mosa, Via Santa Maria in Betlem 11, **t** 0372 411 803 (*moderate*). A tiny family-run place serving delicious traditional *tortelli* stuffed with squash and local sturgeon steamed with herbs and capers. They also concoct a mean *tiramisù*. Best to book. *Closed Sun, and mid-Aug–mid-Sept.*

Hai Xia, Corso Garibaldi 85, **t** 0372 39153 (*cheap*). The Hai Xia serves pizza, Thai and Chinese, and all are delicious. *Closed Mon.*

original state, flanked by two nearly toothless lion telamones and four flat prophets, and crowned by a small portico, where 13th- and 14th-century statues of the Virgin and saints silently but eloquently hold forth above a frieze of the months. The interior is undergoing major restoration, revealing primitive frescoes under the opulent 16th-century works by Romanino, Boccaccino and Pordenone. The choir has exquisite stalls inlaid in 1490 by G.M. Platina, with secular scenes, views of Cremona and still lifes. In the crypt, note the painting of old Cremona with its Manhattan skyline of towers.

Across from the Duomo behind the **Loggia dei Militi** (1292), the 13th-century **Palazzo del Comune** (*open Tues–Sat 8.30–6, Sun and hols 10–6; adm*) holds the town's pride: its violin collection, starring Stradivarius' golden 'Cremonese 1715'. One of Stradivarius' secrets was in the woods he used; he would visit the forests of the Dolomites looking for perfect trees that would one day sing. To hear the violins being played, book a free listening session (***t** 0372 22138*). If you are interested in the art of fiddle-making, visit the **Museo Organologico-Didattico** at the Scuola Internazionale di Liuteria (*Corso Garibaldi 178; **school** open by appointment, **t** 0372 38689; **museum** open Mon–Fri 9–12 and 3–5, Sat 9–12*), where students learn to make violins.

Behind the Palazzo del Comune lie Piazza Cavour and Corso Vittorio Emanuele. They lead to the River Po, passing by way of one of Italy's earliest (1734) and most renowned small-town theatres, the **Teatro Ponchielli** (*reserved visits only, **t** 0372 407 275*).

Mantua (Mantova)

Mantua sits in a table-flat plain, on a thumb of land protruding into three swampy lakes. Its climate is moody; the local dialect is harsh; yet this former capital of the fast-living Gonzaga dukes is one of the most atmospheric old cities in the country: dark, handsome and holding in its hand a royal flush of dazzling Renaissance art.

From the station, Corso Vittorio Emanuele and Corso Umberto I lead straight into the Renaissance heart of Mantua, its cobbled streets lined with inviting porticoes. In Piazza Mantegna rises the **Basilica of Sant'Andrea**, designed by Leon Battista Alberti in 1472 to house the Gonzaga's most precious holy relic: two ampoules of Christ's blood, said to have been acquired from the Roman centurion who pierced Christ's side with his lance. Alberti was briefed to create a truly monumental edifice, and he complied, basing the design on an Etruscan temple, fronted by a triumphal arch. Andrea Mantegna (d. 1506) is buried in the imposing interior, in the first chapel on the left.

On the east side of the basilica are the porticoes and market stalls of the delightful **Piazza dell'Erbe**. An archway leads into the grand cobbled **Piazza Sordello**, traditional seat of Mantua's bosses. At the head of the *piazza*, the **Duomo** hides a lovely interior of 1545 behind a silly 1756 façade topped by wedding-cake figures; inside there is an enormous Trinity in the apse by the Roman painter Domenico Fetti.

On one side of the *piazza* rise the sombre palaces of the Bonacolsi, distinguished by their **Torre della Gabbia**. Opposite stands that of the Gonzaga, the **Palazzo Ducale** (*open Tues–Sun 8.45–7.15; June–Sept open also Sat 8am–11pm; to see **Camera degli Sposi** groups must book on **t** 0376 382 150*), its unimpressive façade hiding one of Italy's most remarkable Renaissance abodes, both for sheer size and the magnificence of its art. The insatiable Gonzaga kept adding until they had some 500 rooms and, although stripped of its furnishings, the palace remains imposing (and seemingly endless). There are fascinating things to be seen: a vivid fresco of Arthurian knights by Pisanello, revealed behind plaster in 1969; *trompe-l'œil* frescoes of the family steeds; a painted ceiling of a labyrinth, each path inscribed 'Maybe Yes, Maybe No'. In the old Castello San Giorgio section of the palace is the famous **Camera degli Sposi**, with its remarkable frescoes painted by Mantegna in 1474. Like a genie, he captured the essence of the Gonzaga in this bottle of a room, creating portraits alike to a family photo album, not for public display. His fascination with the new science of perspective is evident, while his beautiful backgrounds reveal his love of classical architecture.

South of the medieval nucleus, Via Acerbi leads down to Giulio Romano's pleasure dome, the marvellous Palazzo Tè, passing the **Casa di Giulio Romano** (*Via Poma 18*), designed by the artist himself in 1544, and Mantegna's **Casa del Mantegna** (*Via Acerbi 47; open Tues–Sun 10–12.30 and 3–6 when an exhibition is on; otherwise Mon–Fri 10–12.30*), embellished with classical 'Mantegnesque' decorations. Work on the **Palazzo Tè** (*open Tues–Sun 9–6, Mon 1–6; adm exp*) began in 1527 when Federico II had Giulio Romano create a palace for his mistress, then expanded to become a guest house suitable for the emperor Charles V. In this, one of the very first great Mannerist buildings, Romano wished to upset the cool classicism exemplified in Mantua by Alberti. Here he created a Renaissance synthesis of architecture and art, with a bold

Getting There and Around

APAM **buses** (**t** 0376 327 237) leave Brescia (roughly hourly) for Mantua, taking around 1h40mins. There's also an indirect **train** link (change at Verona). Both Mantua's **bus** and **train stations** are near Piazza Porta Pradella, about a 10-min walk from the centre.

Several **boat** companies operate on the lakes and the River Mincio, including Motonavi Andes, Piazza Sordello 8, **t** 0376 322 875, **f** 0376 322 869. A pleasant 1½hr trip is about €10.

Tourist Information

Mantua: Corner of Piazza dell'Erbe/Piazza Mantegna 6, **t** 0376 328 253, **f** 0376 328 253, *aptmantova@iol.it*, *www.aptmantova.it*.

Eating Out

The notorious *stracotto di asino* (donkey stew) heads the list, but Mantuans also have a predilection for adding Lambrusco to soup. The local lake and river fish and deep-fried frog's legs are traditional *secondi*.

Aquila Nigra, Vicolo Bonaclosi 4, **t** 0376 327 180 (*expensive*). A lovely place with its marble and traces of frescoes, serving exquisitely prepared regional dishes and others; the pasta (ravioli filled with truffled duck) is a joy, and there's a wide choice of seafood and meat dishes. A great wine list, cheeses and delicious desserts like chestnut *torte* round off a special meal. *Closed Sun, Mon, Aug*.

Trattoria Quattrotette, Vicolo Nazione, **t** 0376 329 478 (*moderate*). Away from the tourist areas, this restaurant squeezes in hordes of locals who relish the vegetables and salads – *melanzana grillata* and *carciofi alla giudia* – steaming bowls of pasta, and *pasticceria*. In the autumn try the crêpes with pumpkins and the *sugolo*, a vine sorbet. *Closed Sun*.

Ai Garibaldini, Via S. Longino 7, **t** 0376 328 263 (*moderate*). In the historic centre, in a fine old house with a shady garden. The menu features many Mantuan dishes, with especially good risotto and *tortelli di zucca*, fish and meat dishes. *Closed Wed and Jan*.

Due Cavallini, Via Salnitro 5 (near Lago Inferiore, off Corso Garibaldi), **t** 0376 322 084 (*cheap*). The place to bite into some donkey meat – although it has other less ethnic dishes as well. *Closed Tues, and late-July–late-Aug*.

Il Portichetto, Via Portichetto 14, **t** 0376 360 747 (*cheap*). An excellent menu revolves around local river-fish – mixed *antipasti*, tagliatelle with perch or pike in salsa verde – and lots of vegetarian options. *Closed Sun eve, and Mon*.

play between the structure of the room and the frescoes. There are rooms that give an insight into Federico's character and interests; rooms inspired by Ovid and Roman frescoes; rooms that hint at Giulio's love of wacky perspectives; rooms that amaze with their exuberance and intensity of colour. The climax, however, is the startling **Sala dei Giganti**, entirely frescoed from floor to ceiling. Above, Zeus and co. rain thunder, boulders and earthquakes down on the uppity Titans, creating so powerful an illusion of chaos that it seems as if the very room is about to cave in.

Overnighter from Brescia

Verona

Cupid's pilgrims sigh over 'Juliet's balcony', but this rosy-pink city, curling along the banks of the Adige, has far more to offer than Romeo and Juliet and all the other star-crossed lovers singing their hearts out in the Arena: evocative streets and romantic *piazzas*, sublime art, magnificent architecture – and all the gnocchi you can eat.

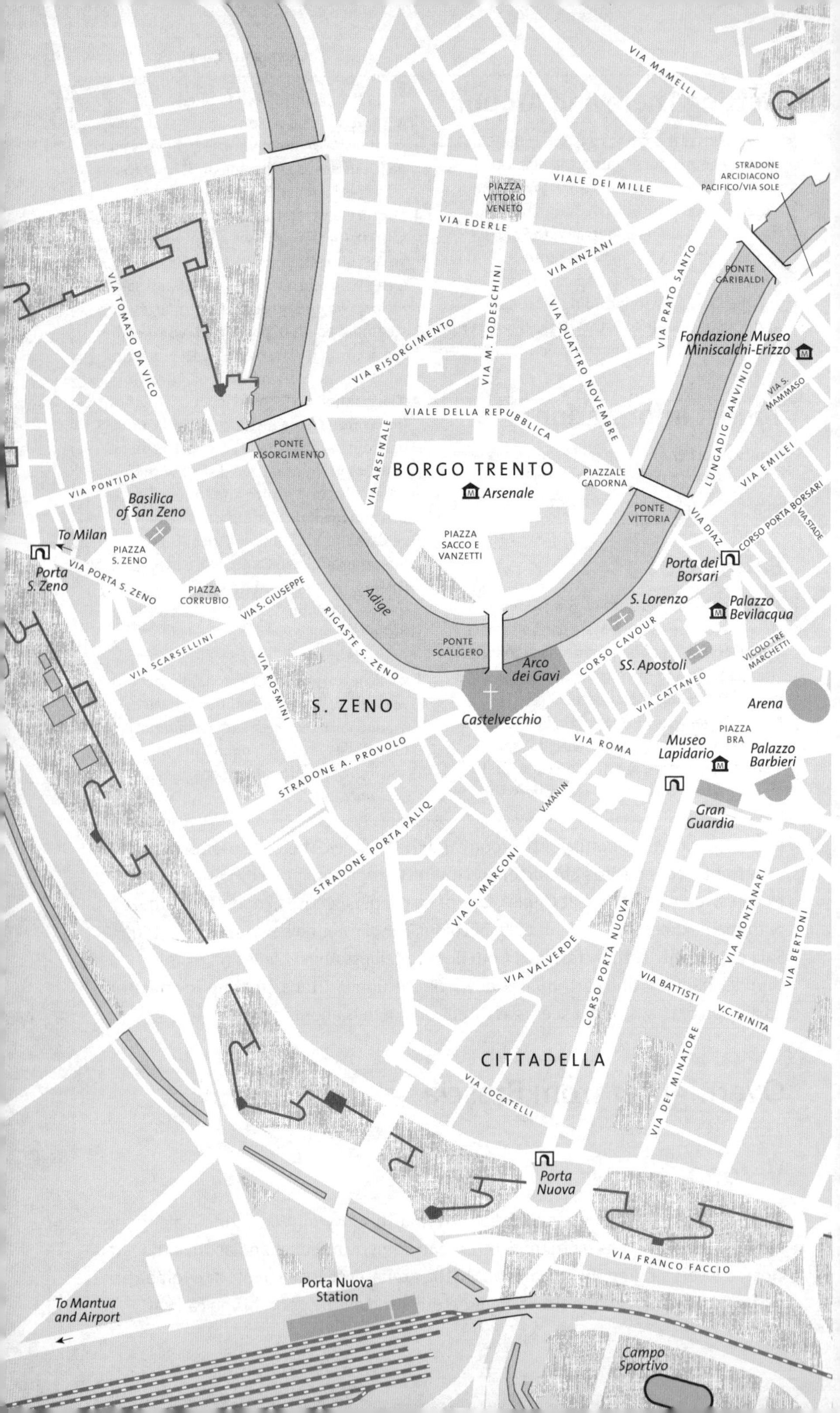

VIA MAMELLI
STRADONE ARCIDIACONO PACIFICO/VIA SOLE
VIALE DEI MILLE
PIAZZA VITTORIO VENETO
VIA EDERLE
VIA ANZANI
PONTE GARIBALDI
VIA TOMASO DA VICO
VIA M. TODESCHINI
VIA PRATO SANTO
VIA QUATTRO NOVEMBRE
VIA RISORGIMENTO
Fondazione Museo Miniscalchi-Erizzo
VIA S. MAMMASO
LUNGADIG PANVINIO
VIALE DELLA REPUBBLICA
PONTE RISORGIMENTO
VIA ARSENALE
BORGO TRENTO
Arsenale
PIAZZALE CADORNA
VIA EMILEI
VIA PONTIDA
Basilica of San Zeno
PONTE VITTORIA
CORSO PORTA BORSARI
VIA STADE
To Milan
PIAZZA SACCO E VANZETTI
VIA DIAZ
PIAZZA S. ZENO
Porta S. Zeno
VIA PORTA S. ZENO
Porta dei Borsari
PIAZZA CORRUBIO
VIA S. GIUSEPPE
Adige
S. Lorenzo
Palazzo Bevilacqua
RIGASTE S. ZENO
VIA SCARSELLINI
PONTE SCALIGERO
CORSO CAVOUR
VICOLO TRE MARCHETTI
Arco dei Gavi
SS. Apostoli
VIA ROSMINI
S. ZENO
Castelvecchio
VIA CATTANEO
Arena
PIAZZA BRA
VIA ROMA
Museo Lapidario
Palazzo Barbieri
STRADONE A. PROVOLO
V.MANIN
Gran Guardia
STRADONE PORTA PALIO
VIA G. MARCONI
VIA MONTANARI
CORSO PORTA NUOVA
VIA BERTONI
VIA VALVERDE
VIA BATTISTI
V.C.TRINITA
CITTADELLA
VIA LOCATELLI
VIA DEL MINATORE
Porta Nuova
VIA FRANCO FACCIO
Porta Nuova Station
To Mantua and Airport
Campo Sportivo

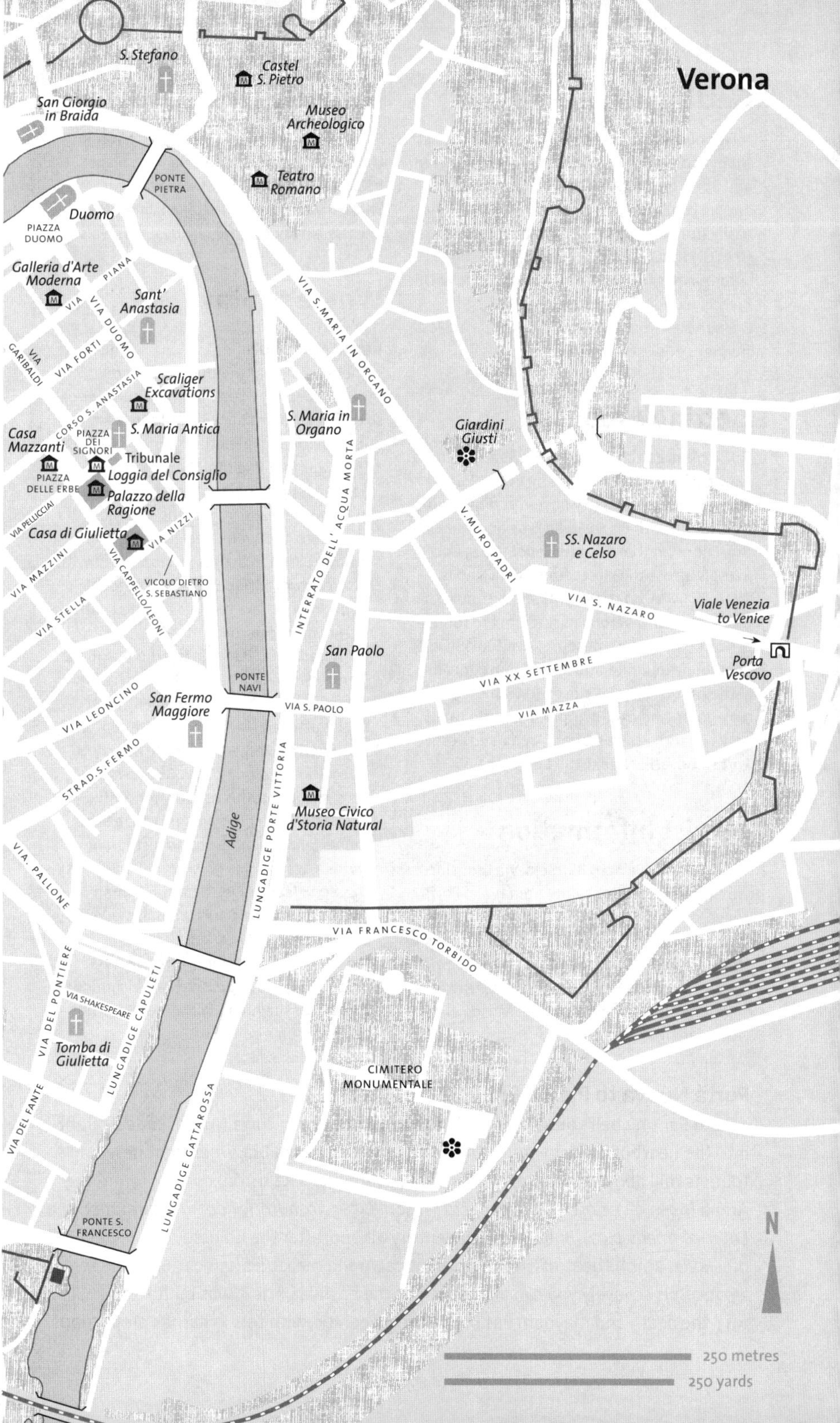

Verona
S. Stefano
Castel S. Pietro
San Giorgio in Braida
Museo Archeologico
Teatro Romano
PONTE PIETRA
Duomo
PIAZZA DUOMO
Galleria d'Arte Moderna
VIA PIANA
VIA DUOMO
Sant' Anastasia
VIA GARIBALDI
VIA FORTI
CORSO S. ANASTASIA
Scaliger Excavations
VIA S. MARIA IN ORGANO
S. Maria in Organo
Giardini Giusti
Casa Mazzanti
PIAZZA DEI SIGNORI
S. Maria Antica
Tribunale
PIAZZA DELLE ERBE
Loggia del Consiglio
Palazzo della Ragione
VIA PELLICCIAI
Casa di Giulietta
VIA NIZZI
VIA MAZZINI
VIA CAPPELLO/LEONI
VICOLO DIETRO S. SEBASTIANO
INTERRATO DELL' ACQUA MORTA
V. MURO PADRI
SS. Nazaro e Celso
VIA S. NAZARO
Viale Venezia to Venice
Porta Vescovo
VIA STELLA
San Paolo
VIA XX SETTEMBRE
PONTE NAVI
VIA S. PAOLO
VIA MAZZA
San Fermo Maggiore
VIA LEONCINO
STRAD. S. FERMO
Museo Civico d'Storia Natural
Adige
LUNGADIGE PORTE VITTORIA
VIA. PALLONE
VIA FRANCESCO TORBIDO
VIA DEL PONTIERE
VIA SHAKESPEARE
LUNGADIGE CAPULETI
Tomba di Giulietta
CIMITERO MONUMENTALE
VIA DEL FANTE
LUNGADIGE GATTAROSSA
PONTE S. FRANCESCO
N
250 metres
250 yards

Getting to Verona

Two **buses** daily (seasonal timetable; now at 10am and 10pm, returning from Verona at 8am and 8pm) go direct to Verona from Brescia's airport (€11). Otherwise, you can reach Verona easily from Brescia's train and bus stations (*see* p.87 for Getting from the Airport).

Verona has frequent **train** connections with Brescia (taking 40–50mins; **t** 147 888 088). **Bus** services from Brescia (**t** 030 34915) are less frequent and take around 2hrs.

Getting Around

The **train** station, **Porta Nuova**, is a 15-min walk south of Piazza Brà, along Corso Porta Nuova; alternatively, city buses no.71 or 72 link the station with Piazza delle Erbe and Piazza Brà. The provincial APT **bus depot** (**t** 045 800 4129) is across the street from Porta Nuova.

Urban (ATM, **t** 045 588 7111) and APT buses offer an ***Invito a Verona*** pass (from the tourist office, bus depot or museums) mid-June–Oct, combining unlimited travel and museum adm.

The *centro storico* is closed to traffic 7.30–10am and 1.30–4.30pm. There are **car parks** near the train station, Arena and Corso Porta Nuova. For a **taxi**, call **t** 045 532 666.

Tourist Information

Verona: In the Palazzo Barbiera, Via Leoncino 61, **t** 045 806 8680 (by the Arena) and Porta Nuova station, **t** 045 800 861, *www.verona-apt.net* (*both open daily, closed Sun in winter*).

Note: on the first Sunday of the month adm is free to the Museo Castelvecchio, Teatro Romano, Juliet's tomb and the Museo Lapidaro Maffeiano.

Festivals

The Verona **opera season** and the **Stagione Lirica** opera and ballet festival take place between July and August. Verona also hosts a **Shakespeare festival** (in Italian), in the Roman Theatre, and one of Italy's oldest **carnivals**.

Where to Stay

Verona ✉ 37100

There aren't really enough nice hotels in the centre, especially in opera season (*July–Aug*), so do book. Rooms are also tight in March, during Verona's agricultural fair.

*****Due Torri Baglioni**, Piazza Sant'Anastasia 4, **t** 045 595 044, **f** 045 800 4130 (*very expensive*). Goethe and Mozart slept here, and would feel just at home today, at least in the rooms appointed with 18th-century antiques. The resplendent public rooms have ceilings adorned with 17th-century frescoes.

****Accademia**, Via Scala 12, **t/f** 045 596 222 (*very expensive*). A restored 16th-century palace housing another excellent, atmospheric place to stay, smack in the centre.

***Giulietta e Romeo**, Vicolo Tre Marchetti 3, **t** 045 800 3554, **f** 045 801 0862 (*expensive*). Near the Arena, this recently renovated hotel is on a quiet street and offers fine rooms (and parking), but no restaurant.

***Italia**, Via Mameli 58, **t** 045 918 088, **f** 045 834 8028 (*expensive*). Near the Roman Theatre: the rooms are tranquil, modern, comfortable and also priced right.

Torcolo, Vicolo Listone 3, **t** 045 800 7512, **f** 045 800 4058 (*moderate*). A welcoming hotel near the Arena, convenient and not too noisy, on a quiet little square.

Porta Nuova to Piazza Brà

From Sammicheli's Renaissance **Porta Nuova**, the Corso Porta Nuova leads straight into the heart of tourist Verona: the large, irregular **Piazza Brà**, where Veronese and tourists mill about a swathe of café-filled pavements (the *Liston*) curving round the **Arena** (*open 9–7, closed Mon; in opera season 8.15–3.30; adm; for opera information* see *Entertainment, p.97*). Built in the 1st century AD and, after the Colosseum, the best-preserved amphitheatre in Italy, the elliptical Arena measures 456 by 364ft and seats 25,000. It is so lovely you can almost forget the brutal sports it was built to host. Since 1913, the death and mayhem has been purely operatic, with sets in Karnak proportions.

★★Scalzi, Via Scalzi 5, **t** 045 590 422, **f** 045 590 069 (*moderate*). South of the Castelvecchio, this family-run place has similar amenities to the Torcolo, in a fairly quiet spot.

★Catullo, Via Valerio Catullo 1, **t** 045 800 2786 (*cheap*). In the centre, this has rooms with or without bath; some have balconies.

Eating Out

The Veronese are very fond of potato gnocchi (with melted butter and sage) and horsemeat, served in a stew called *pastissada de caval*.

Il Desco, Via dietro San Sebastiano 7, **t** 045 595 358 (*very expensive*). The king of Veronese restaurants, within a 15th-century palace, serving exquisite dishes based on seasonal ingredients: gnocchi with ewe's milk cheese; red mullet with black olives and rosemary; goose liver in a sauce of sweet wine and grapes. *Closed Sun, hols, part of Jan and June.*

Arche, Via delle Arche Scaligere 6, **t** 045 800 7415 (*very expensive*). Run by the same family for over a hundred years, this is a classic choice for a special meal in an aristocratic setting. Fresh fish is brought in daily and imaginatively prepared, alongside an excellent wine list. *Closed Sun, Mon lunch.*

I Dodici Apostoli, Corticella San Marco 3, **t** 045 596 999 (*expensive*). Here, a traditional Renaissance setting – complete with frescoes of Romeo and Juliet – sets the scene for dishes adapted from Roman or Renaissance recipes; their *salmone in crosta* is famous. *Closed Sun eve, Mon, two weeks June and July.*

Nuovo Marconi, Via Fogge 4, **t** 045 591 910 (*expensive*). For gourmet glamour, sit out in Piazza dei Signori and enjoy truly traditional food: crab tagliolini, gnocchi with pumpkin, or scampi. *Closed Sun, part of June and July.*

Greppia, Vicolo Samaritana 3, **t** 045 800 4577 (*moderate*). Serves traditional and Veronese favourites in a quiet square. *Closed Mon, June.*

Alla Strueta, Via Redentore 4 (near the Roman Theatre), **t** 045 803 2462 (*moderate*). Prices are lower in Veronetta, where this workers' *osteria* features delights such as smoked goose breast, gnocchi and, yes, *pastissada de caval. Closed Mon and Tues lunch, Aug.*

Giardino, Via G. Giardino 2, **t** 044 834 330 (*cheap*). In Borgo Trento, this exceptionally friendly *trattoria* serves home-made *tortelli di formaggio*, grilled cutlets and Italian cheesecake (*tortine di ricotta*). Tables are few, so book.

Osteria Morandin, Via XX Septembre 144, off Interrato dell'Acqua Morta (*cheap*). Another standby in Veronetta, with a good choice of wines and a few dishes. *Closed Sun.*

Cordioli, Via Cappello 39 (*cheap*). It's hard to beat their Veronese pastries. *Closed Wed.*

Entertainment

All **listings** are in the tourist office's free *Passport Verona*. A weekly broadsheet fly-posted around town, *Siri-Sera*, has information on clubs, films and more casual artistic events.

When it comes to **opera**, **classical music** and **theatre**, big events take place in the Arena. If you're on a tight schedule, it's best to reserve your seat before coming to Italy. Contact **Ente Lirico Arena di Verona**, Piazza Brà 28, **t** 045 805 1811, *www.arena.it* for programme details and bookings; ticket sales are next to the Arena at Via Dietro Anfiteatro 6/b, **t** 045 800 5151, **f** 045 801 3287. If your seat is unnumbered, plan to arrive an hour early. And bring a cushion.

Liaisons Abroad, London, **t** 020 7376 4020. Will arrange tickets before you go.

Piazza delle Erbe, Piazza dei Signori, the Arche Scaligere and Around

The core of medieval and Roman Verona is the **Piazza delle Erbe**, occupying the old forum; it still fulfils its original purpose, selling souvenirs and pricey vegetables. Above the rainbow lake of parasols, a colourful panoply of buildings encases the square, including the **Casa Mazzanti**, bright with 16th-century frescoes, and the 12th-century **Torre de Lamberti** (*open Tues–Sun 9–6; adm*), reached from the court of the striped **Palazzo della Ragione**. The palace's eastern façade looks onto stately **Piazza dei Signori**, Verona's civic centre, presided over by a grouchy statue of Dante (1865).

Behind him, the **Loggia del Consiglio** (1493) is the city's finest Renaissance building. From the adjacent **Tribunale**, you can peer through glass into Verona's Roman streets.

The arch adjoining the Tribunale leads to the grand Gothic pantheon of the della Scala family, the **Arche Scaligere**. The three major tombs portray their occupants in war-like, equestrian poses on top, and reposing in death below; the crowned dogs next to the effigy of Cangrande stand holding ladders, the della Scala emblem.

The plain 14th-century house in the same street belonged to the Montecchi family (Shakespeare's Montagues), but it's the **Casa di Giulietta** (*Via Cappello 23; open 9–6.30, closed Mon; adm*) that swarms with tour groups. The association is slim (it was once called 'Il Cappello', reminiscent of the Capulet family), but the exterior has been restored to fit the Shakespearian bill, with *de rigueur* balcony; inside you can peruse lovelorn graffiti of modern youth and a well-fondled, busty statue of Juliet.

Sant'Anastasia, Modern Art and the Duomo

North of the Scaliger Tombs, it's hard to miss Gothic **Sant'Anastasia**, begun in 1290 but never completed; only the fine portal, with frescoes and reliefs of St Peter Martyr, hints at its builders' good intentions. As you enter, don't be alarmed by the two men loitering under the holy water stoups; these are the *gobbi*, or hunchbacks. The interior is beautiful, supported by massive marble columns and decorated by an all-star line-up of artists: there's the beautiful Fregoso altar by Sammicheli (first on the right), and excellent frescoes from 1390 by Verona native Altichiero, in the Cavalli Chapel. The next chapel has 24 terracottas by Michele da Firenze on the Life of Jesus; to the left of the high altar, the tomb of Cortesia Serego (1429) has an equestrian statue by Tuscan Nanni di Bartolo and frescoes by Michele Giambono. Best of all, the sacristry holds a fairytale fresco, *St George at Trebizond* (1438) by Pisanello, one of his finest works, although his watchful, calculating princess seems more formidable than any dragon.

Down by the river stands Verona's **Duomo**. The portal, supported by griffons, was carved by the great 12th-century Master Nicolò of San Zeno (*see* below). Look for the chivalric figures of Roland and Oliver guarding the west door and, on the south porch, a relief of Jonah being swallowed by the whale. Inside, there's the beautiful Tomb of St Agatha (1353), an *Assumption* (1540) by Titian and, in the baptistry, an eight-sided font (1200) big enough to swim in, wonderfully carved from a single piece of marble.

North of the Adige: Veronetta

The north bank of the Adige, known as 'Veronetta', deserves a whole morning to itself. Crossing the Ponte Garibaldi, you'll see the large dome of **San Giorgio in Braida** (1477) on your right, worth a look inside for Paolo Veronese's *Martyrdom of St George*. Follow the Adige down to **Santo Stefano**, pieced together from 5th- –10th-century columns and capitals, and brightened with 14th-century frescoes. As in ancient times, the citizens of Verona still trot over the Ponte Pietra to attend plays at the nearby **Teatro Romano** (*open summer 9–6.30, winter 9–3 adm*), carved out of the hill in the time of Augustus. Further up, beyond the **Archaeology Museum**, the **Castel San Pietro** affords famous views over Verona at sunset. South, on the Interato dell'Acqua Morta, **Santa Maria in Organo** has a façade (1533) by Fra Giovanni da Verona. The talented friar also made the extraordinary *intarsia* choir stalls, lectern and cupboards (in the sacristy) depicting scenes of old Verona, *trompe-l'œil* birds, animals, musical instruments and flowers. Behind the church lie the cool and romantic **Giardini Giusti**.

East of Piazza Brà: San Fermo Maggiore and Juliet's Tomb

East of the Arena, by the riverbank, rises the splendid vertical apse of **San Fermo Maggiore**, consisting of two churches, one on top of the other. The bottom was begun in 1065 by the Benedictines, while the upper church, with its red and white patterns, was added by the Franciscans in 1320. Inside, the upper church is covered by fine 14th-century frescoes; there are also works by Liberale da Verona and Stefano da Verona and, in the **Cappella delle Donne**, one of Caroto's best altarpieces, as well as the beautiful *Monumento Brenzoni* (1439) by Nanni di Bartolo, with statues and a graceful fresco by Pisanello (1462).

You'll find the so-called **Tomba di Giulietta** (*open 9–6.30, closed Mon; adm*) further south on Via del Pontiere. No one claims any connection with tradition here, except that the Romanesque cloister and the 14th-century marble sarcophagus would make a jolly good stage set for Shakespeare's tragedy. Be prepared to queue, nevertheless.

West of Piazza Brà: Castelvecchio and San Zeno

Northwest of the Arena, the elegant thoroughfare of **Corso Cavour** is embellished with palaces from various epochs, including Sammicheli's refined **Palazzo Bevilacqua** (1588, no.19), with its rhythmic alteration of windows, columns and pediments. At its western end the Corso opens out into a small square by the simple Roman **Arco dei Gavi**. Next to the arch, Cangrande II's fortress of **Castelvecchio** (1355) has weathered the Venetians, Napoleon and the Nazis to become Verona's excellent **museum of art** (*open Tues–Sun 9–6.30; adm*). Exhibits are arranged chronologically: you'll find goldwork from the 4th–7th centuries, expressive 14th-century Veronese sculpture, and excellent 14th-century paintings by the likes of Tommaso da Modena, Altichiero and Turone. There are fine works by Carlo Crivelli and Andrea Mantegna, and several lovely Madonnas, beginning with the fairy-tale *Madonna of the Quail* by Pisanello.

A 15-minute walk west from here will take you to one of the finest Romanesque buildings anywhere. The **Basilica of San Zeno** (*bus no.32 or 33 from Corso Porta Borsari; open 7–12.30 and 3.30–6.30*) took its present form between 1120 and 1398 and its rich façade has a perfect centrepiece: a 12th-century rose window by Maestro Brioloto. Below, the beautiful porch (1138) by Masters Nicolò and Guglielmo shows scenes from the months, the miracles of San Zeno, the Hunt of Theodoric and other allegories. The bronze doors with their 48 panels are a 'poor man's Bible' – one of the wonders of 11th-century Italy. Even after a millennium, they have an unmatched freshness and vitality: at the Annunciation Mary covers her face in fear and anguish while the angel Gabriel does his best to comfort her. The vast interior, divided into three naves by Roman columns, has a beautiful Gothic ceiling, 13th- and 14th-century frescoes and a magnificent altarpiece (1459) by Andrea Mantegna – a work that brilliantly combines his love of classical architecture and luminous colouring. In the crypt below, the body of St Zeno glows in the dark.

Touring from Brescia and Bergamo

Day 1: Roman Baths, Battlefields and a Garden Vale

Morning: Drive east to **Desenzano del Garda**, on the shore of Lake Garda, joining the A4 motorway at either Bergamo or Brescia and getting off at the Desenzano exit, just beyond Lonato. Find out about Desenzano's ancient amber trade and Bronze Age inhabitants at the **Museo Rambotti** (*Via Anelli 7; open Tues, Fri, Sat, Sun and hols 3–7*). See the Roman **Villa Romana** (*Via Crocifisso 22; open Mar–mid Oct Tues 8.30–7, Sat and Sun 9–6; end Oct–Feb Tues–Fri 8.30–4.30, Sat and Sun 9–4.30; adm*), fitted with sumptuous baths, a *triclinium* (dining room) and extensive mosaic floors.

Lunch: In Desenzano del Garda, *see* below.

Afternoon: Drive east 3.5km along the shore, then turn right to **San Martino della Battaglia**, where in 1859, the Italians pounded their Austrian occupiers. Climb the **Torre Monumentale** (*open end Mar–Sept Mon–Sat 9–12.30 and 2–7; Sun and hols 9–7; Oct–mid Mar daily 9–12.30 and 2–7; closed Tues and 1–15 Dec; adm*), full of mementos from the historic battle. In summer, continue to **Pozzolengo** and turn left to **Ponti sul Mincio**. Follow the river Mincio south towards **Valeggio sul Mincio** to walk through the amazing **Sigurtà Gardens** (*open Mar–Nov daily 9–7; adm*), created over 40 years and extending for 7km. From Valeggio take the S249 north to Peschiera, then follow the lake shore west to spend the evening on the peninsula of **Sirmione**.

Dinner and Sleeping: In Sirmione, *see* below.

Day 1

Lunch in Desenzano del Garda

Bagatta alla Lepre, Via Bagatta 33, **t** 030 914 2259 (*very expensive–expensive*). Classy place with a table of truffles and delicacies, also for sale, serving creative Mediterranean fare. Their Wine Bar offers cheaper fare in a more informal, if trendy, ambiance. *Closed Tues.*

Caffè Italia, Piazza Malvezzi 19, **t** 030 914 1243 (*moderate–cheap*). Wine bar and restaurant offering hot and cold dishes, including selected Chianina meat, under the porticoes near the Duomo. Good selection of wines. Open 7.30am–2am. *Closed Mon, Jan–Feb.*

Dinner in Sirmione

Vecchia Lugana, Via Verona 71, **t** 030 919 012 (*expensive*). One of Garda's finest restaurants, with an exquisite seasonal menu – try the asparagus tagliatelle in a ragoût of lake fish, or the mixed grill of fish and meat (*menus* €35/€45). Sip away on the veranda, in the cellar or in the old stables. Dining is in the hall overlooking the lake, or on a lakeside terrace in summer. *Closed Mon eve and Tues.*

Osteria al Torcol, Via San Salvatore 30, **t** 030 990 4605 (*cheap*). For a snack or meal and excellent wines – and oils! – to taste. Try local cheeses and *affettati*, or home-made pasta or *ravioli al bagoz* close to the old wine press inside or outside, your table set in the kitchen garden. *Open 6pm–2am; closed Wed.*

Sleeping in Sirmione

*****Catullo**, Piazza Flaminia 7, **t** 030 990 5811, **f** 030 916 444 (*expensive*). In the old town, with good-sized rooms, beautiful views, a terrace and all mod cons. *Open April–Nov.*

*****Pace**, Piazza Porto Valentino 5, **t** 030 990 5877, **f** 030 919 6097 (*moderate*). In the old city centre; a charming veranda over the lake and the nice turn-of-the-last-century décor compensate for the lack of a/c.

****Grifone**, Via Bocchio 4, **t** 030 916 014, **f** 030 916 548 (*cheap*). More attractive outside than in the rooms, but has a great location overlooking the Rocca. *Open April–Oct.*

Day 2: Romantic Ruins and Lovely Lakeside Towns

Morning: Go out to the very tip of the rocky promontory to enjoy magnificent views from the romantic **Grotte di Catullo** (*open Mar–mid-Oct Tues–Sat 8.30–7, Sun 9–6; end Oct–Feb Tues–Sun 9–6; adm*), once a Roman bath complex, now ruins entwined with ancient olive trees. Look into the **museum**, with mosaics and frescoes. Next visit the fairy-tale **Rocca Scaligera** (*open Nov–Mar Tues–Sun 8.30–4.30; April–Oct 9–6; adm*), built in the 13th century and surrounded almost entirely by water, with more fine views from its swallowtail battlements. The best swimming is off the rocks on the west side of the peninsula. Drive east along the lake shore, picking up the S249 at Peschiera and continuing north to learn all about **Bardolino**'s lively red wine at the **Museo del Vino** (*Via Costabella 9; open Mar–Oct daily 9–1 and 2–6*), before stopping for lunch a bit further on in **Garda**.

Lunch: In Garda, *see* below.

Afternoon: Have a wander through the fine old town, dotted with Renaissance *palazzi* and villas, then continue north to Laurence Olivier's haven of old, the enchanting **Punta di San Vigilio**, occupied by Sammicheli's Villa Guarienti and the Mermaid Bay, reached through a park shaded by olive trees. Beyond, a sparsely populated stretch of shore leads you to **Malcésine**, with its lovely web of medieval streets. Visit the magnificent **Rocca Scaligera** (*open April–Oct 9.30–7; until 9 in summer; winter Sat and Sun only; adm*) rising up on a sheer rock over the water, or take the vertiginous cableway up **Monte Baldo** (***t*** *045 740 0206; adm exp*); the views are ravishing.

Dinner and Sleeping: In Malcésine, *see* below.

Day 2

Lunch in Garda

Stafolet, Via Poiano 12, **t** 045 725 5427 (*moderate*). On the landward side of Garda; it's worth asking directions to this place for its tagliolini with truffles and grilled meat dishes. Pizza also available.

Al Pontesel, Via Monte Baldo 71, **t** 045 725 5419. Less distinguished, but good and cheap, featuring stout local cooking.

Dinner in Malcésine

Trattoria Vecchia Malcesine, Via Pisort 6, **t** 045 7400469 (*expensive*). A charming escape on a panoramic terrace. The high quality food leans towards smoky flavours and spices: try *canederli di speck* (ham-flecked dumplings), sardines with tagliolini mint and pine nuts, or poached pike with caper sauce; warm lobster salad with pineapple and curry, duck legs with caramelized oranges. More Alto Adige in the desserts: strudel, warm poppy seeds pies with date cream centres, fruit tarts. Over 400 wines to select. Various menus. Best to book. *Closed lunch, Wed, Feb.*

Trattoria la Pace, **t** 045 740 0057 (*moderate*). By the Porto Vecchio; a popular place with outdoor tables for seafood by the lake.

Hippopotamus, Piazza Disciplina. A small wine bar open until late where you can taste and buy a vast array of local wines. *Closed Wed.*

Sleeping in Malcésine

********Uphill Park Hotel**** at Campiano, **t** 045 740 0344, **f** 045 740 0848 (*lower end of very expensive*). South of the centre, this is a romantic place to stay, with lovely views, a pool, garden and one of the best restaurants in the area. *Closed Nov–Mar.*

*****Vega**, Viale Roma, **t** 045 657 0355, **f** 045 740 1604 (*expensive–moderate*). An inviting lake-front hotel in the city centre with big, modern rooms, all with satellite TV, minibar, safe and a/c, and a private beach.

***Erika**, Via Campogrande 8, **t/f** 045 740 0451 (*moderate–cheap*). Behind the centre; offers family-run, cosy hospitality and has a garage.

Day 3: Cities with a Rich Past – and a Shower

Morning: Continue north along the lake shore to the charming town of **Riva**, prized by the likes of Stendhal, Thomas Mann, D. H. Lawrence and Kafka. Visit the lakefront **Rocca**, housing Riva's **Museo Civico** (*open Tues–Sun 9.30–6.30, until later in July and Aug; adm*), with finds from the Bronze Age settlement at Lake Ledro, statue-*stele* from the 4th and 3rd millennia BC, Roman finds, paintings, frescoes and sculpture. Stop in at Riva's best church, the **Inviolata** (1603), by an unknown but imaginative Portuguese architect, who was given a free hand with the gilt and stucco inside. It also has paintings by Palma Giovane. Take the S45bis northeast to **Arco**, a popular resort in the 1800s, prized for its climate with a public garden full of Mediterranean plants and a pretty 19th-century casino.

Lunch: In Arco, *see* below.

Afternoon: Follow the lovely path up to the **Castello d'Arco** (*open April–Sept 10–7 (lawn) 10–6 (upper towers); Oct and Mar 10–5 and 10–4; Nov and Feb 10–4 and 10–3; adm*), dramatically crowned with ancient, dagger-sharp cypresses and swallowtail crenellations; it hangs on to a few frescoes, including one of a courtly game of chess. Drive back to Riva, then take the windy road 3km north via Albola to **Varone**, where the dramatic **Cascata del Varone** (287ft) crashes down a tight grotto-like gorge; walkways allow visitors to become mistily intimate with thundering water (*open May–Aug daily 9–7; April and Oct daily 10–12.30 and 2–5; Nov–Feb Sun and hols only 10–12.30 and 2–5; Mar daily same hours; adm*).

Dinner and Sleeping: In Riva del Garda, *see* below.

Day 3

Lunch in Arco

★★★**Al Sole**, Via Sant'Anna 35, **t** 0464 516 676, **f** 0464 518 585, *www.hotelsole.net* (*moderate*). The hotel restaurant features local produce – try gnocchi with local prunes. Wine bar recently opened.

Belvedere, Via Serafini 2, in Varignano, **t** 0464 516 144 (*cheap*). The best place to eat. The specialities are salted meat and Trentine dishes such as *canederli* (meat and bread dumplings in broth), also home-grown vegetables, local salami, fresh pasta and roast meats. *Closed Wed, July and Aug.*

Dinner in Riva del Garda

Villa Negri ai Germandri, Via Bastione 31, **t** 0464 555 061 Overlooking the lake in a historical villa, just below the castle (golf carts take guests from Riva's car park). The exclusive restaurant (*very expensive, eves only*) offers a creative 9-dish menu (€80). The terrace bistrot, less expensive, has a grill and holds Mozart evenings (Fri in summer). Visit the cellar, with over 800 labels. *Closed Wed out of season.*

La Colombera, Via Rovigo 30, **t** 0464 556 033 (*moderate*). In an 18th-century castle, 500m from the lake path. Specializes in grilled meats accompanied by home-produced wine. Outside dining with views over the mountains. *Closed Wed.*

Sleeping in Riva del Garda

★★★★**Grand Hotel Riva**, Piazza Garibaldi 10, **t** 0464 521 800, **f** 0464 552 293 (*expensive*). A turn-of-the-century hotel positioned on the square; the modern rooms look over the lake. The rooftop restaurant offers fine food and incomparable views. *Open Mar–Oct.*

★★★**Centrale**, Piazza III Novembre 27, **t** 0464 552 344, **f** 0464 552 138 (*moderate*). By the harbour, with fully equipped, spacious rooms.

★**Restel de Fer**, Via Restel de Fer 10, **t** 0464 553 481, **f** 0464 552 798 (*moderate*). Built in 1400; only five rooms and a good restaurant, with summer dining in the cloister.

Day 4: Bronze-Age Finds and an Eccentric's Dream

Morning: Just southwest of Riva, take the exciting Ponale Road (S240) to **Lake Ledro** to the remains of a Bronze-Age settlement (*c.* 2000 BC). One pile dwelling has been reconstructed near the ancient piles around **Molina di Ledro**, where the **Museo delle Palafitte** (*open mid-June to mid-Sept daily 10–1 and 2–6; end Sept–Nov and Mar–mid-June Tues–Sun 9–1 and 2–5; Dec Sat and Sun only, same hours; closed Jan–Feb; adm*) houses the pottery, weapons and amber jewellery from the site. Drive back to Lake Garda and continue south along the S45bis, passing the citrus town of **Limone sul Garda**, distinguished by its tiny port and lemon terraces with their white square pillars. Further south, the cliffs plunge sheer into the water and the road pierces tunnel after tunnel like a needle. For tremendous views, take one of the turnings that wind precipitously up to **Tignale** or **Tremósine**. Stop for lunch in **Gargnano**.

Lunch: In Gargnano, *see* below.

Afternoon: Continue south, passing the 18th-century **Villa Bettoni**, used as a set in a dozen films, to **Gardone Riviera**, its promenade lined with sumptuous old villas, gardens and hotels. Visit the **Giardino Botanico Hruska** (*open Mar–Oct daily 9–6.30; adm*), with 8,000 exotic plants growing between imported tufa cliffs and artificial streams. Above it lies the home and private garden of Gabriele D'Annunzio (*see* p.213), a luxurious Liberty-style (Art Nouveau) villa filled with quirky, desirable and hilarious junk, left as it was in 1938, when a brain haemorrhage put an end to the poet's hoarding. Drive on to spend the evening in **Salò**.

Dinner and Sleeping: In Salò, *see* below.

Day 4

Lunch in Gargnano

La Tortuga, Via XXIV Maggio 5, **t** 0365 71251 (*expensive*). A celebrated gourmet haven near the port, serving delicate seasonal dishes and lake fish; there are also delicious vegetable soufflés, innovative meat courses, mouth-watering desserts and fruit sherbets, and an excellent wine cellar. *Closed Mon eve, Tues and mid-Jan–Feb.*

Lo Scoglio, Via Barbacane 3, in Bogliaco di Gargnano, **t** 0365 71030 (*expensive–moderate*). Highly recommended, specializing in lake fish, home-made pasta and cakes. *Closed Fri.*

Dinner in Salò

Osteria dell'Orologio, Via Butterini 26, **t** 0365 290 158 (*moderate*). Extremely good value: an old, beautifully restored inn to indulge in dishes such as *tonno del Garda* (pork in wine and spices), lake fish and skewered wild birds. Very popular; book in advance and be prepared to wait to be served. *Closed Wed.*

Cantina San Giustina, Salita S. Giustina, **t** 0365 520 320 (*cheap*). For cheeses, local *affettati*, salted *coregone* or grilled vegetables and excellent local wines. The vaulted *cantina* features books, wines and a beautiful old slicing machine. The charming host guides you through local delicacies. *Open 8pm–5am.*

Sleeping in Salò

******Laurin**, Viale Landi 9, **t** 0365 22022, **f** 0365 22382, *www.laurinsalo.com* (*expensive*). An enchanting villa with charming grounds including a pool and beach. You can dine in style (*expensive*), amid frescoes and Liberty-style windows. *Closed Jan.*

*****Vigna**, Lungolago Zanardelli 62, **t** 0365 520144, **f** 0365 20516, *www.hotelvigna.it* (*moderate*). Comfortable and modern rooms, and views that really steal the show.

****Lepanto**, Lungolago Zanardelli 67, **t** 0365 20428, **f** 0365 20428 (*cheap*). Salò's best kept secret, on the lake. The sign advertises the garden restaurant, but there are six rooms too, overlooking the lake; book in advance.

Day 5: Salò, Iseo's Sailboats and Plenty of Wine

Morning: Before setting off, visit Salò's late Gothic **cathedral**, with a Renaissance portal stuck in its unfinished façade; among the paintings by Romanino and Moretto there's a golden polyptych by Paolo Veneziano. From Salò, drive west across green valleys to **Lake Iseo**, taking the road northwest out of town via Vobarno to **Sabbiò**. Continue west to **Sarezzo**, passing Lumezzane, famous for its guns; take the road north of Sarezzo towards Gardone, turning left at **Ponte Zanano** onto the road for **Iseo**, the lake's low-key and thoroughly fetching 'capital', with flowers spilling from every window. The long, curved promenade, shaded with ancient plane trees, is the perfect place to laze and watch the sailboats and little steamers dart to and fro.

Lunch: In Iseo, *see* below.

Afternoon: Between Brescia and Iseo lies the charming wine-growing region of **Franciacorta**. This area paid no taxes, thus endearing it to villa-building patricians. Today it is synonymous with sparkling wine, a fine DOC red and Pinot Bianco. Ask the Iseo tourist office for information on Franciacorta's **Via dei Vini**, a guided tour of the local vineyards. In nearby Colombaro is the **Villa Lana da Terzo**, with Italy's oldest cedar of Lebanon; further south you can visit Bornato's **Castello di Bornato** (*open Easter–Sept Sun 10–12 and 2.30–6; Oct Sun 10–12 and 2.30–5; adm*), where Dante once slept; there are rooms frescoed with Olympian gods and landscapes, and the wine is good, too. Drive back to Iseo to spend the evening on the lakeshore.

Dinner and Sleeping: In Iseo, *see* below. In the morning, take the S510 south to Brescia, from where you can pick up the A4 back to Bergamo.

Day 5

Lunch in Iseo

Il Volto, Via Mirolte 33, **t** 030 981 462 (*expensive–moderate*). Dine in an old-fashioned inn, serving a mix of Italian and French cuisine. Dishes feature lake fish (excellent with tagliolini) and tasty dishes such as roast pigeon in a mustardy cream sauce. Best to reserve. *Closed Wed and Thurs lunch and two weeks in July and Jan*.

Osteria dei Poveri, Via Pieve 4/a, **t** 030 984 0936 (*cheap*). Run by a local doctor with a passion for gastronomy and his wife: local cuisine, both fish and meat. *Closed Tues*.

Dinner and Sleeping in Iseo

********I Due Roccoli**, 4km from Iseo in the hills in Fraz. Invino (towards Polaveno), **t** 030 982 2977, **f** 030 982 2980, *www.idueroccoli.com* (*expensive*). In an old hunting lodge with its own gardens; the beautifully designed rooms have garden or lake views. There's a terrace, pool and a dining room with an open fire, offering impeccable service and superb food from the hotel's farm. Try *antipasto* of salad and truffles, delicious green pasta with mushrooms known as *pappardelle verdi con funghi porcini* and a *mousse di cioccolato bianco* that's one of the best in the country. *Closed Oct–Mar; restaurant open to non-residents Thurs–Mon only*.

******Iseolago**, Via Colombera, **t** 030 98891, **f** 030 988 9299, *www.iseolagohotel.it* (*expensive*). An ideal retreat for families, close to the Lido Sassabenek sports centre south of Iseo's centre. Amenities include a gym, tennis, pool and sauna, a pizzeria, a restaurant and an *enoteca*. Canoes, pedalos and bikes to hire; cycling paths are nearby.

****Milano**, Lungolago Marconi 4, **t** 030 980 449, **f** 030 982 1903, *hotel.milano@tmz.it* (*cheap*). A pleasant, convenient place on the lake, with small, old-fashioned rooms, many with lake views. Has a small restaurant/bar.

****Albergo Rosa**, Via Roma 47, **t** 030 980 053, **f** 030 982 1445 (*cheap*). A neat family-run hotel, recently refurbished.

The Veneto

07

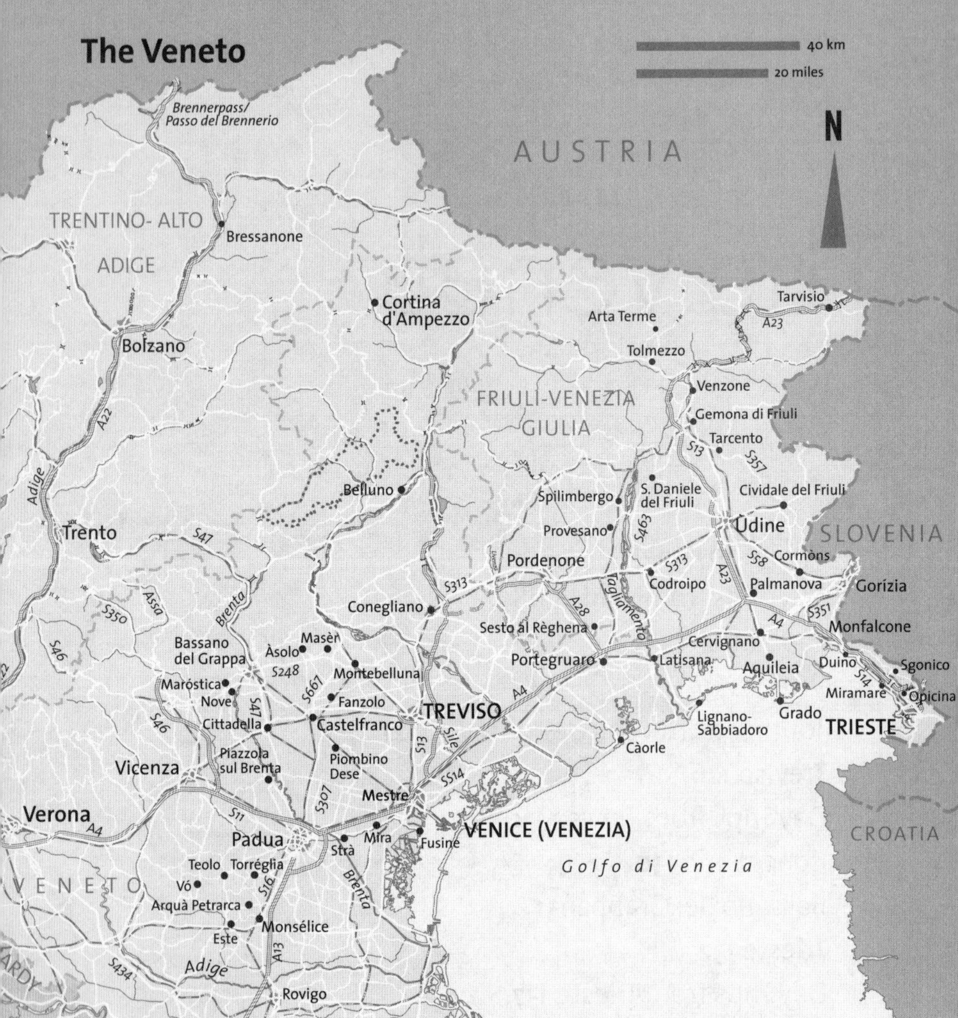

Venetia – or the *Tre Venezie* – encompasses three regions: the Veneto, the autonomous region of Trentino-Alto Adige and Friuli-Venezia Giulia, stretching east to Slovenia. As the local economic powerhouse for over a thousand years, the Venetian influences are strong everywhere. In wealth Venetia rivals Lombardy, while in culture it rivals Tuscany itself: Venice, Verona, Vicenza, Treviso, Padua, Trento and Ùdine are major art cities. Lagoons and sandy beaches line the coast, while the Dolomites, arguably the most beautiful mountains in the world, are dotted with fairy-tale castles and vineyards, as well as resorts equipped for every summer and winter sport. In between, landscapes are lush and green, and littered with thousands of villas built between the 16th and 18th centuries, including 18 by Andrea Palladio, the master of the genre. Friuli is one of Italy's top wine regions, and has a variety of other attractions, especially its Roman-medieval capital Aquileia, the most important archaeological site in northern Italy, and the fascinating Lombard town of Cividale.

Venice (Venezia)

In a world racked by stress, Venice is *la Serenissima*, a fairy-tale city on the sea, a lovely mermaid with the gift of eternal youth. Founded in mud flats by refugees fleeing Attila the Hun, on the surface she is little changed from the days when she dazzled the world with her wealth and pageantry, her magnificent fleet and luminous art, her silken debauchery and decline and fall into a seemingly endless carnival. Credit for this unique preservation goes to the Lagoon, the formaldehyde that has pickled her more thoroughly than many more venerable cities on the mainland.

The Grand Canal

There's no finer introduction to Venice than a ride down her bustling main artery. The Grand Canal has always been Venice's status address and along its looping banks the patricians of the Golden Book, or *Nobili Homini*, built a hundred marble palaces, framed by peppermint-stick posts where they moored their watery carriages. Halfway along, Antonio da Ponte's **Ponte di Rialto** (1592) spans 157ft in an audacious single arch while holding up two rows of shops. Guarding the southern entrance to the Canal is the **Dogana di Mare**, crowned by a weathervane of Fortune; a little beyond, on the north bank, is the landing-stage of San Marco.

Piazza San Marco

Napoleon described this asymmetrical showpiece as 'Europe's finest drawing-room', and no matter how often you've been there, its charm never fades. Lining the *piazza* and its two flanking *piazzette* are the long, arcaded **Procuratie Vecchie** (1499) and **Procuratie Nuove** (1540), filled with jewellery, embroidery and lace shops, and graced by Venice's rival 18th-century grand cafés: **Caffè Quadri** and **Florian's**.

St Mark's Basilica

Open to visitors Mon–Sat 9.30–5, Sun and hols 2–4.30. No shorts; women must cover their shoulders and show a minimum of décolletage; the queue can be diabolically long in season. Separate adm for many of the smaller chapels and individual attractions; different sections frequently closed for restoration. Ramp access from Piazzetta dei Leoncini.

This was the holy of holies of the Venetian state, built to house the relics of its patron saint, the evangelist St Mark, whose winged lion symbol became the city's own. A law decreed that all merchants trading in the East had to bring back an embellishment for the basilica, and the result is a glittering robbers' den. The present structure was consecrated in 1094. Five rounded doorways, five upper arches and five round Byzantine domes are the essentials of the **exterior**, all frosted with a sheen of coloured marbles, ancient columns and sculpture. Ready to prance off the façade, the controversial 1979 copies of the **horses of St Mark** masquerade well enough from a distance. The **interior** dazzles with the intricate splendour of a thousand details: golden mosaics on New Testament subjects cover the domes and atrium; ancient

Venice

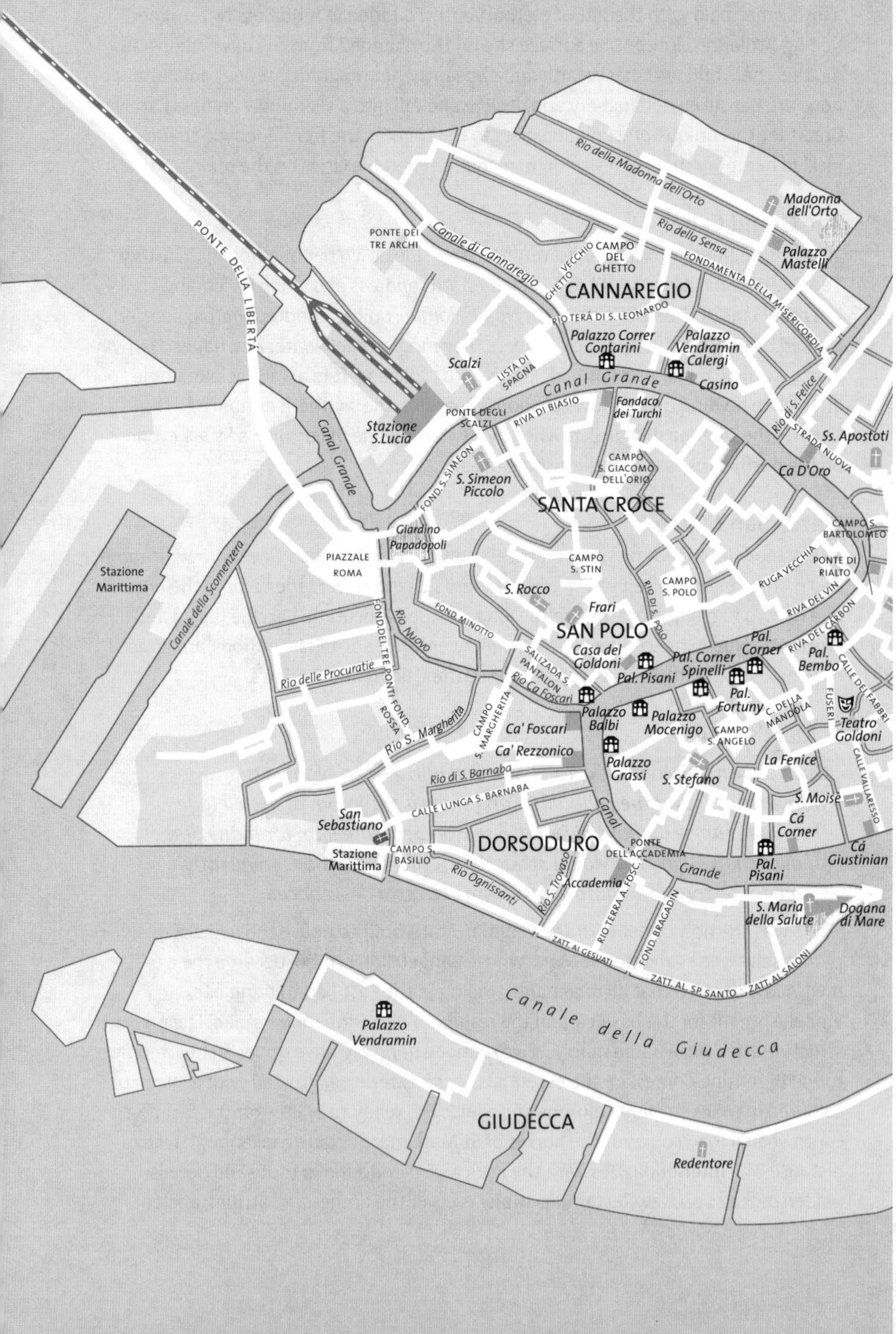

Ponte della Libertà
Ponte dei Tre Archi
Canale di Cannaregio
Rio della Madonna dell'Orto
Madonna dell'Orto
Rio della Sensa
Palazzo Mastelli
Fondamenta della Misericordia
Campo del Ghetto
Ghetto Vecchio
CANNAREGIO
Rio Terá di S. Leonardo
Palazzo Correr Contarini
Palazzo Vendramin Calergi
Casino
Scalzi
Lista di Spagna
Canal Grande
Stazione S.Lucia
Ponte degli Scalzi
Riva di Biasio
Fondaco dei Turchi
Rio di S. Felice
Strada Nuova
Ss. Apostoti
Ca D'Oro
Fond. S. Simeon
S. Simeon Piccolo
Campo S. Giacomo dell'Orio
SANTA CROCE
Campo S. Bartolomeo
Ponte di Rialto
Ruga Vecchia
Riva del Vin
Stazione Marittima
Canale della Scomenzera
Giardino Papadopoli
Piazzale Roma
Campo S. Stin
S. Rocco
Campo S. Polo
Frari
Rio di S. Polo
Fond. Minotto
Rio Nuovo
SAN POLO
Riva del Carbon
Casa del Goldoni
Pal. Corner
Pal. Bembo
Calle dei Fabbri
Salizada S. Pantalon
Pal. Pisani
Pal. Corner Spinelli
Rio delle Procuratie
Fond. del Tre Ponti
Fond. Rossa
Rio Ca Foscari
Palazzo Balbi
Palazzo Mocenigo
Pal. Fortuny
C. della Mandola
Fuseri
Teatro Goldoni
Campo S. Margherita
Rio S. Margherita
Ca' Foscari
Campo S. Angelo
Ca' Rezzonico
Palazzo Grassi
La Fenice
Calle Vallaresso
Rio di S. Barnaba
S. Stefano
S. Moisè
Calle Lunga S. Barnaba
San Sebastiano
Cá Corner
Stazione Marittima
Campo S. Basilio
DORSODURO
Ponte dell'Accademia
Pal. Pisani
Cá Giustinian
Rio Ognissanti
Rio S. Trovaso
Accademia
Rio Terra A. Fosc.
Fond. Bragadin
S. Maria della Salute
Dogana di Mare
Zatt. al Gesuati
Zatt. al Sp. Santo
Zatt. al Saloni
Canale della Giudecca
Palazzo Vendramin
GIUDECCA
Redentore

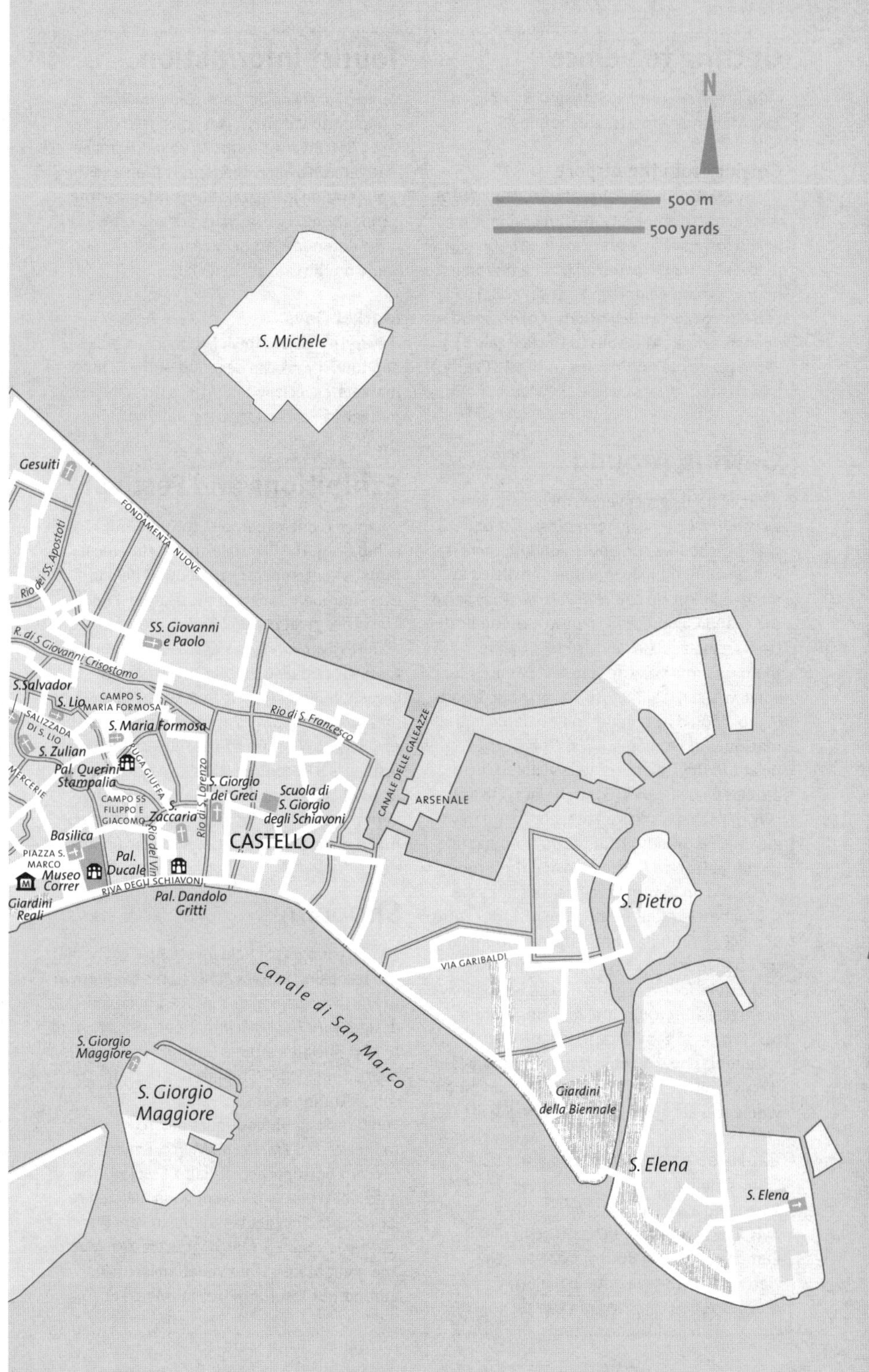
N
500 m
500 yards
S. Michele
Gesuiti
FONDAMENTA NUOVE
Rio dei SS. Apostoli
SS. Giovanni
e Paolo
R. di S Giovanni Crisostomo
S.Salvador
S. Lio
CAMPO S.
MARIA FORMOSA
SALIZZADA
DI S. LIO
S. Maria Formosa
S. Zulian
RUGA GIUFFA
Pal. Querini
Stampalia
MERCERIE
CAMPO SS
FILIPPO E
GIACOMO
Rio di S. Lorenzo
S. Giorgio
dei Greci
Scuola di
S. Giorgio
degli Schiavoni
Rio di S. Francesco
CANALE DELLE GALEAZZE
ARSENALE
S.
Zaccaria
Rio del Vin
Basilica
CASTELLO
PIAZZA S.
MARCO
Pal.
Ducale
Museo
Correr
RIVA DEGLI SCHIAVONI
Giardini
Reali
Pal. Dandolo
Gritti
S. Pietro
VIA GARIBALDI
Canale di San Marco
S. Giorgio
Maggiore
S. Giorgio
Maggiore
Giardini
della Biennale
S. Elena
S. Elena

Getting to Venice

Go flies from London Stansted, Bristol and East Midlands airports (2hrs 10mins).

Getting from the Airport

Venice's Marco Polo airport (**t** 041 260 9260), is 13km north of the city near the Lagoon. It is linked to Venice by **water-taxi** (**t** 041 966 170) for over €45; or by ***motoscafi*** (taking 1hr 10mins, hourly, 4.50am–midnight; **t** 041 541 5084) to San Marco (Zecca). Buy **tickets** (€9) on board. There is also an **ATVO bus** to the Piazzale Roma (€2.70), taking 25mins, or the **ACTV city bus** no.5 (€0.77), which passes twice an hour.

Getting Around

Public transport in Venice means by water, by ***vaporetti***, or the faster ***motoscafi*** (**t** 041 528 7886). Most lines run until midnight; there is also an all-night line. Schedules are listed in the free guide, *Un Ospite di Venezia*. They serve the Grand Canal, the Rio Nuovo, the Canale di Cannaregio and Rio dell'Arsenale; between them, you must rely on your feet; Venice is so small you can walk across it in an hour. **Tickets** (€3.10) should be bought and validated in the machines at landing-stages; it's best to stock up at *tabacchi* (blocks of 10 available). There are also passes: **24hrs** (€9.30), **3-days** (€18.80).

Water-taxis work like taxis, but their fares are de luxe. Stands are at the station, Piazzale Roma, Rialto, San Marco, Lido and the airport. They hold up to 15 passengers, and fares are set for destinations beyond the historic centre, or pay €73/hr. In the centre the minimum fare for up to four people is €73; there are also surcharges for extra people, baggage, holidays or service after 10pm, and for using a **radio taxi** (**t** 041 522 2303 or 041 723 112).

Gondolas now operate frankly for tourists (€62/50mins; €77.50 after 8pm). Agree first on where you are going and how long it will take.

Car Hire

The following have branches at Piazzale Roma and at the airport.

Avis, **t** 041 523 7377 or **t** 041 541 5030.
Europcar, **t** 041 523 8616 or **t** 041 541 5654.
Hertz, **t** 041 528 3524 or **t** 041 541 6075.
Maggiore, **t** 041 277 1205 or **t** 041 541 5040.

Tourist Information

Venice: Palazzina dei Santi, Giardini Reali, Vaporetto Vallarosso, **t** 041 522 5150 or **t** 041 529 8730, *www.turismovenezia.it*. Branches at Venice Pavilion, the train station and the bus station in Piazzale Roma offer accommodation services. There are also offices on the Rotonda Marghera, Marco Polo Airport, and on the Lido at Gran Viale 6.

Market Days

Everything from fresh fish to inlaid boxes and tourist junk can be found at the **Rialto markets**; especially colourful is the fish market, La Pescheria (*closed Sun and Mon*).

Exhibitions and Festivals

Venice is one of Europe's top cities for exhibitions: the **Biennale**, the world's most famous contemporary art show, is held in even-numbered years in the Giardini Pubblici. The other great cultural junket is the **Venice Film Festival** (*late Aug–Sept*). Venice's famous **Carnival**, first held in 1094, attracts huge crowds, but dressing up in costume and taking each other's picture is as much as most of the revellers now get up to. The most spectacular festival is **Il Redentore** (*third Sun of July*), with its bridge of boats. On the Saturday before, Venetians row out for a picnic on the water, manoeuvring for the best view of the fireworks.

Shopping

Venice is a fertile field for shoppers, whether you're looking for tacky bric-à-brac (walk down the Lista di Spagna) or the latest in Italian design – but be warned that bargains are hard to find. The area around Campo San Maurizio, near Campo Santo Stefano, has the largest concentration of **antique** shops. Most of Venice's **designer boutiques** are in the streets to the west of Piazza San Marco; **Emilio Ceccato**, Sottoportico di Rialto, S. Polo, is the place for typically Venetian gondoliers' shirts, jackets, etc. The greatest name in Venetian **leather** is Vogini, S. Marco 1300, Via XXII Marzo. The great place to find **Venetian lace** is on **Burano**, but **Jesurum**, Piazza S. Marco 60/61, has Venetian lace and linen of all kinds. **Codognato**, S. Marco 1295, Calle dell'Ascensione, is one of the oldest **jewellers** in Venice; at **Missiaglia**, Piazza S. Marco 125, you can see pieces produced by Venetian gold and silversmiths working today.

Good places to pick up **local specialities** include **Pastificio Artigiano**, Cannaregio 4292, Strada Nuova, for Venice's most exotic pastas. For **wines and spirits, Cantinone Già Schiavi**, Dorsoduro 992, Fondamenta S. Trovaso, has plenty to choose from.

Anyone seeking **unusual gifts** will find plenty in Venice, though prices may need to be handled with care. For an overview, the **Consorzio Artigianato Artistico Veneziano**, S. Marco 412, Calle Larga, has a fair selection of handmade Venetian crafts. The most renowned of Venice's ancient crafts is, of course, **Venetian glass**. **Murano** is still the place to go, but in the city **Paolo Rossi**, S. Marco 4685, Campo S. Zaccaria has attractive reproductions of ancient glassware.

A **Carnival mask** can make a good souvenir. For the traditionally crafted item, try **Giorgio Clanetti**, Castello 6657, Barbaria delle Tole. Masks of every shape and size are made at **Tragicomica**, S. Polo 2800, Calle dei Nomboli, who also supply theatres with masks. Prices start at €12.50 but the sky's the limit.

Where to Stay

Wherever you stay in Venice, expect it to cost around a third more than it would on the mainland. Booking is near-essential April–Oct and for Carnival; many hotels close in winter.

★★★★★**Danieli**, Castello 4196, Riva degli Schiavoni, **t** 041 522 6480, **f** 041 520 0208, (*luxury*). The most famous hotel in Venice, in the most glorious location, overlooking the Lagoon next to the Palazzo Ducale. Formerly a Gothic *palazzo*, it has been a hotel since 1822; Dickens, Proust, George Sand and Wagner checked in here. Nearly every room has a story to tell, amid silken walls, Gothic stairs, gilt mirrors and oriental rugs. The new wing is comfortable but lacks the stories.

★★★★**Ca' Pisani**, Dorsoduro 979/a, Rio Terrà Foscarini, **t** 041 240 1411, **f** 041 277 1061 (*luxury*). In a 17th-century *palazzo* behind the Zattere, this is designer-minimalist; original 1930s pieces are scattered throughout, blending in with contemporary items. There is a roof terrace, Turkish bath and wine bar.

★★★**Accademia**, Dorsoduro 1058, Fondamenta Bollani, **t** 041 521 0188, **f** 041 523 9152 (*very expensive*). A generous dollop of slightly faded charm in a 17th-century villa with a garden, off the Grand Canal. Its 26 rooms are furnished with a menagerie of antiques. Book well in advance. Off-season discounts.

★★★**Pausania**, Dorsoduro 2824, San Barnabà, **t** 041 522 2083, **f** 041 522 2989 (*very expensive*). Just up-canal from a floating vegetable shop in the picturesque San Barnabà area, this gothic *palazzo* has a breakfast room overlooking a quiet garden. Bedrooms are refreshingly unfussy.

★★**Agli Alboretti**, Dorsoduro 884, Rio Terrà Foscarini, **t** 041 523 0058, **f** 041 521 0158 (*expensive*). A charming little hotel, recently refurbished, on a rare tree-lined lane.

★★★**La Calcina**, Dorsoduro 780, Fondamente delle Zattere, Dorsoduro, **t** 041 520 6466, **f** 041 522 7045 (*expensive*). Overlooking the Giudecca canal, this was Ruskin's *pensione* in 1877. Totally refurbished with all mod cons, and a beautiful breakfast terrace.

★★**La Residenza**, Castello 3608, Campo Bandiera e Moro, **t** 041 528 5315, **f** 041 523 8859 (*expensive*). In a lovely 14th-century palace in a quiet square. The public rooms are flamboyantly decorated with 18th-century frescoes, paintings and antique furniture, though the bedrooms are simpler.

Most of the cheaper hotels are around the Lista di Spagna, though they can be tacky and noisy. Dorsoduro is more attractive, particularly around Campo S. Margherita.

★★**Seguso**, Dorsoduro 779, Zattere, **t** 041 528 6858, **f** 041 522 2340 (*moderate*). Book ahead for this old-fashioned, cosy hotel overlooking the Giudecca. Rooms are small.

★**Ca' Foscari**, Dorsoduro 3887B, Calle della Frescada, **t** 041 710 401, **f** 041 710 817 (*moderate*). In a bustling residential area, this is a cut above other one-stars. Modest, pretty rooms are spotless; not all have bath.

★**Dalla Mora**, S. Croce 42, Salizzada S. Pantalon, **t** 041 710 703, **f** 041 723 006 (*moderate–cheap*). A simple but inviting hotel down a narrow alleyway just off the *salizzada*. Four rooms have canal views; two have a/c.

Eating Out

Venetians are traditionally the worst cooks in Italy, and prices tend to be about 15 per cent higher than elsewhere, but the restaurants below have a history of being decent or better.

Danieli Terrace, Castello 4196, Riva degli Schiavoni, **t** 041 522 6480 (*luxury*). The hotel's rooftop restaurant is renowned for classic cuisine and perfect service in an incomparable setting.

Da Fiore, S. Polo 2202, Calle del Scaleter, **t** 041 731 308 (*luxury*). Begin with *misto crudo* before moving on to classic *bigoli in salsa* (handmade spaghetti in a sauce of anchovies and onions), or a silky black squid ink risotto. *Secondi* include *involtini* of sole wrapped round radicchio, and a superb tuna steak with rosemary. *Closed Sun and Mon.*

Harry's Bar, S. Marco 1323, Calle Vallaresso, **t** 041 523 5777 (*luxury*). A favourite of Hemingway, this is a Venetian institution for its celebrity atmosphere. Avoid the food and flit in to sample the justly famous cocktails (a Bellini, Tiziano or Tiepolo). *Closed Mon.*

Trattoria Vini da Arturo, S. Marco 3656, Calle degli Assassini, **t** 041 528 6974 (*expensive*). Near La Fenice, this tiny *trattoria* has not a speck of seafood on the menu. Try *pappardelle al radicchio* or Venice's best steaks – and a famous *tiramisù*. *Closed Sun and half Aug.*

Le Bistrot, S. Marco 4685, Calle dei Fabbri, **t** 041 523 6651 (*expensive*). A cosy place with live music and poetry readings, serving historical Venetian dishes full of unusual herbs and spices: try pumpkin and cheese gnocchi with cinnamon, spicy pheasant soup, sturgeon cooked with prunes and balsamic vinegar and Turkish rice pudding. *Open until 1am.*

Altanella, Giudecca 268, Calle della Erbe, **t** 041 522 7780 (*moderate*). A delightful seafood restaurant on the Rio del Ponte Longo. Any of the grilled fish will be superb, and the *risotto di pesce* is worth the trip in itself. Book. *Closed Mon eve, Tues, and half of Aug.*

Alle Testiere, Castello 5801, Calle del Mondo Novo, **t** 041 522 7220 (*moderate*). This *osteria* seats 20, so book well ahead. If you can get a table, the fish-based dishes here are a bit different: delicious and varied *antipasti*, *gnocchetti* with squid, monkfish tails with capers and turbot with radicchio. And do leave room for pudding. *Closed Sun and three weeks in Aug.*

L'Incontro, Dorsoduro 3062, Rio Terrà Canal, **t** 041 522 2404 (*moderate*). An unusual restaurant for Venice on two counts: the food is Sardinian, and there's no fish, just succulent meat dishes and a choice of Sardinian pasta.

Al' Aciugheta, Castello, Campo SS. Filippo e Giacomo, **t** 041 522 4292 (*cheap*). One of the best cheap restaurants near the Piazza San Marco, with good pizzas and atmosphere to boot. Go with a local and get in early to the back room for *cicheti*, cheese and excellent wines. *Closed Wed; open daily in summer.*

Vino Vino, S. Marco 1983, Campo S. Fantin, **t** 041 523 7027 (*cheap*). A trendy offspring of the next door élite Antico Martini, where, for a lot less, you can eat a well-cooked, filling dish (cooked by the same chefs!) washed down by a glass of good wine. *Closed Tues.*

The classic **cafés** face each other across Piazza San Marco: **Florian's** and **Quadri**, both beautiful, and both exorbitant. For ice cream, head to tiny **Boutique del Gelato** on Salizada San Lio, or **Paolin**, on Campo Santo Stefano.

Entertainment

The main source in English on any current events is the fortnightly ***Un Ospite di Venezia***, free from tourist offices and hotels. The local papers *Il Gazzettino* and *Nuova Venezia* both have listings of films, concerts, etc.

Venice's **music programme** is heavily oriented to the classical. While La Fenice undergoes restoration, opera (*Dec–May*), ballet and concerts are being staged in the Pala Fenice at Tronchetto; for **tickets**, contact the **Cassa di Risparmio**, Campo S. Luca, **t** 041 521 0161.

Nightlife

Sadly, life after dark is notoriously moribund. You might like to spend less more memorably on a moonlit gondola ride, or do as most people do – wander about. The hotblooded may go on to bars and discos in Mestre, Marghera or the Lido. Venice's few late-night **bars** and music venues can be fun, or just posy and dull; what you find is a matter of luck.

columns, sawn into slices of rich colour, line the lower walls; the 12th-century pavement is a magnificent mosaic of marble, glass and porphyry. The 14th-century **baptistry** (*ask a caretaker to show you the 'Ufficio Technico'*) is famous for its mosaics on the life of John the Baptist, with a Salome who could probably have had just as many heads as she pleased. You can't visit the relics of St Mark, safe in the **sanctuary** (*open Mon–Sat 9–5, Sun 2–4; adm*), but you can see the altar's retable, the fabulous, glowing Pala d'Oro, a masterpiece of medieval gold and jewel work. Before leaving, climb up to the **Museo Marciano, Galleria and Loggia dei Cavalli** (*open summer 9.30–5*) to see the original ancient Greek bronze horses, and get a better view of the dome mosaics from the women's gallery, along with a visit to the loggia, where you can inspect the replica quadriga and look down on the swarming *piazza* below.

The Campanile, the Torre dell'Orologio and Piazzetta San Marco

St Mark's 332ft **bell tower** (*open summer 9–7; adm*) can seem rather alien, a Presbyterian brick sentinel in the otherwise delicately wrought *piazza*. But it has been there since 912; when it gently collapsed in 1902, the Venetians felt its lack so acutely that they constructed an exact replica. Another famous ornament, at the head of the Procuratie Vecchie, is the **Torre dell'Orologio** (*under scaffolding*), built in 1499 and crowned by two bronze 'Moors' who sound the hours. Of elaborate astronomical clocks, none is as beautiful as this; according to rumour, the Council of Ten blinded the builders to prevent them from creating such a marvel for any other city.

To the south of the basilica, the **Piazzetta San Marco** was the republic's foyer, where ships would dock under the watchful eye of the doge. One of its pair of Egyptian columns bears an ancient Assyrian or Persian winged lion, under whose paw the Venetians adroitly slid a book to create the symbol of St Mark. The columns frame the famous view out to the Lagoon towards the islet of **San Giorgio Maggiore**, crowned by Palladio's church of the same name. Built according to his theories on harmonic proportion, it seems to hang between the water and the sky.

Piazza San Marco Museums and the Biblioteca Marciana

One ticket will get you into the Museo Correr, the Biblioteca Marciana, the Museo Archeòlogico and Ducal Palace (*entrance to all except the Palazzo Ducale is via the Museo Correr*). The **Museo Correr** (*facing the basilica in the corner of the piazza; open April–Oct daily 9–7; Nov–Mar daily 9–5; last tickets 90mins before closing; adm to all €9.50*) contains an engaging collection of Venetian memorabilia, and many fine Venetian paintings upstairs. These include Carpaccio's *Courtesans* (or Ladies – in Venice it was hard to tell) and his *Visitation*; there are also works by Antonello da Messina, Cosme Turà, Bellini, Canova and Il Civetta.

Opposite the Doges' Palace stands Sansovino's superb **Biblioteca**, where scholars with permission can examine such treasures as the 1501 *Grimani breviary*, Homeric *codices* and Marco Polo's will. Next to the library, the **Archaeology Museum** has an excellent collection of Greek sculpture, including a violent *Leda and the Swan* and ancient copies of the *Gallic Warriors of Pergamon*. By the waterfront, the **Zecca**, or Old Mint, once stamped out thousands of gold *zecchini*, giving English the word 'sequin'.

The Palace of the Doges (Palazzo Ducale)

Open 15 April–Oct 9–7; Nov–Mar 9–5; adm exp – includes entry to the Museo Correr. Ticket office (closes 5.30 summer, 3.30 winter) through Porta della Carta and in the courtyard.

What St Mark's is to sacred architecture, the **Doges' Palace** is to secular – unique and audacious, an illuminated storybook of Venetian history and legend. Its weight is partly relieved by the white and red diamond pattern on the façade, which from a distance gives the palace its wholesome, peaches-and-cream complexion. Some of Italy's finest medieval sculpture crowns the columns of the lower colonnade. Beautiful sculptural groups adorn the corners, most notably the 13th-century *Judgement of Solomon*, near the grand **Porta della Carta** (1443), a Gothic symphony in stone by Giovanni and Bartolomeo Bon. Just within the Porta, don't miss Antonio Rizzo's delightful courtyard and his **Scala dei Giganti**. Visitors enter the palace via Sansovino's **Scala d'Oro**. The first floor is used for special exhibitions (*separate adm*), while the golden stairway continues up to the Secondo Piano Nobile, from where the Venetian state was governed. After a fire, Veronese and Tintoretto were employed to paint the newly remodelled chambers with mythological themes and scores of allegories and apotheoses of Venice. Among the highlights are the **Sala del Consiglio dei Dieci**, where the Council of Ten deliberated under Veronese's ceiling, and the magnificent **Sala del Maggior Consiglio**, capable of holding the 2,500 patricians of the Great Council. By the entrance is Tintoretto's *Paradiso*, the biggest oil painting in the world, from which all the Blessed look up at Veronese's great *Apotheosis of Venice* on the ceiling. At the end the **Bridge of Sighs** (Ponte dei Sospiri) takes you to the 17th-century **Palazzo delle Prigioni**, where those to whom the Republic took real exception were dumped into uncomfortable *pozzi*, or 'wells'. Celebrities like Casanova, meanwhile, got to stay up in the rather cosier *piombi* or 'leads', just under the roof. These, and the rooms where the real nitty-gritty business of state took place, can only be seen on the 1½-hour **Itinerari Segreti** (*mornings at 10 and 12; 20 people only; book at least a day in advance at the director's office on the first floor, or call* **t** *041 522 4951*).

San Marco to Rialto

The streets between the *piazza* and the Rialto are the busiest in Venice, especially the **Mercerie**, lined with some of the city's smartest shops. The Mercerie continue past two churches in which Sansovino had a hand: **San Zulian**, with a façade most notable for Sansovino's statue of its pompous benefactor; and **San Salvatore**, containing his monument to Doge Francesco Venier. An 89-year-old Titian painted one of his more unusual works for this church, the *Annunciation*, which he signed with double emphasis *Titianus Fecit – 'Fecit'* because his patrons refused to believe that he had painted it. Humming, bustling **Campo San Bartolomeo** has for centuries been one of the social hubs of Venice, and still gets packed daily with after-work crowds. Follow the signs up to the **Ponte di Rialto** (*see* p.107), the geographical heart of Venice. The city's central markets have been just across the bridge for a millennium, divided into sections for vegetables and for fish.

San Marco to the Accademia

Following signs 'To the Accademia' from Piazza San Marco, the first *campo* belongs to Baroque **San Moisè** (1668), Italy's most grotesque church. Detour up Calle Veste to see **La Fenice** (1792; *closed for restoration after a fire in 1996*), Venice's renowned opera house, which saw the premières of Verdi's *Rigoletto* and *La Traviata*. Back en route to the Accademia, the signs lead past the fancy façade (1680) of **Santa Maria Zobenigo** to the **Campo Santo Stefano**, one of the most elegant squares in Venice; at one end, a gravity-defying campanile leers over the church of **Santo Stefano**, which has a striking wooden ceiling like the keel of a ship.

Just over the Grand Canal stands the **Accademia** (*open Mon 9–2, Tues–Fri 9–9, Sat 9am–11pm, Sun 9–8; adm exp. Arrive early; only 300 visitors at a time*), the grand cathedral of Venetian art, ablaze with light and colour. The collection is arranged chronologically, beginning with fine altarpieces, including Giovanni Bellini's *Pala di San Giobbe*, one of the key works of the *quattrocento*. The next rooms are small but, like gifts, contain the best things: works by Mantegna, Giovanni Bellini and Piero della Francesca. The climax of the Venetian High Renaissance comes in **Room X**, with Veronese's *Christ in the House of Levi* (1573), its ghostly imaginary background in violent contrast to the rollicking feast in front. Here, too, is *La Pietà*, Titian's last painting (at age 90); he intended it for his tomb, and smeared the paint on with his fingers. Alongside several Tintorettos, the following few rooms mainly contain work from the 17th and 18th centuries. Canaletto and Guardi are represented in **Room XVII**, and the final rooms house more luminous 15th-century painting by Alvise Vivarini, Giovanni and Gentile Bellini, Marco Basaiti and Crivelli. There's a compelling *Cycle of S. Ursula* by Carpaccio and, in the last room, Titian's striking *Presentation of the Virgin* (1538).

Dorsoduro

The Accademia lies in the *sestiere* of Dorsoduro, which can also boast the **Peggy Guggenheim Collection** (*open Wed–Mon 10–6; April–Oct also Sat 10–10; adm exp*), an impressive quantity of brand-name 20th-century art: Bacon, Brancusi, Braque, Calder, Chagall, Dali, De Chirico, Duchamp, Max Ernst (her second husband), Giacometti, Gris, Kandinsky, Klee, Magritte, Miró, Moore, Mondrian, Picasso, Pollock, Rothko and Smith. From here it's a short stroll to the elegant, octagonal basilica of **Santa Maria della Salute** (1631–81, *open daily 9–12 and 3–5.30*), the masterpiece of Baldassare Longhena, with its snow-white dome and marble jelly rolls. The interior is a relatively restrained Baroque, and contains the *Marriage at Cana* by Tintoretto and several works by Titian. Almost next to the basilica stands the distinctive **Dogana di Mare**, the Customs House. The long **Fondamenta delle Zattere** skirts the Canale della Giudecca (*or vaporetto no.5 to San Basegio*) to the church of **San Sebastiano**, embellished with magnificent ceiling frescoes and illusionistic paintings by Veronese. Back towards the Grand Canal to the north is the delightful **Campo Santa Margherita**, traditionally the marketplace of Dorsoduro; it's also a good spot to find restaurants and cafés. A red campanile marks the 14th-century church of the **Carmini**, next to the **Scuola dei Carmini** (*open summer Mon–Sat 9–6, Sun 9–1; winter Mon–Sat 9–4; adm; also open for concerts*), which has one of Tiepolo's best and brightest ceilings, *The Virgin in Glory*.

San Polo and Santa Croce

From the Ponte di Rialto, the yellow signs lead through the pretty **Campo of San Polo** to a venerable Venetian institution: the severe medieval brick **Frari** (*open Mon–Sat 9–6, Sun and hols 1–6; adm*), celebrated for its paintings, especially for the most overrated painting in Italy, Titian's *Assumption of the Virgin* (1516–18). Marvel at the revolutionary use of space and movement, but the Virgin herself has as much artistic vision as a Sunday school holy card. His less theatrical *Madonna di Ca' Pésaro*, in the north aisle, had a greater influence on Venetian composition. In the sanctuary is the beautiful Renaissance **Tomb of Doge Nicolà Tron** (1476) by Antonio Rizzo. Titian is buried here too, as is Monteverdi, one of the founding fathers of opera. Next to the Frari, the **Scuola Grande di San Rocco** (*open 9–5.30; adm*) holds one of the wonders of Venice – or rather, 54 wonders – all painted by Tintoretto between 1562 and 1585. Tintoretto had the eye of a 16th-century Orson Welles, creating audacious 'sets' with unusual lighting effects, and here he achieved what is considered by some to be the finest painting cycle in existence, culminating in the *Crucifixion*.

East of San Marco to Castello

From Piazzetta San Marco, the ever-thronging **Riva degli Schiavoni** curves gracefully east beyond the Palazzo Ducale. To the northeast, the tiny **Scuola di San Giorgio degli Schiavoni** (*open Tues–Sat 9.30–12.30 and 3.30–6.30, Sun 9.30–12.30; adm*) is decorated with the most beloved art in all Venice: Vittore Carpaccio's frescoes on the lives of the Dalmatian patron saints, among them George charging a petticoat-munching dragon in a landscape strewn with maidenly leftovers from lunch. Further east lies the first of all arsenals, the **Arsenale**, founded in 1104; today it is occupied by the Italian military, but up until the 17th century these were the greatest dockyards in the world. Nearby, Venice's glorious maritime history is the subject of the fascinating artefacts and models in the **Museo Storico Navale** (*open Mon–Fri 8.45–1.30, Sat 8.45–1; closed Sun and hols; adm*).

North of San Marco

You can trace your way through the web of alleys north of San Marco to Campo San Zanipolo and **Santi Giovanni e Paolo** (*open Mon–Sat 8–12.30 and 3–6, Sun 3–5.30*), the pantheon of the doges. Some 25 of them lie here in splendid Gothic and Renaissance tombs; the finest is that of Doge Andrea Vendramin, by Tullio and Antonio Lombardo (1478). From here, Largo G. Gallina leads to the Renaissance church of **Santa Maria dei Miracoli** (*open Mon–Sat 10–5, Sun and hols 1–5; adm*), an exquisite jewel box built by Pietro Lombardo in the 1480s. Further north, the enchanting Gothic fantasy *palazzo*, the **Ca' d'Oro**, houses the **Galleria Franchetti** (*open Mon 8.15–2, Tues–Sun 8.15am–9.15pm; adm*); among its treasures are Mantegna's *St Sebastian* and Guardi's series of Venetian views, as well as Renaissance bronzes and medallions by Pisanello and Il Riccio. The palace itself is famous for the intricate traceries of its façade, best appreciated from the Grand Canal. Due north, near the Fondamenta Nuove, stands the unloved, unrestored church of the **Gesuiti** (*open Mon–Sat 9–6, Sun 1–6; adm*), a Baroque extravaganza from 1714–29, full of *trompe-l'œil* of white and green-grey marble draperies.

Cannaregio

Crumbling, piquant Cannaregio is the least visited *sestiere* in Venice and here, perhaps, you can begin to feel what everyday life is like behind the tourist glitz. This was Tintoretto's home base, and he is buried in the beautiful Venetian Gothic **Madonna dell'Orto** (*open Mon–Sat 10–7, Sun and hols 1–5; adm*), alongside several of his jumbo masterpieces. Here, too, was the cramped **Ghetto**, with its five synagogues; all Jews were confined here in 1516, in part for their own protection, surrounded by a moat-like canal and shut in tight at night. In contrast, towards the station to the north runs the **Lista di Spagna**, Venice's famous tourist highway, lined with restaurants, hotels and souvenir stands that are not as cheap as they should be.

The Lagoon and its Islands

Pearly and melting, iridescent blue or murky green, a sheet of glass in the dawn or leaden, opaque grey: Venice's Lagoon is a wonderful, desolate 'landscape' with a hundred personalities. It is 56 kilometres long and averages eight kilometres across; to navigate it, the Venetians have developed an intricate network of channels that keep their craft from running aground on the mud flats.

Nearest to the centre, next to the little islet of San Giorgio Maggiore (*vaporetto 82; see* p.113), the string of eight islands that make up **La Giudecca** (*vaporetti 41, 42, 82, N*) is seldom visited. Those who can come to rub shoulders with the rich and famous at the luxurious **Cipriani Hotel**; others to visit Palladio's best church, **Il Redentore** (*open Mon–Sat 10–5, Sun 1–5; adm*), its temple front providing a fitting backdrop for one of the most exciting events on the Venetian calendar, the *Festa del Redentore* (*see* p.110).

The **Lido**, with its 12 kilometres of beach, was the pinnacle of Belle Epoque fashion, and it's still Venice's playground today, with its bathing concessions, riding clubs, tennis courts, golf courses and shooting ranges. The free beach (**Spiaggia Comunale**) is on the north side, a 15-minute walk from the *vaporetto* stop at San Nicolò.

Murano (*vaporetti Nos.41 and 42 from Ferrovia or Fondamenta Nuove, 71 and 72 from Piazzale Roma, Ferrovia, S. Zaccaria and F. Nuove*) has been synonymous with glass ever since all the forges in Venice were relocated there in 1291. Can you visit them? You bet! There's the inevitable tour of the 'Museum Show Rooms', but it is free and there's not much pressure to buy. The **Museo Vetrario** (*open April–Oct Thurs–Tues 10–5; Nov–Mar Thurs–Tues 10–4; included in San Marco museums adm*) has a choice collection of 15th-century Murano glass. Nearby, a marvellous mosaic incorporating ancient Murano glass paves the floor of **Santi Maria e Donato** (*open daily 9.15–12 and 4–7*).

In **Burano** (*vaporetto no.12 from Fondamenta Nuove*), everything is painted with a Fauvist sensibility in brightly coloured miniature. Traditionally the men fish and the women make Venetian point, 'the most Italian of all lace work'; beautiful, intricate, and murder on the eyesight. You can see it being made at the **Scuola dei Merletti** (*open April–Oct Wed–Mon 10–5; Nov–Mar 10–4; included in San Marco museums adm*).

Once a rival to Venice, **Torcello** (*vaporetto no.12*) is now overgrown with weeds, but its **Cathedral of Santa Maria Assunta** (*open April–Oct 10.30–5.30; Nov–Mar 10–5; adm*) contains Venice's finest mosaics. All are by 11th- and 12th-century Greek artists, from a wonderful floor to a spectacular *Last Judgement* and the heart-rending *Teotoco*.

Day Trips from Venice

Padua (Padova)

Padua refuses to be overshadowed by Venice, and can rightly claim a place among Italy's most interesting and historic cities. Its university, one of the oldest in Europe, was attended by Petrarch, Dante and Galileo; its churches, under the brushes of Giotto, Altichiero, Giusto de' Menabuoi and Mantegna, were virtual laboratories in the evolution of fresco. But above all, Padua attracts pilgrims of a more pious nature; its exotic, domed mosque of a basilica is the last resting place of St Anthony of Padua.

It's a short walk from the station to the jewel in Padua's crown: Giotto's extraordinary frescoes (1304–7) in the **Cappella degli Scrovegni** (*open 9–6, until 7 in summer,* ***museum*** *closed Mon; adm exp; visits to the chapel timed, book in advance;* **t** *0498 204 550*). In sheer power and inspiration, the cycle was as revolutionary as Michelangelo's Sistine Chapel: a fresh, natural, narrative composition, with three-dimensional figures solidly anchored in their setting. In the adjacent convent, Padua's vast **Museo Civico** (*same hours and ticket as Cappella degli Scrovegni*) combines archaeology (coins, vases, and funerary *stelae* from the 6th to 1st centuries BC) with acres of fine art. Here you'll find Giotto's *Crucifixion*, works by Guariento, founder of the medieval Paduan school, and others by nearly every Venetian who ever applied brush to canvas: Bellini, Tintoretto, Titian, Vivarini, Veronese, Tiepolo and others down the line. The small Renaissance bronzes were a speciality of Padua, especially those by Il Riccio. Next to the museum, the church of the **Eremitani** (1306; *open Mon–Sat 8.15–12.15, 4–6; Sun 9.30–12, 4–6; same ticket as the Cappella Scrovegni*) was shattered in a Second World

Getting There

Padua is easily reached by **train** from Venice (30mins), leaving every half hour or so. A booth outside Padua's station on Piazzale Stazione gives tickets and directions for the city buses.

There are also **buses** from Venice every half hour, arrving at Padua's **bus station** in the Piazzale Boschetti (**t** 049 820 6844), a 10-min walk from the train station.

Tourist Information

Padua: In the train station, **t** 049 875 2077 (*open Mon–Sat 9–7.30, Sun 8.30–12.30; Nov–Mar 9.20–5.45, Sun 9–12*); Riviera Mugnai 8, **t** 049 875 0655, **f** 049 650 794, *apt@padovanet.it.* or *www.padovanet.it.*

Museum ticket: A *biglietto unico* will save you money on adm to many of the main sites; buy it from any participating site.

Eating Out

La cucina padovana features *carni di cortile*: chicken, duck, pheasant, goose and pigeon.

La Corta Dei Leoni, Via Pietro D'Abano 1, **t** 049 815 0083 (*moderate*). For a truly sumptious meal in a walled courtyard in the historic centre. The seasonal menu is changed weekly, while the wine list reflects the best Italy has to offer. Specialities include *lardo di colonata* (wafer-thin lard, spiced and salted) and *scaloppa di rombo con finocci gratinata. Closed Sun eve, Mon; good disabled access.*

Bertolini, Via Antichiero 162, **t** 049 600 357 (*cheap*). This has been a favourite for 150 years; go for the hearty vegetarian dishes and home-made desserts. *Closed Sat.*

Bastioni del Moro, Via Bronzetti 18, **t** 049 871 0006 (*cheap*). This serves delicious gnocchi beyond Padua's western walls (take Corso Milano). The tourist menu is cheap, though prices soar if you order fish. *Closed Sun.*

War air raid, but what could be salvaged of the frescoes has been painstakingly pieced together, most importantly Mantegna's remarkable Ovetari chapel (1454–7).

A short walk from the Eremitani takes you to **Piazza Cavour**, the historic heart of Padua. Here, the Palazzo del Bo' was the seat of the **University of Padua**, where Galileo delivered his lectures from an old wooden pulpit. To the west are the bustling market squares of **Piazza delle Erbe** and **Piazza delle Frutta**, separated by the massive **Palazzo della Ragione** (*open 9–7 closed Mon; adm*). A little further west, Padua's **Duomo** is rather neglected, but the **baptistry** (*open 9.30–1 and 3–6, adm*) was beautifully frescoed by Florentine Giusto de' Menabuoi in the 1370s, its awesome, chilling dome painted with a multitude of saints in the circles of paradise.

Below the commercial heart of Padua, an exotic, fantastical cluster of seven domes rises up around a lofty cupola, two campanili and two minarets: this is the **Basilica di Sant'Antonio**, begun in 1232, the same year that St Anthony was canonized. Inside, pilgrims queue patiently to press their palm against his tomb; no one pays much attention to the 16th-century marble reliefs lining his chapel, but they are exquisite: the fourth and fifth are by Sansovino, the sixth and seventh by Tullio Lombardo, and the last by Antonio Lombardo. The high altar is the work of Donatello and his helpers (1445–50), while the great Paschal Candelabrum is the masterpiece of Il Riccio. In the ambulatory, don't miss the treasury of gold reliquaries, one containing Anthony's tongue and larynx, found intact when his tomb was opened in 1981.

In front of the basilica, a bit lost among the pigeons and souvenirs, is Donatello's **statue of Gattamelata** (1453), the first large equestrian bronze since antiquity.

Vicenza

'The city of Palladio', prettily set under the Monte Bérico, is an architectural pilgrimage shrine, and knows it. Although heavily damaged in the Second World War, restorers have tidied up all the scars; now, thanks to its gold-working, tool-manufacturing, textile-weaving and shoe-making, Vicenza is one of Italy's wealthiest cities.

From the station, Viale Roma enters the historic centre through the **Porta Castello**, near Piazza Castello. The Gothic **Duomo**, housing a beautiful polyptych (1356) by Lorenzo Veneziano, lies east of here along Contra Vescovado. Beneath the *piazza* outside lies a *cryptoporticus* (subterraean gallery) from a palace of the 1st century AD.

To the north lies the regal **Piazza dei Signori**, Vicenza's heart and soul. In the 1540s the Vicentines decided that the *piazza*'s crumbling medieval Palazzo della Ragione needed a facelift, and hired a young unknown called Palladio to do it. The city would never be the same. In 1549 Palladio began working on the **Basilica** (*open Tues–Sun 9–5; adm*), and kept at it off and on until his death. Two tiers of arches interspersed with Doric and Ionic columns give an appearance of Roman regularity, while the roof is concealed behind a pediment lined with life-size statues. Sharing the *piazza* is the needle-like **Torre di Piazza** (12th–15th century), and Palladio's **Loggia del Capitanato** (1571). Step behind the Loggia to **Corso Palladio**, once called 'the most elegant street in Europe, not counting the Grand Canal in incomparable Venice'. Just to your right is Vincenzo Scamozzi's **Palazzo Trissino**, with an Ionic portico and superb courtyard.

Getting There

Trains leave Venice for Vicenza every hour (journey 1hr). The station is on the south side of the town, at the end of Viale Roma.

The FTV **bus station** (**t** 0444 223 115) is alongside it.

Tourist Information

Vicenza: Piazza Matteotti 12; also Piazza Duomo 5, **t** 0444 320 854, **f** 0444 327 072 (*open Mon–Sat 9–1 and 2.30–6, Sun 9–1*).

Eating Out

This is polenta and *baccalà* (salt cod) country; *baccalà alla vicentina* is sprinkled with cheese and browned in butter, anchovies and onions, then seasoned with parsley, pepper and milk.

Nuovo Cinzia e Valerio, Piazza Porta Padova, **t** 0444 505 213 (*expensive*). For perfectly prepared seafood, this serves tagliatelle with salmon, cuttlefish risotto or grilled sole, followed by home-made ice cream and crisp biscuits. *Closed Sun eve, Mon, Aug.*

Antica Decchio Trattoria Tre Visi, Corso Palladio 25, **t** 0444 324 868 (*moderate*). The author of the original Romeo and Juliet was born in this 15th-century palace, which, with its fireplace and rustic fittings, is a charming place to enjoy good, high quality Veneto cooking and home-made pasta. Be sure to try the local delicacies; the ambience, while busy, is very friendly. *Closed Sun eve, Mon, July.*

Trattoria Framarin, Via Battista Framarin 48, **t** 0444 570 407 (*moderate*). Just west of the walls, with delicious home-made pasta and a warm welcome. *Closed Sun and some of Aug.*

Righetti, Piazza Duomo (*cheap*). A popular, bustling self-service canteen with seats spilling on to the *piazza*. *Closed Sat and Sun.*

There is more Palladio on **Contrà Porti**; on the corner of Contrà Riale, **Palazzo Barbaran-da Porto**, built from scratch by Palladio in 1570, now holds the **Museo Palladiano** (*to visit, contact the Institute for Palladian Studies, **t** 0444 323 014*). Opposite, the vast **Palazzo Thiene** (now the Banca Popolare) was another facelift project; Palladio was to make it the most imposing residence in all Vicenza, though it was never completed. The Contrà Porti side is by Lorenzo da Bologna. Around the corner is Palladio's work, with its weighty sculpted windows and Mannerist classicizing. Some of the interior retains its original and rather magnificent decoration; if the bank isn't too busy, ask to see the Rotonda with a domed vault and statues.

Diagonally across the Contrà Zanella from the Palazzo Thiene, the church of **Santo Stefano** contains one of Palma Vecchio's most beautiful paintings, *Madonna with SS. George and Lucy and Musical Angel*. More fine art waits nearby in **Santa Corona**, with Veronese's *Adoration of the Magi* (1573) and Giovanni Bellini's *Baptism of Christ*.

At the north end of the Corso, Palladio's open, airy **Palazzo Chiericati** (1550–1650) houses the **Pinacoteca** (*open Tues–Sat 9–5 June-Aug 9–9; adm*), retaining original frescoes on the ground floor and a collection of 14th- –20th-century art upstairs. Among the artists represented are Paolo Veneziano, Memling, Cima da Conegliano, Lotto, Sansovino, Tintoretto, Van Dyck, Jan Brueghel the Elder, Bassano, Veronese, Tiepolo *père* and *fils*, and the irrepressible Francesco Maffei.

Across Piazza Matteotti, the **Teatro Olimpico** (*open Tues–Sun 9–5; June–Aug 9–9; adm*) was Palladio's swansong, a unique masterpiece of the Italian Renaissance and the oldest operational indoor theatre in the world (1580). Scamozzi's original stage-set, a Renaissance dream city meant to represent the city of Thebes, was so perfect that no one ever thought, or bothered, to change it.

Touring from Venice and Treviso

Day 1: La Malcontenta and a Fiendish Maze

Morning: From Venice, take the S11 to **Mestre** (from Treviso, you can reach Mestre quickly on the southbound S13). South of Mestre, the S11 follows the **Brenta Canal** west towards Padua, sprinkled along its length with 16th-century villas of Venetian patricians. Start at the east end of the S11, between Fusina and Oriago, at Palladio's celebrated **La Malcontenta** (1560) (*open May–Oct, Tues and Sat 9–12 or call* ***t*** *041 520 3966; guided tours; adm exp*), a vision begging for Scarlett O'Hara to sweep down the steps – numerous American plantations were modelled on it. Inside are some delicate frescoes, including the sad lady to whom the villa owes its name. Take the S11 west, past **Oriago**'s Villa Gradenigo, and stop for lunch in **Mira**, or beyond, in **Dolo**.

Lunch: In Mira or Dolo, *see* below.

Afternoon: Take a look at Mira's post office, the **Palazzo Foscarini**, where Byron lived (1817–1819) while working on *Childe Harold*. Then drive on to **Strá** to see the grandest villa in the Veneto: the **Villa Nazionale** (1760) modelled on Versailles (*1-hr guided tours June–Sept Tues–Sun 9–6; Oct–May Tues–Sun 9–1.30; adm*). Tackle the fiendish maze in the park, and don't miss Giambattista Tiepolo's shimmering *Apotheosis of the Pisani Family* in the ballroom. Continue west to Padua, and take the S16 south to **Monsélice**, spilling like an opera set down the slopes of the Euganean Hills.

Dinner and Sleeping: In Monsélice or Este (9km west on the S10), *see* below.

Day 1

Lunch in Mira

Nalin, Via Nuovissimo 29, **t** 041 420 083 (*expensive–moderate*). One of the traditional places to round off an excursion along the Brenta Canal, with a lovely poplar-shaded veranda. The emphasis is on Venetian seafood, finely grilled. *Closed Sun eve, Mon and Aug.*

Lunch in Dolo

Locanda alla Posta, Via Cà Tron 33, **t** 041 410 740 (*expensive*). This restaurant has been around a long time, and it now has a wonderful new chef to wake it from its hibernation: you'll be offered great fish, delicately prepared, alongside other dishes. *Closed Mon.*

Dinner in Monsélice

La Torre, Piazza Mazzini 14, **t** 0429 73752 (*moderate, expensive for truffles*). An elegant place where *funghi* fiends can head for gratification. *Closed Sun eve, Mon, and part of July and Aug.*

Sleeping in Monsélice

*****Ceffri Villa Corner**, Via Orti 7, **t** 0429 783 111, **f** 0429 783 100 (*moderate*). A modern hotel, with a swimming pool and well equipped rooms, plus a good restaurant featuring home-made pasta and an economical tourist menu.

Venetian Palace Hostel, 'Città di Monsélice', Via Santo Stefano Superiore 33, **t** 0429 783 125 (*cheap*). For somewhere rather more stylish, try this hostel, which was once used by the dukes of Padua as a guest house. It now offers comfortable rooms fitted with modern conveniences.

Dinner and Sleeping in Este

****Hotel Beatrice d'Este**, Via le Rimembranze 1, **t** 0429 600 533, **f** 0429 601 957 (*cheap*). This hotel has a lovely little *trattoria* attached serving all the standard dishes of the Veneto.

Day 2: Euganean Musings and Grandiose Gardens

Morning: Explore the citadel of **Monsélice**, and look at the superb medieval and Renaissance arms and antiques in Ezzelino da Romano's **Castello Monsélice** (*open April–11 Nov; tours from 9–12 and 3–6 all year; adm*). Zig-zag your way up the **Via Sacra delle Sette Chiese** past the sumptuous **Villa Nani**, the **Duomo**, seven **chapels** by Scamozzi (frescoed by Palma Giovane), and the elegant **Villa Duodo**. Then visit Monsélice's old rival, **Este** (9km west down the S10), bristling with the towers of the 1339 **Castle**. Next door, the **Museo Nazionale Atestino** (*open 9–7; adm*) covers the Paleoveneto civilization from the 10th century BC up to Roman times; don't miss the outstanding bronze vase, the *Situla Benvenuti*. Muse over the **Villa De Kunkler**, where Shelley, as Byron's guest, penned *Lines written among the Euganean Hills*. Drive up into the Hills themselves to have lunch in the medieval gem of **Arquà Petrarca**.

Lunch: In Arquà Petrarca, *see* below.

Afternoon: Visit Petrarch's villa, the charming **Casa del Petrarca** (*open Feb–Sept 9–12 and 3–7; Oct–Jan 9–12.30 and 2.30–5.30; adm*), which has kept many of its 14th-century furnishings. Then continue north some 9km to the **Villa Barbarigo** at **Valsanzibio** (*open 9–1 and 1.30 until sunset Mar–Nov; adm exp*) for the grandest gardens in the Veneto, laid out with fountains, waterfalls, nymphaeums and another wicked maze. From here, wiggle your way north to **Torréglia**, where a road leads west to **Teolo**, Livy's birthplace. Visit the **Museo di Arte Contemporanea** (*open Tues, Thurs, Sun 3–7*), housing works from many of Italy's finest living artists.

Dinner and Sleeping: Torréglia's the spot to dine, but return to sleep in Teolo; *see* below.

Day 2

Lunch in Arquà Petrarca

La Montanella, Via Costa 33, **t** 0429 718 200 (*expensive–moderate*). Near the centre, this offers a garden and views, and also exquisite *risotti* and duck with fruit; select your wine, oil and vinegar from special menus. *Closed Tues eve, Wed, 2 weeks each in Aug and Jan.*

*****Roncha**, Via Costa 132, **t** 0429 718 286 (*moderate*). Just down from La Montanella, serving local specialities and fine wines.

Dinner in Torréglia

Join the hungry Paduans at their favourite country restaurants in Torréglia, 9km east.

Da Taparo, Via Castelletto 42, **t** 049 521 1060 (*moderate*). This restaurant has a beautiful terrace overlooking the hills to match its delicious Veneto cuisine. *Closed Mon.*

Antica Trattoria Ballotta, Via Carromatto 2, **t** 049 521 2970, **f** 049 521 1385 (*moderate*). In business since 1605 and one of the oldest restaurants in Venetia, with fine dining either inside or out in the garden. *Closed Tues.*

Rifugio Monte Rua, Via Mone Rua 29, **t** 049 521 1049 (*moderate*). Come here for a panoramic location and a seasonal menu. *Closed Tues.*

Sleeping in or around Teolo

*****Lussana**, V. Chiesaeolo 1, **t** 049 992 5530, **f** 049 992 5530 (*moderate–cheap*). A charming Art Nouveau villa in Teolo, with bright rooms and lovely views over a terraced garden.

Bacco e Arianna, 5km west in Vò, **t** 049 994 0187 (*cheap*). A delightful bed and breakfast in the middle of a vineyard.

Praglia Abbey, 9km east, near S. Biagio, **t** 049 990 0010. If you call ahead you can stay in this Benedictine abbey, founded in 1117 but given the Renaissance treatment by Tullio Lombardo, Montagna and others (*tours every half hour, 3.30–5.30 in summer; closed Mon*). There's a dormitory for men, and another for both sexes in the grounds. It's free, but make a donation when you leave. Be sure to hear their famous Gregorian Mass.

Day 3: A Holy Hill, More Villas and Human Chess

Morning: Drive west out of Teolo to pick up the S247 north to **Vicenza**, aiming for its holy hill, **Monte Bérico**, just south of the city. Take the pilgrims' way up the half-mile-long **Portici** to the **Basilica di Monte Bérico** (*open weekdays 6.15–12.30 and 2.30–7.30*), where the refectory has paintings by Bartolomeo Montagna and Veronese. On your way back down, pause by Via M. D'Azeglio; just down on the right is an alley to the **Villa Valmarana** (*open 15 Mar–April daily 2.30–5.30; May–Sept Wed, Thurs, Sat, Sun 10–12 and daily 3–6; Oct–15 Nov daily 2–5; adm exp*), adorned with stone dwarfs and Tiepolo's sumptuous frescoes. Five more minutes along the Stradella Valmarana brings you to Palladio's most famous creation, the **Villa Rotonda** (*gardens open 15 Mar–4 Nov, Tues, Wed and Sat 10–12; interior open Wed only; adm*): a circle in a cube.

Lunch: In Vicenza, *see* below.

Afternoon: Drive east out of Vicenza along the S11 to Padua, turning left after Torri di Quartieri towards **Camisano Vicentino**, from where a road leads east to **Piazzola sul Brenta**. Here, visit the imposing **Villa Contarini** (*garden only, open 9–12 and 3–7, mid-Oct–Mar 9–12 and 2–5, closed Mon; adm*), especially notable for its elaborate interior featuring Music Rooms with excellent acoustics. Follow the Brenta north to **Nove** (just before Bassano), brimful of colourful ceramics; it's only 4km west to **Maròstica**, enclosed in 13th-century walls, a perfect setting for its fairy-tale human chess match (*second weekend in Sept in even-numbered years*), played in medieval costume on a 72sq ft board. You can see the finery in the **Museo dei Costumi** (*ask at Pro Loco; adm*).

Dinner and Sleeping: In or around Maròstica, *see* below.

Day 3

Lunch in Vicenza

See also restaurant choices under **Day Trips from Verona**, p.120.

Vecchia Guardia, Contrà Pescherie Vecchie 11, **t** 0444 321 231 (*cheap*). Located near Piazza dell'Erbe, this offers pizza and straightforward meals. *Closed Thurs.*

Antica Casa della Malvasia, Contrà delle Morette 5, near Piazza dei Signori, **t** 0444 543 704 (*cheap*). Basic, lively and very popular, with real home cooking.

Antica Offelleria della Meneghi, Contrà Cavour 18. For something sweet and stylish, Vicenza has two historic *pasticcerias* near the Basilica: this one, and **Soraru**, Piazzetta Palladio 17.

Dinner and Sleeping in or around Maròstica

Look out for Maròstica's famous cherries and a rather unusual dish, *paetarosta col magaragno*, young turkey roasted on a spit and served with pomegranate sauce.

Be sure to try some of the local firewater while you're here; Bassano, just 7km east, is a major grappa producer. It can be drunk unaged and white, or aged in oak barrels, where it takes on a rich, amber tone.

★★★**Europa**, Via Pizzamano 19, **t** 0424 77842, **f** 0424 72480 (*moderate*). In Maròstica proper. An up-to-date place to stay, its restaurant serving not only Italian but Spanish dishes – one of your few chances for paella in the region.

Ristorante al Castello, **t** 0424 73315 (*moderate*). You might find the delicious *paetarosta col magaragno* on the menu here. Located in a newly renovated upper castle, there are lovely views and food to match, with an emphasis on fresh local ingredients. Top it off with a *caffè corretto*, 'corrected' with one of a score of different grappas.

★★★**La Rosina**, 2km north in Valle San Florian, Contrà Narchetti 4, **t** 0424 75839, **f** 0424 470 290 (*moderate*). In a superb hilltop setting, this has modern, comfortable rooms, and a restaurant with a talented chef. *Closed Aug.*

Day 4: Masèr and the View of a Hundred Horizons

Morning: Drive east through Bassano along the S248 towards Montebelluna, taking a left fork at **Casella** (just south of Àsolo) to **Masèr**. Visit the lovely **Villa Barbaro** (*open Mar–Oct, Tues, Sat, Sun and hols 3–6; Nov–Feb, Sat, Sun and hols, 2.30–5; adm exp*), begun in 1568 for brothers Daniele and Marcantonio Barbaro and a unique synthesis of two great talents: Palladio and his friend Veronese. Palladio taught Veronese about space and volume, and nowhere is this so evident as in these ravishing, architectonic *trompe-l'œil* frescoes, featuring the villa's original owners and their pets. Signora Barbaro and her sons gaze down from painted balconies; painted windows offer views of imaginary landscapes; the huntsman in the far bedroom is Veronese, gazing at his mistress. Behind the villa, the nymphaeum is guarded by giants sculpted by Marcantonio himself.

Lunch: Near Masèr, *see* below.

Afternoon: Drive to the old walled hilltown of **Àsolo**, and succumb to the charms that inspired both Pietro Bembo's dialogues on love, *Gli Asolani*, and Robert Browning's last volume of poems, *Asolando*. Some people never get beyond Àsolo's perfect *piazza* with its 16th-century **Fontana Maggiore**, but every passing celebrity has had a drink at the historic **Caffè Centrale** (*Via Roma 72*), and you should too, for it's a great place to watch the world go by. Stroll to the **Castello** with its watch tower, and step inside the **Duomo** to see its works by Lotto, Jacopo da Bassano and Vivarini. Finally, for the famous view of 'a hundred horizons', climb (or drive) up to the **Rocca**.

Dinner and Sleeping: In Àsolo, *see* below.

Day 4

Lunch near Masèr

Da Bastian, Via Cornuda, **t** 0423 565 400 (*moderate*). Just up the road from Palladio's villa; dine in enchanting surroundings, where the pâté, risotto, Venetian-style snails and desserts are renowned. *Closed Wed eve and Thurs, some of Aug.*

Al Ringranziamento, Via S. Pio X 107, **t** 0423 543 271 (*expensive–moderate*). Just north in Cavaso del Tomba, the chef at this romantic restaurant is a master at concocting delicious dishes. *Closed Mon, Tues lunch, some of Aug.*

Dinner in Àsolo

Hosteria Ca' Derton, Piazza D'Annunzio 11, **t** 0423 52730 (*moderate*). In one of Àsolo's oldest houses, featuring traditional specialities to match the setting. *Closed Mon.*

Ai Due Archi, Via Roma 55, **t** 0423 952 201 (*moderate*). Wood-panelled, intimate, elegant and antique, with delicious polenta in various guises. *Closed Wed eve and Thurs.*

Sleeping in Àsolo

Àsolo is a wonderful place to spend a night in style, but it doesn't do cheap; if you'd prefer somewhere more reasonable, **Castelfranco** is just 15km south (*see* Day 5, opposite).

*****Villa Cipriani**, Via Canova 298, **t** 0423 952 166, **f** 0423 952 095 (*very expensive*). One of Italy's most charming and evocative hotels, in a house dating from the 16th-century that belonged to Robert Browning, decorated with Persian carpets owned by Eleonora Duse. Overlooking a paradise of hills and cypresses, it has an enchanting garden filled with roses and songbirds.

****Al Sole**, Via Collegio 33, **t** 0423 528 111, **f** 0423 528 399 (*expensive*). Also in the *centro storico*, this celebrated hotel is both very comfortable and very charming, whispering with memories of famous past guests. It has an agreement with the local country club.

***Duse**, Via Browning 190, **t** 0423 55241, **f** 0423 950 404 (*expensive, but the cheapest in town*). Overlooking Àsolo's central *piazza*, with a little garden behind it.

Day 5: Masonic Codes and Big George

Morning: Take the road south of Àsolo via San Vito and Riese to join the S667 to **Castelfranco Vèneto**. Then continue south on the S307 towards Padua, turning left at **Resana** for **Piombino Dese**, a Palladiophile must-see for its **Villa Cornaro** (*garden only; interior open by appointment*, **t** *049 936 5017*) of 1553. This is one of the master's most innovative structures, the first with a double loggia. It's also the only one to preserve much of its original cladding and tile floors. See what you make of the frescoes (1716) by Bortoloni; Cornaro eschewed the usual allegories for biblical scenes, but they may have been a vehicle to smuggle in a forbidden message: those on the east wall of the main room abound with Masonic symbols. Puzzle them on your way to lunch, either in **Castelfranco** itself, or just west down the S53 in **Galliera Vèneto**.

Lunch: In or near Castelfranco, *see* below.

Afternoon: Castelfranco basks in the glory of having given the world Giorgione, in 1478, and the **Duomo** holds the masterpiece he gave the town in return: the *Castelfranco Madonna* (1504). There's more Big George next door in the **Casa del Giorgione** (*open Tues–Sun 9.30–12.30 and 3–6 in summer; adm*), which keeps copies of all his works. If you're not villa-ed out, you can nip up the road to **Fanzolo** (5km northeast), for another of Palladio's finest: **Villa Emo** (*open April–Oct 3–7, Sun and hols 10–12.30 and 3–7; Oct–Mar Sat and Sun only 2–6; adm exp*), designed as a working farm and containing bright mythologies by Giambattista Zelotti.

Dinner and Sleeping: In Castelfranco or Fanzolo, *see* below. In the morning, the S53 will return you to Treviso, while the S245 leads back via Piombino Dese to Venice.

Day 5

Lunch in or near Castelfranco Vèneto

Alle Mura, Via Preti 69, **t** 0423 498 098 (*expensive–moderate*). An elegant place situated next to the walls in Castelfranco, with well-prepared seafood dishes and a garden. *Closed Thurs.*

Palazzino, Via Roma 29, **t** 049 596 9224 (*expensive–moderate*). In Galliera Vèneto, on the road between Castelfranco Vèneto and Cittadella, with a former patrician hunting lodge serving as its setting. A great place to try Renaissance dishes such as pheasant stuffed with truffles. *Closed Tues eve, Wed, and Aug.*

Dinner in Castelfranco Vèneto

Barbesin, at the Hotel Ca' delle Rose, on the Circonvallazione Est at Salvarosa, **t** 0423 490 446 (*moderate*). At this famous restaurant, the setting is as idyllic as the cuisine, based entirely on fresh, seasonal ingredients; the veal with apples melts in your mouth. You can also stay here. *Closed Wed eve and Thurs.*

Dinner in Fanzolo

******Villa Emo**, Via Stazione 5, **t** 0423 476 414, **f** 0423 487 043 (*expensive*). There's fine dining to be had in the restaurant at Palladio's villa. If you wish, you could even stay in one of the wings, where a handful of elegant rooms and suites come with a pool; quiet guaranteed. *Closed Mon and Tues lunch.*

Sleeping in Castelfranco Vèneto

******Al Moretto**, Via S. Pio X 10, **t** 0423 721 313, **f** 0423 721 066 (*moderate*). In the centre of Castelfranco, set in a 17th-century palace.

******Roma**, Via Fabio Filzi 39, **t** 0423 721 616, **f** 0423 721 515 (*moderate*). Situated outside the fortifications but offering a good view of them; all rooms have TV and a/c.

*******Fior**, Via dei Carpani 18, **t** 0423 721 212, **f** 0423 498 771 (*expensive*). In the same area, occupying an old villa and park, with tennis, pool and sauna.

Treviso

Famous for radicchio, cherries and Benetton, Treviso is one of the Veneto's best kept secrets, laced with little canals (*canagi*), languorous with willows and water wheels, yet humming with more than a little discreet prosperity. Colours were an obsession in Treviso long before Benetton united them. Attractive building stone was scarce, so it became the custom to cover the humble brick: with simple patterns in the 1300s; with mythologies and allegories by the 1500s. Although faded and fragmented – Treviso endured 35 air raids during the last war – one of the delights here is to pick out frescoes in the shadows under the eaves. Another is to take a stroll along the outside of the city walls, the canals and *corsos*, or the leafy banks of the River Sile to the south.

Piazza dei Signori and the Duomo

From the stations, it's a 10-minute walk over the Sile along the Corso del Popolo and Via XX Settembre to the **Piazza dei Signori**, the heart of Treviso. Here stands the great brick **Palazzo dei Trecento**, rebuilt after it took a bomb on the nose; Treviso café society shelters underneath its loggia. Behind, the **Monte di Pietà** contains the Renaissance **Sala dei Reggitori** (*open for group tours only, Mon–Fri 9–12 and 3–5*), with walls of gilt leather, a painted, beamed ceiling and canvases by Sebastiano Ricci and Luca Giordano.

The elegant and arcaded main street, the **Calmaggiore**, was the *decumanus* of the Roman town, Tarvisium. It leads to the **Duomo**, a Venetian Romanesque building with a cluster of domes, founded in the 12th century. Besides some fine Renaissance tombs, much of the cathedral's brand-name art is concentrated in the **Cappella Malchiostro**, designed by Tullio and Antonio Lombardo, with works by Paris Bordone and Girolamo da Treviso the elder. The frescoes are by Pordenone, while his mortal enemy Titian contributed *The Annunciation* on the altar; Vasari wrote that Pordenone always painted with a sword at his hip in case Titian showed up while he was working. Behind the cathedral, the **Museo Diocesano** (*open Mon–Thurs 9–12, Sat 9–12 and 3–6*) contains Tommaso da Modena's masterly *Cristo Passo*, and fine marble reliefs from the 1200s.

From the Piazza Duomo, Via Canova leads past the 15th-century **Casa Trevigiana** (*open for special exhibitions*) to meet Borgo Cavour near the **Museo Civico Luigi Bailo** (*open Tues–Sat 9–12.30 and 2.30–5, Sun 9–12; adm*). Here, the archaeological collection includes Bronze Age swords (*c.* 1000 BC) and unusual 5th-century BC bronze discs. Upstairs there's an excellent collection of masters from the Veneto.

Borgo Cavour makes a grandiose exit through the great **Porta dei Santi Quaranta** (1517), encompassed by an impressive stretch of the ramparts. However, turn down Via S. Liberale and turn right in Via Absidi, and you'll come to Treviso's best church: the enormous Gothic **San Nicolò**. The interior is a treasure house of lovely frescoes, from a huge *St Christopher* on the south wall to the charming pages by Lorenzo Lotto on the monument of Senator Agostino d'Onigo, sculpted by Giovanni Buora. Tommaso da Modena contributed the saints standing at attention on the columns, but even better are his perceptive portraits of 40 Dominicans (1352), some using medieval reading glasses, in the **Capitolo dei Domenicani** in the adjacent Seminario (*open April–Sept 8–6; Oct–Mar 8–12.30 and 3–5.30; ring the bell at the porter's lodge*).

Getting to Treviso

Ryanair flies from London Stansted (2hrs).

Getting from the Airport

Treviso's San Giuseppe airport (**t** 0422 230 393) lies southwest of the town. ACTT **bus no.6** serves links it to Treviso's **train station** (every 30mins until about 9.30pm; journey 20mins). Buy your ticket (€1) before boarding the bus from the airport terminal. A **taxi** to the centre costs about €13 (10mins).

Getting Around

Treviso is small and easily negotiable on foot, though there are also urban buses. Both the **train** and **bus stations** (**t** 0422 412 222) are in Via Roma south of the centre.

For a **taxi**, call **Radio Taxi**, **t** 0422 400 152.

Don't take a **car** into Treviso; it's mayhem.

Car Hire

Avis, Piazzale Duca D'Aosta 1, **t** 0422 542 287; at the airport, **t** 0422 542 287.

Europcar, at the airport, **t** 0422 22807.

Hertz, at the airport, **t** 0422 264 216.

Maggiore, at the airport, **t** 0422 210 115.

Tourist Information

Treviso: Piazza Monte di Pietà 8, **t** 0422 547 632, **f** 0422 419 092, *tvapt@sevenonline.it*.

Market Days

Besides the lovely **fish market** (*Mon–Sat*) in Treviso's east end, central **Piazzale Matteotti** sees a morning market (*Tues and Sat*).

Shopping

The main shopping area is in the streets around the **Piazza dei Signori**, such as Via XX Settembre and Via Calmaggiore.

Where to Stay

Treviso ✉ 31100

***Al Foghèr**, Viale della Repubblica 10, **t** 0422 432 950, **f** 0422 430 391 (*expensive–moderate*). The pick of the bunch, outside the walls but near the centre, with well-equipped rooms, a warm welcome, and a good restaurant.

****Continental**, Via Roma 16, **t** 0422 411 662, **f** 0422 411 620 (*expensive*). A modern hotel conveniently near the station, with a/c.

Campeol, Piazza Ancillotto 8, **t** 0422 56601, **f** 0422 540 871 (*moderate*). Smack in the historical centre, a hospitable and long established hotel with good views.

Eating Out

Radicchio trevignana is not only a local obsession, but also a vegetable with quality control; to be DOC it must have sprouted up in one of eight *comuni* and be grown under certain organic conditions. Another speciality is *sopa coada*, a baked pigeon casserole.

Alfredo, Via Collalto 26, **t** 0422 540 275 (*expensive*). If money's no object, try *sopa coada* here at Treviso's most acclaimed restaurant, in a lovely, elegant Belle Epoque setting. The imaginative menu has an emphasis on seafood. Book. *Closed Sun eve, Mon and Aug.*

Al Bersagliere, Via Barberia 21, **t** 0422 579 902 (*moderate*). Set in a beautiful 12th-century building, this offers delicious *antipasti*, *sopa coada* and other Venetian specialities such as squid in its own ink, risotto and liver. *Closed Sun, Sat lunch and Aug.*

Beccherie, Piazza Anchillotto 10, **t** 0422 540 871 (*moderate*). A local bastion of atmosphere and cooking – great for *pasta e fagioli* with radicchio. *Closed Sun eve, Mon and July.*

Toni del Spin, Via Inferiore 7, **t** 0422 543 829 (*moderate–cheap*). An old favourite for its Veneto dishes (*bigoli, risi e bisi*, etc.), topped off by apple pie. *Closed Sun and Mon lunch.*

The East End

Treviso's east end, the Oltrecagnàn, is separated from the rest of the city by the Cagnàn stream. On its little islet (take Via Trevisi–Via Pescheria from Monte di Pietà), the lively **Pescheria** or fish market (*open mornings Mon–Sat*) is a colourful, appetizing delight. Just up Via S. Parisio is San Nicolò's near twin, the tall Romanesque–Gothic

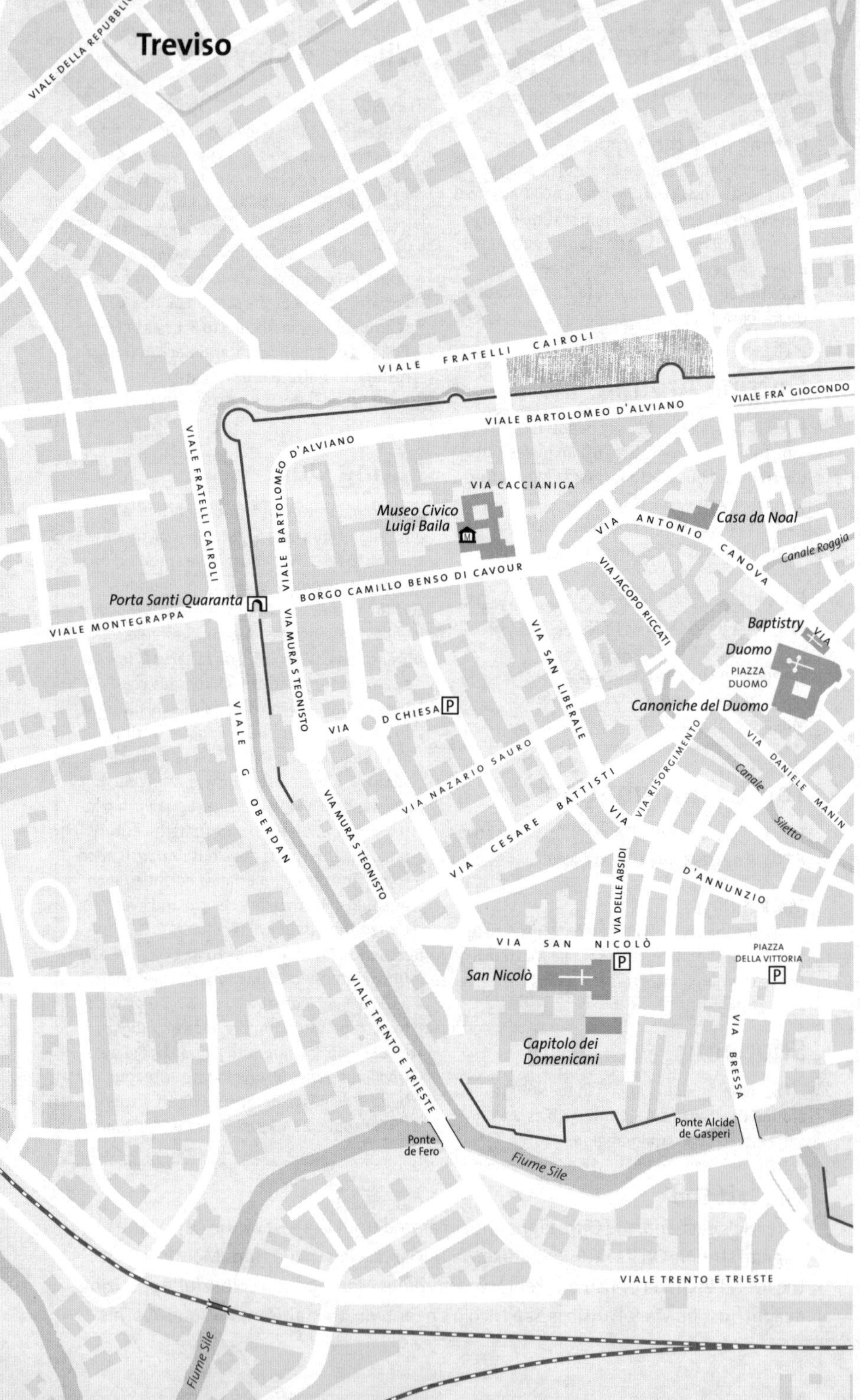

Treviso
VIALE DELLA REPUBBLICA
VIALE FRATELLI CAIROLI
VIALE FRA' GIOCONDO
VIALE BARTOLOMEO D'ALVIANO
VIALE BARTOLOMEO D'ALVIANO
VIALE FRATELLI CAIROLI
VIA CACCIANIGA
Museo Civico Luigi Baila
Casa da Noal
VIA ANTONIO CANOVA
Canale Roggia
BORGO CAMILLO BENSO DI CAVOUR
Porta Santi Quaranta
VIALE MONTEGRAPPA
VIA JACOPO RICCATI
VIA SAN LIBERALE
Baptistry
VIA
Duomo
PIAZZA DUOMO
Canoniche del Duomo
VIA MURA S TEONISTO
VIA D CHIESA
VIALE G OBERDAN
VIA NAZARIO SAURO
VIA RISORGIMENTO
VIA DANIELE MANIN
Canale Siletto
VIA CESARE BATTISTI
VIA
VIA MURA S TEONISTO
VIA DELLE ABSIDI
D'ANNUNZIO
VIA SAN NICOLÒ
PIAZZA DELLA VITTORIA
San Nicolò
VIALE TRENTO E TRIESTE
Capitolo dei Domenicani
VIA BRESSA
Ponte de Fero
Ponte Alcide de Gasperi
Fiume Sile
VIALE TRENTO E TRIESTE
Fiume Sile

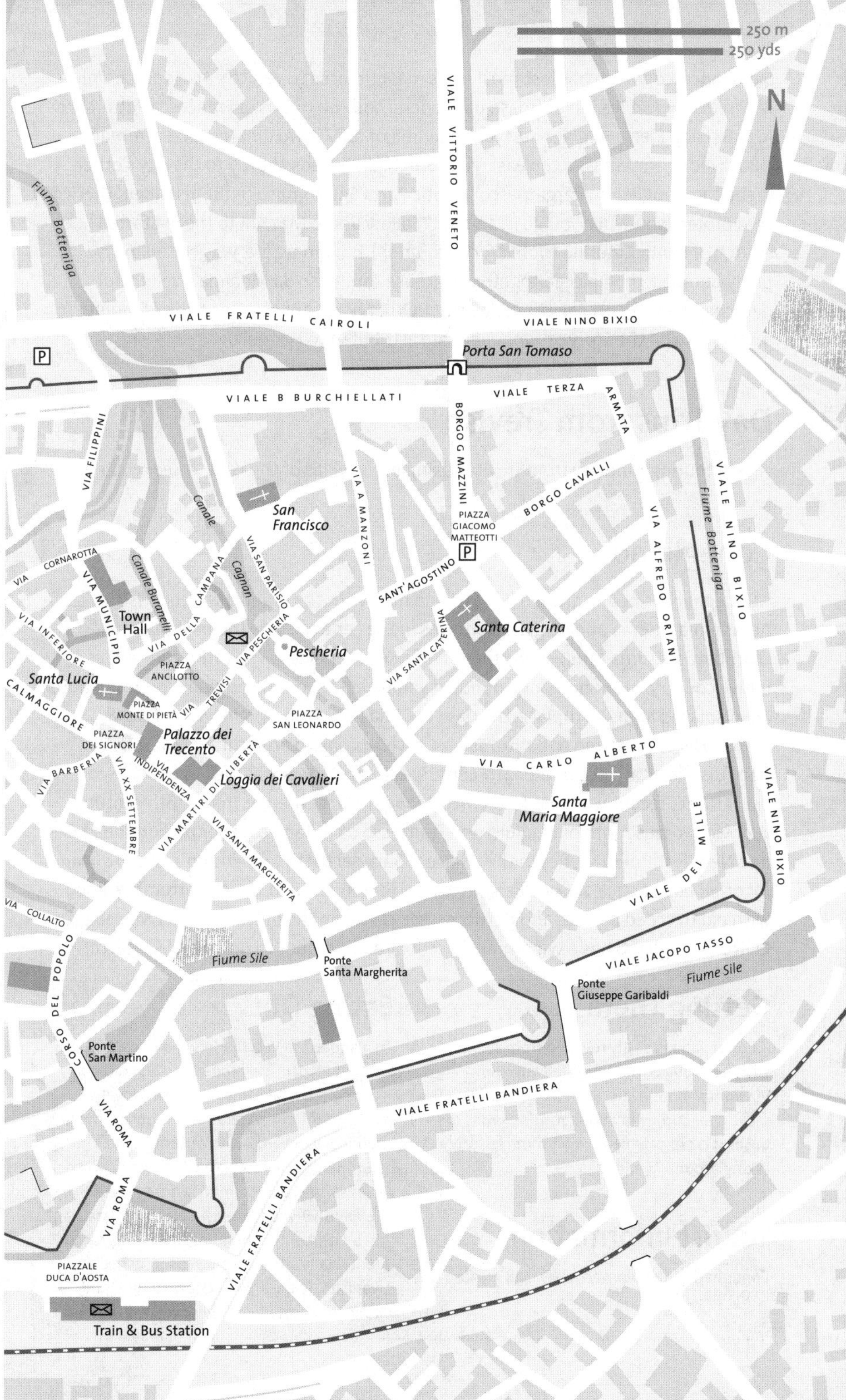

250 m
250 yds
N
Fiume Botteniga
Viale Vittorio Veneto
Viale Fratelli Cairoli
Viale Nino Bixio
P
Porta San Tomaso
Viale B Burchiellati
Viale Terza Armata
Borgo G Mazzini
Via Filippini
Canale
Cagnan
San Francisco
Via A Manzoni
Borgo Cavalli
Piazza Giacomo Matteotti
P
Via Alfredo Oriani
Fiume Botteniga
Viale Nino Bixio
Via Cornarotta
Via Municipio
Canale Buranelli
Via della Campana
Via San Parisio
Sant' Agostino
Town Hall
Via Inferiore
Via Pescheria
Pescheria
Via Santa Caterina
Santa Caterina
Piazza Ancilotto
Santa Lucia
Calmaggiore
Piazza Monte di Pietà
Via Trevisi
Piazza San Leonardo
Piazza dei Signori
Palazzo dei Trecento
Via Barberia
Via XX Settembre
Via Indipendenza
Via Martiri di Libertà
Loggia dei Cavalieri
Via Carlo Alberto
Santa Maria Maggiore
Viale dei Mille
Via Santa Margherita
Via Collalto
Fiume Sile
Ponte Santa Margherita
Viale Jacopo Tasso
Ponte Giuseppe Garibaldi
Fiume Sile
Corso del Popolo
Ponte San Martino
Via Roma
Viale Fratelli Bandiera
Viale Fratelli Bandiera
Via Roma
Piazzale Duca d'Aosta
Train & Bus Station

San Francesco, which has lost most of its masterpieces to Venice's Accademia. Only a *Madonna and Saints* by Tommaso da Modena and the tombs of Francesca Petrarch (d. 1384) and Pietro Alighieri (d. 1364), children of Italy's two greatest poets, remain.

Back along the walls to the east, Viale Burchiellati leads shortly to the city's other great gate, Guglielmo Bergamasco's exotic **Porta San Tomaso** (1518), inscribed 'The Lord protect you while you go in and out'. Follow Borgo Mazzini to the ill-starred church of **Santa Caterina** (*closed for restoration*), built in 1346. It was closed in 1772, badly bombed, then pieced together to house Tommaso da Modena's delightful detached frescoes on *The Life of St Ursula*. Other beautiful paintings, the *Madonna and Saints* and the *Story of Sant'Eligio*, are attributed to Pisanello.

Day Trips from Treviso

For a **touring itinerary** from Treviso taking in the villas of the Veneto, *see* pp.121–5.

Conegliano

Conegliano is neatly divided into old and new, with the grandiose neoclassical Accademia cinema and its giant sphinxes in the centre. It was the birthplace of Giambattista Cima (1460–1518), the son of a seller of hides, who often painted his native countryside in his backgrounds. If you haven't seen the originals, reproductions are displayed at his birthplace, the **Casa di Cima** (*Via Cima 24; call ahead,* **t** *0438 21660*). His original and beautiful *Sacra Conversazione*, in an architectural setting (1493), is the altarpiece of the 14th-century **Duomo**; look out as well for Francesco Beccaruzzi's recently restored *SS. Marco, Leonardo and Caterina*. In the 16th century, Ludovico Pozzoserrato of Belgium and Francesco da Milano collaborated on the 27 Old and New Testament scenes in the adjacent **Sala dei Battuti** (*open Sun 3–7; call ahead for other days,* **t** *0438 22606*). Be sure to stroll down arcaded **Via XX Settembre**, lined with old frescoed palaces and porticoes; the **castle** on the hill has a small **Museo Civico**. Conegliano has a wine-making school, and produces a delightful Prosecco.

Getting There

Conegliano is easily reached from Treviso, with both buses and trains leaving from Via Roma about every 30 mins. The **trains** make the journey in about 20mins, while **buses** (**t** 0422 577 311) are a bit more leisurely, taking around 35mins.

Tourist Information

Conegliano: Via Colombo 1, **t/f** 0438 21230.

Eating Out

Tre Panoce, Via Vecchia Trevigiana 50, **t** 0438 60071 (*expensive–moderate*). Just outside Conegliano, take bus no.1 to this lovely restaurant in a *seicento* farmhouse crowning a hill of vineyards, with outdoor tables in summer. *Closed Sun eve, Mon and Aug.*

Al Salisà, Via XX Settembre 2, **t** 0438 24288 (*expensive–moderate*). An elegant restaurant in a 13th-century building, featuring succulent snails and game in season, especially venison. There are good local wines, and lunch menus. *Closed Tues eve, Wed and Aug.*

Bassano del Grappa

Sprawled over the foothills of the Alps, the bustling town of Bassano celebrated its first millennium in 1998. In the past 1,000 years it has given the world lovely ceramics, white asparagus, firewater and a dynasty of painters who adopted Bassano's name as their own and rather sombrely influenced 17th-century painting across Europe.

The first houses, back in 998, were clustered high around the **Castello Ezzelino**, but most of the action these days happens in Bassano's three central squares: **Piazzotto Montevecchio**, where the old municipal pawn shop is covered with the coats-of-arms of 120 Venetian *podestàs*; the piquant **Piazza Libertà**; and **Piazza Garibaldi**, guarded physically and spiritually by the **Torre Civica** and the Gothic church of **San Francesco**. Inside the cloister, Bassano's **Museo Civico** (*open 9–6.30 Tues–Sat, 3.30–6.30 Sun; adm; same ticket for the ceramics museum*) has an excellent Chini collection of vases from Magna Grecia, studies by Canova, and paintings with an emphasis on the dark and stormy; look out for Jacopo Bassano's twilit *Baptism of St Lucia*. There are calmer works as well: Michele Giambono's *Madonna* and a beautiful *Crucifix* by Guariento.

Palladio designed Bassano's **Ponte degli Alpini**, the unique covered wooden bridge that spans the unruly Brenta. At one end, in the Palazzo Beltrame-Menarola, the grappa distillery Poli operates a **Museo della Grappa** where you can taste and buy (*open 9–1 and 2.30–7.30; closed Mon am; adm free*). Grappa can be drunk unaged and white, or aged in oak barrels, where it takes on a rich, amber tone. There are methods for drinking it, too, the idea being to take a little to cleanse your tastebuds (or prepare them for the shock) and then to drink the glass. Wincing is not an option.

In the mid-17th century, Bassano and nearby Nove became the Veneto's top ceramic manufacturers, a status they maintain to this day. In the 18th-century Palazzo Sturm, the **Museo della Ceramica** (*open April–Oct 9–12.30 and 3.30–6.30, closed Sun morning and Mon; June–Sept Sun 10–12.30; Nov–Mar 9–12.30, Fri, Sat and Sun 3.30–6.30; same adm as Museo Civico*) keeps a fine display of local porcelain knick-knacks and majolica.

Getting There

Bassano is linked directly to Treviso by **bus** (journey 1hr15; **t** 0422 577 311); note that there is usually only one bus to Bassano in the morning (currently at 9.50am), though the service is a lot more frequent after midday. **Trains** are generally less convenient, requiring a change in Castelfranco.

Bassano's **bus station** is in the Piazzale Trento, **t** 0424 30850, while the **train station** is at the top of Via Chilesotti.

Tourist Information

Bassano: Largo Corona d'Italia 35, **t** 0424 524 351, **f** 0424 525 301.

Eating Out

Bassano del Grappa ✉ 36061

Besides mushrooms, honey and *grappa*, Bassano deals in white asparagus: try it *alla bassanese*, with a hollandaise-type sauce, or simply *alla parmigiana*.

Belvedere Hotel restaurant, Viale delle Fosse 1, **t** 0424 524 988 (*expensive*). The elegant hotel restaurant delivers Bassano's finest gastronomic delights, Veneto and other Italian classics and the promised view. *Closed Sun*.

Al Sole-Da Tiziano, Via Vitorelli 41, **t** 0424 523 206 (*moderate*). This beautiful dining room offers a perfect risotto, delicious duck and Bassano's favourites: mushrooms, asparagus and radicchio. *Closed Mon and July*.

Trieste

Once the main seaport of the Austro-Hungarian Empire, two world wars left Trieste a woebegone widow of the Adriatic. But all this has changed, and Trieste is quickly regaining its old cosmopolitan lustre: the shops bubble with a babel of Slovene, Czech, German, Serbo-Croat and Hungarian, and an exotic bouquet of numberplates clog up the straight, central European 19th-century streets. Don't come to Trieste for art or beautiful buildings: its profits have been firmly invested in banks, shipping-lines and stocks. Come to sense the energy of a city shaking off decades of nostalgic sloth and picking up from where it left off, in the vibrant days just before the First World War.

Getting to Trieste

Ryanair flies from London Stansted (2hrs).

Getting from the Airport

Trieste's Ronchi dei Legionari airport (**t** 0481 773 224) is 35km north near Monfalcone; APT **buses** (**t** 0481 593 511) run to and from Trieste's main bus station in Piazzale Libertà (every 30mins or so), taking 50mins–1hr (tickets €2.55 from the airport bar or post office).

A **taxi** to the centre will cost about €50.

Getting Around

Trieste's long, straight Habsburger streets mean that finding one's way around on foot is relatively simple, although use the crossings carefully; these streets make even Rome appear pedestrian. **City buses** (**t** 167 016 675) are frequent, and most routes run from or by the main bus station. A **funicular railway** (*tranvia*) runs every 22mins from Piazza Oberdan to Villa Opicina. The train station, **Stazione Centrale**, is on Piazza della Libertà. The **bus station** (**t** 040 425 001) is in front of it.

Cars have been banished from the centre and parking can be diabolical; surrender your *macchina* to one of the car parks. For a **taxi**, call **Radio taxi**, **t** 040 307 730.

Car Hire

Avis, Piazza Libertà, **t** 0481 421 521; at the airport, **t** 0481 777 085.

Budget, at the airport, **t** 0481 779 166.

Europcar, Via Mazzini 1, **t** 0481 367 944; at the airport **t** 0481 778 920.

Hertz, Piazza Libertà, **t** 0481 422 122; at the airport, **t** 0481 777 025.

Tourist Information

Trieste: Piazza Unità d'Italia, **t** 040 347 8312, **f** 040 679 6299; at the Stazione Centrale, **t** 040 420 182 (ask for their Joyce itinerary). Friuli regional office, Via G. Rossini 6, **t** 040 363 952, **f** 040 365 496, *www.triestetourism.it*.

Market Days

Piazza Ponterosso, next to the Canale Grande, is the site of the daily market.

Shopping

Trieste's shopping streets are the **Corso Italia** and the **Via Carducci**. The single most famous Friulian comestible is *prosciutto di San Daniele*, which rivals Parma's famous hams.

Where to Stay

Trieste ✉ 34100

★★★★**Duchi d'Aosta**, Piazza dell'Unità d'Italia 2, **t** 040 760 0011, **f** 040 366 092 (*very expensive*). Trieste's finest hotel is on its finest square, in a neo-Renaissance palace now owned by the CIGA chain. It exudes a dignified Belle Epoque ambience; upstairs, the luxurious rooms are fitted with every comfort and it has an excellent restaurant, **Harry's Grill**.

★★★**Novo Hotel Impero**, Via S. Anastasia 1, **t** 040 364 242, **f** 040 365 023 (*expensive*). Conveniently near the train station and the centre; some rooms are cheaper.

★★★**San Giusto**, Via C. Belli 3, **t** 040 762 661, **f** 040 7606 585 (*moderate*). By the historic hill, a modern hotel with all you need.

Along the Port to Piazza dell'Unità d'Italia

Across from the station, the **Galleria Nazionale d'Arte Antica** (*Piazza della Libertà 7; open 9–1.30, closed Sun; adm*) offers some second division 15th–19th-century Italian paintings. Corso Cavour, meanwhile, leads into the **Borgo Teresiano**, Trieste's business hub, laid out with ruler-straight streets and planted with neoclassical architecture. Just across the **Canale Grande**, an inlet with moorings for small craft, stands the city's oldest coffee house, **Caffè Tommaseo** (1830), restored with its Belle Epoque fittings.

Next along the waterfront opens Trieste's whale of a heart, **Piazza dell'Unità d'Italia**, framed by a hefty **Palazzo del Comune**, topped by two Moors who ring the bell over the clock, and the **Palazzo del Governo** glowing in its bright skin of mosaics.

★★**Al Teatro**, Via Capo di Piazza G. Bartoli 1 (near Piazza dell'Unità), **t** 040 366 220, **f** 040 366 560 (*moderate*). In a neoclassical building, this served as British headquarters after the Second World War and is a bit of a nostalgic trip back to the Trieste of yore.

★★★**Milano**, Via Ghega 17, **t** 040 369 680, **f** 040 369 727 (*moderate*). A comfortable hotel near the station.

★★★**Nuovo Hotel Daneu**, Via Nazionale 11, **t** 040 214 241, **f** 040 214 215 (*moderate*). If you don't like the hurly-burly of a big city, take the tram up to Opicina where this hotel has a good restaurant and indoor pool.

There are many less expensive choices in the centre of Trieste – look around Via Roma, Via della Geppa, or Via XXX Ottobre.

★**Alabarda-Flora**, Via Valdirivo 22, **t** 040 630 269, **f** 040 639 284 (*cheap*). A clean, comfortable, good value hotel.

Eating Out

Slovenian and Hungarian influences are strong and Trieste is a good place to eat dumplings. A famous *primo* is *jota*, a bean, potato and sauerkraut soup, or *kaiserknödel* (bread dumplings with grated cheese, ham and parsley). For *secondo*, there's a wide variety of fish, such as tasty *sardoni* (big sardines), served fried or marinated, or the popular goulash, roast pork and *stinco* (veal knuckle). The Middle European influence, however, is most noticeable in the desserts: lovely strudels, *gnocchi di susine* (plums) or *zavate*, a warm cream pastry.

Antica Trattoria Suban, Via Comici 2, **t** 040 54368 (*expensive*). The place to partake of *cucina Triestina* is this wonderful old inn in the suburb of San Giovanni (take a taxi), maintaining much of its old feel and fine views over Trieste. They offer a famous *jota*, *sevapcici* (Slovenian grilled meat fritters), sinful desserts and good wines. Check when you book, however, that the regular chef is on duty; if not, wait till he is. *Closed Mon lunch, Tues, part of Jan and Aug.*

Hosteria Bellavista, Via Bonomea 52, **t** 040 411 150 (*expensive*). A wine lover's paradise, with hundreds of bottles from around the world to go with delicate renditions of Trieste's favourites and lovely views. *Closed Sun, Mon lunch and some of Jan.*

Città di Cherso, Via Cadorna 6, **t** 040 366 044 (*moderate*). Convenient to Piazza Unità d'Italia, serving delicious seafood Friulian-style, topped off with heavenly desserts. *Closed Tues, some of July and Aug.*

Buffet da Pepi, Via Cassa di Risparmo 3, **t** 040 366 858 (*cheap*). Founded in 1903 and has been thriving ever since, serving up Trieste's specialities. *Closed Sun and half of July.*

Birreria Forst, Via Galatti 11, near Piazza Oberdan, **t** 040 365 276 (*cheap*). Another old favourite, serving goulash and lots of beer. *Closed Sun.*

Re di Coppe, Via Geppa 11, **t** 040 370 330 (*cheap*). The waiters still write the orders on the tablecloths at this restaurant, where you can find a classic *jota* and boiled meats. *Closed Sat, Sun and mid-July–mid-Aug.*

Entertainment

The **opera** season at Trieste's Teatro Comunale Verdi runs Nov–Mar; in summer the theatre and the Sala Tripcovich in Piazza della Libertà see an International Operetta festival (**t** 040 672 2500, **f** 040 672 2249).

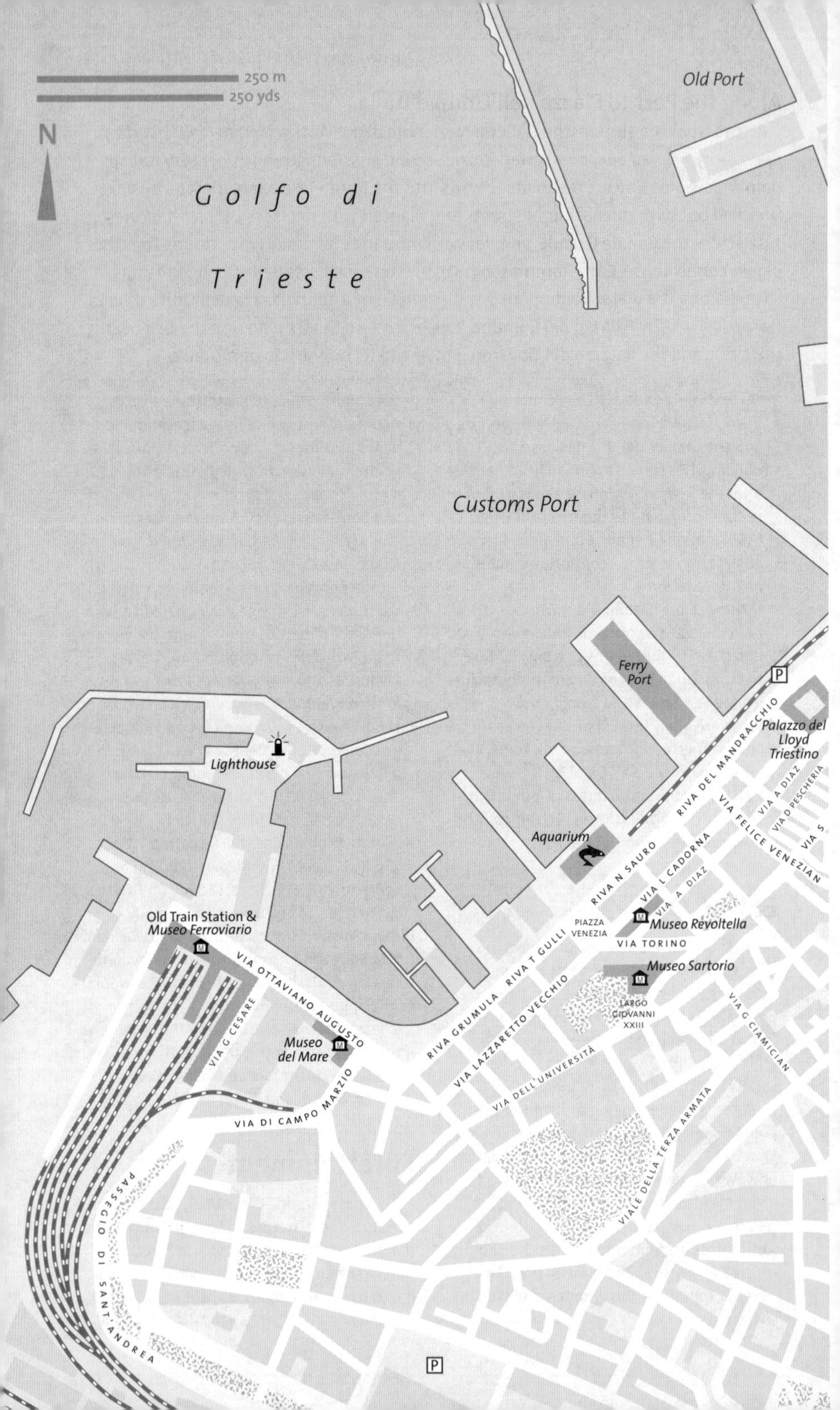
250 m
250 yds
N
Golfo di
Trieste
Old Port
Customs Port
Ferry Port
P
Palazzo del Lloyd Triestino
Lighthouse
Aquarium
RIVA DEL MANDRACCHIO
VIA A DIAZ
VIA D PESCHERIA
VIA S
VIA FELICE VENEZIAN
VIA L CADORNA
RIVA N SAURO
VIA A DIAZ
PIAZZA VENEZIA
Museo Revoltella
RIVA T GULLI
VIA TORINO
Museo Sartorio
LARGO GIOVANNI XXIII
Old Train Station &
Museo Ferroviario
VIA OTTAVIANO AUGUSTO
RIVA GRUMULA
VIA LAZZARETTO VECCHIO
VIA G CIAMICIAN
VIA G CESARE
Museo del Mare
VIA DELL'UNIVERSITÀ
VIA DI CAMPO MARZIO
VIALE DELLA TERZA ARMATA
PASSEGGIO DI SANT'ANDREA
P

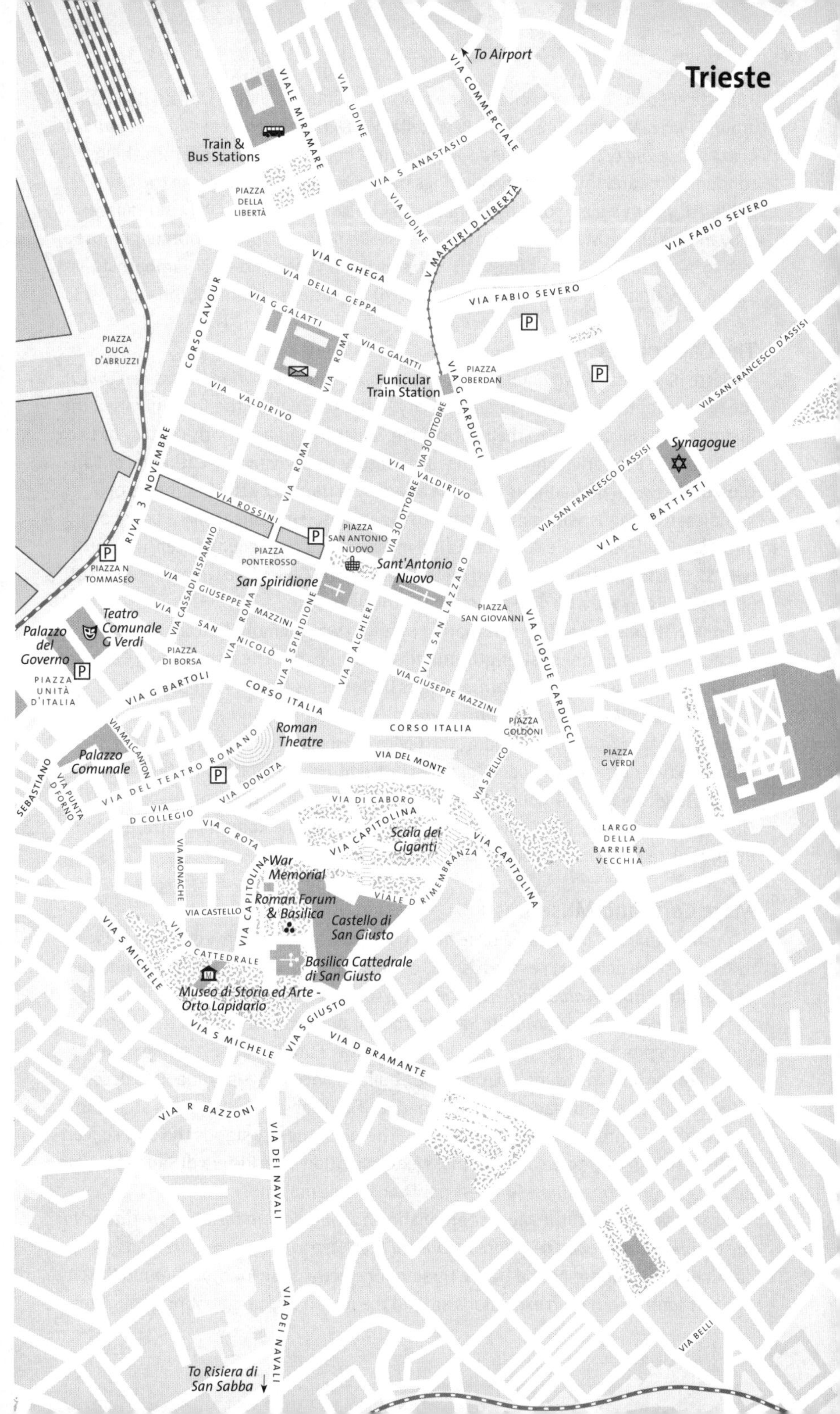
Trieste
To Airport
Train & Bus Stations
Piazza della Libertà
Piazza Duca d'Abruzzi
Funicular Train Station
Piazza Oberdan
Synagogue
Piazza San Antonio Nuovo
Piazza Ponterosso
Piazza N Tommaseo
Sant'Antonio Nuovo
San Spiridione
Teatro Comunale G Verdi
Palazzo del Governo
Piazza di Borsa
Piazza Unità d'Italia
Piazza San Giovanni
Piazza Goldoni
Piazza G Verdi
Roman Theatre
Palazzo Comunale
Largo della Barriera Vecchia
Scala dei Giganti
War Memorial
Roman Forum & Basilica
Castello di San Giusto
Basilica Cattedrale di San Giusto
Museo di Storia ed Arte - Orto Lapidario
To Risiera di San Sabba
Viale Miramare
Via Udine
Via Commerciale
Via S Anastasio
V Martiri d Libertà
Via Fabio Severo
Via C Ghega
Via della Geppa
Via G Galatti
Corso Cavour
Via Roma
Via G Carducci
Via San Francesco d'Assisi
Via Valdirivo
Riva 3 Novembre
Via 30 Ottobre
Via Rossini
Via C Battisti
Via Cassa di Risparmio
Via Giuseppe Mazzini
Via San Nicolò
Via S Spiridione
Via D Alighieri
Via San Lazzaro
Via Giosue Carducci
Via G Bartoli
Corso Italia
Via Malcanton
Via del Teatro Romano
Via Donota
Via del Monte
Via S Pellico
Sebastiano
Via Punta d Forno
Via d Collegio
Via di Caboro
Via Capitolina
Via G Rota
Via Monache
Viale d Rimembranza
Via Castello
Via S Michele
Via d Cattedrale
Via S Giusto
Via D Bramante
Via R Bazzoni
Via dei Navali
Via Belli

Trieste keeps its chief art collections a few blocks south of Piazza Unità d'Italia, around **Piazza Venezia**. The **Museo Revoltella** (*Via Diaz 27; open 9–12 and 3–6, tours at 9, 10.30, 12, 3 and 6; closed Tues and Sun; adm*), in a house full of original furnishings, contains 18th- and 19th-century paintings by Triestine artists that evoke the city's golden days, as well as works by Morandi, De Chirico and Canova. On Largo Papa Giovanni XXIII, the **Museo Sartorio** (*open Tues–Sun 9–1; adm*) offers another glimpse into 19th-century bourgeois life, with works by Paolo Veneziano and Giambattista Tiepolo, ceramics and a wonderful collection of miniatures in some surprising poses.

The Capitoline Hill

Trieste has its very own Capitoline Hill (*bus no.24 from the station/Piazza dell'Unità*), the nucleus of the Roman and medieval city. In the 5th century the Triestini raised the first of two basilicas here to their patron San Giusto. An adjacent 11th-century basilica was linked to the earlier church in the 14th century, thus giving the **Cathedral of San Giusto** (*closed 12–3*) its curious plan. The doorway is framed by the fragments of a Roman sarcophagus, with six funerary busts gazing solemly ahead like a board of directors. Inside, there are some beautiful mosaics, especially the 13th-century *Christ with SS. Giusto and Servulus*. Buried on the right is Don Carlos, the Great Pretender of Spain's Carlist Wars, who died as an exile in Trieste in 1855.

Outside, the view over Trieste is marred by a 1933 **war memorial** extolling the principal Fascist virtues of strength, brutality and vulgarity. The 15th-century **Castello di San Giusto** (*open daily until sunset*) offers better views from its ramparts and a small **Museo Civico** (*open Tues–Sun 9–1; adm*), full of armour and weapons.

Down the lane from the cathedral, the **Civico Museo di Storia ed Arte e Orto Lapidario** (*Via Cattedrale 15; open Tues–Sun 9–1; adm*) houses intriguing finds from Roman Tergeste and a famous 5th-century deer's-head silver drinking vessel from Greek Tarentum (Tàranto). Down the hill, stop to look at the **Roman Theatre**, built during the reign of Trajan and remarkably intact.

More *Caffè* and Museums

Trieste's famous Grand Cafés, once filled with cross-cultural conversation, ideas and spies, still serve delicious pastries as well as dollops of nostalgia. Joyce was a habitué of the **Caffé Pirona** (*Largo Barriera Vecchia 12*), south of the Piazza Goldoni, while on the other side of the *piazza*, **Caffè San Marco** contains Venetian murals that betrayed the owner's pro-Italian sentiments. One street away, Europe's largest **synagogue** (*usually open only to groups;* **t** *040 371 466*), built on ancient Syriac models, is decorated with copper and black and white marble; if you can get in, it really is stunning.

In sombre counterpoint, at the southern extreme of the city stands the only concentration camp in Italy to be used for mass exterminations, the **Risiera di San Sabba** (*bus no.20, 21, 23 or 19; open Tues–Sun 9–1*), now housing a small museum.

On a far lighter note, the **Museo Ferroviario** (*Via G Cesare 1, in the old train station in the Campo Marzio; open 9–1, closed Mon; call* **t** *040 379 4185 for schedules*) runs summer excursions in period trains: three-hour electric train journeys around the city, and day-long steam train excursions around the region and neighbouring countries.

Short Excursions from Trieste

Miramare: Habsburg Folly by the Sea

7km from Trieste; bus no.36 from Piazza Oberdan/Stazione Centrale; open April–Sept 9–6; Oct–Mar 9–4; also open Thurs, Fri, and Sat 8.30–10.30pm in July, Aug, and early Sept; adm exp.
***Park** open daily in summer 9–sunset, winter 8–4; adm free.*

Towering on its own little promontory overlooking the sea, the castle of Miramare hides a dark history behind its white 19th-century façade, having acquired the ominous reputation of laying a curse on anyone who slept within its walls. Once he built his pleasure palace, the Habsburg Archduke Maximilian allowed himself to be conned into leaving it, only to face a firing squad; later, the Archduke Ferdinand stayed here on his way to assassination in Sarajevo. The whole sad story is retold in a **sound and light show** (*in Italian on Mon, Tues and Wed at 9.30 or 10.45 pm in July, Aug and Sept; call **t** 040 679 6111 for possible English performances*). The palace interior retains its overblown Victorian-era décor, some rather cosy rooms designed like ship's cabins and 1920s furnishings. The magnificent **park** was designed by Maximilian; the gardens and coastal waters shelter the rare Stella's otter and marsh harriers.

The Grotta Gigante

Bus no.45 departs every 30mins from Piazza Oberdan; guided tours April–Sept 10–6; closed Mon exc in July and Aug; Oct–Mar 10–12 and 2–4; adm exp.

The famous stalactite **Grotta Gigante**, near Opicina, is the largest cavern in the world open to visitors; its main hall could swallow Rome's basilica of St Peter whole and is graced by a pair of record-breaking 346ft stalactites. The ceiling is so high that drops of water disintegrate before reaching the floor, forming curious leaf-shaped stalagmites; you can follow a path past a belvedere over a vertiginous 360ft drop.

Day Trips from Trieste

Aquileia

Aquileia is unique in that it was the only great Roman city in Italy to die on the vine; once the proud capital of the X Legio Venetia et Histria, it has dwindled from 200,000 to 3,500 inhabitants. No longer receiving emperors, they now tend to vineyards, and to tourists who flock to see the most important archaeological site in northern Italy.

The city's magnificent **Basilica** (*open April–Sept 8.30–7; Oct–Mar 8.30–12.30 and 2.30–5.30*) and its campanile are a landmark for miles around. It was founded in 313 by the Aquileia's first Patriarch, Theodore, and when Patriarch Poppone rebuilt it in 1023, he covered the floor, nicely preserving it for its rediscovery in 1909. At 837 sq yards, this is the largest palaeochristian mosaic in the west, a vivid carpet of portraits, animals

Getting There

The simplest way from Trieste to Aquileia is to take the **train** to **Cervignano** (35mins), then catch a **bus** from outside the station 7km to Aquileia (10mins). Trains leave Trieste roughly hourly, with regular bus links in Cervignano.

Tourist Information

Aquileia ✉ **33051**: Piazza Capitolo, **t** 0431 919 491 (*open April–Nov*).

Eating Out

★**Aquila Nera**, Piazza Garibaldi 5, **t** 0431 91045 (*cheap*). An old hotel with a traditional and homely restaurant, serving good *gnocchi* and basic meat dishes.

La Colombara, Via Zilli 42, **t** 0431 91513 (*moderate*). A family-run restaurant which specializes in fish and seafood, and all sorts of recipes involving asparagus; there's a choice of menus. *Closed Mon.*

and geometric patterns mingling with Christian and pagan scenes. Frescoes from 1031 survive in the apse, showing Patriarch Poppone dedicating the basilica. Next to the left wall of the nave, the 11th-century marble Santo Sepolcro marks the entrance to the **Cripta degli Scavi**, containing more mosaics from 313, sandwiched in between Roman mosaics and others from the 8th century. The crypt under the altar is adorned with 12th-century Byzantine-style frescoes (*one adm for both crypts*).

Opposite the church, the **Museo del Patriarcato** (*open April–Oct 9.30–12.30 and 3–6; closed Mon*) contains fancy medieval reliquaries and other works from the basilica. Down the same road, the **Museo Archeològico** (*open April–Sept Tues–Sun 9.30–7, Mon 9–2; Oct–Mar Tues–Sun 9–2; adm*) houses artefacts from pre-Christian Aquileia. There is a fine set of warts-and-all Republican portrait busts (Tiberius and Trajan among them), as well as amber and gold, glass, coins, a rare, intact Roman chandelier, and a thousand and one household items that breathe life into ancient Aquileia.

A circular walk, beginning on the Via Sacra behind the basilica, takes in what remains of the ancient city, passing **Roman houses** and **palaeochristian oratories** (some with mosaics), then the considerable ruins of the **harbour**: in the 1st century AD this was a bustling commercial port. Continue straight and bear right after the crossroads on Via Gemina to the **Palaeochristian Museum** (*same hours as Museo Archeològico; adm free*), with reliefs, sarcophagi and a walkway over the mossy mosaics of a 4th-century basilica. Return by way of Via Gemina to Via Giulia Augusta; to the right you can see the old Roman road and, to the left, the **Forum** with its re-erected columns. Just off a fork to the right, the **Grand Mausoleum** (1st century AD) was brought here from the suburbs. The meagre ruins of the amphitheatre, baths and **Sepolcreto** (five Roman family tombs) are on Via XXIV Maggio and Via Acidino, north of Piazza Garibaldi.

Ùdine

Ùdine, the culture capital of Friuli, is a charmer, and not half as well known as it deserves to be. Its old streets are interwoven with little canals; Venice left its hand-print on the architecture; while Giambattista Tiepolo brightened many of the walls, thanks to his patron Patriarch Dionisio Delfino, who kept him here between 1726 to 1730, when he took up the brilliant colours that became his trademark.

The heart of Ùdine, **Piazza della Libertà**, has been called 'the most beautiful Venetian square on the *terra firma*', adorned by its striking, candy-striped **Loggia del Lionello**, and the **Loggia di San Giovanni** (1533), with its clock tower and bell rung by Venetian-style Moors. The **Municipio**, all in white, is a bravura piece of Art Deco by Raimondo D'Aronco (1910–31) that manages to blend right in with all the rest.

Palladio's rugged **Arco Bollari** (1556) is the gateway to the sweeping **portico**, built to shelter visitors to the **Castello**. This now houses the **Civici Musei** (*open 9.30–12.30 and 3–6; closed Mon; adm, free Sun am*) with sections on archaeology, designs and prints – by Tiepolo and Dürer, among others – and a notable collection of paintings, beginning in the Salone del Parlamento with its frescoes by Pomponio Amalteo and Giovanni Battista Grassi. Among the highlights are works by Carpaccio, Tiepolo and a bird's-eye view of Ùdine by local boy Luca Carlefarijs (1662–1730).

Just east of Piazza Libertà, the oft-altered **Duomo** has a charming 14th-century lunette of the *Coronation of the Virgin and Saints* over the door. The interior, a dignified Baroque symphony of grey and gold, contains frescoes by Tiepolo in the first two altars on the right and in the Cappella del Sacramento. In the heavy-set campanile, the small **Museo del Duomo** (*open Mon–Sat 9–12 and 4–6, Sun 4–6*) is adorned with excellent frescoes of 1349 by Vitale da Bologna. Tiepolo never forgot Ùdine, and in 1759 he returned to decorate the adjacent **Oratorio della Purità** (1680) with a masterful, partly frescoed, partly painted and recently restored *Assumption* on the ceiling, and an altarpiece of the *Immaculate Conception*; the frescoes on the walls are by his son.

The Tiepolo trail continues in the Piazza Patriarcato, where he frescoed an entire gallery with Old Testament scenes in the **Museo Diocesano** (*open Wed–Sun 10–12 and 3.30–6.30*). More recent art (Arturo Martini, Severini, De Chirico, De Kooning, Segal, Lichtenstein, Dufy and works by the local brothers Afro, Mirko and Dino Basaldell) is on display in the excellent **Galleria d'Arte Moderna** (*take bus 2; open 9.30–12.30 and 3–6; closed Mon; adm, Sun am free*), on the northern fringes of the old town.

The new **Museo Friulano di Storia Naturale** (*Via Grazzano 1; provisionally open 9–12 and 3–6;* **t** *0432 510 221*) offers a mixture of natural history and Friuli culture, showing how the people have developed customs and traditions from the land.

Getting There

Trains to Ùdine from Trieste run roughly every 30mins (1hr15); **buses** (**t** 040 425 020) may take slightly longer (1hr30). Ùdine's **train station** is on Viale Europa Unità. The **bus station** is not far away on the other side of the same street, **t** 0432 506 941.

Tourist Information

Ùdine ✉ **33 100:** Piazza 1 Maggio 7, **t** 0432 295 972, **f** 0432 504 743, *arpt1.ud@adriacom.it*.

Eating Out

*****La' di Moret**, just north of the centre at Viale Tricesimo 276, **t** 0432 545 096, **f** 0432 545 096 (*expensive*). This hotel has one of the best restaurants in the region, featuring seafood Friuli-style. *Closed Sun eve and Mon.*

Vitello d'Oro, Via Valvason 4, **t** 0432 508 982, **f** 0432 508 982 (*expensive*). A historic inn serving traditional specialities; the emphasis is on fish. *Closed Wed and three weeks in July.*

Vecchio Stallo, Via Viola 7, **t** 0432 21296 (*cheap*). A charming restaurant and the best value; good food, and wine by the glass. *Closed Wed.*

Touring from Trieste

Day 1: Karst and Wines of the Collio

Morning: Leave Trieste by the S58, and at Villa Opicina follow signs northeast for **Sgonico**. Trieste province is known as the Carso, after its limestone karst, pocked with caves and resurgent rivers, and covered with sumac; learn more about it at Sgonico's **Carsiana botanical garden** (*open 24 April–15 Oct Tues–Fri 10–12, Sat, Sun and hols 10–1 and 3–7; closed Mon*). Continue northwest to the seaside resorts of **Sistiana** and **Duino**, on two pretty bays. In the latter's 15th-century **Castello Nuovo**, poet Rainier Maria Rilke wrote his *Duino Elegies*; follow his favourite 2km path, the **Rilke walk**, around the promontory. Just above Duino, visit the winsome Romanesque church of **San Giovanni in Tuba**, where the River Timavo resurfaces in a lush setting.

Lunch: In Duino, *see* below.

Afternoon: Head northeast to the frontier city of **Gorízia**, the former 'Austrian Nice', with a medieval **Castle of the Counts of Gorízia** (*open Tues–Sun 9.30–1 and 3–7.30; adm*). Just below, the **Museo Provinciale** (*open 10–8; closed Mon, adm*) has historical and art exhibits, while the adjacent **Museo delle Guerre** (*open 10–1 and 2–6; closed Mon; adm*) has fascinating exhibits on the First World War. From Gorízia explore Friuli's most prestigious wine district, the hilly and pretty **Collio**; go tasting at the Cantina Prodottori Vini del Collio (*closed Sun*) in the medieval **Cormòns**.

Dinner and Sleeping: In or around Cormòns, *see* below.

Day 1

Lunch in Duino

Duino has fashionable seafood restaurants, so prices here tend to be over the odds. If you don't feel like indulging, pack a picnic lunch before leaving Trieste.

Dama Bianca, t 040 298 137 (*expensive*). By the old castle walls, overlooking Duino's bijou port. Highly rated for its absolutely fresh fish, beautifully prepared in pasta dishes and the main course, where the menu depends on the day's catch. Great wine list. *Closed Wed exc summer.*

Ai Cavalluccio, next door to the Dama Bianca, **t** 040 208 133 (*expensive–moderate*). Zuzana Hornakovar's restaurant also has lovely fish (try the sea bass baked in salt), besides Collio wines and great desserts. *Closed Tues.*

Dinner and Sleeping in or around Cormòns

★★★**Felcaro**, Via Giovanni 45, **t** 0481 60214, **f** 0481 630 255 (*moderate*). The nicest place to sleep in the Collio. It began life as an Austrian villa and is spread out among several buildings, with a pool as well as a fine restaurant, specializing in game dishes to set off its enormous wine list.

★★**La Subida**, Monte 22, **t** 0481 60531, **f** 0481 61616 (*cheap*). In a charming rural setting on a hill, with a handful of rooms, many of which sleep up to five; there's an outdoor pool and riding available, too. The hotel's 'Hunter' restaurant, **Il Cacciatore** (*expensive*), is famed for its excellent regional dishes, with extensive borrowings from nearly Slovenia: the cold breast of pheasant in mushroom cream is a popular summer dish. Excellent Collio wines. *Closed Tues, Wed and Feb.*

Il Giardinetto, Via Matteotti 54, **t** 0481 60257, **f** 0481 630 704 (*expensive*). Twin chefs have put this restaurant firmly on the gastronomic map with their innovative Friulian dishes, such as *millefoglie di polenta* and gnocchi with crinkly cabbage and game sauce. *Closed Mon eve, Tues and July.*

Day 2: Dark Age Wonders and Carnia Foothills

Morning: Take the S356 north to **Cividale del Friuli**, a city founded by Julius Caesar that caught the fancy of the invading Lombards, who made it their capital in 568. The **Duomo** has a great 12th-century altarpiece and two wonderful 8th-century Lombard works, the Baptistry of Callisto and the Altar of Ratchis, in the **Museo Cristiano** (*open 9.30–12 and 3–7*). Other Lombard artefacts, along with Roman ones, fill the adjacent **Museo Archeològico Nazionale** (*open Mon 9–2, Tues–Fri 9.30–7.30*). Walk down to the river to see the lofty **Ponte del Diavolo** (1442) spanning the turquoise Natisone; just up the river is the marvellous **Tempietto Longobardo** (*open summer 9–1 and 3–6.30; winter 10–1 and 3.30–5.30; adm*), where a lovely sextet of princesses and female saints in high relief are the finest 8th-century works in Italy, a love letter from the Dark Ages.

Lunch: In Cividale del Friuli, *see* below.

Afternoon: Head for the hills – take the S356 to **Tarcento**, then cross over west to the S13 for **Gemona del Friuli**; its fine 13th-century cathedral has a remarkable portal. Continue north on the S13 to **Venzone**, a double-walled town that had to be rebuilt, twice: after the Second World War and after the 1967 earthquake. North of here, leave the S13 to turn west for **Tolmezzo**, once a great producer of damasks; visit the great ethnographic collection of the Carnia Mountains at the **Museo Carnico Delle Arti Popolari** (*open 9–1 and 3–6; closed Mon*), in a 16th-century palace. And if you need a dose of mountain scenery, drive to **Lake Verzeghis**, 5km south of Tolmezzo.

Dinner and Sleeping: In Tolmezzo or nearby Arta Terme, *see* below.

Day 2

Lunch in Cividale del Friuli

Alla Frasca, Via di Rebeis 8a, **t** 0432 731 270 (*moderate*). A restaurant with a charming Renaissance atmosphere and tasty Friulian dishes, including a *menu di funghi* that offers truffles and mushrooms with everything. In winter, game dishes rule the menu. All year round, though, save room for the many home-made desserts. *Closed Mon.*

Al Fortino, Via Carlo Alberto 46, **t** 0432 731 270 (*moderate*). Another pleasant place for lunch, featuring home-made pasta dishes and typical Friulian fare. *Closed Tues.*

Dinner and Sleeping in Tolmezzo

******Roma**, Piazza XX Settembre 14, **t** 043 32081, **f** 043 343 316 (*rooms moderate, restaurant expensive*). Smack in the heart of town, where Friuli's top chef, Gianni Cosetti, holds forth, giving his clients gastronomic sweet dreams: try the traditional *toc in braide* (polenta with cheese), porcini mushroom dishes, pheasant cooked with fresh herbs and lovely desserts. *Closed Sun eve, Mon and some of June and Nov.*

Dinner and Sleeping in Arta Terme

Arta Terme is just 7km north of Tolmezzo.

******Poldo**, up in Piano d'Arta, Arta Terme, **t** 043 392 056, **f** 043 392 577 (*expensive*). Enjoys a peaceful setting in the trees, with an exotic garden and views down into the valley. You may want to come back: it's also a spa centre, specializing in the treatment of obesity and dietary disorders.

*****Salon**, Via Peresson 70, **t** 043 392 003, **f** 043 392 9364 (*rooms cheap, restaurant moderate*). This hotel has more basic rooms, but an excellent restaurant, serving traditional Carnican dishes, where mushrooms and fresh herbs are plentiful; in summer crêpes with courgette flowers are a speciality. Don't miss the selection of mountain cheeses. *Open May–Oct, restaurant closed Tues exc in season.*

Day 3: Prosciutto, Frescoes and a Really Big Villa

Morning: Retrace your way south, picking up the S463 near Gemona for **San Daniele del Friuli**, the ochre-tinted 'Siena of Friuli', where you can try and buy its famous sweet-cured hams. Don't miss the church of **Sant'Antonio Abate**, containing the finest fresco cycle in Friuli, the masterpiece of Pellegrino di San Daniele, painted between 1498 and 1522. To the right of the Duomo, the **Biblioteca Guarneriana** (*open Tues–Sun 9–12*) was established in 1466 by a canon of Aquileia and has lovely medieval manuscripts. Then drive south and cross the River Tagliamento for **Spilimbergo**, a historic town with plenty of churches and a 12th-century **castle** with exterior frescoes and a **mosaic school** (*open Mon–Sat 9–12 by appointment,* ***t*** *0427 2077,* ***f*** *0427 3903*).

Lunch: In Spilimbergo, *see* below.

Afternoon: Drive south to **Provesano** to see the fine frescoes (1496) inside its church, by Gianfrancesco da Tolmezzo, then turn east for **Codroipo**, where the the last Doge, Ludovico Manin, built the **Villa Manin** (1738) (*open summer Tues–Sun 9–12 and 3–6; winter 9–12 and 2–5; adm free*) the biggest villa in all Venetia. Besides rooms of frescoed fluff, there's a museum of carriages and a handsome park. From here back-track west to **San Vito**, for the 16th-century frescoes by Pompeo Amalteo in **Santa Maria dei Battuti**. Continue west to **Pordenone**, where the **Duomo** and **Museo Civico d'Arte** (*open Tues–Fri 9.30–12.30 and 3–6; adm*) contain works by the famous Renaissance painter named after the town.

Dinner and Sleeping: In or around Pordenone, *see* below.

Day 3

Lunch in Spilimbergo

La Torre, Piazza Castello, **t** 0427 50555 (*moderate*). Dine in the castle on the likes of ravioli, filled with pumpkin in mushroom sauce, and strudels. If you love wine, you'll have a field day with its jam-packed cellar. *Closed Sun eve and Mon.*

Osteria Al Bachero, Via Pilacorte 5, **t** 0427 2317 (*cheap*). The furniture may be simple and wooden, but here you'll find the authentic taste of Friuli. Try the *baccalá con polenta* (salt cod with polenta) or any number of local dishes, and dine around an open fire. They have one menu in English but you won't have to wait for it. *Closed Sun.*

Dinner and Sleeping in and around Pordenone

★★★★Villa Ottoboni, Piazzetta Ottoboni 2, **t** 0434 208 891, **f** 0434 208 148 (*expensive*). An elegant hotel right near the centre, offering fully furnished rooms; the dining room dates from the late 15th century.

Antica Trattoria La Primula, Via San Rocco 47, **t** 0434 91005, **f** 0434 919 280 (*expensive*). For something special, drive 9km north of Pordenone to San Quirino. Here six generations have served up the best food in the province, classic and simply prepared, from the *antipasti* through the fresh seafood to the elegant desserts. It has seven rooms as well, but you'll need to book ahead to nab one. The same talented family also runs the adjacent, frescoed Osteria Alle Nazioni, serving simpler delights at prices that are kinder on the pocket. *Closed Sun eve, Mon, part of Jan and July.*

★★★**Park**, Via Mazzini 42, **t** 0434 27901, **f** 0434 522 353 (*moderate*). For modern, comfortable rooms in the centre of Pordenone.

Alla Cantina, Piazza Cavour 3, **t/f** 0434 520 358 (*cheap*). This is easy to find in the centre. There'll be no surprises, but it's a good bet for well-prepared Italian classics, served in rather opulent surroundings. *Closed Tues.*

Day 4: Romans, a *Pala d'Oro* and Beaches

Morning: Speed south on the A28 to **Sesto al Règhena**, a quaint medieval village built around **Santa Maria in Silvis** (*open 8–8*), an abbey founded by the Lombards. The Romanesque Byzantine basilica dates from the 11th century and has some fine and unusual frescoes, including one of Christ crucified on a pomegranite tree. Continue 9km south to **Portugruaro**, a seductive old town of porticoed streets, palm trees and canals. It has a striking 14th-century **Loggia Comunale** (the Municipio) and the **Museo Nazionale Concordiese** (*open daily 9–8; adm*) is full of bronzes, coins and finds from the Roman glass-and-arrow manufacturing colony of **Concordia Sagittaria**, located just south of Portugruaro. Here you'll find a Romanesque cathedral sitting next to a ruined basilica of 380, and a frescoed Byzantine baptistry of 1089, as well as a **museum** (*open Tues–Sun 9–12 and 3.30–6.30; closed Mon)* with more archaological finds. Next, drive south towards **Càorle**.

Lunch: In San Giorgio di Livenza or Càorle, *see* below.

Afternoon: Visit Càorle – its landmark **church lighthouse** on an isthmus; its **cathedral**, vintage 1028, with a radiant Venetian **Pala d'Oro** (12th–14th centuries) on the altar; and go out watching for birds in its inner lagoon. Then head eastwards, crossing the flatlands; stop in **Latisana** to see Veronese's *Baptism of Christ* (1567) in the cathedral, then drive south to **Lignano-Sabbiadoro**, the fastest growing resort on the whole of the Adriatic, to relax on its long sandy beach and/or birdwatch in the **Laguna di Marano**.

Dinner and Sleeping: In Lignano-Sabbiadoro, *see* below.

Day 4

Lunch in San Giorgio di Livenza

Al Cacciatore, Corso Risorgimento 25, **t** 0421 80331 (*expensive*). Ten km before Càorle, near the Livenza river. A popular family-run restaurant of long standing, featuring the freshest of fish and tasty mushroom dishes in the autumn. *Closed Wed and some of Aug.*

Lunch in Càorle

Duilio, at the Hotel Diplomatic, Via Strada Nuova 19, **t** 0421 81087, **f** 0421 210 089 (*moderate*). In a charming setting overlooking a little port, famed for the heavenly seafood served in the *antipasti*, with the pasta, and as the main course. A huge wine list and reasonably priced menus are added attractions. *Closed Mon and Jan.*

Dinner in Lignano-Sabbiadoro

Bidin, Via Europa 1, **t** 0431 71988. (*expensive*). A small, convivial restaurant, with a separate *menu degustazione* featuring either fish or meat to accompany the fine bottles in its tremendous wine cellar. *Closed Wed, exc in summer.*

Al Bancut, Via Friuli 32, **t** 0431 71926 (*moderate*). In the centre of town, a popular restaurant with a woodsy seaside décor featuring tasty grilled fish, traditionally prepared, followed by delightful home-made desserts. *Closed Tues eve and Wed.*

Sleeping in Lignano-Sabbiadoro

★★★★**Eurotel**, Calle Mendelssohn 13, **t** 0431 71260, **f** 0431 428 992 (*expensive*). A fashionable hotel in Lignano Riviera, enjoying perhaps the most beautiful setting in the whole area and offering lovely rooms, a heated pool and much more. *Open mid-May–mid-Sept.*

★★★**Etna**, Viale Miramare 24, **t** 0431 720 640, **f** 043 172 1649, *www.albergoetna.com* (*moderate*, including breakfast). A tasteful hotel near the sea with well equipped rooms; it's also one of the few that remains open all year.

Day 5: New Towns, Old Towns and Sand Cures

Morning: Have a last swim in Lignano, and then head east for **Palmanova**. In the Renaissance, despite all of its theories on planning, only a handful of new towns ever saw the light of day, and this was one of them, built in 1593 by the Venetians as a bulwark against the Austrians and Turks. Perhaps because it was never actually needed, Palmanova remains intact, a perfect example of an 'ideal' radial military plan: a nine-pointed star with a hexagonal *piazza* in the centre; learn all about it in the **Museo Storico** at Borgo Udine *(open 10–12 and 3–6; closed Wed)*. Then drive south to **Cervignano**.

Lunch: In Cervignano del Friuli, *see* below.

Afternoon: Stop in ancient **Aquileia** (*see* p.137), just south, then continue to **Grado**, Aquileia's old port. In the narrow lanes of the old town, the Castrum Gradense, look for the **Basilica of Sant'Eufemia**, once the seat of the 6th-century Patriarch of Nova Aquileia, as he fashioned himself. Inside it has its original 6th-century mosaic floor, an 11th-century domed pulpit and a silver *pala* donated by the Venetians in 1372; also visit the adjacent **baptistry** and **Basilica of Santa Maria delle Grazie**, both from the 5th century. You might fancy a swim, either at the town beach or at the pine-fringed **Pineta**; or you could take the 'sand cure' (get buried up to your neck in benevolent warm sand, full of curative minerals and micro-organisms) at the **Thermal Bath and Theraputic Department** (**t** *0431 82821*); or simply watch for birds in Grado's **lagoon**.

Dinner and Sleeping: In Grado, *see* below. In the morning, jump on the *autostrada* back to Trieste.

Day 5

Lunch in Cervignano del Friuli

Hotel Internazionale Rotonda, Via Ramazzotti 2, **t** 0431 30751 (*expensive*). An elegant hotel restaurant on the Trieste–Venice road, with a keen attention to detail. Top billing goes to seasonal vegetables and seafood, but everything is delicious, including the exquisite desserts. Excellent wine list, too. *Closed Sun eve, Mon and half of Aug.*

Chichibio, Via Carnia 2, **t** 0431 32704 (*moderate–cheap*). A big, busy place on the Grado crossroads, serving up delicious meat or seafood menus, as well as top notch pizzas. *Closed Wed.*

Dinner in Grado

All'Androna, Calle Porta Piccola 4, **t** 0431 80950 (*expensive*). In the winding streets around the cathedral, with a summer garden and a daily-changing menu of fresh fish, home-made bread and pasta. If it's on the menu, try the *zuppette di frutti di mare* or the *ravioli di scampi in brodo. Closed Tues out of season and Dec–Mar.*

De Toni, Piazza Duca d'Aosta 37, **t** 0431 80104 (*moderate*). A characteristic little resturant overlooking the Roman excavations, offering fresh fish prepared in a variety of local styles with garden vegetables. A long wine list is another bonus, and excellent desserts round things out very nicely indeed. *Closed Wed out of season and Dec.*

Sleeping in Grado

********Antica Villa Bernt**, Via Colombo 5, **t** 0431 82516, **f** 0431 82517 (*very expensive*). There are lots of nice hotels in Grado, but only a couple stand out. Right in the centre of town, this one is a refurbished villa from the 1920s with 22 lovely rooms, equipped with all mod cons. *Open April–Oct.*

*****Ambriabella**, Riva Slataper 2, **t** 0431 81479, **f** 0431 82257 (*moderate*). A pleasant little place facing the Isola della Schiusa, offering welcome personal touches that are sometimes missing from Grado's larger hotels.

Emilia-Romagna

08

This is Middle Italy: agricultural, wealthy, progressive, a barometer of Italian highs and lows – the birthplace of the country's socialist movement, but also of Mussolini and Fascism. In Emilia-Romagna hard-working cities like Modena, Parma and Bologna share space with Rimini, Italy's vast, madcap, international resort, and traditional Apennine villages. This region is the cradle of innovative film directors such as Fellini and Bertolucci; of the musical giants Verdi, Toscanini and Pavarotti; and of such diverse talents as Marconi, Correggio, Savonarola, Ariosto and Ferrari.

The Via Aemilia, built in 187 BC between Piacenza and Rimini, runs almost dead straight for hundreds of kilometres along the Apennines; nearly all of Emilia's cities grew up at intervals along the road, like beads on a string. You'll find remarkable Byzantine art in Ravenna, exceptional Romanesque churches in Parma and Modena, Italy's crookedest towers in Bologna, beautiful Renaissance art in Parma, Bologna and Ferrara, and the Renaissance's strangest building, the Malatesta Temple, in Rimini. You can sunbathe in style on the Adriatic, stock up on plates in Italy's ceramics capital at Faenza, or attend grand opera in Parma, Bologna or Modena. And when it's time for a break, you'll also find Italy's best food.

Bologna

Bologna's sobriquets are *La Dotta*, *La Grassa* and *La Rossa* (the Learned, the Fat and the Red), but a fervent insistence on the plain truth, as opposed to the typical Italian delight in appearance, sets this city apart. Its handsome, harmonic centre disdains marble and stucco, preferring honest red brick. A homespun realism characterizes the Bolognese school of art, and it was the desire for truth that led to the founding of the University of Bologna, whose first scholars occupied themselves with interpreting the law codes of the emperor Justinian.

The city's historic centre is one of the best preserved in Italy, every street lined with miles of *portici*, or arcades; along with the absurdly tilting Due Torri, these are the city's identity. It may be full of socialist virtue, but Bologna is also very wealthy, its bars and squares brimming with youth and life; there's a full calendar of events – from rap to avant-garde ballet to Renaissance madrigals – and *la cucina bolognese* is the best in the country. Beware, though, that in July and August Bologna can be as exciting as the cheap supermarket salami that bears its name.

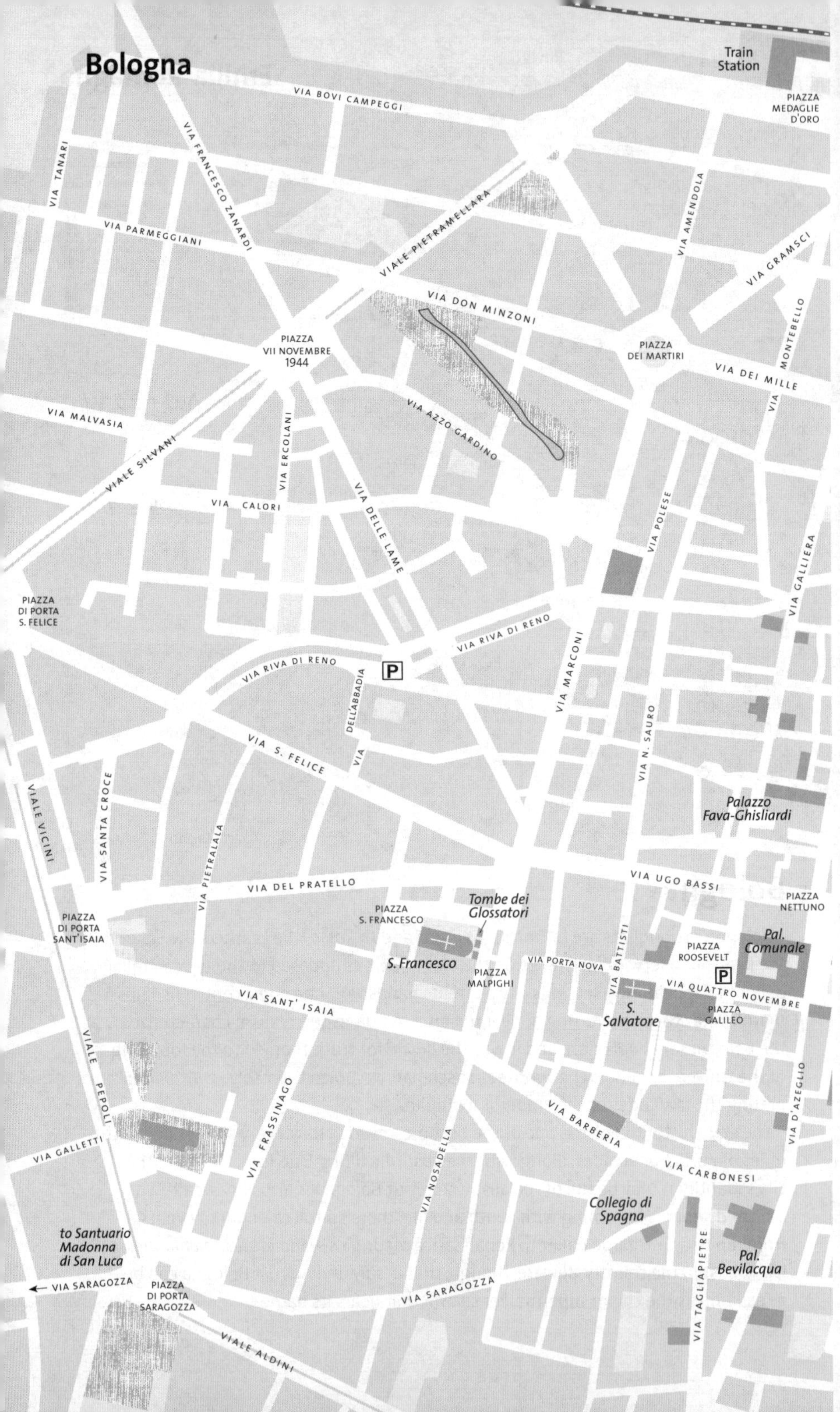
Bologna
Train Station
PIAZZA MEDAGLIE D'ORO
VIA BOVI CAMPEGGI
VIA TANARI
VIA FRANCESCO ZANARDI
VIA PARMEGGIANI
VIALE PIETRAMELLARA
VIA AMENDOLA
VIA GRAMSCI
VIA DON MINZONI
PIAZZA VII NOVEMBRE 1944
PIAZZA DEI MARTIRI
VIA MONTEBELLO
VIA DEI MILLE
VIA MALVASIA
VIA AZZO GARDINO
VIALE SILVANI
VIA ERCOLANI
VIA CALORI
VIA DELLE LAME
VIA POLESE
VIA GALLIERA
PIAZZA DI PORTA S. FELICE
VIA RIVA DI RENO
VIA RIVA DI RENO
VIA DELL'ABBADIA
VIA MARCONI
VIA S. FELICE
VIA N. SAURO
VIALE VICINI
VIA SANTA CROCE
VIA PIETRALATA
Palazzo Fava-Ghisliardi
VIA DEL PRATELLO
VIA UGO BASSI
PIAZZA NETTUNO
PIAZZA DI PORTA SANT'ISAIA
PIAZZA S. FRANCESCO
Tombe dei Glossatori
Pal. Comunale
PIAZZA ROOSEVELT
VIA BATTISTI
S. Francesco
VIA PORTA NOVA
PIAZZA MALPIGHI
VIA QUATTRO NOVEMBRE
VIA SANT' ISAIA
S. Salvatore
PIAZZA GALILEO
VIALE PEPOLI
VIA D'AZEGLIO
VIA BARBERIA
VIA FRASSINAGO
VIA GALLETTI
VIA NOSADELLA
VIA CARBONESI
Collegio di Spagna
to Santuario Madonna di San Luca
Pal. Bevilacqua
VIA TAGLIAPIETRE
VIA SARAGOZZA
PIAZZA DI PORTA SARAGOZZA
VIA SARAGOZZA
VIALE ALDINI

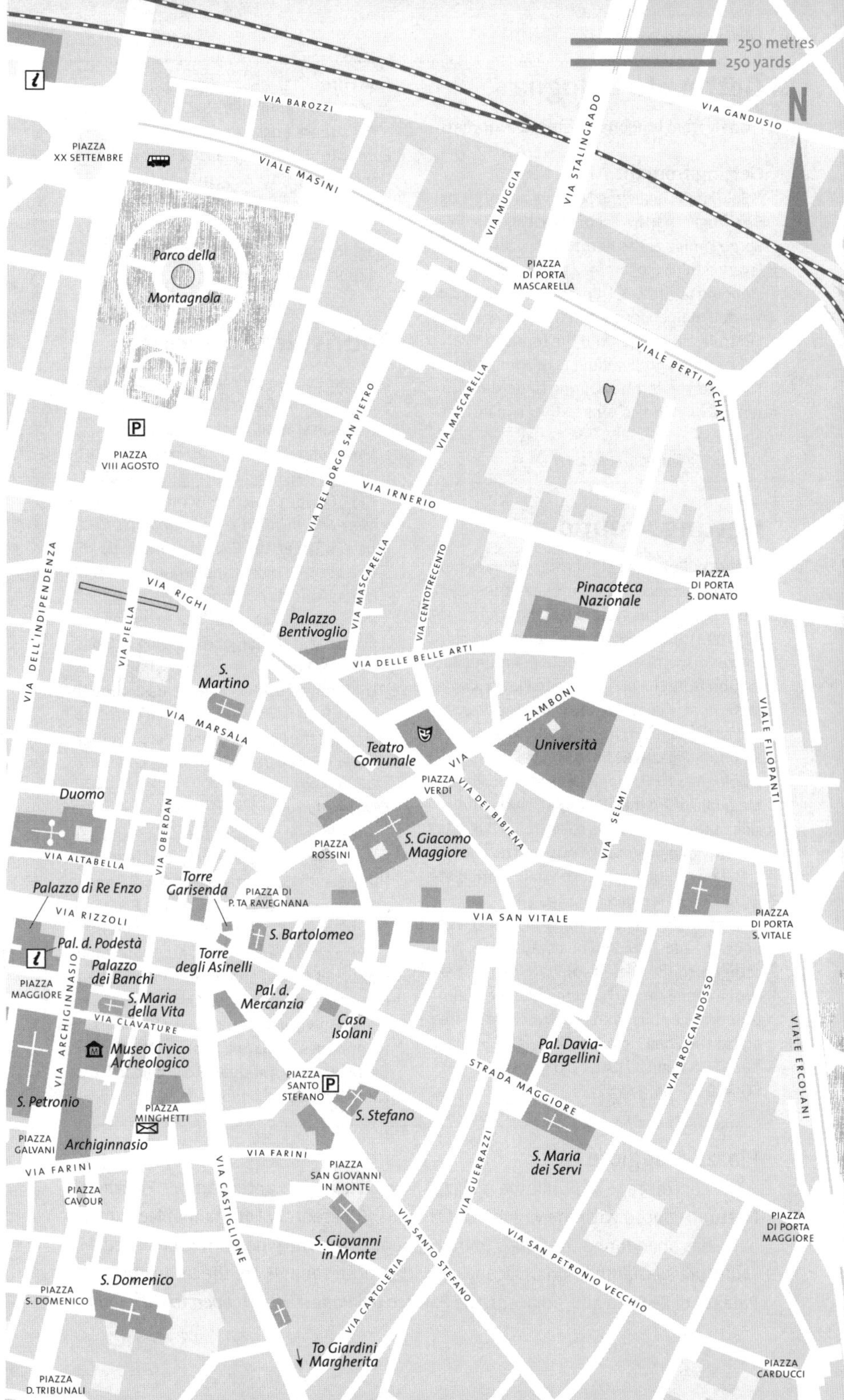
250 metres
250 yards
N
VIA BAROZZI
VIA GANDUSIO
PIAZZA
XX SETTEMBRE
VIALE MASINI
VIA STALINGRADO
VIA MUGGIA
Parco della
Montagnola
PIAZZA
DI PORTA
MASCARELLA
VIALE BERTI PICHAT
VIA MASCARELLA
VIA DEL BORGO SAN PIETRO
PIAZZA
VIII AGOSTO
VIA IRNERIO
VIA MASCARELLA
VIA CENTOTRECENTO
PIAZZA
DI PORTA
S. DONATO
Pinacoteca
Nazionale
VIA DELL'INDIPENDENZA
VIA RIGHI
VIA PIELLA
Palazzo
Bentivoglio
VIA DELLE BELLE ARTI
S.
Martino
ZAMBONI
VIALE FILOPANTI
VIA MARSALA
Teatro
Comunale
Università
VIA
PIAZZA
VERDI
VIA DEI BIBIENA
Duomo
VIA OBERDAN
PIAZZA
ROSSINI
S. Giacomo
Maggiore
VIA SELMI
VIA ALTABELLA
Torre
Garisenda
Palazzo di Re Enzo
PIAZZA DI
P. TA RAVEGNANA
VIA RIZZOLI
VIA SAN VITALE
PIAZZA
DI PORTA
S. VITALE
Pal. d. Podestà
S. Bartolomeo
Torre
degli Asinelli
Palazzo
dei Banchi
PIAZZA
MAGGIORE
VIA ARCHIGINNASIO
S. Maria
della Vita
Pal. d.
Mercanzia
VIA BROCCAINDOSSO
VIA CLAVATURE
Casa
Isolani
VIALE ERCOLANI
Museo Civico
Archeologico
Pal. Davia-
Bargellini
STRADA MAGGIORE
PIAZZA
SANTO
STEFANO
S. Petronio
S. Stefano
PIAZZA
MINGHETTI
PIAZZA
GALVANI
Archiginnasio
VIA GUERRAZZI
VIA FARINI
S. Maria
dei Servi
VIA FARINI
PIAZZA
SAN GIOVANNI
IN MONTE
VIA CASTIGLIONE
PIAZZA
CAVOUR
VIA SANTO STEFANO
PIAZZA
DI PORTA
MAGGIORE
VIA SAN PETRONIO VECCHIO
S. Giovanni
in Monte
VIA CARTOLERIA
S. Domenico
PIAZZA
S. DOMENICO
To Giardini
Margherita
PIAZZA
CARDUCCI
PIAZZA
D. TRIBUNALI

Getting to Bologna

Go fly from London Stansted (2hrs 10mins).

Getting from the Airport

Bologna's Guglielmo Marconi airport (**t** 051 647 9615) is northwest of the city centre in Borgo Panigale. The **Aerobus** *servizio navetta* (every 15mins 6.05am–11.45pm) does a loop, stopping at Arrivals, Departures, Via Ugo Bassi, Via dell'Indipendenza, and the Stazione Centrale; timetable from the tourist office, or **t** 051 290 290. It should take 20mins, but traffic can be terrible. During trade shows, a ***servizio diretto*** also runs to the Fiera district (30mins).

A **taxi** to the centre costs € 12–15.

Getting Around

Most of Bologna's sights are within easy walking distance of each other, but there's an efficient local **bus** system (ATC **t** 051 290 290). Buy **tickets** before you board from *tabacchi*. Offices dispense tickets, route maps and information from the bus station in Piazza XX Settembre, a booth by the train station on Piazza Medaglie d'Oro, at Via IV Novembre 16, and from Palazzo Re Enzo on Via Rizzoli.

Bologna's **FS Stazione Centrale** is in Piazza Medaglie d'Oro (**t** 1478 88088), on the north side of the city centre, a 10–15-min walk from Piazza Maggiore (or take buses 10 or 25).

The **bus station** is near the train station at Piazza XX Settembre, **t** 051 350 301.

Bologna's *tangenziale* ring road encircles a node of pedestrian and one-way streets with complex traffic rules. If you have a car, leave it in one of the car parks on the periphery, all connected by bus to the centre; there's a free one at the Zona Fiera Nord on Viale Europa.

To call a **taxi**, call **CAT**, **t** 051 534 141, or **CO.TA.BO.**, **t** 051 37 27 27.

Car Hire

Avis, Via Pietrammellara 27D, **t** 051 255 024; at the airport, **t** 051 647 2032.

Europcar, Via Amendola 12F, **t** 051 247 101; at the airport, **t** 051 647 2111.

Hertz, Via Amendola 16, **t** 051 254 830; at the airport, **t** 051 647 2015.

Maggiore, Via Cairoli 4, **t** 051 252 525; at the airport, **t** 051 647 2007.

Tourist Information

Bologna: Palazzo del Podestà, Piazza Maggiore, **t** 051 239 660 (*open daily 9–8*). Branches at the train station, **t** 051 246 541 (*open Mon–Sat 9–12.30 and 2.30–7*) and airport. Offers a free hotel booking service, CST, **t** 051 239 660, for 3-star hotels and up (*available Mon–Sat 10–2 and 3–7, Sun and hols 10–2*).

Museum Ticket: the *Biglietto Unico* gets you in free at some places and brings a discount in others (one-day or three-day); the *Biglietto Integrato* also works as a bus pass; all are available at the larger museums, ATC bus ticket outlets and many bookshops.

Look out for posters in the bars around the university to find out about what's on; also check out the **listings** in Bologna's *Il Resto del Carlino*, or the fortnightly *Zero in Condotta*.

Market Days

The lavish products of the local countryside can be found in the bustling **food markets** at the Mercato Coperto, Via Ugo Bassi 2, and in and around Via dei Orefici, off the Piazza Maggiore. *Both open mornings Mon–Sat*.

La Piazzola market sells clothes and more in Piazza VIII Agosto and Via dell'Indipendenza (*open Fri and Sat*); try the **Celò Celò Mamanca** market in Via Valdonica/Piazza San Martino for antiques, old lace and old books (*Thurs*); a big **Mercato di Antiquariato** is held in Piazza Santo Stefano (*second Sun of the month*).

Piazza Maggiore

The centre stage of public life is Piazza Maggiore and its antechamber, **Piazza Nettuno**, graced with the vaguely outrageous 16th-century **Fountain of Neptune**, 'who has abandoned the fishes to make friends with the pigeons', embellished with sculpture by Giambologna. Occupying part of both squares are the 13th-century **Palazzo di Re Enzo** and, adjacent, the **Palazzo del Podestà** (*both open to the public*

Festivals

Apart from its numerous **trade fairs**, Bologna organizes the *Bologna Sogna* festival throughout July and August, featuring concerts, theatre and open-air cinema.

Shopping

Bologna has no lack of small **boutiques**: Via Rizzoli and Via dell'Indipendenza are the main fashion centres, with chic outlets in Via Farini and an arcade of designer shops in Via d'Azeglio and Via Clavature. The city's most characteristic souvenir, however, is food. Apart from the general **food stores** (around Piazza Maggiore, near the Two Towers), **Paolo Atti & Figli**, Via Caprarie 7 or Via Drapperie 6, in business since 1880, sells excellent home-made pasta and pastries; **Al Regno della Forma**, Via Oberdan 45a, has perfect cheeses; while **Tamburini**, Via Caprarie 1, is famous for *salumeria* and other gastronomic highlights from Emilia-Romagna.

Where to Stay

Bologna ✉ 40100

Confirm the room price when you book; prices may vary as much as €150, depending on the room, season, and what's cooking at BolognaFiera. What cheaper accommodation there is tends to be central. You may be asked to pay in cash in the smaller, cheaper hotels.

******Grand Hotel Baglioni**, Via dell' Indipendenza 8, **t** 051 225 445, **f** 051 234 840, *ghb.bologna@bcedit.it* (*luxury*). In an opulent 16th-century *palazzo* and so embedded in history as to be almost a monument. Antiques line the luxurious rooms and there's a beautiful restaurant frescoed by the Carracci, specializing in authentic Bolognese cuisine.

*****Dei Commercianti**, Via Pignattari 11, **t** 051 233 052, **f** 051 224 733, *hotcom.tin.it* (*very expensive*). In the 12th-century town hall, right by San Petronio and the ritziest shopping streets. All rooms are different: most have balconies; the priciest, with beamed ceilings and the odd piece of fresco, are at the top. Excellent buffet breakfast included.

*****Roma**, Via D'Azeglio 9, **t** 051 226 322, **f** 051 239 909 (*expensive*). One of Bologna's nicest hotels, in the medieval centre by Piazza Maggiore, with large soundproofed rooms decorated with floral wallpaper and fabrics.

*****Orologio**, Via IV Novembre 10, **t** 051 231 253, **f** 051 260 552, *hotoro@iperbole.bologna.it* (*expensive*). An atmospheric aged *palazzo* in a pleasant square with a big clock on the façade; cosy rooms with good views of the streets outside. Buffet breakfast included.

*****Palace**, Via Monte Grappa 9/2, **t** 051 237 442, **f** 051 220 689 (*moderate*). In a central, genteely faded old *palazzo*; the large, older rooms are little changed since the early 1900s (but have satellite TV). *Closed Aug*.

*****Donatello**, Via dell' Indipendenza 65, **t/f** 051 248 174 (*moderate*). A typical vintage 1930s hotel, with a variety of rooms with a/c, mostly large, comfortable and quiet.

****Centrale**, Via della Zecca 2, **t** 051 225 114, **f** 051 235 162 (*moderate*). Another old *palazzo*; rooms are simple but pleasant, with a/c, and nearly all en suite; some triples available.

****Rossini**, Via Bibiena 11, **t** 051 237 716, **f** 051 268 035 (*cheap*). In the university quarter and very friendly, with clean, comfortable rooms (some en suite rooms *moderate*).

***Apollo**, Via Drapperie 5, **t/f** 051 223 955 (*cheap*). Rooms are small, and the market outside starts up early, but this is brilliantly placed in the shopping streets off Piazza Maggiore.

***Panorama**, Via Livraghi 1, **t** 051 221 802, **f** 051 266 360 (*cheap*). Central, clean and friendly, with TV; a few rooms without baths.

when hosting exhibitions), remodelled in 1484 by Aristotele Fioravanti, who went on to design parts of the Kremlin. Filling the western side of the Piazza Maggiore, the crenellated **Palazzo Comunale** (*open Tues–Sat 9–6.30, Sun and hols 10–6.30*) holds two museums: the **Collezioni Comunali d'Arte** features works by Bolognese artists, from the medieval Vitale da Bologna and Simone de'Crocefissi to the Carracci brothers and Giuseppe Maria Crespi; the **Museo Morandi** is devoted to Bologna's

Eating Out

Bologna is Italy's self-acclaimed gastronomic capital: besides pasta, the city is known for pâtés, veal and for culinary innovations. It's always worth booking ahead for any good restaurant in the historical centre.

Pappagallo, Piazza delle Mercanzia 3, **t/f** 051 232 807 (*luxury*). Bologna's most famous restaurant, in a *quattrocento palazzo*, with elegant if eccentric touches: bowls of handsome vegetables adorn the tables. The food is Italian with French influences: prawns with red risotto; fresh pasta; a wide range of seafood; Châteaubriand and rabbit (the house speciality). Vast wine list. *Closed Sun.*

Torre de Galluzzi, Corte Galluzzi 5/a, **t** 051 267 638 (*very expensive*). Atmospheric place in a medieval tower behind the Cathedral, serving original dishes with finesse: seafood, tortellini with black truffles, risotto with porcini, glazed rabbit and exquisite desserts. Big wine list. *Closed Sun and most of Aug.*

Da Cesari, Via de' Carbonesi 8, **t** 051 237 710 (*expensive*). The ambience has barely altered in 30 years; classic Bolognese dishes have innovative touches, so you may find ravioli stuffed with rabbit and smoked ricotta alongside standards like tripe *alla parmigiana. Closed Sun, and Sat in June and July.*

Silverio, Via Mirasole 19, **t** 051 585 857 (*expensive*). Delightful place south of San Domenico, with a charming terrace and inventive cuisine: even Parmesan ice cream. Great wine and spirits list. *Closed Sun and Aug.*

Da Leonida, Vicolo Alemagna 2, **t** 0512 39742 (*moderate*). Popular, elegant *trattoria* near the Due Torri, doing everything possible with *tortellini* and tagliatelle; also roast pheasant, rabbit with polenta and a choice of homemade desserts. *Closed Sun.*

Osteria del Palazzo Malvezzi, Via Zamboni 24/f, **t** 051 233 739 (*moderate*). In an old *palazzo* overlooking S. Giacomo Maggiore; enjoy the ambience, eclectic art collection and the excellent local cuisine. The lunch *menu* is much cheaper. *Closed Sun and Mon.*

Godot, Via Cartoleria 12, **t** 051 226 315 (*moderate*). An informal, magnificently stocked wine bar, serving gourmet snacks, lunch and dinner, all made from the finest ingredients. Very popular. *Open until 2am. Closed Sun and Aug.*

Osteria del Sole, Vicolo Ranocchi, off Piazza Maggiore, no phone (*cheap*). A Bologna institution since 1468; long wooden tables where you can sample the excellent wine and eat food bought from the surrounding market. *Weekdays only, open until 9pm; closed Aug.*

La Farfalla, Via Bertiera 12, **t** 051 225 656 (*cheap*). Authentic, rustic *trattoria*: delicious *tortellini in brodo*, aubergine *parmigiana*, stuffed courgettes, *bollito misto* and, for the bold, donkey with polenta, all accompanied by jugs of house wine. Arrive early for a seat. No credit cards. *Closed Sat eve and Sun.*

Pasticceria Majani, Via dei Carbonesi 5. Dates back to 1796; famous for its *cioccolata scorza.*

La Torinese, Piazza Re Enzo 1. A century old and a shrine for hot chocolate and pastries.

Nightlife

An ancient university city like Bologna stays up later than most. People eat late – around 10pm – and plenty of bars and cafés open till 3am. No visitor should leave without sampling one of the traditional ***osterie***, which serve food, have live music, and usually open late.

Cantina Bentivoglio, Via Mascarella 4, **t** 051 265 416. Smart, lively cellar for live jazz, with food and an endless wine list. *Open till 2am.*

Chet Baker Jazz Club, Via Polese 7/a, **t** 051 223 795, *www.chetbaker.com*. Intimate, underground jazz bar: come for dinner and stay, or arrive later for live jazz (€10 with one drink).

greatest modern painter, Giorgio Morandi (1890–1964), whose fierce gaze transforms the mundane with startling intensity; as Umberto Eco put it, he 'made the dust sing'.

Opposite the Palazzo del Podestà, the **Basilica di San Petronio**, begun by Antonio da Vicenza (1390), is the fifth-largest church in Italy. It would have been even larger, but in 1565 Pope Pius IV ordered the Bolognese to spend their money on the university's Archiginnasio instead. Bologna was so miffed that it has never bothered to finish the façade; however, it does have a remarkable portal (1425), with Old and New Testament scenes by Jacopo della Quercia of Siena. His reliefs are landmarks in the evolution of the early Renaissance, and seem strangely modern – almost Art Deco in sensibility. The lofty interior saw the coronation of Charles V as Holy Roman Emperor; here too, in 1655, the astronomer Cassini traced a meridian on the floor and designed the huge astronomical clock, which tells the time by a shaft of light admitted via an *oculus* in the vaulting at noon. Giovanni da Modena contributed some exceedingly strange (and bigoted) frescoes in the first chapel on the left, and filled the fourth with one of the most dramatic, populous *Last Judgement* scenes ever painted (1415).

Via dell'Archiginnasio

The eastern side of Piazza Maggiore is closed by the elegant **Palazzo dei Banchi**; through its archways lies the joyful little district that spreads through **Via Pescherie Vecchie** and **Via Clavature**, full of market stands, restaurants and fancy food shops. Next to the Palazzo dei Banchi, the **Museo Civico Archeològico** (*open Tues–Sat 9–6.30, Sun and hols 10–6.30; adm*) crams one of Italy's best collections of antiquities into its dusty cases. There are beautifully wrought urns and jewellery from the Iron Age Villanova culture; funerary art and spectacular carved tombstones from Etruscan Velzna; a famous embossed urn (the *Situla di Certosa*) and Greek Attic vases, as well as Roman and Egyptian finds. The next long porticoed façade is the **Archiginnasio** (*open Mon–Sat 9–1; adm free*), former seat of the University and now the **Biblioteca Comunale**, its walls covered with the escutcheons and memorials of famous scholars.

Two Leaning Towers

At the eastern end of Via Rizzoli stand a veritable odd couple: the Laurel and Hardy of medieval architecture. In the early Middle Ages, such towers were status symbols, and the **Due Torri** were built in 1119 in a competition between two families. The winner, the svelte 318ft **Torre degli Asinelli** (*open summer daily 9–6; winter daily 9–5; adm*), is still the tallest building in Bologna, tilting about 7ft out of true; there are 500 head-spinning steps to the top, but the view is worth it. Its sidekick, the **Torre delle Garisenda**, sways 3ft more tipsily to the south; in 1360 it became such a threat to public safety that its top was lopped off, leaving only a squat 157ft stump.

East of the Centre: The Radial Streets

The east end was the fashionable part of medieval Bologna, and remains so today. From the towers four streets fan out to gates in the eastern walls of the old city. The southernmost, **Via Santo Stefano**, leads to a quartet of churches, all part of the monastery of **Santo Stefano** (*open daily 9–12.15 and 3–6.15; adm free*), founded by St Petronius, who planned to reproduce the seven holy sites of Jerusalem here. You can enter this unique and harmonious 8–12th-century ensemble through the **Chiesa del Crocifisso**; to the left is **San Sepolcro**, a strangely irregular temple containing the equally curious Edicola di San Petronio, a large pulpit adorned with reliefs; the saint's bones are visible through a tiny hole at floor level. The circle of columns around it survives from an earlier temple to the Egyptian goddess Isis; a single column outside the circle was claimed to be the column to which Christ was bound during his flagellation. A door behind this leads into **SS. Vitale e Agricola**, Bologna's oldest church, from the 5th century. Beyond it, the Cortile di Pilato contains an 8th-century bathtub with the sinister reputation of being the basin in which Pontius Pilate washed his hands. The fourth church, the 13th-century **Trinità**, contains a wonderful folk-art *Adoration of the Magi* from the 1370s, with figures painted by Simone de' Crocefissi.

Strada Maggiore and Via San Vitale

The palace-lined **Strada Maggiore** follows the route of the Via Emilia. At no.44 the 18th-century **Palazzo Davia-Bargellini** (*museums open Tues–Sat 9–2, Sun 9–1; adm free*) is known as the Palazzo dei Giganti for Gabriele Brunelli's two Baroque telamones around the entrance. It contains a small but excellent collection of early Bolognese painting, including Vitale da Bologna's famous smiling *Madonna dei Denti*, perhaps most characteristic of the 14th-century Bolognese school. Beyond the palace, the *portici* intermingle with the arcades of the city's Gothic jewel, **Santa Maria dei Servi** (*open 7–1 and 3.30–8*), begun in 1346. Inside are fragments of a fresco by Vitale da Bologna, a late work by Crespi and a rare *Madonna* by Giotto's master Cimabue (in the ambulatory), which you'll need to illuminate to see.

Via Zamboni and the University

From the Towers, the **Via Zamboni** leads before long into the Piazza Rossini and the **Conservatorio G.B. Martini** (*open Mon–Sat 9–1; closed Aug; adm*), where the composer Rossini studied from 1806 to 1810. Next door in the 13th-century **San Giacomo Maggiore** (*open daily 7–12 and 4–6*), the Capella Bentivoglio contains frescoes by the Ferrarese Lorenzo Costa and a fine altarpiece by Bologna native Francesco Francia, while the Baroque Cappella Poggi is entirely decorated by Pellegrino Tibaldi. Costa and Francia both had a hand in the lively frescoes in the **Oratory of Santa Cecilia** (*open summer 10–1 and 3.30–6.30, winter 10–1 and 3–6; adm free*), entered from Via Zamboni.

Further up, beyond the **Teatro Comunale** (1763), the **University** is housed in Pellegrino Tibaldi's Mannerist **Palazzo Poggi**, which contains frescoes by Tibaldi in the hall, early illusionistic *quadratura* ceiling painting and more Mannerist paintings in the Library. The university buildings also house a number of small, specialist museums (*all open Mon–Fri 9–5.30; adm free*).

A block north of Via Zamboni, the **Pinacoteca Nazionale** (*Via Belle Arti 56; open Tues–Sun 9–7; adm*) stores Bologna's most important art; the most famous painting is probably Raphael's *Ecstasy of St Cecilia*. Among the 14th-century Bolognese artists Vitale da Bologna emerges as the star with his intense *St George and the Dragon*; there's a Giotto polyptych, and fine Renaissance works by Antonio and Bartolomeo Vivarini and Cima da Conegliano of Venice. Besides works by Parmigianino, Tibaldi, dell'Abate, Perugino and Titian, the Carracci brothers get a room to themselves, as does Guido Reni, whose classical precision and command of colour and composition were a refreshing advance on the fevered exaggeration of the Mannerists. In the rooms that follow, true gems are mixed with a helping of dross; Domenichino, Guercino, Francesco Albani, Donato Creti and Giuseppe Maria Crespi all appear.

North and West of Piazza Maggiore

A block north of Piazza Nettuno, Via dell'Indipendenza passes the **Duomo di San Pietro**, remodelled in the Baroque style and not very interesting. Just opposite, Via Manzoni leads to the *quattrocento* Palazzo Fava-Ghisliardi, site of the **Museo Civico Medioevale e del Rinascimento** (*open Tues–Sat 9–6.30, Sun and hols 10–6.30; adm*), one of the unmissable sights of the city. Aside from armour, ceramics, glass and Renaissance sculpture, there is an outstanding collection of the tombs of medieval scholars, carved with lifelike images of professors expounding to perplexed, earnest, daydreaming students; exceptionally intricate ivories; a colossal bronze propaganda statue of that most arrogant of popes, Boniface VIII; even a 13th-century English cope. Several rooms of the *palazzo* are open to the public, frescoed by all three Carracci and other Bolognese painters with scenes from classical mythology.

Via Ugo Bassi runs west from Piazza Nettuno past the **Mercato Coperto** to the narrow and lively **Piazza Malpighi**, site of the unique **Tombs of the Glossatori**, little pavilions with pyramidal roofs raised on slender columns, built as memorials to four notable professors of law of the 13th century. Backing onto the square is the apse of the lovely Gothic **San Francesco**, begun in 1236 when St Francis was still alive and characteristic of Bologna's medieval churches, its striking interior all white with brick piers and vaulting. On the high altar is a beautiful 14th-century marble *ancona* (1393), with various saints and wonderfully naturalistic scenes from the saint's life.

South of Piazza Maggiore

South of the Archiginnasio, Via Garibaldi leads south to **San Domenico**, built in 1251 to house the relics of St Dominic, founder of the Dominican order of preaching friars, who died here in 1221. Inside is his spectacular tomb, the Arca di San Domenico. Nicolò Pisano and his school executed the beautiful reliefs of the saint's life, while Nicolò dell'Arca added the statues of Bologna's patron saints on top; he died mid-project, leaving a 20-year-old refugee from Florence named Michelangelo to finish them off. The decorative scheme in the chapel opposite is a collaborative effort of several artists, including Guido Reni, Ludovico Carracci and Francesco Albani. Behind the high altar is a set of beautiful wooden *intarsia* choir stalls (1549).

Santuario della Madonna di San Luca

Bus 20 from Via dell'Indipendenza/Via Ugo Bassi takes you as far as the Arco di Meloncello. ***Sanctuary*** *open daily 7–12.30 and 2.30–7; winter until 5.30.*

In the southwestern corner of the *centro storico* is the **Porta Saragozza**, from where the *portico* to beat all porticoes winds four kilometres up the Colle della Guardia, with 666 arches along the way. Beginning at the **Arco di Meloncello** (1732), there are 15 rest stops for prayer, corresponding to the 15 Mysteries of the life of the Virgin Mary. It culminates in the elliptical form of the **Santuario della Madonna di San Luca**, visible from all over Bologna. Built to house a 'Black Madonna', an icon attributed to St Luke, the church is richly decorated within and contains three paintings by Guido Reni and one by Guercino. From outside, there are fantastic views of the Apennines.

Day Trip from Bologna

Ferrara

Thanks to the rather tyrannical Este, this charming city enclosed by 9km of walls was one of the brightest stars of the Renaissance, with its own fine school of art led by the great Cosmè Tura, Ercole de' Roberti, Lorenzo Costa and Francesco del Cossa. Poets patronized by the Este produced three of the Renaissance's greatest epic poems: Boiardo's *Orlando Innamorato* (1483), Ariosto's better-known continuation of the same story, *Orlando Furioso* (1532), and Tasso's *Gerusalemme Liberata* (1581).

The City Centre

At the very centre of Ferrara towers the imposing **Castello Estense** (*castle residence open Tues–Sun 9.30–5; adm*), the very image of suave and intelligent tyranny. Initially a fortress, it was transformed by the Este into a residence in the 1400s. A few decorated rooms survive in the **ducal apartments**, among them some charming allegorical frescoes by Giovanni Settevecchi and Bastianino. The tour also takes in Renée of France's Calvinist chapel and the Torre dei Leoni, where the brothers of Alfonso I spent their lives after attempting a conspiracy in 1506.

Getting There and Around

Around two **trains** each hour serve Ferrara (30–40mins) from Bologna. There are also frequent **buses** (1hr approx.). The **train station** is outside the city walls, about 1km from the centre; city buses 1, 2, 3c or 5 will take you in. The **bus station** is near the corner of Rampari di San Paolo and Corso Isonzo (bus 2 connects it with the railway station).

Tourist Information

Ferrara: in the Castello Estense, **t** 0532 209 370, **f** 0532 212 266 (*open daily 9–1 and 2–6*).

Eating Out

Ferrara's most famous dish is **salama da sugo** – a sausage that is cured for a year, then gently boiled for about four hours and eaten with a spoon. When Renée, daughter of Louis XII of France, came to Ferrara, she brought her own vines, the origin of the local *Vino di Bosco*.

L'Oca Guiliva, Via Boccacanale–Santo Stefano, **t** 0532 207 628 (*moderate*). Good wine and good food with a traditional menu featuring *pasticcio di maccheroni alla ferrarese, salama da sugo* and *cappellacci di zucca*; the other menu changes every two weeks. There are 250 wines to choose from, some served by the glass. *Closed Mon and Tues lunch.*

Quel Fanastico Giovedì, Via Castelnuovo 9 (near Piazza del Travaglio), **t** 0532 760 570 (*moderate*). Intimate, creative restaurant with dishes prepared with an effortlessly light touch – salmon marinated in herbs, or squid stuffed with aubergines in a yellow pepper sauce, and game in season. Save room for dessert. *Closed Wed, late Jan and mid-July–mid-Aug. Booking essential.*

Antica Trattoria Il Cucco, Via Voltacasotto 3, off Via C. Mayr, **t** 0532 760 026 (*cheap*). Good place to indulge in traditional classics: *cappellacci con la zucca* and, if you book ahead, *salama da sugo* or *pasticcio alla ferrarese* for *secondi*, followed by traditional *ciambella* and sweet wine. *Closed Wed.*

Al Brindisi, Via Adelardi, behind the Cathedral (*cheap*). Supposedly one of the oldest *enoteche* in the world. Now a convivial old wood-panelled place with fine cheeses, *salama da sugo* and other treats. *Closed Mon.*

South of the *castello*, Corso dei Martiri leads to the handsome, rose-coloured **cathedral**, begun in 1135 by Wiligelmo of Modena fame (*see* p.160) and his follower Nicolò. Its glory is its marble **portico**, guarded by lions and griffins. Nicolò executed the relief on the tympanum of *St George* and the various Old Testament scenes above; the pediment above the loggia is carved with a magnificent 13th-century *Last Judgement* by an unknown sculptor. The interior suffered a catastrophic remodelling in 1710, but you can see the best works across Piazza Trento e Trieste in the **Museo della Cattedrale** (*open Tues–Sun 9–1 and 3–6; adm*), among them the lovely marble *Madonna of the Pomegranite* by Jacopo della Quercia and two painted organ shutters that rank among the greatest surviving works of Cosmè Tura: a lovely naturalistic *Annunciation* and the remarkable, surreal *St George*.

East of the Centre

From behind the cathedral, Via Voltapaletto will take you out to the east end of Ferrara, its streets full of beautifully restored palaces. The most famous of these is the **Palazzo Schifanoia** (*open Tues–Sun 9–6; adm; joint ticket available*) on Via Scandiana. The reason for visiting is a single bare room, the **Salone dei Mesi**, frescoed *c.* 1475 for Borso d'Este by Ferrara's finest: Cosmè Tura, Ercole de' Roberti and Francesco del Cossa, and probably other hands too. The scenes of mythological and allegorical subjects, peopled by amiable 15th-century aristocrats, are believed to have been inspired by Petrarch's *Triumphs* – in each month a different god 'triumphs', most famously in April's *Triumph of Venus*, showing a rare Renaissance kiss.

South of the Schifanoia, the elegant **Palazzo di Lodovico Il Moro** (*Via XX Settembre 124*) contains the excellent **Museo Archeològico Nazionale** (*open Tues–Sun 9–2; adm*), with a collection of finds from the ancient necropolis of the Graeco-Etruscan seaport of Spina, including Attic vases, some by noted painters of Athens. Down by the city walls, the convent of **Sant'Antonio in Polesine** (*ring the bell by the door; open Mon–Fri 9.30–11.30 and 3–5, Sat 9.30–11.15 and 3–4; donation*) hides a lovely surprise: three chapels entirely covered with some of the best medieval painting in Ferrara.

The Herculean Addition

North of the Castello Estense stretches the Herculean Addition, laid out by Biagio Rossetti for Ercole I in the 15th century. Corso Ercole I was intended to be the district's 'noble street', and attracted many to build palaces there. At the junction with Corsos Rossetti and Porta Mare, Rossetti built three big palaces: the **Palazzo Prosperi-Sacrati**; the **Palazzo Turchi di Bagno**; and the home of the Este dukes, the **Palazzo dei Diamanti** (*open Mon–Sat 9–2, Thurs till 7, hols 9–1; adm*), named for the 8,500 diamond-shaped stones that stud the façade. The *palazzo* houses the **Pinacoteca Nazionale**, beginning with fine 14th-century and early Renaissance painting by the likes of Mantegna, Giovanni Bellini, Gentile da Fabriano, Giovanni da Modena and Ercole de' Roberti. Next come rooms of Ferraresi: from the *quattrocento*, Cosmè Tura and several little-known artists; from the *cinquecento*, the Raphaelesque Garofalo, Bastianino, Girolamo da Carpi and Girolamo Marchesi. Later paintings include works by Scarsellino. Among many fine works by non-Ferrarese artists is Carpaccio's *Death of the Virgin*.

Overnighters from Bologna

Parma

Besides its prosperity and quality of life, Parma's admirers cite her splendid churches and elegant lanes, her artworks and antiquities, the lyrical strains of grand opera that waft from her Teatro Regio and the glories of her famous cheese and ham as reasons not only to visit, but to return again and again. With Parma's baptistry, the sculptor Benedetto Antelami (1177–1233) introduced the Italians to the idea of a building as a unified design, while the sensuous, subtle painting of Correggio (1494–1534) had a profound influence on many, most notably on Parmigianino.

Piazza Pilotta and Piazza della Pace

On **Piazza Pilotta**, the patched-together shell of the Palazzo della Pilotta contains Parma's greatest treasures. In the **Museo Archeològico Nazionale** (*open Tues–Sun 9am–1.30pm; adm*), the prize exhibit is the *Tabula Alimentaria*, a bronze tablet that records the contributions of private citizens to a special dole, sharing space with finds from Roman Velleia, Egyptian sarcophagi, Greek vases and Roman statues. Pass through the 17th-century wooden **Teatro Farnese** to reach the **Galleria Nazionale** (*open daily 9–1.45; adm*), featuring works mainly from Tuscany and Emilia-Romagna. Among the early Renaissance artists are Agnolo Gaddi, Giovanni di Paolo, Fra Angelico, Simone de' Crocifissi and Jacopo Loschi – star of the Parma *quattrocento*. Local talent of the late Renaissance is represented by Bartolomeo Schedoni. Some of Correggio's most celebrated works are here, including the *Madonna della Scadella*, as well as Parmigianino's *Marriage of St Catherine* and flirtatious *Turkish Slave*. Among the non-Italians are El Greco, Brueghel the Younger, Van Dyck and Holbein.

The south side of **Piazza della Pace** is occupied by the celebrated **Teatro Regio** (*entrance in Via Garibaldi, **t** 0521 218 910; open only by appointment*), one of operatic Italy's holy-of-holies. Its audiences are legendary, submitting the singers either to avalanches of flowers or catcalls from the upper balconies. Toscanini played in the orchestra here, now named in his honour. Across from the theatre is the church of **Madonna della Steccata** (*open daily 9–12 and 3–6*), its sumptuous interior chiefly prized for the hyper-elegant frescoes by Parmigianino on the arch to the sanctuary. To the north, bordering the graceful **Palazzo della Riserva**, the ex-convent of San Paolo contains the remarkable **Camera di San Paolo** (*open daily 9–1.45; adm*). In the 1510s its worldly abbess hired Correggio and Alessandro Araldi to fresco the refectory with mythological allegories representing 'the conquest of moral virtue'; Correggio portrayed the abbess herself as a sensuous Diana. The possibly heretical concepts expressed in these mysterious paintings led the pope to cloister the nuns in 1524.

Piazza Duomo

Strada Pisacane connects Piazza della Pace to Piazza Duomo, the heart of medieval Parma and the site of its superb cathedral and baptistry. The ambitious Romanesque

Getting There

Parma is easily reached by **train** from Bologna with about two trains each hour (55mins). There are **buses** (**t** 0521 273 251), but they're much less convenient. Both **train** and **bus stations** are north of the centre, on Piazzale Alberto Della Chiesa; take bus 1 or 8 to the centre (a 10-min walk).

Tourist Information

Parma: Strada Melloni 1/6, off the main Strada Garibaldi, **t** 0521 218 889, **f** 0521 234 735 (*open Mon–Sat 9–7, Sun 9–1*).

Shopping

Around Borgo Angelo Mazza you'll find perfume shops selling Borsari's ***Violetti di Parma***. The main **market** in Piazza Ghiaia is the most convenient place for local specialities.

Where to Stay

Parma ✉ 43100

Book two months ahead in May and Sept.

******Hotel Verdi**, Via Pasini 18 (facing the Parco Ducale) **t** 0521 293 539, **f** 0521 293 559, *hotelverdi@netvalley.it* (*very expensive*). A refined and intimate hotel in an elegant Liberty-style building, complete with marble floors, Murano lamps and marble baths. There are free bicycles, and an adjacent gourmet restaurant, the **Santa Croce**. *Hotel and restaurant closed for two weeks in Aug.*

*****Torino**, Borgo A. Mazza 7, **t** 0521 281 046, **f** 0521 230 725 (*moderate*). This has ample, comfortable rooms and very friendly staff; have breakfast in a Liberty-style room or out in the flower-filled courtyard. Free bicycles. *Closed most of Aug, and two weeks in Jan.*

***Brozzi**, Via Trento 11, **t** 0521 272 717 (*cheap*). A popular budget hotel with a good restaurant (*cheap*); rooms without bath.

Eating Out

Parizzi, Via Repubblica 71, **t** 0521 285 952 (*very expensive*). A large, cheerful place to dip into Parma's specialities, with delicious *prosciutto di Parma*, *crêpes alla parmigiana*, or *cappelletti*, as well as *scaloppe Parizzi*, with fontina and ham, and great desserts. Book ahead. *Closed Sun eve, Mon and most of Aug.*

Trattoria dei Corrieri, Strada del Conservatorio 1, **t** 0521 234 426 (*cheap*). Traditional Parma cuisine amid walls of old Parma photos and relics. The menu usually features salami and ham *antipasti*, *carpaccio* with rocket, pasta *alla parmigiana*, quail and a tasty *bollito misto* (boiled meats). This is *the* place, and everybody knows it. *Closed Sun.*

Antica Osteria Fontana, Via Farini 24a, **t** 0521 286 037 (*cheap*). This has been here for donkey's years. Wine is the main focus, with a good selection of charcuterie to make up a light meal around a bottle. *Closed Sun, Mon and most of Aug.*

Entertainment

Opera and **theatre** mobilize Parma more than anything, and September sees the **Verdi Festival**; contact Fondazione Verdi Festival, Via Farini 34, **t** 0521 289 028, **f** 0521 282 141. The main season at the **Teatro Regio** (**t** 0521 218 678; *box office open weekdays 10–2 and 5–7, Sat 9.30–12.30 and 4–7*) runs Dec–Mar.

For **listings**, seek out *Parmagenda* in shops or at the tourist office.

Duomo (*open daily, outside Mass times, 9–12.30 and 3–7; adm free*) is embellished with rows of shallow arches; the Labours of the Months decorate the central portal. Frescoes cover every inch of the interior, which has two masterpieces: a relief of the *Deposition from the Cross* by Antelami and, in the dome, Correggio's *Assumption* (1526–30), celebrated for its three-dimensional qualities.

The rosy octagonal **Baptistry** (*open daily 9–12.30 and 3–6; adm*) is a jewel of the Italian Romanesque, designed in 1196 by Antelami, who also carved the remarkable and elusive ribbon frieze of animals and allegories encircling it. Inside are his famous reliefs of the Months, with the Labours and zodiacal signs. The interior is one of the most complete ensembles of Italian medieval art, covered with paintings. The vault is divided into six zones with a starry heaven, with a grab-bag of biblical figures below.

The Oltratorrente

Across the river in the **Otratorrente** you can make two musical pilgrimages. The first is to the **tomb of Paganini** (a *15-min walk from the centre; open daily all year 7.45–12.30; May–Sept also 6–7; Oct and Feb–April also 2.30–5.30; Nov–Jan also 2–5*). He lies decked out in virtuoso splendour in Villetta cemetery, after the rest of Europe, suspecting his talents were diabolic, refused him Christian burial. The modest **birthplace of Toscanini** (1867–1957) is at Borgo Rudolfo Tanzi 13 (*open Tues–Sat 10–1 and 3–6, Sun 10–1; adm*), containing memorabilia and a copy of every record he ever made.

Modena

Modena puts on a class act; sleek and speedy, it also has a lyrical side of larger-than-life proportions. Luciano Pavarotti was born here, and its scenographic streets take on an air of mystery and romance when enveloped in the winter mists rising from the Po.

Via Aemilia is Modena's main thoroughfare, and it picks up one of its loveliest gems: the cobbled and partially porticoed Piazza Grande, site of the Lanfranco's celebrated Romanesque **Duomo di San Geminiano**, a living museum of medieval sculpture featuring magnificent carvings by the 12th-century sculptor Wiligelmo. His friezes around the **Lion Portal** illustrate scenes from the medieval mystery play on the Book of Genesis, while his **South Portal** depicts the life of Modena's patron, St Geminiano. A contemporary executed the fascinating reliefs on top of the buttresses: among them, a hermaphrodite and a nude woman with a dragon; a three-armed woman; a giantess with an ibis and a sphinx; a fork-tailed siren. These are copies; the originals are in the adjacent **Museo Lapidario** (*soon to reopen after restoration, ask at the tourist office or* **t** *059 216 078*). Lanfranco's charming interior is adorned with the great Pontile by the Campionese masters of Lake Lugano, carved with lion pillars and polychromed reliefs of the life of Christ, and incorporating a pulpit with excellent capitals.

Modena's other main sight is the **Palazzo dei Musei** (west along Via Aemilia), where the **Galleria Estense** (*open Tues, Fri, Sat 9–7, Wed and Thurs 9–2, Sun 9–1; closed Mon; adm*) houses works by Modena's greatest medieval painter, Tommaso da Modena, as well as bronzes by Il Riccio of Padua, a good Flemish collection, works by Palma Vecchio, Cima da Conegliano, Veronese and Tintoretto, even Velázquez. The Florentines really steal the show, especially Botticelli's ripe *Madonna con il Bambino*, but the painting you can't stop staring at will be the last known work of the *quattrocento* eccentric Cosmè Tura. His cadaverous, beautiful, horrific *St Anthony of Padua* (1484) is a life-sized vision of spiritual and anatomical deformity. Elsewhere in the *palazzo*, the **Biblioteca Estense** (*open Mon–Thurs 9–7.15, Fri and Sat 9–1.45*) displays a famous collection of illuminated manuscripts, including the *Bible of Borso d'Este*, a gorgeously coloured marvel illustrated in the 15th century by Taddeo Crivelli and Franco Rossi.

From Piazza Grande, Via C. Battisti leads to the huge Baroque **Palazzo Ducale**, once the home of the Este dukes and now the **National Military Academy**; some surviving frescoes and 18th-century rooms are on the guided tours (*open Sun only, except in Aug or when the Sunday is also a holiday; guided tours at 10 and 11; reservations necessary, book at the tourist office, or call* **t** *059 206 660*).

The streets south of the Piazza Grande are some of Modena's oldest and loveliest. In this neighbourhood you'll also find the city markets, including the delightful glass and iron **Mercato Coperto**, on Piazza XX Settembre, just south of Piazza Grande.

Getting There

Modena has frequent **train** connections with Bologna (25–30mins). The station is on Piazza Dante, a 10-min walk from the centre.

Tourist Information

Modena: Piazza Grande 17, **t** 059 206 660, **f** 059 206 659, *www.comune.modena.it*.

Market Days

There are **markets** held in Parco Novi Sad (*Mon morning*) and in Piazza XX Settembre (*Mon–Sat*).

Where to Stay

Modena ✉ 41100

****__Canalgrande__, Corso Canalgrande 6, **t** 059 217 160, **f** 059 221 674, *www.canalgrandehotel.it* (*expensive*). Once the *palazzo* of the Marchesi Schedoni, this hotel has 18th-century public rooms with crystal chandeliers and ceiling frescoes, and plush bedrooms with a/c. Ancient trees grace the pretty garden.

***__Milano__, Corso Vittorio Emanuele 68, **t** 059 223 011, **f** 059 225 136 (*moderate*). This is modern and functional, soundproofed, with posh bathrooms; you can also have a/c for a fee.

***__Centrale__, Via Rismondo 55, **t** 059 218 808, **f** 059 238 201 (*moderate*). Near the cathedral, with comfortable modern rooms.

Ask about the *cheap* rooms without bath at the Centrale and the Milano (*see* above).

*__Sole__, Via Malatesta 45, **t** 059 214 245 (*cheap*). A clean, old-fashioned *locanda* with seven basic but spacious rooms without bath.

Eating Out

Modena ✉ 41100

As well as balsamic vinegar, Modena prides itself on its *salumeria* and *prosciutto*. It is also the best place to taste *Lambrusco*.

Fini, Largo San Francesco, **t** 059 223 314 (*very expensive*). Founded in 1912, Fini has an almost endless menu of hearty regional pasta (the *pasticcio di tortellini* is exceptional), meat dishes (the famous *zampone* or *bollito misto*), and appetizers, all deliciously prepared. *Closed Mon, Tues and most of Aug.*

Cucina del Museo, Via Sant'Agostino 5, **t** 059 217 429 (*expensive*). A charming, intimate restaurant serving lovely artichoke ravioli, foie gras with balsamic vinegar, succulent pigeon with rosemary and melon and ginger sorbet. *Closed Mon and mid-July to mid-Aug.*

Osteria Ruggera, Via Ruggera 18, **t** 059 211 129 (*moderate*). A 150-year-old establishment near the cathedral; try the gnocchi with gorgonzola and walnuts, chops made with balsamic vinegar, and the famous *cotoletta alla Ruggera*. *Closed Tues and Aug.*

Aldina, Via Albinelli 40, opposite the Mercato Coperto, **t** 059 236 106 (*cheap*). Resolutely old-fashioned but good, and attracts a wide range of customers, all happy to plonk down €13 for a plate of fresh pasta, roast meat, dessert and a bottle of *Lambrusco*. *Open for lunch only, closed Sun and Aug.*

Entertainment

Modena is nearly as mad for culture as Parma and there is a full schedule of plays, ballet and concerts at venues around town. A weekly handout called *News Spettacolo* has all the listings; it's available just about anywhere.

Forlì

The Roman town of Forum Livii on the Via Emilia was elided over the centuries into Forlì, a city of over 100,000 people that has been around for 2,000 years without calling attention to itself in any way – a rare achievement in Italy. It did produce one outstanding Renaissance painter, Melozzo da Forlì, but as luck would have it the only frescoes he left in town were blasted to bits in the war. However, Forlì does have one little secret: Benito Mussolini was born in nearby Predappio and, favouring his home area, he left Forlì an open-air museum of Mussolinian architecture.

Forlì has an old sprawling *centro storico*, centred around Piazza Aurelio Saffi. Here, on the **Palazzo del Municipio**, rises the medieval **Torre Civica**, a victim of Allied bombing which was entirely rebuilt in the 1970s. In the corner of the square, the striking 12th-century **Basilica di San Mercuriale** is dominated by an impressive 235ft **campanile** (1180), Forlì's other landmark tower. On the main portal there's a fine lunette of the Magi by the school of Antelami, but the interior, buffeted by repeated renovations between the 17th and 19th centuries, has little to show besides the lovely *quattro-cento* tomb of Barbara Manfredi and an ocean of preposterous painting.

Corso della Repubblica leads east to the worthy **Museo Archeològico e Pinacoteca Saffi** (*open Tues and Thurs 9–1.30 and 3–5, Wed and Fri–Sat 9–1.30, Sun 9–1; adm free*),

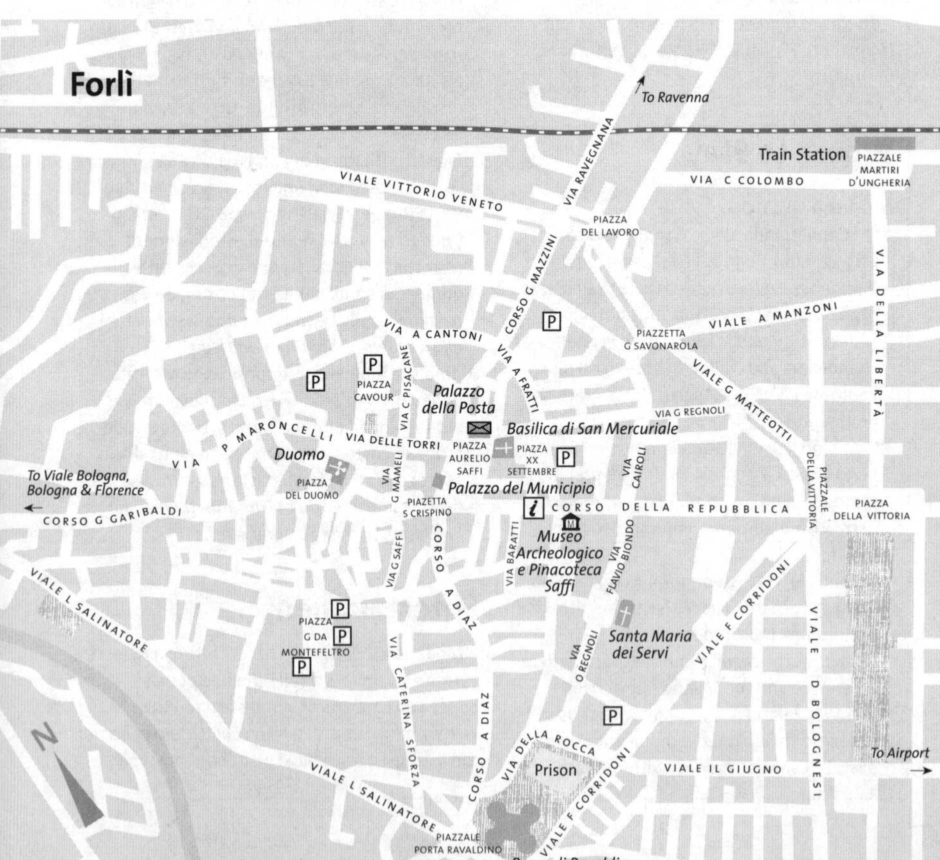

Getting to Forlì

Ryanair flies from London Stansted (2hrs10).

Getting from the Airport

Forlì's Ridolfi airport (**t** 0543 474 990) is on Via Seganti, 6km southeast of the centre. Buses (**t** 0543 27821) link the airport and Forlì's train station every 20mins (15mins; under €1).

A **taxi** to the centre costs about €11.

Getting Around

Forlì is small and it's easy to get around on foot, but there are buses (ATR; **t** 0543 27821). The **bus station** is on Via Oriani, 200m from the **train station**, on Piazza Martiri d'Ungheria. **Tickets** cost less than €1 and are available from tabbaco shops and from the train station.

For a **taxi**, call **Radio Taxi t** 0543 31111.

Car Hire

All the following are based at the airport.

Avis, **t** 0543 781 835.
CarFo, **t** 0543 473 507.
Europcar, **t** 0543 473 241.
Hertz, **t** 0543 782 637.

Tourist Information

Forlì: Piazzetta XC Pacifici 1/2, in the municipal offices, Piazza Saffi, **t** 0543 712 435, **f** 0543 712 434, *www.delfo.forli-cesena.it/prov/turismo*.

Market Days

Markets are held in **Piazza Saffi** (*Mon and Fri*).

Shopping

Forlì isn't known for any particular speciality, but you can pick up a range of *prodotti tipici* from the Romagna region around the town.

Where to Stay and Eat

Forlì ✉ 47100

★★★★**Principe**, Via Bologna 153, **t** 0543 701 570, **f** 0543 702 270 (*expensive–moderate*). Just out of the centre, with comfortable modern rooms (a/c) and a restaurant serving fine dishes such as salmon with tarragon.

★★★**Vittorino**, Via Baratti 4, **t** 0543 21521, **f** 0543 25933 (*cheap*). In the centre, with small and simple rooms.

La Volpe e l'Uva, Via. G. Saffi, **t** 0543 33600 (*moderate*). Based near the *pinacoteca*, serving a wide variety of reliable traditional dishes, including *tigelle*, green *garganelli*, fish and salads. *Closed Mon, and July–Aug.*

La Casa Rusticale dei Cavalieri Templari, Via Bologna 275, **t** 0543 701 888 (*moderate*). In a house built as a Templar lodge in the 13th century. It's *the* place for delicious *piadine*, home-made pasta and classic Romagnoli *secondi*. Lunchtime *menus di degustazione* at €20 and €30. *Closed Sun and Mon.*

a rare chance to see (minor) paintings by Fra Angelico outside Tuscany, as well as works by local artist Marco Palmezzano, Il Francia, Francesco del Cossa and others. There are also Flemish tapestries, ethnographic exhibits and ceramics, but pride of place is held by Antonio Canova's marble *Hebe*, a rarefied neoclassical fantasy. The nearby **Santa Maria dei Servi** merits a stop for the finely sculpted tomb of Luffo Numai (1502) and a frescoed chapel of the 1300s. West of Piazza Saffi, the **Duomo** on Corso Garibaldi was completely rebuilt in 1841; note the painting inside of 15th-century firemen. South of the centre, the picturesque 15th-century **Rocca di Ravaldino** belonged to Caterina Sforza and now serves as a prison.

We promised you Mussolini Deco, and you'll find it at the eastern edge of the centre, on and around **Piazza della Vittoria**, centre of an entire district laid out between 1925 and 1932. A little Bauhaus, a little Chicago World's Fair, and a touch of travertine Roman monumentalism are the main ingredients, with recurring conceits like the porticos of square columns. The entire ensemble is wonderfully evocative, a reminder of just how much Fascism depended on mass spectacles and settings appropriate to them.

Day Trip from Forlì

Faenza

'Faïence ware' was born here in the 16th century with the invention of a new style of majolica: a piece was given a solid white glaze then rapidly, almost impressionistically, decorated with two tones of yellow and blue. It caused a sensation, and was in such demand throughout Europe that Faenza became a household name.

Today Faenza has regained much of its renown as a ceramics centre, with 500 students enrolled in its Istituto d'Arte per la Ceramica, as well as some 60 artists with workshops in the town. The **Associati Ente Ceramica** (*Voltone della Molinella 2*) exhibits their work and has a list of studios to visit (*see* Shopping, below). The **Museo Internazionale delle Ceramiche** (*Viale Baccarini 19; open April–Oct Tues–Sat 9–7, Sun 9.30–1 and 3–7; Nov–Mar Tues–Fri 9–1.30, Sat and Sun 9.30–1 and 3–6; adm*) houses a magnificent collection of ceramics, centred on 16th- and 17th-century Italian works. There are fine Liberty-style pieces, and some by Picasso, Matisse, Chagall and Rouault.

Beyond the plates, Faenza is a shabby old town, but it does have a grand centrepiece, the adjacent **Piazza della Libertà** and **Piazza del Popolo**, with a lovely double portico, the **Voltone della Molinella** (1600s), linking up to Piazzetta Nenni. On Piazza della Libertà, the unfinished Renaissance **Duomo** has some good Renaissance sculpture in its severe interior, notably in the Capella di San Savino, with a beautiful marble arca decorated with reliefs by the Tuscan Benedetto da Maiano, and ceramic work by the masterful Florentine Andrea della Robbia, who did the colourful tondo over the altar.

Faenza has a number of neoclassical buildings, the finest of which is the 1802 **Palazzo Milzetti** on Via Tonducci (*open Mon–Sat 8.30–1.30, Thurs also 2.30–5; adm*). The palace contains some fine rooms with painted and stucco decoration influenced by the discovery of Pompeii; there is also some esoteric Masonic symbolism.

Getting There

There are **trains** from Forlì to Faenza every 20mins (journey 10mins).

Tourist Information

Faenza ✉ **48018**: Piazza del Popolo 1, **t** 0546 25231.

Market Days

Markets are in **Piazza del Popolo** and **Piazza della Libertà** (*Tues, Thurs and Sat mornings*).

Shopping

Particularly good ceramics studios are: **Carlo Zauli**, Via della Croce 6; **Ivo Sassi**, Via Bondiollo 11; **Ceramiche Cortese**, 49 Corso Mazzini; and the **Consorzio Ceramiche**, Via Pietro Borlotti.

Eating Out

Le Volte, Corso Mazzini 54, **t** 0546 661 600 (*moderate*). Hidden away in old wine cellars beneath the Galleria Gessi: specialities include *tortelloni al radicchio*, duck breast roasted with cabbage and pepper, or rack of lamb in a herb crust. *Closed Sun.*

Enoteca Astorre, Piazza della Libertà 16, **t** 0546 681 407 (*moderate*). This offers an array of wines accompanied by bruschetta, *piadine* and tasty snacks; they also do full meals and two-course lunches for €9. *Closed Sun.*

Overnighters from Forlì

Ravenna

Innocently tucked away among the art towns of Emilia-Romagna, there is one famous city that has nothing to do with Renaissance popes and potentates, sports cars or socialists. Little, in fact, has been heard from Ravenna in the last thousand years. Before that time, however, this little city's career was simply astounding: heir to Rome itself and, for a time, the leading city of western Europe. The advancing delta gradually dried out all Ravenna's magic, at least on the outside, but step inside the city's ancient monuments, including five sites on UNESCO's Heritage List, and you'll see things you can't see anywhere else in the world.

San Vitale and the Mausoleum of Galla Placidia

Via San Vitale, near Porta Adriana, the western gate of the centro storico*; open summer daily 9–7; winter daily 9–5.30; adm block ticket (*see *p.166).*

At first this dark old church may not seem like much, but as soon as the lights come on, the 1,400-year-old mosaics ignite into an explosion of colour. The mosaics of San Vitale, Ravenna's best, are one of the last great works of art of the ancient world, and one of Christianity's first. The octagonal church, begun in 525, was a breathtakingly original departure in architecture. Take some time to admire the exterior, with its beautiful interplay of octagons, arches, gables and exedrae. Then step inside, for nowhere in the world will you find anything as brilliant as San Vitale's **mosaics**. The best, in the **choir**, have deep blue skies and rich green meadows, highlighted by brightly coloured birds and flowers. Two lunettes show the hospitality of Abraham and the sacrifice of Isaac, and the offerings of Abel and Melchizedek, set under fiery clouds with hands of benediction extended from Heaven. At the front of the choir the **triumphal arch** has mosaic portraits of the Apostles supported by a pair of dolphins. The **apse** is dominated by portraits of Justinian and Theodora; Justinian's cute daisy slipper steps on the foot (a convention of Byzantine art to show who's boss) of General Belisarius. The mosaics are such an attraction that you might miss the other features of San Vitale – including the **maze** under your feet. Also worthy of note are the lower walls, covered in thin sheets of precious marbles; the alabaster 6th-century altar; the ancient reliefs near the choir; and the sarcophagus of Quintus Bonus.

The modest brick exterior of the **Mausoleum of Galla Placidia**, set in the grounds of San Vitale, makes the brilliant mosaics within that much more of a surprise. Those representing *St Lawrence*, with his flaming gridiron, and Jesus, as the *Good Shepherd*, are as rich as the ones in San Vitale. The vault itself, a deep blue firmament glowing with dazzling golden stars, is the most remarkable feature; in the centre, a golden cross represents the unimaginable, transcendent God above the heavens.

The cloisters attached to San Vitale now house the **Museo Nazionale** (*open summer Tues–Sun 8.30–7.30; winter Tues–Sun 8.30–5.30; adm, individual or joint ticket,* see *p.166*), with Etruscan finds, coins, ceramics, ivories, good Roman plumbing and more.

Getting There

Buses from Forlì go to Ravenna every ½hr or so (40mins). **Trains** are less frequent and take longer, as you have to change. Ravenna's **bus station** is on Via Darsena across the tracks from the **train station** on Piazzale Farini (take the tunnel under the tracks between them). It's a short walk to the centre from the train station.

Tourist Information

Ravenna: APT: Via Salara 8, **t** 0544 35404 or **t** 35755, **f** 0544 35094.

Block ticket: Obligatory for the major sights (€4.50). Includes Mausoleo di Galla Placida, San Vitale, Sant' Appollinare Nuovo, Santo Spirito, Battistero Neoniano and Cappella Arcivescovile. Unless stated, all sights *open summer daily 9–7; winter daily 9–5.30*.

Where to Stay and Eat

Ravenna ✉ 48100

★★★**Cappello**, Via IV Novembre 41, **t** 0544 219 813 (*expensive*). In a 14th-century *palazzo* reputed to have been the home of Francesca da Rimini, with seven big and lovely rooms. Frescoes, wood-panelled ceilings and a romantic restaurant (*open to non-guests*), with *menus* at €35 and €30. *Hotel open all year; restaurant closed Mon lunch, Sun, Aug.*

★★★**Diana**, Via G. Rossi 47, **t** 0544 39164, **f** 0544 30001 (*moderate*). In an 18th-century palace, near the tomb of Galla Placidia. Delightful, comfortable hotel with a Baroque lobby and a/c and TV in every big quiet room. The delicious breakfast is worth the price.

★★★**Centrale Byron**, Via IV Novembre 14, **t** 0544 33479, **f** 0544 34114 (*moderate*). Old favourite, ageing gracefully just off the Piazza del Popolo: with a/c, some very nice rooms and some very plain ones in the *cheap* range.

Taverna San Romualdo, Via Sant' Alberto 364, **t** 0544 483 447 (*moderate*). Not far from San Vitale. Typically Romagnolo *osteria* serving excellent-value hearty dishes. Seasonal *antipasti* include *tortellacci* stuffed with nettles with mascarpone and pine nuts, octopus stewed with balsamic vinegar and served with rocket, or a good choice of game in winter. Desserts are a must: try the nougat *semifreddo*. *Closed Tues.*

La Gardela, Via Ponte Marino 3, **t** 0544 217 147 (*moderate*). Small restaurant with a/c in the centre. Makes its own *tortelloni*; be sure to try *scaloppine* with *taleggio* and rocket, and sample the many grappas. *Closed Thurs.*

Ca' de Ven (the 'house of wine'), Via Corrado Ricci 24, **t** 0544 30163 (*cheap*). An *enoteca* in a beautiful building with painted ceilings, with a huge selection of Emilia-Romagna wines and snacks using local cheeses, hams and sausages. Suitably calm and the perfect place to while away an afternoon after a morning with the Byzantines. *Closed Mon.*

Exceptional works include the 6th-century Byzantine carved screens, a unique sculpture of *Hercules capturing the Cerynean hind*, also 6th-century, and a wonderful set of **frescoes** (*c.* 1320) by Pietro da Rimini, the Romagna's greatest painter of the *trecento*.

Ravenna's Centre

At the centre of Ravenna lies the Venetian-style **Piazza del Popolo**. South of here, a modest pavilion shelters the **Tomb of Dante**; Ravenna will gently but perpetually remind you that it sheltered the storm-tossed poet in his last years. Further south, behind Ravenna's **cathedral** (*open summer daily 9–7; winter daily 9–5.30; adm block ticket*, see *above*), the **Museo Arcivescovile** houses treasures such as the 6th-century ivory throne of Bishop Maximian, and a 6th-century silver reliquary. The biggest surprise is in the **Oratorio di Sant'Andrea**, with some of Ravenna's best mosaics: the finest are the excellent portraits of saints decorating the arches.

East of here, on Via Roma, the 6th-century church of **Sant'Apollinare Nuovo** (*open summer daily 9–7; winter daily 9–5.30; adm block ticket*, see *above*) holds the finest mosaics in Ravenna after San Vitale. Within, on walls that lean outwards rather dangerously, are the mosaics, begun under Theodoric and completed by the Byzantines, on panels that stretch the length of the church. On the left, you see the *City of Classe*, with ships in the protected harbour; on the right is the *Palatium*, Theodoric's royal palace. Beyond these are processions of martyrs bearing crowns.

Just off Via Roma, between Via Paolo Costa and Via Armando Diaz, the **Arian Baptistry** (*open daily summer 8.30–7; winter 8.30–5.30; adm free*) preserves a fine mosaic ceiling, with the Apostles arranged around a scene of the *Baptism of Jesus*. Jesus here is pictured nude, something the orthodox would never have allowed.

Rimini

With its 15km of broad beaches, 1,600 hotels, 751 bars and 343 restaurants, Rimini has been dubbed 'the Beach of Europe'. But the resort has its advantages. Noisy as it is, it's a respectable, family place, relatively cheap for northern Italy, convenient and well organized. Also, tucked away behind the beach is a genuine old city, damaged in the Second World War but inviting, and offering one four-star Renaissance attraction.

The Tempio Malatestiano

Open Mon–Sat 8–12.30 and 3.30–6.30, Sun 9–1 and 3.30–7; adm free.

While the rest of Rimini was shattered by bombs, some special angel seems to have been watching over the city's unique Renaissance monument, the eclectic and thoroughly mysterious work that has come to be known as Tempio Malatestiano. To transform this unfinished 13th-century Gothic Franciscan church into his temple Sigismondo Malatesta called in Leon Battista Alberti to redesign the exterior and Agostino di Duccio for the reliefs inside. Alberti's unfinished exterior grievously feels the lack of the planned cupola that might have tied the composition together. Inside, however, are some of the greatest works of the Renaissance: Agostino's **sculptural reliefs**, an enchanted forest of allegories, putti and enigmatic symbols and mottoes. Some of the best depict the planets and signs of the zodiac; note especially the enchanting Moon – Cynthia in her silver car. Below the reliefs, the recurring devices of the decorative scheme are an omnipresent S and I, for Sigismondo and Isotta, and lots of elephants, the Malatesta's heraldic symbol. Among other works are a crucifix by Giotto and Piero della Francesca's famous fresco of Sigismondo and his patron.

Along the Corso di Augusto

The centre of Rimini around **Piazza Tre Martiri** has been strikingly modernized in recent years, though the new aspects fit in remarkably well with the historic surroundings. Running through the square is the **Corso di Augusto**, the *decumanus* of old Ariminium, with relics of the Roman city at either end. At the southern end stands the well-preserved **Arch of Augustus** (27 BC); at the northern end is the five-arched **Bridge of Tiberius** (AD 21), badly patched up after damage in the Greek–Gothic wars. From here to the sea, along the **Porto Canale**, stretches Rimini's colourful fishing port.

Near the bridge, **Piazza Cavour** was the early medieval centre of town. Here stands the bulky castle **Rocca Sismondo**, built by Sigismondo in 1446. Little survives besides the relief elephant over the gate, Sigismondo's symbol, but one part of the castle has become the temporary home of the extraordinary **Museo delle Culture Extraeuropee** (*open Tues–Fri 8.30–12.30, Sat and Sun 5–7; adm*). This contains over 3,000 pieces of ancient and modern art from Africa, Oceania and the Americas.

Not many of the works of the *trecento* 'school of Rimini' can still be seen in the city, but some of the best are in **Sant'Agostino**, on Via Cairoli just off Piazza Cavour. Otherwise, works by the school can be seen in the **Museo della Città** (*Via L. Tonini 1; open Sept–June Tues–Sat 8.30–12.30 and 5–7, Sun 4–7; June–Sept Tues–Sat 10–12.30 and 4.30–7.30, Sun 4.30–7.30; July and Aug Fri 9–11pm; adm*), east of the Corso di Augusto on Piazza Ferrari. Also present are works by Rimini's most accomplished *seicento* painter, Guido Cagnacci, as well as Guercino, Guido Reni, Ghirlandaio and Giovanni Bellini. Nearby on Via Gambalunga is the **Cineteca del Comune di Rimini** (*Via Gambalunga 27; open Mon–Fri 8–1, Tues and Thurs 8–1 and 3–6, Sat 8.30–12.30, Sun 3–6; adm free*), with a film library devoted to films about Rimini or made by Riminese directors; it also houses drawings by Fellini, who started his career as a caricaturist.

Getting There and Around

Two or three **trains** each hour serve Rimini from Forlì (30mins approx.). The train station is on Piazzale Cesare Battisti, and the Tempio Malatestiano is a 10-min walk away. In summer **buses** run regularly along the beach strip.

Tourist Information

Rimini: Main office, Piazzale C. Battisti, next to the station, **t** 0541 51331, **f** 0541 27927; also on the beach at Piazza Fellini 3, **t** 0541 56902, **f** 0541 56598. The Municipio, on Piazza Cavour, has details on entertainment.

Where to Stay and Eat

Rimini ✉ 47900

Expect a modern room with a balcony, pleasant but unimaginative; in high season you'll probably have to take half board.

*****__Grand Hotel__, Via Ramusio 1, at Marina Centro, **t** 0541 56000, **f** 0541 56866, *ghotel@iper.net* (*luxury*). The palace of dreams that helped make Rimini what it is today. Indecently luxurious, glittering with brass and chandeliers, it has its own orchestra, park, pool, beach, tennis, and fitness centre.

****__Milton__, Via Cappellini 1/a, **t** 0541 54600, **f** 0541 54698 (*expensive*). On the beach with elegant, soundproofed rooms, this has a good restaurant, a garden bar, pool, fitness centre and tennis. *Closed mid-Dec–mid-Jan.*

***__Esedra__, Viale Caio Duilio 3, **t** 0541 23421, **f** 0541 24424 (*moderate*). A handsome seaside 1890s villa, with spacious modern rooms within a garden and a pool; a sauna, a gym and a big buffet breakfast are included.

***__Saxon__, Via Cirene 36, **t/f** 0541 391 400 (*cheap*). Central, pleasant and friendly.

Osteria Saraghina's, Via Poletti 32, **t** 0541 783 794 (*moderate*). A popular and friendly spot in the heart of town, serving seasonal dishes and seafood with a light touch. *Open eves only and Sun lunch; closed Mon.*

Dallo Zio, Via S. Chiara 16, **t** 0541 786 747 (*moderate*). A seafood palace in the old town, offering marine lasagna and other surprises; popular with locals and tourists. *Closed Mon.*

4 Moschetteri, Via S. Maria al Mare, just off Piazza Ferrari, **t** 0541 56496 (*cheap*). A near perfect *trattoria*: excellent pizza and pasta, and Romagna favourites that change daily.

Osteria de Borg, Via Dei Forzieri 12, **t** 0541 56071 (*cheap*). Small *osteria* in San Giuliano; try the imaginative *tortellini* stuffed with carrot or *strozzapreti* with broccoli and spicy sausage. *Open eves only, and lunch on Sun and hols; closed Mon, half of Jan and half of July.*

Tuscany

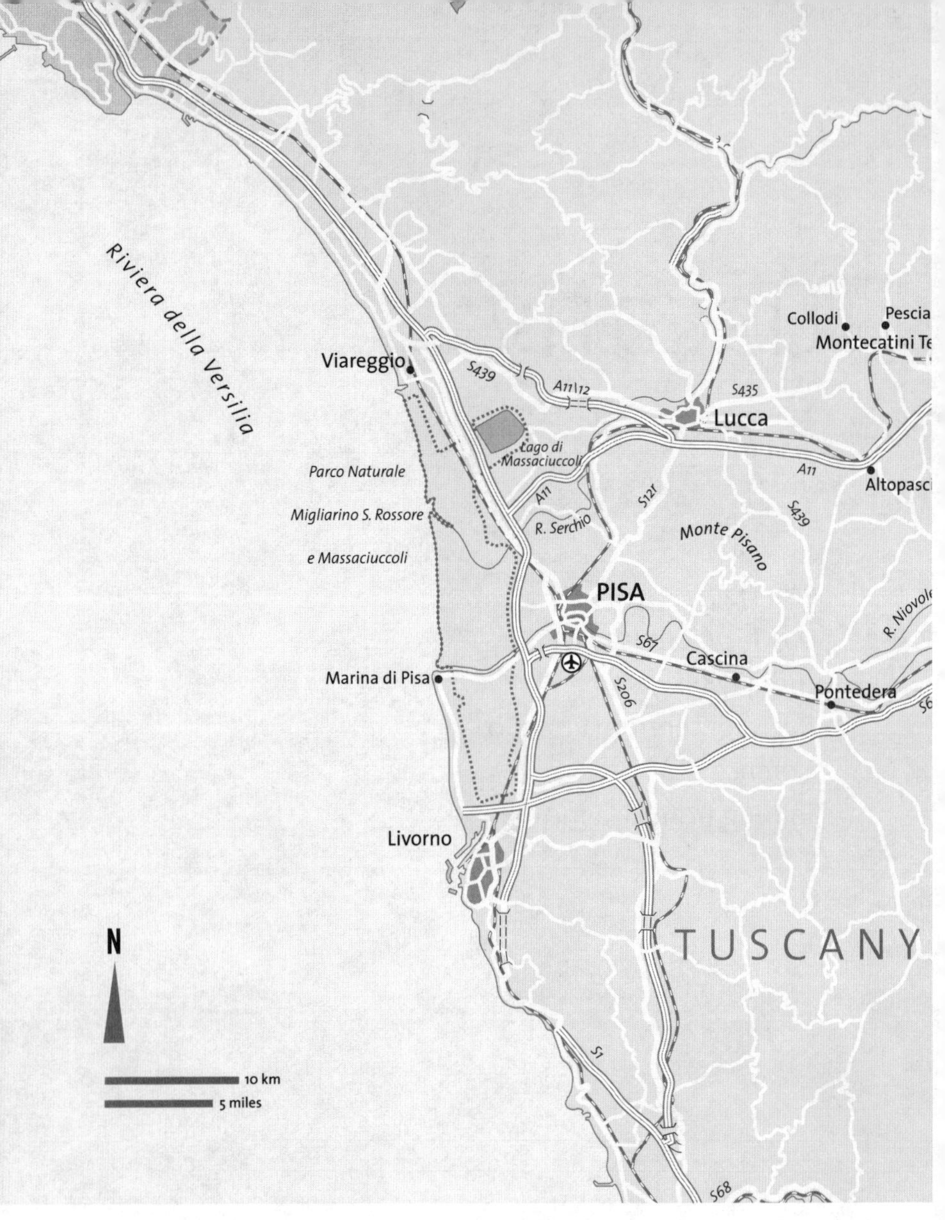

No region could be more essentially Italian. Its Renaissance culture and art became the whole of Italy's, and its dialect, as refined by Dante, cast a hundred other dialects into the shadows to become the Italian language. Nevertheless, Tuscany seems to stand a bit aloof from the rest of the nation; it keeps its own counsel, never changes its ways, and faces the world with a Mona Lisa smile that has proved irresistible to northern Europeans since the days of Shelley and Browning.

For a province that has contributed so much to western civilization since the Middle Ages, Tuscany's career remains slightly mysterious. Out of the Dark Ages, inexplicably,

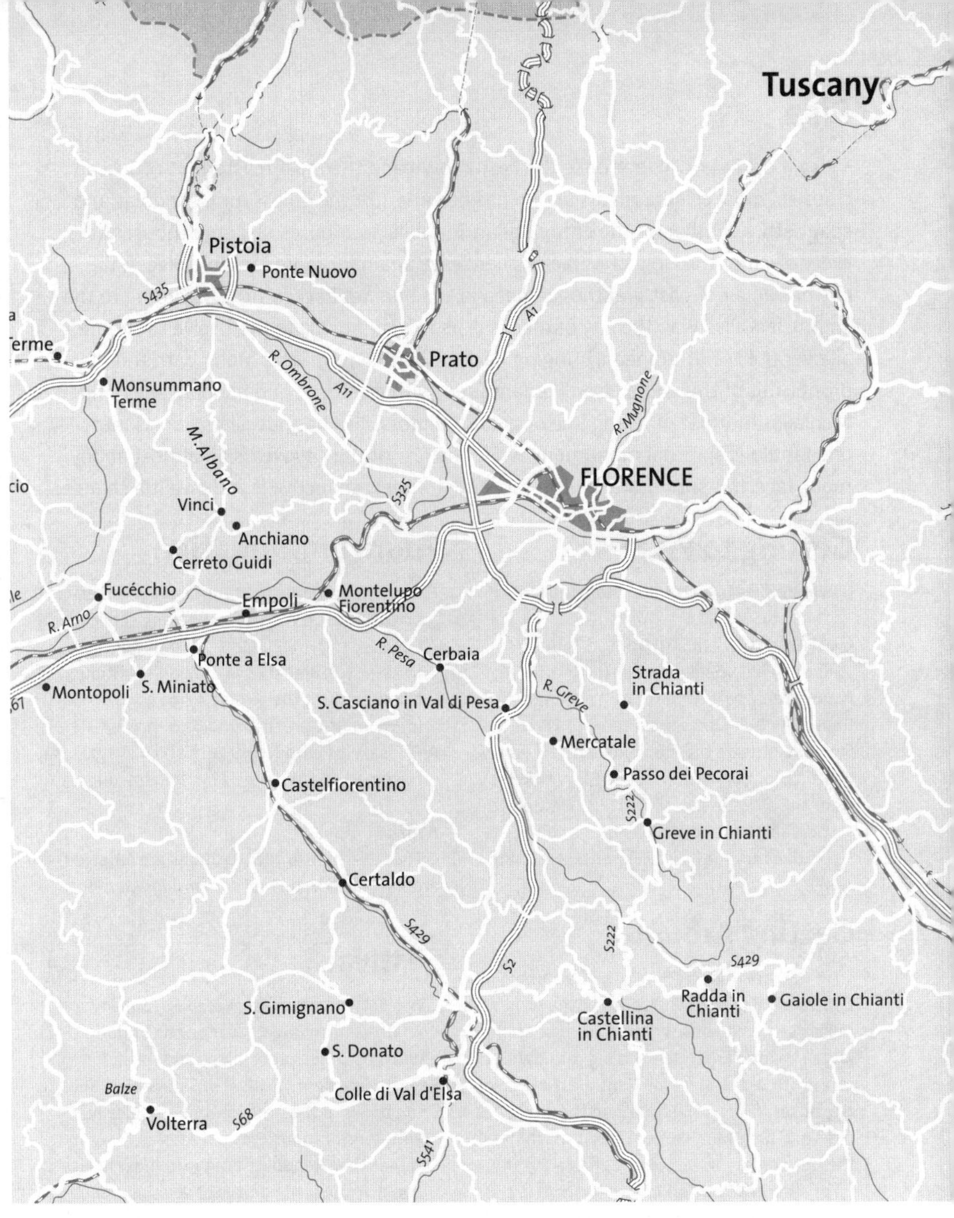

new centres of learning and art appeared, first in Pisa and Florence and then in a dozen other towns, inaugurating a cultural Renaissance that really began as early as the 1100s. As abruptly as it began, this brilliant age was extinguished in the 16th century, but Tuscany's cities and their art treasures have been preserved with loving care. So has the countryside; each year thousands of foreigners jostle to spend a month in a classic Tuscan farmhouse, with a view over a charmed, civilized landscape of cypresses and parasol pines, orderly rows of vines and olives, and a chapel on the hill with a *quattrocento* fresco.

Pisa

Pisa (pop. 104,000) is at once the best-known and the most mysterious of Tuscan cities. Its most celebrated attraction has become, like the Colosseum, gondolas and spaghetti, a symbol for the entire Italian Republic. Tour buses disgorge thousands every day into the Field of Miracles, then leave again for more tangible places; the city has an air of past greatness nipped in the bud. Yet back in 1100, according to the chroniclers, Pisa was 'the city of marvels'; its merchants made themselves at home all over the Mediterranean, bringing back influential new ideas along with their fat profits: out of this came Pisan Romanesque, with its stripes and blind arcades, and Nicola Pisano, first of a long line of great sculptors. Pisa has put all its efforts into one fabulous spiritual monument, while the rest of the city wears an almost anonymous face. It is subtle, and a little sad, but strangely seductive if you give it a chance.

Getting to Pisa

Ryanair flies from London Stansted (2hrs 15).

Getting from the Airport

Pisa's Galileo Galilei airport (**t** 050 500 707, *www.pisa-airport.com*) is 3km to the south of town. **City bus 3** links the airport to Piazza Stazione outside the Stazione Centrale (every 20 mins; journey 10mins; €0.77). Buy **tickets** from the office in the airport. Pisa Aeroporto **station** also has a few **trains** to the centre.

If you're on your way to **Florence**, *see* p.184.

Getting Around

Pisa's main **train station** is the **Stazione Centrale** (**t** 848 888 088) south of the Arno. All of Pisa's intercity **buses** depart from near Piazza Vittorio Emanuele II, a big roundabout just north of the Stazione Centrale. **Tickets** for **city buses** (€0.77; valid for 1hr on the city network) are available from ticket machines in the bus station or the airport office.

For a **taxi**, call **CO.TA.PI**, **t** 050 541 600 (€4–8 within the city). There are ranks at the airport, Stazione Centrale and Piazza Duomo.

Car Hire

The following have offices at the airport.

AutoEuropa, **t** 050 506 883.
Avis, **t** 050 42028.
Europcar, **t** 050 41081.
Hertz, **t** 050 43220.
Maggiore, **t** 050 42574.

Tourist Information

Pisa: Via Cammeo 2, near the Leaning Tower, **t** 050 560 464. With hotel booking service, **t** 050 830 253 (*open Mon–Sat 9–6, Sun 10.30–4.30*). Branches at Stazione Centrale, **t** 050 42291; at the airport, **t** 050 503 700 (*open daily 10.30–3.30 and 6.30–9.30*).

APT Pisa, Via Pietro Nenni 24, **t** 050 929 777, **f** 050 929 764, *www.pisa.turismo.toscana.it*.

Market Days

The city's mercantile traditions are renewed around **Piazza Vettovaglie** (*mornings Mon–Sat*).

Festivals

Gioco del Ponte, Ponte de Rezzo, *last Sun in June*. A 13th-century tug-of-war on the bridge, with costumes, processions and music.

Regatta and lights festival of San Ranieri. See the banks of the Arno glimmer magically with tens of thousands of bulbs.

Old Maritime Republics boat race (next in Pisa 2003). Hotly contested each year between four old sea rivals: Pisa, Venice, Genoa and Amalfi; hosted by Pisa every four years.

Shopping

Pisa is a great place for tacky **souvenirs**, particularly near the Campo dei Miracoli; Light-up Leaning Towers in pink and yellow are an amazingly good buy. If it's **boutiques** you're after, try Via Oberdan and Corso Italia.

The Field of Miracles (Campo dei Miracoli)

Joint ticket available for museums and monuments on the Field of Miracles.

Almost from the time of its conception, this was the name given to medieval Italy's most ambitious building programme. The cathedral was begun in 1063, the famous Leaning Tower and the baptistry in the middle 1100s, at the height of Pisa's fortunes, and the cloistered cemetery of the Campo Santo in 1278. Of all the unique aspects of this complex, its location strikes one first. Whether their reasons were dictated by aesthetics or land values – probably both – the Pisans built their cathedral on a broad expanse of green lawn at the northern edge of town, just inside the walls. And the leaning campanile is hardly the only oddity. The longer you look, the more you notice: little monster-griffins, dragons and such, peeking out of the sculptural work; a rhinoceros by the cathedral door; or Muslim arabesques in the Campo Santo.

Where to Stay

Pisa ✉ 56100

Pisa isn't known for fine hotels, but there's usually enough room for those who elect to stay. Many of the middle-range hotels are around the train station, south of the Arno.

****__Grand Hotel Duomo__, Via S. Maria 94, **t** 050 561 894, **f** 050 560 418 (*very expensive*). Very close to the Campo dei Miracoli, this is a modern yet richly appointed luxury hotel, with a roof garden; all rooms have a/c.

****__D'Azeglio__, Piazza Vittorio Emanuele II 18b, **t** 050 500 310, **f** 050 28017 (*expensive*). This modern place is convenient for buses and trains, offering comfortable rooms with a/c.

***__Royal Victoria__, Lungarno Pacinotti 12, **t** 050 940 111, **f** 050 940 180 (*moderate*). A tasteful place, managed by the same family since 1837; its best assets are rooms overlooking the Arno and its own garage.

***__Verdi__, Piazza Repubblica 5, **t** 050 598 947, **f** 050 598 944 (*moderate*). Another good choice in this price range, this time in the centre, set in a well-restored historic palace.

__Di Stefano__, Via Sant'Apollonia 35, **t 050 553 559, **f** 050 556 038 (*moderate*). Central and recently upgraded, with a TV in every room.

*__Gronchi__, Piazza Arcivescovado 1, **t** 050 561 823 (*cheap*). A decent, convivial pad, within a few blocks of the cathedral.

*__Helvetia__, Via Don Boschi 31, **t** 050 553 084 (*cheap*). Close by and similar to the Gronchi.

Other inexpensive places are spread throughout town – and often full of students.

Eating Out

Strolling around Pisa, you can find eels and squid, *baccalà*, tripe, wild mushrooms and 'twice-boiled soup' along with other dishes that waiters cannot satisfactorily explain.

Ristoro dei Vecchi Macelli, Via Volturno 49, **t** 050 20424 (*very expensive*). A gourmet stronghold on the north bank, with imaginative dishes based on coastal Tuscan traditions. *Closed Wed and Sun lunch and 15–31 Aug.*

Cagliostro, Via del Castelletto 26–30, **t** 050 575 413 (*expensive*). An extraordinary wine bar/restaurant/art gallery and general trendy hang-out; cuisine is 'Tuscan Creative', but throws in other dishes from all over Italy. Lunch is a bit more modest. *Closed Tues.*

Pisa is well endowed with unpretentious *trattorias*; many are around the university.

Osteria La Grotta, Via San Francesco 103, **t** 050 578 105 (*moderate*). A cosy place with a simulated grotto and comforting, traditional dishes, imaginatively prepared and without pretensions. Meat-lovers are well catered for; try the *Gran Padellata del Maremmano*, a rich stew of three kinds of meat cooked with spicy sausage and vegetables. *Closed Sun.*

Il Nuraghe, Via Mazzini 58, **t** 050 443 68 (*moderate*). Among many tempting options is a ricotta ravioli; the chef is Sardinian, so Tuscan and Sard specialities rub shoulders. *Closed Mon and 5–25 Aug.*

Numero Undici, Via Cavalca 11, **t** 050 544294 (*cheap*). A diminutive *trattoria* with no frills; but prices are rock bottom and the limited menu delicious. *Closed Sat lunch and Sun.*

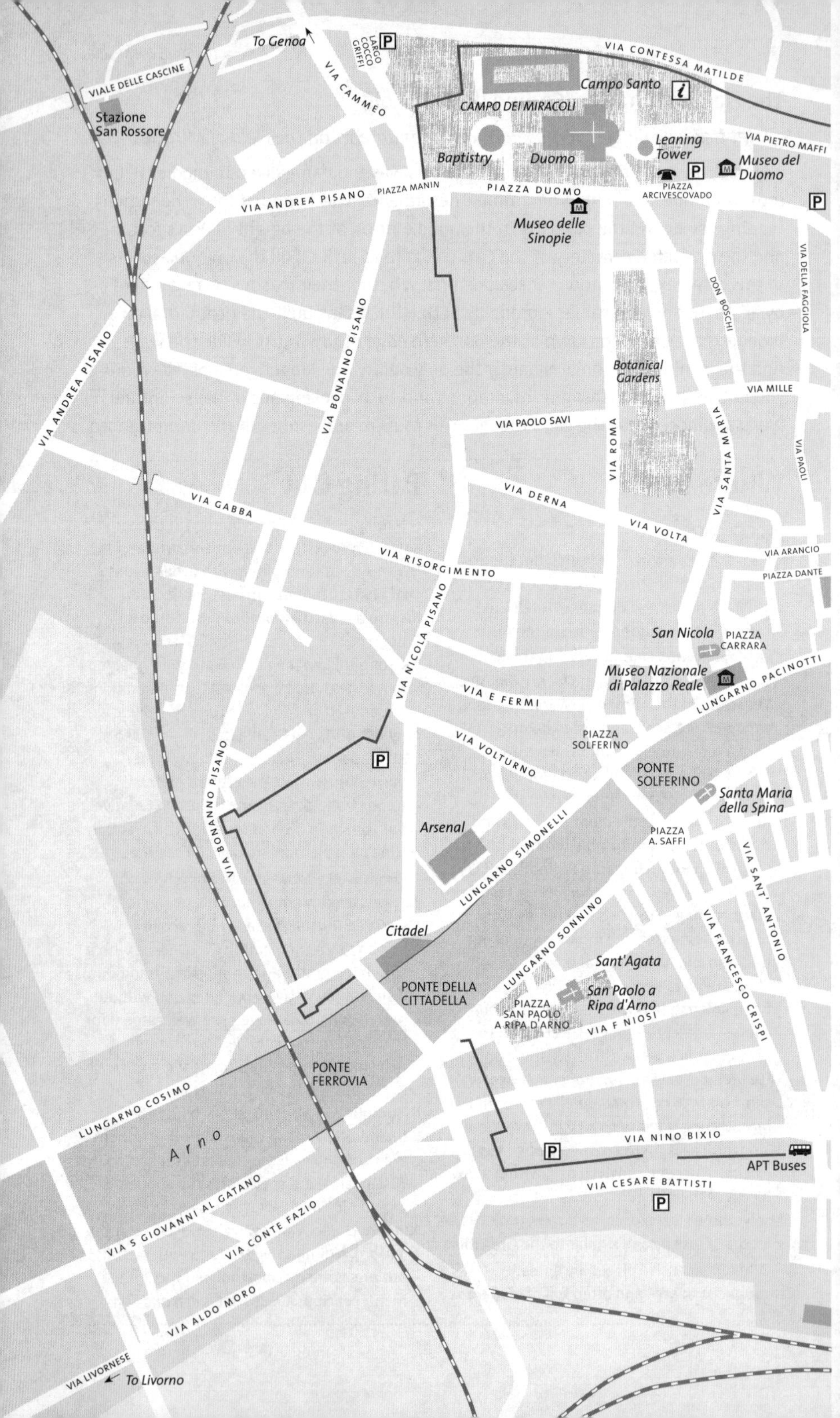

To Genoa
LARGO COCCO GRIFFI
VIA CONTESSA MATILDE
VIALE DELLE CASCINE
Campo Santo
CAMPO DEI MIRACOLI
VIA CAMMEO
Stazione San Rossore
Leaning Tower
VIA PIETRO MAFFI
Baptistry
Duomo
Museo del Duomo
PIAZZA ARCIVESCOVADO
VIA ANDREA PISANO
PIAZZA MANIN
PIAZZA DUOMO
Museo delle Sinopie
DON BOSCHI
VIA DELLA FAGGIOLA
VIA BONANNO PISANO
VIA ANDREA PISANO
Botanical Gardens
VIA MILLE
VIA PAOLO SAVI
VIA ROMA
VIA SANTA MARIA
VIA PAOLI
VIA DERNA
VIA GABBA
VIA VOLTA
VIA ARANCIO
VIA RISORGIMENTO
PIAZZA DANTE
VIA NICOLA PISANO
San Nicola
PIAZZA CARRARA
Museo Nazionale di Palazzo Reale
LUNGARNO PACINOTTI
VIA E FERMI
PIAZZA SOLFERINO
VIA VOLTURNO
VIA BONANNO PISANO
PONTE SOLFERINO
Santa Maria della Spina
Arsenal
LUNGARNO SIMONELLI
PIAZZA A. SAFFI
VIA SANT' ANTONIO
VIA FRANCESCO CRISPI
Citadel
LUNGARNO SONNINO
Sant'Agata
PONTE DELLA CITTADELLA
PIAZZA SAN PAOLO A RIPA D'ARNO
San Paolo a Ripa d'Arno
VIA F NIOSI
PONTE FERROVIA
LUNGARNO COSIMO
Arno
VIA NINO BIXIO
APT Buses
VIA CESARE BATTISTI
VIA S GIOVANNI AL GATANO
VIA CONTE FAZIO
VIA ALDO MORO
VIA LIVORNESE
To Livorno

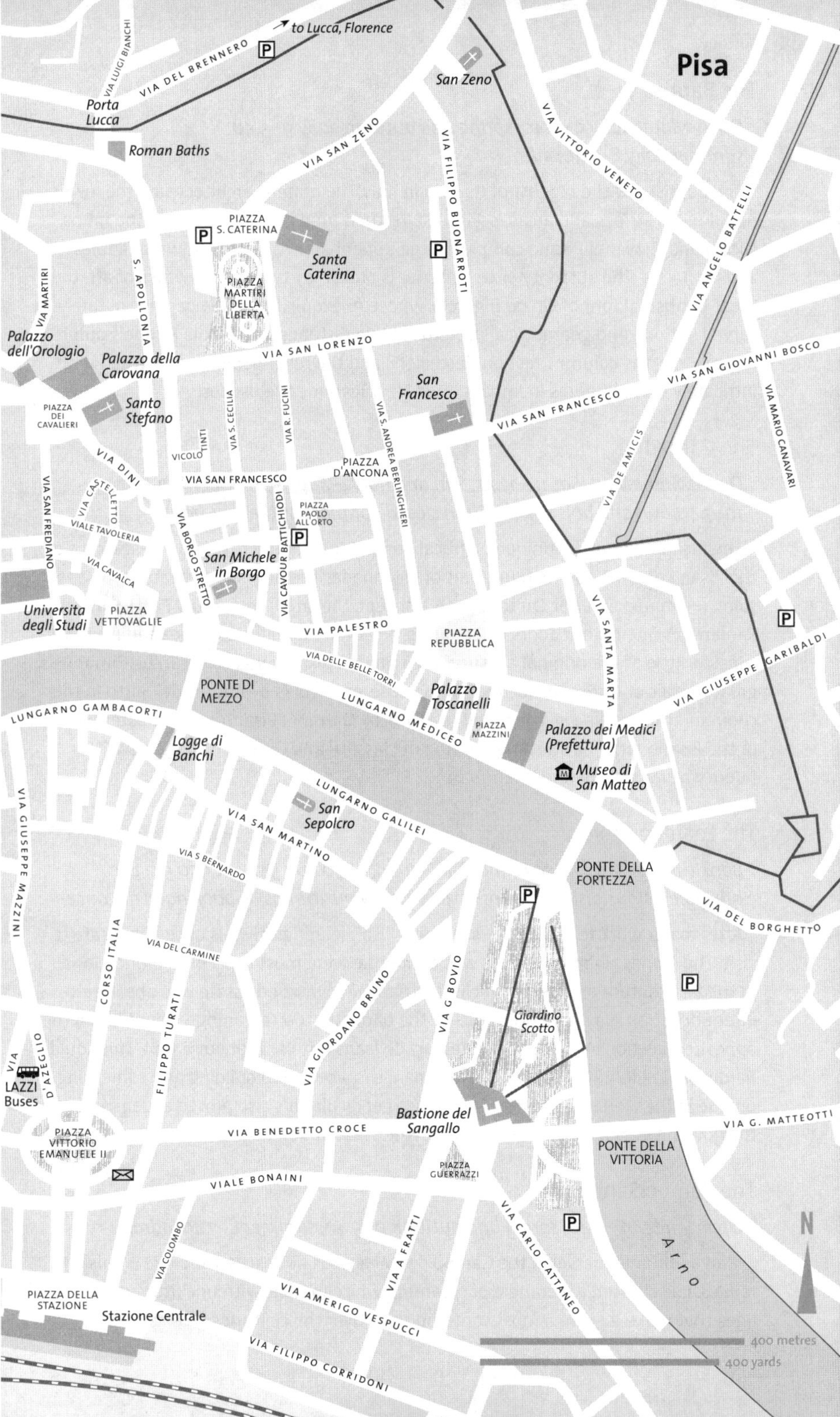

Pisa
to Lucca, Florence
Via del Brennero
Via Luigi Bianchi
Porta Lucca
San Zeno
Roman Baths
Via San Zeno
Via Filippo Buonarroti
Via Vittorio Veneto
Piazza S. Caterina
Santa Caterina
Piazza Martiri della Libertà
S. Apollonia
Via Martiri
Via Angelo Battelli
Palazzo dell'Orologio
Palazzo della Carovana
Via San Lorenzo
Piazza dei Cavalieri
Santo Stefano
San Francesco
Via San Francesco
Via San Giovanni Bosco
Via Mario Canavari
Via S. Cecilia
Via R. Fucini
Via S. Andrea Berlinghieri
Vicolo Tinti
Via Dini
Via de Amicis
Via San Francesco
Piazza d'Ancona
Via San Frediano
Via Castelletto
Viale Tavoleria
Piazza Paolo all'Orto
Via Borgo Stretto
Via Cavour Battichiodi
Via Cavalca
San Michele in Borgo
Via Santa Marta
Universita degli Studi
Piazza Vettovaglie
Via Palestro
Piazza Repubblica
Via delle Belle Torri
Via Giuseppe Garibaldi
Ponte di Mezzo
Palazzo Toscanelli
Lungarno Gambacorti
Lungarno Mediceo
Piazza Mazzini
Palazzo dei Medici (Prefettura)
Logge di Banchi
Museo di San Matteo
Via Giuseppe Mazzini
Lungarno Galilei
San Sepolcro
Via San Martino
Via S Bernardo
Ponte della Fortezza
Via del Borghetto
Via del Carmine
Corso Italia
Via Giordano Bruno
Via G Bovio
Filippo Turati
Giardino Scotto
Via d'Azeglio
LAZZI Buses
Bastione del Sangallo
Via Benedetto Croce
Via G. Matteotti
Piazza Vittorio Emanuele II
Ponte della Vittoria
Piazza Guerrazzi
Viale Bonaini
Via Colombo
Via A Fratti
Via Carlo Cattaneo
Arno
N
Via Amerigo Vespucci
Piazza della Stazione
Stazione Centrale
400 metres
400 yards
Via Filippo Corridoni

The Baptistry

Open winter daily 9–4.40; spring and autumn daily 9–5.40; summer daily 8–7.40; adm.

The Baptistry is the biggest of its kind in Italy. The original architect saw the lower half done in stripes and arcades, Pisan style; then funds ran short, and in the 1260s, Nicola and Giovanni Pisano completed the upper half in a Gothic crown of gables and pinnacles. The austerity of the interior is broken by two superb works of art: the great **baptismal font** of Guido Bigarelli, whose 16 exquisite marble panels are finely carved in floral and geometrical patterns of inlaid stones, and Nicola Pisano's **pulpit** (1260). Here, the columns rest on fierce lions and the relief panels are crowded with intricately carved figures in impassioned New Testament episodes.

The Cathedral

Open winter Mon–Sat 10–12.45, Sun and hols 3–4.45; April–Oct Mon–Sat 10–7.40, Sun and hols 1–7.40; often closed for most of the day; adm.

The façade, below the unique elliptical dome, is one of the first and finest works of the Pisan Romanesque, its four levels of colonnades the only showy features on the calm, restrained exterior. On the south transept, the late 12th-century **Porte San Ranieri** has fine bronze doors by Bonanno, one of the architects of the Leaning Tower.

Inside, little of the original art survived a fire in 1595, but you can still see Cimabue's great mosaic of Christ Pantocrator in the apse, and works by Andrea del Sarto in the choir and the right nave. The **pulpit** (*c.* 1300), by Giovanni Pisano, is the masterpiece of the Pisano family, a startling mixture of classical and Christian elements with a fluency never seen before Pisano's time.

The Leaning Tower

Book through the Opera Primaziale Pisana, **t** *050 560 547, or* **t** *050 561 820, priaziale@sirius.pisa.it; groups of 30 enter every 30mins by booking in advance.*

After major work to secure the structure, Pisa's leaning tower is once again safe to visit. The stories claiming the tilt was accidental were most likely pure fabrications; in the last century, architects concluded that the tower's odd state was absolutely intentional. You may have noticed that the baptistry, too, is leaning – about 5ft, in the opposite direction. And the cathedral façade leans outwards about a foot. This could hardly be accidental. Whatever, the campanile is a beautiful building and something unique in the world – at some 16½ft off perpendicular, it's also proved expensive for the government: $80 million since 1990, when restoration began.

The Campo Santo

Open winter 9–4.40; spring and autumn 9–5.40; summer 8–7.40; adm.

If an additional marvel in the Campo dei Miracoli is not excessive, there is this remarkable cloister: a rectangle of gleaming white marble, with uncluttered, simple lines that make it seem almost contemporary. Over the centuries an exceptional hoard of frescoes and sculpture accumulated here. Unfortunately, much of it went up in flames when a bomb hit the roof in 1944, but there remain two 14th-century frescoes of the *Triumph of Death* and the *Last Judgement* by an unknown artist: some of the best paintings of the *trecento*. Another curiosity is the *Theological Cosmography* by Piero di Puccio (*under restoration;* ***t*** *050 560 547*). This vertiginous diagram depicts 22 spheres of the planets and stars; the circle trisected by a T was a common medieval pattern for the known earth. The three sides represent Asia, Africa and Europe, while three lines show the Mediterranean, the Black Sea and the Nile.

The Museo delle Sinopie and Museo del Duomo

Both open winter 9–4.40; spring and autumn 9–5.40 (Museo del Duomo 5.20); summer 8–7.40 (Museo 7.20); adm.

Opposite the cathedral, the **Museo delle Sinopie** contains the pre-painting sketches of the frescoes lost in the Campo Santo fire. Many of them are works of art in their own right and give an idea as to how the frescoes once looked. Among the treasures of the **Museo del Duomo**, in Piazza Arcivescovado, are beautiful fragments from the cathedral façade and altar and two Islamic works: the very strange, original **Griffin** from the top of the cathedral, and an intricate 12th-century bronze basin. Among the sculptures, Giovanni Pisano's grotesque faces stand out, the lovely *Madonna del Colloquio* named because she speaks to her child with her eyes; there are also fine works by Tino di Camaino, Nino Pisano and, in Rooms 11–12, the Cathedral Treasure, where Giovanni Pisano's ivory *Madonna and Child* steals the show.

North Pisa

With the cathedral on the very edge of town, Pisa has no real centre. Near the Campo dei Miracoli, a long street leads down into the **Piazza dei Cavalieri**, where Duke Cosimo I had Vasari build the outlandishly ornate **Palazzo della Carovana** for his crusading order of knights. Across from the palace, the **Palazzo dell'Orologio** was built around the 'Hunger Tower', where Dante claimed the Pisan commander Ugolino della Gherardesca was imprisoned after his fickle city began to suspect him of intrigues with the Genoese. Pisa's **University**, founded by his family in 1330, is just south of here, while Via dei Mille leads west to the **Botanical Gardens** (*open Nov–Feb Mon–Fri 8–5, Sat 8–1; Mar–Oct Mon–Fri 8–5.30, Sat 8–1; closed Sun*). Just east of the university are the twisting alleys of the lively market area around **Piazza Vettovaglie**.

Along the Arno

Here the **Museo di San Matteo** (*Lungarno Mediceo; open Tues–Sat 9–7, Sun 9–2; closed Mon; adm*) immures much of the best Pisan art from the Middle Ages and Renaissance. It contains works by Giunta Pisano, believed to be the first artist to sign his work (early 1200s); an excellent, well-arranged collection of 1300s paintings by Pisans and other schools; sculptures by the Pisanos; also medieval ceramics from the Middle East. In Room 7, the Early Renaissance comes as a startling revelation: here is Neri di Bicci's wonderfully festive *Coronation of St Catherine*, a sorrowful *St Paul* by

Masaccio, and a beautifully coloured *Crucifixion* by Gozzoli, more like a party than an execution. The last great work is Donatello's gilded reliquary bust of *San Lussorio*.

West along the Lungarno, Pisa's **Prefettura** is housed in the lovely 13th-century Palazzo Medici, not far from the 16th-century **Palazzo Toscanelli**, where Lord Byron lived betweem 1821 and 1822 and wrote six cantos of *Don Juan*. Further down, the **Museo Nazionale di Palazzo Reale** (*Lungarno Pacinotti 46; open Mon–Fri 9–2.30, Sat 9–1.30; adm*) houses a collection of old armour which gets dusted off every June for the *Gioco del Ponte*, as well as pieces from the 15th–17th centuries, and art and collectables from the Medici and Lorraine archducal hoards. Just behind the Palazzo Reale rises Pisa's other famous bell tower, belonging to the 12th-century church of **San Nicola**: this one is cylindrical at the bottom, octagonal in the middle and hexagonal on top. Designed by Nicola Pisano, it was built to lean forward before curving back again towards the perpendicular. Within the church is a fine *Madonna* by Traini and a wooden sculpture by Nino Pisano.

South of the Arno

The languidly curving stretch of the Arno is an exercise in Tuscan gravity. Lined by two mirror-image lines of blank-faced yellow and tan buildings, its uncanny monotony is broken by only one landmark: **Santa Maria della Spina** (*open Oct–Mar Tues–Sun 10–2; April, May and Sept Tues–Fri 10–1.30 and 2.30–7; June–Aug Tues–Fri 11–1.30 and 2.30–6, Sat and Sun 11–1.30 and 2.30–8; adm*), which sits on the bank like a precious Gothic jewel box, rebuilt as an extravaganza of pointed gables and blooming pinnacles in 1323. All of the sculptural work is first class, especially the figures of Christ and the Apostles facing the streets. The luminous zebra interior holds statues by Andrea and Nino Pisano. Just down from here, the church of **San Paolo a Ripa del Arno** has a beautiful 12th-century façade. Behind it, the 12th-century chapel of **Sant'Agata** has an unusual eight-sided prismatic roof like an Ottoman tomb.

Day Trip from Pisa

Lucca

Of all Tuscany's great cities, Lucca (pop. 92,500) is the most cosy, a tidy gem encased within its walls; at first glance it seems almost too bijou, a good burgher's daydream. The old ramparts are now full of lawns and trees; where soldiers once patrolled, citizens ride their bicycles and walk their dogs. Like paradise, Lucca is entered by way of **St Peter's Gate**. Once inside, Corso Garibaldi leads to the Pisan-style **Duomo** (*open summer 7–7; winter 7–5*), begun in the 11th century. The singular porch has Lucca's finest 12th- and 13th-century reliefs and sculpture; look out for Nicola Pisano's Tree of Life, with Adam and Eve crouched at the bottom, and a host of fantastical animals and other carvings by unknown masters. The dark interior offers an introduction to Lucca's only great artist, **Matteo Civitali** (1435–1501), whose famous octagonal

Tempietto (1484) in the left aisle contains Lucca's holy relic, a *Crucifix* said to be a true portrait of Jesus, sculpted by Nicodemus, an eyewitness to the crucifixion. Besides works by Fra Bartolomeo, Giambologna, Ghirlandaio and the high altar carved by Civitali, Lucca's real icon is the remarkable **Tomb of Ilaria del Carretto** (1408) in the sacristy, a beautifully tender effigy by Jacopo della Quercia.

Across the *piazza*, Lucca's original cathedral, **San Giovanni** (*open Apr–Oct daily 10–6; Nov–Mar Mon–Fri 10–3, Sat and Sun 10–6; adm*), stands on the site of a 5th-century basilica. Under the huge square **baptistry** you can see the original Roman font – a walk-in model for total immersion baptisms. Just west, Lucca's twin squares, **Piazza del Giglio** and **Piazza Napoleone**, are the focus of the Lucchesi evening *passeggiata*.

A little north in Piazza San Michele, the ambitious façade of **San Michele in Foro** (*open 7.40–12 and 3–6*) rises high above the roof, each column in the Pisan arcading different: twisted like corkscrews, inlaid with mosaic Cosmati work, or carved with myriad fanciful figures and beasts. Inside are a terracotta attributed to Luca della Robbia and a painting of plague saints by Filippino Lippi. Across the street in the **Puccini Museum** (*entrance in Corte San Lorenzo 9; open winter Tues–Sun 10–1 and 3–6; summer daily 10–6; adm*) you can see mementos of the great composer Giacomo Puccini, including the piano he used to compose his opera *Turandot*.

East of San Michele, medieval **Via Fillungo** and its surrounding lanes make up the busy shopping district, a tidy nest of straight and narrow alleys. Beyond the **Torre delle Ore** stands the tall church and taller campanile of **San Frediano**, shimmering with the colours of a large mosaic showing Christ and the Apostles in an elegant, flowing style. The palatial interior houses Tuscany's most remarkable baptismal font, the 12th-century *Fontana lustrale* carved with reliefs and, behind, an equally beautiful lunette by Andrea della Robbia. Across Via Fillungo, arches lead to the ancient site of Lucca's **Anfiteatro Romano**. Not a stone remains, but you can clearly see the outline of the amphitheatre; where the grandstands were, you now see a complete ellipse of medieval houses, with a *piazza* where the gladiators once slugged it out.

Getting There

Pisa has several **trains** each hour to Lucca (25–30mins). Trains from Florence to Lucca run roughly hourly (1hr15). LAZZI (**t** 0583 584 876) operates **buses** to Lucca from both Pisa (40mins) and Florence (1hr15).

Lucca's **train station** (**t** 848 888 088) is south of the walls on Piazza Ricasoli. **Buses** go to Piazzale Verdi, inside the walls to the west.

Tourist Information

Lucca: Piazza Santa Maria 35, **t** 0583 419 689, **f** 0583 469 964, *www.lucca.turismo.toscana.it* (*open Mar–Oct daily 9–7; Nov–Feb daily 9–1 and 3–7*).

Eating Out

Il Giglio, Piazza del Giglio 2, **t** 0583 494 058 (*moderate*). Lucca's best seafood, in Hotel Universo. *Closed Tues eve and Wed, first two weeks of Feb and last two weeks of July.*

Canuleia, Via Canuleia 14, **t** 0583 467 470 (*moderate*). Near the amphitheatre in a medieval workshop, serving local food with some surprises such as aubergine soufflé and usually a choice of vegetarian dishes. *Closed Mon lunch and Sat.*

Vecchia Trattoria Buralli, Piazza S. Agostino 10, **t** 0583 950 611 (*cheap*). Around the corner from Sant'Agostino church, this offers plain Lucchese home cooking on a good bargain buffet; or pay a bit more for house specialities like the beef *tagliata* with rocket.

Overnighter from Pisa

Florence (Firenze)

Florence is a museum city *par excellence*. Her visitors are not so much tourists of leisure, but cultural pilgrims who throng the Uffizi, the Accademia, the Bargello, to gaze upon the holy mysteries of our secular society; to buy postcards and replicas, the holy cards of our day. Florence only blossoms if you apply your mind as well as your eyes. To understand this capital of contradiction, remember one historical constant: it always takes both sides, its schizophrenia epitomized by the irreconcilable differences between Botticelli's graceful *Primavera* and Michelangelo's cold, perfect *David*.

The Baptistry

Open Mon–Sat 12–7, Sun 8.30–2; adm.

This ancient, mysterious building is the egg from which Florence's golden age was hatched. Scholarship sets its date of construction between the 6th and 9th centuries, and though the builders remain unknown, their strikingly original exercise in geometry provided the model for all of Florence's great church façades. Under the cupola, the glittering gold-ground mosaics of the 13th and 14th centuries show a strong Byzantine influence; over the apse is a *Last Judgement*, while the other bands portray the *Hierarchy of Heaven, Story of Genesis, Life of Joseph, Life of Christ* and the *Life of St John the Baptist*. Below, the mosaics are matched by an intricate tessellated marble floor, with signs of the Zodiac; otherwise the Baptistry is uncluttered; only the tomb of Anti-Pope John XXIII by Donatello and Michelozzo stands out, while the remarkable walls combine influences from the ancient world with modern inspiration.

Historians used to pinpoint the beginning of the 'Renaissance' as the year 1401, when Lorenzo Ghiberti defeated Brunelleschi in a competition to finish the baptistry's **bronze doors**. The **East Doors** (1425–52) are his masterpiece, and one of the most awesome achievements of the age: Old Testament scenes reinterpreting the forms of antiquity with a depth and drama that have never been surpassed. Michelangelo is said to have judged them 'worthy to be the Gates of Paradise'. Near the centre, the balding figure with arched eyebrows and a little smile is Ghiberti himself.

The Duomo

Open Mon–Wed and Fri 10–5, Thurs 10–3.30, Sat 10–4.45, Sun 1–4.45.

In the 1290s, the sculptor Arnolfo di Cambio was charged to create something 'so magnificent in size and beauty as to surpass anything built by the Greeks and Romans'. In response, Arnolfo confidently laid the foundations for an octagonal crossing 146ft in diameter, then died before working out a way to cover it. Beyond its size, the cathedral shows little interest in contemporary innovations, its ponderous bulk garbed in an eccentric green, white and red pattern of rectangles and flowers. Yet if this St Mary of the Floral Wallpaper was created purely as a base for its dome, it would be more than enough. **Brunelleschi's dome**, more than any landmark, makes Florence Florence. Losing the competition for the baptistry doors was a bitter disappointment to Brunelleschi, and when proposals were solicited for the dome in 1418, he was ready with a brilliant *tour de force*. Not only would he build the biggest, most beautiful dome of his time, but he would do it without any expensive supports during construction, making use of a cantilevered system of bricks.

After the façade, the austerity of the **interior** is almost startling, with simple arches and counterpoint of grey stone and white plaster. There is surprisingly little religious art – the Florentines have carted most of it off into the Cathedral Museum (*see* below), though the terracotta scene of the Resurrection over the north sacristy is one of Luca della Robbia's best works. More memorable, however, are the two lifesized *trompe-l'oeil* frescoes of equestrian statues: of the *condottiere Sir John Hawkwood* by Uccello, and *Niccolò da Tolentino* by Andrea del Castagno. A door on the left aisle, near Michelino's well-known fresco of Dante, leads up into the **dome** (*open Mon–Fri 8.30–7, Sat 8.30–5.40; closed Sun and first Sat of the month; adm*). The network of stairs and walks between the inner and outer domes (not too difficult, if a little claustrophobic) was designed by Brunelleschi, and there is no better place to get a sense of the dome's scale. From the gallery you can get a good look at the lovely **stained glass** by Uccello, Donatello, Ghiberti and Castagno. Further up, views through small windows offer tantalizing hints of the breathtaking panorama from the lantern at the top.

The dome puts Giotto's beautiful 280ft **campanile** in the shade, both figuratively and literally. Giotto's design was completed after his death by Andrea Pisano and Francesco Talenti, and its major fame rests with their **sculptural reliefs** (originals in the Museo del Duomo) – a veritable encyclopaedia of the medieval world view.

Museo dell'Opera del Duomo

Piazza del Duomo 9; open Mon–Sat 9–7.30, Sun 9–1.40; adm.

The Cathedral Museum is one of Florence's finest, housing both relics from the actual construction of the cathedral and the masterpieces that once adorned it. Look out for the section of the Porta della Mandorla, the first representation of the adult male nude, and the *Pietà* that Michelangelo intended for his own tomb. Other highlights include two marble choir balconies with bas-reliefs made in the 1430s by Luca della Robbia and Donatello, and Donatello's *Mary Magdalene*, one of the most jarring figures ever sculpted. There is also a **new section** with a fascinating collection of instruments used in the construction of the cathedral; you can descend from here to the **courtyard** to see eight of Ghiberti's panels from the *Gates of Paradise*.

Between the Duomo and the Uffizi

Across from the beautiful campanile of the Badia Fiorentina looms the **Museo Nazionale del Bargello** (*open daily 8.15–1.50; closed first and third Sun and second and fourth Mon of month; adm*), once Florence's prison. Today its only inmates are men of marble, meeting to form Italy's finest collection of sculpture. Downstairs, there are early works by Michelangelo, a fine bronze by Benvenuto Cellini, and Giambologna's

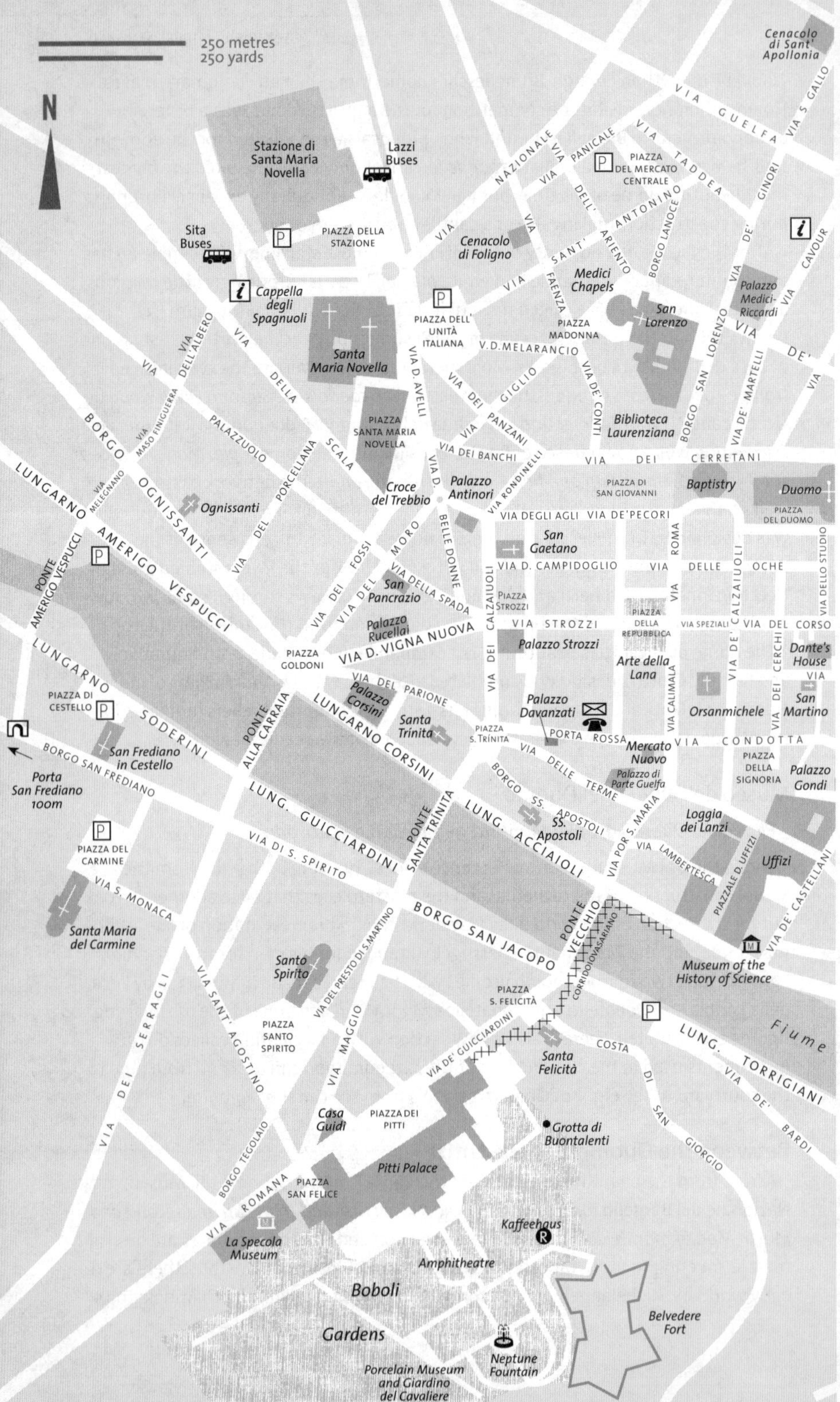
250 metres
250 yards
N
Stazione di Santa Maria Novella
Lazzi Buses
Sita Buses
Piazza della Stazione
Cappella degli Spagnuoli
Santa Maria Novella
Piazza Santa Maria Novella
Piazza dell' Unità Italiana
Cenacolo di Foligno
Medici Chapels
San Lorenzo
Piazza Madonna
Biblioteca Laurenziana
Piazza del Mercato Centrale
Cenacolo di Sant' Apollonia
Palazzo Medici-Riccardi
Ognissanti
Croce del Trebbio
Palazzo Antinori
Piazza di San Giovanni
Baptistry
Duomo
Piazza del Duomo
San Gaetano
San Pancrazio
Palazzo Rucellai
Piazza Strozzi
Piazza della Repubblica
Palazzo Strozzi
Arte della Lana
Dante's House
Piazza Goldoni
Palazzo Corsini
Santa Trinita
Palazzo Davanzati
Orsanmichele
San Martino
Piazza S. Trinita
Mercato Nuovo
Palazzo di Parte Guelfa
Piazza della Signoria
Palazzo Gondi
SS. Apostoli
Loggia dei Lanzi
Uffizi
Piazza di Cestello
San Frediano in Cestello
Porta San Frediano 100m
Piazza del Carmine
Santa Maria del Carmine
Santo Spirito
Piazza Santo Spirito
Museum of the History of Science
Piazza S. Felicità
Santa Felicità
Fiume
Casa Guidi
Piazza dei Pitti
Grotta di Buontalenti
Pitti Palace
Piazza San Felice
La Specola Museum
Kaffeehaus
Amphitheatre
Boboli Gardens
Belvedere Fort
Neptune Fountain
Porcelain Museum and Giardino del Cavaliere
Via Nazionale
Via Panicale
Via Guelfa
Via S. Gallo
Via Taddea
Via dell' Ariento
Via Sant' Antonino
Borgo Lanoce
Via de' Ginori
Via Cavour
Via Faenza
Via de' Conti
Via de' Martelli
Borgo San Lorenzo
V. D. Melarancio
Via del Giglio
Via dei Panzani
Via dei Banchi
Via dei Cerretani
Via Rondinelli
Via D. Avelli
Via della Scala
Via dell' Albero
Via Palazzuolo
Via Maso Finiguerra
Borgo Ognissanti
Via Melegnano
Via del Porcellana
Lungarno Amerigo Vespucci
Ponte Amerigo Vespucci
Via dei Fossi
Via del Moro
Via della Spada
Via D. Belle Donne
Via degli Agli
Via de' Pecori
Via D. Campidoglio
Via Roma
Via delle Oche
Via dello Studio
Via dei Calzaiuoli
Via Strozzi
Via Speziali
Via del Corso
Via D. Vigna Nuova
Via del Parione
Via Calimala
Via dei Cerchi
Porta Rossa
Via Condotta
Via delle Terme
Borgo SS. Apostoli
Via Por S. Maria
Via Lambertesca
Piazzale d. Uffizi
Via de' Castellani
Lungarno Soderini
Borgo San Frediano
Ponte alla Carraia
Lungarno Corsini
Ponte Santa Trinita
Lung. Acciaioli
Lung. Guicciardini
Via di S. Spirito
Via S. Monaca
Borgo San Jacopo
Ponte Vecchio
Corridoio Vasariano
Lung. Torrigiani
Via del Presto di S. Martino
Via Maggio
Via Sant' Agostino
Via dei Serragli
Via de' Guicciardini
Costa di San Giorgio
Via de' Bardi
Borgo Tegolaio
Via Romana

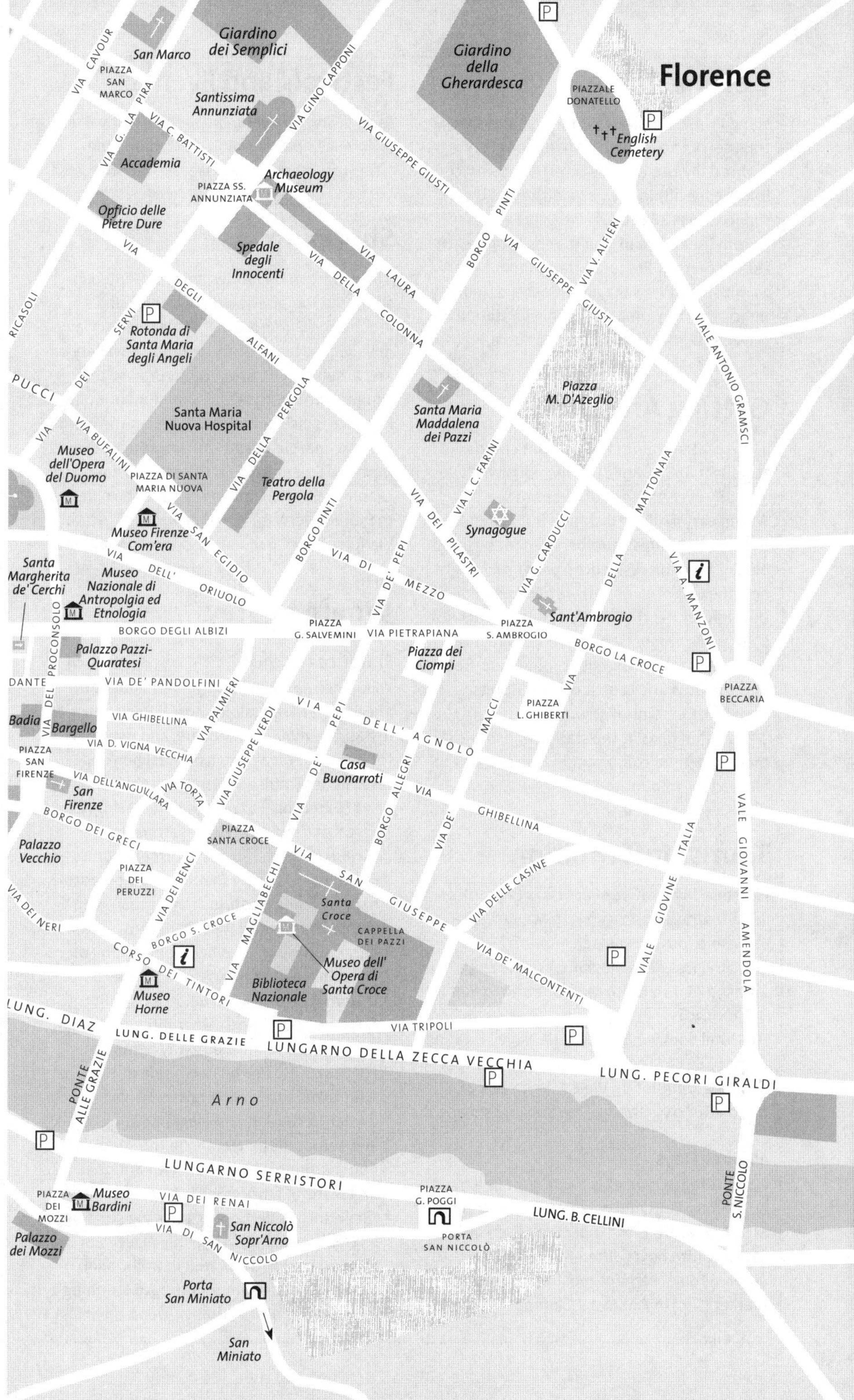

Florence
Giardino dei Semplici
Giardino della Gherardesca
San Marco
Piazza San Marco
Via Cavour
Via G. La Pira
Via C. Battisti
Via Gino Capponi
Santissima Annunziata
Piazzale Donatello
English Cemetery
Accademia
Via Giuseppe Giusti
Piazza SS. Annunziata
Archaeology Museum
Opficio delle Pietre Dure
Spedale degli Innocenti
Via Laura
Via della Colonna
Borgo Pinti
Via V. Alfieri
Via degli Alfani
Via dei Servi
Ricasoli
Rotonda di Santa Maria degli Angeli
Viale Antonio Gramsci
Piazza M. D'Azeglio
Pucci
Santa Maria Nuova Hospital
Via della Pergola
Santa Maria Maddalena dei Pazzi
Via Bufalini
Museo dell'Opera del Duomo
Piazza di Santa Maria Nuova
Teatro della Pergola
Via L. C. Farini
Mattonaia
Via dei Pilastri
Synagogue
Via G. Carducci
Museo Firenze Com'era
Via San Egidio
Via di Mezzo
Via de' Pepi
Via della
Via A. Manzoni
Santa Margherita de' Cerchi
Via dell' Oriuolo
Museo Nazionale di Antropolgia ed Etnologia
Via del Proconsolo
Sant'Ambrogio
Borgo degli Albizi
Piazza G. Salvemini
Via Pietrapiana
Piazza S. Ambrogio
Borgo la Croce
Piazza dei Ciompi
Palazzo Pazzi-Quaratesi
Piazza Beccaria
Dante
Via de' Pandolfini
Via dell' Agnolo
Piazza L. Ghiberti
Via Palmieri
Badia
Bargello
Via Ghibellina
Via Giuseppe Verdi
Via Macci
Piazza San Firenze
Via D. Vigna Vecchia
Casa Buonarroti
Via dell'Anguillara
Via Torta
San Firenze
Borgo Allegri
Vale Giovanni Amendola
Borgo dei Greci
Piazza Santa Croce
Via de'
Via Ghibellina
Viale Giovine Italia
Palazzo Vecchio
Via San Giuseppe
Piazza dei Peruzzi
Via dei Benci
Via delle Casine
Via dei Neri
Santa Croce
Cappella dei Pazzi
Borgo S. Croce
Via Magliabechi
Via de' Malcontenti
Corso dei Tintori
Museo dell' Opera di Santa Croce
Museo Horne
Biblioteca Nazionale
Lung. Diaz
Lung. delle Grazie
Via Tripoli
Lungarno della Zecca Vecchia
Lung. Pecori Giraldi
Ponte alle Grazie
Arno
Lungarno Serristori
Ponte S. Niccolò
Piazza dei Mozzi
Museo Bardini
Via dei Renai
Piazza G. Poggi
Lung. B. Cellini
Palazzo dei Mozzi
Via di San Niccolò
San Niccolò Sopr'Arno
Porta San Niccolò
Porta San Miniato
San Miniato

Getting There

The Pisa Aeroporto rail station has a special **train** service to Florence (taking 1hr, every 1–2hrs daily). An off-and-on SITA **bus** service to Florence fills in the gaps left by the train service (**t** 055 483 561).

From the centre of Pisa, it's easiest to reach Florence by rail. Frequent **trains** (about every 25 mins) link Pisa's Stazione Centrale (journey 1hr30mins) to Santa Maria Novella station. To travel by **bus** you need to go via Lucca.

Getting Around

The central **train station** is **Santa Maria Novella** (**t** 8488 88088), in the northwest.

Nearly everything you'll want to see is within easy walking distance. But Florence has two sets of **address numbers**: red for business, blue or black for residences; your hotel might be either. Helpful maps have been posted throughout the city. ATAF city **buses** (**t** 055 565 0222, *www.ataf.net*) can inch you across the city and supply an excellent route map, from ticket booths and tourist offices. **Tickets** €1.03/1hr, €1.81/3hrs, €4.13/24hrs.

You'll find **taxis** at the station and in the major *piazze*, or call: **t** 055 4798 or 4390 (€2.21 plus extras; minimum €3.65).

Tourist Information

Florence: Main office near Piazza Beccaria on Via Manzoni 16, **t** 055 23320, *www.firenze.turismo.toscana.it*, (*open Mon–Fri 8–6, Sat 8–2*); Piazza della Stazione, **t** 055 212 245, **f** 055 238 1226 (*open Mon–Sat 8.30–7, Sun 8.30–1.30*).

ITA Hotel Booking: Santa Maria Novella station, **t** 055 282 893 (*open 9–9, in winter until 8*).

Florence Promhotels: Viale A. Volta 72, **t** 055 570 481, **f** 055 587 189. Free booking service.

Market Days

San Lorenzo market is the largest and most boisterous; **Sant'Ambrogiois** bustles for food; **Mercato Nuovo** is the most touristic. **Piazza Santo Spirito** hosts different markets on different days. Perhaps most fun is the **flea market** (*Sun*) in Piazza dei Ciompi.

Festivals and Events

Festa di San Giovanni, *24 June*. The festival of Florence's patron saint, marked by a big firework display near Piazzale Michelangelo.

Shopping

The big **fashion** names are represented in smart Via Tornabuoni, Via Calzaiuoli and around the Duomo. You'll see **leather** in Via della Vigna Nuova, and Florentine **jewellery** on and around the Ponte Vecchio. Browse the Lungarni and Borgo Ognissanti for **antiques**. Florence is also one of few places in the world to make **marbled paper**, an art brought over from the Orient in the 12th century. Giulio Giannini e Figlio, Piazza Pitti 37r, is the oldest manufacturer here. For ***alimentari***, Il Procacci, Via Tornabuoni 64r, sells regional specialities.

Where to Stay

Florence ✉ 50100

Florence has some lovely hotels, but book ahead as far as possible. Most hotels with a restaurant require half-board, and many try to charge for breakfast. (For hotel booking services, *see* Tourist Information, above).

★★★★★**Excelsior**, Piazza Ognissanti 3, **t** 055 2715, **f** 055 210 278, *www. westin.com/excelsiorflorence* (*luxury*). Former address of Napoleon's sister Caroline. Lots of marble, neoclassically plush, lush and green with plants, immaculately staffed, with decadently luxurious bedrooms, many of which have river views (for a price).

★★★**Hermitage**, Vicolo Marzio 1, **t** 055 287 216, **f** 055 212 208, *florence@hermitagehotel.com* (*very expensive*). Tucked away behind the Ponte Vecchio on the north side of the river. A lift takes you up to a ravishing roof garden, reception and elegant sitting room. The bedrooms below are on the small side, but charmingly furnished with antiques and tasteful fabrics. Some have river views.

★★**Belletini**, Via de' Conti 7, **t** 055 213 561, **f** 055 283 551 (*moderate*). A friendly place near the Medici chapels, decorated in traditional Florentine style; two rooms have stunning views of the nearby domes. Good breakfast.

Residenza Johlea Uno, Via San Gallo 80, **t** 055 4633292, **f** 055 4634552, *www.johanna.it* (*moderate*). Remarkable value, 10 mins' walk north of the central market, its comfortable rooms furnished with taste and style; all have excellent bathrooms. On the top floor is a small sitting room and a roof terrace affording 360° views of the city.

*__Scoti__, Via Tournabuoni 7, **t/f** 055 292 128 (*cheap*). A simple, friendly *pensione* with a fairly upmarket address, offering basic, large rooms (up to four beds) and no private bath, but bags of atmosphere, starting with the floor-to-ceiling frescoes in the sitting room.

Eating Out

Florence has plenty of fine restaurants; even in the cheaper places standards are high. Many close for all or part of Aug; it's also wise to book ahead, even a day or two in advance.

Cibreo, Via dei Macci 118r, **t** 055 234 1100 (*very expensive*). One of the most Florentine of restaurants; décor is simple – food is the main concern, and all of it is market-fresh. Go native and order tripe *antipasto*, or play safe with prosciutto or leg of lamb stuffed with artichokes. Booking is essential. *Open 12.50–2.30 and 7.30–11.15, closed Mon and Aug.*

Buca Lapi, Via del Trebbio 1r, **t** 055 213 768 (*expensive*). Located since 1800 in the old wine cellar of the lovely Palazzo Antinori, serving traditional favourites, from *pappardelle al cinghiale* (wide pasta with boar) and a *bistecca fiorentina con fagioli* that is hard to beat, downed with many different Tuscan wines. *Closed Sun and Mon lunch*.

Il Latini, Via dei Palchetti 6r, **t** 055 210 916 (*moderate*). Something of an institution (prepare to queue) and noisy but fun, where you eat huge portions of Florentine classics at long tables. The *primi* aren't great; so go for the *bistecca* or the *gran pezzo* – a vast rib-roast of beef. The house wine is good; try a *riserva*. *Closed Mon and all of Aug.*

Buca Mario, Piazza degli Ottaviani 16r, **t** 055 214179 (*moderate*). One of Florence's 'cellar restaurants'; full of Florentine atmosphere with a menu to match. The soups here are superb, as is the tagliatelle with porcini. *Ossobuco* and *bistecca* are also excellent. *Open Thurs–Tues 12.30–2.30 and 7.30–10.30.*

Trattoria del Carmine, Piazza del Carmine 185, **t** 055 218 601 (*cheap*). A traditional, bustling *trattoria* in San Frediano district. The long menu includes such staples as *ribollita*, *pasta e fagioli* and roast pork; also seasonal dishes such as risotto with asparagus, pasta with wild boar and *osso buco*. *Closed Sun.*

Il Pizzaiuolo, Via dei Macci 113r, **t** 055 241 171 (*cheap*). One of the best pizzerias, boasting a real Neapolitan pizza maker. *Open Mon–Sat 12.30–3.30 and 7.30–1am, closed Aug.*

Caffè Ricchi, Piazza Santo Spirito. An institution for excellent light lunches and wonderful ice cream out in the beautiful square.

Vivoli, Via Isola delle Stinche 7r, between the Bargello and S. Croce. Decadently delicious ice cream and rich *semifreddi*. *Closed Mon.*

Entertainment

Look for **listings** of films, concerts and events in Florence's daily, *La Nazione*. The tourist office's free *Florence Today* contains bilingual monthly information, as does *Florence Concierge Information*. The monthly *Firenze Spettacolo* is most comprehensive (from newsstands), and has a brief section in English.

The Teatro Comunale offers **opera** and **ballet** (*Sept–Dec*) and **concerts** (*Jan–April*). There's also the **Maggio Musicale festival**, featuring all three (*mid-April–June*). The Roman theatre hosts performances for the **Estate Fiesolana** (*late June–Aug*).

Contact **Box Office**, Via Alamanni 39, **t** 055 210 804, a ticket agency for all major events in Tuscany, including classical, rock, jazz, etc.

Nightlife

Nightlife is still awaiting its Renaissance – 1am is late in this city. Many **clubs** have themed evenings; keep an eye out for posters or handouts or buy *Firenze Spettacolo*. Venues are somewhat seasonal, but **Universale**, Via Pisana 77r, offers designer décor, a restaurant, bars and a pizzeria year round, all accompanied by live music and a giant film screen. *Open 8.30pm–2am; closed Mon*. In summer, **Central Park**, in Parco delle Cascine, is possibly the trendiest place in Florence, full of serious clubbers on its three dance floors.

famous *Mercury* (1564). Upstairs, the **Salone del Consiglio Generale** contains the greatest masterpieces of Early Renaissance sculpture, including three of Donatello's most celebrated works; his androgynous *David* explores depths of the Florentine psyche the Florentines probably didn't know they had. Besides excellent reliefs and busts by di Duccio, da Settignano and Luca della Robbia, you can see and judge for yourself the famous trial reliefs for the baptistry doors, by Ghiberti and Brunelleschi. The museum also has fascinating collections of **decorative arts**, small Renaissance bronzes, fine della Robbia terracottas and works by Antonio Pollaiuolo and Verrocchio.

West of the Bargello, the eccentric **Orsanmichele** (*open Mon–Fri 9–12 and 4–6, Sat and Sun 9–1 and 4–6; closed first and last Mon of month*) is a showcase of 15th-century Florentine sculpture. All around the exterior, the guilds erected statues of their patron saints, commissioning the finest artists of the day in an effort to outdo each other.

To the south, the city's civic stage, **Piazza della Signoria**, is a grand space, populated by a lively gathering of more of the best and worst of Florentine sculpture. Dominating the square is Arnolfo di Cambio's **Palazzo Vecchio** (*open Mon–Wed, Fri and Sat 9–7, Thurs, Sun 9–2 (15 June–15 Sept Mon and Fri 9am–11pm); adm*) now the city hall. Most of the interior decorations are by Cosimo I's court artist, Giorgio Vasari, known for his speed over quality; in league with Cosimo's propaganda machine Vasari's fresco factory produced room after room of self-glorifying Medicean puffery.

The Uffizi and the Museum of the History of Science

Queues in the summer are common. Open summer Tues–Fri 8.30–9, Sat 8.30–midnight, Sun 8.30–8; winter Tues–Sun 8.15–6.50; adm exp. You can pre-book on **t** *055 294 883: pay when you pick up your ticket.*

The Uffizi ('offices') were built as Cosimo's secretariat, and as usual we have the Medici to thank for the collection inside it; there are galleries in the world with more works of art, but the Uffizi overwhelms by the fact that everything in it is worth looking at. Rooms may be closed when you visit; there is a list at the ticket counters. All the Florentine masters are represented, but there are also masterpieces from other parts of Italy and abroad. In the early rooms look out for the *trecento* masterpieces by Cimabue, Duccio di Buoninsegna and Giotto and, from the early Renaissance, those by Domenico Veneziano, Piero della Francesca and Paolo Uccello. Elsewhere, Fra Filippo Lippi, Botticelli and Raphael have rooms dedicated to them, although it's Botticelli (Rooms 10–14) who attracts the most onlookers with his mysterious *La Primavera* and *Birth of Venus*. Room 15 has the Florentine works of Leonardo da Vinci's early career, and Room 25 has Michelangelo's one and only oil painting, the ambiguous *Tondo Doni* (1506), which draws crowds of confused admirers.

From the back of the Uffizi, Vasari's **Corridoio Vasariano** (*open for limited periods; booking obligatory,* **t** *055 2654 321; adm exp*), built for the Medici, leapfrogs over the Ponte Vecchio to link up with their Pitti Palace. Besides offering interesting views, it is hung with a celebrated collection of artists' self-portraits, starting with Vasari himself.

Behind the Uffizi the **Museum of the History of Science** (*Piazza Giudicci; open summer 9.30–5, Tues and Sat 9.30–1, closed Sun; winter 9.30–5, Tues 9.30–1; adm exp*) pays tribute to all that Tuscany contributed to the birth of science. Among the artful sundials and armillary spheres, microscopes and models, Galileo's instruments take pride of place, including the lens with which he discovered the four moons of Jupiter.

The Ponte Vecchio and Ponte Santa Trínita

Often at sunset the Arno becomes a stream of molten gold, confined in its walls of stone and laced in with the curving arches of its spans. The **Ponte Vecchio** crosses the Arno at its narrowest point; like old London Bridge, it is covered with shops and houses and has long been the haunt of Florentine goldsmiths. To the west, Florence's beautiful **Ponte Santa Trìnita**, built on a low sweeping arch designed by Michelangelo, was a tragic victim of Nazi bombing in 1944, but the Florentines set about replacing it exactly as it was, replicating not only the old stones but the old ways of cutting them.

Northwest of the Duomo: Santa Maria Novella

In the northwest corner of the city, by the station, the church of **Santa Maria Novella** (*open Mon–Thurs and Sat 9.30–5, Fri, Sun and hols 1–5; adm*) redeems the blandness of its square with its stupendous black and white marble façade. Its upper half, completed in 1456 by Alberti, perfects the original Romanesque section with geometrical harmonies to create a kind of Renaissance Sun Temple. The vast, lofty **interior** is a treasure trove of frescoes: Masaccio's famous *Trinità* is in the left aisle; excellent scenes by Domenico Ghirlandaio adorn the Sanctuary; the Filippo Strozzi Chapel contains the finest work ever to come from the brush of Filippino Lippi; while the raised Cappella Strozzi is one of the most evocative corners of 14th-century Florence, frescoed entirely by Nardo di Cione and his brother, Andrea Orcagna. Nearby, in the Capella Gondi, you'll also find Brunelleschi's only wooden sculpture: a crucifix.

More great frescoes await in the Cloisters (*entrance to the left of the church; open Sat–Thurs 9–2; closed Fri; adm*). Those in the **Green Cloister** are the masterpiece of Paolo Uccello and his assistants; though deteriorated, they are still striking for their Uccellian obsessions: perspective and animals. Best known, and in better condition than the others, is the surreal *Universal Deluge*. The **Spanish Chapel** is also famous for its frescoes, the masterpiece of a little-known 14th-century artist, Andrea di Buonaiuto.

North of the Duomo: San Lorenzo and the Palazzo Medici-Riccardi

North of the Duomo and east of Santa Maria is the lively neighbourhood around San Lorenzo's flamboyant street market. Here you'll find the ancient church of **San Lorenzo**, parish church of the Medici and a shrine to the art of Brunelleschi and Michelangelo. The **interior** is true to Brunelleschi's design, a contemplative repetition of arches and columns in grey and white. Its artistic treasures are few but choice; most riveting are Donatello's unbalanced, emotional pulpits. Off the left transept, Brunelleschi's **Old Sacristy** is often cited as one of the first and finest works of the early Renaissance, designed with his characteristic mathematical precision. In contrast, Michelangelo's celebrated **Biblioteca Laurenziana** (*entered from the cloister; open Mon–Sat 8.30–1.30*) is something of a Mannerist prototype, its architectural elements stuck on for effect rather than for any structural purpose.

San Lorenzo is most famous, however, for the **Medici Chapels** (*open 8.15–5; closed second and fourth Sun and first, third and fifth Mon of month*), outside and behind the church. The main monument, designed according to the best Medici taste, is the **Chapel of the Princes**, a stupefying, fabulously costly octagon of death, lined in *pietra dura*. From here a corridor leads to Michelangelo's **New Sacristy**, a silent, closed-in mausoleum calculated to depress even the most chatty tour groups. Nor are the famous tombs guaranteed to cheer. *Night and Day* belongs to Giuliano Medici, Duke of Nemours, symbolizing the Active Life; *Dawn and Dusk* is that of Lorenzo, Duke of Urbino, symbolizing Contemplative Life. Idealized statues of the two men, in Roman patrician gear, represent these states of mind, while draped on their sarcophagi are Michelangelo's four allegorical figures of the Times of Day, so heavy with weariness and grief they seem ready to slide off onto the floor. The most finished figure, *Night*, has always impressed the critics; she is almost a personification of despair.

A block from the Piazza del Duomo, the **Palazzo Medici-Riccardi** offers an antidote in Benozzo Gozzoli's 1459 *Procession of the Magi* in the **Cappella dei Magi** (*open Thurs–Tues 9–7; closed Wed; adm; only a few people allowed at a time; in summer you can book,* ***t*** *055 276 0340*), a merry pageant of beautifully dressed kings, knights and pages, accompanied by greyhounds and a giraffe, amid jewel-like trees and castles.

Piazza San Marco, the Accademia and the Archaeology Museum

In the northeast corner of the city lies **Piazza San Marco**, a lively square full of art students from the nearby Accademia. The north side of the square is occupied by the **church and convent of San Marco** (***convent*** *open 8.15–1.50, Sat 8.15–6.50; closed first and third Sun of month and second and fourth Mon of month; adm;* ***church*** *open 7–12 and 4–7 daily*), unchanged from the 1400s and best known for the works of the other-worldly Fra Angelico, who turned Michelozzo's simple cloister into an exposition of his faith, expressed in bright playroom colours and soft angelic pastels. Among the works gathered here are his great *Last Judgement* (1430), the charming *Thirty-five Scenes from the Life of Christ* and an *Annunciation* that must have earned him his beatification. The church-like **Library** is one of Michelozzo's greatest works, radiating a spirit of serenity.

From the Piazza San Marco, Via Ricasoli makes a beeline for the Duomo, but on most days the view is obstructed by the crowds around **the Galleria dell'Accademia** (*open Tues–Sun 8.15–6.50 and summer Sat 8.15–10pm; closed Mon; adm exp*), anxious to get a peek at Michelangelo's overweening *David*. Michelangelo completed the statue in 1504, and it established the overwhelming reputation he had in his own time; as a symbol of Renaissance aspirations, it is unsurpassed. Nearby are Michelangelo's famous *nonfiniti*, the four *Prisoners* or *Slaves*, left in various stages of completion. Other rooms contain good *quattrocento* painting, including works by Botticelli and Perugino, and the delightful Adimari chest, which pops up in half the books ever written about the Renaissance.

East of the Accademia, beautiful Piazza Santa Annunziata is the address of Brunelleschi's celebrated **Spedale degli Innocenti** (1420) and its famous portico; to this day it still functions as an orphanage. Nearby up Via della Colonna is the impressive **Museo Archeològico** (*open Mon 2–7, Tues and Thurs 8.30–7, Wed and Fri–Sun 8.30–2;*

adm). Besides a beautifully lit Egyptian collection, the museum has a cases full of wonderful Etruscan finds, including a famous 5th-century bronze Chimera; there's also a vast collection of Greek pottery, bronzes and fabulous Greek marble sculptures.

Santa Croce

Santa Croce (*open summer Mon–Sat 9.30–5.30, Sun 3–5.30; winter Mon–Sat 9.30–12.30 and 3–5.30, Sun 3–5.30*), the big Franciscan church on Florence's east end, is Italy's 'Westminster Abbey', filled with monuments to illustrious men. The rule is, the greater the person, the uglier the tomb: Vasari's **Tomb of Michelangelo** (1570) is one of the least attractive. There are, however, beautiful contributions by Donatello, Canova, Antonio and Bernardo Rossellini and da Settignano, and Benedetto da Maiano's **marble pulpit** (1476) is one of the most beautiful of the Renaissance. Santa Croce is especially rich in *trecento* frescoes, providing a unique chance to compare the work of Giotto with his followers. There are later compositions (1380s) by Agnolo Gaddi in the **Castellani Chapel**, while the beautiful **Baroncelli Chapel** was painted by Agnolo's father Taddeo, Giotto's assistant in the 1330s. The **Peruzzi** and **Bardi Chapels** were frescoed by Giotto himself in the 1330s, now restored more or less as Giotto painted them. The **Pazzi Chapel** (*open Thurs–Tues 10–5, later in summer; closed Wed; adm*) is well worth the entrance fee, containing some of Brunelleschi's best work.

The Oltrarno

Once over the Ponte Vecchio, a greener, quieter Florence reveals itself, squeezed against the river by a chain of hills that afford some of the best views over the city.

The **Pitti Palace** remained the residence of the Medici until 1868 and houses eight **museums** – a tribute to Medici acquisitiveness in the centuries of decadence. Most people visit the Galleria Palatina (*open Tues–Sun 8.15–6.50; adm*), containing the State Apartments and a famous collection of 16th- –18th-century paintings (by the likes of Titian, Raphael and Botticelli). Other museums feature later art, jewellery, clothes, ceramics and carriages. Stretching back invitingly from the Pitti, the **Boboli Gardens** (*open 9–one hour before sunset; adm*) are full of shady nooks and pretty walks.

Piazza Santo Spirito, the centre of the Oltrarno, becomes lively at night but is quiet by day, with a few market stalls and cafés. On one side stands Brunelleschi's last and perhaps finest church, **Santo Spirito**. Further west, the Oltrarno's other great church, **Santa Maria del Carmine** (*open 10–5, Sun and hols 1–5; closed Tues; adm; only 30 people at a time, for 15mins*) houses wonderful frescoes in the **Cappella Brancacci**. Three artists worked on them, but it's the scenes by Masaccio, from the early 1400s, that were studied by all subsequent artists for his precocious rendering of light and space.

At the eastern end of the Oltrarno it's worth climbing up to **San Miniato** (*open daily summer 8–7.30; winter daily 8–12.30 and 2.30–7.30*) for a wonderful panorama and one of the finest Romanesque churches in Italy. Besides its delicate *intarsia* floor of animals and zodiac symbols, it holds Michelozzo's unique **Cappella del Crocifisso**, magnificently carved and adorned with terracottas by Luca della Robbia. Elsewhere there are works by Antonio Rossellino, Alesso Baldovinetti and Piero Pollaiuolo, while the **cloister** has remarkable frescoes by Paolo Uccello.

Touring from Pisa

Day 1: Gardens, a Spa and Zebra Stripes Galore

Morning: Take the S12(r) northeast to **Lucca** (*see* p.178) and from there, look for the S435 east; in 9km you'll see a turn to **Collodi**, home of Carlo Collodi, author of *Pinocchio*; there's a **Parco di Pinocchio** (*open 8.30–sunset; adm*) for the kids but, even better, superb 17th-century Italian gardens, complete with labyrinth, at the **Castello Garzoni** (*open 9–one hour before sunset; mid-Nov–mid-Mar Sun only; adm*). **Pescia**, 5km west, is the cut-flower capital of Italy; visit the 14th-century church of **San Francesco**, with a portrait and scenes of Francis' life (1235) believed to be an authentic likeness. Then continue east to the delicious spa of **Montecatini Terme**, in the 'Valley of Mists'.

Lunch: In Montecatini Terme, *see* below.

Afternoon: Continue east on the S435 to **Pistoia**, full of medieval zebra stripes; its Piazza del Duomo is one of the most perfect squares in Italy. Visit the 12th-century **Duomo**, with its fabulous silver altar of St James (*open daily 8–12 and 3.30–5.30*), the Gothic **Baptistry** by Andrea Pisano and the art-filled **Museo Civico** (*open Tues–Sat 10–7, Sun 9.30–12.30; closed Mon; adm*) in the Palazzo Comunale. Other jewels are the 12th-century **Sant'Andrea** (*open daily 8–12.30 and 3.30–6*), with a fabulous pulpit by Giovanni Pisano (1297), and the 12th-century **San Giovanni Fuoricivitas** (*open daily 8–12 and 4–6.30*), the stripiest church in all Christendom.

Dinner and Sleeping: In or near Pistoia, *see* below.

Day 1

Lunch in Montecatini Terme

Enoteca da Giovanni, Via Garibaldi 25, **t** 0572 71695 (*expensive*). A unique, time-honoured place, where game dishes – hare, venison and wild duck – turn into impeccably haute cuisine in the hands of a master chef. Next door, at **Cucina da Giovanni**, you can dine on simpler fare at more modest prices; the *antipasti* and *maccheroni* with duck sauce are divine. *Closed Mon.*

Ristorante il Cuco, Via Salsero 3, **t** 0572 72765 (*expensive–moderate*). Elaborate Tuscan cooking, at some of the more reasonable prices in Montecatini.

Dinner in or around Pistoia

See also 'Sleeping in or around Pistoia', below.

Rafanelli, Via Sant'Agostino 47, Sant'Agostino, **t** 0573 532 046 (*moderate*). Tuscan home cooking, including *maccheroni* with duck, games dishes and lamb, served in a pretty country villa. *Closed Sun eve, Mon, and Aug.*

Locanda degli Elfi, Via della Chiesa 3, Loc. San Felice, **t** 0573 416 700 (*expensive–moderate*). A beautiful 18th-century villa, offering fish and local dishes. *Closed Tues.*

Sleeping in or around Pistoia

Pistoia, inventor of pistols in the Renaissance, is now the ornamental plant capital of Italy, and most of its hotels and restaurants are geared to businessmen. But there are some good bets just outside of town.

*****Il Convento**, Via S. Quirico 33, 5km east at Pontenuovo, **t** 0573 452 651, **f** 0573 453 578 (*moderate*). A former convent, preserving its exterior if not all of its interior. The setting is quiet, with views over Pistoia; there's a pool and one of the city's better restaurants.

Villa Vannini, 6km north of town, **t** 0573 42031, **f** 0573 26331 (*moderate*). Even more rural, this delightful villa is set amongst fir trees; wonderful walks await on the doorstep. Rooms are elegant, comfortable and excellent value and there's also a good restaurant for dinner.

Day 2: Leonardo, *Trecento* Frescoes and Chianti

Morning: Drive south on a narrow winding road through lovely countryside to **Vinci**, the birthplace in 1452 of the great Leonardo, illegitimate son of a notary and a peasant girl. In his honour the town's castle has been converted into a **Museo Leonardiano** (*open daily 9.30–6; in summer until 7; adm*), full of models of the inventions he designed in his *Codex Atlanticus* notebooks. Leonardo's actual birthplace is a simple stone house 3km away in **Anchiano** (*open daily 9.30–6; summer until 7; adm*). Continue south to **Empoli** – try to arrive in time to see the **Collegiata Sant'Andrea** and the **museum** (*open Tues–Sun 9–12 and 4–7; closed Mon; adm*) in its cloister. Though small, it is full of beautiful works by Masolino, Starnina, Lorenzo Monaco and Mino da Fiesole.

Lunch: In Empoli, *see* below.

Afternoon: Take the S67 east to **Montelupo**, and turn south for **San Casciano in Val di Pesa**, the largest town in Chianti, with more good *trecento* art in **Santa Maria del Prato** (1335). Continue southeast to **Mercatale**, surrounded by villas and castles from the days when Chianti was a war zone between Florence and Siena rather than a wine region. From here, drive east towards **Passo dei Pecorai**, where you can pick up the scenic **Chiantigiana** (aka S222). Follow this south to **Greve in Chianti**, packed with shops selling you know what; take the side road east to visit the lovely towns of the Monti del Chianti, **Radda** and **Gaiole**, and end up back on the S222 at **Castellina in Chianti**.

Dinner and Sleeping: In Castellina in Chianti, *see* below.

Day 2

Lunch in Empoli

Empoli has no pretentions, and you won't have any trouble finding a place to eat.

La Panzanella, Via dei Cappuccini 10, **t** 0571 922 182 (*moderate–cheap*). An old-fashioned *trattoria* by the station, which does wonderful things with porcini mushrooms in season, and sometimes snails, too. In summer don't miss the *panzanella* – a kind of Tuscan gazpacho. *Closed Sun.*

Il Galeone, Via Curtatone e Montanara 67, **t** 0571 72826 (*moderate*). A good place for fresh fish dishes. *Closed Sun.*

Dinner in Castellina in Chianti

Castellina, one of the prettiest hill towns in Chianti, is a fine place to spend the night, with several good hotels and restaurants.

Albergaccio di Castellina, Via Fiorentina 35, on the road to San Donato, **t** 0577 741 042 (*expensive*). On the outskirts of town, this serves fresh food, attractively presented, with a glass of *spumante* and free rolls with every meal. Excellent value. *Closed Sun.*

Antica Trattoria Le Torre, Piazza del Comune, **t** 0577 740 236 (*moderate*). A popular family-run place with a cosy atmosphere, serving tasty dishes like risotto with mushrooms and an exceptional *fagiano alla Torre*, prepared to an ancient Chianti recipe. *Closed Fri.*

Sleeping in Castellina in Chianti

****__Villa Casalecchi__**, **t** 055 740 240, **f** 055 741 111 (*very expensive*). A comfortable old house set among trees and vineyards on a slope, with some elegant rooms full of antiques, and some that aren't so elegant; from either, however, you can enjoy the big pool and the enchanting views over the hills. *Open April–Oct.*

***__Salivolpi__**, Via Fiorentina, **t** 055 740 484, **f** 055 740 998 (*moderate*). Two old farmhouses have been combined to create this smart establishment just outside Castellina; a garden and pool are added attractions.

Day 3: A Sienese Interlude

Morning: Drive 22km south to **Siena**, the most beautiful city in Tuscany, a flamboyant medieval ensemble of palaces and towers in warm brick. Start near the top at the glorious striped **Duomo** (*open Nov–mid-Mar Mon–Sat 7.30–1 and 2.30–5, Sun 2–5; mid-Mar–Oct Mon–Sat 7.30–7.30, Sun 2–5*), begun in 1200, with its intricate marble pavement and stained glass. Off the left aisle, the delightful **Piccolomini Library** (*open winter 10–1 and 2.30–5; summer 9–7.30; Sun all year only 2.30–5; adm*) was frescoed by Pinturicchio with the life of Aeneas Silvius, who became Pope Pius II. Down the steps, the **Baptistry** (*open summer 9–7.30; winter 10–1 and 2.30–5; adm*) holds another trove of art; look out especially for the font, covered with reliefs by the likes of Donatello, Ghiberti and della Quercia. The **Ospedale di Santa Maria della Scala** (*open Mar–Oct 10–6; Nov–Feb 10.30–4.30; adm*), opposite the cathedral, was once the best and largest hospital in the world; inside it has a wonderful frescoes.

Lunch: In Siena, *see* below.

Afternoon: Stroll around Siena's **Campo**, the beautiful scallop-shell central square where the famous Palio horse race takes place every year. Visit the **Palazzo Pubblico** (1310), still the city hall, under the tremendous 332ft **Torre di Mangia** (*open Nov–mid-Mar 10–4; mid-Mar–Oct 10–7; July–Aug 10am–11pm; adm*). The lower part is now the **city museum** (*open daily 10–7; adm*), home to Ambrogio Lorenzetti's famous fresco cycle, the *Allegories of Good and Bad Government*. Wander along Siena's lovely streets until the light fades, then head northwest 27km to **Colle di Val d'Elsa**.

Dinner and Sleeping: In or near Colle di Val d'Elsa, *see* below.

Day 3

Lunch in Siena

Siena specializes in sweets, including two rich cakes you'll see for sale everywhere: *panforte*, laced with fruits, nuts, orange peel and secret ingredients; and *panpepato*, similar, but containing pepper.

Tullio ai Tre Cristi, Vicolo Provenzano, **t** 0577 280 608 (*moderate*). Established *c.* 1830 and perhaps the most authentic of all Sienese restaurants; the menu includes dishes such as *ribollita*, tripe with sausage and roast boar. Their *pici* (Sienese fat spaghetti) is home-made. In the summer, there are tables outside. *Closed Mon.*

Ristorante-Pizzeria, Via dei Fusari, hidden around the corner from Santa Maria della Scala (*cheap*). A good informal no-name restaurant, perfect for lunch after slogging through the Duomo. There's an excellent value set-price menu with a wide choice of dishes, and you can get pizza even at lunch time; just get there early.

Dinner and Sleeping in or near Colle di Val d'Elsa

*****Villa Belvedere**, Loc. Belvedere, **t** 0577 920 966, **f** 0577 924 128 (*expensive*). Located a kilometre or so east of town, near the Siena highway, this pretty villa has a big garden, a restaurant and 15 simple rooms.

*****Arnolfo**, Via Campana 8, **t** 0577 922 020, **f** 0577 92224 (*moderate–cheap*). Simple and comfortable, this is in the town itself, and has a popular restaurant (*see* below).

Arnolfo restaurant, Via XX Settembre 52, **t** 0577 922 549 (*very expensive–expensive*). Just around the corner from the hotel, this now occupies a Renaissance palace, the perfect setting for what is widely considered one of the top restauarants in all Italy. Menus are seasonal, but you can always choose from two menus: one 'traditional'; one 'creative'. *Closed Tues.*

Ristorante lo Sfizio, Via Graco del Secco 86, **t** 0577 922 115 (*expensive–moderate*). A good value alternative, only slightly less upmarket than the Arnolfo. *Closed Fri.*

Day 4: Medieval Towers and Etruscans

Morning: Take a walk around the striking hill town of **Colle di Val d'Elsa**, birthplace of the great sculptor Arnolfo di Cambio and today Italy's top producer of fine glass. Then make the short drive north to **San Gimignano**, Italy's best-preserved medieval city, famed for its medieval towers – 15 of the original 70 survive. The tallest of these, belonging to the **Palazzo del Popolo**, rises high (177ft) over the Piazza del Duomo. The palace houses the **Museo Civico** (*open Nov–Feb 10–5.30; Mar–Oct 9.30–7.30; adm*), with an excellent collection of Florentine and Sienese art. The same lovely *piazza* has the **Collegiata**, begun in the 12th century and full of frescoes, including the most perverse *Last Judgement* ever (by Taddeo di Bartolo) and, in the **Chapel of Santa Fina** (*open April–Oct Mon–Fri 9.30–7.30, Sat 9.30–5, Sun and hols 1–5; Nov–Mar Mon–Sat 9.30–5, Sun and hols 1–5; adm*), some foolish, pretty ones by Ghirlandaio, dedicated to one of the most absurd holy legends in Christendom.

Lunch: In San Gimignano, *see* below.

Afternoon: Head south through San Donato to the S68 for **Volterra**. The Etruscans were the first to settle its spectacular site, and you can learn all about them in the excellent **Museo Etrusco Guarnacci** near the main gate (*open 16 Mar–2 Nov daily 9–7; 3 Nov–15 Mar daily 9–2; adm exp; a joint ticket covers Volterra's other museums*). South of the museum you can have a walk through the pretty **Parco Archeològico** (*open 11–5*), a lush English garden of manicured lawns and shady groves unlike anything else in Tuscany.

Dinner and Sleeping: In Volterra, *see* below.

Day 4

Lunch in San Gimignano

Dorando, Vicolo del Oro 2, **t** 0577 941 862 (*expensive*). For the adventurous; the chef attempts to recreate authentic Etruscan cuisine: *cibreo* (a truly rich chicken liver pâté); *pici* with mint-leaf pesto; and crème caramel flavoured with coriander. The combinations are often surprisingly tasty. *Closed Mon.*

Le Terrazze, in Hotel La Cisterna, Piazza della Cesterna, **t** 0577 940 328 (*moderate*). This is very popular, both for its views and for the cuisine. The *medaglione al vinsanto* is a treat, or else try *osso buco 'alla Toscana'*, followed by classics like *zuppa sangimignese* or *pappardelle alla lepre* (wide noodles with hare). *Closed for lunch Tues and Wed.*

Il Pino, Via San Matteo 102, **t** 0577 940 415, **f** 0577 942 225 (*moderate–cheap*). At the opposite end of town, the main attraction to be savoured here is the *antipasti*; but it can be pricier if you indulge in the dishes with truffles that are Il Pino's pride. *Closed Thurs.*

Dinner in Volterra

Il Sacco Fiorentino, Piazza XX Settembre 18, **t** 0588 88537 (*expensive–moderate*). This combines a vast assortment of *crostini*, wonderful gnocchi, roast pork with olives and more, on a seasonal menu.

Il Porcellino, Vicolo delle Prigioni 18, **t** 0588 86392 (*moderate*). Here you'll find seafood and local favourites such as roast pigeon and boar with olives. *Closed Oct–Mar.*

La Tavernetta, Via Guarnacci 14, **t** 0588 87630 (*moderate*). This offers hearty Tuscan fare. *Closed Tues and two weeks in Feb.*

Sleeping in Volterra

********San Lio****, Via San Lio 26, **t** 0588 85250, **f** 0588 80620 (*expensive–moderate*). A fairly upscale place, with tastefully remodelled rooms set around an old cloister; it's the only hotel in the city which has parking.

*****Villa Nencini**, Borgo S. Stefano, **t** 0588 86386, **f** 0588 80601 (*moderate, some rooms cheaper without bath*). A 16th-century house with beautiful views just north of the centre.

Day 5: A Bevy of Tuscan Hill Towns

Morning: Explore the rest of Volterra, along with its numerous alabaster shops. The same stone went into Mino da Fiesole's tabernacle, over the high altar in the **Duomo**; the cathedral also has a good carved pulpit by the Pisani. Near here, in Via Porta all'Arco, is an **Etruscan arch** from *c.* 600 BC, adorned by three gods, now worn by time into garden slugs. Pop into the **Pinacoteca** (*hours and ticket as for archaeology museum*; see *Day 4, p.193*), which has a small but choice collection starring Rosso Fiorentino's startling Mannerist *Deposition*. Next, head north out of Volterra, passing the striking, eroded formations known as the **Balze**, and continue northeast through stunning scenery to **Certaldo**, hometown of Boccaccio.

Lunch: In Certaldo, *see* below.

Afternoon: Visit Certaldo's 14th-century **Palazzo Pretorio**, now the town museum (*open summer 10–1 and 2.30–7.30; winter 10–1 and 3–5.30; adm*) and Boccaccio's tomb in **SS. Michele ed Iacopo**. Then carry on north to **Castelfiorentino**, a handsome hill town rebuilt after the war, with a fine **Pinacoteca** (*open Mon–Sat 4–7, Sun 10–12 and 4–7, but times may vary*) in the church of Santa Verdiana. Continue north and turn left at **Ponte a Elsa** for **San Miniato**, another hill town, famous for its national kite-flying contest; on a clear day the views are tremendous. Here you can have a look in the **Duomo** and its **museum** (*open summer Tues–Sun 9–12 and 3–5; winter Sat and Sun only 9–12 and 2.30–5; adm*), as well as other pretty churches.

Dinner and Sleeping: In or around San Miniato, *see* below. In the morning drive back west to Pisa (38km).

Day 5

Lunch in Certaldo

Osteria del Vicaro, Via Rivellino 3, **t** 0571 668 228 (*expensive*). This is in a 12th-century ex-monastery, now converted into a hotel and serving delicious fresh fare.

Dolci Follie, Piazza Bocaccio (*cheap*). A fancy *pasticceria*, a wine bar, but also a fine little restaurant, where the cuisine is more than a simple prelude to the exquisite desserts.

Dinner and Sleeping in San Miniato

******Miravalle**, Piazza Castello 3, **t** 0571 418 075, **f** 0571 419 681 (*moderate*). Sleep in Emperor Frederick II's 12th-century palace, near the top of the town.

Il Canapone, Piazza Bonaparte 5, **t** 0571 418 121 (*moderate*). A simple place where you can try the local white truffles on spaghetti, in risotto, or with veal *scaloppine*; in the spring, try the rice with asparagus. The square is named for the local Bonaparte family, reputedly the ancestors of Napoleon.

Dinner and Sleeping in Montópoli in Val d'Arno

*****Quattro Gigli**, Piazza Michele 2, 10km west of San Miniato, **t** 0571 466 878, **f** 0571 466 879 (*moderate; cheap without bath*). In this little place, the old town hall has been converted into an inn with 28 rooms of varying quality. The hotel **restaurant** (*moderate*), situated beyond the permanent display of Montópoli's painted ceramics, has a delightful terrace and features an imaginative menu, based on Tuscan traditions and seasonal ingredients. You'll find plenty of mushrooms, vegetables and salads, and an Italian rarity: roast potatoes. The duck and game are excellent. *Closed Sun eve and Mon.*

Dinner in Fucécchio

Le Vedute, Via Romana-Lucchese 121, 5km north of San Miniato, **t** 0571 297 498 (*expensive*). A good seafood restaurant in the country, where you can linger on the veranda over your favourite denizen of the deep; there are also good meats in the autumn. *Closed Mon.*

The Marches

10

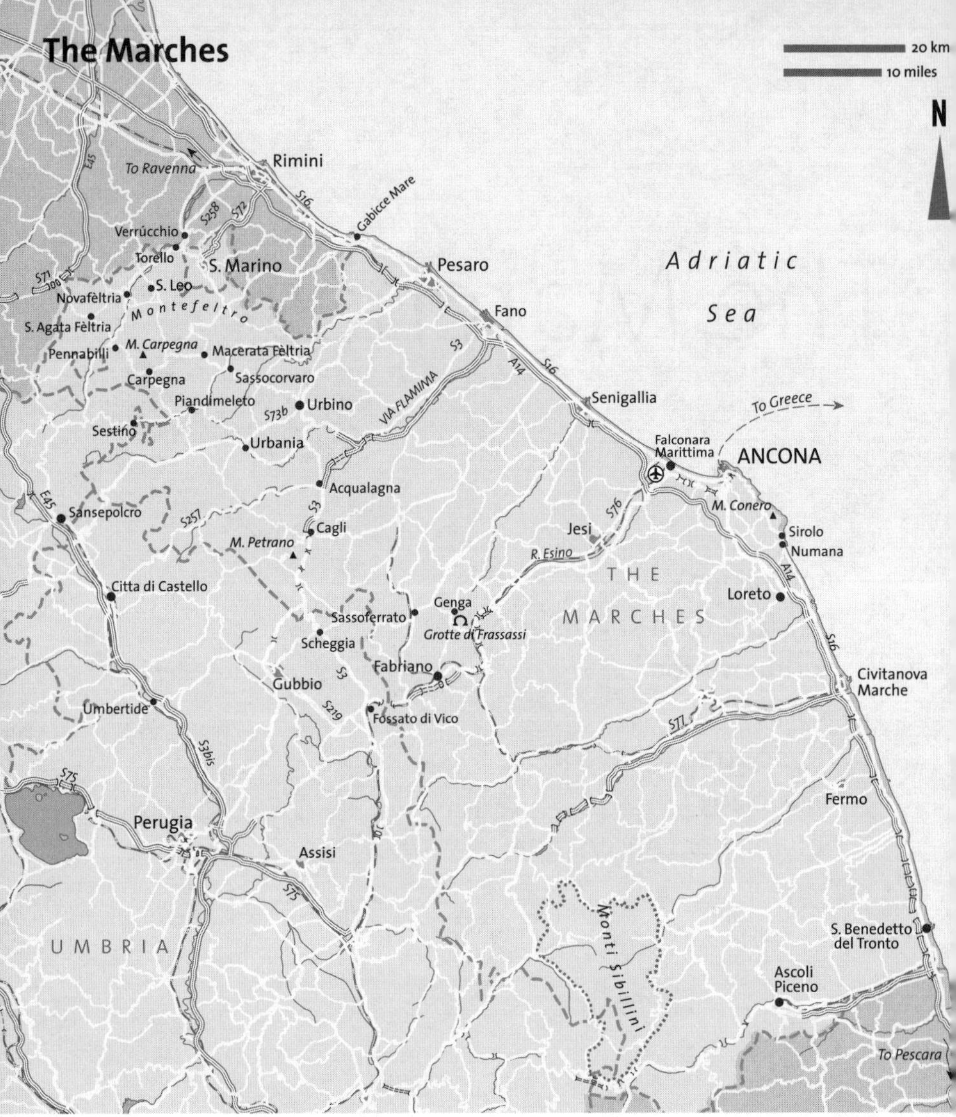

In the Middle Ages, a *march* was a border province of the Holy Roman Empire. With no better name than that, one might expect the Marches to be lacking in personality, but in fact, this is one of the greenest, prettiest and most civilized corners of Italy. Tucked between the Apennines and the sea, it has lovely Renaissance art towns such as Urbino, lots of beaches, art and scores of fine old rosy-brick towns in the valleys that lead up to the snowy peaks of the Sibilline Mountains, one of the highest sections of the Apennines. Today, what every Italian knows about the Marchigiani is that they have a new-found talent for business, and it's given the region a fresh sense of pride. They use their natural Italian talent to find something they can make better or more cheaply than anyone else – from shoes to electric guitars – and the results are often spectacular.

Ancona

A patch of mountains on an otherwise pancake coast provides the mid-Adriatic's biggest port with a splendid crescent-shaped harbour under the steep promontory of Monte Guasco. Ancona never had the leisure to blossom in the style of Italy's other maritime republics: it was too busy battling rival Venice and various emperors; then the 20th century thought to inflict it with a rash of bombings, earthquakes and even a landslide, causing the abandonment of parts of the old town. But for all its troubles, Ancona (pop. 101,000) has come up smiling. The port is prospering, and the city is now devoting its attention to restoring the historic centre.

Around the Port

Most of Ancona's monuments have survived the recent misfortunes. At its western end, the long curve of the port is anchored by the fortress-like **Mole Vanvitelliana**, a pentagonal building designed in 1733 by the Neapolitan Luigi Vanvitelli, which now holds temporary exhibitions. At the other end of the port, the tall, graceful **Arco di Traiano** was built in AD 115 in honour of Trajan, Ancona's imperial benefactor; nearby, Pope Clement XII had Vanvitelli erect an **Arco Clementino** (1733) to himself, as papal benefactor (he declared the city a duty-free port). At the heart of the port, the elegant 15th-century Venetian Gothic **Loggia dei Mercanti** recalls Ancona's maritime heyday.

Getting to Ancona

Ryanair flies from London Stansted (2hrs25).

Getting From The Airport

Ancona's Raffaello Sanzio airport (**t** 071 28271 or 071 282 7233), 12km north of the city at Falconara. **Bus 9** runs every half hour (6.15am–6.30pm), then at 10.45 and 11.35pm, to the train station at Piazza Rosselli (25mins). **Trains** also run from Castelferretti station, outside the airport, to the station at Piazza Rosselli. A **taxi** into the centre (**t** 071 918 221) takes only 10mins and costs about €20–25.

Getting Around

You can get around town on foot, but Ancona has a network of buses/trams that also serve the Cònero Riviera. **Tickets** (€0.80) are available from *tabacchi*, from machines in the stations, and on board (more expensive).

Ancona's **train** station is west of the port on Piazza Rosselli (bus no.1 or 3 to or from Piazza Repubblica near the port). A few trains go on to Ancona Marittima station on the port itself.

Car Hire

Avis, Via Bruno 1, **t** 071 43988, or at the airport, **t** 071 44241.

Europcar, Piazza Rosselli 16, **t** 071 203 100, or at the airport, **t** 071 916 2240.

Hertz, Via Flaminia 16, **t** 071 41314, or at the airport, **t** 071 207 3798.

Maggiore Buget, Via Marconi 215, **t** 071 4264, or at the airport, **t** 071 918 8805.

Tourist Information

Ancona: Via Thaon de Revel 4, **t** 071 358 991, **f** 071 358 0592. Branches at the train station (no phone); in the port, **t** 071 201 183.

Market Days

Markets are held on Corso Mazzini (*Tues and Fri*) and on Piazza Medaglie d'Oro (*Wed and Sat*).

Shopping

Look out for ***beccute*** (biscuits with nuts and raisins), and don't miss the wines: celebrated **Verdicchio**, a delicate white born to wash down *stocco*, and **Rosso Cònero**, a full-bodied red.

Piazza della Repubblica and Via Gramsci

Just in from the Loggia, the 19th-century **Teatro delle Muse** and the church of **Santissimo Sacramento** dominate Piazza Repubblica. From here, Corso Garibaldi leads east to Piazza Cavour and Ancona's business district, while Via Gramsci climbs to the oldest quarters of Ancona. On the right, under the Renaissance arch of the handsome **Palazzo del Governo** (1484), the elongated **Piazza del Plebiscito** extends past Clement XII to the church of **San Domenico** (*open daily 8–12 and 3–7.30*), worth a step inside to see Titian's *Crucifixion* (1558) on the high altar, and Guercino's *Annunciation*, to the left. Below the church, on Corso Mazzini, Ancona is proud of its pretty **Fontana del Calamo** with its 13 spouts designed by Pellegrino Tibaldi in 1560.

Off the continuation of Via Gramsci, the 13th-century church of **Santa Maria della Piazza** (*open 7.30–7*) has a great late Romanesque façade, carved with musicians, soldiers and strange animals by a 'Master Phillippus'. Under the pavement are the ruins of the church's predecessors, from the 5th and 6th centuries. To the left of the church, the late Renaissance **Palazzo Bosdari** houses a small **Pinacoteca Comunale** (*Via Pizzecolli 17; open Tues–Sat 9–7, Mon 9–1, Sun 3–7; adm*), with a masterly *Madonna col Bambino* by the eccentric Carlo Crivelli, the tidiest of all Renaissance painters, complete with his trademark apples and cucumbers hanging overhead. Other Madonnas include one by Lorenzo Lotto (a good one), and one of Titian's, floating smugly on a cloud.

Where to Stay

Ancona ✉ 60100

****Grand Hotel Palace**, Lungomare Vanvitelli 24, **t** 071 201 813, **f** 071 207 4832, *palace.ancona@tiscalinet.it* (*expensive*). Ancona's finest hotel, near the Arco di Traiano. Comfy and small, in a 17th-century palace, with a roof garden and magnificent views over the port, but no restaurant.

****Grand Hotel Passetto**, Via Thaon de Revel 1, **t** 071 31307, **f** 071 32856 (*very expensive–expensive*). Similar; central but modern, with a pool in summer.

***Fortuna**, Piazza Rosselli 15, **t** 071 42663, **f** 071 42662 (*moderate*). The nicest place near the station; convenient and comfortable.

***Della Rosa**, Piazza Rosselli 3, **t** 071 42651, **f** 071 41388 (*moderate*). Near the station, this has pleasant rooms, not all en suite.

Gino, Via Flaminia 4, **t/f** 071 42179, *hotel.gino@tiscalinet.it* (*cheap*). A straightforward place, but the restaurant has excellent fresh seafood. *Closed Sun.*

Dorico, Via Flaminia 8, **t/f** 071 42761 (*cheap*). On the same road, this offers simple rooms, with or without bath.

Eating Out

The dish to try is *stoccafisso all'anconetana*, dried cod exquisitely prepared in a casserole with tomatoes, potatoes and marjoram, or *brodetto*, a soup made with a variety of fish.

Passetto, Piazzale IV Novembre, **t** 071 33214 (*expensive*). An excellent seafood place with a seaside terrace. *Closed Sun eve, Mon and second and third weeks in Aug.*

La Moretta, Piazza Plebiscito 52, **t** 071 202 317 (*expensive*). This is a long-established local favourite for excellent *stoccafisso all'anconetana* and *spaghetti agli scampi*. *Closed Sun.*

Corte, Via della Loggia 5, **t** 071 200 806 (*moderate*). Set in an elegant 18th-century palace near the port, with a very pretty summer garden and excellent gourmet dishes, including fish. *Closed Sun and Jan.*

Osteria del Pozzo, Via Bonda 2, **t** 071 207 3996 (*cheap*). In the middle of the port, this is elegant but absurdly cheap; try the mixed fry or pasta of the day. *Closed Sun and Aug.*

La Cantinetta, Via Gramsci, **t** 071 201 107 (*cheap*). A popular, atmospheric place, famed for its *stoccafisso* (on Fridays), its nightly fish fry, *vincisgrassi* and lemon sorbet. *Closed Sun.*

On Monte Guasco

Further up towards Via del Guasco is the area hardest hit by the earthquake and landslide; bits of decorative brickwork from Roman Ancona's **theatre** peek out between the ruined buildings. In the ripe interior of a 16th-century palace, the **Museo Archeologico Nazionale delle Marche** (*Via Feretti 6; open Tues–Sun 8.30–7.30; closed*

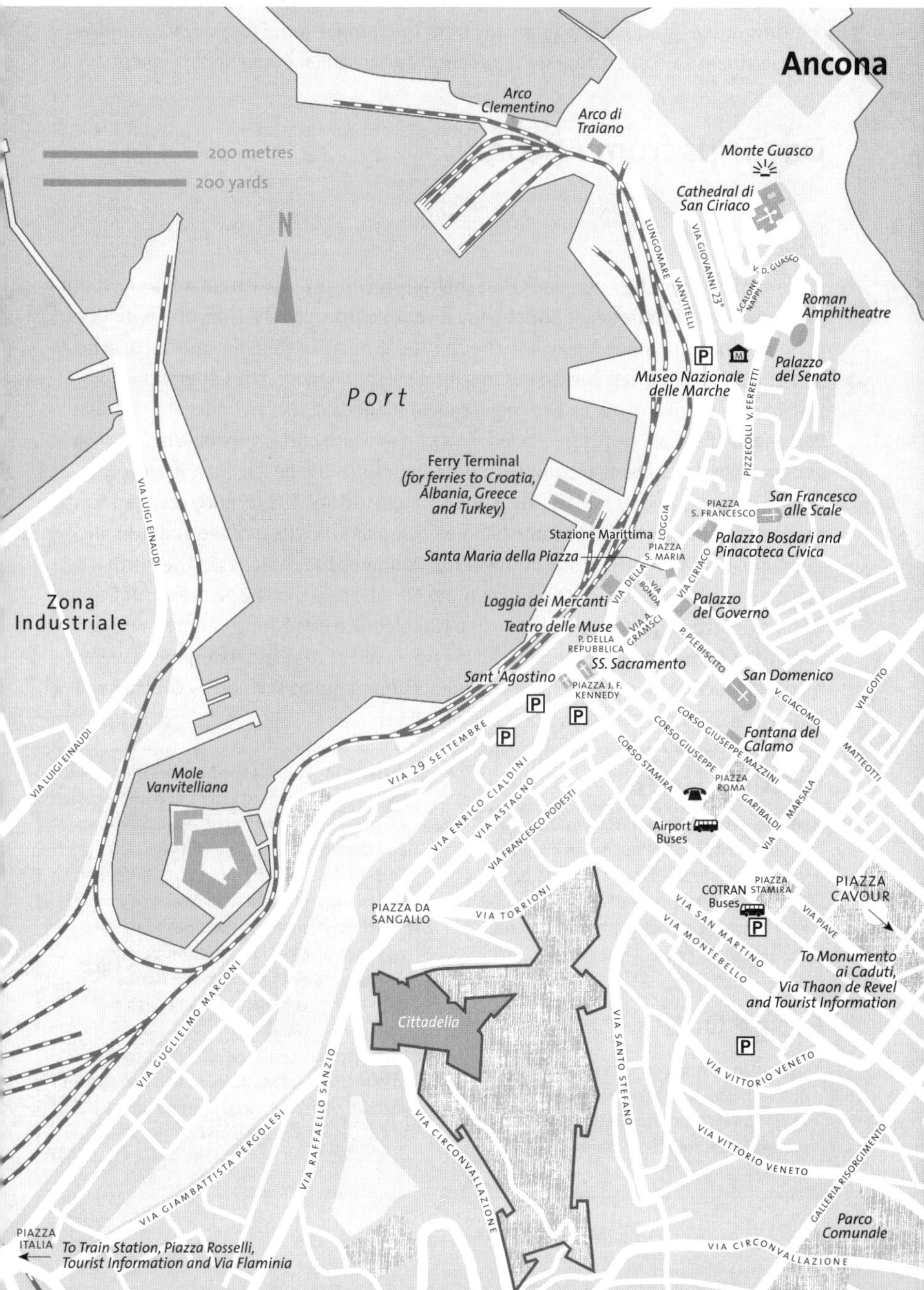

Mon; adm) has a rich archaeological collection, including some exceptional Greek vases and metalwork, beautiful Etruscan bronzes, gold and amber from Gaulish and Piceni tombs, and an extensive collection of Roman finds. Crowning the ancient Greek acropolis of Monte Guasco is the pink and white **Cattedrale di San Ciriaco** (*open autumn and winter 8–12 and 3–6; spring and summer 8–12 and 3–7*), facing out to sea on the site of a famous temple of Venus. Beyond the fancy Gothic porch, the marble columns of the interior come originally from the temple, some topped by Byzantine capitals; there's also an elaborate 12th-century altar screen in the right transept.

Day Trips from Ancona

Portonovo

The same arm of the Apennines that shelters Ancona's port also creates a short but uniquely beautiful stretch of Adriatic coast south of the city. The cliffs of Monte Cónero (1,876ft) plunge steeply into the sea, isolating a number of beautiful beaches and coves that are often packed out in summer. From Ancona, the Cónero road threads the narrow corniche between sea and mountain; tucked under the cliffs is **Portonovo**, the most beautiful place for a swim in these parts, its pebble beach clean and unspoiled despite its proximity to the city. Besides the beach, there's a lovely church of the 1030s, built in the style of Ancona cathedral. The recently restored **Santa Maria di Portonovo**, with the same blind arcading around the roofline and a distinctive cupola in the centre, is one of the better Romanesque churches in the north, mentioned as 'the House of Our Lady on the Adriatic coast' in the 21st canto of Dante's *Paradiso*. Portonovo's fortress, the **Fortino Napoleonico** (*see* Eating Out, below), has a watch-tower built by Pope Clement XII in 1716 – even at that late date, pirates were a menace. Much earlier, some of the local pirates hung out at the nearby **Grotta degli Schiavi**, facing a sheltered cove popular with divers.

Getting There

Portonovo is only 30mins from the city centre. RENI **buses** to the Cónero Riviera depart from Piazza Cavour, **t** 071 804 6430. CONERO bus no.94 serves Portonovo from Piazza Rosselli, **t** 071 280 2092, with around 10 buses each way daily.

Eating Out

******Fortino Napoleonico**, **t** 071 801 450, **f** 071 801 454 (*very expensive–expensive*). The hotel incorporates part of a fortress built in the Napoleonic Wars and its restaurant is one of the Marches' finest, with two beautiful dining rooms and immaculate service. Eight superb courses include olives and scampi, sole stuffed with spinach, cream and smoked salmon, shrimps with fennel and orange, gnocchi with caviar, and more.

*****Internazionale**, Via Portonovo 149, **t** 071 801 001, **f** 071 801 082 (*moderate*). A sturdy stone building in the trees, with ravishing views, its own beach and a good restaurant.

Il Laghetto, near Portonovo's lake, **t** 071 801 183 (*moderate*). A great place to feast on fish and *frutti di mare*, prepared in some unusual ways. *Closed Mon and mid Jan–mid Mar.*

Getting There

Several **trains** a day on the Ancona–Rome line stop at Jesi. CONERO **buses** (**t** 071 919 8623 or 071 280 2092) to Jesi leave from Piazza Cavour; many stop at the train station. Crognaletti **buses** (**t** 0731 59280) operate between Ancona and Jesi (at least once an hour Mon–Sat, several times daily on Sun).

Tourist Information

Jesi: Piazza Repubblica 11, **t** 0731 59788, **f** 0731 58291, *prolocoj@tiscali.it*, *www.comune.jesi.an/proloco*.

Eating Out

Tana Liberatutti, Piazza Baccio Pontelli I, **t** 0731 59237 (*moderate, expensive with truffles*). Set in a pretty medieval building with a garden. *Closed Sun and part of Aug*.

Hostaria Santa Lucía, Via Marche 2/b (500m from centre; ask for directions), **t** 0731 64409 (*moderate*). Delectable seafood classics, carefully but simply prepared. Book ahead. *Closed Mon and some of Aug; open eves only in winter*.

Da Antonietta, Via Garibaldi 19, **t** 0731 207 173 (*cheap*). The best kind of simple, Italian home cooking. *Closed Sun and eves*.

Jesi

The busy Valle dell'Esino is named for the hill town of **Jesi** ('Yea si'), set on a narrow ridge with houses built on and over its walls. The *centro storico* evolved around a necklace of theatrical squares: in 1194, the uppermost was thrust into the limelight when Constance de Hauteville, passing through on her way to Sicily, found herself assailed by labour pains; she promptly pitched her tent and gave birth then and there to the future Emperor Frederick II *Stupor Mundis*. The square was renamed **Piazza Federico II** and the exact spot of the tent marked by an obelisk. Further down, in Piazza Colocci, the elegant **Palazzo della Signora** has a clock tower, and wears Jesi's proud *stemma* over the portal: a giant lion rampant, paws up, ready to box all comers.

Besides the most extraordinary of medieval emperors, Jesi also gave birth to the composer Giambattista Pergolesi in 1710, who, although he died aged only 26, managed to produce some perennial favourites of the Italian repertoire: the *Stabat Mater*, the *Frate 'nnammorato* and *La Serva Padrona*. Next door to the late 18th-century **Teatro Pergolesi** (*open Mon, Wed and Sat 9–12.30, Tues and Thurs 3.30–6.30;* ***Sale*** *open Mon–Sat 10–1, Tues, Thurs and Sun also 4–7; tours available Sun; adm free*), the **Sale Pergolesiane** exhibits odds and ends relating to his life and works.

Jesi's real treasure, however, is the **Pinacoteca e Musei Civici** (*open Tues–Sat 10–1 and 4–7; adm*) in Via XX Settembre, housed in the Palazzo Pianetti. This has a delightful rococo gallery – 230ft of exuberant stuccoes on the 'human adventure in time and space' – a catch-all for lobsters, drums, camels and anything else its creator Placido Lazzarini felt like throwing in. Pride of place goes to a set of paintings by Lorenzo Lotto, including a strange, beautifully lit *Annunciation* (1526) and a luxurious *Sacra Conversazione*. A small **Museo Civico** holds Renaissance sculpture, ceramics and archaeological finds, and a modern art gallery which is mainly an excuse to see more frescoed ceilings. Outside the walls the church of **San Marco** (*open Mon–Sat 8.30–11.30 and 4–5.30, Sun 9–11.30 and 4.30–5.30*) has exceptional 14th-century frescoes in the manner of Giotto.

Loreto

Loreto, a small but concentrated dose of fine art from the Renaissance, has been one of the most popular pilgrimage sites in Europe since the 1300s, when Mary's house from Nazareth – site of the Annunciation – miraculously flew across the sea and landed in the laurel woods (*loreti*) south of Ancona. Doubting Thomases are referred to the Hebrew-Christian graffiti on its walls, similar to that in the Grotto of Nazareth.

Corso Boccalini, lined with the inevitable souvenir stands, leads from the town centre up to the **Santuario della Santa Casa** (*www.santuarioloreto.it;* ***Basilica*** *open daily 6.45am–7pm (8pm in summer);* ***Santa Casa*** *closed 12.30–2.30*), which materializes in all its glory when you turn a corner and enter the Piazza della Madonna. The understated façade is typical early Roman Baroque (1587): one of the best features is the series of reliefs on the bronze doors; another is the circle of radiating brick apses on the east end, turreted like a Renaissance castle. The only unfortunate element is the ungainly neoclassical campanile, topped with a bronze-plated garlic bulb and designed to hold a 15-ton bell.

Chapels line the walls inside, embellished by the faithful from nations around the world. Under the dome you'll see the object of the pilgrims' attention: the **Santa Casa**, a simple brick room with traces of medieval frescoes, sheathed in marble by Bramante to become one of the largest, most expensive sculptural ensembles ever attempted – the better to make the flying house stay put. Its decoration includes beautiful reliefs by Sansovino, Sangallo, della Porta and others, showing scenes from the *Life of Mary*. The reliefs on the back show the airborne house-removal that made Loreto's Virgin the patroness of the airline industry. A good deal of Loreto's art was swiped by Napoleon, but the **sacristies** on the right aisle have fine frescoes by Luca Signorelli and Melozzo da Forlì, and the **Sala del Tesoro** (1610) has a ceiling frescoed with the *Life of Mary* by Pomarancio. Upstairs in the Apostolic palace, the **Museo-Pinacoteca** (*open April–Oct Tues–Sun 9–1 and 4–7; Nov–Mar Sat and Sun 10–1 and 3–6; mid-June–mid-Sept also Thurs and Fri 9–11pm; contribution requested*) has excellent, dramatic late paintings by Lorenzo Lotto, Flemish tapestries from cartoons by Raphael and a superb collection of ceramics.

Getting There

After 11am, there are around two **trains** hourly to Loreto from Ancona, taking 20mins. CONERO **buses** (**t** 071 919 8623) also operate a frequent service to Loreto from Piazza Cavour (taking about 45mins). Local buses link Loreto station (**t** 071 978 668) with the town centre.

Tourist Information

Loreto ✉ 60025: Via Solari 3, **t** 071 970 276, **f** 071 970 020, *iat.loreto@regione.marche.it. Open Mon–Sat 9–1 and 4–7, Sun 9–1 only.*

Eating Out

Zì Nene, at the hotel Villa Tetlameya, Via Villa Costantina 187, Loreto Archi, **t** 071 978 863, **f** 071 976 639 (*expensive*). In an elegant 19th-century villa, this excellent restaurant specializes in classic seafood and historical Marchigiano recipes. *Closed Mon.*

Andreina, Via Buffolareccia 14, **t** 071 970 124 (*moderate–cheap*). This place has been here for donkey's years, continuing to serve wonderful grilled meats and Marchigiano specialities. *Closed Tues and some of July.*

Pésaro

Although it doesn't have many exceptional monuments, **Pésaro** (pop. 88,900) is none the less lovely to walk through, both in its older quarters and arcaded streets, and in the new streets by the beach. These are full of trees and little villas from the 19th century – many in the Liberty (Art Nouveau) style, including the small but outrageous **Villino Ruggieri** (1907) with a cornice supported by terracotta lobsters.

The Sforzas of Milan ruled Pésaro for a time, endowing the central Piazza del Popolo with the big, crenellated **Palazzo Ducale** (*open for tours by appointment only,* **t** *0721 387 474*). In their time, Pésaro rivalled Faenza as a producer of fine ceramics; beautiful examples are displayed in the nearby **Pinacoteca and Museo delle Ceramiche** (*Piazza Toschi Mosca 29; open Sept–June Thurs–Sun 9.30–12.30 and 4–7, Tues and Wed 9.30–12.30; July and Aug Tues and Thurs 9.30–12.30 and 5–11, Wed and Fri–Sun 9.30–12.30 and 5–8*), as well as a few good pictures, including the great *Coronation of the Virgin* (1474) by Giovanni Bellini. Pésaro also produced the composer Gioacchino Rossini in 1792, and mementos of the maestro are displayed in the nearby **Casa Rossini** (*Via Rossini 34; same hours as museums above*). The town hosts an annual Rossini festival, focused on performances in the grand **Teatro Rossini** (*closed for restoration*) in the Piazza Olivieri. In the adjacent Via Mazza, the **Museo Oliveriano** (*no.97; open Sept–June Mon–Sat 9–12; July and Aug Mon–Sat 4–7 on request; adm free*) has an intriguing collection; look out for two Greek bronze ornaments from the 5th century BC, an elegant 3rd-century Roman sarcophagus, a rare Etruscan-Latin inscription and the *stele* of Novilara, with a peculiar Iron-Age relief of a sea battle.

Getting There

Frequent **trains** serve Pésaro from Ancona's station in Piazza Rosselli (journey 35–45mins). Pésaro's station is on Viale Roma, ½km from the centre; city buses link it to the centre.

Tourist Information

Pésaro ✉ *61100*: Piazzale Libertà II, **t** 0721 69341, in Italy **t** 800 563 800, *iat.pesaro@regione.marche.it*.

Eating Out

Local cuisine includes delectables such as *garagoli in porchetta* (shellfish with olive oil, garlic, rosemary and wild fennel) and stuffed cuttlefish; a local recipe is *olivette alla pesarese* (slices of veal in prosciutto, rolled and fried). All of the above go very nicely with the local white wine, Bianchello del Metauro.

Alceo, Strada Panoramica Ardizio 101, **t** 0721 51360 (*very expensive*). This has fresh fish, home-made pasta and desserts, a friendly atmosphere and tables outside with sea views. *Closed Sun eve and Mon.*

Lo Scudiero, Via Baldassini 2, **t** 0721 64107 (*expensive*). In the cellar of a 17th-century palace, serving imaginative seafood and pasta: ravioli with sole, or *tagliatelle marine*; also good roast lamb. *Closed Sun and July.*

Teresa, at the Hotel Principe, Viale Trieste 180, **t** 0721 30222, **f** 0721 31636 (*moderate*). This excellent hotel restaurant on the waterfront serves enticing risotto with wild herbs (picked locally) and fried calamari with sage.

Antica Osteria La Guercia, Via Baviera 33, **t** 0721 33463 (*cheap*). Offers all the classics, including home-made *strozzapreti* ('priest-chokers'). *Closed Sun.*

Il Cantuccio di Leo, Via Perfetti 18, **t** 0721 68088 (*cheap*). An *enoteca* with pasta, meat dishes, boar terrines and cheeses to go with its wines. *Open until 2am. Closed Tues and July.*

Touring from Ancona

Day 1: Karstic Complexes and Paper Craft

Morning: Take the N16 north from Ancona, turning left at **Falconara Marittima** onto the S76. This winds up beyond Jesi past rolling vineyards and castles before the looming mountains are sliced by a dramatic gorge, the **Gola della Rossa**. At the western end, take the Genga-Sassoferato motorway exit to explore the magnificent 18km-long **Grotte di Frasassi** (*t 0732 97211 or t 0732 90090; open Nov–Feb Mon–Fri 11–3, Sat 11–4.30, Sun and hols 9.30–6; Mar–July and Sept daily 9.30–6; Aug daily 8–6.30; closed 4 Dec, 25 Dec, 1 Jan and 10–30; tours 70mins; adm exp, includes adm to museums*), with a spectacular display of pastel stalactites reflected in calcareous pools. Drive south to medieval **Fabriano**, famous for manufacturing paper.

Lunch: In Fabriano, *see* below.

Afternoon: Stroll through the beautiful, arcaded Piazza del Comune and visit the 14th-century **Cattedrale Basilica di San Venanzio**, glisteningly restored and containing frescoes by Allegretto Nuzi, one of Fabriano's 14th-century school of painters. Discover the art of papermaking at the **Museo della Carta e della Filigrana** (*open Tues–Sat 10–6, Sun 10–12 and 2–5; closed Mon; adm*), which also displays works of art from the town's **Pinacoteca** while it is being restored after earthquake damage. Take the S76 west to Fossato di Vico, picking up the S219 northwest to **Gubbio**.

Dinner and Sleeping: In Gubbio, *see* below.

Day 1

Lunch in Fabriano

La Pérgola, at the Hotel Janus, Piazzale Matteotti 45, **t** 0732 4191, **f** 0732 5714 (*moderate*). Connected to an ugly hotel is Fabriano's finest restaurant; try *agnolotti* with courgettes and truffles. *Closed Fri.*

Osteria da Fortino, Piazza dei Partigiani 10, near Bar Otello, **t** 0732 24455 (*moderate*). A traditional *osteria* with an array of home-made pasta, as well as meatier dishes such as wild boar (*cinghiale*). *Closed Mon.*

Dinner in Gubbio

Taverna del Lupo, Via Ansidei 21a, **t** 075 927 4368 (*expensive*). An atmospheric medieval setting, with excellent traditional fare like boar sausage, game and *risotto dei tartufi*, as well as delicious pasta and *frico*, a local dish of mixed meats with cress. *Closed Mon.*

Funivia, on Monte Ingino, **t** 075 922 1259 (*moderate*). An exceptional experience on a clear day, offering fabulous views as well as delicious pasta with truffles or porcini, and tasty *secondi*: grilled lamb or stuffed pigeon. Good desserts and local wines. *Closed Wed.*

S. Francesco e Il Lupo, Via Cairoli 24, **t** 075 927 2344 (*moderate*). Local products – among them porcini and truffles – are on offer, or you can order the cheaper pizza. *Closed Tues.*

Sleeping in Gubbio

Reservations are essential July–Aug, when visitors come looking for authentic Umbria.

****Park Hotel ai Cappuccini**, Via Tifernate, 3km out of town, **t** 075 9234, **f** 075 922 0323 (*expensive*). A beautifully restored, award-winning Franciscan monastery, in its own grounds, with pool, sauna and fitness centre.

***San Marco**, Via Perugina 5, **t** 075 922 0234, **f** 075 927 3716 (*moderate*). Mod cons in an ex-convent, with a pretty garden terrace. Rooms are all en suite and there's parking nearby.

Dei Consoli, Via dei Consoli 59, **t** 075 927 3335 (*cheap*). Small and simple; their restaurant, in a medieval cellar, serves tasty *spiedini* (meat on a spit).

Day 2: Medieval Gubbio v. Renaissance Urbino

Morning: Wander through Gubbio's resolutely medieval lanes, adorned with carved doors or windows, and discover the local ceramics, a craft inherited from the 16th-century Mastro Giorgio, who added a secret ruby lustre to his majolica. Gubbio also produced a master painter, Ottaviano Nelli; step into the church of **San Francesco** to see his 15th-century frescoes in the left apse. Hovering over a steep drop is the magnificent **Piazza della Signoria**, where Gattapone's beautiful **Palazzo dei Consoli**, now the **Museo Civico** (*open April–Sept daily 10–1 and 3–6; Oct–Mar daily 10–1 and 2–5; closed 14–15 May, 25 Dec and 1 Jan; adm*) houses a unique treasure: the bronze Eugubian Tablets, the most important inscriptions ever found in the old Umbrian language. From the Porta Romana, a *funivia* (*open winter 10–1 and 2.30–5; summer 8.30–7.30*) lifts you up to the sanctuary of **San Ubaldo**, for more spectacular views. Take the S298 northeast of Gubbio to Scheggia, turning north onto the S3 to **Cagli**.

Lunch: In Cagli, *see* below.

Afternoon: Continue north along the S3, turning off at Acqualagna to the lively university town of **Urbino**, a Renaissance monument combining elegance, learning and intelligent patronage. Here Raphael was born; here there are beautiful frescoes to be sought out in the churches; but the crown jewel is Duke Federico's twin-towered **Palazzo Ducale** (*open Tues–Sun 8.30–7, Mon 8.30–2; visits every 15 mins in winter; adm*), famed for its amazing art collection and wonderful interior décor embellished by the likes of Piero della Francesca, Paolo Uccello and Botticelli.

Dinner and Sleeping: In Urbino, *see* below.

Day 2

Lunch in Cagli

Guazza, Piazza Federico da Montefeltro, **t** 0721 787 231 (*moderate–cheap*). You can't do better for a country lunch than here, at the entrance to this village. The chef is a dab hand with fragrant porcini mushrooms and a local speciality called *fricò* – a mixture of lamb, chicken and rabbit doused in wine and vinegar and fried with garlic; try it with the house wine. *Lunch only, closed Fri and July.*

Pizzeria el Paso, Pianello di Cagli 123, **t** 0721 785 181 (*cheap*). Besides pizza, this friendly place offers a seasonal menu of typical regional dishes; you might find home-made tagliatelle, grilled meats or porcini. *Closed Tues.*

Dinner in Urbino

Vecchia Urbino, in the historic centre at Via Vasari 3/5, **t** 0722 4447 (*moderate*). An elegant option which will treat you to a feast in the autumn/winter *tartufi* and porcini season. *Closed Tues in winter.*

L'Angolo Divino, Via Sant'Andrea 14 (off Via Battisti), **t** 0722 327559 (*cheap*). Occupies a pretty room in an old palace and specializes in old Urbino specialities – pasta with chick-peas, bacon, lamb or breadcrumbs, and tasty *secondi* from the grill; some vegetarian dishes. *Closed Sun eve and Mon lunch.*

Sleeping in Urbino

Urbino's few hotels can be very crowded, so book ahead. Much of the civilized air of Duke Federico's time has survived into our own – you may end up staying longer than planned.

*******Bonconte**, Via delle Mura 28, **t** 0722 2463, **f** 0722 4782 (*expensive*). Sitting on the walls of the city, this is the most luxurious place in town short of the palace itself. Lovely views.

*****Italia**, Corso Garibaldi 32, **t** 0722 2701, **f** 0722 322 664 (*moderate*). Good and central, one block from the Ducal Palace.

*****Tortorina**, northeast of the centre at Via Tortorina 4, **t** 0722 3081, **f** 0722 308 372 (*moderate*). Has a large panoramic terrace and rooms furnished with antiques.

Day 3: Striking Crags, Castles and Churches

Morning: Start early, following signs northwest of Urbino to **Sassocorvaro**; the roads grow increasingly scenic as you approach the town, topped by the striking 15th-century Rocca Ubaldinesca (*open daily Oct–Mar Sat and Sun 9.30–12.30 and 2.30–6; daily April–Sept 9.30–12.30 and 3–7; adm*), with exhibits on country life and crafts. Continue west past **Macerata Féltria** towards the majestic **Monte Carpegna** (4,641ft), in a natural park noted for its rare wild orchids and falcons. From **Carpegna**, detour up a to a track below the summit for grandiose views. Just west, the market town of **Pennabilli** lies under two crags, each capped by an 11th-century castle. See the pretty frescoes in its Renaissance **Santuario della Madonna delle Grazie**, where a **museum** (*open on request*) displays art from the Montefeltro's churches; look out for contemporary art too, decorating houses across the town. Pause for lunch here, or go a little further north along a narrow mountain road to **Sant'Agata Féltria**, guarded by the fantastical **Rocca Fregoso** and famous for its white truffle market in October.

Lunch: In Pennabilli or Santa Agata Féltria, *see* below.

Afternoon: Visit the **Rocca** (*open winter daily 10–1 and 3–6.30; summer 10–1 and 3–7.30; adm*) to see its Renaissance frescoes, some rather unexpected stained glass from various periods, and Liberty-style (Art Nouveau) ads and posters. Drive northeast to **Novaféltria** and take the S258 four kilometres south to visit **Santa Maria Antico**, a 13th-century sandstone church with a marble lunette and a Madonna inside by Luca della Robbia. Just north of the church, a road leads east to **San Leo**.

Dinner and Sleeping: In San Leo, *see* below.

Day 3

Lunch in Pennabilli

Piastrino, Via Parco Begni 9, **t** 0541 928 569 (*moderate, cheaper without truffles*). This offers the best food in town, located in a pretty country house with a garden, just outside the *centro storico*. Truffles are their forte, though they push up the prices. *Closed Tues lunch.*

Lunch in Sant'Agata Féltria

Antenna, Monte Benedetto 32, **t** 0541 929 626 (*moderate; more expensive with truffles*). This has been renowned for nearly half a century as the best *trattoria* in the neighbourhood, situated up in the *frazione* Monte Benedetto. Come here for their excellent home-made pasta and tasty oven-baked ham; they also do a good value menu, which includes wine. If you call ahead in the autumn you can feast on their *pièce de résistance* – chestnut-stuffed pheasant. *Closed Mon exc July and Aug.*

Dinner and Sleeping in San Leo

****Castello**, Piazza Dante Alighieri 11–12, **t** 0541 916 214, **f** 0541 926 926 (*moderate*). The most comfortable place to sleep; made all the better by its excellent restaurant.

Locanda San Leone, Strada Sant'Antimo 102, **t** 0541 912 194, **f** 0541 912 348 (*expensive–moderate*). There are some rooms here as you head towards Sant'Igne; but the farm restaurant (*open to all*) serves lovely pasta with eggs and other home-grown ingredients. *Restaurant closed Mon–Wed and Jan.*

La Lama, Strada per Pugliano 4, **t** 0541 926 928 (*expensive–moderate*). At the foot of San Leo, this charming *agriturismo* is run personally by the Conti Nardini; rooms are individually decorated with wrought-iron beds, and the restaurant (*book*) uses ingredients grown on site; dine on pasta with truffles, roast meats, game and cheeses, all washed down by fine wines. Horse-riding is also available.

Il Bettelino, Via Montefeltro 4, **t** 0541 916 265 (*cheap*). A bar-pizzeria-restaurant, with inexpensive rooms available. *Closed Wed.*

Day 4: San Leo's Alcatraz and San Marino's Shops

Morning: Dante slept and St Francis preached in **San Leo**, but for all that, it is tiny, a huddle of stone houses balanced on the gentle slope of the stupendous crag. Visit the most extraordinary of all the area's extraordinary castles, the **Rocca di San Leo** (*open Mon–Sat 9–6, Sun 9–6.30; adm*), which became the Alcatraz of its day; inside you can see Renaissance weapons, illustrations from Dante's *Inferno* and the cell where the popes kept one of their most famous prisoners, Count Cagliostro, until he went mad and died. San Leo's churches are also worth a look: the **Pieve** (*open daily 9–12.30 and 3–7; adm free*) is one of the oldest in the Marches; the ciborium over the altar has an inscription from the year 882. In the **Palazzo Mediceo** (*open Mon–Sun 9–6; adm*) the **Museo d'Arte Sacra** displays 14th- to 18th-century artworks.

Lunch: In San Leo, *see* below.

Afternoon: Drive north to **Villanova**, picking up the S258 towards Verúcchio for 3km, then turn right at **Torello** to **San Marino**, the world's only sovereign roadside attraction and a mecca for duty-free shopping. From **Borgo Maggiore**, take the funicular up to the citadel of **San Marino**, a steep medieval village preserved in aspic, with wonderful views over the coast. A cheesy batch of **museums** (*open Jan–Mar and Oct–Dec 8.50–5; April–Sept 8–8; closed 25 Dec, 1 Jan and 2 Nov*) have been conjured up to extract money from the tourists, but the best thing to do is walk through Monte Titano's forests to the three medieval (rebuilt) tower fortresses that give San Marino its famous silhouette, long the symbol of the republic.

Dinner and Sleeping: In San Marino, *see* below.

Day 4

Lunch in San Leo

****La Rocca**, Via G. Leopardi 16, **t** 0541 916 241, **f** 0541 926 914 (*moderate*). The Rossi family offer good home cooking; truffles and mushrooms in season, and *secondi* such as *pasticciata alla Cagliostro* – beef marinated in wine, with vegetables and cloves. *Closed Mon Sept–June; also closed Dec 12–early Feb.*

La Quercia, Via Leontina, **t** 0541 916 282 (*moderate*). Offers *tagliatelle al ragù* and other typical dishes. *Closed Tues.*

Dinner in San Marino

La Taverna Righi, Piazza Libertà 10, **t** 0549 991 196 (*expensive*). For the best food in the republic, go straight to the centre, where you'll find refined versions of the traditional *passatelli*, seafood and vegetarian dishes, as well as some fancier innovative ones with foie gras: be bold and order the house wine, grown in San Marino – it's not bad at all. *Closed Wed in winter, also three weeks in Jan.*

La Fratta, Salita alla Rocca, **t** 0549 991 594 (*cheap*). An old favourite with grand views from the terrace. *Closed Wed exc June–Oct.*

Sleeping in San Marino (t 0549 from Italy; t 00 378 549 from elsewhere).

******Grand Hotel San Marino**, Viale Onofri 31, **t** 0549 992 400, **f** 0549 992 951 (*expensive*). A modern hotel with luxurious rooms and lovely views, close to the Rocche.

******Titano**, Contrada del Collegio 31, **t** 0549 991 006, **f** 0549 991 375 (*expensive–moderate*). Situated in the historic centre, this has kept much of its 1890s décor, along with a pretty restaurant terrace. *Closed Jan–Mar 10.*

*****Panoramic**, Via Voltone 91, **t** 0549 992 359, **f** 0549 990 356 (*moderate–cheap*). The views assure this family-run place lives up to its name, though the rooms are fairly functional.

*****Quercia Antica**, corner of Via Capannaccia and Via Cella Bella, **t** 0549 991 257, **f** 0549 990 044 (*moderate*). A little pricier, this newer hotel is just out of the *centro storico*, with more views and a good restaurant.

Day 5: Elephants, Allegories and Beaches

Morning: Drive down the S72 to **Rimini**, Italy's biggest resort, with a colourful fishing port and, tucked behind the beachfront, a genuine old city possessing one first-rate Renaissance attraction: the tyrant Sigismondo Malatesta's **Tempio Malatestiano** (*open 8–12.30 and 3.30–6.30; Sun 9–1 and 3.30–7; adm free*). This eclectic, thoroughly mysterious work is full of indecipherable sculptural allegories. Most famous are the **sculptural reliefs** by Agostino, on blue backgrounds, depicting angels and musicians, the Arts and Sciences, St Michael, putti, Sigismondo himself and the Triumph of Scipio. Some of the best are allegorical panels of the planets and signs of the zodiac. Note the tombs of Sigismondo and Isotta, adorned by their omnipresent monograms S and I (like a dollar sign), together with elephants, the Malatesta symbol.

Lunch: In Rimini, *see* below.

Afternoon: Drive back towards Ancona down the coast along the S16; for the best views, opt for the corniche road hugging the coast from **Gabbice Mare**. South of Pésaro, the string of resorts continues; break off at **Fano**, not merely a seaside playground but a fine old town retaining a perfect provincial Roman town plan. Stroll along its long, broad beach, or visit the 15th-century **Palazzo Malatestiano** (*open Tues–Sun 9.30–12.30 and 4–7; 15 June–15 Sept also 9–11pm; closed Mon; adm*), with a lovely crenellated courtyard and mullioned windows, and a picture gallery starring Michele Giambono and Guercino. Look into the church of **Santa Maria Nuova**, decorated with stuccoes and altarpieces by Perugino and Giovanni Santi.

Dinner and Sleeping: In Fano, *see* below.

Day 5

Lunch in Rimini

Dallo Zio, Via S. Chiara 16, **t** 0541 786 74 (*moderate*). An excellent seafood palace in the old town, offering marine *lasagne*, fishy vol-au-vents and other surprises; popular with locals and tourists alike. *Closed Mon.*

4 Moschetteri, Via S. Maria al Mare, just off Piazza Ferrari, **t** 0541 5649 (*cheap*). The practically perfect *trattoria* in the centre, with excellent pizza and pasta, and a menu of Romagna favourites that changes every day.

Dinner in Fano

Ristorantino (Giulio), Viale Adriatico 100, **t** 0721 805 680 (*expensive*). A reliable favourite, serving tasty, extra fresh seafood in the Marchigiano style: try the *fusilli con le canocchie* (a local shrimp). *Closed Tues and Nov.*

Pesce Azzurro, near the port at Viale Adriatico 48, **t** 0721 803 165 (*cheap*).This was founded by the local fishermen's cooperative to promote the glories of 'blue fish' – a variety of sardines, anchovies, mackerel and other small fish, all, despite their diminutive size, very tasty! They're harder to find each year, but at this self-service restaurant you can try them in three courses, with the local Bianchello del Metauro to wash them down. *Closed Mon and Oct–Mar.*

Sleeping in Fano

********Augustus**, Via Puccini 2, **t** 0721 809 781, **f** 0721 825 517 (*moderate*). A central, family-run hotel, which has had a facelift from head to toe and offers all mod-cons; the restaurant serves fish as well as some more creative dishes. *Restaurant closed Mon.*

*****Astoria**, Viale Cairoli 86, **t/f** 0721 803 474 (*moderate–cheap*). A pleasant hotel, on the best part of the beach. *Open Easter–Oct.*

****Mare**, Viale C. Colombo 20, **t/f** 0721 805 667 (*cheap*). This place just off the beach is like a homely *pensione* of 20 years ago, where *mamma* Anna cooks up some of the best and most affordable seafood in Fano. *Restaurant* (*cheap*) *closed Sun eve.*

Abruzzo and Molise

11

In Italy's narrow peninsula, dense with cities and art, packed with *autostrade* and sultry *signorinas*, Abruzzo and Molise are a breath of fresh air. Of course there's the Adriatic: long sandy beaches and resorts, and more sandy beaches and resorts – most catering to Italian-style beach holidays, where you pay for your umbrella in its neat little row and watch everyone else do the same. But beyond the beach strip, Abruzzo has one-third of its land reserved for nature, with four national or regional parks. Sparsely populated and marginal to great affairs of state, Abruzzo and Molise stand out for their majestic beauty; vast tracts of wilderness encompass the highest peaks of the Apennines, the habitat of Italy's unique species of bear. Yet from this mountain-bound land of country tradition came two of Italy's most urbane, sophisticated and passionate poets, Ovid and Gabriele d'Annunzio.

Pescara

Pescara wears many hats: it is Abruzzo's biggest city and its most popular resort, its most prosperous town, a fishing port and provincial capital. In ancient times it was a modest port, but Pescara never made much of itself until 1927, when the government merged the sleepy little fishing village with the equally inconsequential Castellamare Adriatica across the River Pescara, and started pumping money into it. Such efforts

Getting to Pescara

Ryanair flies from London Stansted (2hrs 30).

Getting from the Airport

City bus 38 connects Liberi airport (**t** 085 432 4200) to Pescara Centrale station every 10 mins (5.30am–11pm; journey 15mins). Buy **tickets** (€0.70) from the airport news-stand or bar.

A **taxi** to the centre will cost about €15.

Getting Around

The centre of Pescara is easily tackled on foot, but there are also local **buses** (€0.70).

The main **train station**, Pescara Centrale, is on Piazza delle Stazione; the **bus station** is close by. For a **taxi**, call **CO.TA.PE**, **t** 085 421 6363.

Car Hire

The following have branches at the aiport:

Avis, **t** 085 421 2442.
Europcar, **t** 085 421 1022.
Hertz, **t** 085 53900.
Maggiore, **t** 085 389 167.

Tourist Information

Pescara: Via Nicola Fabrizi 171, **t** 085 421 0188.

Market Days

There's a weekly market in **Via Pepe** (*Mon*).

Festivals

Pescara's week-long **Jazz festival** usually takes place in the first half of July.

Shopping

It's probably most fun to browse around the fish market, but Pescara is also a good place to pick up a bottle of the region's famous red wine, **Montepulciano d'Abruzzo**. Abruzzo is also well known for its ceramics.

Where to Stay and Eat

Pescara ✉ 65100

There's no shortage of hotels and restaurants, but tranquillity is a rare in the summer, and full board is usually required July–Aug.

******Carlton**, Viale Riviera 35, **t** 085 373 125, **f** 085 421 3922 (*expensive*). A very comfortable resort palace on the sea, with a private beach that almost absorbs the racket.

*****Bellariva**, Viale Riviera 213, **t/f** 085 471 2641 (*moderate*). This is unpretentious, and a good, friendly place to stay for families.

*****Salus**, Lungomare Matteotti 13/1, **t** 085 374 196, **f** 085 374 103 (*moderate*). Offers good standard rooms and a private beach.

Guerino, Viale della Riviera 4, **t** 085 421 2065 (*expensive*). Elegant, with a seafront terrace, this is the city's best seafood restaurant: the Adriatic speciality – fillets of John Dory (*pesce San Pietro*) with *prosciutto* – go down especially well. *Closed Tues and 22 Dec–5 Jan.*

Duilio, Via Regina Margherita 11, **t** 085 378 278 (*moderate*). Serves delicately prepared dishes, most of which feature seafood. *Closed Sun eve, Mon and Aug.*

La Terrazza Verde, Largo Madonna 6, **t** 085 413 239 (*moderate*). One restaurant that doesn't serve fish at all; in a panoramic setting with a beautiful garden terrace up in the hills, it serves delicious *gnocchi* and duck, a popular dish in Abruzzo, prepared in various ways. *Closed Wed and 10 days in July.*

Trattoria Roma, Via Trento 86, **t** 085 295 374 (*cheap*). Tucked away, this is a good place for hearty Abruzzese cooking. It's very popular with locals, and the menu changes daily – there's always at least one good fish choice. *Closed Sun and one week in July.*

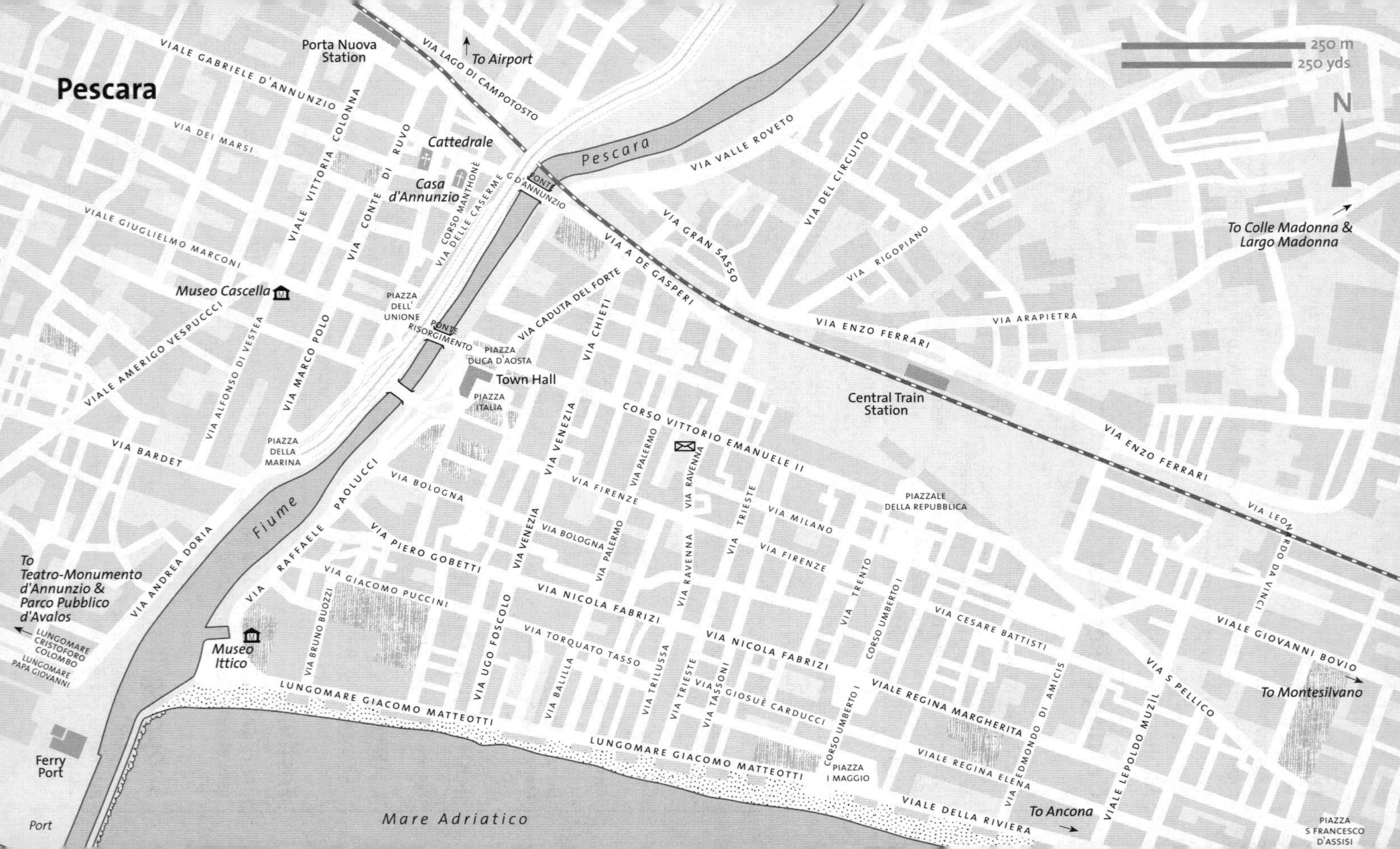

Pescara
250 m
250 yds
N
Porta Nuova Station
To Airport
Via Lago di Campotosto
Viale Gabriele d'Annunzio
Via dei Marsi
Viale Vittoria Colonna
Via Conte di Ruvo
Cattedrale
Casa d'Annunzio
Corso Manthonè
Via delle Caserme
Ponte G. D'Annunzio
Pescara
Via Valle Roveto
Via del Circuito
Via Gran Sasso
Via Rigopiano
To Colle Madonna & Largo Madonna
Viale Giuglielmo Marconi
Museo Cascella
Viale Amerigo Vespucci
Via Alfonso di Vestea
Via Marco Polo
Piazza dell' Unione
Ponte Risorgimento
Piazza Duca d'Aosta
Town Hall
Piazza Italia
Via Caduta del Forte
Via A de Gasperi
Via Chieti
Via Enzo Ferrari
Via Arapietra
Central Train Station
Via Bardet
Piazza della Marina
Fiume
Via Andrea Doria
To Teatro-Monumento d'Annunzio & Parco Pubblico d'Avalos
Lungomare Cristoforo Colombo
Lungomare Papa Giovanni
Ferry Port
Port
Via Raffaele Paolucci
Museo Ittico
Via Bologna
Via Venezia
Corso Vittorio Emanuele II
Via Palermo
Via Ravenna
Via Firenze
Via Trieste
Via Milano
Piazzale della Repubblica
Via Leonardo da Vinci
Via Piero Gobetti
Via Giacomo Puccini
Via Bruno Buozzi
Via Ugo Foscolo
Via Nicola Fabrizi
Via Torquato Tasso
Via Balilla
Via Trilussa
Via Tassoni
Via Giosuè Carducci
Via Trento
Corso Umberto I
Via Cesare Battisti
Viale Giovanni Bovio
Via S Pellico
To Montesilvano
Lungomare Giacomo Matteotti
Viale Regina Margherita
Viale Regina Elena
Via Edmondo di Amicis
Viale Lepoldo Muzil
Piazza I Maggio
Viale della Riviera
To Ancona
Mare Adriatico
Piazza S Francesco d'Assisi

were largely due to the influence of the city's most famous son, Gabriele D'Annunzio, who was born here in 1864. Today Pescara is the metropolis of the central Adriatic, with a population of 120,000. It isn't the most charming of cities, but its splendid Lungomare and miles of broad beaches make up for the monotonous streets behind.

Pescara's golden egg is its 16-kilometre stretch of sandy beach, broad and safe for the youngest child, almost solid with hotels, cafés and fish restaurants between the River Pescara and Montesilvano to the north. Any old buildings it had were decimated during the Second World War. Still, this is no Rimini; if you need excitement, there are riding stables, go-kart tracks, tennis courts, fishing and, for some real thrills, the **Museo Ittico** (*closed for restoration*) in the bustling fish market on Lungofiume Paolucci, offering aquariums and fossils. From here Via Paolucci follows the river to **Piazza Italia**, Pescara's Mussolinian, somewhat uninspiring civic centre.

The original fishing village of Pescara lies on the southern bank of the river, now spoilt by an elevated motorway. Here, the **Museo delle Genti d'Abruzzo** (*Via delle Caserme 22; open Mon–Sat 9–1, Tues and Thurs also 3.30–6.30, Sun 10–1; adm*) has a comprehensive collection dedicated to everyday life and traditions in the Abruzzo over the centuries. The **Casa Cascella** (*Via G Marconi 45; open daily 9–1, Tues and Thurs also 4.30–6.30; adm*) features sculptures, ceramics and other works of art by three generations of the Cascella family. One of them made *The Nave*, the ship fountain along the Lungomare at Piazza 1 Maggio.

This otherwise resolutely normal town must have a bit of kryptonite in it to have produced Gaetano Rapagnetto, the son of a local merchant. He left Pescara for Rome and France, only to re-emerge as the 'Angel Gabriel of the Annunciation', Gabriele D'Annunzio, and went on to become the greatest poet of his generation. Decadent, deeply political and deeply passionate, he was an inspiration to many of his fellow Italians. You can see where he got his start in life, at the **Casa D'Annunzio** (*Corso Manthonè 101; open Mon–Sat 9–1, Sun 9–12.30; adm*), housing memorabilia of the poet.

Day Trips from Pescara

Chieti

For something a bit weightier than gills and beachballs, head up to **Chieti**, some 13km up the River Pescara. Another provincial capital, Chieti was the Roman town of Theate Marrucinorum, and its star attraction is the **Museo Nazionale Archeòlogico di Antichità** (*Villa Comunale; open daily 9–7; adm*), the chief repository of pre-Roman and Roman artworks unearthed in the Abruzzo. These include the shapely 6th-century BC **Warrior of Capestrano**, accompanied by an inscription in the language of the Middle Adriatic Bronze Age culture; items found in Bronze Age tombs; Hellenistic and Roman sculptures, portraits, coins, jewellery and votive offerings, many of which were discovered in Alba Fucens, in the Parco Nazionale d'Abruzzo, and Amiternum, near L'Aquila. The documentation of material from Abruzzo's many Upper Palaeolithic caves is displayed with ancient ceramics and artefacts from Italic necropolises.

Getting There

Trains run from Pescara Centrale to Chieti roughly every hour (more in the middle of the day) taking 10–15mins. **ARPA buses** (**t** 085 421 5099) and **SATAM buses** (**t** 085 421 0733) also connect Chieti with Pescara several times a day; buy bus tickets from Piazza Repubblica.

Tourist Information

Chieti ✉ **66100**: Palazzo INAIL, Via B. Spaventa 29, **t** 0871 63640.

Eating Out

Venturini, Via De Lollis 10, **t** 0871 330 663 (*moderate*). For a fairly priced, fairly cooked meal, try this local institution, whose speciality is mushroom *risotto* with *mozzarella*. *Closed Tues.*

Nonna Elisa, Località Brecciarola, Via Peropoli 267 (near the motorway exit), **t** 0871 684 152 (*moderate*). Offers a delicious, strictly Abruzzese experience. *Closed Mon, one week in July and first week of Oct.*

Out of doors, Chieti's best feature is its lovely views, stretching from the sea to the Gran Sasso and Maiella Mountains. However, it also retains a dramatic 12th–14th-century Gothic **cathedral** and a couple of traces of old Theate Marrucinorum: the ruins of three little temples on Via Spaventa, and, in the eastern quarters of town, the **Terme Romane** (*closed for restoration; to visit ask at the Museo Archeològico*), with a mighty cistern.

Sulmona

Sulmona, in a green basin surrounded by mountains, is best remembered as the birthplace of Ovid (43 BC–AD 17), who is commemorated with a large 20th-century statue in **Piazza XX Settembre**. Much later, the town was a minor centre of learning and religion, home of the Celestine Order's main abbey, and in the early Renaissance its craftsmen were celebrated for their goldwork, although they have since learned a sweeter skill: what the Italians call *confetti*.

Getting There

Sulmona is a major **rail** junction and there are trains to and from Pescara roughly every hour (more in the middle of the day), taking 1hr–1hr10. ARPA **buses** (**t** 085 421 5099) also serve Sulmona around three times daily.

Tourist Information

Sulmona: Corso Ovidio 208, **t** 0864 53276.

Shopping

Any number of shops in the centre sell *confetti*, but **William di Carlo**, near the station, reckons it is the oldest manufacturer here.

Eating Out

*****Europa Park**, on S17 (off Bivio Badia), just north of town, **t** 0864 251 260, **f** 0864 251 317 (*moderate*). Sulmona's largest hotel has a bar and a good restaurant.

Italia, Piazza XX Settembre 22, **t** 0864 33070 (*moderate*). Restaurant of the same name. Prepares winning variations on traditional local cuisine: home-made pasta and lamb with rosemary. *Closed Mon.*

Clemente, Vico della Quercia 5, **t** 0864 52284 (*cheap*). Serves up home-made sausages and delicious local dishes: fresh pasta with lamb sauce, saffron or wild mushrooms, roast kid, and good desserts. *Closed Thurs, Christmas period and 10 days in July.*

Traditionally given out at weddings, *confetti* has been a speciality of Abruzzo since the Middle Ages. The original sweets were sugared almonds, but today they come in a variety of fillings. All over town, lavish window displays show off confectionery made up to look like flowers or ornate gold and silver ornaments.

The main street, Corso Ovidio, holds Sulmona's loveliest monument, the church and palace of **Santa Maria Annunziata**, a Gothic and Renaissance ensemble begun in 1320. The three portals on the façade were done at different periods, but the result is as harmoniously sweet as *confetti*: the left one is finely carved florid Gothic, while the middle one is pure symmetrical Renaissance; the plain portal on the right was built last, in 1522. Doctors of the Church and saints stand sentry along the façade; above them runs an intricate ribbon frieze; above that are three lacy Gothic windows. The palace's two small **museums** (*open Tues–Sun 9–1, Sat–Sun also 4–6.30*) contain traditional Abruzzese costumes, work by the goldsmiths of Renaissance Sulmona, and sculpture and paintings from the 16th–18th centuries. The Baroque **church** façade, rebuilt after the 1703 earthquake, still complements the palace. Running through the centre of Sulmona is an unusual Gothic **aqueduct** (1256); it can be seen in the huge Piazza Garibaldi, site of the 1474 **Fontana del Vecchio**. Over the road stands the carved Romanesque portal of **San Francesco delle Scarpe**; the rest tumbled in an earthquake.

Térmoli

Just over the River Trigno in Molise, Térmoli is a bright little fishing town on a promontory, with a long sandy beach, palms and oleanders. The diva of the old town, or at least the part that survived a Turkish raid in 1566, is the exotic 13th-century **cathedral**, its façade undulating with Puglian-style blind arcades and Moorish horseshoe arches; inside is a marble floor of twisting mythological beasts. From the old town, Via Roma leads to **Piazza San Antonio**, where the old church of Sant'Antonio has become the **Galleria Civica d'Arte** (*open summer daily 6–10pm*), housing the best works from Térmoli's biennial art competition. Térmoli also boasts a **castle** and walls from the same period, built by Emperor Frederick II. After enjoying the view from the castle and poking around the old lanes, there's nothing more demanding to do than relax on the beach and decide which seafood restaurant to try.

Getting There

Although there are frequent **trains** from Pescara Centrale to Térmoli after midday, there is only one in the morning, at around 9.30am. The journey takes 1hr–1hr20mins. There are also around three **buses** daily, but on the whole it's easier to opt for the train.

Tourist Information

Térmoli: Piazza Bega, **t** 0875 706 754.

Eating Out

Z'Bass, Via Oberdan 8, **t** 0875 706 703 (*expensive*). Has a tempting fish menu and a lively atmosphere. *Closed Mon Oct–May.*

Da Noi Tre, Via Ruffini 47, **t** 0875 703 639 (*cheap*). Modest, but serving good fish. *Open daily in summer; closed Mon in winter.*

Cian, Lungomare Colombo 136, **t** 0875 704 436 (*cheap*). On a rock above the coast, this hotel offers a decent fish restaurant and lovely views. *Closed Mon and Nov.*

Touring from Pescara

Day 1: Abruzzese Hill Towns of Distinction

Morning: From Pescara, follow the coast north to **Montesilvano Marina**; from here, the S16bis and 151 will take you inland to the hills and **Loreto Aprutino**, a town of ancient distinction with several small **museums** (*open Sat and Sun 10.30–12.30 and 3.30–6.30 or call* **t** *0339 441 1319; adm*). Just below Loreto, don't miss the church of **Santa Maria in Piano**, with a very unusual *Last Judgement*. If there's time before lunch, carry on to **Penne**, another sleepy medieval town 7km west, with some exceptional medieval sculpture in its **Museo Civico** (*open daily 10–1 and 4–7; adm*). Just outside town, the **Riserva Naturale Lago di Penne** is a WWF preserve for waterfowl with nature trails.

Lunch: In Loreto Aprutino or Penne, *see* below.

Afternoon: From Penne, take the S81 north through this rollercoaster landscape of the eastern Apennines; follow signs for **Atri**. It may not make the best impression from afar, surrounded by strange eroded rock formations (*calanchi*), but on top you'll find one of central Italy's most attractive hill towns. There are views over the countryside and the sea, and a majestic 13th-century **cathedral** with some remarkable frescoes by a *quattrocento* Abruzzese painter named Andrea di Litio. In the cloister, the **Museo Diocesano** (*open June–Sept daily 10–12 and 4–8; Oct Thurs–Tues 10–12 and 3–5; adm*) has a fine collection of Abruzzo majolica.

Dinner and Sleeping: In Atri, *see* below.

Day 1

Lunch in Penne

Tatobbe, Corso Allessandrini 37, **t** 085 827 9512 (*moderate–cheap*). A traditional *trattoria* in the centre of Penne serving classic Abruzzese cuisine such as *carne alla brace* (meats grilled over embers). *Closed Mon and 20 Dec–3 Jan.*

Lunch in Loreto Aprutino

Bilancia, 5km outside the centre of Loreto Aprutino at Contrada Palazzo, **t** 085 828 9610 (*cheap*). Join the locals who flock to this popular restaurant in the hotel Bilancia; it's a good place to come to try regional dishes prepared with Loreto's famous olive oil; look out particularly for their soups and roast goose. *Closed Mon.*

Dinner in Atri

Aside from the eateries listed below, it's worth visiting the restaurant in the Hotel Du Parc (*see* Sleeping in Atri, below), which also serves a range of good regional dishes.

Taverna del Posto, Via A. Probi 10, **t** 085 878 0034 (*moderate*). Right in the centre of Atri, off the Corso near San Francesco, the *taverna* is devoted to fish of all sorts. *Closed Mon.*

Alla Campana d'Oro, Piazza Duomo 23, **t** 085 870 177 (*cheap*). This straightforward but enjoyable *trattoria* offers the usual standards, and turns into something of a pizzeria by night (pizza served eves only). *Closed Sun lunch and Mon.*

Sleeping in Atri

*****Du Parc**, Viale Umberto I 6, **t** 085 870 260, **f** 085 879 8326 (*moderate–cheap*). A peaceful place with a swimming pool as well as a good restaurant.

***San Francesco**, Corso Adriano 38, **t** 085 87287 (*cheap*). This tidy, ancient hotel in the historic centre of Atri makes for an interesting alternative.

Day 2: Romanesque Gems and a Hidden Art City

Morning: From Atri, it's back on the rollercoaster hill roads for a while; take the S553 north for a look at two Romanesque gems: **San Clemente a Vomano**, with some frescoes and an unusual and lovely 12th-century ciborium; and just up the S150 towards the coast, **Santa Maria di Propezzano**. Continue on this road to **Roseto** on the Adriatic and turn north; you have a choice of spending the rest of the morning on the beach, or exploring **Giulianova**, the most interesting of the chain of little resorts lining this coast, with a medieval centre and another Romanesque church.

Lunch: In Giulianova, *see* below.

Afternoon: A few km inland from Giulianova on the S80 takes you to the A14 motorway, which in turn will get you to **Ascoli Piceno** in half an hour. Ascoli is a delightful city, with the air of a Tuscan art town that has somehow escaped to this out-of-the way corner of the southern Marches. Travertine-paved **Piazza del Popolo** is one of Italy's most beautiful *piazzas*, bounded by the Renaissance **Loggia dei Mercanti**, the 13th-century church of **San Francesco** and the Art Nouveau **Caffé Meletti**. Wandering the back streets will take you past a number of interesting churches, medieval walls and palaces and a Roman theatre. The fine art, meanwhile, is concentrated around Piazza dell'Arringo, in the **Museo Diocesano** (*open Tues–Sun 10–1 and 3.30–7.30; adm*), the **Pinacoteca Civica** (*open Mon–Sat 9–1 and 3–7, Sun and hols 9.30–12.30 and 4–7;adm*) and in the **Cathedral**, with an excellent altarpiece by Carlo Crivelli.

Dinner and Sleeping: In Ascoli Piceno, *see* below.

Day 2

Lunch in Giulianova

★★★**Beccaceci**, Via Zola 28, **t** 085 800 3550 (*expensive*). The Abruzzo's most celebrated seafood restaurant, where the menu features seafood and pasta inventions so good that they're copied elsewhere; try the *linguine alla giuliese* or the squid stuffed with prawns. *Closed Sun eve, Mon and 27 Dec–10 Jan.*

Osteria della Stracciavocc, Via Trieste 124, **t** 085 800 5326 (*moderate–cheap*). This is one of the best *trattorias* around for traditional regional cuisine, serving outstanding pasta and seafood. *Closed Mon, Tues lunch and two weeks in Sept.*

Dinner in Ascoli Piceno

The speciality here is *ulivi all'ascolana* (stuffed, breaded and fried olives). They're wonderful, but so tedious to prepare that you won't often find them outside Ascoli.

Tornasacco, Piazza del Popolo 36, **t** 0736 254 151 (*cheap*). This is one place to find *ulivi all'ascolana*; it's also good for local cheeses and *charcuterie*, and tagliatelle with lamb sauce. *Closed Fri and part of July.*

Gallo d'Oro, Corso Vittorio Emanuele 13, **t** 0736 253 520 (*cheap*). Another local favourite, with three dining rooms, a good tourist menu and fresh seafood on Wed and Fri. *Closed Sun.*

Sleeping in Ascoli Piceno

★★★★**Gioli**, Via Alcide di Gasperi 14, **t/f** 0736 255 550 (*moderate*). A thoroughly pleasant, modern hotel near the cathedral with parking – a real blessing in this crowded town – and a garden.

The Cantina dell'Arte, Rua della Lupa 8, **t** 0736 251 135 (*cheap*). Here in an old palace in the centre near the post office, you can find a handful of rooms and abundant servings of local dishes, grilled meats and pitchers of wine in the restaurant (*cheap*).

Day 3: The Great Gran Sasso, Ceramics and L'Aquila

Morning: Leave Ascoli on the S81, south for Téramo. On the way you'll pass under the curious mountaintop castle of **Civitella di Tronto**, last redoubt of the Bourbon Kings of Naples in the wars for Italian unification in 1861. **Téramo**, the provincial capital, has little to detain you besides a good cathedral and the strange Byzantine church of Santa Anna. Stop here for lunch, or go on along the motorway (A24) towards the looming snow-capped presence on the horizon: the highest massif of the Apennines, the **Gran Sasso d'Italia**. At the San Gabriele-Colledara exit, you can make a short detour to the village of **Castelli**, famed for centuries for its hand-painted ceramics; these decorate the village church and the **Museo della Ceramica Abruzzese** (*open Oct–May Tues–Sun 9–1; June–Sept Tues–Sun 10–1 and 3–7; adm*).

Lunch: In Téramo or Camarda, *see* below.

Afternoon: In a feat of road-building bravura, the A24 burrows right under the highest peak of the Gran Sasso, the 9,554ft **Corno Grande**. From the exit on the southern end of tunnel at **Assergi**, you can take a brief tour of the mountains on the route through the grand, solemn plain between the peaks called the **Campo Imperatore**. Otherwise, continue on to **L'Aquila**. This gracious mountain city, founded by Emperor Frederick II in the 13th century, has a lovely 12th-century church, **Santa Maria in Collemaggio**, with a typically Abruzzese facade of stone in geometrical patterns, and a Renaissance Castello housing the extensive collections of the **Museo Nazionale d'Abruzzo** (*open Tues–Sun 9–8; adm*).

Dinner and Sleeping: In L'Aquila, *see* below.

Day 3

Lunch in Téramo

Il Duomo, Via Stazio 9, **t** 0861 241 774 (*moderate*). In the centre of town, the 'Cathedral' offers such specialities as *maccheroni alla chitarra* and fine meat dishes, including grilled kid. *Closed Mon, two weeks in Jan and two weeks in Aug.*

Sotto le Stelle, Via dei Mille 59, **t** 0861 247 126 (*cheap*). An informal local hangout with local cuisine to match. *Closed Sun and two weeks in Jan.*

Lunch in Camarda

Elodia, in the village of Camarda, on the S17bis towards L'Aquila, on the southern edge of the Gran Sasso (after the tunnel, Assergi exit), **t** 0862 606 024 (*cheap*). This serves up all manner of tasty local dishes, using Abruzzo-grown saffron, wild mushrooms and local cheeses. *Closed Mon and two weeks in July.*

Dinner in L'Aquila

Antiche Mura, Via XXV Aprile 2, **t** 0862 62422 (*moderate*). This specializes in Abruzzese cuisine: homely soups, home-made pasta, rabbit with peppers and saffron. Don't miss the *ferratelle*, a waffle dessert. *Closed Sun.*

L'Antico Borgo, Piazza San Vito 1, **t** 0862 22005 (*cheap*). A restaurant offering delicious vegetarian *ravioli* and, in season, 'truffled' treats. *Closed Tues Oct–May; open daily in summer.*

La Cantina del Boss, Via Castello 3, **t** 0862 413 393 (*cheap*). A great place to snack on stuffed pizza or *frittata*. *Closed Sat lunch, Sun and 15 July–15 Aug.*

Sleeping in L'Aquila

*****Castello**, Piazza Battaglione Alpini, **t** 0862 419 147, **f** 0862 419 140 (*moderate*). A classy hotel opposite the castle.

*****Duomo**, Via Dragonetti 6, **t** 0862 410 893, **f** 862 413 058 (*moderate*). A 17th-century palace off Piazza Duomo, with 28 rooms, some with a view of the square.

Day 4: A Scenic Drive Into Bear Territory

Morning: Leave L'Aquila by the S17, and turn south at Caporciano for **Bominaco**, a tiny village with wonderful medieval frescoes in its church; just to the west, there are underground waterfalls and stalactites to explore in the **Grotte di Stiffe** (*50-min guided tours daily 10–1 and 3–6; adm exp, includes visit to speleological museum in town; call ahead on* **t** *0862 86142 to arrange a tour in English*). From here, backtrack towards L'Aquila and look for signs for Celano; it's a scenic drive south on the S5, passing through the heart of the **Parco Regionale Sirente-Velino** between the two big mountains that give the park its name. **Celano**, at the southern end, has an excellent little museum in its **Piccolomini Castle** (*open winter daily 9–1.30, Sat and Sun 9–8; summer daily 9–8; adm*). From here the S5 continues on to **Avezzano**.

Lunch: In Avezzano, *see* below.

Afternoon: Just north of Avezzano at **Albe**, you can visit the unusual ruins of Roman **Alba Fucens**. The Piano del Fucino, east of Avezzano, is one of the oddest landscapes in Italy: an eight-mile-long vanished lake, first drained by the ancient Romans, it now it has a radiotelescope in the middle. Cross it on the road for **San Benedetto dei Marsi**, and then head south on the S83 into the **Parco Nazionale d'Abruzzo**, home of the famous Abruzzo bear and many lovely forests and Apennine meadows. **Pescasséroli**, the largest village in the park, has the main **visitors' centre** (*open daily 10–12 and 3–7*) and a cable car up to the summit of Monte Vitelle. A little further on, take the S479 north for the lovely lakeside resort village of **Scanno**.

Dinner and Sleeping: In Scanno, *see* below.

Day 4

Lunch in Avezzano

Vecchi Sapori, Via Montello 3, **t** 0863 416 626 (*cheap*). A good, fairly priced restaurant with local specialities, including particularly fine pasta and lamb, and fish on Tues and Fri.

La Locanda, Via XX Settembre 359, **t** 0863 26523 (*moderate*). This place is devoted to maritime delicacies, including *frittura* and scampi. *Closed Sun.*

Dinner in Scanno

Gli Archetti, Via Silla 8, **t** 0864 74645 (*moderate*). Scanno's best offers refined old elegance and dishes made from home-grown ingredients; try the grilled lamb with pears. *Closed Tues from Oct to May.*

Sleeping in Scanno

***Del Lago**, Viale del Lago 202, **t** 0864 74343, **f** 0864 74343 (*moderate*). A small, tranquil hotel with a garden in a lovely setting on the lake. *Open mid-Dec–mid-Jan and Mar–Oct.*

***Margherita**, Via D. Tanturri 100, **t** 0864 74353 (*cheap*). Scanno hotels tend to be slightly more expensive than those in the surrounding area, but this one is good value.

Dinner and Sleeping in Pescasséroli

****Grand Hotel del Parco**, **t** 0863 912 745, **f** 0863 912 749 (*expensive*). The grandest hotel in the area, with a beautiful setting, a garden and a pool in summer. *Open Christmas–Easter and June–Sept.*

***Il Pinguino**, Via Collacchi 2, **t** 0863 912 580, **f** 0863 910 449 (*moderate*). Another good choice in the national park, with rooms that are far too snug for a real penguin. *Full or half board only July–Aug.*

Plistia, Viale Principe de Napoli 28, **t** 0863 910 732 (*rooms cheap, restaurant moderate*). This place offers a few simple rooms as well as a restaurant with Abruzzese cooking. *Closed Mon.*

Day 5: Back to the Coast Through Parks and Peaks

Morning: Retrace your steps southwards to escape Scanno's isolated valley, then take the S83 east and the S17 north to another mountain resort, **Roccaraso**. A beautiful drive north from here, along the S84, escorts you through yet another park, the Parco Nazionale della Maiella, to **Guardiagrele**, a sweet, peaceful hill town known for centuries for its metalworking. You can see a work of its Renaissance sculptor Nicola da Guardiagrele in the treasury of Santa Maria Maggiore (*open mid-July–Aug daily 10–12.30 and 4–7.30; otherwise call* ***t*** *0871 82117*), while the more modest contributions of today's artisans can be found in the streets around Porta San Giovanni. Next, drive to **Lanciano**, 23km east of here on the S36, an interesting market town with a cathedral built over a Roman bridge and four separate medieval quarters.

Lunch: In Guardiagrele or Lanciano, *see* below.

Afternoon: The S524 from Lanciano will take you to **Fossacésia Marina** on the coast. Just off the coastal road, pause for a look at **San Giovanni in Venere** (*open daily 8–8*) a remarkable 11th- –12th-century monastic church built over what had once been a seaside temple to Venus. There is some fine medieval sculpture outside and some Byzantine-style frescoes in the crypt. From here, follow the coastal road south to **Vasto**, home of Gabriele Rossetti, poet and father of Dante Gabriel and Christina Rossetti. Set on a low natural terrace above its port, it is a popular family resort with plenty of broad beaches, while at its centre you'll fine one of the most attractive old towns on the Adriatic coast, full of palm trees and old *palazzi* with iron balconies.

Dinner and Sleeping: In Vasto, *see* below.

Day 5

Lunch in Guardiagrele

★★★**Villa Maiella**, just outside the town on Via Sette Dolori, **t** 0871 809 362 (*moderate*). This hotel is worth stopping at for one of the most popular restaurants in the whole area. The chef has concocted an imaginative menu based on traditional preparations (including some interesting pasta variations, such as the wide, squarish *toccole* and *trenette di farro*, made with spelt) and excellent mountain trout. You'll also find careful and enthusiastic service, and a very tempting dessert cart. *Closed Mon and last two weeks of July.*

Lunch in Lanciano

La Ruota, Via Per Fossacesia 62 (400m from town centre), **t** 0872 44590 (*expensive*). Very popular with the locals, this serves lovely seafood and also a few meat dishes. *Closed Sun and two weeks in July.*

Dinner and Sleeping in Vasto

Vasto has plenty of hotels along the beaches, and as long as it's not high season you can take your pick. Otherwise, one or two good options are listed below.

★★★★★**Villa Vignola**, Marina di Vasto on the S16c, 6km from Vasto's centre, in Vignola, **t** 0873 310 050, **f** 0873 310 060 (*expensive*). This offers five spacious rooms in an enchanting seafront villa, with a private beach and an excellent restaurant, where you can dine out in summer by candlelight.

★★★**La Panoramica**, Via Smargiasi 1, **t** 0873 367 700 (*moderate*). A pleasant hotel in a tranquil setting near the belvedere gardens, in the centre of Vasto; some rooms have views over the coast.

All'Hostaria del Pavone, Via Barbarotta 15, **t** 0873 60227 (*moderate*). Here you can taste a wonderful *brodetto* – the local fish soup that has nourished generations of sailors – as well as many other fish specialities. *Closed 10 Jan–10 Feb and Tues from Oct–May.*

Lazio

12

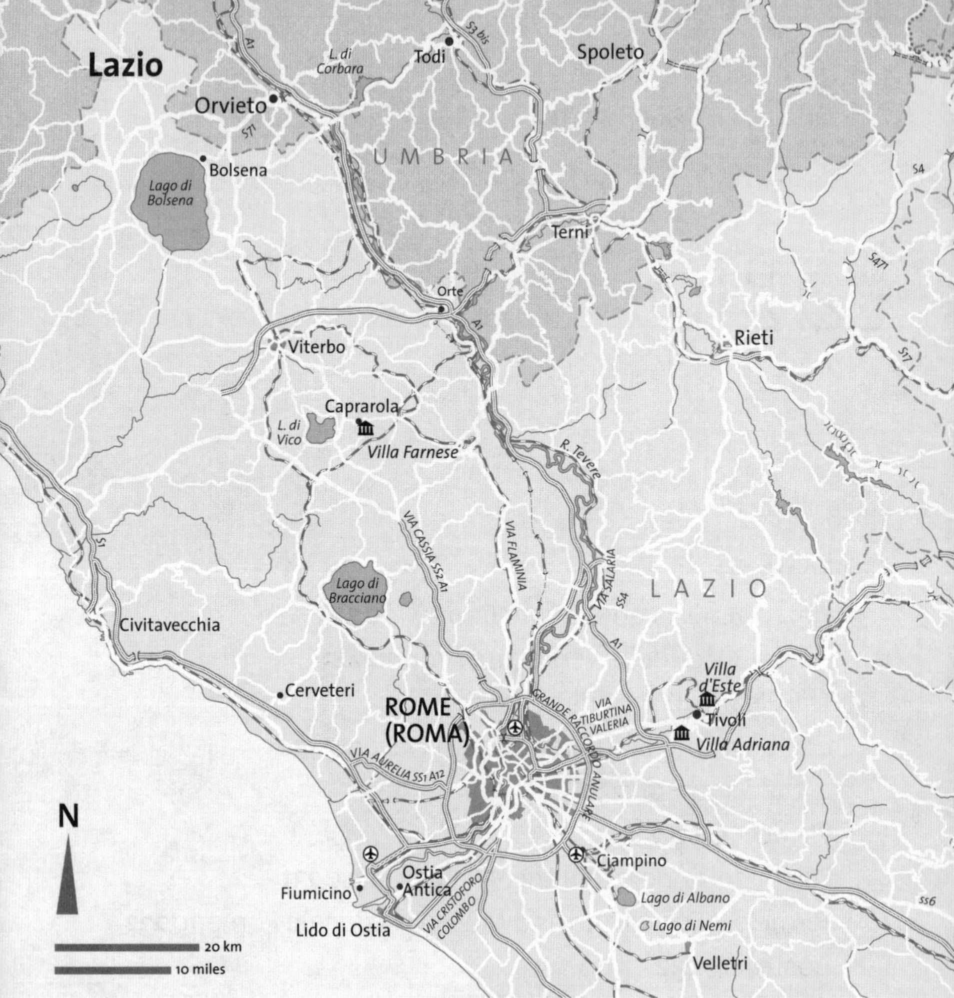

Lazio does not get much respect from the average Italian, who thinks of it as a sort of vacuum, half swamps and half poor mountain villages, that needs to be crossed to get to Rome. Lazio's problem is a simple one: Rome. Before there was Rome this was probably the wealthiest and most densely populated part of non-Greek Italy, but the Romans who proved such good governors elsewhere caused utter ruin to their own back yard. To finance their grandiose building projects, Renaissance popes literally taxed Lazio into extinction; whole villages and stretches of land were abandoned and reverted to malarial swamps. Modern Rome has begun to mend its ways; the government considers Lazio a development area, and pumps a lot of money into it.

Rome (Roma)

You won't get to the bottom of this city, whether you stay for three days or a month. With its legions of statues, acres of paintings, 913 churches and megatons of artistic sediment, the name Rome passed into the plane of legend some 2,200 years ago. Ancient Rome at the height of its glory had perhaps a million and a half people; today there are four million, and at least half of them will be pushing their way into the metro while you are trying to get off. Don't concern yourself; the present is only one snapshot from a 2,600-year history, and no one has ever left Rome disappointed.

Piazza Venezia and Monte Capitolino (The Capitoline Hill)

This traffic-crazed *piazza* may be a poor introduction to Rome, but it's a good place to start, with the ruins of old Rome on one side and the boutiques and bureaucracies of the new city on the other. The *piazza* is named after the **Palazzo Venezia**, residence of Mussolini, who left a light on all night to make the Italians think he was working. The approach to the Capitoline Hill is now entirely blocked by the **Altar of the Nation** (Vittoriano or 'Wedding Cake'), a megaton apotheosis of dubious taste; the man who commissioned it in the 1880s happened to have a marble quarry in his home district.

Behind the Vittoriano, a stairway will lead you up the hill into the real heart of Rome, Michelangelo's **Piazza del Campidoglio**, a triumph of Renaissance design bordered by a formidable cast of statues and centred around an equestrian one of the Emperor Marcus Aurelius (now a copy). Facing each other across the square, the matching **Palazzo dei Conservatori** and the **Palazzo Nuovo** (*both open Tues–Sat 9–7, Sun 9–6.45, hols 9–1.45; adm, free last Sun of every month*) make up the **Capitoline Museums** (*open Tues–Sun 9.30–7, Sat until 11pm; adm*), founded by Pope Clement XII in 1734, making it the oldest true museum in the world. The heights and depths of ancient society and culture are reflected here, with roomfuls of statuary in between, including the *Capitoline She-Wolf*, the very symbol of Rome, and the *Muse Polyhymnia*, one of the most delightful statues of antiquity. You'll also find lots of papal paraphernalia, and, in a *pinacoteca*, some dignified Velázquez gentlemen and major works by Caravaggio.

Piazza Bocca della Verità and Around

At the foot of the Capitoline Hill, the streets west of the **Teatro di Marcello** contain some of Rome's oldest houses, mixed in with new buildings that have replaced the old walled Jewish **ghetto**. Opposite the theatre, ancient bridges join the lovely **Isola Tiberina** to both banks of the Tiber. A single arch decorated by dragons is all that remains of the 2nd century BC Pons Aemilius, or **Ponte Rotto** ('broken bridge'). Here, on the east bank, there are two well-preserved Roman temples in the **Piazza Bocca della Verità** and, across from them, the handsome medieval church of **Santa Maria in Cosmedin** (*open 10–7, in winter until 5*), where medieval Romans would swear oaths by the Bocca della Verità (Mouth of Truth) in the portico. If you tell a lie with your hand in the spooky image's mouth, he'll bite your fingers off. Try it.

The Heart of Ancient Rome

The **Imperial Fora** of Augustus, Nerva and Trajan were built to relieve congestion in the original Roman Forum. **Trajan's Forum** (*Foro di Traiano*), built with the spoils of his conquest of Dacia (modern Romania), was perhaps the grandest architectural and planning conception ever built in Rome, a broad square surrounded by colonnades,

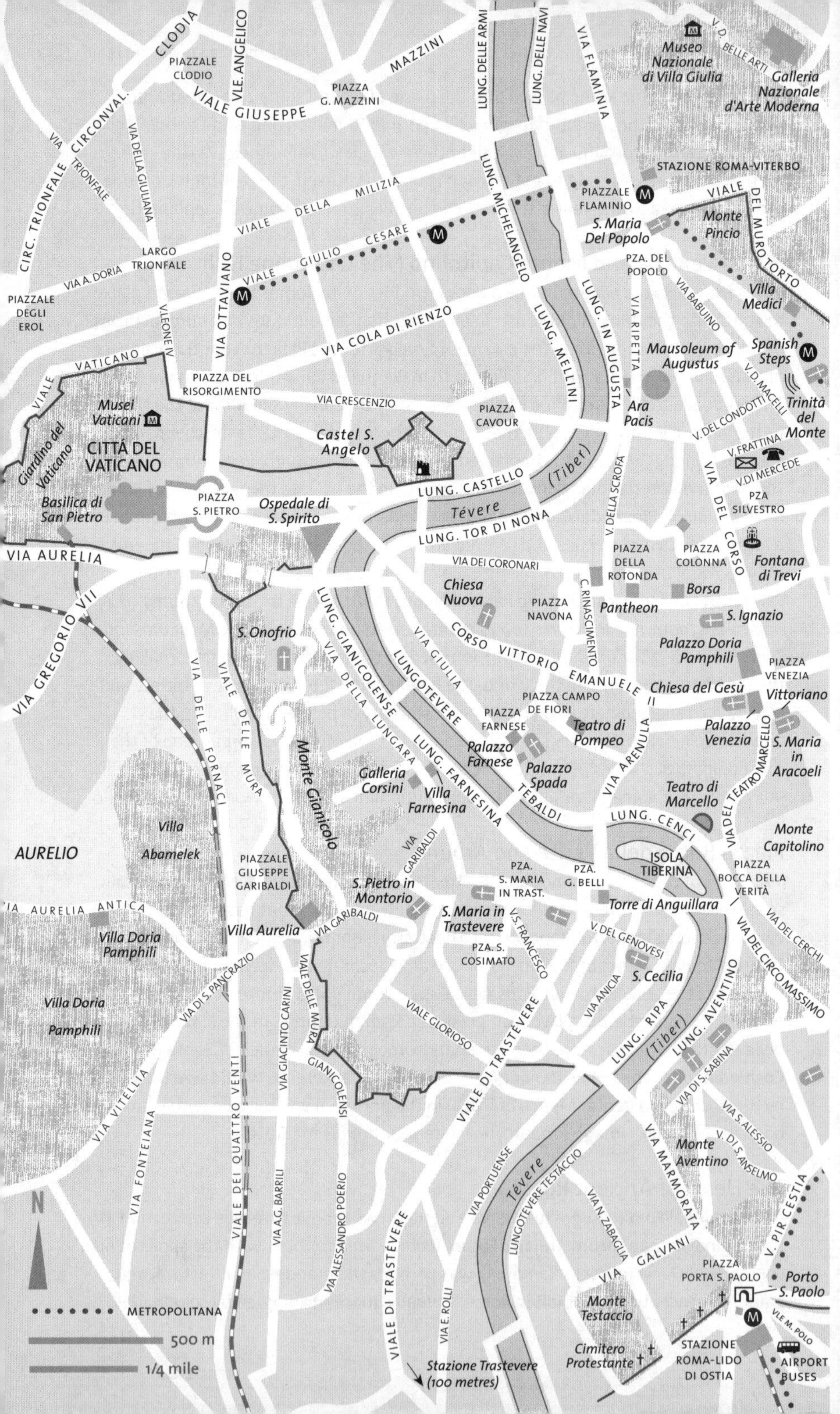

Museo Nazionale di Villa Giulia
Galleria Nazionale d'Arte Moderna
PIAZZALE CLODIO
PIAZZA G. MAZZINI
VIALE GIUSEPPE MAZZINI
STAZIONE ROMA-VITERBO
PIAZZALE FLAMINIO
S. Maria Del Popolo
Monte Pincio
PZA. DEL POPOLO
Villa Medici
Spanish Steps
Mausoleum of Augustus
Trinità del Monte
Ara Pacis
PIAZZA CAVOUR
Castel S. Angelo
Musei Vaticani
CITTÁ DEL VATICANO
Giardino del Vaticano
Basilica di San Pietro
PIAZZA S. PIETRO
Ospedale di S. Spirito
PIAZZA DEL RISORGIMENTO
LARGO TRIONFALE
PIAZZALE DEGLI EROI
Tévere
(Tiber)
PIAZZA DELLA ROTONDA
PIAZZA COLONNA
Fontana di Trevi
Borsa
Pantheon
Chiesa Nuova
PIAZZA NAVONA
S. Ignazio
Palazzo Doria Pamphili
PIAZZA VENEZIA
Chiesa del Gesù
Vittoriano
PIAZZA CAMPO DE FIORI
PIAZZA FARNESE
Teatro di Pompeo
Palazzo Farnese
Palazzo Spada
Palazzo Venezia
S. Maria in Aracoeli
S. Onofrio
Monte Gianicolo
Galleria Corsini
Villa Farnesina
Teatro di Marcello
Monte Capitolino
ISOLA TIBERINA
PIAZZA BOCCA DELLA VERITÀ
Villa Abamelek
AURELIO
PIAZZALE GIUSEPPE GARIBALDI
S. Pietro in Montorio
PZA. S. MARIA IN TRAST.
PZA. G. BELLI
Torre di Anguillara
S. Maria in Trastevere
Villa Aurelia
Villa Doria Pamphili
PZA. S. COSIMATO
S. Cecilia
Monte Aventino
PIAZZA PORTA S. PAOLO
Porto S. Paolo
Monte Testaccio
Cimitero Protestante
STAZIONE ROMA-LIDO DI OSTIA
AIRPORT BUSES
Stazione Trastevere (100 metres)
METROPOLITANA
500 m
1/4 mile
N

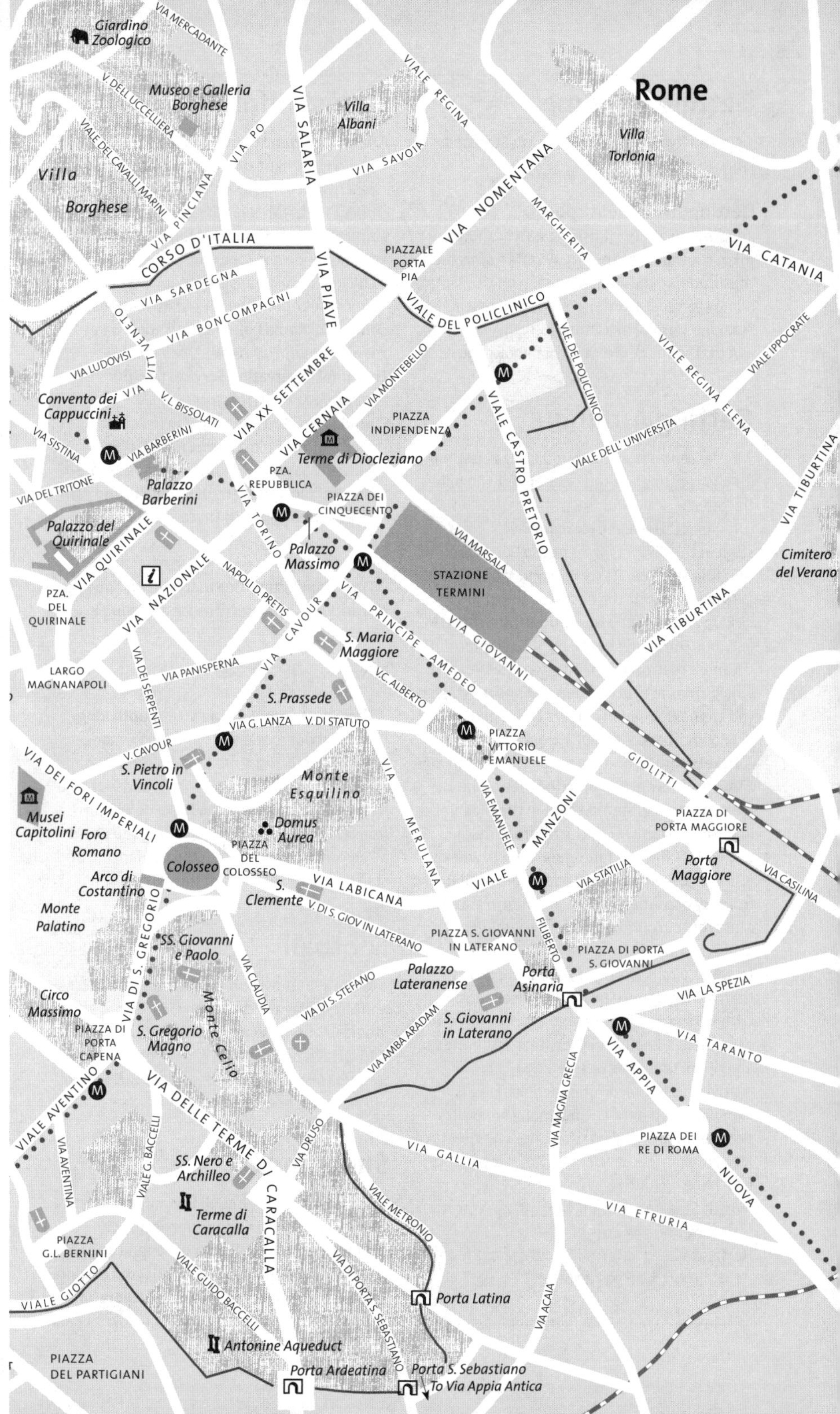
Rome
Giardino Zoologico
Museo e Galleria Borghese
Villa Borghese
Villa Albani
Villa Torlonia
VIA MERCADANTE
V. DELL'UCCELLIERA
VIALE DEL CAVALLI MARINI
VIA PINCIANA
VIA PO
VIA SALARIA
VIALE REGINA
VIA SAVOIA
VIA NOMENTANA
MARGHERITA
CORSO D'ITALIA
PIAZZALE PORTA PIA
VIA PIAVE
VIA CATANIA
VIA SARDEGNA
VIA BONCOMPAGNI
VIA VENETO
VIALE DEL POLICLINICO
VLE. DEL POLICLINICO
VIALE REGINA ELENA
VIALE IPPOCRATE
VIA LUDOVISI
VIA XX SETTEMBRE
VIA MONTEBELLO
Convento dei Cappuccini
V. L. BISSOLATI
VIA CERNAIA
PIAZZA INDIPENDENZA
VIALE CASTRO PRETORIO
VIALE DELL' UNIVERSITA
VIA TIBURTINA
VIA SISTINA
VIA BARBERINI
Terme di Diocleziano
PZA. REPUBBLICA
Palazzo Barberini
VIA DEL TRITONE
PIAZZA DEI CINQUECENTO
Palazzo del Quirinale
VIA TORINO
Palazzo Massimo
VIA MARSALA
STAZIONE TERMINI
Cimitero del Verano
VIA QUIRINALE
VIA NAZIONALE
NAPOLI D. PRETIS
PZA. DEL QUIRINALE
VIA CAVOUR
VIA PRINCIPE AMEDEO
VIA GIOVANNI
S. Maria Maggiore
LARGO MAGNANAPOLI
VIA PANISPERNA
VIA DEI SERPENTI
V.C. ALBERTO
S. Prassede
VIA G. LANZA
V. DI STATUTO
PIAZZA VITTORIO EMANUELE
V. CAVOUR
S. Pietro in Vincoli
VIA DEI FORI IMPERIALI
Monte Esquilino
VIA MERULANA
VIA EMANUELE
GIOLITTI
Musei Capitolini
Foro Romano
Domus Aurea
VIALE MANZONI
PIAZZA DI PORTA MAGGIORE
Porta Maggiore
Colosseo
PIAZZA DEL COLOSSEO
VIA LABICANA
VIA STATILIA
VIA CASILINA
Arco di Costantino
S. Clemente
V. DI S. GIOV IN LATERANO
Monte Palatino
VIA DI S. GREGORIO
SS. Giovanni e Paolo
PIAZZA S. GIOVANNI IN LATERANO
FILIBERTO
PIAZZA DI PORTA S. GIOVANNI
VIA CLAUDIA
Palazzo Lateranense
Porta Asinaria
Monte Celio
VIA LA SPEZIA
Circo Massimo
VIA DI S. STEFANO
VIA AMBA ARADAM
S. Giovanni in Laterano
PIAZZA DI PORTA CAPENA
S. Gregorio Magno
VIA APPIA
VIA TARANTO
VIALE AVENTINO
VIA DELLE TERME DI CARACALLA
VIA MAGNA GRECIA
VIA DRUSO
PIAZZA DEI RE DI ROMA
VIA AVENTINA
VIALE G. BACCELLI
SS. Nero e Archilleo
VIA GALLIA
NUOVA
Terme di Caracalla
VIALE METRONIO
VIA ETRURIA
PIAZZA G.L. BERNINI
VIALE GUIDO BACCELLI
VIA DI PORTA S. SEBASTIANO
VIALE GIOTTO
Porta Latina
VIA ACAIA
PIAZZA DEL PARTIGIANI
Antonine Aqueduct
Porta Ardeatina
Porta S. Sebastiano
To Via Appia Antica

Getting to Rome

Go and **Ryanair** fly from London Stansted (2hrs 30mins).

Getting from the Airport

Ciampino airport (**t** 06 794 941) is about 16km southeast of the city. A COTRAL bus links the airport to the Agnanina stop on the Metro A line (30mins); from there, you can reach Stazione Termini in 20mins (6.15am–10.20pm).

A **taxi** to the centre will cost about €30–40.

Getting Around

In the *centro storico* around Piazza Navona, it's easy getting around on foot, but the hills, the outsize scale and the traffic make Rome a tiring place. However, you can have a pleasant stroll in the districts west of the Corso, around the Isola Tiberina, Trastevere and Monte Celio.

Buses are by far the best way to get around. Pick up a map of the bus routes from the **ATAC** (city bus company) booth by Stazione Termini.

Rome's **metro** system has two lines, A and B, which cross at Stazione Termini and will take you to the Colosseum, Piazza di Spagna, Piazza del Popolo, or within eight blocks of St Peter's.

Tickets cost €1, and are valid for travel on any ATAC city bus or tram and one metro ride (within 75mins); stamp them in the machines in buses or trams, or in the metro turnstile. **Day tickets** (BIG, including metro; €3), **weekly** (CIS €12.50) and **monthly passes** are available, from *tabacchi*, bars, kiosks and metro stations. Most routes run frequently (*5.30–midnight*).

Official **taxis** (white) are plentiful and easier to get at a rank in one of the main piazzas than to flag down. They are quite expensive, with surcharges for luggage etc., but fares are explained in English in every taxi. To phone for a taxi, call **t** 06 3570, or **t** 06 4994.

Driving is not recommended! Parking is expensive and hard to find; many areas are pedestrian and riddled with one-way streets.

Car Hire

Avis, at Stazione Termini, **t** 06 481 4373; at the airport, **t** 06 793 40195.

Hertz, at Stazione Termini, **t** 06 474 0389; at the airport, **t** 06 793 40616.

Tourist Information

Azienda di Promozione Turistica (APT), Via Parigi 11, 00185, **t** 06 488 991, **f** 06 4889 9238 (*open Mon–Fri 9.30–12.30, Mon and Thurs also 2.30–4.30*). Near the Baths of Diocletian.

Comune di Roma Tourist Information Office, Stazione Termini (*open daily 8–8*). Provides city and public transport maps (free) and brochures about the tourist attractions.

Comune di Roma helpline, t 06 3600 4399, *www.romaturismo.com*. *Open daily 8–7*.

The Hotel Reservation Service, t 06 699 1000 (*open daily 8am–10.45pm*).

Cumulative Site Ticket: a 5-day ticket includes the Palatino, Colosseum, Cripta Balbi, Palazzo Massimo, Palazzo Altemps, Terme di Diocleziano and Baths of Caracalla and can be acquired at any of these sites.

Market Days

The Porta Portese **flea market** (*Sun dawn–1*) has antiques and pretty much anything else.

Festivals

The ***Estate Romana*** is a three-month long festival of outdoor events and performances, and most museums run longer hours. Ask at the tourist office, check *Romac'e'* and look out for posters. Far older is the **Festa de' Noantri** (*16–31 July*) in Trastevere, including music from all across the spectrum, acrobats, dancing and stall upon stall all around the piazzas.

Football

Rome's first-division **football** clubs, AS Roma and Lazio, play on Sat or Sun (*Sept–May*) at the Stadio Olimpico, Viale dei Gladiatori 2 (Ⓜ Linea A to Ottaviano, then bus 32). Tickets €18–110; for sale 10–14 days ahead; contact **Lazio Point**, Via Farini 34, **t** 06 6482 6688.

Shopping

Rome isn't Milan, but all the major labels are well represented. High **fashion** is on the streets between the Piazza di Spagna and the Corso. Some highlights: **Massoni**, Largo Goldoni 48, sells some of Rome's finest **jewellery**; for

menswear, try **Testa**, Via Borgognona 13, or **Valentino Uomo**, Via Condotti 12, or for **custom tailoring** go to **Battistoni**, Via Condotti 61/a. For **women's clothes** try **Missoni**, Via del Babuino 96; **Giorgio Armani**, Via Condotti 76–7, and Via del Babuino 140; or **Fendi**, Via Borgognona 36/e. For **leather**, you'll find **Gucci** at Via Condotti 8, and don't miss **Fausto Santini**, Via Frattina 120. **Discounted designer fashion** may be had at **Il Discount dell'Alta Moda**, Via Gesù e Maria 16/a; for **high-fashion shoes**, try Barrilà, Via Condotti 29.

For **wine**, try **Enoteca Costantini**, Piazza Cavour 16, or stock up on **coffee** at **Tazza d'Oro**, Via degli Orfani 84. For **antiques**, look between the Tiber and Piazza Navona off Via Monserrato, Via dei Coronari and Via dell'Anima.

Where to Stay

Rome ✉ 00100

Prices tend to be higher and service and quality lower than elsewhere in Italy. Breakfast is often extra and places with a history, a view or quiet gardens are rare. Many hotels are in the streets around the Stazione Termini, but these are now dingy and down-at-heel, as well as inconvenient for most of the sights.

*******Hassler-Villa Medici**, Piazza Trinità dei Monti 6, 00187, **t** 06 699 340, **f** 06 678 9991, *www.hotelhasslerroma.com* (*luxury*). One of Rome's élite hotels, located atop the Spanish Steps with wonderful views if you book far enough ahead. It has a beautiful courtyard, deferential service and wood-panelled rooms.

*******Excelsior**, Via Veneto 125, 00187, **t** 06 47081, **f** 06 482 6205, *www.westin.com* (*luxury*). Also in a choice area, though it lacks the aura it had in the 1950s. The reception areas have thicker carpets, bigger chandeliers and more gilded plaster than anywhere in Italy, and most of the rooms are just as good; don't let them give you a modern one. It offers saunas, a famous bar and all the personal attention you could ask for.

******Raphael**, Largo di Febo 2, 00186, **t** 06 682 831, **f** 06 687 8993, *www.raphaelhotel.com* (*very expensive*). Near Piazza Navona, this is a vine-covered old charmer, decorated with antiques. Top-floor rooms have views, and it offers TV, bar, restaurant and a/c.

*****Fontana**, Piazza di Trevi 96, 00187, **t** 06 678 6113, **f** 06 679 0024 (*very expensive*). This would be a good hotel anywhere, but it also happens to overlook the Trevi Fountain.

*****Gregoriana**, Via Gregoriana 18, 00187, **t** 06 679 4269, **f** 06 678 4258 (*very expensive*). Close to the Spanish Steps; small, tasteful and gratifyingly friendly, with a devoted clientèle – it has just 19 rooms, so book early.

******La Residenza**, Via Emilia 22, 00187, **t** 06 488 0789, **f** 06 485 721, *www.venere.it/roma/laresidenza* (*very expensive*). A very pleasant base, with beautifully appointed rooms in an old town house, and some luxuries.

*****Villa San Pio**, Via Santa Melania 19, 00153, **t** 06 578 3214, **f** 06 578 3604, *www.aventinohotels.com* (*very expensive*). A glorious Aventine villa with a gorgeous, secluded statue-studded garden. Bar and TV.

****Croce di Malta**, Via Borgognona 28, 00187, **t** 06 679 5482, **f** 06 678 0675, *www.crocedimalta.com* (*expensive*). Well located on a designer shopping street, with smart bedrooms, some with opulent furniture.

****Casa Kolbe**, Via di San Teodoro 44, 00186, **t** 06 679 4974, **f** 06 6994 1550 (*moderate*). Large rooms in a former monastery in one of Rome's most central but remote corners, with a garden, bar and restaurant.

***Perugia**, Via del Colosseo 7, 00184, **t** 06 679 7200, **f** 06 678 4635 (*moderate*). Small, fairly quiet, fairly basic hotel near the Colosseum. Cheaper rooms available without bath.

The area around **Stazione Termini** offers a wide choice of inexpensive hotels.

***Restivo**, Via Palestro 55, **t** 06 446 2172, **f** 06 445 2629 (*cheap*). Immaculate *pensione* run by a sweet old lady, whose hall is cluttered with gifts from affectionate visitors.

Mari, **t** 06 446 2137, **f** 06 6482 8313 (*cheap*). If Restivo is full, try this in the same *palazzo*.

Eating Out

Rome attracts talented chefs from all over Italy, creating a microcosm of Italian cuisine you'll find nowhere else. Roman specialities include *saltimbocca*, paper-thin slices of veal cooked with *prosciutto*, *stracciatella* (a soup with eggs, parmesan cheese and parsley), fried artichokes and veal *involtini*. The wine will probably be from the Castelli Romani.

La Pergola dell'Hotel Hilton, Via Cadlolo 101, **t** 06 35091 (*very expensive*). High above the city, this is one of Rome's top restaurants, offering elegant surroundings with all of Rome at your feet. Book well ahead. *Open Feb–Dec Tues–Sat 7.30–11.45pm.*

Alberto Ciarla, Piazza San Cosimato 40, **t** 06 581 8668 (*very expensive*). In Trastevere; everything is delicately and perfectly done, and graciously served: oysters, ravioli and adventurous *pesce crudo*. *Open Mon–Sat 7.30–midnight, except two weeks in Jan.*

Checchino dal 1887, Via di Monte Testaccio 30, **t** 06 574 3816 (*very expensive*). The temple of old Roman cooking, owned by the family for 107 years. Both the fancy and humble are represented, including plenty of powerful offal, and the setting is unique: on the edge of Monte Testaccio, with a brilliant cellar. *Open Sept–July Tues–Sat 12–3 and 8–11.30.*

Il Toscano, Via Germanico 58, **t** 06 397 25717 (*expensive*). A good option in the touristy Vatican area: family-run and popular with Roman families, offering well-prepared *pici* (rough spaghetti rolled by hand) in game sauce, *fiorentina* steak and home-made desserts. Book. *Open Sept–July Tues–Sat 12.30–3 and 8–11, except last week of Dec.*

Il Convivio, Vicolo dei Soldati 31, **t** 06 686 9432 (*expensive*). Some of Rome's most innovative cuisine: unbeatable chilled fruit soups, baked *zucchini* flowers and exquisite pastries. Book. *Open Tues–Sat 1–2.30 and 8–10.30, Mon 8–10.30 only, except one week in Aug.*

Dal Bolognese, Piazza del Popolo 1, **t** 06 361 1426 (*expensive*). With tables on the grand *piazza* and a view of the Pincio, this features Emilian specialities – don't miss the fresh pasta, and finish with *fruttini*, a selection of real fruit shells each filled with its own sorbet flavour. *Open Sept–June Tues–Sat 12.45–3 and 8.15–11, July–Aug Tues–Fri only.*

Grappolo d'Oro, Piazza della Cancelleria 80, **t** 06 689 7080 (*moderate*). Near Campo de' Fiori, with great value, traditional Roman fare; it's one of the best places to sit out at night. *Open Sept–July Mon–Sat 12–3 and 8–11.*

Armando al Pantheon, Salita dei Crescenzi 31, **t** 06 6880 3034 (*moderate*). An authentic Roman *trattoria* famous for *spaghetti cacio e pepe* (with pecorino and black pepper). *Open Mon–Fri 12.30–3 and 7–11, Sat 12.30–3.*

Ditirambo, Piazza della Cancelleria, **t** 06 687 1626 (*moderate*). A favourite with Roman youth; you'll have to take the noise along with the good food: home-made dishes such as ricotta and almond ravioli. *Open Sept–July Tues–Sun 1–3.30 and 8–11.30, Mon 8–11.30 only.*

Semidivino, Via Alessandria 230, **t** 06 4425 0795. A classy, intimate wine bar with excellent salads, interesting cheeses, cured meat and soups at reasonable prices. *Open Sept–July Mon–Fri 12.30–2 and 7.30–11.30, Sat 7.30–11.30.*

La Montecarlo, Vicolo Savelli 12, **t** 06 686 1877. Sit elbow to elbow with your neighbours and duck as brilliant pizzas (€3–7), chairs and tables are whipped over your head. *Open May–Oct daily 12–3 and 6.30–1, except 2 weeks in Aug; Nov–April Tues–Sun only.*

Caffè Greco, Via Condotti 86, **t** 06 678 5474. Rome's oldest café (1760), where Keats and Casanova sipped their java – the chance for a quick fix of *ancien régime* luxury.

Il Gelato di San Crispino, Via della Panetteria 42, near the Trevi Fountain. It's easy to succumb to *gelato* on every corner here, but hold out for the best the city has to offer.

Entertainment

The best sources of **listings** are two weeklies available from news-stands, *Romac'e'* (with a short English section) and *Time Out* (in Italian).

Try to get **tickets** early for events or concerts. **Orbis**, Piazza Esquilino 37, **t** 06 474 4776, *www.ticketone.it*, is reliable for concerts, opera and theatre (*open Mon–Sat 9.30–1 and 4–7.30*).

Nightlife

The best entertainment in Rome may be in the passing cosmopolitan spectacle of its streets. If you're determined, the back streets around the **Piazza Navona** or **Campo de' Fiori** swarm in the evenings, and leaflets are always being handed out. For serious posing, head to **Bar della Pace**, Via della Pace 5, an ultra-hip bar frequented by celebrities. Otherwise, Rome has a select band of clubs with live music – *Romac'e'* will have up-to-date details. For serious **dancing**, look out for *di tendenza* clubs, which keep up with current UK and US trends. Most indoor venues close late July–Aug.

with a huge basilica flanked by two libraries and a covered market outside. A large part of **Trajan's Markets** still stands (*open Tues–Sun 9–6.30; adm*). All that remains of the great square is the paving and **Trajan's Column** (*Colonna Traiana*); its amazing spiralling bands of reliefs, illustrating the Dacian Wars, reach some 96ft to the top.

The Roman Forum

Entrances on Via dei Fori Imperiali (Via Cavour); or by the ramp that approaches the Forum from the Colosseum; open daily 9–1hr before sunset.

For a place that was the centre of the Mediterranean world, there is surprisingly little to see; centuries of use as a quarry have seen to that. The **Via Sacra**, ancient Rome's most important street, runs the length of the Forum. At the end of it beneath Capitoline Hill stands the **Arch of Septimius Severus** (AD 203), in front of which lies the **Lapis Niger**, the legendary tomb of Romulus. To the right is the **Curia** (Senate), heavily restored after centuries' use as a church, while to the left are the remains of the **Rostra**, the speakers' platform, decorated with ships' prows (*rostra*). The mastodontic **Basilica of Maxentius** remains the largest ruin of the Forum, its clumsy arches an illustration of the ungainly but technically sophisticated 4th century. Nearby, a church is built over a corner of Rome's largest temple, that of **Venus and Rome**, one side devoted to the Goddess Roma, the other to Venus, mythical ancestress of the Caesars. Near the exit, the **Arch of Titus** commemorates the victories of Titus over the rebellious Jews (AD 60–80), with reliefs showing the booty being carted through Rome in the triumphal parade.

South of the arch a path leads up to the **Monte Palatino** (*open daily 9–one hr before sunset; adm*), the imperial *Palatium* that was once a complex half a mile long. Most of the stone has been cannibalized, but there are good views across the Circus Maximus and the gardens are one of the most peaceful spots in the city.

The Colosseum

Piazza del Colosseo; open daily 9–1hr before sunset; adm.

Its real name was the Flavian Amphitheatre, after the family of emperors who built it, beginning with Vespasian in AD 72; Colosseum refers to the *Colossus*, a huge gilded statue of Nero that stood in front. Gladiatorial contests began under the republic, designed to make Roman soldiers indifferent to the sight of death. However hideous its purpose, the Colosseum ranks with the greatest works of Roman architecture; all modern stadia follow its basic plan. Originally there were statues in every arch and a ring of bronze shields around the cornice. Outside, the **Arch of Constantine** marks the end of the ancient Triumphal Way (Via di San Gregorio) where victorious emperors and their troops would parade their captives and booty.

The Domus Aurea, the Monte Esquilino and San Clemente

Nero's palace, the **Domus Aurea** (Golden House; *Colle Oppio;* **t** *06 3996 7700; open daily 9–8; advance booking essential; adm*), was probably the most sumptuous palace ever built in Rome. Realizing that this symbol of imperial decadance had to go, his successors demolished it, and great bath complexes were erected on its foundations. However, in the 1500s some beautifully decorated rooms of the Domus Aurea were discovered underground, and these are now open for guided visits.

The **Monte Esquilino**, much of it covered with parks, surrounds the Domus Aurea. On the northern slope, **San Pietro in Vincoli** (*open daily 7–12.30 and 3.30–6*) houses the ill-fated **tomb of Julius II**, so ambitious that of the 40 statues originally planned, Michelangelo only completed *Leah*, *Rachel* and the powerful figure of *Moses*, perhaps the closest anyone has ever come to capturing prophetic vision in stone.

East of the Colosseum, the church of **San Clemente** (*Via San Giovanni in Laterano; open 9–12.30 and 3.30–6; adm to excavations*) is a fascinating illustration of Rome's many layered history. The original basilica of *c.* 375 burned in 1084, to be rebuilt soon afterwards, but the lower half of the first church remains, containing remarkable 9th- and 12th-century frescoes. Steps lead down to the lowest stratum of 1st and 2nd century AD buildings, including a fascinating *mithraeum* (temple to Mithras), and underneath, you can see yet a fourth building level, from the republican era.

Corso Vittorio Emanuele, Piazza Navona and the Pantheon

This ragged, smoky traffic tunnel will come in handy when you find yourself lost in the tortuous, meandering streets of Rome's oldest quarter. Going west from Piazza Venezia, Vignola and della Porta's church of **Il Gesù** (1568–84) (*open 7–12 and 3–7.30*) was the Jesuit headquarters and a landmark in *cinquecento* Roman architecture, laying down Baroque's first law: an intimation of paradise through decorative excess. The string of grand Baroque churches and palaces continues along the length of the Corso, ending at its western end with the **Chiesa Nuova** (*open 8–12 and 4.30–7*) of 1584, another flagrant offering with an altarpiece by Rubens.

Off the Corso, Rome's chaotic **Campo de' Fiori** is easily the liveliest corner of the city, best seen by night, or during the morning market (*Mon–Sat dawn–1*). A heap of buildings over the *cavea* of the **Teatro di Pompeo** marks the spot where Julius Caesar was assassinated in 44 BC. South of here, the florid **Palazzo Spada** (*Via Capo di Ferro 13; open Tues–Sat 9–7, Sun 9–6; adm*) contains one of Rome's great collections of 16th- and 17th-century painting, with Guido Reni, Guercino and other favourites of the age.

North of the Corso is **Piazza Navona**, one of Rome's most beautiful *piazzas*, famed for its fountains by Bernini. The **Fontana dei Fiumi** is his masterpiece, Baroque at its flashiest and most lovable, representing the four great rivers amid grottoes and fantastical flora and fauna; it is especially lovely at night when it's illuminated. At the square's north end, the **Palazzo Altemps** houses part of the **Museo Nazionale Romano** (*see* p.232). Nearby, the great dome of the **Pantheon** (*open Mon–Sat 8.30–7.30, Sun 9–6*) looms over the Piazza della Rotonda, built by the Emperor Hadrian in AD 119–128. Through the great bronze doors is the grandest and best-preserved building from the ancient world, an interior of precious marbles and finely sculpted details. The coffered dome is the crowning audacity; at 141ft in diameter it is probably the largest in the world (St Peter's is 6ft less). The statues of gods around the perimeter are all gone, leaving only an *Annunciation* attributed to Melozzo da Forlì, and the tombs of eminent Italians such as Raphael and kings Vittorio Emanuele II and Umberto I.

Via del Corso

Leading north from the Piazza Venezia, the **Via del Corso** has been the main axis of Roman society ever since it was laid out by the popes of the 14th and 15th centuries. Much of its length is taken up by the overdone palaces of the age, such as the 1780 **Palazzo Doria-Pamphili** (*open Fri–Wed 10–5; adm*), which contains fine paintings by the likes of Velazquez, Caravaggio, Rubens, Titian, Brueghel. Continuing north, the palaces have come down in the world somewhat, now tired-looking blocks housing banks and offices. A little way east of Piazza Colonna is the grand **Fontana di Trevi** (1762), into which you can throw your coins to guarantee your return trip to Rome.

Further north, the Corso approaches the Tiber and the burial chamber of all the Julian emperors except Nero, the dilapidated **Mausoleo di Augusto** (*closed to the public*). Across the street, Augustus' **Ara Pacis** (*closed for restoration*) has had a better fate, recreated almost in its entirety, with fine mythological reliefs. East of here, the supremely sophisticated **Piazza di Spagna** has been a favourite with foreigners ever since it was laid out in the early 16th century. The Spaniards came first in 1646, giving the square its name; later, the English Romantic poets moved in; today it's bursting with refreshingly Philistine gawkers, caught between the charms of McDonald's and the fancy shops around Via Condotti. In 1725, the popes built them somewhere to sit: the exceptionally beautiful, and exceptionally Baroque, **Spanish Steps**, culminating with Carlo Maderno's effective 16th-century church of **Trinità dei Monti** (*open 9–8*).

Piazza del Popolo and the Villa Borghese

Via del Babuino connects Piazza di Spagna with **Piazza del Popolo**, where Nero's ashes were originally interred at the foot of Monte Pincio, giving rise to rumours that he was sending out evil spirits from beyond the grave. The church of **Santa Maria del Popolo** (*open Mon–Sat 7–7, Sun 8–1.30 and 4.30–7.30*), said to have been built to complete the exorcism, contains some of the best paintings in Rome: Caravaggio's stunning *Crucifixion of St Peter* and *Conversion of St Paul*, and frescoes by Pinturicchio. The Chigi Chapel was designed by Raphael, including its mosaics.

From the *piazza* a winding ramp leads up to Rome's great complex of parks. On one side of the Aurelian wall, the **Monte Pincio** has been redesigned by Valadier as a lovely formal garden, offering rare views over Rome; on the other, the **Villa Borghese** (*open dawn–sunset*) is a haven of charming vales and rococo avenues, with a dated **zoo** (*open daily Mar–Oct 9.30–5; Oct–Mar 9.30–5; adm*). On the northern edge the **Galleria Nazionale d'Arte Moderna** (***t** 06 322 981; open Tues–Sun 8.30–7.30; adm; guided tours in English by reservation, Sun 11am*) includes some great works of Modigliani and the Futurists, as well as a fair sampling of other 19th- and 20th-century European artists.

Nearby, the **Museo Etrusco Nazionale di Villa Giulia** (*open Tues–Sun 9–7.30; adm*) is the place to get to know the Etruscans. Perhaps most compelling is their effortless, endearing talent for portraiture; look out for the charming couple on the *Sarcophago dei Sposi* from Cerveteri, and the roof statues from the Temple of Portonaccio at Veii.

To the east is the fantastic trove of ancient relics and late-Renaissance and Baroque art amassed by Cardinal Borghese in the **Museo e Galleria Borghese** (***t** 06 32810; open Tues–Sun 9–7; adm, advance booking (€1 fee) recommended*). Among the highlights are the sensuous showpieces of Bernini, Canova's *Conquering Venus*, the famous *Sleeping Hermaphrodite* and several Caravaggios. Upstairs many of the finest 16th- and 17th-century painters appear, including Titian, Bernini, Raphael, Correggio and Rubens.

Terme di Diocleziano and Museo Nazionale Romano

Rome's Stazione Termini takes its name from the nearby **Terme di Diocleziano**, a bath complex which once covered some 11 hectares; its outer wall followed the lines of Via XX Settembre and Piazza dei Cinquecento, while the **Piazza della Repubblica**, with its mouldering *palazzi* and huge fountain, occupies the site of the exercise ground (*palaestra*). Michelangelo (not on one of his better days) converted part of the central bathhouse into the church of **Santa Maria degli Angeli**, adding a new cloister (*open Tues–Fri 9–7.45; Sun 9am–11pm; adm free*). This now houses inscriptions, lapidaries and sarcophagi from the **Museo Nazionale Romano**, the greatest Italian collection of Roman antiquities after the museum in Naples – recently relocated to five different sites. Most impressive is the **Palazzo Massimo alle Terme** (*open Tues–Sun 9–7.45; adm exp*) opposite the station, with astonishingly vivid frescoes and mosaics that once decorated villas in Rome and its suburbs, as well as fine Roman statuary, coins and gold jewellery. The nearby **Aula Ottagona** (*Via Parigi/Giuseppe Romita; open Tues–Sat 9–2, Sun 9–1; adm free*) displays remarkable bronze statues; **Palazzo Altemps** (*open Tues–Fri 9–7.45, Sun 9am–11pm; adm*) near Piazza Navona (*see* p.230), houses sculpture, including the famous Ludovisi throne; the 1st-century **Crypta Balbi** (*Via dell Botteghe Oscure; open Tues–Sun 9–7.45; adm*) is its newest addition.

West of Piazza Repubblica on Via Barberini, the showy **Palazzo Barberini** houses the **Galleria Nazionale d'Arte Antica** (*open Tues–Fri 9–7, Sat and Sun 9–8; adm*), devoted to Italian works of the 12th–18th centuries, although the interior decoration often steals the show. Beyond it, the president's residence, the **Palazzo del Quirinale**, stretches on for a dreary half kilometre.

Trastevere

So often just being on the wrong side of the river encourages a city district to cultivate its differences and its eccentricities. The people of Trastevere are more Roman than the Romans, and the quarter remains the liveliest and most entertaining in Rome, attracting a young crowd whose trendy clothes are somehow a perfect match for the medieval alleys. Just over Ponte Garibaldi is Piazza Sonnino, with the **Torre degli Anguillara**, one of the city's few surviving medieval defence towers. East down Via dei Genovesi stands the church of **Santa Cecilia in Trastevere** (*open daily 9.30–6.30*), the 2nd-century martyr whose body, on being disinterred in 1599, was found entirely uncorrupted. Maderno sculpted an exact copy from sketches made before her body dissolved into thin air, a charming work now situated near the altar. Up in the gallery (*open Tues and Fri 10.30–11.30; adm*) are the remains of a wonderful fresco of the *Last Judgement* by Cavallini.

The heart of old Trastevere lies to the west across Viale di Trastevere, around **Piazza Santa Maria in Trastevere** and its medieval church, a treasure-house of Roman mosaics, starting with the frieze on the façade, and continuing with the remarkable series by Cavallini in the apse (*c.* 1290). This area has long been one of Rome's most popular spots to eat out, with tables spread out wherever there's room; there's always a crowd in the evening.

Castel Sant'Angelo

Lungotevere Castello 50; open Tues–Sun 9–7; **t** *06 681 9111; adm; guided visits by reservation (extra adm): of* **castle** *Tues–Fri 10.30am, Sat and Sun 10.30, 12.15 and 4.30; adm; of* **prisons** *Tues–Fri 3pm; adm.*

The castle was intended as a resting place for the Emperor Hadrian, but in about 590, its high, steep and pretty well impregnable cylinder caught the eye of Pope Gregory the Great, who fancied it might prove more valuable as a fortress. So it did; not only did the popes use it (regularly) as a safe haven during rebellions, but they also used it as a prison; Tosca tosses herself off the top at the end of Puccini's opera. Inside, the **Papal Apartments** are are as lavishly decorated as anything in the Vatican, with frescoes by Perin del Vaga in the Sala Paolina, and frescoes of grotesques in the Sala di Apollo, attempting to reproduce the decorations of Nero's Golden House. The views from the roof are some of the best in Rome, and there's a café on the 4th floor.

Vatican City

St Peter's

No arrangement of streets and buildings could really prepare you for Bernini's **Piazza San Pietro**. Capable of holding 300,000 people with no crowding, the open space almost exactly meets the size and dimensions of the Colosseum. Bernini's **Colonnade** (1656), with 284 massive columns and statues of 140 saints, stretches around it like 'the arms of the Church embracing the world' – perhaps the biggest cliché in Christendom. Stand on either of the two dark stones at the foci of the *piazza* and you will see Bernini's forest of columns resolve into neat rows.

The original St Peter's, begun over the Apostle's tomb by Constantine in 324, was falling to pieces by the 1400s, but it was not until the time of Julius II that Bramante was commissioned to begin the new church. His original plan called for a great dome over a centralized Greek cross; Michelangelo, who took over in 1546, basically agreed. Unfortunately, over 120 years of construction too many artists got their hand in, encouraged by Baroque popes who mistook size and virtuosity for art. Passing through Maderno's façade, the best is on the right: Michelangelo's *Pietà*, sculpted when he was only 25, helped to make his reputation, with the realities of death and grief sublimated onto some ethereal plane. Not much else really stands out. Scores of popes and saints are remembered in assembly-line Baroque; the famous bronze of St Peter by Arnolfo di Cambio, his foot worn by millions of pilgrims, is by the right front pier; but Bernini's great, garish *baldacchino* over the high altar steals the show. Many visitors head straight for Michelangelo's **dome** (*open 9–5.45; adm*). Don't miss the **Sacred Grottoes** below, where dozens of popes are buried, including John XXII and Sixtus IV.

Vatican Practicalities

The **museums** are open Mar–Oct Mon–Fri 8.30–3.30, Sat 8.30–12.30; Nov–Feb Mon–Sat 8–12.30; adm exp (€9); also open (and free) the last Sun of each month 8.30–12.30. The entrance is on Viale Vaticano, north of Piazza San Pietro. **St Peter's** is open daily 8–7; the basilica is closed for official ceremonies in the *piazza*, but visitors are allowed during mass. The dome is open 9–5.45 and the Treasury 9–6.15. The dress code – no shorts, short skirts or sleeveless dresses – is strictly controlled.

The **Vatican Information Office**, **t** 06 6988 4466, in Piazza San Pietro (*open daily 8–7*), is very helpful, and there are Vatican post offices on the opposite side of the square and inside the museums. The information office arranges 2hr morning tours of the **gardens**, easily Rome's most beautiful park, with a remarkable Renaissance jewel of a villa within (*tours May–Sept Mon–Tues and Thurs–Sat; Oct–April on Sat; €8.50 per person; reserve a few days in advance with the information office*).

Underneath the crypt of St Peter's, archaeologists discovered a **street of Roman tombs**, perfectly preserved with many beautiful paintings (*open by reservation only for 1½-hr guided visits (in English); adm €8. Call the Ufficio degli Scavi, just to the left of St Peter's,* **t** *06 6988 5318, for information; then fax them,* **f** *06 6988 5518, with your name, nationality, the language you want a tour in, the dates you are in Rome, an email address and contact number in Rome – they will confirm a date and time for the tour.* The rest of the Vatican is off limits, patrolled by Swiss Guards (recruited from the three Catholic Swiss cantons).

Michelangelo also designed the **wall** that since 1929 has marked the Vatican boundaries. Behind it are things most of us will never see: a printing press, Vatican Radio, even a shop. The Papal Apartments are in a corner of the Vatican Palace overlooking Piazza San Pietro; John Paul II usually appears to say a few words from his window at noon on Sundays.

For the Wednesdsay **papal audience**, usually at 11am in the *piazza* (*May–Sept*) or in the Nervi Auditorium (*Oct–April*), apply in advance at the Papal Prefecture – through the bronze door in the right-hand colonnade of Piazza San Pietro (*open Mon–Sat 9–1.30,* **t** *06 6988 3114,* **f** *06 6988 5863; collect tickets Mon–Sat 3–8 at Portone del Bronzo on Piazza San Pietro*).

The Musei Vaticani (Vatican Museums)

The admission may be the most expensive in Italy, but for that you get 10 museums in one, with the Sistine Chapel and the Raphael rooms thrown in free. Unfortunately for you there isn't much dull museum clutter, but there is a choice of colour-coded itineraries, which you may follow according to the hours you have to spend.

The first big challenge is the large **Museo Egizio**; then the **Museo Chiaramonti**, full of Roman statuary (including famous busts of Caesar, Mark Antony and Augustus). The **Museo Pio Clementino** contains the dramatic *Laocoön* from Nero's Domus Aurea, while the best thing in the **Museo Etrusco** is a truly excellent collection of Greek vases. If it weren't for Michelangelo, Raphael's frescoes in the **Stanza della Segnatura** would be the highlight of anyone's itinerary. Among those displayed here, you'll find his famous apotheosis of philosophy, the *School of Athens* and, across from it, a Triumph of Theology to keep the clerics happy: the *Dispute of the Holy Sacrament*.

Michelango painted the ceiling of the **Sistine Chapel** against his will, on the orders of Julius II. No one can say what inspired him to turn his master's whim into a masterpiece, but he spent four years (1508–12) on the ceiling, and refused all assistance. Julius II had asked for nothing more than virtuoso interior decoration, but what he got was a new vocabulary of images, the way the Old Testament looks in the deepest recesses of the imagination. Michelangelo's tremendous, harrowing vision of the *Last Judgement* (1534–41), on the rear wall, was painted after the Sack of Rome and reflects the darker mood of the age. Most visitors overlook the frescoes on the lower walls, great works in their own right: the *Exodus* by Botticelli, Perugino's *Donation of the Keys*, and Signorelli's *Moses Consigning his Staff to Joshua*.

Beyond, there's still the **Vatican Library**, with endless precious manuscripts, reliquaries, and every sort of globe, orrery and astronomical instrument. If you survive this, the **Museo Gregoriano** has a hoard of classical statuary, mosaics and inscriptions; beyond that are the collections of **carriages**, **early Christian art** and **ethnology**.

The **Pinacoteca** is the finest picture gallery in Rome, a representative sampling of Renaissance art from its beginnings, with fine works by Giotto, Gentile da Fabriano, Sano di Pietro, Filippo Lippi, Fra Angelico and Melozzo da Forlì. Perhaps best-known are the *Transfiguration of Christ*, Raphael's last work, and the *St Jerome* of Da Vinci.

Outside the Centre

The Patriarchal Basilicas

Besides St Peter's there are three Patriarchal Basilicas, ancient and revered churches under the care of the pope that have always been a part of the Roman Pilgrimage.

Santa Maria Maggiore (*open daily 7–7*), on Monte Esquilino, was probably begun *c.* 352, though it took its current form in the 1740s. Beyond its fine façade, the most conspicuous feature inside is the coffered ceiling by Giuliano da Sangallo, gilded with the first gold brought back from the New World by Columbus. The prize relic is no less than the genuine manger from Bethlehem.

South of Santa Maria, at the other end of the Via Merulana, lies the true seat of the Bishop of Rome, **San Giovanni in Laterano** (*open daily 7–7.30*), established by emperor Constantine himself. Almost nothing remains of the original basilica, but it has a miraculously good 18th-century exterior and, within, you'll find a striking example of Rome's highly individual architectural style of the late Middle Ages: the Lateran **cloister** (*open daily 9–5; adm*), with its pairs of spiral columns and 13th-century Cosmatesque mosaics, upstages everything else. Constantine's **Lateran Baptistry** (*open daily 8–12.30 and 4–6.30*), meanwhile, is the oldest one in Christendom.

San Paolo Fuori le Mura, now lost amid factories and gasworks along the Ostia road, was once the grandest of all the basilicas, but thanks to a good sacking, a few earthquakes and a catastrophic fire, few old features survive: an 11th-century door made in Constantinople, a Gothic baldaquin by Arnolfo di Cambio, a beautiful 13th-century Cosmatesque cloister and 5th-century mosaics over the arch in front of the apse.

Monte Aventino and Monte Testaccio

Under the republic, when legislation seriously threatened the interests of the people, they retired *en masse* to the Monte Aventino and laid low until the plan was dropped. Down by the river, Via Santa Sabina has a string of interesting early churches worth exploring; further south, the **Porta San Paolo** stands in one of the best preserved stretches of the Aurelian Wall. Inside the walls, the lovely **Cimitero Protestante** (*open Tues–Sun 9–6, in winter until 5; ring the bell at the gate; donation* *expected*) is a popular point of Romantic pilgrimage, where you'll find the graves of Shelley and Keats. Just to the west, **Monte Testaccio** has a plethora of wine cellars and nightclubs, making it a swinging area after dark.

Monte Celio

South of the Colosseum, the Monte Celio is one of the least known and most delightful corners of Rome, where some of the city's most ancient churches repose, all worth a look inside if they are open. A broad green lawn is all that's left of the **Circus Maximus**, where once 300,000 Romans would cram in to place their bets on chariot races. To the south lie the remains of the lavish baths, the **Terme di Caracalla** (AD 206–220) (*open Tues–Sun 9–one hour before sunset, Mon 9–2; adm, or* see *cumulative ticket p.226*), where much of the central building survives, with its hot and cold rooms, great hall and pool, all decorated with mosaics.

The Via Appia: Rome's Catacombs

Over the centuries the Via Appia, leading south from the Monte Celio, became lined with cemeteries of the wealthy: burials were prohibited within the sacred ground of the city itself. Over generations some catacombs grew into enormous termitaries extending for miles. Among the many you can visit are the **Catacombe di San Callisto** (*open for guided tours, summer Thurs–Tues 8.30–12 and 2.30–5.30; winter 8.30–12 and 2.30–5; adm*), notable for the 'Crypt of the Popes', with some well executed frescoes and inscriptions, and, largest of all, the **Catacombe di San Sebastiano** (*open for guided tours only Fri–Wed 8.30–12 and 2.30–5.30; adm*), featuring intriguing paintings and incised symbols throughout, left behind by early Christians.

Day Trips from Rome

Orvieto

Orvieto owes much of its success to an ancient volcano, which first created the city's magnificent pedestal, then enriched the hillsides with a mixture of minerals that form part of the alchemy of Orvieto's famous white wine. The medieval town, crowned by its stupendous cathedral, looks much as it has for the last 500 years.

The 'Golden Lily of Cathedrals' was built in honour of the Miracle of Bolsena. A priest, passing through on his way to Rome, was asked to celebrate Mass in Bolsena, just to the south. Father Peter had long been sceptical about the doctrine of the Host becoming the body of Christ but, during this Mass, the Host itself answered his doubts by dripping blood on the altar linen. The Pope declared it a miracle and instituted the feast of Corpus Christi, and Orvieto was promised a magnificent new cathedral to enshrine the blood-stained relic. Begun in 1290, the **Duomo** (*open Nov–Feb 7.30–12.45 and 2.30–5.15; Mar and Oct 7.30–12.45 and 2.30–6.15; April–Sept 7.30–12.45 and 2.30–7.15; for* ***Cappella di San Brizio***, see *below*) is the masterpiece of

Getting There and Around

Orvieto Scalo lies on the Florence–Rome **rail** line, with regular departures from Stazione Termini (1hr–1hr15). From the station, take the scenic *funivia* (every 15 mins, 7.15am–8.30pm, Sun 8am–8.30pm) from the station to Piazza Cahen next to the Fortezza. From here shuttle **bus A** will take you to the cathedral, or **bus B** will take you around the *centro storico* (save your ticket for a discount at the Museo Faina).

Tourist Information

Orvieto: Piazza del Duomo 24, **t** 0763 341 772, **f** 0763 344 433, *www.umbria2000.it* or *www.comune.orvieto.tr.it*. Enquire about their money-saving *Carta Orvieto Unica* (€12.50), covering adm to the Capella San Brizio, Museo Faina, Orvieto Underground and the Torre del Moro, including a round trip on the *funivia* plus minibus A or B. Buy it from the tourist office or the museums.

Eating Out

Besides the town's famous wine, look for *cinghiale in agrodolce* (sweet and sour boar) and *gallina ubriaca* ('drunken chicken').

Etrusca, Via Lorenzo Maitani 10, **t** 0763 344 016 (*expensive*). Not as ancient as the name might suggest, but there's lovely traditional food in this *cinquecento* building near the cathedral; it comes top among the *trattorias. Closed Mon and 6 Jan–8 Feb.*

La Volpe e l'Uva, Via Ripa Corsica 1, **t** 0763 341 612 (*cheap*). A busy place with a seasonal menu, including some unusual *secondi. Closed Mon, Tues in winter and Jan.*

L'Asino d'Oro, Vicolo del Popolo 9, **t** 0763 344 406 (*cheap*). A wine bar with a few outside tables in a lane off Piazza del Popolo, where you can have a snack or something more substantial accompanied by a glass of local wine. Tables under a pergola in a quiet lane. Charming, humorous waiters and simple, stylish presentation. *Closed Mon, 20 Oct–30 Nov and 15 Jan–15 Mar. Open till midnight.*

Lorenzo Maitani of Siena, striking one with its dazzling mosaics, prickly spires, and rich sculptural detail. Some 152 sculptors contributed, but it was Maitani who gave us the celebrated **bas-reliefs** on the lower pilasters, capturing the essence of the Christian story with their vivid drama and detail. Within, the greatest treasures are in the chapels, especially the **Cappella della Madonna di San Brizio** (*open Nov–Feb Mon–Sat 10–12.45 and 2.30–5.15; also Oct–June Sun and hols 2.30–5.45; open later in summer; buy tickets at the tourist office or shops in Piazza del Duomo; to reserve tickets, call* **t** *0763 342 477; only 25 admitted at a time*), embellished with one of the finest fresco cycles of the Renaissance. The vaults, with the serene *Christ in Judgement* (1447–9), are the work of Fra Angelico and Benozzo Gozzoli. The walls (1499) we owe to Luca Signorelli: breathtaking compositions of the *Last Judgement*, the *Preaching of the Antichrist* and the *Resurrection of the Dead*, with tremendous power. To the left, the **Cappella del Corporale** shelters fine *trecento* frescoes by Lippo Memmi and Ugolino of Siena, the remarkable silver gilt **Reliquario del Corporale** (1338), echoing the façade of the cathedral and decorated with enamelled scenes from the Life of Christ, and the venerated blood-stained linen.

Outside, the **Piazza del Duomo** has a couple of wine bars where you can try Orvieto's vintages. Opposite, the **Museo Claudio Faina e Civico** (*open Oct–Mar Tues–Sun 10–1 and 2.30–5; closed Mon; April–Sept daily 9.30–6; adm*) contains one of Italy's top private archaeological collections and Orvieto's excellent Etruscan collection, excavated from local tombs. On the south side of the Duomo, the **Palazzo Papale** (1297–1500s; *closed for restoration*) houses art from the cathedral, including statues by Arnolfo di Cambio and the Pisanos, and a rich polyptych by Simone Martini.

The rest of Orvieto is unpretentious and worldly, a solid, bourgeois, medieval town. The main drag, Corso Cavour, leads from the funicular west towards the city's main square, **Piazza della Repubblica**, where beneath the 12th-century church of **Sant'Andrea**, a 6th-century mosaic pavement has been revealed, and below that an Etruscan street (*the sacristan has the key to the excavations*). Beyond the *piazza*, some of Orvieto's most ancient streets will lead you to the northwestern corner of town, where the church of **San Giovenale** is crammed full of frescoes from the 12th–15th centuries. More frescoes cover the walls of **San Lorenzo de Arari**, reached by Via Maitani from the Piazza Duomo, or on Via Scalza from Corso Cavour. At Orvieto's northeastern end (near the funicular), there are lovely views from the ramparts of Cardinal Albornoz's **citadel** (1364). Beside it is the amazing **Pozzo di San Patrizio** (*open daily summer 10–7; winter 10–6; adm*), designed in the 1530s to supply Orvieto in times of siege, with two spiral stairs of 248 steps for the water carriers.

Tivoli and the Villa Adriana

Ancient Tibur, set in a cliff with a beautiful view over the Roman Campagna, first became popular as a sort of garden suburb for the senatorial class in the early days of the Empire. Come the Renaissance, a number of cardinals decided the ancients had been onto a good thing, and one, Cardinal Ippolito d'Este, created perhaps the most fantastically worldly villa and gardens Italy has ever seen. The **Villa d'Este** (*open Tues–Sun 8.30–two hrs before sunset; adm*), designed by Pietro Ligorio and decorated with Mannerist frescoes, is upstaged by the gardens, laid out on terraces with palms, cypresses, flowers and lawns. Every turn exposes a confectionery fountain – Bernini's 'Fountain of Glass', the 'Grotto of Diana' – along with artificial waterfalls and pools.

Tivoli has a gaudy 17th-century **cathedral** and a Romanesque church, **San Silvestro**, with early medieval frescoes, which you will pass on the way to another Renaissance cardinal's fantasy, the **Villa Gregoriana** (*open daily 9–one hour before sunset; adm*). Built in a natural chasm, the shady paths and gardens are irresistible to visitors. It's worth the trip for the spectacular natural waterfall on the River Aniene and a smaller,

Getting There and Around

Tivoli (31km) and the Villa d'Este are most easily reached by COTRAL **bus** from metro Ponte Mammolo; buses leave every 20 mins (journey 30mins). For Villa Adriana the bus drops you a 20-min walk away on the Via Prenestina at the Bivio Villa Adriana; local buses from Tivoli will take you much nearer the entrance.

Tourist Information

Tivoli: **t** 0774 312 070.

Eating Out

Hadrian's Villa is a great place for a picnic lunch, and Tivoli has no lack of restaurants:

Sibilla, next to the Temple of the Sibyl on Via della Sibilla, **t** 0774 335 281 (*moderate*). The Sibilla is admittedly touristy, but it's also fun, in a great setting and moderately priced – and serves good grilled trout. *Open Tues–Sat.*

Antica Hostaria de' Carrettieri, Via Giuliani 55, **t** 0774 83243 (*moderate*). In Tivoli's centre, run by two sisters who'll guide you through the day's specials. You might find onion soup, gnocchi, or beef with balsamic vinegar. Save room for dessert. *Open Thurs–Tues.*

artificial one by Bernini. On the edge of the abyss, you'll notice two small, remarkably well preserved Roman temples, called the **Temples of the Sibyl** and **Vesta**.

Just outside the town, signs direct you to **Hadrian's Villa**, the grandest palace complex ever built in Italy (*open daily 9–90mins before sunset; adm*). Hadrian was an architect, whose design credits include the Pantheon; he travelled widely through the empire gathering inspiration for his villa, creating reproductions of the Canopic Temple of Alexandria, the Platonic Academy and Stoa Poikile of Athens, set among huge baths, libraries, temples and theatres. Most charming of all is the 'Naval Theatre', a little palace on an island in an artificial lagoon, which may have been Hadrian's private retreat. Near the entrance, a model of Hadrian's dream house shows the excess that even an intelligent and useful emperor was capable of: all marble and travertine, and the same size as the ancient centre of Rome, with such surprises as a heated beach with steam pipes under the sand.

Caprarola and the Villa Farnese

The smallest and perhaps loveliest of Lazio's lakes, Vico is ringed by rugged hills. Unspoiled marshes line some of its shore and its ancient crater has a younger volcano (also extinct) poking up inside it: **Monte Venere**. Just over the hills from the lake you'll find one of Italy's most arrogantly ambitious late Renaissance palaces, the **Villa Farnese**, in Caprarola (*open daily 8.30–6.30 (5.30 in winter), guided tours of the villa and gardens every 30 mins; adm*), built by Alessandro Farnese as the family headquarters with the fantastic wealth accumulated by his grandfather, Pope Paul III. Vignola, the family architect, turned the entire town of Caprarola into a setting for the palace, ploughing a new avenue through the town as an axis that led to a grand stairway, and then another stairway up to the huge pentagonal villa. The palace is empty today, but it remains an impressive place. The tour takes in Vignola's elegant courtyard, a room with uncanny acoustic tricks, one decorated with frescoes of the *Labours of Hercules*, another with a wonderful ceiling painted with figures of the constellations, and Vignola's decorative masterpiece: an incredible **spiral staircase** of stone columns and frescoes. The best part, however, is the 'secret garden', a park full of azaleas and rhododendrons leading up to a sculpture garden of grotesques and fantastical *telamones* and, finally a delightful, smaller villa, the **Palazzina del Piacere**.

Getting There

COTRAL **buses** make the journey from Rome's metro station Saxa Rubra (1hr). Call (free within Italy) **t** 800 431 784 for times.

Eating Out

Catch a bus to Lake Vico for a picnic on the shore, or try one of the following, in Caprarola.

Trattoria del Cimino, Via F Nicolai 44, **t** 0761 646 173 (*expensive*). A stylish place by the cathedral offering a range of central Italian classics, including *pappardelle alla lepre* and *cinghiale* (wild boar), as well as grills. *Closed Mon and also eves on Tues and Wed.*

Bella Gioia, Via Tempest 1, **t** 0761 646 963 (*cheap*). Also near the Farnese villa, this specializes particularly in home-made pasta, served with *funghi* in season. *Closed Tues.*

Ostia, the Port of the Empire

Open Tues–Sun 9–one hour before sunset; adm.

After Pompeii and Herculaneum, Ostia Antica is the best preserved Roman town in Italy, a fascinating lesson on everyday life in ancient Rome. Set amid parasol pines and wild flowers, it is as lovely as it is interesting; its walls festooned with garlands of ivy, its ruins home to scores of lizards and tiny blue butterflies. According to the archaeologists, Rome's port was founded in the 4th century BC, 400 years after Rome itself. But in the centuries of conquest Ostia grew into a major city in its own right, with a population of *c.* 100,000 and nearly 2km of *horrea* (warehouses). By the 1st century AD, the port could no longer handle Rome's insatiable demands and the trade flow slowed; Ostia lost its *raison-d'être*, malaria thrived and by AD 800 the site was abandoned. The River Tiber obliged the future, preserving Ostia in sand and mud.

As in Pompeii (*see* p.252), you can imagine life in a big, ancient city; the temples, baths, frescoed houses, barracks and warehouses are amazingly intact. Ostia's **Forum**, with its columns of temples, is set around a little hill wistfully called the 'Capitol'. The small **theatre** has an interesting ***mithraeum***, like the one under San Clemente in Rome (*see* p.230); there's a police station (**Caserma dei Vigili**) and the oldest **synagogue** in Italy. One vast square, the **Piazzale delle Corporazione**, preserves mosaics symbolizing the trades. A floor mosaic in **Fortunatus' Tavern** boasts an early specimen of advertising: 'Fortunatus says: if you're thirsty, have a bowl of wine.'

Near the ruins, spare a few minutes for the sleepy hamlet of **Ostia Antica** or 'Borgo'. It was founded as a fortress town in 830 by Pope Gregory IV, but it wasn't sufficient to keep the Saracens out when they sacked Rome 19 years later. There is a small Renaissance church dedicated to **Sant'Aurea** (a 3rd-century Ostian martyr) and the elegant **castello**, erected in 1483 by Julius II (still only a cardinal), to keep out the Turks.

Getting There and Around

Overland **Metropolitana trains** run to Ostia Antica and Ostia Lido from Porta San Paolo or EUR-Magliana metro stops, every 30 mins throughout the day (20mins). The excavations are a 5-min walk from the Ostia Antica station.

Tourist Information

Ostia Antica: **t** 06 5635 8099.
Ostia Lido: **t** 06 562 7892.

Eating Out

One option is to buy supplies in the village of Ostia, and picnic amid the ruins. Other options are unashamedly touristy.

Allo Sbarco di Enea, Viale dei Romagnoli 675, **t** 06 565 0034 (*moderate*). 'Aeneas's Landing', between excavations and station, has a Ben Hur chariot in the yard, and there's dining under the trellis in summer. *Open Tues–Sun, except three weeks in Jan.*

In **Lido di Ostia** there are plenty of pizzerias and fish restaurants, but don't expect to find any bargains. The places listed below are worth a try.

Sporting Beach, Lungomare A. Vespucci 8, Ostia Lido, **t** 06 5647 0256 (*moderate*). You can dine on the beach at this reasonably priced fish restaurant, which also offers a few meat dishes. *Open daily.*

Il Segreto di Pulcinella, Via Rutilio Namaziano 31, **t** 06 567 2194 (*cheap*). No credit cards. Genuine Neapolitan pizza 'al fresco'. *Open Oct–May Tues–Sun, June–Sept daily.*

Campania

13

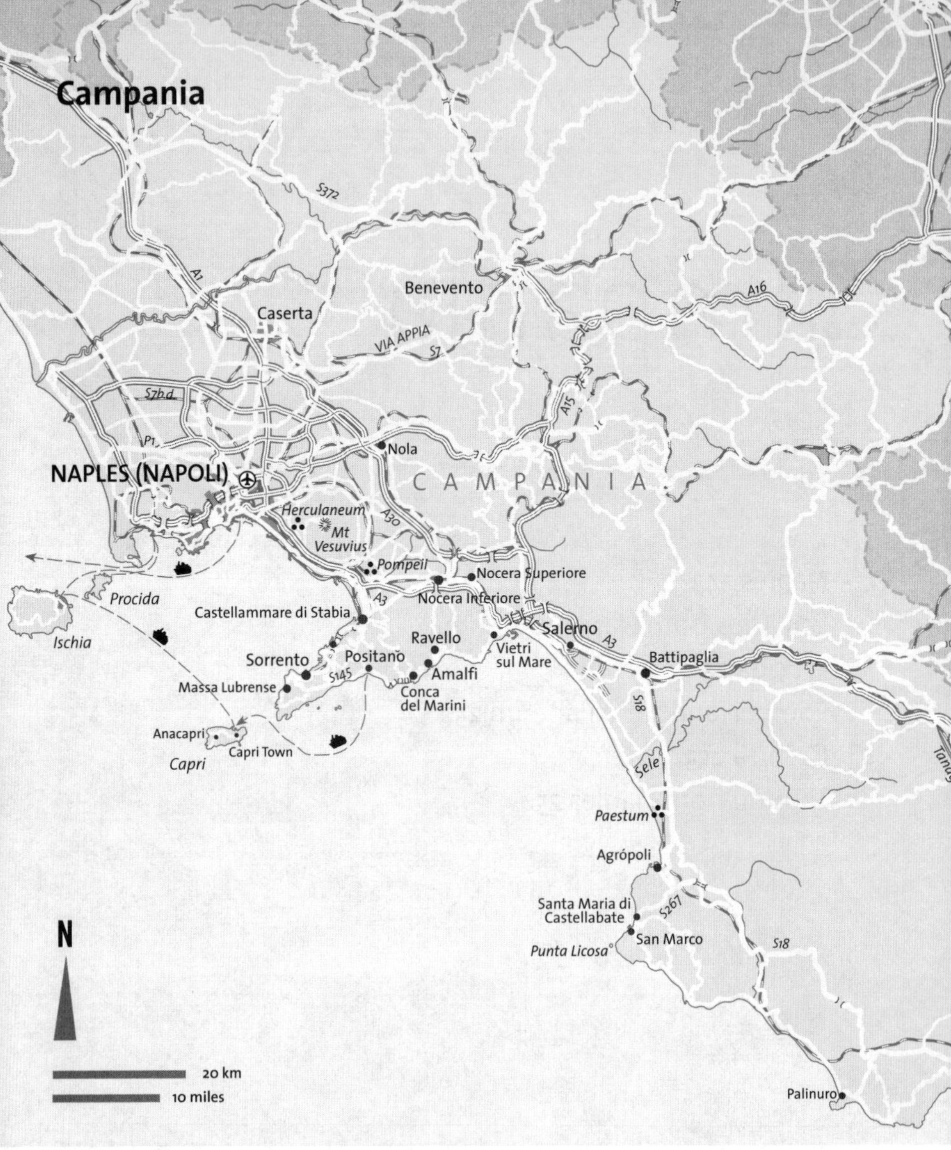

Campania's charm starts with one of the most captivating stretches of coastline in Italy – the Amalfi Coast – followed by Capri and Ischia, Sorrento, Vesuvius and the beautiful but lesser-known Cilento Coast. Roman emperors and senators spent as much time here as business would allow, and even today it is said that the dream of every Italian is to have a villa at Capri or Sorrento overlooking the sea. In the middle of all this, of course, sprawls Italy's third-largest city, Naples, which might be either your favourite or least favourite Italian city – or both at once. Campania has new industries and ambitious planning schemes, but it is also battling against poverty, corruption and crime. Though the potential certainly exists, there is a long way to go before the region can reclaim the position it held in the days of the Caesars.

Naples (Napoli)

For many, Naples is the homeland of an Italian fantasy, the last bastion of singing waiters and red-checked tablecloths, operatic passion and colourful poverty. But mention Naples to any modern north Italian, and you'll get a first-hand lesson in the dynamics of Italy's 'Problem of the South'. Crime is so well organized here that smugglers have formed a trade union to protect their interests against the police. Naples, the city that has given the world Enrico Caruso, Sophia Loren, pizza and syphilis, may also be the first city to make social disorder into an art form. Don't let its current degradation spoil your visit, though; the only thing subtle about Naples is its charm, and the city may win your heart at the same time as it deranges your senses.

Piazza del Plebiscito and Via Toledo

The immense, elegant **Piazza del Plebiscito** marks the centre of modern Naples, embraced by the curving colonnades of **San Francesco di Paola** and flanked by the **Palazzo Reale** (*open weekdays and hols 9–8, Sat 9–12; adm*), residence of the Bourbons and retaining some chambers in 18th-century style. The Bourbons were great opera buffs and in 1737 they built Italy's largest opera house, the prestigious **Teatro San Carlo** (*guided tours,* ***t*** *081 797 2111*), right next to their palace.

For some 700 years, the port of Naples has been protected by the odd, beautiful **Castel Nuovo** (*offices open Mon–Fri 8–1;* ***museums*** *Mon–Fri 9–7, Sat 9–1.30; adm*), looming behind the San Carlo and distinguished by Alfonso V's Triumphal Arch. Inside, two museums display 14th- and 15th-century frescoes, paintings and 15th–20th-century silver and bronzes; ask to see the Sala dei Baroni, with its unusual cupola.

From Piazza del Plebiscito, the imposing **Via Toledo** runs northwards beyond Piazza Carita towards Capodimonte. Laid out by Don Pedro de Toledo in the 16th century, Stendhal rightly called it 'the most populous and gayest street in the world', and it is still the city's commercial hub. Immediately to the left, a dense grid of narrow streets marks the inner sanctum of the Neapolitan soul, the **Quartieri Spagnuoli**, which is fascinating to walk around – at least by day. To the right, the confusion of Naples' half-crumbling, half-modern business centre conceals the **church of Monteoliveto** (*open Tues–Sat 8.30–12.30*) a little treasure house of late Renaissance art, with tombs and altars by Giovanni da Nola and Antonio Rosellino, and frescoes by Vasari.

Once past Spaccanapoli, Via Toledo/Roma continues north through the delightfully animated **Piazza Dante** to the **Museo Archeològico Nazionale** (*open Wed–Mon 9am–7.30pm; adm*), the most important collection of Roman-era art and antiquities in the world. (Unfortunately, at any one time half of it will be closed for 'restorations', and the rest may well be the worst-exhibited major museum in Europe.) On the **first floor**, room after room of ancient sculpture competes for your attention, with many of the best existing Roman-era copies of lost Greek statues, such as the heroic Farnese Hercules that decorated the Baths of Caracalla. **Upstairs**, most of the rooms are given over to Pompeii. The collection of Roman mosaics is one of the best anywhere, providing a priceless insight into the life of the ancients, and nowhere will you find a larger collection of Roman mural painting, much of it fascinatingly modern in theme

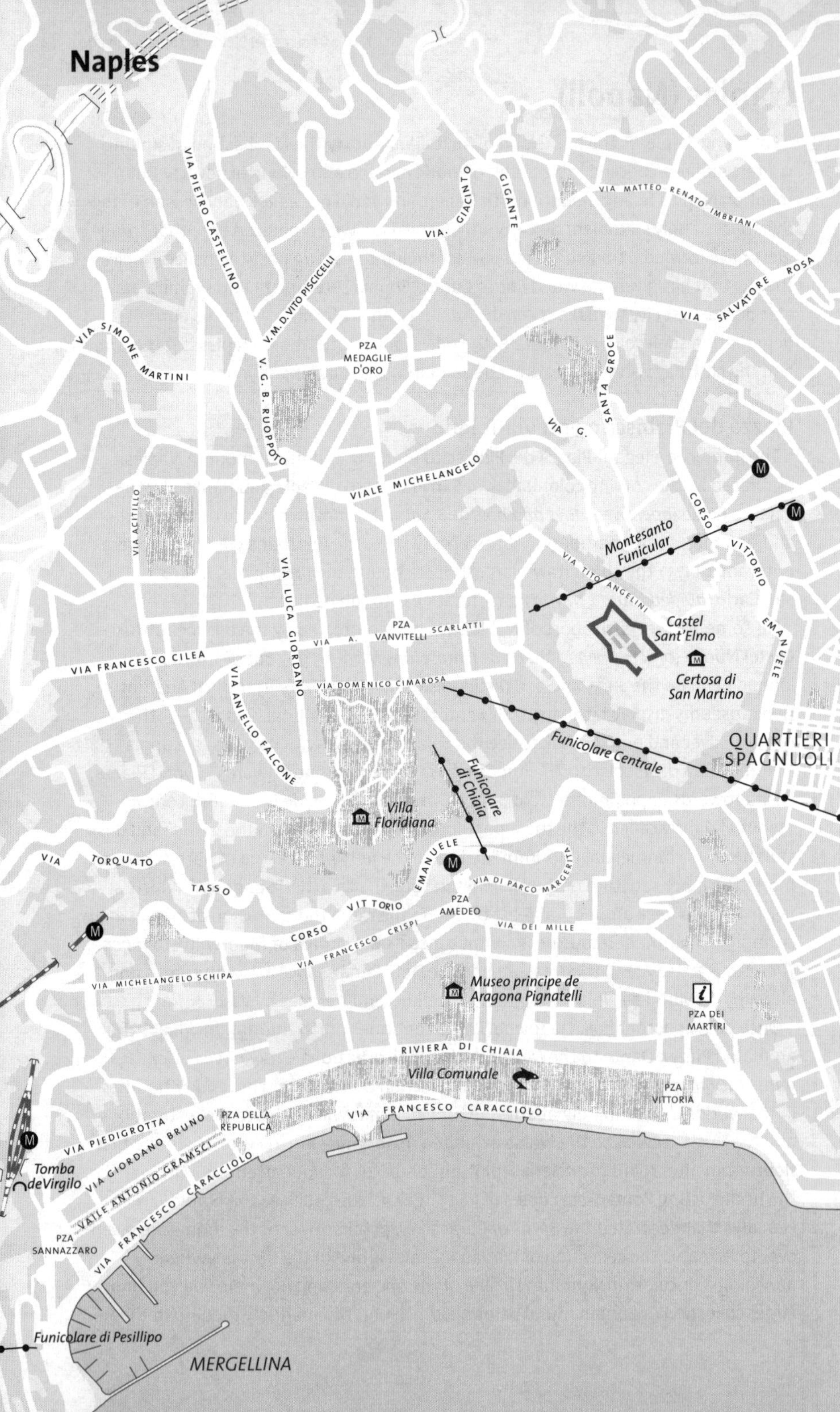
Naples
VIA PIETRO CASTELLINO
VIA GIACINTO GIGANTE
VIA MATTEO RENATO IMBRIANI
VIA SALVATORE ROSA
V. M. D. VITO PISCICELLI
VIA SIMONE MARTINI
PZA MEDAGLIE D'ORO
V. G. B. RUOPPOLO
SANTA CROCE
VIA G.
VIALE MICHELANGELO
CORSO VITTORIO EMANUELE
Montesanto Funicular
VIA ACITILLO
VIA LUCA GIORDANO
VIA TITO ANGELINI
Castel Sant'Elmo
Certosa di San Martino
PZA VANVITELLI
VIA A. SCARLATTI
VIA FRANCESCO CILEA
VIA DOMENICO CIMAROSA
VIA ANIELLO FALCONE
Funicolare Centrale
QUARTIERI SPAGNUOLI
Funicolare di Chiaia
Villa Floridiana
VIA TORQUATO TASSO
VIA DI PARCO MARGHERITA
PZA AMEDEO
VIA DEI MILLE
VIA FRANCESCO CRISPI
VIA MICHELANGELO SCHIPA
Museo principe de Aragona Pignatelli
PZA DEI MARTIRI
RIVIERA DI CHIAIA
Villa Comunale
PZA VITTORIA
VIA FRANCESCO CARACCIOLO
PZA DELLA REPUBLICA
VIA PIEDIGROTTA
VIA GIORDANO BRUNO
VIALE ANTONIO GRAMSCI
Tomba deVirgilo
PZA SANNAZZARO
Funicolare di Pesillipo
MERGELLINA

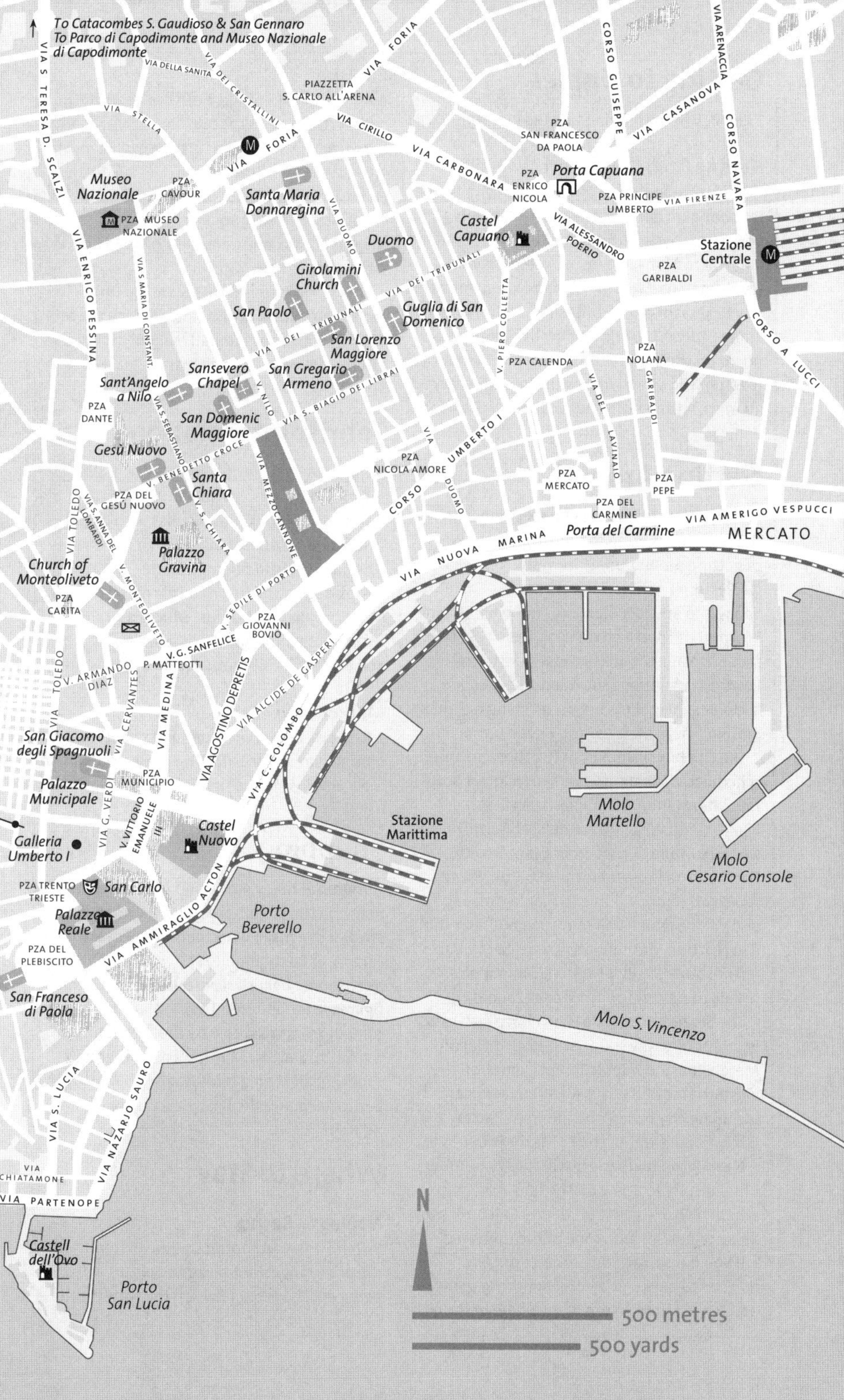

To Catacombes S. Gaudioso & San Gennaro
To Parco di Capodimonte and Museo Nazionale di Capodimonte
VIA S TERESA D. SCALZI
VIA DELLA SANITA
VIA DEI CRISTALLINI
VIA FORIA
PIAZZETTA S. CARLO ALL'ARENA
VIA STELLA
VIA CIRILLO
CORSO GUISEPPE
VIA ARENACCIA
VIA CASANOVA
CORSO NAVARA
PZA SAN FRANCESCO DA PAOLA
VIA CARBONARA
PZA ENRICO NICOLA
Porta Capuana
PZA PRINCIPE UMBERTO
VIA FIRENZE
Museo Nazionale
PZA CAVOUR
Santa Maria Donnaregina
PZA MUSEO NAZIONALE
VIA DUOMO
Duomo
Castel Capuano
VIA ALESSANDRO POERIO
Stazione Centrale
PZA GARIBALDI
VIA ENRICO PESSINA
VIA S MARIA DI CONSTANT.
Girolamini Church
VIA DEI TRIBUNALI
San Paolo
Guglia di San Domenico
V. PIERO COLLETTA
CORSO A LUCCI
San Lorenzo Maggiore
PZA NOLANA
PZA CALENDA
GARIBALDI
Sansevero Chapel
San Gregario Armeno
Sant'Angelo a Nilo
V. NILO
VIA S. BIAGIO DEI LIBRAI
VIA DEL LAVINAIO
PZA DANTE
VIA S. SEBASTIANO
San Domenic Maggiore
VIA DUOMO
CORSO UMBERTO I
Gesù Nuovo
V. BENEDETTO CROCE
PZA NICOLA AMORE
PZA MERCATO
PZA PEPE
Santa Chiara
VIA MEZZOCANNONE
PZA DEL GESÙ NUOVO
VIA TOLEDO
VIA S. ANNA DEI LOMBARDI
V. S. CHIARA
CORSO
PZA DEL CARMINE
VIA AMERIGO VESPUCCI
Porta del Carmine
MERCATO
VIA NUOVA MARINA
Palazzo Gravina
Church of Monteoliveto
V. MONTEOLIVETO
V. SEDILE DI PORTO
PZA CARITA
PZA GIOVANNI BOVIO
V. G. SANFELICE
P. MATTEOTTI
VIA TOLEDO
V. ARMANDO DIAZ
VIA CERVANTES
VIA MEDINA
VIA AGOSTINO DEPRETIS
VIA ALCIDE DE GASPERI
VIA C. COLOMBO
San Giacomo degli Spagnuoli
PZA MUNICIPIO
Palazzo Municipale
VIA G. VERDI
V. VITTORIO EMANUELE III
Castel Nuovo
Stazione Marittima
Molo Martello
Galleria Umberto I
Molo Cesario Console
PZA TRENTO TRIESTE
San Carlo
Palazzo Reale
VIA AMMIRAGLIO ACTON
Porto Beverello
PZA DEL PLEBISCITO
San Franceso di Paola
Molo S. Vincenzo
VIA S. LUCIA
VIA NAZARIO SAURO
VIA CHIATAMONE
VIA PARTENOPE
N
Castell dell'Ovo
Porto San Lucia
500 metres
500 yards

Getting to Naples

Go flies from London Stansted (2hrs55).

Getting from the Airport

Naples' Capodichino airport (**t** 081 789 6111) is about 8km north of the centre. **City bus 3** links the arrivals terminal to Stazione Centrale and Piazza Municipio near the ferry harbour (every 15 mins, 6.30am–11.30pm; 20–45mins). Buy tickets for all city buses (€0.77) from news-stands, *tabacchi* or ticket booths before you board (in the airport or in town). The **Alibus** (€2 from the driver) makes the journey every 30 mins. A **taxi** should not cost more than €20.

Getting Around

Such is the state of most public transport that walking is often the most practical way of getting around, apart from the *funicolari*. Naples' dominant landmarks are the Castel Sant'Elmo and San Martino, on the hill sloping down to the port and dividing the city in two. Modern Naples is on the west side; to the east lies the centre along Via Toledo; beyond are the oldest neighbourhoods, reaching a climax around Piazza Mercato and Piazza Garibaldi.

The **city bus** system is awful. There are no schedules, no maps and nowhere to get accurate information. Most lines start at either Piazza Garibaldi or Piazza del Plebiscito. The **Metropolitana FS** runs from Gianturco to Pozzuoli and is useful for the station. Three ***funicolari*** (from Via Toledo, Piazza Amedeo and Via Morghen) will bring you out near the San Martino Museum and Castel Sant'Elmo (*all run daily till about 10pm*). '**Giranapoli**' tickets cost €0.77 (90mins) or €3 (one-day).

The **Stazione Centrale** is on Piazza Garibaldi. In addition, many trains also stop at **Napoli Mergellina** and **Napoli Campi Flegrei**, on the western side of the city. Most **bus services**, including **city buses**, operate from Piazza Garibaldi, in front of the FS Stazione Centrale.

Neapolitan **taxi** drivers will try any number of scams. Try to agree on the fare in advance, whether there is a meter or not. Call **t** 081 556 4444, or get one from one of the taxi ranks.

If you have a **car**, you are categorically advised to park it at a hotel or private garage, and not attempt to use it anywhere in the city.

Car Hire

Avis, Stazione Centrale, **t** 081 554 3020; at the airport, **t** 081 780 5790.

Europcar, Via Scarfoglia 10, **t** 081 570 8426; at the airport, **t** 081 780 5643.

Hertz, Piazza Garibaldi 91/B, **t** 081 206 228; at the airport, **t** 081 780 2971.

Maggiore, Stazione Centrale, **t** 081 287 858; at the airport, **t** 081 780 3011.

Check that hotels have **secure parking** (*parcheggio custodito*). If not, opt for a private car park. For scant sympathy about stolen cars, call the police on **t** 081 794 1111.

Tourist Information

Naples: AAS, Piazza del Gesù Nuovo, **t** 081 552 3328 or **t** 081 551 2701 (*open Mon–Sat 9–8, Sun and hols 9–3*); the EPT has an office at Stazione Centrale, **t** 081 268 779, which may be some help in finding a hotel.

Look out for the free monthly handbook *Qui Napoli*, available at tourist offices and some hotels, with information, timetables, listings and events. The EPT produce good maps (free).

Market Days

Don't miss the *bancarelle* and street markets around **Piazza Garibaldi**. The daily catch of fish is a must, just to the right off Corso Garibaldi.

Shopping

There are many pretty and unusual things here and the streets around Spaccanapoli are still full of **artisan workshops**. The Royal Factory at Capodimonte still makes what may be the most beautiful **porcelain and ceramic figures** in Europe. Another old tradition is **cameos** from seashells; try the shops outside the Certosa di San Martino. For **clothes and shoes** the best area is off Piazza dei Martiri, in particular along the flashy Via Chiaia.

Where to Stay

Naples ✉ 80100

There are many options at the extremes of the price ranges, but few good places in between. The best area is on the waterfront where you have easy access to shopping, museums and good restaurants. Many of the cheap places around the station are horrible dives. Stick to those here and you shouldn't go too wrong; at least you'll be safe.

****Excelsior, Via Partenope 48, t 081 764 0111, f 081 764 9743 (*very expensive*). Naples' finest hotel faces Vesuvius, with beautiful suites and a tradition of perfect service since 1909. You pay for space – elegant lounges, a rooftop solarium and restaurant, rooms with large beds and antique-style furniture.

****Vesuvio, Via Partenope 45, t 081 764 0044, f 081 764 4483 (*very expensive*). In spite of its name, this grandiose hotel lacks the head-on view of Vesuvius, but otherwise provides the same stuff as the Excelsior. It also has a lovely roof garden for dining.

****Miramare, Via Sauro 24, t 081 764 7589, f 081 764 0775 (*expensive*). A gem of olde-worlde charm, with thoughtful personal touches in each room and a cosy, intimate atmosphere. Some rooms are too small, but the old lift and the lavish breakfast on the rooftop solarium more than compensate.

****Paradiso, Via Catullo 11, t 081 761 4161, f 081 761 3449 (*expensive*). A good bet, with stunning views over the bay.

****Parker's, Corso Vittorio Emanuele 135, t 081 761 2474, f 081 663 527 (*expensive*). A delightful hotel; the airy rooms have ample charm, polished wood, chandeliers and comfortable furniture. Choose a sea-facing room for the vista of Vesuvius and Capri. The view is even more spectacular from the award-winning roof restaurant.

***Cavour, Piazza Garibaldi 32, t 081 283 122, f 081 287 488 (*moderate*). Near the Stazione Centrale, this is a well-run, decent hotel in an otherwise desperate area. Book the top-floor suites (only slightly pricier), with ample terraces and views over Vesuvius; they're a respite from the bustle below. Rooms are nicely decorated in the omnipresent Liberty style, bathrooms are unusually good and the restaurant gets two Michelin *fourchettes*.

***Canada, Via Mergellina 43, t 081 682 018, f 081 681 594 (*moderate*). This is good value, with comfortable rooms, TV, safe, minibar and fans. It has no pretensions and a poor excuse for a breakfast area, but is well placed for the *passeggiata*.

**Ausonia, Via Caracciolo 11, t/f 081 682 278 (*moderate*). A clean, comfortable *pensione* with a nautical character. The owner is kind and cheerful and rooms are well-appointed, with TV and video recorder. In a *palazzo*, looking on to an interior courtyard, this is the quiet option for the Mergellina area.

The cheaper hotels around the Piazza Garibaldi are at best a place to sleep. Also try Via Mezzocannone, south of Spaccanapoli.

**Fontane al Mare, Via N. Tommaseo 14, t 081 764 3470 (*cheap*). Book ahead for one of 21 rooms on the last two floors of an old *palazzo* next to the Chiaia gardens. Ask for rooms without a bathroom since they enjoy the great sea view and are better value.

**Zara, Via Firenze 81, t 081 287 125 (*cheap*). With only 10 rooms, two with baths, this is sadly the best Naples can do in this category.

*Fiore, Via Milano 109, t 081 553 8798 (*cheap*). This Polish-Italian *pensione* is barely acceptable, but good for the area.

Eating Out

Neapolitan cuisine is simple and even in some of the more pretentious places you will see favourites of the Neapolitan *cucina povera*, like *pasta e fagioli*. For **pizza**, look for the real Neapolitan pizza oven: a built-in, bell-shaped affair made of stone with a tile floor; the fire is at the back, close to the pizza, not underneath. Watch out for the **house wines**; in cheaper places this is likely to be rough stuff. Try Greco di Tufo, a good dry white, and Taurasi, a distinguished red – as well as Falerno.

For harbourside dinners, it's difficult to beat the Borgo Marinara beside the Castel Dell'Ovo; the whole marina area is set aside for dining. Many of the cheapest, homeliest places can be found around Via Speranzella in the Tavoliere. The area around Piazza Mercato and the station is an open bazaar, with stands selling pizza and flaky pastries called *sfogliatelle*.

La Cantinella, Via Nazario Sauro 23, **t** 081 464 8684 (*expensive*). Near the Castel dell'Ovo on the esplanade, this is believed by many to be Naples' finest, with telephones on the tables. Their *linguine Santa Lucia*, with home-made pasta, octopi, prawns, clams and baby tomatoes, takes some beating. The atmosphere is smart but relaxed. the service welcoming.

Ciro, Via Santa Brigida 71, **t** 081 552 4072 (*expensive*). A smart place between the civic centre and the Castel Nuovo. Order *pasta e fagioli* or any other humble pasta dish; that's what the place is famous for, Naples cuisine at its best. They also do pizzas. *Closed Sun.*

La Sacrestia, Via Orazio 116, **t** 081 761 1051 (*expensive*). Run for generations by the same family, this temple of Neapolitan gastronomy is in a superb position over-looking the bay from on high at Mergellina. Try the risotto with baby squid (*risotto con neonati di seppietta*). *Closed Mon.*

La Cantina di Triunfo, Riviera di Chiaia 64, **t** 081 668 101 (*moderate*). On the north side of Piazza della Repubblica, this is *cucina povera* raised to an art form: wintry soups of chest-nuts and lentils; *polpette di baccalà* – small balls of salt-cod, fried or served in a fresh tomato sauce – and mouth-watering pasta. The *crostata d'arance e mandorle* (orange and almond tart) is excellent. The wine list is also exceptional and many of the grappas – there are 80 – are home-made. Do book, as space is very limited. *Closed Sun.*

Taverna e Zi Carmela, Via Niccolò Tommaseo 11/12, **t** 081 764 3581 (*moderate*). Track down this restaurant on the esplanade of Via Partenope beyond the Castel dell'Ovo. Aunt Carmela does much of the excellent home-cooking herself. The speciality here is once more seafood. *Closed Sun.*

O Sole Mio, Via Tommaso Campanella 7, **t** 081 761 2323 (*moderate*). Run by a fisherman's family up near the Mergellina end, you'd be best advised to go straight for the seafood, in all its forms, though you will find some meat on the menu. Try the wonderfully tasty *cassuola di pesce* (fish casserole). *Closed Tues.*

Da Pasqualino, Piazza Sannazzaro 78/9, **t** 081 681 524 (*cheap*). A long established pizzeria in Mergellina where you can get two superb pizzas and lots of easy-drinking local wine.

Da Michele, Via Sersale 1, **t** 081 553 9204 (*cheap*). For a quick snack, join the cluster of Neapolitans outside here and queue to taste the superb massive pizzas. They only come in two models: *margherita* and *marinara*.

Lombardi a Santa Chiara, Via Benedetto Croce 59, **t** 081 552 0780 (*cheap*). Only slightly more upmarket, this busy restaurant off Piazza del Gesù Nuovo offers memorable *antipasti* of fried courgettes, baby mozzarella and artichokes, before you ever get to your pizza, wonderfully cooked in a classic wood oven. If you can't stomach more pizza the *bucatini al pomodoro* is a simple treat. It's noisy but friendly; book ahead or be prepared to wait. *Closed Sun.*

Trattoria Nennella, Vico Lungo Teatro Nuovo 103–5 (*cheap*). An amazing bargain in the Quartieri Spagnuoli, with true Neapolitan food and spirit in a simple setting. *Open weekdays for lunch only.*

Naples has its crop of elegant 19th-century *gran caffè*, mostly around the Galleria and the Piazza del Plebiscito. **Gambrinus**, on Piazza Trieste e Trento, has the best position, but **Ciro**, on the waterfront, is considered the best. Naples also produces some great **ice cream**. *Gelaterie* can be found all over town, but **Scimmia**, Piazza della Carità 4, just off the Via Toledo, has long been highly acclaimed.

Entertainment

For opera lovers one of the ultimate experiences is a night at the **San Carlo** (**t** 081 797 2111), but tickets are very hard to come by, and very pricey. If you get one, be sure to dress up. For concerts and other cultural events – Naples has plenty – the best information on programmes and times will be found in the newspaper *Il Mattino*, or *Qui Napoli*. Look out for billboards with details of coming events. **Tickets** for major events are issued at the **Box Office**, Galleria Umberto I 15–16, **t** 081 551 9188, or **Concerteria**, Via Schipa 23, **t** 081 761 1221.

Nightlife

Neapolitans are night-owls and many don't even think about dinner until 10pm. That doesn't leave much time for partying, but there are some reasonable clubs and bars. After midnight, steer clear of the Piazza Garibaldi area and the narrow side streets that run off the Via Toledo. The popularity of haunts changes with the current fads, but a list of **clubs** can be found in *Qui Napoli*. The **bars** of Via Paladino are where it all happens, and **Piazza Bellini** is the spot where the young and trendy come to see and be seen.

and execution. Among the most famous paintings are *The Astragal Players* and the *Portrait of an Unknown Woman*. Other attractions include jewellery, coins, gladiators' armour, Greek vases, Egyptian finds and the famous *sezione pornografica* (*open by reservation; book when you buy your ticket at the entrance*).

Spaccanapoli

This street's familiar name means 'Split-Naples', and that is exactly what it has done for the last 2,600 years. And what a street it is, the heart of old Naples, lined with grocery barrows and bookshops, haunted by Neapolitan characters and brightened by a hundred clothes-lines swelling between impossibly tall tenements. Off Via Toledo is the most characteristic of Neapolitan squares: **Piazza del Gesù Nuovo**. Here an unsightly, unfinished façade of dark basalt belongs to the **church of Gesù Nuovo**, its Baroque interior gloriously overdone in acres of coloured marbles and frescoes, with one of Solimena's best works (1725) above the door inside. Across the piazza, step into the **Complesso di Santa Chiara** (*open Mon–Sat 9.30–1 and 3.30–5.30, Sun and hols 9.30–1; adm*) to see the Majolica Cloister, where someone in the 1740s created an Andalucian fairyland of gaily coloured arbours and columns; there are also inspired 16th-century scenes of the Last Judgement to be seen via the back of the church.

Further down Via Benedetto Croce is tiny **Piazza San Domenico**, where **Sant'Angelo a Nilo** (*closed for restoration*) houses Michelozzo's tomb of Cardinal Brancaccio, with a relief by Donatello. Around the corner on Via F. de Sanctis, you can inspect Neapolitan rococo at its most peculiar in the **Sansevero Chapel** (*open Mon–Sat 10–8, Sun and hols 10–1.30; closed Tues; adm*), where Raimondo di Sangro (b. 1701) had his family chapel adorned with a grand allegorical scheme of sculptures and frescoes, often executed with a breathtaking virtuosity; rarely has an artist attempted to carve a fishing net from marble. Continuing east to Via San Gregorio, you can have a fascinating glimpse of ancient Greek and Roman Naples, revealed beneath **San Lorenzo Maggiore**.

Around Piazza del Duomo

After Spaccanapoli, **Via dei Tribunali** is the busiest street of old Naples, its ancient arcades forming a sort of continuous covered market. Just north near **Via Anticaglia**, a few unusually crooked streets follow the outline of the **Roman Theatre**, much of which survives among the tenements. Via dei Tribunali opens onto the wide Via del Duomo, where the fine medieval **Cathedral of San Gennaro** conceals its best assets behind an awful façade of 1905: the Renaissance Cappella Minùtolo; the tomb of Charles of Anjou; and the glittering **Cappella San Gennaro**, dedicated to Naples' patron saint and adorned with frescoes by Domenichino and Lanfranco. Here the Napoletani keep the saint's head, along with two phials of his blood that miraculously liquefy three times a year to prove that he's still looking out for them. Tacked onto the side is the **Basilica Santa Restituta**, with ceiling frescoes by Luca Giordano and a collection of archaeological remains (*open daily 9–12 and 4.30–7, Sun and hols 9–12; adm*).

To the east, some of Naples' shabbiest streets lie between the **Piazza Garibaldi** and the **Piazza Enrico de Nicola**, once the city's main gate. Naples' market tradition is as vibrant today as it was in the Middle Ages; the **Forcella market district** lies to the south of here, concentrated around Piazza Mercato. You'll find everything from stereos to light bulbs, and plenty of designer labels – just don't ask where they came from.

Capodimonte

To the north of the city, the neighbourhoods along Via Toledo – briefly named Via Santa Teresa degli Scalzi – begin to lose some of their Neapolitan intensity as they climb to the suburban heights. Three Christian burial vaults have been discovered here, the most interesting of which is the **Catacombe di San Gennaro** (*enter through the Basilica dell'Incoronata; look for the yellow signs; tours daily at 9.30, 10.15, 11 and 11.45; adm*), containing extensive early (2nd century AD) Christian mosaics and frescoes.

Beyond lies the exotic **Parco di Capodimonte**, originally a hunting preserve of the Bourbons, and the site of Charles III's palace (1738), now the **Museo Nazionale di Capodimonte** (*open Tues–Sun 8.30–7.30; adm*). The picture collection is the best in the south of Italy, and especially rich in works of the late Renaissance. Among the works you shouldn't miss are an *Assumption* by Lippi, a Botticelli *Madonna* and others by the elder Brueghel, Masaccio and Mantegna. Other rooms are devoted to Caravaggio and Titian. The Bourbons maintained a porcelain factory at Capodimonte, and among the royal apartments you'll find their **Salotto di porcellana**, entirely lined with the stuff. Elsewhere a whole wing is filled with delightfully frivolous porcelain figurines.

Up on the highest point overlooking Naples, hogging the best view, stands the poshest monastery in Italy, the **Certosa di San Martino**, only marginally smaller than the **Castel Sant'Elmo** next door. The **Museo Nazionale di San Martino** (*open Tues–Fri and Sun 8.30–7.30, Sat 9–11; closed Mon; adm*) is apparently devoted to Naples' history, art and traditions, but only parts are ever open and no one knows exactly what is in it. However, the views and the architecture are worth the funicular ride in themselves, and you can always see the *presepi*, the Christmas cribs the Neapolitani have turned into an art form. Inside the **church**, an excess of lovely coloured marble sets off the overabundance of painting, including a fine work by José Ribera. The **Chiostro Grande** (cloister), even in its state of neglect, is a masterpiece of elegant Baroque, gloriously original and a bit creepy, its garden lined by gleaming marble skulls. Most of the collections surround the cloister: costume, painting and every sort of curiosity.

Pizzofalcone, the Villa Comunale and Mergellina

Behind the Piazza del Plebiscito rises the hill called **Pizzofalcone**; around it was the site of Parthenope, the Greek town that predated Neapolis. The island that formed its harbour is almost totally covered by the strangely shaped fortress of the **Castel dell'Ovo**, so-named because Master Virgil is said to have built it balanced on an egg.

Once past the Egg Castle, a handsome sweep of coastline opens up the districts of **Chiaia** and **Mergellina**, the most pleasant parts of the new city. Following the shore is the long, pretty park of the **Villa Comunale**, where the city's old **Aquarium** (*open winter Tues–Sat 9–5, Sun 9–2; summer Tues–Sat 9–6, Sun 10–6; adm*) is filled with a host of fascinating (and appetizing) marine delicacies. Deeper into Chiaia, the **Museo Principe di Aragona Pignatelli Cortes** (*open Tues–Sun 8.30–7.30; adm*) and the **Villa Floridiana** (*open Tues–Sun 8.30–7.30; adm*) will show you more decorative porcelain.

A few streets beyond the Villa Comunale, Mergellina is one of the brightest and most popular quarters of Naples – a good place for dinner or a *passeggiata* around the busy Piazza Sannazzaro. From the **Marina**, the district rises steeply up the surrounding hills (*funicular every 15 mins*), passing the **Tomb of Virgil** (*open Tues–Sun 9–1*), who wrote most of the *Aeneid* here in Naples. Just below lies the entrance to the **Crypta Neapolitana**, a 1,988ft road tunnel built during the reign of Augustus, the longest such work the Romans ever attempted.

Day Trips from Naples

Procida

Lovely, uncomplicated and tiny, Procida is in many ways the archetypal image of all that an 'Italian island' evokes: scented by lemon groves (the *granita* served in the bars is a treat) and embellished with colourful houses as original as they are beautiful. It was the setting for the Oscar-wining film *Il Postino* and its main port, overlooked by the village of **Corricella**, is a pastel fantasy with the undulating rhythm of a hundred arches, riddled with steep stone stairways cascading between them. Perched up on the promontory above, the **Terra Murata** (298ft) is the old walled town, where you can visit the 16th-century **Castello d'Aragona** and the church of **San Michele Arcangelo**.

Beyond this minimal urban centre, Procida is an enchanting Ruritania of lemon groves and crumbling old villas, rural beauty spots, shaded walkways and narrow roads, old farmhouses and crumbling small *palazzi* – you can walk around it in a day or take the bus to **Chiaiolella**, a small fishing port, where a long stretch of sand faces the tiny wooded **islet of Vivara**. The areas around **Centane** are especially pretty, with views over the entire east coast of the island from the belvedere.

Getting There and Around

There are frequent **ferry** and **hydrofoil** services from Naples to Procida. All are very short rides. Among the principle operators, **Caremar** (**t** 081 551 3882) runs ferries and hydrofoils from Molo Beverello, in the centre of the port; **SNAV** (**t** 081 761 2348) operates hydrofoils from Mergellina, further west. Check with the operators for timetables, or look in the daily newspaper *Il Mattino*.

The harbour in Procida itself is tiny and, if you want to explore further afield, jump on one of the colourful **buggies** that serve as taxis. Alternatively, there is a **bus service** about every 30 mins between the harbour and the other end of the island at Chiaiolella, stopping at more or less every point in between.

Tourist Information

Procida: Marina Grande, Via Roma 92, **t** 081 810 1968, **f** 081 981 904 (*open summer 9–1 and 3.30–7.30, winter 9–1*), beside the ticket office near the ferry departure point.

Eating Out

There are several good restaurants along the port at Marina Grande; it's probably most fun to stroll along and see what you fancy.

La Medusa, Via Roma 116, **t** 081 896 7481 (*moderate*). The house speciality is *spaghetti ai ricci di mare* (spaghetti with sea urchins). To accompany it, try the excellent local wine – literally 'on tap'.

Pompeii and Herculaneum

Despite its fearsome reputation, no one even suspected Vesuvius was a volcano until it surprised the people of Pompeii, Herculaneum and Stabiae on 24 August AD 79, burying Herculaneum in mud and coating most of Italy with a layer of dust.

Unlike Pompeii, an important commercial centre, ancient **Herculaneum** (*open daily Mar–Sept 8.30–7.30, Oct–Feb 8.30–5; last tickets 90mins earlier; adm*) seems to have been a wealthy resort. It drowned under a sea of mud, which hardened to a soft stone, preserving the city and nearly everything in it as a sort of fossil – furniture, clothing and even some of the goods in the shops have survived. Only about eight blocks of shops and villas have been excavated; the rest is covered by rock, but also by a dense modern neighbourhood. The **Suburban Baths**, near the entrance, are probably the best preserved baths of antiquity, with stucco reliefs and a central furnace that is perfectly intact. Many of the most interesting houses are along **Cardo IV**, in the centre of the excavated area. Look out for the **House of the Wooden Partition**; the **House of the Neptune**, with a mythological mosaic; the **House of the Deer**, with its infamous statue of a drunken Hercules relieving himself; and the ***palaestra***, with its serpent fountain and rather elegant swimming pool in the shape of a cross.

Herculaneum may have been better preserved, but to see an entire ancient city come to life, you must experience **Pompeii** (*open Mar–Sept 8–6 and Oct–Feb 8.30–3.30; adm*). Walking down the old high street, you can peek into shops, read graffiti on the walls, then wander down the back streets to explore the homes of the inhabitants and appraise their taste in painting. You can either spend a few hours on the main sights or devote the day to scrutinizing details (guidebooks at the stands outside will help). Your ticket (hang on to it) also entitles you to enter the **Villa of the Mysteries**, five minutes' walk up the Viale Villa dei Misteri, and best left to the end of your sightseeing.

Getting There

The refreshingly efficient **Circumvesuviana** (every 30 mins, 5am–10.45pm) is the best way to reach Pompeii and Herculaneum (**Ercolano**). It has its own station (**t** 081 772 2444) on Corso Garibaldi, just south of the Piazza Garibaldi, but all of its trains also make a stop at the Stazione Centrale. At Centrale the station is underground; there are no timetables posted and ticket windows aren't marked – ask someone to check you are going for the right train. For **Pompeii** take the Sorrento line to the Scavi di Pompeii/Villa dei Misteri stop.

Tourist Information

Pompei town: Via Sacra 1, **t** 081 850 7255, **f** 081 863 2401 (*open Mon–Sat 9–3*); branch near the Porta Marina entrance to the site.

Eating Out

At **Ercolano** there are no on-site facilities apart from toilets, but there are places nearby:

Bar degli Amorini, opposite the entrance to the ruins. Good for a snack or pizza.

Cagnano, Via Roma 17 (*cheap*). A short walk from the ruins, serving huge bowls of pasta.

If you spend the day in **Pompeii** there is a restaurant on-site near the Arch of Tiberius. Opt for the waiter service and sit out under the colonnade adjoining the baths. Otherwise, **modern Pompei** has several options:

Zi Caterina, Via Roma 20, **t** 081 850 7447 (*moderate*). With live lobsters in the tank, this is a good spot for Lacrima Christi wine from the slopes of Vesuvius. *Closed Tues eve.*

Anfiteatro, Via Plinio 9, **t** 081 863 1245 (*cheap*). Here you'll see *baccalà* (salt cod), along with truly good *spaghetti alle vongole*. Right outside the excavations' exit. *Closed Fri.*

Just inside the gate, the **Antiquarium** displays the art that hasn't been spirited off to Naples, as well as some truly gruesome casts of fossilized victims of the eruption. The **Forum** beyond has been poorly preserved, but you can see the once-imposing **Basilica** (law courts), temples to Apollo and Jupiter, a public latrine and a **Macellum** decorated with frescoes. North of here, the key attractions are the lavish villas off on the side streets: the enormous **House of Pansa**; the **House of the Faun**; and the wonderful **House of the Vettii**, containing a famous picture of Priapus. Three blocks east of the Forum lies the **Via dell'Abbondanza**, probably the city's most important thoroughfare. Along its length it passes a smith's, a grocer's, a weaver's, a laundry and a typical Roman tavern with its modest walk-up brothel. Bordering the southern walls is the **Triangular Forum**, where there are two **theatres** and a small **Temple of Isis**. The two most impressive structures occupy a corner just within the eastern walls: the ***palaestra***, a big colonnaded exercise yard, and the **Amphitheatre**, the best-preserved in Italy, with seating for about 20,000. Finally, the famous **Villa dei Misteri** is thought to have been a place of initiation into the forbidden Bacchic (or Dionysiac) Mysteries, one of the cults most feared by the Roman Senate and, later, by the emperors. Scenes from the myth of Dionysus and of the rituals themselves are painted on the walls.

Caserta

In one shot, you can see the biggest palace in Italy and also the most wearisome; both distinctions belong incontestably to the **Reggia** (Royal Palace), built here by the Bourbon King of Naples, Charles III (*Royal Apartments open Tues–Sat 9–2, Sun and hols 9am–10pm; adm*). His architect, Luigi Vanvitelli, spared no expense; the Reggia, begun in 1752, has some 1,200 rooms (it's larger than Versailles) and the façade is 804ft across. Inside, everything is tasteful, ornate and soberingly expensive; the only good touches from Vanvitelli's heavy hand are the elegant grand staircases. The **Park** (*open Tues–Sun 9–one hour before sunset; adm*) makes the trip worthwhile, an amazingly long axis of pools and cascades climbing up to the famous **Diana fountain**, with a life-like sculptural group of the goddess and her attendants catching Actaeon in the act. There is also an **English garden** of the sort fashionable in the 18th century.

Getting There

There are two or three **trains** every hour to Caserta from Stazione Centrale (30–40mins), conveniently stopping right in front of the Royal Palace. There is also a frequent service by CTP **buses** (**t** 081 700 5104); these leave from outside the train station in Piazza Garibaldi, taking about 50mins.

Tourist Information

Caserta: in the Royal Palace, **t** 0823 322 170.

Eating Out

The park is lovely, so you're best off bringing a picnic but, if not, try the following places:

Rocca di Sant'Andrea, Via Torre 8, **t** 0823 371 140 (*moderate*). In the centre of Casertavecchia, this offers delicious pasta and a variety of *secondi*, including meat grilled on the open fire in front of you. There is also a good selection of home-made desserts. *Closed Mon.*

La Massa, Via Mazzini 55, **t** 0823 444 096 (*cheap*). A simple and convenient place for lunch near the Reggia. *Closed Fri.*

Touring from Naples

Day 1: The Lost City on the Cilento Coast

Morning: Start early, taking the S18 (or A3) south of Naples towards Paestum. There's little to see en route, but you can pause in the hamlet **Nocera Superiore**, in the hills above Nocera Inferiore, to see its unusual 4th-century church. Back on the S18, make sure you stop in **Battipaglia** to buy the local buffalo mozzarella – you won't taste anything else like it. Then follow the last stretch of the S18 (23km) to **Paestum**.

Lunch: In Paestum, *see* below.

Afternoon: Explore the lost city of **Paestum** (*site open daily 9–one hour before sunset; closed first and third Mon of month; museum open Tues–Sun 9–2 only; adm*), founded in the 7th century BC; famous for its roses, it prospered until the end of the Roman era. Of its celebrated Doric temples, the **Temple of Neptune** (450 BC) is the best preserved: 200ft long, the whole structure survives except for the roof and internal walls. The **Basilica**, a century older, is connected with Hera. Elsewhere you can see the **Forum**, the ruins of an amphitheatre and the smaller **Temple of Ceres**. In the **museum** you'll see finds from the site, as well as the only examples of Greek fresco painting in existence. Afterwards, follow the coastal road south alongside long sandy beaches, passing through **Agrópoli**, with a warren of medieval streets above a lively marina. From here the S267 will lead you to **Santa Maria di Castellabate**.

Dinner and Sleeping: In or near Santa Maria di Castellabate, *see* below.

Day 1

Lunch in Paestum

Nettuno, t 0828 811 028 (*moderate*). In the archaeological zone, under the city walls near Porta Giustizia, the excellent Nettuno has been a family-run restaurant specializing in seafood for over 70 years.

Museo, t 0828 811 135 (*moderate*). Next door to the museum, this seafood restaurant is excellent value, with an informal dining room and outdoor terrace.

Bar Anna, t 0828 811 196 (*moderate*). If you are just seeking a tasty snack by the museum, this bar offers a good selection of cold *antipasti*, as well as local buffalo mozzarella in a tomato salad (*insalata alla caprese*). *Closed Mon in winter.*

Dinner and Sleeping in or near Santa Maria di Castellabate

Most of the restaurants are in the hotels, and in summer you'll be stuck on full or at least half board.

****Castelsandra, t/f** 0974 966 021 (*expensive*). Further south, high on the point above the towns of San Marco and Santa Maria di Castellabate, this has a pretty setting and outstanding views towards the Amalfi coast. The hotel proffers a Club Med-style complex of landscaped villas and innumerable sports facilities, as well as evening entertainment. Unsurprisingly, it's popular with package holiday operators.

***Sonia**, Via Gennaro Landi 25, **t/f** 0974 961 172 (*cheap*). This is an authentic Cilentan hotel on the seafront, with pleasant rooms and obliging, courteous management.

****Hotel Hermitage**, Via Catarozza, **t** 0974 966 618, **f** 0974 966 619, *hermi@costacilento.it* (*moderate*). About 1km from San Marco, this pretty hotel is bedecked with flowers, retaining a traditional rustic façade but completely renovated inside to ensure a comfortable and relaxing visit; there's even a complimentary bus to their private beach. Traditional Cilentan cooking is served in the restaurant and on the delightful terrace.

Day 2: '1,000 Bends' to Amalfi – via a Tiled Carpet

Morning: Drive back north to Agrópoli, from where you can skirt the coast all the way to **Salerno**, an orderly town memorably set before a backdrop of mountains, its shoreline graced with a pretty park. In the centre, stroll along Via dei Mercanti, the most colourful of Salerno's old streets, then visit the **cathedral** on Via del Duomo, surrounded by Corinthian columns from Paestum. Step inside to see the overwhelming mosaic floor: 1,968 sq ft of marble and polychrome tiles. Many of the original details are in the adjacent **Museo del Duomo** (*open daily 9–6*).

Lunch: In Salerno, *see* below.

Afternoon: Follow the coast west to **Vietri sul Mare**, a steep, pretty town famous for its beautiful majolica ware, with innumerable ceramics shops where you can watch craftsmen at work. From here the **Amalfi Drive** begins in earnest – a spectacular corniche road of 'a thousand bends' through an amazing vertical landscape, so narrow that every oncoming vehicle is an adventure. Wend your way via **Atrani** to experience the legendary **Amalfi**, beautiful almost to excess. Marvel at the delicate façade of the **cathedral** (9th–12th centuries), striped with interlaced arches, and its bronze doors (1066) from Constantinople, cast with portraits of Christ, Mary, St Peter and Amalfi's patron, St Andrew. The old **Chiostro del Paradiso** (*open summer daily 9–9, winter 9–5; adm*) has an African air while, to the side, you can see fragments of old Amalfi in the **Basilica del Crocifisso**, including bright Cosmatesque mosaics. Don't miss the lovely 16th-century *Madonna col Bambino* by the stairs to the Crypt.

Dinner and Sleeping: In Amalfi, *see* below.

Day 2

Lunch in Salerno

Al Cenacolo, Piazza Alfano I, **t** 089 228 818 (*moderate*). At the foot of the cathedral, this serves excellent seafood; recommended by the locals. *Closed Mon and Sun eve.*

Ristorante Pinocchio, Lungomare Trieste 56–58, **t** 089 229 964 (*cheap*). Another local favourite for good pizza and seafood; it's also great value. *Closed Fri.*

Dinner in Amalfi

Da Gemma, Via Fra Gerardo Sasso 9, **t** 089 871 345 (*expensive*). Established in 1872, this has an attractive terrace and an excellent fish-based menu. *Zuppa di pesce* is a wonderfully rich mixture of fish and seafood (but not cheap). Leave room for *melanzane al cioccolato* (grilled aubergines in chocolate sauce), an oddly heavenly combination. *Closed Wed.*

Lo Smeraldino, Piazzale dei Protontini 1, **t** 089 871 070 (*moderate*). On the water's edge at the far end of the port. You'll be offered *scialatielli ai frutti di mare* – fresh pasta with mixed seafood – and a range of *secondi*, most notably an excellent *fritto misto*. Good food and bustling waiters. *Closed Wed.*

Da Baracca, Piazza dei Dogi, **t** 089 871 285 (*cheap*). What a *trattoria* should be: tables spill out onto a tranquil leafy piazza, shaded by an awning, and friendly waiters proffer tasty snacks and plates of steaming pasta.

Sleeping in Amalfi

****Lidomare**, Largo Duchi Piccolomini 9, **t** 089 871 332, **f** 089 871 394 (*moderate*). A pleasant hotel away from the crowds; bright rooms, a cosy breakfast area and very obliging staff.

****Sole**, Largo della Zecca 2, **t** 089 871 147, **f** 089 871 926 (*moderate*). Further along the Corso Roma, this is in a quiet piazza; it's clean and airy, with parking. It's small, so book ahead.

****Sant'Andrea**, Via Santolo Camera 1, **t** 089 871 145 (*cheap*). This tiny and elaborately furnished hotel is one of a number of inexpensive places with good views of the cathedral. Expect an effusive welcome.

Day 3: Exotic Ravello and Pastel-Pretty Positano

Morning: Take the road back east out of Amalfi, turning inland to **Ravello**, a balcony overlooking the Amalfi coast and a treasure house of exotic medieval art and tropical botany (be aware that parking is a nightmare). Its chief glories are the **Villa Cimbrone** (*open daily 9–8; adm*), one of the most beautiful properties in all Italy, and the **Villa Rùfolo** (*open daily 9–8; adm*), an 11th-century pleasure palace with a semi-tropical paradise of a garden. The **cathedral** is named after Ravello's patron, San Pantaleone, whose blood 'boils' like that of San Gennaro in Naples (*see* p.249) whenever the saint is in the mood. Besides its bronze doors (1179), it has an exquisite pair of marble pulpits that rank among the outstanding examples of 12th- and 13th-century sculptural and mosaic work.

Lunch: In Ravello, *see* below.

Afternoon: Fortified by lunch, drive back to the coast to tackle the next stretch of the Amalfi Drive to the west. Beyond Conca dei Marini you'll notice a lift leading down to the **Grotta Smeralda** (*open April–Oct daily 9–5; Nov–Mar daily 10–6; adm*), a sea-level cavern diffused with a strange emerald-green light. Look out for the steep, impenetrable **Furore Gorge** as you make your way to **Positano**, spilling down from the corniche like a waterfall of pink, cream and yellow villas. After the Second World War, the village became a hideaway for artists and writers; fashion was not slow to follow. You can walk down to the pebbly, grey beach and the town's **church**, with a pretty tiled dome; only the alpinists make it back up (luckily there's a regular bus).

Dinner and Sleeping: In Positano, *see* below and Day 4.

Day 3

Lunch in Ravello

Cumpà Cosimo, Via Roma 44–46, **t** 089 857 156. Framed recommendations line the walls enthusing over the traditional recipes and the warm, homely atmosphere you find here.

Vittoria, Via dei Rufolo 3, **t** 089 857 947. This large *trattoria* just off the main *piazza* serves good food at reasonable prices – a rarity in Ravello. The servings are generous. Head to the back for the shady patio.

Dinner in Positano

La Cambusa, Spiaggia Grande, **t** 089 875 432 (*expensive*). With a terrace looking out onto the beach, this is a Positano favourite. The chef serves excellent fresh fish and seafood in every way you can think of, and more.

Lo Guarracino, Via Positanesi d'America 12, **t** 089 875 794 (*moderate*). In one of the loveliest spots, on a terrace over the sea, reached by a short walk along the cliff path towards Fornillo beach. This *pizzeria-cum-trattoria* is pleasantly informal after the modish Spiaggia Grande, and is a favourite with the Positanesi. Meals are straightforward and the atmostphere very friendly.

Sleeping in Positano

****Palazzo Murat**, Via dei Mulini 23, **t** 089 875 177, **f** 089 811 419 (*very expensive–expensive*). This 18th-century *palazzo* has plenty of old-world ambience, with a courtyard shaded by palms staging summer concerts.

***Tramonto d'Oro**, Via Capriglione 119, **t** 089 874 955, **f** 089 874 670 (*moderate*). An exceptional bargain offering a pool, beach access and great views. Staff are friendly and helpful and the rooms are decorated with attractive tiling and bright materials.

California, Via Cristoforo Colombo 141, **t** 089 875 382, **f** 089 812 154 (*cheap*). One of the best bargains in Positano, with 15 very pleasant rooms and a lovely terrace for breakfast and other meals. Set slightly back from the sea, it is still well located, and charmingly run.

Day 4: Eden on the Water

Morning: Take a ferry from Positano (*call **Alicost**, **t** 089 871 483, for schedules*) to the enchanting isle of **Capri**, a delicious garden of Eden cascading over a sheer chunk of limestone. Arriving in the Marina Grande, you can take a bus or funicular (*every 15 mins throughout the day*) up to **Capri Town**, a charming white village packed with jewellery shops and designer boutiques. The town is the base for several lovely walks. From Via Tragara, aim for the **Faraglioni**, three great limestone pinnacles towering from the sea; a stairway descends to the point where, for a price, you can take a swim. Or head for **La Certosa**, a golden-hued 14th-century Carthusian charterhouse topped by a 17th-century tower. Nearby are the **Gardens of Augustus**, founded by Caesar himself, where a wide variety of plants grow on the fertile terraces, overlooking one of the most striking views in the world.

Lunch: In Capri Town, *see* below.

Afternoon: Take the Via Roma for buses to **Anacapri**, on the island's top shelf; the town retains a rustic air, with its olive trees and surrounding vineyards, and its simple architecture. Look into the **church of San Michele** (*open April–Oct daily 9–7; Nov–Mar daily 10–3*), containing a magnificent floor of majolica tiles, showing Adam and Eve in the Garden of Eden. A chairlift (*12-min ride; summer 9.30–dusk; Nov–Feb 10.30–3; closed Tues*) will whisk you up to **Monte Solaro**, for a fabulous view over the Bay of Naples. From Anacapri, buses will take you to the fabled **Blue Grotto**, **Faro** and **Marina Piccola**. In the evening, return to spend another night in Positano.

Dinner and Sleeping: In Positano, *see* below and Day 3.

Day 4

Lunch in Capri Town

La Capannina, Via delle Botteghe 12–14, **t** 081 837 0732 (*expensive*). In a secluded garden, this has long been Capri's best restaurant, with delicate shellfish, pasta and fish.

Da Paolino, Via Palazzo a Mare 11, **t** 081 837 6102 (*moderate*). Look out for this restaurant on the way down from Capri Town to Marina Grande. Eat in an arbour of lemon trees, tasting dishes mainly inspired by the fruit.

Da Gemma, Via Madre Serafina 6, **t** 081 837 0461, **f** 081 837 8947 (*moderate*). Up the steps past the cathedral and down a tunnel to the right, this friendly *trattoria*, its walls decked with brass pans and plates, serves superb local dishes including a *risotto alla pescatore*, delicious mozzarella and very good pizza.

Dinner in Positano

Buca Di Bacco, Via Rampa Teglia 8, **t** 089 875 699 (*expensive*). Across the road from La Cambusa, this is a Positano institution and the place to stop for a drink on the way back from the beach. The fish is always well cooked here and you'd be crazy to go for anything else. It also has a few rooms.

O'Caporale, Via Regina Giovanna 12, **t** 089 811 188 (*moderate*). Just off the beach, this offers simple, well-cooked seafood. The succulent swordfish and *zuppa di pesce* are particularly highly recommended.

Sleeping in Positano

****Covo dei Saraceni**, Via Regina Giovanna 5, **t** 089 875 400, **f** 089 875 878 (*expensive*). A comfortable hotel beautifully set on the edge of the harbour, with views up through town and out to sea. Rooms are simple, spacious and furnished with antiques.

***Casa Albertina**, Via Tavolozza 3, **t** 089 875 143, **f** 089 811 540 (*moderate*). Furnished in a lovely understated manner to accentuate the views over Positano and the sea, this is a quiet, family-run place near the beach, with a nice restaurant on the rooftop terrace. Half board only in high season. *Closed Nov–Mar.*

Day 5: Strolling the Streets of Sorrento

Morning: Negotiate the infamous bends for the last time as you head west along the S145 to spend a day in the lovely, civilized old town of **Sorrento**. It began drawing the crowds in the 19th century, when Naples started to grow too piquant for English tastes, and the English have never forsaken it. Built on a long cliff along the shore, a narrow ravine cuts the town in half, between a quiet suburban area and the old town itself, which preserves its grid of Roman streets. The major draw here is the pleasant walk through the old streets, browsing through shops full of *intarsia* (fine pictures done in inlaid woods), a local craft for centuries. For the classic Sorrentine view, with the sea and Vesuvius in the distance, stroll up to the **Public Gardens**. From here you can take the lift down to the *stabilimenti* – piers jutting into the sea.

Lunch: In Sorrento, *see* below.

Afternoon: Be sure to stop for an ice cream at the truly exceptional **Davide** (*Via P. R. Giuliani 39*), with at least 50 flavours at any one time (try the *tiramisù* or *pistacchio*). This is also a good place to pick up the distinctive liqueur, *limoncello*, made with lemons from the lush groves around the town; look out for the 'laboratories', which are open to the street. Follow the winding path west from town to the **Bagni Regina Giovanna**, a natural seapool where you can see the ruins of a Roman Villa. Or drive down the little coast road to **Massa Lubrense**, a refreshingly simple fishing village with more fine views as far as the tip of the peninsula. Whatever you do, make sure you're in Sorrento at dusk, when the town comes alive for its *passeggiata*.

Dinner and Sleeping: In Sorrento, *see* below.

Day 5

Lunch and Dinner in Sorrento

Don Alfonso, Piazza Sant'Agata, in Sant'Agata Sui Due Golfi, **t** 081 878 0026, **f** 081 533 0226 (*very expensive–expensive*). This Michelin-starred restaurant, reckoned by some to be the best in southern Italy, turns food into an art form: beautifully cooked and stylishly presented. It's 9km outside Sorrento, but well worth the trip. *Closed Sun eve Sept–May and Mon all year.*

O'Parrucchiano, Corso Italia 71, **t** 081 878 1321 (*moderate–cheap*). If setting is what you're after, this is the place to be. Choose from a large but modest menu and dine among a riot of tropical greenery.

La Lanterna, Via S. Cesareo 23–25, **t** 081 878 1355 (*moderate–cheap*). Right in the middle of it all, with tables in the alley area which are a little quieter. It has tasteful décor, friendly and efficient service and, most important, impeccable *risotto alla pescatore*. *Closed Jan, Feb and Mon exc July–Aug.*

Da Gigino, Via Degli Archi 15, **t** 081 878 1927 (*moderate–cheap*). A bustling family-run *trattoria* serving pizza and pasta alongside more sophisticated dishes, such as *salmone e pesce spada affumicato con rucola* (smoked salmon and smoked swordfish with rocket).

Sleeping in Sorrento

★★★★**Excelsior Vittoria**, Piazza T. Tasso 34, **t** 081 807 1044, **f** 081 877 1206 (*very expensive*). For the Grand Tour atmosphere, this the place to stay, set in its own plush park overlooking the sea. Wagner, Princess Margaret, Sophia Loren and Pavarotti have all stopped by.

★★**La Tonnarella**, Via Capo 31, **t** 081 878 1153, **f** 081 878 2169 (*moderate*). In an attractive villa with some of the best views in Sorrento, with a pleasant private beach and a good restaurant to boot, this is a real bargain. It's advisable to book well ahead.

★★★**Minerva**, Via Capo 30, **t** 081 878 1011, **f** 081 878 1949 (*moderate*). On the road east out of town, this has nice rooms, some with stunning sea views. *Closed Nov–Mar.*

Sardinia

14

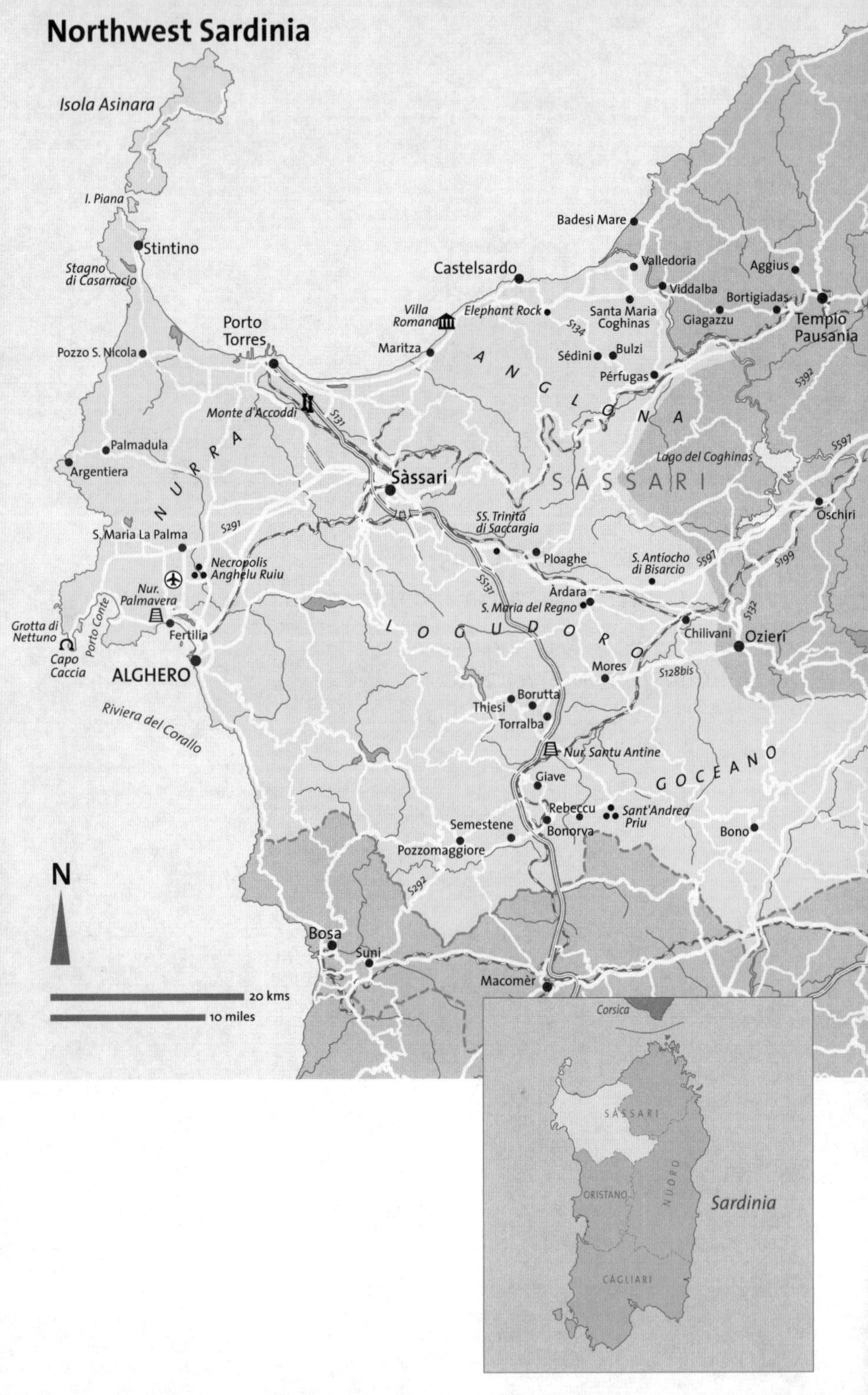
Northwest Sardinia
Isola Asinara
I. Piana
Stintino
Stagno di Casarracio
Porto Torres
Pozzo S. Nicola
Castelsardo
Villa Romana
Maritza
Elephant Rock
Badesi Mare
Valledoria
Viddalba
Aggius
Bortigiadas
Santa Maria Coghinas
Giagazzu
Tempio Pausania
S134
Sédini
Bulzi
Pérfugas
ANGLONA
Monte d'Accoddi
S131
Palmadula
Argentiera
NURRA
Sàssari
SÁSSARI
Lago del Coghinas
S392
S597
Oschiri
S291
S.Maria La Palma
Necropolis Anghelu Ruiu
SS. Trinità di Saccargia
Ploaghe
S. Antíocho di Bisarcio
S199
Nur. Palmavera
Porto Conte
Grotta di Nettuno
Capo Caccia
Fertilia
ALGHERO
SS131
Àrdara
S. Maria del Regno
LOGUDORO
Chilivani
Ozieri
S132
Mores
S128bis
Riviera del Corallo
Borutta
Thiesi
Torralba
Nur. Santu Antine
GOCEANO
Giave
Rebeccu
Sant'Andrea Priu
Bonorva
Semestene
Pozzomaggiore
Bono
S292
N
Bosa
Suni
Macomèr
20 kms
10 miles
Corsica
SÁSSARI
ORISTANO
NUORO
Sardinia
CAGLIARI

There is no place in Italy that is less Italian than Sardinia. While the rest of the country is clothed in a thousand gorgeous Baroque artifices, Sardinia remains as artless and unaffected as Eve in the garden. Her beauty is natural, sculpted by the wind rather than a chisel; her music is ancient and polyphonic; her cuisine is simple and genuine, full of flavours nearly forgotten elsewhere. Her greatest monuments are stone megaliths that fit organically into their natural surroundings: the castle-like *nuraghi*, menhirs and 'giants' tombs'. But what tourists most know her for are her spectacular beaches, washed by a sea that comes in every shade of turquoise and sapphire. The Sards, a *simpatico* and attractive people, look on their visitors as just the latest and least worrisome in a long series of invasions that began with the Phoenicians. Politics are their passion and their greatest talent, and they'll be glad to bend your ear about NATO or philosophy as well as *nuraghi* and seafood.

Sássari is the largest province in Italy and, while its eastern half has become known as Sardinia's seaside playground, its western half remains essentially Sard. This is the land of lovely medieval Pisan country churches and of the island's most attractive cities, Sássari and Alghero and Castelsardo, each with a medieval core like a delicious chocolate filling. The seaside Grotta di Nettuno is among the most spectacular caves in all Italy, the astonishing Santu Antine is one of the very best *nuraghi*, and there beaches galore: a sandy stretch east of Porto Torres to Castelsardo, beautiful coves west of Alghero but, fairest of all, the Spiaggia della Pelosa by Stintino.

Alghero

Alghero (pop. 41,000) is a beautiful city in a beautiful setting, and one of the most popular destinations on the island. In a sense, however, it isn't Sard at all. Founded by the Arabs, and later controlled by the Doria family of Genoa, it was considered so valuable by the Catalans that their whole army turned up in 1355 to stake their claim in the name of the pope. When the Algherese proved to be less than docile subjects, King Pere the Ceremonious simply deported the entire population to the interior and replaced them with loyal Catalans. Walls went up, and 'Little Barcelona' became a de facto foreign concession on the island. It still has a marked Catalan flavour and is determined to maintain it; the *comune* even offers free classes in the language. Today, restored to just the right degree of habitation, Alghero has all the appearances of a town built for noblemen – which suits it perfectly as a town for tourists.

Old Alghero

Alghero's Gothic *centro storico* is at its best in the evening, when the street lights lend it a rich vanilla tone and the shops in the cobbled medieval lanes glitter like Ali Baba's caverns (provided that the Forty Thieves went in for coral). Overhead, laundry that no one has bothered to take in floats like banners, and everyone is out and about, shopping and strolling and meeting friends at the cafés and *gelaterie*.

Two towers are all that survive of the land walls: the most important, the **Torre del Porta a Terra** (or Torre del Portal) marks the site of the old main gate, erected in 1360. It

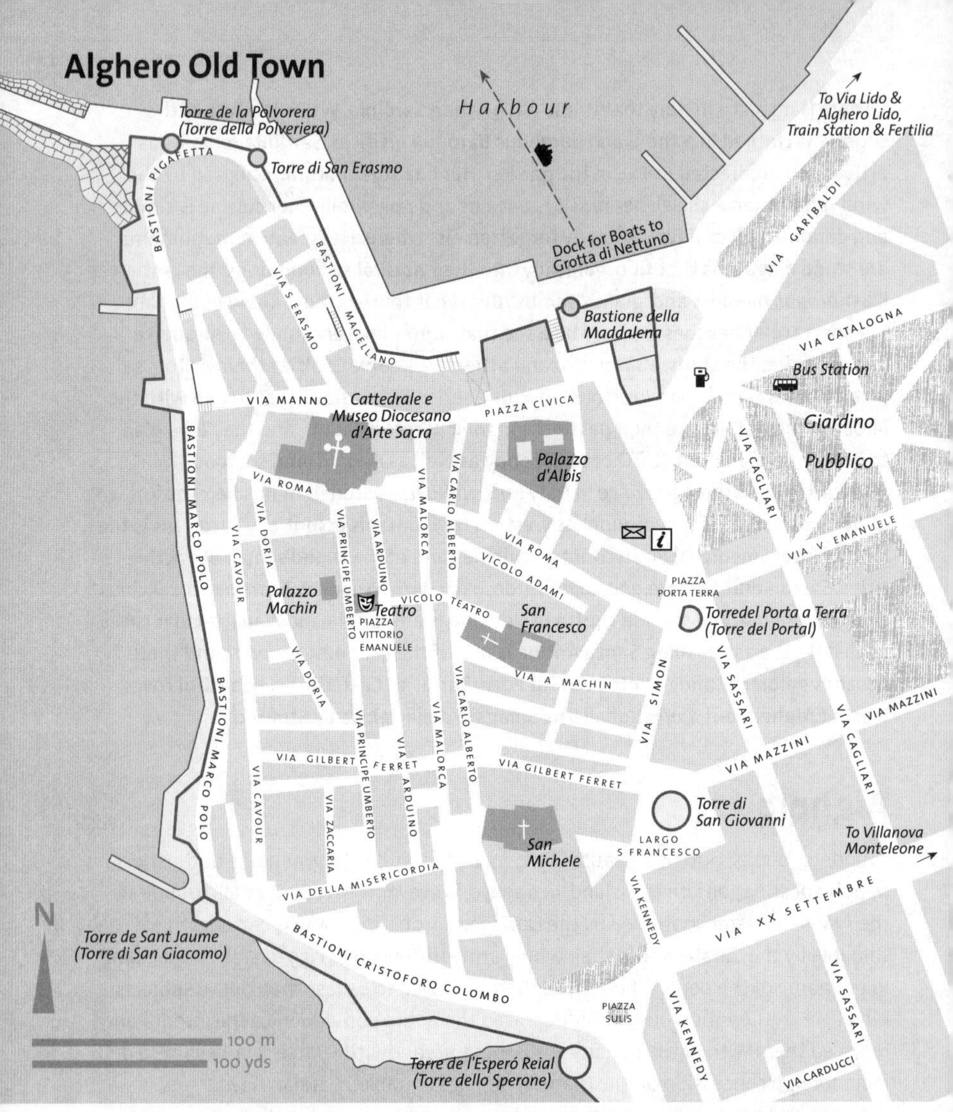

once had a drawbridge, which was closed every evening until 1848 with the warning cry: *'Chi es arrinz es arrinz, chi es a foras resta!'* (Whoever is in is in; whoever is out stays there!). The **Torre di San Giovanni**, in Largo San Francesco, marks a pair of good pizzeria-*tavola caldas*. From here pedestrian Via Gilbert Ferret (or Carrer del Quarter) leads to Via Carlo Alberto, coral necklace central HQ. Just left on Carlo Alberto, the Baroque church of **San Michele** (1612) features a beautiful multicoloured tile dome and a fine interior while, to the right, the 14th-century **San Francesco** is distinguished by a graceful bell tower. The façade has two rose windows, one Romanesque, one Renaissance, and inside there's a lavish polychrome marble altar from the 1700s. The cloister, not a complete success, dates from the original church. A bit further up Via Carlo Alberto, the Vicolo Teatro leads into Piazza Vittorio Emanuele; both the square and the Corinthian-pilastered **Teatro** are prime examples of Alghero's austere side.

Alghero's landmark is the 16th-century **cathedral** on Via Manno, its plain façade (1730) marked by four outsized Doric columns. Its lovely Catalan **campanile** (*open for guided tours in July and Aug every Wed and Fri 5.30–9pm*) dominates the skyline, best appreciated from Via Roma; there is a finely sculptured portal at its base. The new **Museo Diocesano d'Arte Sacra** is next door. Down the street extends the elegant, funnel-shaped **Piazza Civica**, address of Alghero's finest palace, the 16th-century Catalan Gothic **Palazzo d'Albis**, where Emperor Charles stayed in 1542, when he

Getting to Alghero

Ryanair flies from London Stansted (2hrs35).

Getting from the Airport

Fertilia airport (**t** 079 935 082) lies 10km out of Alghero. A **taxi** into the centre costs about €23, or you can take the **FdS bus** from Piazza della Mercede which coincides with regular flights (**t** 079 950 458; about 20mins); buy tickets from the bars or *tabacchi*.

Getting Around

You can get around all of Alghero's sights easily on foot. FdS (**t** 079 950 179) and ARST **buses** (**t** 079 263 9220), for the surrounding area and Sássari, depart from Via Catalogna. The **FdS train station** (**t** 079 950 785) is at Via Don Minzoni.

For a **taxi**, call Alghero Aereoporto, **t** 079 975 396.

Car Hire

Avis, Piazza Gulis 9, **t** 079 979 577; at the airport, **t** 079 935 064.
Europcar, at the airport, **t** 079 935 032.
Hertz, at the airport, **t** 079 935 054.
Maggiore (**Budget**), Via Sássari 87, **t** 079 979 375; at the airport, **t** 079 935 045.
Sardinya, at the airport, **t** 079 935 060.
Thrifty, at the airport, **t** 079 935 167.

Tourist Information

Alghero: Piazza Portaterra 9, ✉ 07041, **t** 079 979 054, **f** 079 974 881, *infoturism@infoalghero.it*, *www.infoalghero.it*. They can provide a list of operators who hire out boats. There's also an **EPT** point at the airport, **t** 079 935 124.

Market Days

The weekly market is held in **Via dei Gasperi** (Wed morning), and there's an **antiques** fair in Piazza Civica (last Sat of month).

Shopping

Alghero is the best spot to shop in Sardinia. The *centro storico* is filled with a wide array of attractive boutiques where you can buy just about anything made on the island. **Enodolciaria di Renzo Dettori**, Via Simon 24, has a fine selection of sweets, wines and other goodies to eat and drink, while **Domenico Manca**, Via Carrabufas, offers Alghero's best olive oil, artichoke cream and herbs. Among many places featuring arty creations in coral, **Antonio Marogna**, Via Don Minzoni 208, has a good reputation.

Where to Stay

Alghero ✉ 07041

****__Villa Las Tronas__**, Lungomare Valencia 1, **t** 079 981 818, **f** 079 981 044 (*very expensive*). Built in the 1940s as a villa for the King of Italy, this is beautifully located on the coast south of the centre, surrounded by gardens, with luminous public areas, a pretty veranda and restaurant (*summer only, by reservation*). Each of the rooms is different; most are spacious, all luxurious. Amenities include a gym, pool, private beach and bicycles.

****__Carlos V__**, Lungomare Valencia 24, **t** 079 979 501, **f** 079 980 298 (*expensive*). One of Alghero's best regarded hotels, on the coast road with fine views overlooking the town. It also has tennis, a large, pretty pool, a large terrace and activities for children.

****__Rina__**, Via delle Baleari 34, **t** 079 984 240, **f** 079 984 297, *rinahotel@algherovacanze.*

announced to the Algherese, 'You are all knights' – a declaration they recall with pride. The modern Algherese do their shopping along tree-lined **Via XX Settembre**, which begins in Piazza Sulis and extends into the new town; you can duck into the underground **Mare Nostrum Aquarium** (*Via XX Settembre 1; open June and Oct daily 10–1 and 4–9; July and Sept daily 10–1 and 5–11; Aug 10–1.30 and 5–12.30am; Nov–May Sat, Sun and hols only 4–9; adm*), which has most Mediterranean species, plus white sharks, moray eels, piranhas, rare alligator pikes and other denizens of the deep.

com (*expensive–moderate*). By the Lido di Alghero and a minute's walk from the sea, this offers large, comfortable modern rooms, a pool and a private beach. Near the airport.

★★★**Florida**, Via Lido 15, **t** 079 950 500, **f** 079 985 424 (*expensive–moderate*). A typical beach hotel, with a pool, gym, garden and a/c.

★★**San Francesco**, Via Ambrogio Machin 2, **t/f** 079 980 330 (*cheap*). One of the few places to stay in the historic centre – simple rooms in an old building on a quiet street. Breakfast is served in the cloister.

Eating Out

Alghero's Catalan heritage has given it a head start in preparing delightful seafood and its waters are full of *aragosta*: Mediterranean lobster. The Algherese also like spicy hot sauces, served with *polpagliara* (octopus) and *il peutxus* (boiled lamb or kid's foot, served cold and slightly redeemed by hot sauce).

La Lépanto, Via Carlo Alberto 135, **t** 079 979 116 (*expensive*). Right in the centre and *the* place for seafood: Moreno Cecchini, the *padrone*, is famous all over Sardinia for his stylish, luminous dining room and innovative, masterly touch; no one prepares a tastier lobster, and the wines are all from the nearby estate of Sella & Mosca. *Closed Mon Nov–Feb.*

Il Pavone, Piazza Sulis 3/4, **t** 079 979 584 (*expensive*). Near the Torre de l'Esperó Reial, with a lovely outdoor terrace, or a/c inside. Well prepared food from land and sea, good rice dishes and desserts with a Sard or Catalan twist, such as goat's milk yoghurt with arbutus honey. *Closed Wed.*

Nettuno, Bastione della Maddalena, **t** 079 979 774 (*expensive*). A trendy place in a wonderful location, with tables on a little outdoor terrace, or up on the third floor with views over the port. Stylish laid-back atmosphere, simply prepared fish, or pizza; the €18 menu offers good value, though *à la carte* the bill can go haywire. *Closed Wed.*

Palau Reial, Via Sant'Erasmo 14, **t** 079 980 688 (*expensive*). Elegant restaurant in a medieval Jewish *palazzo* featuring local fare including sea-urchin mousse. *Closed Wed in winter.*

Ristorante Andreini, Via Arduino 45 (just off Via G. Ferret), **t** 079 982 098 (*expensive*). Vaulted dining room offering varied menus according to the season. Good wine list. *Closed Mon lunch and 15–30 Oct.*

Ristorante Borgo Antico, Via Zaccaria 12, **t** 079 982 649 (*expensive*). In the *centro storico*, with a terrace, this serves Mediterranean cuisine; fish dishes are highly recommended.

Posada del Mar, Vicolo Adami 29, **t** 079 979 579 (*moderate–cheap*). Famous for sea urchins (*ricci*) – though the chef insists they only taste right in cool weather. At other times you can rely on well prepared fresh fish or pizza and wonderful *sebadas* for dessert. *Closed Sun, exc in summer.*

La Muraglia, Bastioni Marco Polo 7, **t** 079 977 254 (*moderate*). Choose from variously priced menus and eat outside on the old city walls. Their speciality is *paella valenziana* (must be ordered in advance).

Da Pietro, on corner of Via A. Macchin and Via Simon, **t** 079 979 645 (*moderate*). This offers an excellent value €18 menu with wine, but the tempting *à la carte* dishes (a fragrant *bucatini* with clams, capers and olives, grilled mushrooms, or lobster) can double your bill. Sella & Mosca wines accompany the meals. *Closed Wed and 10–28 Dec.*

Casabianca, Via Principe Umberto 76, **t** 079 980 165 (*cheap*). The best pizzas in town, served by young, friendly staff. Outdoor tables on a lovely square. *Closed Wed and two weeks in Nov and Feb.*

Caffé Latino, Piazza Duomo 6. A very popular terrace café overlooking the harbour. Also serves pasta, *panini* and ice creams.

Along the Walls

The **sea walls**, beautifully illuminated at night, are the focus of Alghero's finest promenade. Seven sturdy towers remain: the bleached **Torre de l'Esperó Reial**, the southernmost, is also called the Torre di Sulis after the 19th-century revolutionary Vincenzo Sulis who was imprisoned there following Angioy's rebellion. The main hall on the ground floor, with its dramatic rib vaulting, is a fine example of Catalan late Gothic. The next tower west is the octagonal **Torre de Sant Jaume**, built in the 15th century and recently restored; within, a covered stair once offered access to the sea. If you continue north along the **Bastioni Marco Polo** you'll come to the 18th-century **Torre de la Polvorera**. Through the **Bastione della Maddalena**, steps lead down to Alghero's small harbour – no longer the haven for fat galleys from Barcelona, but for the town's coral and lobster fleet, plenty of yachts and the boats to the Grotta di Nettuno. Across from the Bastione della Maddalena, the **Giardino Pubblico** is a pretty park patrolled during the summer by a horde of beautiful but audacious caterpillars. A long walk north of here is Alghero's beach, the **Lido**.

Day Trips from Alghero

Porto Conte and Capo Caccia

West of Alghero, horseshoe **Porto Conte**, is so beautiful that the Romans called it Nimpharum Portus, the 'port of nymphs'; it has a diving centre and excellent beaches, especially **Spiaggia Mugoni** and **Spiaggia La Stalla**. The western side of the bay is framed by **Capo Caccia**, sloping up gradually 350ft only to plummet sheer down to the sea; take the little *strada panoramica* half-way up to peer over the vertiginous lip of the **Cala dell'Inferno**. Further up, at the end of the road, is the land entrance to the **Grotta di Nettuno** (*open for guided tours on the hour, April–Sept 8–7; Oct 10–5; Nov–Mar 9–1; adm exp; if the weather's rough, call* **t** *079 946 540: it may be closed*): the 650-step Escala del Cabriol, cut in 1954. It's more than worth the effort; this is one of the world's most beautiful caves, extending two and a half kilometres into the cliff. Its narrow entrance is only a few feet above sea level, and the sea surges against it.

Getting There and Around

FdS **buses** (three a day in summer, one in winter; **t** 079 950 179) leave from Via Catalogna in Alghero for Porto Conte and Capo Caccia (50mins), from where you can walk down the long stair to the cave. Otherwise, **Compagnia Marittima Navisarda**, Via IV Novembre 6, by the port (**t** 079 978 961), issues tickets for the 2½hr sea excursion to the cave (*June–Sept hourly departures 9–5; April, May and Oct at 9, 10, 3 and 4*). If it's rough, they won't go out.

Eating Out

There's a **snack bar** by the entrance to the caves. Otherwise, the silvery sands are shared by a few restaurants, such as **La Baia**, **t** 079 949 034, or **La Nuvola**, **t** 079 946 533 (both *moderate*). All will dish up some fine maritime delicacies from the Coral Riviera.

Alternatively, you could pop into one of the hotel restaurants; try the **El Faro**, **t** 079 942 010 (*very expensive*). *Open May–mid Oct.*

Inside, calm reigns around the shores of **Lake Lamarmora**, one of the largest salt-water lakes in Europe. Neptune's Grotto is remarkable not only for the subterranean lagoons and delicate stalactites – they look like a forest drawn by Gaudí – but for the colours, ranging from white to orange. Most spectacular is the **Palace**, a chamber which seems to be supported by 30ft columns rising out of the water. Among the concretions are some beautiful eccentrics: crystal 'pears' suspended on filaments of stone, and tangles made of nearly transparent stone threads.

Sássari

Sássari, provincial capital and home to over 120,000 people, is Sardinia's second-largest city and a place of great character. It somehow manages to be very Sard in atmosphere, yet different from anywhere else on the island. At the same time, there is still very much the air of a medieval free city here, a civic spirit reflected in the 'Festival of the Candlesticks' (*see* opposite) organized each year by the ancient guilds.

Sássari is built on a long gentle slope, linked from top to bottom by the **Corso Vittorio Emanuele**. Three almost contiguous squares connect the newer town with the older town down below. The southernmost, **Piazza Italia**, is Sássari's main square; descending into the old town, the Corso widens before entering the pretty triangular **Piazza Azuni**, a busy shopping area. The very bottom of the street is closed by Piazza Sant'Antonio and the **Colonna Sant'Antonio**, made in 1954 and wound around with reliefs depicting scenes from the city's history. West of here at the end of Corso Vico is **Santa Maria di Betlem**, the special church of the guilds, where the giant 'candlesticks', *li Candaleri*, are kept between festivals. The interior underwent a major 19th-century remodelling but the chapels, each belonging to a different guild, escaped. Of them, the Cappella dei Muratori (bricklayers) is the best preserved, with a sculptural group of seven statues in wood and stone from the 1500s.

The *centro storico*, for the most part, has been neither restored nor gentrified. North of the Corso, charming **Piazza Tola** was the main square of the medieval town, where the Spaniards held their *autos-da-fé* and the locals their market (the latter still takes places on weekday mornings). At one end, the very Spanish-looking **Palazzetto Usini** is the oldest Renaissance palace in Sardinia (1577), with rusticated doors and windows.

South of the Corso in Via Santa Caterina, the church of **Santa Caterina**, built in 1580 in the late Renaissance Counter-Reformation style, has a fine interior, a single nave lined with deep chapels and an octagonal cupola lit by pretty windows. Beyond, Sássari's 'giant flower of grey stone' rises up: the **Duomo di San Nicola** (*open 9–12 and 4–7*), completely rebuilt in 15th-century Catalan Gothic style. In the 1700s, the famous Baroque façade was added, a work of rare beauty; the underlying simplicity and sense of proportion make the profuse decoration an integral part of the building. The Gothic interior isn't quite as grandiose, but there are some fine details: the altarpiece by the baptismal font, by Corrado Giaquinto; a painting of *SS. Cosma e Damiano*, attributed to Carlo Maratta; also the neoclassical tomb of Placido Benedetto of Savoy, watched over by allegories of Faith, Military Genius and a teary-eyed Sardinia.

Getting There and Around

Both **FS trains** (**t** 079 260 362) and **FdS narrow-gauge trains** (**t** 079 241 301) from Alghero serve Sássari's **train station**, at Piazza Stazione on the western edge of the old town. ARST **buses** (**t** 079 263 9220) and FDS **coaches** (**t** 079 241 301) from Alghero (55mins) arrive nearby, on Via XXV Aprile. City bus no.8 will take you from the train station to Corso Vittorio Emanele; buy tickets from *tabacchi*.

Tourist Information

Sássari: **EPT**, Viale Caprera 36, **t** 079 299 544 or **t** 079 299 546, **f** 079 299 415 (*closed Sat and Sun*); **AAST**, Viale Umberto 72, **t** 079 231 331 or **t** 079 233 534, **f** 079 237 585.

Festivals

Li Candaleri (*14 Aug*) evokes the spirit of a medieval free city, with a procession of the nine medieval guilds from Piazza Castello to Santa Maria di Betlem. Each guild carries a great 'candlestick' to the rhythm of the drum and whistling of the *pifferario* (pipe).

Eating Out

The Ligurian legacy includes *fainé*: baked chickpea flour and olive oil, served plain, with onions or with sausage. The town also has a weakness for horse and donkey meat and *cordula* (lamb intestines, tripe and stomach). Nearly everything closes on Sunday.

Giamaranto, Via Alghero 69, **t** 079 274 598 (*moderate*). A bit hard to find, but the stylish horseshoe-shaped room is a perfect backdrop for dishes prepared using the finest seasonal ingredients. Try ravioli filled with artichokes or wild mushrooms; the wine list is excellent too. *Closed Sun and 10–20 Aug.*

Antica Hostaria, Via Cavour 55, **t** 079 200 066 (*moderate*). An intimate place serving imaginative and delicate cuisine based on ancient recipes (terrine of wild herbs, fettuccine with clams and courgette flowers, red mullet with saffron). The wine list is cosmopolitan; there's a fine cheese board and desserts such as a *torta* made with cocoa and bitter orange. Book. *Closed Sun and 15–31 Aug.*

Oasi and **Fainé alle Genovese**, Via Usai, near Piazza Tola (*cheap*). Both of these are very popular and both serve *fainé*. Oasi also serves plenty of pasta dishes.

South of Piazza Italia, the Corso continues as Via Roma into the new part of town. Here, just beyond an elaborate palace decorated with stucco tondos, reliefs and tiles, a lemon-coloured neoclassical temple façade conceals the **Museo Archeològico-Etnografico Sanna** (*Via Roma 64; open Tues–Sun 9–8; closed Mon; adm*), its insides now modernized and beautifully laid out. The first stop is the conference room, with four beautiful Roman mosaics. To the left, look into the small **Pinacoteca** for a 14th-century Pisan triptych, a *Madonna* (1473) by Bartolomeo Vivarini, a *St Sebastian* by the Maestro di Ozieri and two *Crucifixions* by anonymous Sard painters. Archaeology, however, is the main course on the menu, and art and artefacts from all periods of early Sardinian history are represented, starting in the **Sala Preistorica** (around 500,000–4000 BC). A whole room is devoted to the remarkable **sanctuary of Monte d'Accoddi**, a unique late Neolithic/Copper Age temple (*see* p.269); another is dedicated to ***domus de janas***, with exhibits on the shadowy Ozieri culture, Copper Age and early Bronze Age people. Upstairs, you can learn about nuraghe-building techniques in the **Sala Nuragica**, while the **Sala Romana** contains pots and pans, glass, fine jewellery and inscriptions. The latter includes the **Tavola di Esterzili** of AD 69, a decree of the Roman Proconsul Lucius Elvius Agrippa seeking to suppress a border dispute in south-east Sardinia. Elsewhere, an excellent **ethnographic collection** features folk art, costumes and traditional music.

Touring from Alghero

Day 1: Neolithic Tombs, Wine and Beaches

Morning: Drive north towards Porto Torres for 10km to visit the **necropolis of Anghelu Ruiu** (*open Oct–Feb 9.30–4; Mar–Sept 9–7; adm, joint with Palmavera; bring a torch*), with its brilliantly preserved Neolithic tombs: the earliest (3300 BC) are narrow and well-like; later ones are more refined, and many are decorated. Just up the road (at km8 marker), drop in to buy a bottle at the prestigious **Sella & Mosca winery** (*shop open Oct–May Mon–Sat 8.30–1 and 3–6.30; June–Sept daily 8.30–8*) before heading back towards Alghero; turn right on the edge of town towards Porto Conte, passing **Fertilia** on your way to the **Nuraghe Palmavera** (*same hours as Anghelu Ruiu*), a key Bronze-Age site (15th–7th century BC), with its circular 'meeting hut'.

Lunch: In or near Fertilia, *see* below.

Afternoon: Drive north of Fertilia towards S. Maria La Palma for 7km, then turn right onto the S291; after 5km, turn left onto the Porto Torres road, turning left again after 7km to dusty **Palmadula**. From here, follow the road north to Pozzo S. Nicola and up into the narrow peninsula. Once past the Stagno di Casarracio, look out for a little *strada panoramica* to **Stintino**, a fishing village with boxy pink and ochre houses and a pair of bijou ports, famous for the Caribbean fantasy colour of the sea at **Saline beach**. Just north, the luminous white curl of **La Pelosa beach** is even more beautiful.

Dinner and Sleeping: In Stintino, *see* below.

Day 1

Lunch in Fertilia

Da Bruno, at the Hotel Fertilia, near crossroads for Santa Maria La Palma, **t** 079 930 098 (*expensive*). A highly acclaimed hotel restaurant; game and mushrooms are the speciality in season; at any time of year the succulent lamb, kid or suckling pig more than live up to their reputation. Wines are from Santa Maria La Palma and Sella & Mosca. *Closed Tues, exc in summer.*

Sa Mandra, Strada Aeroporto Civile, Sa Segada, Podere 21 (look for signs), **t/f** 079 999 150 (*cheap*). An excellent option by the airport with lovely home-grown food; book ahead.

Dinner and Sleeping in Stintino

★★★★**Rocca Ruja**, Loc. Capo Falcone, **t** 079 529 200, **f** 079 529 785 (*expensive*). One of the best of the holiday villages occupying the outskirts of Stintino. Within walking distance of Pelosa Beach – offering a pool, tennis and watersports. *Open May–mid-Oct.*

★★★**Silvestrino**, Via Sássari 14, **t** 079 523 007, **f** 079 593 192 (*moderate–cheap*). Small and friendly with adequate rooms with TV, and attached to the best restaurant in Stintino. Their *riso al tonno mantecato* is famous, followed by a choice of fish, a few meat dishes, or *baci alla Silvestrino* – light fritter 'kisses' filled with spinach and ricotta in a cheese sauce. *Closed Thurs, exc in summer.*

★★**Lina**, Via Lepanto 38, **t** 079 523 071, **f** 079 523 192 (*cheap*). In the centre of town, away from the big resort compounds, with 10 simple, tidy rooms overlooking the sea.

La Pelosetta, overlooking La Pelosa beach, **t** 079 527 140 (*very expensive–expensive*). With a staggeringly beautiful view and an enchanting terrace: seafood rules, and the wine list has bottles from Sardinia's finest growers. *Open daily in season; closed winter.*

Da Antonio, Via Marco Polo 14, **t** 079 523 077 (*moderate*). Tuna and their roe (*bottarga*) may star here in spring. Try *tonno all'acqua pazza*, cooked with a little water and lots of *vernaccia* wine. *Closed Wed, exc in summer.*

Day 2: Romans, Ancient Sanctuaries and a Castle

Morning: Take a 'boat bus' (***t*** *079 500 886*) over to the **Isola Asinara**, now a national park. Drive back down the peninsula; once you reach Pozzo S. Nicola and head east, the coast becomes a squelchy industrial ghetto, yet as you draw nearer to Porto Torres, keep an eye peeled for a 440ft **Roman bridge**, so well preserved that it was used by cars until the 1970s. Take the S131 from Porto Torres towards Sássari, turning off at km222.3 to see the remarkable pre-*nuraghic* sanctuary at **Monte d'Accoddi**, built in the 3rd millennium BC. The truncated pyramid-like structure, some 40ft high, has two levels, which were possibly for small and large sacrifices, and very likely for star-gazing as well. A dolmen-like structure found next to it has been identified as the western world's only known **megalithic altar**. Return to **Porto Torres** for lunch.

Lunch: In or near Porto Torres, *see* below.

Afternoon: Have a look at the remains of Roman Turris at the **Palazzo di Re Barbaro**, including the massive baths, before taking the S200 east alongside sandy beaches. Pause beyond Marritza by the ruined seaside **Roman villa**, where a pool and mosaic survive, then go on to the beautiful and dramatic fortress town of **Castelsardo**, renowned for its baskets made of wild palm leaves. Follow the cobbled lane up to the **Castello Doria** (*open Nov–Mar Tues–Sun 9.30–1 and 3–5.30; longer hrs in summer; adm*), offering a **museum** devoted to basketry besides its views. Watch the sun go down from the **Cathedral of Sant'Antonio Abate**, set on a platform over the sea, but only after stepping in to see the Maestro di Castelsardo's wonderful *Madonna*.

Dinner and Sleeping: In Castelsardo, *see* below.

Day 2

Lunch in Porto Torres

Cristallo, Piazza XX Settembre, **t** 079 514 909 (*moderate*). Offering just about anything you fancy in the food department, with a bar and vast pastry shop on the ground floor, and a seafood restaurant-pizzeria upstairs; views across the port. *Closed Mon in winter.*

Li Lioni, 3km outside Porto Torres on the S131, on the way to Monte d'Accoddi, **t** 079 502 286 (*moderate*). Traditional restaurant run by the Pintus family. In a tranquil setting and serving all the right stuff, from *malluredus* to lamb and suckling pig roasted slowly over an open fire, finished off with a fiery glass of *filu 'e ferru*. *Closed Wed.*

Dinner in Castelsardo

La Guardiola, Piazza del Bastione 4, **t** 079 470 428 (*very expensive–expensive*). Just within the old town gate, and stalwartly defying the old Italian saying 'If you have a beautiful view, you eat like a dog'. The terrace is splendid, but be aware that they only serve seafood. *Closed Mon, exc in summer.*

Fofò, in the Hotel Riviera, *see* below (*expensive*). Another good seafood restaurant. *Open to non-guests.*

Maria Giuseppa, Via Nazionale 20, **t** 079 470 611 (*moderate–cheap*). A warm, traditional place serving a range of typical Sard *piatti*, including *pane carasau* with local pecorino and *funghi* in season. *Closed Mon.*

Sleeping in Castelsardo

A few small hotels are set in the sweeping curve of the bay, overlooking the promontory.

********Riviera****, Via Lungomare Anglona 1, **t** 079 470 143, **f** 079 471 312 (*moderate*). The fanciest of the bayside hotels: soundproofed rooms with a/c, a pool and a good restaurant.

*****Castello**, Lungomare Anglona 15, **t** 079 470 062, **f** 079 479 163 (*moderate–cheap*). Offers nice rooms with TVs and views. It's also very close to the sea, and has an open-air solarium and reserved parking. *Open April–Sept and Dec.*

Day 3: Petrified Trees and Granite Pinnacles

Morning: Head up the road east of town to see the peculiar **Elephant Rock**, chiselled with *domus de janas* 'fairy houses' (really neolithic tombs), 300m beyond the Elephant Bar near the crossroads to Tempio Pausania. Take the S134 south of here towards **Bulzi**, passing **Sèdini**, with its impressive *domu de janas*; beyond Bulzi you'll see the lovely zebra façade of the 11th-century church of **San Pietro di Simbranos**, showing an abbot praying with two monks. Stop in the next town, **Pérfugas**, to visit the **Museo Archeologico e Paleobotanico** (*open 8–2, Sun and hols 8–8*) with examples from the petrified forest of Anglona, Neolithic statuettes and fine Attic and Carthaginian vases. It also possesses the oldest human artefacts on the island, from the early Palaeolithic era. From Pérfugas, take the road north to **Santa Maria Coghinas**, a one-horse town with a cute little granite church, and pause for lunch.

Lunch: In Santa Maria Coghinas, *see* below.

Afternoon: After lunch, drive east to **Viddalba** where a turn right will take you south-east through green forests via Giagazzu and Bortigiadas towards Tempio Pausania. Shortly before Tempio, turn left to **Aggius**, a striking village under a mini range of prickly granite peaks and Gothic spires nicknamed 'the Dolomites of the Gallura'. Aggius is also known for its rugs, still made on looms today; call the village centre (*t 079 620 488*) to see its display of carpets. Before returning to **Tempio Pausania**, follow the *strada panoramica* up into the surreal kingdom of granite where, beyond a tiny lake, the **Valle de la Luna** is strewn with boulders and pale, wild formations.

Dinner and Sleeping: In or around Tempio Pausania, *see* below.

Day 3

Lunch in Santa Maria Coghinas

*****Montiruju**, Via Terme di Casteldoria 1, **t** 079 585 400, **f** 079 585 725 (*cheap*). A very pleasant little hotel with a garden and a popular restaurant-pizzeria. Situated up by the spa in a panoramic position, it makes a lovely place to stop for lunch.

****Doria**, Via San Nicola 17, **t/f** 079 585 842 or **t** 079 585670 (*cheap*). A simple place just off the main road, with a restaurant serving typical Sardinian cuisine.

Dinner and Sleeping in or around Tempio Pausania

*****Petit Hotel**, Piazza De Gasperi 9/11, **t** 079 631 134, **f** 079 631 760, *petithotel@tiscalinet.it* (*moderate*). A serene little place located near the spa, with comfortable rooms and a panoramic dining room.

Agriturismo L'Agnata, outside of town at Loc. L'Agnata, **t/f** 079 671 384 (*cheap*). This is a hospitable *agriturismo* with 10 rooms in a restored farm; it also has a fine restaurant, serving delicious country cooking – try the fantastic artichokes and tender lamb. The restaurant is also open to non-guests if they book. *Closed Tues, no credit cards.*

Agriturismo Muto di Gallura, Fraiga (✉ 07020), between Tempio and Aggius, **t** 079 620 559 (*cheap*). Another good *agriturismo* offering double and triple rooms on a farm with a riding stable. This also has a restaurant open to non-guests, serving locally grown food, much of which has been raised organically on the farm. *Open all year, and they also speak English.*

Il Giardino, Via Cavour 1, **t** 079 671 247 (*moderate*). An 18th-century *palazzo* with a terrace for dining *al fresco* in the summer. Service is friendly and recipes are based around produce available locally, as well as some seafood dishes. Plus, it's all accompanied by carafes of wine from the local *cantina. Closed Wed, exc in summer.*

Day 4: Pastries and Romanesque Churches

Morning: Take the S392 south of Tempio through the mountains of Monte Acuto, passing the **Lago Coghinas**; just south of the S597, pause in **Oschiri** to pick up some of its famous cheeses and *panadas*, savoury pastries filled with eel or pork. Follow the S199 to explore **Ozieri**, a distinguished-looking town associated with the late Neolithic era (3000–2000 BC) ever since the excavation of the **Grotte di San Michele** (signposted near the top of town). You can see some of the finds in the impressive **Museo Archeològico** (*open Tues–Sat 9–1 and 4–7, Sun 9.30–12.30; closed Mon; adm*).

Lunch: In Ozieri, *see* below.

Afternoon: Follow the 'Way of the Churches' by driving north out of Ozieri and fork left towards Chilivani to join the S597 east of Àrdara. **Sant'Antíoco di Bisarcio** stands a little east of the junction on a rocky bluff; a meld of Pisan and French Romanesque, its entrance is decorated with little human figures. Drive west to **Àrdara** for the classic Sard Romanesque **Santa Maria del Regno**, made entirely of black lava; inside is a beautiful retablo in the form of a Gothic cathedral (1515), with over 30 paintings, all by Sards. Further west, the most spectacular church awaits right by the road near **Ploaghe**: the **Basilica della SS. Trinità di Saccargia** (*open summer 9–1 and 3.30–7; in winter call* **t** *079 236 565 or* **t** *079 435 019*) is gloriously decorated with black basalt, limestone stripes and festive coloured stones in geometric rondels, squares and lozenges. Take the road south of Àrdara to meet the S128bis at **Mores**; sleep here, or in **Thiesi**, 14km west of Mores, across the S131 beyond Bonnanaro and Borutta.

Dinner and Sleeping: In Mores or Thieri, *see* below.

Day 4

This region may have its fair share of wonderful churches and five-star archaeological sites, but it doesn't offer much choice when it comes to food and accommodation. Finding lunch can be hard, but there's no shortage of pretty picnic places, so it may be a good idea to stock up on some traditional goodies from the local villages and find yourself a nice spot out on the plain between the nuraghi. Besides **Oschiri** (*see* above), **Thiesi** also makes cheese for its living.

Lunch in Ozieri

Ozieri is the metropolis of the Monte Acuto but it still doesn't have much in the way of eateries. There's a good and cheap ***spaghetteria*** right above the bus station in Piazza Garibaldi, and plenty of bars, but besides the restaurant in the Hotel Mastino (*see* below), that's pretty well it.

If you fancy something sweet, sample the local speciality, called *sospiri* or 'sighs', made of almond paste covered in sugar or chocolate; you'll find them at **La Copuletta di Mario Cappai**, Via Alagon 19.

*****Mastino**, Via Vittorio Veneto 13, **t** 079 787 041, **f** 079 787 059, *hmastino@hotmail.com* (*moderate–cheap*). A simple, family-run hotel in the centre of the village, which also has a good restaurant serving regional dishes; unsurprisingly, it is much patronized by the locals.

Dinner and Sleeping in Mores

***Asfodelo**, Loc. Baddingusti, **t** 079 706 726 (*cheap*). Here you'll find a handful of rooms with a/c, surrounded by a garden; there's also a restaurant.

Dinner and Sleeping in Thiesi

*****Cavallino Rosso**, Via F.lli Chighine, **t** 079 886 643, **f** 079 889 710 (*cheap*). Thiesi's option is pleasant and modern, with comfortable enough rooms, a restaurant and, if you can summon up the energy, the local disco.

Day 5: *Nuraghi* and Renaissance Frescoes

Morning: Visit the best preserved and most astonishing of the island's *nuraghi*, the **Nuraghe Santu Antine** (*open 8.30–7.30; 9–5 in Oct–April; adm includes Torralba museum*), some 12km south of Mores next to the S131. Surrounded by 10 huts, the central tower (16th century BC) is surrounded by three smaller towers; from the top you can spot other *nuraghi* over the plain. Then drive north to **Torralba**'s **Museo della Valle dei Nuraghi** (*open May–Sept 9–8; Oct–April 9–5; same ticket as Santu Antine*) to see what Santu Antine looked like when it was built. Drive back south to have lunch in **Bonorva**, just east of the S131, a village known for its traditional weaving.

Lunch: In or near Bonorva, *see* below.

Afternoon: Follow the road to Bono east for 9km, then turn right onto an unpaved road for the **'Grotte' di Sant'Andrea Priu** (***t*** *079 867 988; guided tours 15 Mar–June and 1–15 Oct daily 9.30–1 and 3–half an hour before sunset; July–Sept daily 9.30–7.30; 16 Oct–14 Mar by appointment only; adm*), one of the most fascinating and evocative necropoli on the island. Then, drive back west towards the coast, passing under the S131 and following the road to **Pozzomaggiore**, where you can pick up the S292 southwest via **Suni** to the charming, ancient city of **Bosa**. Explore the steep, narrow lanes of the old quarter, **Sa Costa**, and climb to the rosy **Castello di Serravalle** to visit the castle chapel (***t*** *0785 373 030*), housing the finest fresco cycle in all Sardinia.

Dinner and Sleeping: In Bosa, *see* below. In the morning, return to Alghero along the spectacular coastal road, a corniche that goes on for 45km over volcanic cliffs. Fill up your car and stomach first, however – there isn't a garage or restaurant in sight.

Day 5

Lunch in or near Bonorva

Su Cozziglia. A reliable little *trattoria* on the main street.

Su Lumarzu, in Rebeccu, on the road to Bono, **t** 079 867 933 (*cheap*). A restaurant-pizzeria by the nuraghic well.

Agriturismo Coronas, at Loc. Coronas, **t** 079 866 842, **f** 079 867 511 (*cheap*). This serves traditional Sard cuisine.

Dinner in Bosa and Bosa Marina

Da Tatore, Via Mannu 13, **t** 0785 373 104 (*moderate*). In business for over 50 years, with a fine reputation for Catalan-influenced versions of local recipes. Moray eel and tamer fish are cooked in salt, on the grill or with *vernaccia*. *Closed Wed, exc in summer.*

Borgo Sant'Ignazio, Via Sant'Ignazio 33, in the Sa Costa quarter, **t** 0785 374 662 (*moderate*). Atmospheric place to linger over authentic local dishes: *alizansas* (the local pasta), *culinzones 'e calameda* (aubergine and ricotta ravioli in a meat sauce), smoked fish, and *impanate* (fried pasta filled with meat and greens); good choice of wines. *Closed Sun eve and Mon Oct–May, 1 Nov–15 Dec.*

La Griglia d'Oro, Via Genova 19, Bosa Marina, **t** 0785 373 157 (*moderate*). Set back behind a garden in a typical house and serving good, non-fussy fare in welcoming surroundings. No credit cards. *Open summer only.*

Sleeping in Bosa and Bosa Marina

★★★**Al Gabbiano**, Viale Mediterraneo, Bosa Marina, **t** 0785 374 123, **f** 0785 374 109 (*moderate–cheap*). Right by the beach, with balconies and rooms with a/c; an adjacent family-run restaurant serves a magnificent array of tempting seafood, including a tasty *zuppa di pesce* flavoured with sun-dried tomatoes. *Restaurant open Easter–Oct only.*

★★★**Mannu**, Via Alghero, near turn-off for Bosa Marina, **t** 0785 375 306 or **t** 0785 375 307, **f** 0785 375 308 (*moderate–cheap*). Cosy and fairly new; rooms are a touch small, but the restaurant's good and the owners are helpful.

Language

The fathers of modern Italian were Dante, Manzoni and television, and each played their part in creating a national language from an infinity of regional and local dialects. The Florentine Dante, the first to write in the vernacular, did much to put the Tuscan dialect into the foreground of Italian literature. Manzoni's revolutionary novel, *I Promessi Sposi*, heightened national consciousness by using an everyday language that everyone could understand in the 19th century. In the last few decades, television has performed an even more spectacular linguistic unification; although many Italians still speak a dialect at home, school and work, their TV idols insist on proper Italian.

Italians are not especially adept at learning other languages. English lessons, however, have been the rage for years, and at most hotels and restaurants there will be someone who speaks some English. In small towns and out-of-the-way places, finding anybody Anglophone may prove more difficult. The words and phrases below should help you out in most situations, but the ideal way to come to Italy is with some Italian under your belt; your visit will be richer, and you're much more likely to make some Italian friends.

Pronunciation

Italian words are pronounced phonetically. Every vowel and consonant except 'h' is sounded. **Consonants** are the same as in English, with the following exceptions.

The ***c***, when followed by an 'e' or 'i', is pronounced like the English 'ch' (*cinque* thus becomes cheen-quay). Italian ***g*** is also soft before 'i' or 'e' as in *gira*, or jee-rah. ***Z*** is pronounced like 'ts'. The consonants ***sc*** before the vowels 'i' or 'e' become like the English 'sh, as in sci, pronounced 'shee'. The combination ***ch*** is pronouced like a 'k', as in *Chianti*, 'kee-an-tee'. The combination ***gn*** is pronounced as 'nya' (thus *bagno* is pronounced ban-yo). The combination ***gli*** is pronounced like the middle of the word million (so *Castiglione* is pronounced Ca-steel-yoh-nay).

Vowel pronunciation is as follows:

A is as in English *father*.

E when unstressed is pronounced like 'a' in *fate* (as in *mele*); when stressed it can be the same or like the 'e' in *pet* (*bello*).

I is like the 'i' in *machine*.

O, like 'e', has two sounds, 'o' as in *hope* when unstressed (*tacchino*), and usually 'o' as in *rock* when stressed (*morte*).

U is pronounced like the 'u' in *June*.

The **stress** usually (but not always!) falls on the penultimate syllable. Accents indicate if it falls elsewhere (as in *città*). Also note that in the big northern cities, the informal way of addressing someone as you, *tu*, is widely used; the more formal *lei* or *voi* is commonly used in provincial districts, *voi* more in the south.

Useful Words and Phrases

yes/no/maybe *si/no/forse*
I don't know *Non (lo) so*
I don't understand (Italian) *Non capisco (l'italiano)*
Does someone here speak English? *C'è qualcuno qui che parla inglese?*
Speak slowly *Parla lentamente*
Could you assist me? *Potrebbe aiutarmi?*
Help! *Aiuto!*
Please *Per favore*
Thank you (very much) *Grazie molte/mille*
You're welcome *Prego*
It doesn't matter *Non importa*
All right *Va bene*
Excuse me/I'm sorry *Permesso/Mi scusi/Mi dispiace*
Be careful! *Attenzione!/Attento!*
Nothing *Niente*
It is urgent! *È urgente!*
How are you? *Come sta?*
Well, and you? *Bene, e Lei?/e tu?*

What is your name? *Come si chiama?/Come ti chiami*
Hello *Salve or ciao (both informal)*
Good morning *Buongiorno (formal hello)*
Good afternoon, evening *Buonasera*
Good night *Buona notte*
Goodbye *Arrivederla (formal); Arrivederci/Ciao (informal)*
What do you call this in Italian? *Come si chiama questo in italiano?*
What?/Who?/Where? *Che?/Chi?/Dove?*
When?/Why? *Quando?/Perché?*
How? *Come?*
How much (does it cost? *Quanto (costa)?*
I am lost *Mi sono perso*
I am hungry/thirsty/sleepy *Ho fame/ sete/sonno*
I am sorry *Mi dispiace*
I am tired *Sono stanco*
I feel unwell *Mi sento male*
Leave me alone *Lasciami in pace*
good/bad *buono/cattivo*
well/badly *bene/male*
hot/cold *caldo/freddo*
slow/fast *lento/rapido*
up/down *su/giù*
big/small *grande/piccolo*
here/there *qui/lì*

Days

Monday *lunedì*
Tuesday *martedì*
Wednesday *mercoledì*
Thursday *giovedì*
Friday *venerdì*
Saturday *sàbato*
Sunday *doménica*
holidays *festivi*
weekdays *feriali*

Numbers

one *uno/una*
two/three/four *due/tre/quattro*
five/six/seven *cinque/sei/sette*
eight/nine/ten *otto/nove/dieci*
eleven/twelve *undici/dodici*
thirteen/fourteen *tredici/quattordici*
fifteen/sixteen *quindici/sedici*
seventeen/eighteen *diciassette/diciotto*
nineteen *diciannove*
twenty *venti*
twenty-one/twenty-two *ventuno/ventidue*
thirty *trenta*
forty *quaranta*
fifty *cinquanta*
sixty *sesanta*
seventy *settanta*
eighty *ottanta*
ninety *novanta*
one hundred *cento*
one hundred and one *centuno*
two hundred *duecento*
one thousand *mille*
two thousand *duemila*
one million *un milione*

Time

What time is it? *Che ore sono?*
day/week *giorno/settimana*
month *mese*
morning/afternoon *mattina/pomeriggio*
evening *sera*
yesterday *ieri*
today *oggi*
tomorrow *domani*
soon *fra poco*
later *dopo/più tardi*
It is too early/late *È troppo presto/tardi*

Public Transport

airport *aeroporto*
bus stop *fermata*
bus/coach *autobus*
railway station *stazione ferroviaria*
train *treno*
platform *binario*
taxi *tassì/taxi*
ticket *biglietto*
customs *dogana*
seat (reserved) *posto (prenotato)*

Travel Directions

One (two) ticket(s) to ..., please *Un biglietto (due biglietti) per ..., per favore*
one way *semplice/andata*
return *andata e ritorno*
first/second class *Prima/seconda classe*
I want to go to... *Desidero andare a...*

How can I get to...? *Come posso andare a...?*
Do you stop at...? *Si ferma a...?*
Where is...? *Dov'è...?*
How far is it to...? *Quanto è lontano...?*
What is the name of this station? *Come si chiama questa stazione?*
When does the next ... leave? *Quando parte il prossimo...?*
From where does it leave? *Da dove parte?*
How much is the fare? *Quant'è il biglietto?*
Have a good trip *Buon viaggio!*

Driving

near/far *vicino/lontano*
left/right *sinistra/destra*
straight ahead *sempre diritto*
forward/backwards *avanti/indietro*
north/south *nord/sud*
east *est/oriente*
west *ovest/occidente*
crossroads *bivio*
street/road *strada/via*
square *piazza*
car hire *autonoleggio*
motorbike/scooter/moped *motocicletta/Vespa/motorino*
bicycle *bicicletta*
petrol/diesel *benzina/gasolio*
garage *garage*
This doesn't work *Questo non funziona*
mechanic *meccanico*
map/town plan *carta/pianta*
Where is the road to...? *Dov'è la strada per...?*
breakdown *guasto*
driving licence *patente di guida*
driver *guidatore*
speed *velocità*
danger *pericolo*
parking *parcheggio*
no parking *sosta vietata*
narrow *stretto*
bridge *ponte*
toll *pedaggio*
slow down *rallentare*

Shopping, Services, Sightseeing

I would like... *Vorrei...*
Where is/are...? *Dov'è/Dove sono...?*
How much is it? *Quanto costa?*
open/closed *aperto/chiuso*
cheap/expensive *a buon prezzo/caro*
bank *banca*
beach *spiaggia*
bed *letto*
church *chiesa*
entrance/exit *ingresso/uscita*
hospital *ospedale*
money *soldi*
newspaper *giornale*
pharmacy *farmacia*
police station *commissariato*
policeman *poliziotto*
post office *ufficio postale*
sea *mare*
shop *negozio*
room *camera*
tobacco shop *tabaccaio* (pl. *tabacchi*)
WC *toilette/bagno/servizi*
men *Signori/Uomini*
women *Signore/Donne*

Useful Hotel Vocabulary

I'd like a double room please *Vorrei una camera doppia (matrimoniale), per favore*
I'd like a single room please *Vorrei una camera singola, per favore*
with/without bath *con/senza bagno*
for two nights *per due notti*
We are leaving tomorrow morning *Partiamo domani mattina*
May I see the room, please? *Posso vedere la camera, per cortesia?*
Is there a room with a balcony? *C'è una camera con balcone?*
There isn't (aren't) any hot water, soap, *Manca (Mancano) acqua calda, sapone,* **...light, toilet paper, towels** *...luce, carta igienica, asciugamani*
May I pay by credit card? *Posso pagare con carta di credito?*
May I see another room please? *Per favore, potrei vedere un'altra camera?*
Fine, I'll take it *Bene, la prendo*
Is breakfast included? *E' compresa la prima colazione?*
What time do you serve breakfast? *A che ora è la colazione?*
How do I get to the town centre? *Come posso raggiungere il centro città?*

Glossary

Ambones: twin pulpits in southern churches, often elaborately decorated.
Atrium: entrance court of a Roman house or early church.
Badia: *abbazia*, an abbey or abbey church.
Baldacchino: baldaquin, a columned stone canopy above the altar of a church.
Basilica: a rectangular building usually divided into three aisles by rows of columns. Roman Christians adapted it for their early churches.
Borgo: a suburb.
Calvary chapels (Sacro Monte): a series of outdoor chapels, usually on a hill, commemorating the stages of the Passion of Christ.
Campanile: a bell tower.
Camposanto: a cemetery.
Cardo: the transverse street of a Roman *castrum*-shaped city, perpendicular to the Decumanus Major (*see* below).
Carroccio: a wagon carrying the banners of a medieval city and an altar, serving as the rallying point in battles.
Cartoon: the initial sketch for a fresco/tapestry.
Caryatid: pillar carved into a standing female form; male versions are called *telamones*.
Castrum: a Roman military camp, neatly rectangular, with straight streets and gates at the cardinal points. Later the Romans founded or refounded cities in this form.
Cavea: a semicircle of seats in a classical theatre.
Ciborium: a tabernacle.
Comune: commune, referring to the governments of the free cities of the Middle Ages. Today it denotes any local government.
Condottiere: leader of a band of mercenaries in the late Middle Ages and Renaissance.
Cosmati work: where inlaid marble or enamel chips are used in architectural decoration.
Cyclopean walls: fortifications built of enormous, irregular polygonal blocks.
Decumanus: street of a Roman *castrum*-shaped city parallel to the central, main avenue called the Decumanus Major.
Forum: the central square of a Roman town, with its most important public buildings.
Fresco: wall painting; first the artist draws the *sinopia* (q.v.) on the wall. This is covered with plaster, but only a little at a time, as the paint must be on the plaster before it dries.
Gonfalon: the banner of a medieval free city.
Grotesques: carved or painted faces used in Etruscan and later Roman decoration.
Hypogeum: underground burial cavern, usually of pre-Christian religions.
Intarsia: work in inlaid wood or marble.
Narthex: the enclosed porch of a church.
Palazzo: not just a palace, but any large, important building.
Palio: a banner, and the horse race in which city neighbourhoods contend for it in their annual festivals.
Pantocrator: Christ 'ruler of all', a common subject for apse paintings and mosaics.
Pietra dura: rich inlay work using semi-precious stones.
Predella: smaller paintings on panels below the main subject of a painted altarpiece.
Presepio: a Christmas crib.
Putti: flocks of plaster cherubs that infested much of Italy in the Baroque era.
Quattrocento: the 1400s – the Italian way of referring to centuries (*cinquecento*: 1500s).
Risseu: a figurative black-and-white pebble pavement, often in a parvis outside a church.
Sinopia: the layout of a fresco (q.v.) etched on the wall before the plaster is applied.
Telamon: *see Caryatid*.
Thermae (Terme): Roman baths.
Tondo: round relief, painting or terracotta.
Transenna: marble screen separating the altar area from the rest of a Christian church.
Travertine: hard, light-coloured stone, sometimes flecked or pitted with black.
Triclinium: the main hall of a Roman house, used for dining and entertaining.
Triptych: a painting in three sections.
Trompe-l'œil: art that uses perspective effects to deceive the eye.
Tympanum: the semicircular space, often decorated, above the portal of a church.

Index

Main page references are in **bold**. Page references to maps are in *italics*.